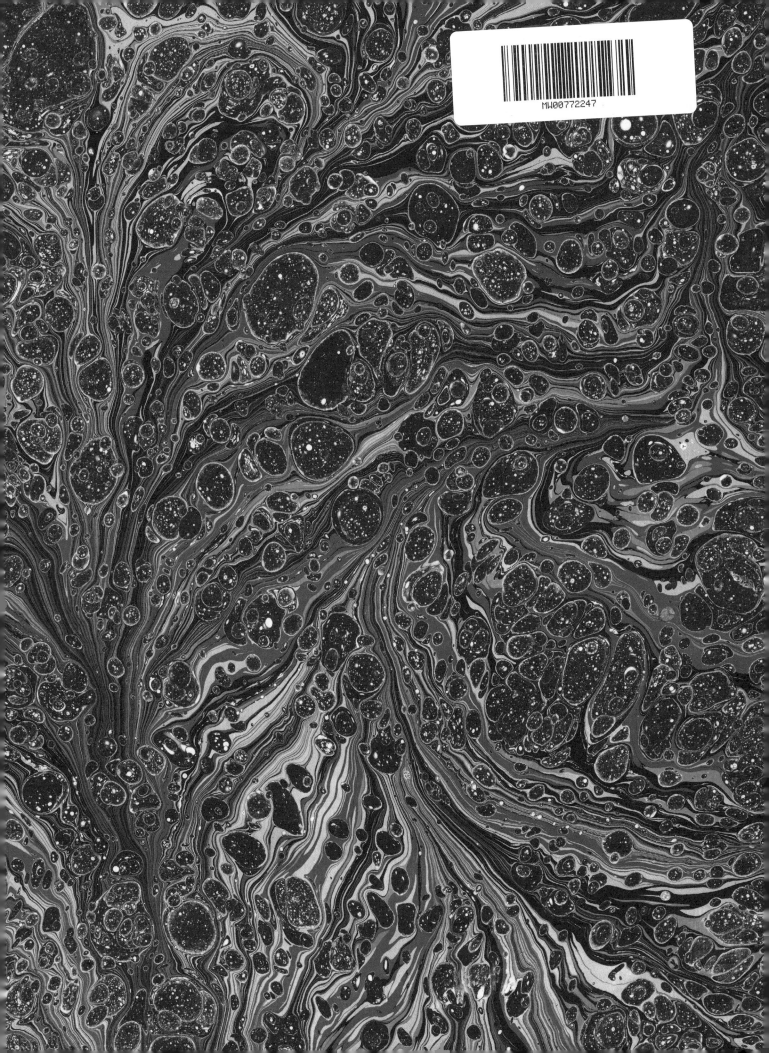

The 5th Fighter Command
in World War II
Volume 3

The 5th Fighter Command
in World War II

William Wolf

Volume 3:
5th FC vs. Japan:
Aces, Units, Aircraft
and Tactics

Schiffer
Publishing Ltd

4880 Lower Valley Road • Atglen, PA 19310

Dedication

To the brave, unheralded men of the Fifth Fighter Command who gave up their youth and often their lives to win the relentless air war over New Guinea and the Philippines.

Copyright © 2014 William Wolf

Library of Congress Control Number: 2014944373

Printed in China
ISBN: 978-0-7643-4738-2

We are interested in hearing from authors with book ideas on related topics.

Published by Schiffer Publishing Ltd.
4880 Lower Valley Road
Atglen, PA 19310
Phone: (610) 593-1777
FAX: (610) 593-2002
E-mail: Info@schifferbooks.com

Visit our web site at: www.schifferbooks.com
Please write for a free catalog. This book may be purchased from the publisher. Try your bookstore first.

Contents

Preface

After completing the history of the 5th Fighter Command in two volumes, I realized that a third volume—actually a giant Appendix—would expand and explain parts of the first two volumes. The aces of the 5FC were mentioned many times in terms of their combat exploits, but were not personalized, while Japanese aces were not mentioned at all. American and Japanese pilot training and its importance to the outcome of the war is now discussed and compared in Part 1. The 5FC Groups and Squadrons needed to be detailed and organized, as did those of the Japanese Naval and Army Air Forces. In Part 3, the aircraft of the two combatants are detailed and compared. The vulnerability of Japanese aircraft is discussed in detail. Flying the six fighters of the 5th Fighter Command is first described from Pilot Flight Manuals, then by aces who flew them. When describing the various air combats from the Individual Combat Reports, there were many references to combat maneuvers and tactics which, not being a pilot, I did not fully understand, and with the input of pilots, I have included Part 4 on Air Tactics and Combat. Also, I have included in-depth descriptions of the AAF and Japanese aircraft involved in SWPA air combat. The importance of logistics and the construction of airfields are discussed in Part 5. Finally, after two volumes on the air war from the perspective of the 5th Fighter Command, I decided to present the air war from the Japanese viewpoint and discuss the causes for the defeat of its air forces.

Foreword

Bill Wolf is indeed an accomplished author of many books on World War II aviation, and I have appreciated his work since meeting him at an American Fighter Aces Association meeting many years ago, after he wrote my biography for the Ace's Album. It is with great pleasure that I write this foreword to his homage to the Fifth Fighter Command.

Following Pearl Harbor, with the war raging in Europe, our leaders had to make tough decisions as to priorities in manpower and equipment. The fighter force in the Southwest Pacific was woefully inadequate. The 5th Air Force was forced to engage the Japanese with the P-39 and P-40, neither of which was capable of meeting the demands of combat in this environment. The P-39 was no match for the Japanese fighters and could not reach altitudes to engage enemy bombers. The P-40 could hold its own, but did not have the range required to engage the enemy over this territory.

General George Kenny, the commander of all Allied Air Forces in the Southwest Pacific, made a plea to MacArthur for P-38s and finally, in 1943, his request was heard and the decision was made to send him P-38s. The 475th Fighter Group was the only all P-38 equipped Group in the theater and was formed in Australia, filling its ranks with personnel already in theater, as well as replacements from the U.S. For the first time, American pilots in the Southwest Pacific believed they had a fighter able to combat the Japanese, who were at Australia's front door, threatening to capture Port Moresby, New Guinea.

Historians relate that for all intents and purposes, the successes at the Battle of the Coral Sea, Midway, and Guadalcanal pretty much spelled the demise of the Japanese efforts to dominate the entire Pacific region. However, somebody forgot to tell the Japanese that the war was over, so the fierce and bloody battles on the ground and in the air continued, as our forces island hopped toward the Philippines, starting in mid-1943.

I arrived in the Pacific in October 1943, flying with the 432nd Fighter Squadron of the 475th Fighter Group, "Satan's Angles." From the outset, living conditions in the Pacific were miserable and never did improve as we moved west. Aircrews and support personnel did not experience the comparative luxuries provided in the European theater. We lived in damp tents, ate awful food, struggled with the disheartening conditions associated with tropical high temperatures, humidity, and monsoon rains, and endured snakes, insects, and critters of every description.

The P-38, with its heavy firepower, speed, and durability, was ideally suited for this theater and gave us confidence that we would win the war. I shot down nine Japanese aircraft while in combat from New Guinea and on into the Philippines. Fighting was tough, and in the process I managed to lose four of my P-38s, ranging from a mid-air collision to just plain being shot down. My Group Commander informed me that if I lost one more I would be a Japanese ace!

Writing this foreword brings back many memories of the air war and makes me realize that a history of the Fifth Fighter Command and its valiant fight over the Southwest Pacific and the Philippines has been neglected for far too long. I thank Bill for his efforts to bring proper credit to my comrades in the Fifth Fighter Command and their historic efforts in his excellent, massive, three-volume history.

Perry J. Dahl
Colonel, USAF (ret)

Acknowledgments

My lifelong hobby has been WWII aerial combat, and over the past forty years, I have collected over 20,000 books and magazines, along with hundreds of reels of microfilm on the subject. I probably have nearly every book written on WWII aviation and complete collections of every combat aviation magazine published since 1939. Also included in my collection are hundreds of aviation unit histories; intelligence reports; pilot, crew, flight, and training manuals; and technical, structural, and maintenance manuals for aircraft ordnance, armament, engines, and equipment. My microfilm collection includes vintage intelligence reports; hundreds of USAF, USN, and USMC group and squadron histories, After Combat Reports (ACRs), Narrative Combat Reports (NCRs), and Individual Combat Reports (ICRs); complete Japanese Monograph series; and complete U.S. Strategic Bombing Surveys, as well as complete USAF Historical Studies. I wish to thank the hundreds of persons, museums, and libraries that contributed photos and materials to my collection during the past forty years. I apologize for any photos that may be miscredited. Also, some of the photos are not of the best quality, because of their age and sources, especially those copied from microfilm and contemporary publications, but were used with permission because of their uniqueness and importance to the book.

My appreciation again goes to my editor, Ian Robertson, who reads and rereads the lengthy text and hundreds of captions, making corrections and suggestions. Ian does a great job of editing my fourteen books published by Schiffer. I also wish to thank Steve Ferguson again, for his great profiles, cover paintings, and for his drawings of air combat principals and tactics, which prove that a picture is worth a thousand words. Steve has become a friend over the years and has been a pleasure to work with and spend time talking about our passion for WWII aircraft and pilots. Thanks also go to pilot, fellow aviation enthusiast, and friend John Vick, for his help in my understanding flight principals and maneuvers.

Again, my thanks go to my persevering wife, Nancy, who allows me to spend many hours researching and writing, and patiently (mostly) waits while I browse bookstores and visit air museums in search of new material and photos. Also, I thank her because her car sits out in the hot Arizona sun as my library luxuriates in the remodeled, air conditioned, three-car garage

Author with Bong and Rickenbacker autographs, models of their fighters, and a Bong *Marge* P-38 cowling in the background.

PART 1:
Aces and Pilots

1

The Ace

Fighter Pilots: Aces and Others

There were two types of fighter pilots: those whose priority was to fight the war and those who only sought to survive the war. The bottom line of air combat was, no matter how much faster, more powerful, or potent a fighter plane became, it depended on a combination of skill and aggressiveness in its pilot to be effective.

During combat in WWII, it was essential that a fighter pilot be totally aware of his surroundings: monitoring his own aircraft, looking after his Wingman, and remaining vigilant for threats around him, all the while not allowing uncertainty and apprehension to affect him. An inexperienced pilot was at a great disadvantage in combat if he had to be alert for the enemy and also keep his high-performance fighter in the air. On the other hand, while some men were naturally good pilots, a well trained and experienced pilot who was able to fly his fighter by instinct was far more prepared to react to the deadly and rapidly evolving situation of air combat.

An ace can be defined as a talented pilot being in the right place at the right time to encounter enemy aircraft. Then, possessing the physical and mental characteristics which gave him the ability to fly and shoot better than the enemy and by utilizing this skill and superior tactics, often aided by luck, he was able to shoot down five or more enemy aircraft. The highest scoring aces were by nature aggressive and determined pilots who were also in the right place at the right time, but scored more frequently because they sought out the enemy and went in for the kill, often without regard for personal safety.

The total number of aces was not high, but a very high percentage of those who became aces totaled between five and seven kills. These aces were not necessarily more highly skilled than a pilot with three or four victories, as much of their success again had to do with the luck of being in the right place at the right time. For example, a pilot might encounter a particularly inexperienced Japanese unit and shoot down several aircraft or be on patrol and shoot down relatively defenseless Japanese reconnaissance, float planes, or trainers. The number of pilots scoring more than 15 victories was low and indicated that these pilots were particularly skilled, rather than lucky. However, for most pilots, the number of kills was very secondary to their primary goal of self preservation by landing safely after a mission, especially with their Wingman.

The Ace: A History

Throughout history, the inherent competitive nature of men has led to the scorecard ranging from notches on his six shooter handle or his bedpost to sports statistics listing who is the best batter, rusher, or rebounder. In today's "Top Gun" age of the automated electronic jet fighter jockey, boys sit in

Capt. Eddie Rickenbacker was America's top ace in WWI with 26 victories and he won the Medal of Honor while flying with the 94th "Hat-in-the-Ring" Squadron. (AFHRC)

front of their computers playing air combat video games, dreaming of becoming an air ace by shooting down five alien spaceships. The air ace, the twentieth century's equivalent of the medieval knight in armor, is the unofficial designation bestowed on the military pilot who officially shoots down five or more aircraft in aerial combat. World War I lent itself to the glorification of air warfare, as airmen fought chivalrously, man against man, pitting individual expertise against individual expertise in the clean, clear skies, far above the horror of the muddy and bloody trenches which had produced indescribable carnage. In wartime, both the military and the public crave heroes, so during WWI, when French morale was at low ebb, their air Escadrilles provided these heroes called "L'as," the French word for ace—the highest card in a suit. The word was initially used as a casual title for a pilot of superior skill and courage, but soon certain pilots became proficient in shooting down enemy aircraft and those scoring ten or more kills were designated as "L'as." When the United States belatedly entered the Great War, its press arbitrarily set America's "ace total" at five rather than ten, in order to catch up to the French and British pilots who had a three-year head start. During WWI, American pilots accounted for 776 German aircraft and 72 balloons for a loss of 289 aircraft. A product of these victories was 111 aces. The top American ace was Edward Rickenbacker, with 26 victories, who trailed the top aces of World War I: Manfred von Richtofen (Germany) with 80 victories, Rene Fonck (France) with 78 victories, and William Bishop (Great Britain) with 72 victories.

In 1920, a policy statement by the U.S. Air Service affirmed:
"The USAS does not use the title 'ace' in referring to those who are credited officially with five or more victories over enemy aircraft. It is not the policy of the Air Service to glorify one particular branch of aeronautics, aviation, or aerostation at the expense of another."

This statement went on to state that bombardment and observation aviation was considered equally dangerous as pursuit aviation, but nonetheless received no recognition.

In World War II and Korea, the three American air services continued to shy away from creating individual heroes, stressing teamwork and squadron performance. *Stars & Stripes* and *Yank*, the armed services weeklies, also emphasized group over individual accomplishments. A research paper, issued in 1975 by the USAAF's Albert E. Simpson Historical Research Center at Maxwell AFB, reiterated the 1920 stand on aces of WWII and Korea, stating that: "….as far as the Air Force was concerned, there are no aces….These men have been applauded and feted and acclaimed by the public as heroes; but from the Air Force they have no special reward, not even in a medal, a ribbon, or badge to signify that they are aces. Nonetheless, people persist in using the title. The Air Force never has prohibited, or even discouraged, the informal or unofficial use of the title within its own organization."

However, in World War II and Korea, the American press was able to create aces and races for the top scorers from the extensive official air statistics collected by the Army (later the Air Force), Navy, and Marines.

The Air Combat Equation
In the air combat equation, with all personal skill factors being equal, a pilot in a superior aircraft *should* be able to outfight a pilot in an inferior aircraft. Early in the Pacific War, many American pilots had extensive prewar flying experience, but many were shot down while flying obsolete fighters, such as the Navy's F2A Buffalo or the Army's P-39 Airacobra, against the then-modern Japanese Zero, which, early in the war, were also flown by highly experienced pilots. With the introduction of the F6F Hellcat, F4U Corsair, and P-38 Lightning, the average American pilot could be more than a match against the same Zero flown by increasingly less well trained and experienced pilots. Of course, utilizing the superior characteristics of

an aircraft while not allowing the enemy to utilize his aircraft's strengths was the key to achieving success. Gen. Claire Chennault's "no dogfighting but dive in, fire, dive away" edict to his Flying Tigers when flying their superior diving P-40s against the much more maneuverable Zero is a prime example of this philosophy. The AVG totaled a phenomenal 11:1 kill to loss ratio over better Japanese pilots flying a better fighter in greater numbers. Therefore, tactical doctrine entered the air combat equation and strict adherence to its tenets gave the pilot, who understood the limitations and strengths of their aircraft, command of a situation. For this reason, Marine pilots, like Joe Foss (26 victories), John Smith (19), and Marion Carl (16½), flying the F4F Wildcat over Guadalcanal and Air Force P-40 10-victory double aces, like Ernest Harris and Robert DeHaven flying over New Guinea, were able to combine ability and tactics suited to their aircraft to shoot down the superior Zero piloted by above average Japanese pilots, or to evade them to get at the bombers they were escorting.

Gen. Claire Chennault, shown with the Chinese Aeronautical Commission at Kunming, issued his "no dogfighting but dive in, fire, dive away" edict to his Flying Tigers when flying their superior diving P-40s against the much more maneuverable Zero, to gain an 11 to 1 victory ratio. (AFHRC)

Most air combats did not result in an aerial victory, and the true measure of success of any encounter with the enemy was for the pilot and his Wingman to return to base safely. Thus, the robustness and reliability of the pilot's fighter came into the equation. The Japanese fighter aircraft sacrificed pilot protection (armor plate and self-sealing fuel tanks) for quickness and maneuverability. American aircraft, particularly the P-47 and the Grumman-built Navy fighters, were renowned for their ruggedness and ability to return to base despite heavy damage.

A change in a fighter could transform it from an ordinary to an extraordinary aircraft. An outstanding example is the replacement of the Allison with the Rolls Royce engine in the P-51 Mustang, which made it arguably the best fighter in WWII. Other more subtle modifications in a fighter could give it an advantage in combat, albeit often temporary, as it usually was not long before the enemy made similar changes or developed new innovations which countered them. The introduction of superchargers and water methanol power boosters, the bubble canopy, better communications, and the gyroscopic K-14 (USAAF) and Mark 18 (USN) gun sights all made for better aircraft, and in turn better pilots.

Combat Documentation and Victory Credits
The air war over the Pacific was reasonably well documented on the Squadron level, as after every mission Squadron Intelligence debriefed as

many participants as possible and tried to reconstruct a narrative of events. The procedures involved to claim and verify a victory were done separately. Squadrons sent their reports up the chain of command and most After Action Reports survived the slapdash handling of paperwork that characterized bureaucracy in the Pacific. These Reports were collected at a higher headquarters for analysis, then distribution to other squadrons. The events described by the pilots in their Individual Combat Reports (ICRs) were honest and basically accurate, but described actions that had occurred very rapidly and much was missed and predictive. If a pilot fired at and hit an enemy aircraft, it was his natural tendency to want to see it go down, but braggarts were not tolerated by squadron mates and most men did their best to report reality as they saw it. ICRs claiming victories were forwarded to HQ with a short description and signed confirmation by a witness. On 3 March, Capt. Richard Bong shot down two Sally bombers for his 23rd and 24th victories near Tadji, while flying with Maj. Thomas Lynch on one of their famous two-man "Flying Circus" sweeps. Bong's ICR witnessed by Lynch and Lynch's ICR shooting down a Tony and another unidentified fighter for his 18th and 19th victories are presented on the next two pages.

Air victory claims procedure has always been a controversial system. In World War I, victory credits in the U.S. Air Service (USAS) were awarded only upon confirmation by a balloon observer, or if the wreckage was found. Sometimes confirmation by three disinterested observers would be accepted as evidence of a claim.

Early in WWII, it was obvious that many claims were exaggerated, or in the case of the Luftwaffe seemed to be exaggerated. The admitted losses by the Japanese in the early war seem very low when compared to "official" American victory claims. It is often asserted that early American claims in the Pacific were exaggerated, which they probably were, but many genuine victories were also lost due to lack of proper verification or claims procedure, or when a badly damaged enemy aircraft did not arrive back at its base after flying hundreds of miles.

The vulnerability of Japanese aircraft to catch on fire was well known, as Allied pilots derisively referred to them as "Ronsons," after the popular cigarette lighter of the time, so upon seeing flames after firing, a pilot could be inclined to claim his victory and break off his attack to save his ammunition for another enemy aircraft and not see the fire go out. Another occurrence was the Zero's proclivity to leave a trail of smoke when its pilot put his fighter into increased engine boost for maximum performance. The Zero's engine also produced a flash of flame during a backfire with a sudden advance of its throttle when trying a high-speed escape. These factors also could have played a role in some pseudo/inflated victory claims.

Claims System Established

On 7 May 1943, the War Department announced a claims policy based on the RAF system:

"There are only three circumstances in which an enemy plane is definitely counted as lost. These are:
1) If the plane is seen descending completely enveloped in flames.
2) If the plane is seen to disintegrate in the air, or if a complete wing or tail assembly is seen to be shot away from the fuselage.
3) If the plane is a single seater and the pilot is seen to bail out.
"Enemy aircraft are not counted as having been destroyed on the basis of the fact that flames are licking out from the engine or wheel, or some other similar part of the plane is seen to be shot away.

"After each combat mission, every fighter pilot and member of a bombardment crew is interrogated by Intelligence Officers. When any crewmember or pilot claims to have shot down or damaged an enemy plane, he is questioned about pertinent details. He is questioned also about the

claims of other crewmembers or pilots. After the debriefing is completed, the intelligence officers make a complete breakdown and their official reports are to be on the conservative side.

"Taken into consideration by the Commanding and Intelligence Officers are the following:
1) The number and type of enemy planes attacking
2) The direction and angle of attack
3) The range at which the gunner or pilot is believed to have opened fire and the distance at which he destroys the plane
4) The rounds fired and results
5) The time, place and altitude of our planes and their positions relative to other factors
"A plane is counted as having been probably destroyed if it is sufficiently in flames to preclude the chance of extinguishing the fire or when damaged to the extent where it is believed it must have crashed, but where there is not 100% certainty. A plane is counted as having been damaged when parts are seen to be shot away. The commanding and intelligence officers, in analyzing the claims, are cognizant that as long as the enemy has a plane in the air, some skeptics will doubt the accuracy of the claims of the enemy planes destroyed. Consequently, the first thought of the officers is to eliminate duplicate claims. They do so whenever there is any doubt."

Capt. Richard Bong was America's top ace with 40 victories, but also had the AAF's most Probable claims with eight and the most Damaged claims in the Pacific with seven. (AAF)

(**Note:** Top American ace Dick Bong, with 40 victories, also had the most probable claims with eight—high for the AAF. Ray Wetmore (AAF-17 ETO victories) followed with six probables. Donald Aldrich (USMC-20 victories) had six probables, while Thomas Blackburn (USN-11 victories), David McCampbell (USN Top Ace with 34 victories), and James Rigg (USN-11 victories) each had five probables and were high for their branch of service. ETO Air Force aces Glenn Eagleston (10½ victories) and Steven Gerrick (5 victories) each damaged nine enemy aircraft, followed by Gerald Tyler (11 ETO victories) with eight and Bong with seven—high for the AAF in the Pacific. For the Navy, Howard Hudson (5 victories) and Rigg each had five damaged. For the Marines, Francis Terrill (6 victories) and Franklin Thomas (9 victories) each had four damaged credits.)

The Intelligence Officer

The duties of the Fighter Squadron Intelligence Officer (IO or S-**2**) were described in the *AAC Field Manual 1-40, 9 September 1940: Intelligence Procedures in Aviation Units*. *Field Manual 30-5* gave the IO methods to

HEADQUARTERS
V FIGHTER COMMAND
APO 713, UNIT #1

3 March, 1944

AG 373

SUBJECT: Credit for Destruction of Enemy Aircraft.

TO   : Commanding General, Fifth Air Force, APO 925, (Thru Channels).

1. Request official confirmation for the destruction of two (2) SALLY type aircraft in aerial combat near TADJI, New Guinea, at 1745/L - 1800/L, on 3 March, 1944, by Captain RICHARD I. BONG, 0-433784.

2. I was a member of a 2-plane formation on a fighter swoop to TADJI, New Guinea on 3 March, 1944. Took off at 1610/L and arrived TADJI at 1740/L. Sighted 1 SALLY headed east by TADJI Strip and dove down for a tail attack when he was about 2 miles east of strip. Major Lynch damaged this SALLY and I followed in on it and shot him down into the trees. Went back over the strip at 6,000 feet and sighted 5 fighters about 12 o'clock same level about mile offshore. Made a tail attack on a TONY and damaged him. Dove away from other Zeros and saw pilot bail out of Major Lynch's first plane. Pulled up again in time to see Major Lynch shoot down the TONY I damaged and joined Major Lynch. Sighted 2 SALLYS down below. Major Lynch made a tail attack on one but he ran out of ammunition before he could knock it down. I followed up and fired from close range and his tail blew off and he crashed to the ground and exploded and burned. Both bombers crashed within 100 yards of each other about 2 miles east of strip. I claim two (2) SALLY bombers definitely destroyed. Left the area due to lack of ammunition and landed at 1930/L.

RICHARD I. BONG,
Captain, Air Corps.

WITNESS:

I was a member of the formation mentioned in the above communication and observed the first SALLY attacked by Captain BONG to crash into the trees. I observed the second SALLY attacked by Captain BONG to start burning after which it crashed to the ground.

THOMAS J. LYNCH,
Major, Air Corps.

010413
181159

Capt. Richard Bong's request for a victory confirmation for 3 March 1944

80FS Unit Narrative Combat Report for 30 March 1944

Enemy objective - Enemy objective was obviously to break up bombing attack but his attempts generally appeared poor and half-hearted.

Own objective - To protect bombers and at same time to destroy maximum number of enemy as possible.

Enemy tactics - Enemy tactics seemed to be almost totally lacking in any organized manner. Except in very few cases they appeared unwilling to mix with our fighters. Their favorite maneuver was the half-roll or split. The majority of enemy contacted were in disorganized bunches or in pairs and occasionally alone. Most of the fighters sighted were slightly below bomber level and to northwest of target area where they seemed to mill around with no apparent purpose.

Own tactics - Four-ship flight formations were maintained throughout with attacks being made upon any enemy fighters which presented themselves as targets. Three flights remained at altitudes of fifteen to eighteen thousand feet throughout most of time over target area and the three lead flights went down to altitudes ranging from six to ten thousand feet where enemy fighters appeared to be more numerous.

End of engagement - Combat ended over target area and slightly to northwest of target area. Our P-38's broke off combat without difficulty as enemy never appeared to want combat. Combat was broken off as bombers were already clear of target area and because gas supply was a little uncertain as this was first time over this target and the longest range mission yet attempted by P-38's in this area.

Evaluation of enemy - The enemy can not be admired for his actions in this combat. He appeared disorganized. He was unwilling to make head-on passes at our fighters and many of his action appeared to be purposeless. Perhaps too little warning of the Allied attack was the cause of this as many of the planes apparently never did get formed into flights. Gunnery appeared very poor but because of the few attacks attempted by the enemy an accurate evaluation could not be made. His split S is an effective evasive maneuvers when in combat with P-38's and good use was made of this evasive action.

Evaluation of own forces - It is believed by this squadron that best method of protecting bombers is to attack before enemy can start passes on bombers and by doing so disorganize and split up enemy attackers. This was briefly the method used by this squadron. It is believed that by doing this many fighters which might have made attacks on escorted bombers were kept from their objective. Attacks which might be made by the enemy under these conditions were found to be uncoordinated and generally ineffective.

OWN LOSSES:

Airplanes - 1 P-38 received what appeared to be a .50 cal. hole through right reserve gas tank.

Personnel - Nil.

ENEMY LOSSES: 5 Oscars and 2 Tonies were definitely destroyed and one Oscar and one Tony probably destroyed. Damage was inflicted on one Tony and six Oscars.

AMMUNITION EXPENDED: 6990 rds of .50 cal.
886 rds of 20 mm.

SIGHTINGS: Because of combat over target area sightings of bombing were very scanty. Pilots reported a huge fire burning on north side of Holland Strip with black smoke rising several thousand feet in the air. No other sightings were reported.

MALFUNCTIONING OF EQUIPMENT: Nil.

George C Ruke

ICR of Capt. J.T. Robbins (80FS) for 30 March 1944

80TH FIGHTER SQUADRON
8TH FIGHTER GROUP
APO 713
UNIT #1

30 March 1944

INDIVIDUAL COMBAT REPORT OF CAPTAIN JAY T. ROBBINS, O-504112.

A. Mission No. 391   80th Fighter Squadron   30 March 1944   23 P-38's.
B. Top cover for B-24's to Hollandia.
C. Over target area from 1030 to 1105 at 7,000 to 18,000 feet.
D. I took off at 0800 leading the squadron of 23 planes. We met the
   bombers just north of rendezvous point at 0930. There were no snafu's.
   We reached the target area around 1030 at 18,000 feet and I saw seven Jap
   fighters above and to my right. I called them in to Hades and Clover
   and dropped my tanks. The fighters (Oscars and Tonies) were just be-
   ginning to split S on the bombers. I got a direct tail shot at an
   Oscar, got hits as he half-rolled out of range. He was smoking slightly
   Then I went down through light ack-ack and drove off several Jap
   fighters. One dived and turned right and I had a 30 degree deflection
   from rear. I got numerous hits and he burst into flames and crashed.
   I made another pass down fairly low but the Oscar half-rolled away.
   I could see no results. Then I climbed with my flight back to 11/12,000
   feet into numerous Jap fighters. I got on one's tail. He half-rolled
   very far out of range. I made a very fast diving turn to left and
   got on his tail again and immediately he started a turn and half-rolled
   again. The Oscar was too low and crashed as he attempted to pull out
   of the dive. My altimeter read 2300 feet and I was about 300 feet
   above tree tops. My wingman saw him as he crashed. Then I climbed
   back to 7/8,000 feet and gradually gained altitude as we maneuvered for
   good passes. I made four passes in all. Most of the fighters were
   fairly low and NW of Hollandia strip on which numerous planes were
   burning. Left target area at 1105, landed Nadzab at 1315. I claim
   two definites; one probable.

                                        Jay T. Robbins
                                        JAY T. ROBBINS,
                                        Captain, Air Corps.

acquire intelligence for his unit to insure the success of a mission. After a mission, the IO would debrief the Flight Leaders and pilots making claims. A written report, the *Unit Narrative Combat Report*, would be submitted by the Mission Leader, which included:

1) Mission number and date
2) Designation of the Unit performing the mission and its base
3) Type and number of aircraft involved
4) Objective or Task of the mission
5) Times and Routes
6) Weather and Visibility
7) Air Combat
   a) Initial observation
   b) Number, position, formation of enemy planes
   c) Own altitude and formation (Relation to escorted aircraft, if applicable)
   d) Initial attack
   e) Objective (Own and enemies)
   f) Tactics (Own and enemies)
   g) End of engagement
   h) Evaluation of Enemy forces (characteristics and tactics of enemy aircraft and surface anti-aircraft units)
   i) Evaluation of own forces
   j) Casualties suffered and aircraft or equipment lost or damaged
8) Enemy casualties, enemy aircraft destroyed (damaged), and enemy surface material damaged, other than that listed in the objective of the mission
9) Ammunition and pyrotechnics expended and malfunction of equipment
10) Sightings of combat results in a brief chronological account of items of information obtained visually; of any photographs taken; of messages sent; of enemy aircraft observed or encountered; and of enemy surface anti-aircraft fire observed or encountered
   Signed (Mission or Flight Leader)"

Every participating pilot would submit his Individual Combat Report (ICR) to the IO. From early 1943, Army Air Force participants in air combat were required to complete an Individual Combat Report describing their involvement as per a standardized format:

General

Aircraft type and number; own position in formation; take off time.

   Mission assigned by order of Controller; course followed; rendezvous time and place; arrival time at target.

Approach

Own height when enemy first sighted; height of enemy; time; position of enemy relative to own; height at which combat began; number and positions of own fighter aircraft (and bombers, if present).

   Number, type, and formation of enemy aircraft seen or engaged (Give time, course, and altitude)

Combat Tactics

Orders by Control, formation leader, etc
   Type of attack made.
   Action taken by our formation: tactics, evasive action, use of cloud cover, etc.
   Action taken by enemy aircraft attacked and by enemy aircraft not attacked.
   Range at which fire opened; deflection shots, and duration of our fire in each attack (approximate length of bursts).
   Number and types of each enemy aircraft destroyed and probably destroyed, with details and witnesses.
   Estimation of own and enemy tactics

Miscellaneous
Observation of other friendly aircraft
Amount and type of enemy anti-aircraft fire
Positions of guns on enemy aircraft (caliber and type etc.) and effectiveness
Enemy camouflage and markings
Comments on ground control
Defects of own equipment
Weather, sightings (air, land, and sea)
Damage to own plane
Time combat ended, route home, time of landing
Criticisms and recommendations

Gun Camera

Although this stated policy for establishing claims gave pilots a set of stringent guidelines, it remained imperfect. In the heat of combat, excitement and fear stimulated the imagination and events tended to become confused, especially during multiple combats. The requirement to have a witness, usually a Wingman, see the claimed aircraft crash, burn, or break up in flight was not always strictly followed. A pilot might fire on an enemy aircraft and believe he saw evidence of hits or damage; his witness might see an aircraft crash and believe it to be the aircraft claimant fired upon. This often sufficed for verification, even if neither pilot had actually observed the aircraft continuously from damage to crash. In other cases, smoke rising from the jungle or "disturbances on the water" were accepted as adequate evidence of a crash. The utilization of the gun camera greatly aided in authenticating victory claims.

Morse Gunsight Aiming Point Camera (GSAP) Type An-6. (Author's Collection)

The camera gun, officially titled the Gunsight Aiming Point Camera (GSAP), was manufactured by the Fairchild Camera and Instrument Company of Jamaica, NY, and the Morse Instrument Company of Hudson, OH. The Type AN-N-4 and AN-N-6, Type AN-6N, and KB-3 16mm motion film gun camera body consisted of a shutter, motor, drive mechanism, a reset film footage indicator, and a Type A-6 film magazine containing 50 feet of film.

Two types of camera mounts were used in fighter aircraft: the early North American Aviation type and the later Type C-1 mount. On early fighter aircraft, the opening on the leading edge of the wing for the gun camera was covered by glass. On later fighters, the opening was sealed by a Spring-loaded metal plate that was actuated by a cable attached to the landing gear. The cable opened the plate when the gear was raised and closed the plate when the gear was lowered, which protected the camera from damage from

Fairchild Navy Gun Camera Magazine MG-1. (Author's Collection)

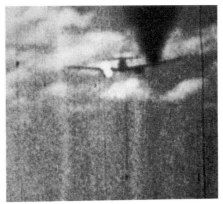

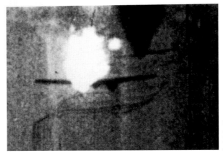

Gun Camera photo of a JAAF **Ki-46 Dinah** in the sights of a P-38. (AAF)

debris during takeoff and landing. Cameras used in turret guns were mounted directly on the gun or on a turret structure near the gun.

Before takeoff, a new film magazine was inserted into the camera by releasing the camera magazine access cover by pressing the knobs forward and pulling the cover open. The magazine was inserted with the film opening toward the lens and its footage indicator toward the side of the camera that was mounted toward the turret or guns. The magazine latch was pulled up as far as possible, then the access cover was closed. The footage indicator knob on the camera body was pushed in until the dial read "50," which was the number of feet of film available in a fresh magazine. After the camera had been used, the dial showed how many feet had been exposed during the mission. The lens and filter were to be kept clean. Dust was to be removed with a camel hair brush and the lens and filter cleaned with lens tissue or a clean dry lint-free cloth. A puff of breath could be used to moisten the lens or filter but never water, cleaning fluid, or alcohol.

The AN-N-6 camera had a built-in overrun mechanism, while the AN-N-4 camera had a separate overrun mechanism. The amount of overrun control could be set for the amount of time the camera would run after triggers were released. This time was usually determined by the combat theater or by special mission instructions. The plain lens consisted of an f/3.5 telephoto lens, a sunshade, and a No.12 minus blue interchangeable glass filter. The bore sight adapter focused the camera on the bullet convergence point. The electrically operated drive mechanism could be set

for 16, 32, or 64 frames per second. The diaphragm stops were marked "B" (Bright), "H" (Hazy), and "D" (Dull) to allow for various light conditions. Before takeoff, the diaphragm ring on the camera was preset for one of three types of lighting conditions (weather) expected on the mission. However, in practice, lighting conditions varied and the camera was unable to adjust and would often provide unclear footage that was either over- or under-exposed.

The camera switch on the control box was turned ON to activate the gun camera system. The guns and camera were controlled by a three-way toggle switch (GUNS, CAMERA, and SIGHT). When the trigger(s) was pressed, the guns fired and the cameras operated if the toggle was in the GUN position. The CAMERA and SIGHT positions on the toggle took motion pictures when the trigger was pressed but did not fire the guns. The camera was sighted by a boresighting adapter slightly below the gunsight line so that the camera remained on the target for a longer period after the pullout from the gunnery run. The camera could be set to stop operating as soon as the trigger was released, but it was usually set to continue to operate for three seconds after firing to show the fate of the intended target. With this extended running time, there would not be enough film available before all the ammunition was fired. So as not to waste film, the gunner would turn off the camera switch when he test fired the gun. When the gun switch was ON, self contained automatic heaters kept the camera mechanism warm.

After the combat film was processed, each unit did its own evaluation and would forward conclusive film and a written Encounter Report describing the combat, including the angle, distance, and duration of the gunfire, and describe observable hits to Group or Wing Headquarters.

Even the use of gun cameras did not make the claims system anywhere near perfect. Gun cameras were not in general use until late 1943, and then the availability of gun camera film was often the exception rather than the rule. Vibration from an aircraft's guns often made film useless, which was particularly common in the P-38. Also, the hot and humid environment of the tropics often ruined film. Moreover, claims were almost always verified by the claims system immediately after the mission, while gun camera film was not available for review until days later, and then camera evidence often proved inconclusive.

2

The Pacific "Ace Races"

Pacific Ace Race (USMC/USN/USAAF)

In a time when heroes were needed, the veneration of the air ace was a natural extension of the number one nation's personality. The fighter pilot, an all-American boy, fighting a gallant man-to-man war, became the new star to the American public, who were accustomed to coverage of the famous via the media of that time: newspapers, magazines, radio, and movie newsreels.

The Pacific Theater air race began on the first day of the war, when the Army Air Corps' 1Lt. George Welch of the 47th Pursuit Group quickly jumped into the lead by scoring four victories defending Pearl Harbor. Nine days later, on the other side of the Pacific, another AAC pilot, 1Lt. Boyd "Buzz" Wagner of the 17th Pursuit Group of the 5th Interceptor Command, became the first American ace when he destroyed a Japanese fighter taking off from a Philippines airdrome. Perhaps there were other victories and aces in these early days of the war, but they were lost in the general chaos and marginal communications of the time.

Early Pacific Aces

It was not until two months later, on 20 February 1942, that America's second ace appeared, one whose spectacular "instant ace" feat could be savored by the American public. Navy 1Lt. Edward "Butch" O'Hare was credited with saving the carrier *Lexington* by intercepting the determined attack of eight Japanese bombers and single-handedly downing five of them. In April, the handsome, modest O'Hare returned to the States a celebrated hero, whom the media pursued across the country as he traveled to Washington to receive the Medal of Honor. His Medal award was widely publicized in word and picture as his wife draped the ribbon around his neck in the presence of President Roosevelt. The hype surrounding O'Hare created the ace charisma that was to carry through the war.

It was only five days after O'Hare's victories, 24 February, that 1Lt. George Kiser of the 17PS tied Wagner and O'Hare with five victories. Subsequently, Kiser, flying P-40s over Java, destroyed three more enemy aircraft over the next two months to lead the ace race with eight.

"Buzz" Wagner, now a Major and Director of Fighters of the Fifth Fighter Command and flying P-39s out of Port Moresby, got three victories, his last of the war, on 30 April 1942, to tie Kiser with eight.

On 16 June, there was a new leader with nine victories: 2Lt. Andrew Jackson Reynolds of the 49FG. Reynolds, who had flown in George Kiser's unit over Java, was flying P-40s for the 9FS out of Darwin, Australia, when his squadron intercepted 27 bombers escorted by 15 Zeros. Leading his flight, Reynolds found the enemy 30 miles west over Point Charles at 23,000 feet. Making diving attacks, he hit the #1 and #3 bombers, setting them on fire, but only getting a "confirmed" on one. An errant bullet hit Reynolds's engine, damaging the lubricating and coolant systems, but Reynolds was able to make a crash landing on an auxiliary strip near Darwin.

The war and the ace race heated up as the Marines went ashore at Guadalcanal on 17 August 1942. There was no shortage of air targets for the beleaguered "Cactus Air Force," as it was dubbed, because Cactus was the code for Guadalcanal. The Japanese dispatched land-based bombers, escorted by fighters, from its Rabaul bastion, some 600 miles to the northwest. To meet the Japanese threat, Marine Squadron VMF-223 was launched from the carrier *Long Island* to reinforce Henderson Field, Guadalcanal, on 20 August. The group had recently exchanged its lacking F2A Brewster Buffalos for the chubby F4F Grumman Wildcat. The -223 CO, 27-year-old John L. Smith, was an "old" veteran, being a former Army artillery man-cum-dive bomber pilot. Smith, newly promoted to Major, was assessed (rightly so) as an ambitious, arrogant, and generally difficult individual. Joining Smith was an easy going Oregonian, Marion Carl, who had served with VMF-221 at Midway, where he scored his first victory, and Montanan 2Lt. Eugene Trowbridge. The Squadron had been at Henderson Field for less than 24 hours when they scrambled to meet six Zeros over Iron Bottom Sound. In the air battle, Smith got one Zero while Trowbridge got two confirmed. The next day, Trowbridge added another enemy to his total. On 24 August, VMF-223 got into the carrier battles between the *Saratoga* and *Enterprise* and the Japanese carrier *Ryujo*, which was escorting transport carrying reinforcements. In the skirmish, Carl got two Kate bombers and two Zeros to make him the Marine Corps' first ace. Trowbridge got two Japanese (unconfirmed) to become an ace. In the next 15 days, Carl got eight more victories to become the war's first double ace, totaling 13. During this time, both Smith and Trowbridge became double aces with ten victories each. The big day in this period was 30 August, when 18 experienced Japanese Naval pilots from the carriers *Shokaku* and *Zuikaku* headed toward Cactus. The scrambled Wildcats gained the altitude advantage on the Hamps, enabling Smith to shoot down four, while Carl got three. The good hunting continued for Smith for four days from 10-13 September, as he got four bombers and a fighter to put him in the ace race lead with a triple ace total of 16. Marion Carl was shot down on 9 September, when an unnoticed Zero

Early Pacific Aces

2Lt. Andrew Reynolds of the 49FG became the new scoring leader with nine victories while flying over Darwin. (AFAA)

1Lt. Boyd "Buzz" Wagner, of the 17th Pursuit Group, became the first American ace when he destroyed a Japanese fighter taking off from a Philippines airdrome. (AFAA)

1Lt. George Welch of the 47th Pursuit Group quickly jumped into the scoring lead by scoring four victories defending Pearl Harbor. (AFAA)

1Lt. George Kiser of the 17PS tied Wagner and O'Hare with five victories and subsequently Kiser destroyed three more enemy aircraft over the next two months over Java to lead the ace race with eight. (AFAA)

1Lt. Edward "Butch" O'Hare was credited with saving the carrier *Lexington* by intercepting the determined attack of eight Japanese bombers and single-handedly downing five of them. (AFAA)

set his F4F on fire and forced him to bail out. Carl missed five days of combat getting back to base, and in the process allowed Smith to gain the lead. When Brig.Gen. Roy Geiger was told that Carl was safe, he asked to meet the young ace. During the meeting, in jest, Geiger informed Carl that Smith now had 16 victories to his 13 and asked, "What are you going to do about that?" Without hesitation Carl replied, "Damn it, General, ground Smitty for five days." But Carl was never able to catch Smith, even though Smith, too, was shot down. On 2 September, Smith was bounced by three Zeros. He managed to flame one, but the odds forced Smith to make a forced dead stick landing. After months of difficult times on the ground and in the air, the final ace standing was: Smith 19, Carl 15½. Carl subsequently returned to combat in December 1943, flying F4U Corsairs over New Britain

and adding three more victories. When VMF-223 was rotated out of combat in mid-October from Guadalcanal, only six of the original twenty pilots who left Hawaii in July remained. Upon their departure on 12 October, the Squadron claimed 110 victories, including 47 Zeros. Smith and Carl, with eight and ten bomber victories, respectively, shot down more multi-engine bombers than any other Marine pilots. The VMF-223 roster showed eight aces in its ranks. Smith was awarded the Medal of Honor for his tactical skill and leadership qualities.

VMF-223 was replaced by VMF-121, which was commanded by Maj. "Duke" Davis and his XO, another old man at 27 years old named Joseph Jacob Foss, who was to succeed Smith as the top ace. The initial meeting between Smith and the 20 new pilots of VMF-121 was inauspicious, to say

USMC Captains **John Smith** (L) and **Marion Carl** (R) (with VMBS-232 CO Maj. Richard Mangrum) battled each other for the top Pacific ace lead while flying F4F Wildcats for VMF-223 over Guadalcanal. (AFAA)

USMC **Capt. Joseph Foss**, CO of VMF-121, broke Rickenbacker's record of 26 victories flying F4Fs over Guadalcanal and would remain the top ace for 15 months. (AFAA)

the least. The ever-sardonic Smith met the group as they landed at Henderson and sarcastically apprised them that they had landed at the wrong field, and that "The Marine fighter strip was over there." So VMF-121, which would become the top Marine unit of the war, humbly got back into their Wildcats and flew another three-quarter mile to begin their war.

The scope of the Pacific war had narrowed to Guadalcanal and the media people had congregated there. It was easier to interview a flier over a beer in the relative comfort of Henderson Field behind the lines than to brave the dangers and discomforts of a fox-

hole. Besides, fliers made good copy, as generally they were intelligent, loquacious, and exuded an aura of dash and bravura. The affable Foss, a graduate of the state university of his native South Dakota, definitely made good copy, but his skills in the F4F Wildcat spoke for him. He shot down 26 Japanese aircraft, 20 of which were the maneuverable Zero, which was still flown by experienced pilots. His rapid assault on Eddie Rickenbacker's WWI American record of 26 enemies (which included five balloons, two tethered) destroyed took only three months, and the record, once toppled, made Foss a national hero. The mission earned Foss the nickname "Swivel Neck Joe"; Foss learned the hard way that a fighter pilot must constantly look out for bounces. Foss became an ace in less than a week when he got two Zeros and a bomber on 18 October. His biggest months and the record once toppled made Foss a national hero. A marksman from his hunting days

as a farm boy carried over to his aerial gunnery expertise, both as an instructor at Pensacola and as a fighter pilot. Foss's first 23 victories were compressed into 33 days, scoring daily victories at first, then scoring multiple daily victories seven times during his first tour. He also crash landed six times, but credited the rugged F4F and his protecting Wingman, Lt. Thomas Furlow, for his survival.

Foss's first sortie was almost his last. During the afternoon of 30 October, while leading three divisions of Wildcats against 15 incoming Betty bombers, Foss suddenly found himself left alone when his fellow VMF-121 pilots dove to evade Jap Zeros diving from above. The first eager Zero pilot overshot Foss and presented himself as an easy target as Foss's first victory. In the battle, Foss's P&W engine was hit and lost oil, causing Foss to sweat out reaching Henderson safely. His best scoring days came on the 23rd, when he downed four Zeros, and on the 25th, when he became the first Marine Corps pilot to become an ace in a day. On the 25th, on his morning mission, as his flight was climbing after takeoff, it was bounced by diving Zeros. By skilful flying the Marines escaped and Foss got two Zeros. On his afternoon mission, he got three more Japanese, giving him five victories for the day and 16 in 13 days. On 7 November, he downed a Zero and two float planes covering a Japanese convoy 120 miles NW of Henderson. These victories tied Foss with John Smith for top gun in the Pacific with 19. But the celebration had to wait, as Foss ran out of gas while getting lost in a thunder squall. He ditched off Malaita and spent the night with a coast watcher before boarding a PBY bound for Cactus the next morning.

On 12 November, the Japanese made earnest attempts to bloody the American reinforcement of Guadalcanal by Adm. Kelly Turner's troop transports. Flying CAP at 29,000 feet, Foss and six other VMF-121 pilots spotted approximately 20 torpedo-carrying Bettys running in on Turner's vulnerable transports which were unloading off Kukum Point. Going into power dives from their high altitude, Foss's men found their windscreens frosted over. To make matters worse for Foss, the increased pressure of his dive blew his canopy off. The Bettys were closing on the transports and the Wildcats, abetted by some Army P-400s, were desperately trying to catch them from astern. Wind howling around him, Foss fired within 100 yards of a bomber, hitting its starboard engine and causing it to crash into the sea. The determined American pilots disrupted the Japanese attack and little damage was done to the transports. While chasing a fleeing bomber, Foss was bounced by a Zero. He quickly turned into the attack and the surprised Jap became the victim of an expert snap deflection shot. Foss returned to the fray, flaming his previous interrupted target. This three-victory mission made Foss the first American to score 20 victories in the war. The next day, he got a "Pete" float plane for victim #23. As were most VMF-121 personnel, Foss was racked by malaria and dysentery, dropping his weight from 197 to 160lbs. The squadron was sent on a well-earned R&R to New Caledonia and Sydney.

Upon recuperating Foss, three victories short of Rickenbacker's 26, returned to a secured Guadalcanal; the crisis had passed and the American Air Forces would become hunters. During the afternoon of 3 January 1943, Foss's outfit and a few Army P-39s escorted Dauntless dive bombers that were to finish off a Japanese destroyer force near New Georgia. Upon approaching the enemy warships, three Wildcats led by William Morontate dove on Zeros which were on CAP while Foss and three others circled at altitude. The air battle moved upwards as Foss fired a short burst, missing a fleeing Zero. He turned to help 2Lt. Oscar Bate shake some Zeros off his tail. As Foss turned, a Jap fighter dove in front of him and was dispatched in an explosion as Foss's .50 caliber bullets hit. Quickly, another Zero following on the tail of another Wildcat dove in front of Foss, who snapped off a few hasty but highly effective rounds, sending the enemy into a flaming spin. Bate's persistent attacker was only a 100 yards astern, lining up a fatal firing run. Foss dove and began desperately firing at the Zero at long

1Lt. Richard Bong being presented the DSC for his 16th victory on 26 August, when he shot down four Japanese fighters. (AFAA)

Maj. Thomas Lynch, CO of the 39FS, would mentor newcomer Bong, and the two would form the "Flying Circus" duo, but Lynch's career was cut short when he was KIA with 20 victories. (AFAA)

USMC **Capt. Gregory "Pappy" Boyington** scored 22 victories (plus a questionable three with the AVG) before being shot down and made a POW on 3 January 1944, while shooting down his last enemy aircraft (which was not credited then) to tie Rickenbacker's record. (AFAA)

range, persuading its pilot to break off his attack on Bate. The Zero then pulled up and came head-on at Foss. Both pilots fired and missed, passed each other, and both again turned into each other, with Foss above and the Jap below. Both adversaries were on a nerve racking head-on firing run when the Jap gave in and broke right, allowing Foss to put machine gun rounds into his cockpit area. The tenacious Jap broke into a dive, circling back toward Foss, who was being menaced by approaching Zeros. Foss broke off and headed for the safety of nearby clouds. Just as he entered the clouds, Foss saw his wounded Jap burst into flames and head down. Foss had gotten his 26th victory to tie Rickenbacker's record of 25 years.

On 26 January 1943, VMF-121 left Guadalcanal and flew to New Zealand, where the Squadron sailed for America on 25 March and landed in San Diego on 19 April. On the long voyage home, Foss almost died of his ongoing malaria and was in poor physical condition to meet the hectic schedule awaiting him. After initial appearances in Washington and New York, the Marine Corps had scheduled a nationwide tour for him. The exhausting, well-publicized tour was interrupted by a visit to his Sioux Falls home and on 18 May, by the presentation of the Medal of Honor. Accompanied by his mother and wife, June, Foss was personally awarded

the Medal by FDR—twice, in fact, so all the photographers could get their pictures. The frantic agenda continued, as Foss was to remain the top American ace for nearly 15 months. But even before the Marine Wildcats left the Solomons, new and superior American fighters were appearing over the Pacific battlefronts. The Army Air Force's twin-boomed Lockheed P-38 Lightning had arrived in the Solomons and New Guinea. It would not be too long before Foss would be reading in his morning newspaper of the exploits of such new aces as Tommy Lynch, Neel Kearby, and a young, unassuming Wisconsin farm boy named Richard Ira Bong.

P-38s were shipped to the SWPA in late Summer 1942, but numerous mechanical problems postponed their entry into combat. Finally, at mid-day on 27 December 1942, 12 P-38s of the 39FS under Capt. Thomas Lynch left 14 Mile Drome, New Guinea, to meet a formation of more than two dozen Japanese bombers and escorts heading toward Buna Mission. Lynch destroyed two Ki-43 Oscar escorts to become an ace after previously bagging three Zeros while flying the P-400 in May 1942, over New Guinea. Also scoring a double that day was Dick Bong, who was on temporary duty from the 9FS. Thus began another ace derby, but one which appeared as though it might be rather one-sided. On 31 December, Bong fired on six Japanese aircraft, gaining only one "probable" while expending a large amount of ammunition. Bong became an ace during an anti-shipping attack on Lae Harbor on 8 January 1943, when he splashed an Oscar in a diving attack. During this time, Bong flew on Lynch's wing and the two developed a close friendship; their rivalry was based on that friendship. Lynch excelled as a combat pilot and leader and was genuinely admired by his men. Bong, while on the ground, was modest and reserved, but was a Mr. Hyde in the air. He came to the Pacific with a flying attitude which bordered on undisciplined, but Lynch's influence put restraints on Bong's enthusiasm and directed them into life preserving aerial tactics.

The next combat for the two occurred in March, when the group escorted B-17s against well-protected Japanese shipping in Huon Harbor. By mid-April, Bong surpassed Lynch in victories, with Bong scoring his tenth victory to become the AAF's first double ace in the Pacific and leading Lynch by one. But Lynch went ahead again on 10 June—11 to 10—by downing a bomber. Then Bong tied him two days later, when he got an Oscar. On 26 August, Bong had his biggest single day of his career when he encountered 20 enemy fighters over Markham Valley, south of Lae. In 20 minutes Bong had downed two Tonys and two Zeros to total 16 victories, collecting a few bullet holes in his Lightning and the DSC.

In 17 days in January 1944, in only six missions, **1Lt. Robert Hanson** tallied an incredible 20 Japanese aircraft to threaten Foss, Bong, and Rickenbacker, but was KIA on 26 January with 25 victories. (AFAA)

Bong went on leave to Brisbane, Australia, in August. When he returned, his missions in September were unproductive and his victory total remained at 16. Meanwhile Lynch, losing weight and becoming exhausted from the effects of Dengue Fever, managed to score five separate single daily victories to creep into a tie with Bong, but was sent back to his Pennsylvania home and wife, Rosemary, to recuperate. The long leave put him out of the ace race for the time being, as he did not return to combat until early January 1944. While Lynch was gone Bong found slim pickings and only scored five victories, increasng his total to 21. This total made him America's third ranking ace behind the Marine Corp's Foss with 26 and Gregory "Pappy" Boyington with 25. There is some controversy over Boyington's career total, as during his tour with the AVG (Flying Tigers), he was credited with six victories which were included in his later totals. But later inquiries found that four of the victories were gained by strafing and destroying ground targets, which were accepted and given bonuses by Chennault as victories.

Bong was also sent on the States on leave, so both of America's active leading aces were on the home front. Bong did extensive PR work, which was well covered by the media. While back home in Poplar, Wisconsin, Bong was asked to crown the Homecoming Queen of Wisconsin State Teacher's College and afterward met Marjorie Vattendahl, and it was love at first sight. When he returned to combat, the infatuated Bong's P-38 would bear the name Marge.

During the months that Lynch and Bong were gone, a Marine Lieutenant born in India of missionary parents would make one of the most spectacular and concentrated victory runs of the war which would him earn his nickname, "Butcher Bob." In 17 days in January 1944, in only six missions, 1Lt. Robert Hanson tallied an incredible 20 Japanese aircraft to threaten Foss, Bong, and Rickenbacker. After Pearl Harbor, Hanson left Hamline College in Minnesota to enter Navy flight training in May 1942 and earned his wings in mid-February 1943. In June, he was flying F4U Corsairs for Marine Squadron VMF-215 in the northern Solomons and was credited with only five victories in his first two combat tours in 1943.

On 1 November 1943, the American landings on Bougainville were taking place and Hanson was flying CAP for Lt.Col. Herbert Williamson's VMF-215. He spotted six torpedo-carrying Kates heading low over Empress Augusta Bay toward the American fleet. Hanson dove through the enemy formation, knocking down two and breaking up the attack. A Japanese rear gunner hit Hanson's Corsair, forcing him to ditch, and the Marine spent several hours floating on a life raft before a destroyer picked him up.

Hanson's next big day occurred on 14 January 1944, when he and his Wingman, 2Lt. Richard Bowman, were escorting Navy TBF Avenger torpedo bombers over Simpson Harbor, Rabaul. Spotting 60-70 Japanese Zeros, Hanson's group went into a swirling, cloud-to-cloud dogfight. Hanson became separated from Bowman and got five enemy fighters in the clash, making him a double ace and earning him the sobriquet, "Master of Individual Combat." On his next two sorties over Rabaul, on 20 and 22 January, he got one and three victories, respectively, to total 14. On the 24th, he again became separated from his squadron and was surrounded by Zeros. Aggressive tactics saved his life and added four more victories and a probable to his total. On the 26th, he got three, and on the 30th four more to give him 25 victories—20 over Rabaul.

On 3 January, the day before his 24th birthday and near the end of his tour, Hanson took off on an escort and strafing mission on New Ireland, north of Rabaul. On a strafing run on gun emplacements on Cape St. George, ground fire apparently killed him, as his guns were seen to have ceased firing. His Corsair, with 25 Jap flags under its cockpit, crossed the target area and slowly lost altitude and crashed into the sea. On 24 January, Maj. Gen. Lewis Merritt presented the Medal of Honor to Hanson's mother for his actions on 1 November 1943. Hanson was the third Corsair pilot to win the MOH (with Gregory Boyington and Kenneth Walsh) and was the top-scoring Corsair pilot (followed by Boyington with 22, Walsh 21, and Donald Aldrich 20).

Hanson was not the only pilot to take advantage of Bong and Lynch during their R&R. A 32-year-old Texan, Col. Neel Kearby, CO of the 348 FG, ran his total up to 20 victories in four months. The 348th, a P-47 Thunderbolt group, was slated to go to Europe, but Gen. George Kenney, Commander of the 5th Air Force, used his influence to divert them to his command. The seven-ton P-47 was an unproven entity in the Pacific, being considered too big and heavy to successfully engage the light and maneuverable Japanese aircraft. It was fitted with the most powerful aircraft engine in the world, the 2,000hp Pratt & Whitney R-2800 radial, which gave it a high operational ceiling and a great diving speed. Its rugged construction and

Col. Neel Kearby, CO of the 348 FG, ran his total up to 20 victories in four months, but on 5 March 1944, while shooting down a Nell bomber, Kearby neglected to watch his tail and was shot down by an Oscar. Kearby's victory total ended at 22. (AFAA)

On 12 April 1944, **Capt. Richard Bong** became the first pilot to surpass Rickenbacker's record when he shot down two Oscars to give him 27 victories. (AAF)

Rickenbacker and **Bong** meeting before Bong broke the WWI American record. (AFAA)

heavy armament could be used to advantage, but the P-38 remained the favorite fighter in the theater. The 348ᵗʰ shared Dobodura airfield with the 9FS and their P-38s, where constant speculation and arguments broke out over the relative merits of each aircraft. Shortly before Bong went on leave, Kearby scheduled several mock dogfights, pitting his P-47s against the seasoned P-38 pilots. While the initial results in mock combat went to the experienced Kearby and the P-47, in combat the overall results were mixed, perhaps with the edge going to the P-38.

On 1 October 1943, Kearby distinguished himself and the P-47 by destroying six Japanese aircraft in one mission. Flying Fiery Ginger in a sweep over Jap airfields at Borum, Kearby destroyed two Zekes, two Tonys, and two Haps. These victories, added to his previous three, made him an ace and more. For this action Kearby was awarded the Medal of Honor, which he personally received from Gen. MacArthur in Brisbane, Australia, on 24 January 1944. By that time, despite heavy staff duties at 5AF HQ, he had achieved 21 victories to tie Bong. When Kenney queried Kearby on his combat ambitions, the ace had set 50 victories as his goal. On 5 March, while shooting down a Nell bomber, Kearby neglected to watch his tail and was shot down by an Oscar. Kearby's victory total ended at 22 to supposedly tie Bong, but Kearby never knew that Bong had scored two victories two days previously to bring his total to 24.

Throughout the years, accusations of favoritism have arisen concerning Gen. Kenney's treatment of Bong. Kenney's sugary biography *Dick Bong, Ace of Aces*, written in 1960, tends to confirm these allegations, as did the 5AF Commander's book, *General Kenney Reports* (1949), which is filled with references to the Bong-Lynch-Kearby and later Bong-McGuire ace races. For example, in December 1942, Kenney commented to Brig.Gen. Whitehead: "Watch that boy Bong. There is the top American ace of aces of this war. He just started to work today." Kenney went so far as to have a diver confirm Bong's "probable" of 12 April 1944, which had gone into the water off Hollandia. This victory was an Oscar, which gave him victory #28 of his triple victory day when Kenney's "tow-headed cherub" broke Rickenbacker's record. Kenney also had an evident fondness for "Tommy" Lynch, but a neutrality toward the hard working, business-like Kearby. When Lynch and Bong returned to combat, Kenney had his three top aces (Bong, Lynch, and Kearby) assigned to the 5ᵗʰ Fighter Command in HQ positions. Kenney allowed Lynch and Bong to fly as a duo, which they christened the "Flying Circus." Unlike Kearby, their desk work was limited and they were allowed to fly missions at their discretion. They could accompany other squadrons on bomber escort missions or fly sweeps as a team. They were assigned personal P-38s stripped down for combat. Kenney

was very PR conscious, as he felt the Pacific Army Air Forces were being treated as the war's stepchild when compared to the 8AF in Europe. He gave both Lynch and Bong free rein so that their victory totals would keep his Command in the pubic eye. This was especially evident as Rickenbacker's record was coming into reach. The "Flying Circus" scored its first victory on 10 February on a sweep of Tadji airfields, when Lynch got a Lily bomber. The two aces continued to score victories, with Bong closing in on Rickenbacker with 24 and Lynch with 20.

As discussed previously, by March 1944, Kearby had 22 kills to his credit and on 5 March 1944, Kearby and two other pilots attacked a formation of 15 Japanese aircraft near Wcwak. After shooting down one of the aircraft, Kearby was shot down by an Oscar and escaped by parachute, but died of his wounds.

After celebrating Lynch's promotion to light Colonel the previous evening, the morning of 8 March saw the two pilots sweep the New Guinea coast, looking for targets. While strafing luggers and barges, Lynch's P-38 was hit by small arms fire at wave-top level. With the aircraft's nose damaged and the right engine on fire, Lynch attempted to bail out at 100 feet, but his parachute failed to open completely and he fell to his death. In three days, Kenney had lost two-thirds (Lynch and Kearby) of his ace race. After the death of two of "his boys," Kenney ordered Bong to Australia to ferry a new P-38 back to New Guinea, but more importantly, to compose himself, but Bong flew eight more missions before obeying the order at the end of March.

Returning to combat on 3 April, Bong got an Oscar in two firing passes over Sentani Lake to give him his 25ᵗʰ victory. Joe Foss and Pappy Boyington were tied with Rickenbacker with 26. Again, Boyington had 20 victories with the USMC and six with the AVG (later downgraded down to two). Boyington's three victories on 3 January 1944 were not known at this time, as both he and his Wingman were shot down and confirmation would not be made until after the war, when Boyington was released from a Japanese POW camp in Japan.

Earlier in the war, on a visit to the 5AF, Rickenbacker promised a case of whiskey to the first pilot to break his record, but now Bong, a non-drinker, was the only challenger. On 12 April, 20 P-38s of the crack 80FS "Headhunters" were flying escort for B-24s over Hollandia. Flying without a Wingman and freelancing like the pilots of WWI, Bong attached himself to Capt. C.M. Smith's Flight as a "tail end Charlie." Bong was flying a loaner aircraft, *Down Beat*, when his flight arrived over the target area at 1145 and was intercepted by 12 to 15 Jap fighters in groups of three or four. In the next 45 minutes, Bong destroyed three Oscars to give him the record. He knew

Navy Ace Gallery

Lt. Stanley Vejtasa of VF-10 was the high scorer for the Navy at the end of January 1944 with only 10¼ victories, and he scored seven of these victories in one day, way back on 26 October 1942. (USN)

In 24 days, **Ens. Ira Kepford** would score 12 victories, and after he scored 16 victories he was shipped back to the States as the Navy's leading ace. (AFAA)

Lt. Alexander Vraciu of VF-16 ended his Navy career by briefly leading the USN scorers with 19 victories, including 10 during the "Marianas Turkey Shoot". (AFAA)

Cdr. David McCampbell, AGC of VF-15, would score nine victories during the Turkey Shoot; this gave him 30 to tie him briefly with Bong for the victory lead in the Pacific. (AFAA)

speeches, and attending breakfasts, luncheons, and dinners. Also during the time Bong, a self-confessed poor shot (27 victories in 25 combats, indicating few multiple victories), attended gunnery school. The leave time was made easier by his visits with his family and his engagement to Marge. During this time, Bong feared he, like Foss, would be pulled from combat forever. But at gunnery school Bong heard of Kenney's intention to have him learn and then serve as a gunnery instructor, and as an "observer" in combat areas he would be allowed only to shoot in "self defense."

At the time Bong broke the record the next challenger, a Navy flier, had not yet flown a mission! In fact, for naval aviators, the opportunities to score against the Japanese had been scarce. The large, early naval battles at Midway and the Coral Sea, unlike the later great battles, did not pit vast numbers of aircraft against aircraft. During the Guadalcanal Campaign, the Navy needed to be prudent in exposing its few remaining carriers and their aircraft to superior Japanese forces. The Navy's high scorer at the end of January 1944 was Lt. Stanley Vejtasa of VF-10 with only 10¼ victories, and he scored seven of these victories on one day way back on 26 October 1942, during the Battle of Santa Cruz. He was the first of six aces to score seven or more victories in one day. Flying a Wildcat for VF-10 (the "Grim Reapers") off the carrier *Enterprise*, Vejtasa joined his CO, the redoubtable Jim Flatley, on CAP when a large wave of Japanese torpedo bombers attacked the U.S. fleet. In the battle, Vejtasa destroyed two Aichi Val dive bombers and five Nakajima Kate torpedo bombers. Previously, Vejtasa had three victories while flying a Dauntless dive bomber and these victories made him the leading Navy ace for 15 months.

It was not until early 1944 that Vejtasa's total was challenged. In October 1943, VF-17—called "Blackburn's Irregulars" after their Commander, Tommy Blackburn—landed their F4U Corsairs at Ondonga, New Georgia. Their assignment was to protect Navy shipping and attack enemy land and maritime targets. On 11 November 1943, Ens. Ira Kepford was flying top cover for a task force that included two carriers, the *Essex* and *Bunker Hill*.

he had several eyewitness confirmations of at least two of the victories, but became worried upon landing when he found he had set his gun cameras wrong. By the next morning, two official confirmations were received, with the third Oscar listed as a "probable" (later confirmed as downed by the diver Kenney dispatched). Kenney immediately promoted Bong to Major and also grounded him to be sent back to the States as a celebrity being heralded in the newspapers, radio, and newsreels. Much of Bong's five-month leave was filled with public relations and war bond sales appearances. He flew a P-38 over towns and cities, meeting dignitaries, making uncomfortable

By October 1944, **Capt. Thomas McGuire** (L) of the 475FG would be seven victories (21 to 28) behind **Bong** (R), who had just returned to combat. (AFAA)

Maj. Thomas McGuire's officer's cap, the same one worn in the photo taken with Maj. Bong.

McGuire's beat up officer's dress hat as displayed at the National Museum of the USAF. (NMUSAF)

A mixed group of 30 Japanese dive and torpedo bombers attacked the carriers in Empress Augusta Bay, off Bougainville, in the Solomons. Diving through intense AA fire, Kepford destroyed three Vals and a Kate and damaged another to win the Navy Cross. It was not until 27 January 1944 that he became an ace when he got two Zeros on an escort mission to Tobaro Airbase, Rabaul. In the next 24 days, Kepford would score 12 victories, including four on his next mission on 29 January. After Kepford scored 16 quick victories he was shipped back to the States as the Navy's leading ace.

The Navy's next top ace was Lt. Alexander Vraciu—the son of Rumanian immigrants—who gained his first victory on 5 October 1943, during the raid on Wake Island. He was an Element Leader in one-time leading Navy ace Butch O'Hare's Fighting Six when he got a Zero. The carrier raids on the Gilberts in November and Kwajalein in January 1944 netted him four Betty bombers to make him an ace. The carrier strike on the Carolines on 17 February got him four more victories to give him nine. VF-6 headed home, but Vraciu managed to transfer to VF-16, aboard the *Lexington*. He scored three victories before his biggest career day during the "Great Mariana's Turkey Shoot" on 19 June 1944. That day, he destroyed six Judy dive bombers in eight minutes. The next afternoon, he claimed a Zeke for his 19th and last victory to lead Navy pilots in victories.

During the "Turkey Shoot," when Vraciu scored his six, another Navy pilot got seven; Cdr. David McCampbell, another "old man" at 34. The Annapolis graduate from Alabama was the AGC of VF-15 on the carrier *Essex*. The "Fabled 15" was to be in combat for five months (mid-June to mid-November 1944), participating in the greatest air-sea battles in history: the Battle of the Philippines Sea (Turkey Shoot) and Battle of Leyte Gulf. In these massive air battles, McCampbell was able to grab victories in large chunks. During two missions during the Turkey Shoot, 19 June, he destroyed five Judys in the morning and then got two Zekes in the afternoon to make him an ace with nine victories. On 12 September he got four, and the next day he got three; by the 24th he had tied Vraciu with 19.

The evening of 24 October 1944 would see the end of the greatest victory in naval aviation history: a total of 270 Japanese aircraft had been destroyed and nine Navy fliers had scored five or more victories in a single day. One of these aces in a day was McCampbell, who was the only American to accomplish this feat twice (the Luftwaffe's August Lambert scored 17, 14, and 12 victories in single-day missions). During the battle, he would get credit for five Zekes, two Oscars, two Hamps, and two probables, while his Wingman, Roy Rushing, would get six. These nine victories would give

McCampbell 30, tying him with Bong. Since so many victories came so fast for McCampbell, and since Bong regained the lead three days later, the tie was never publicized and it is virtually unknown even today. In November, McCampbell got four more victories to give him a career 34 and the Medal of Honor, but Bong had 36 at the time and McCampbell was headed back to the States. In any event, the press which created and perpetuated the ace race became more interested in a new, brash, and self-proclaimed pretender to Bong's title: Capt. Thomas McGuire of the 475FG/5AF.

While Bong was on his five-month leave from April to October 1944, McGuire, whose trademark was his old, beat up officer's dress hat, was closing in on Bong's 28 with 21 of his own. McGuire made his intentions known that he was out to pass Bong. McGuire's flying skills were unquestioned, but his contemporaries almost unanimously disliked the man. He was variously described by his Squadron mates as "a pain in the ass," "self centered," "abrasive," "constantly pulling rank," "certainly no intellectual," and "constantly running off at the mouth."

When Bong returned to the Pacific, he continued to fly "observation missions" to oversee results of his gunnery lectures to his students in combat. In "self defense" he managed to shoot down enough Japanese to always keep McGuire's total about eight to ten behind:

Month	Bong*	McGuire*
October 1944	5 (33)	3 (24)
November 1944	3 (36)	3 (27)
December 1944	4 (40)	3 (30)

*Monthly victories and (total victories)

Bong flew only nine missions in November and December, as Kenney was afraid he would lose his Ace of Aces. On 28 November, Capt. John Davis, while flying Bong's P-38, had its engine catch fire and crash on take off, killing Davis. At first it was thought Bong was in the aircraft, but the incident caused Kenney to resolve to remove Bong from combat after his 40th victory.

As McGuire often publicly asserted his intention to pass Bong, it was surprising that Bong chose McGuire's 431FG as his next combat assignment, then chose to room with McGuire! On 7 December, McGuire was leading a flight over Ormoc Bay in which Bong was leading the second Element. McGuire came back with two victories, but gained no ground on Bong, who matched him. On 12 December, Bong was away receiving the Medal of Honor from MacArthur and McGuire narrowed Bong's lead to eight with a victory over a Jack fighter on the 13th, but Bong returned to down an Oscar on the 15th.

On the 17th, Bong logged his 40th and last victory. He left Dulag airstrip at 1450, climbing to 9,000 feet while leading a sweep over the Mindoro beachhead. At 1615, he spotted two incoming Oscars at 12 o'clock and dropped his auxiliary fuel tanks to climb towards the enemy, who were fleeing north toward home. The chase lasted ten minutes, as Bong closed astern on the frantically evading Oscar. Bong fired and flamed the enemy fighter, which crashed into the jungle. Kenney immediately ordered Bong to go off operations. On 29 December, he boarded an Air Transport Command C-54, heading home for marriage and a career as a jet test pilot. McGuire was now the leading active ace with 32 victories and needing nine more victories to become America's Ace of Aces.

Now unopposed and no longer frustrated by matching victories, McGuire became almost obsessed with the record. On Christmas morning, McGuire led a volunteer mission escorting B-24s that were to bomb Malacat. McGuire got three Zeros before his guns malfunctioned, and despite being virtually defenseless, the frustrated McGuire continued to attack enemy fighters, supposedly "forcing them into his Wingman's line of fire." The next day, he volunteered again for a B-24 escort mission over Clark Field. He lured three Zeros off a crippled B-24 and with remarkable flying skill and marksmanship he got two to run his score to 38. Kenney did not want Bong to be second before reaching America and ordered McGuire not to fly any more missions until further notified that Bong had arrived in the States and completed the planned ceremonies to honor him as the Ace of Aces. The impatient McGuire, beset with malaria and incipient battle fatigue, was forced to remain inactive until 7 January, when Kenney lifted the ban. As

PR photo of top ETO ace **Capt. Robert Johnson** (L) seen with AAF Chief **Hap Arnold** (C) and **Richard Bong** (R). (AAF)

soon as possible, McGuire led a four-ship Element from Dulag in marginal weather for a sweep over Japanese airfields at Fabrica and Manapla, on the Los Negros Islands. Flying under the low overcast at 1,400 feet, McGuire's Wingman, Capt. Edwin Weaver, spotted a solitary Ki-84 Oscar below the P-38s returning to Fabrica. McGuire pulled around, but the experienced Jap pilot turned into the American formation. The Oscar fired on McGuire's #3 man, Lt. Douglas Thropp. McGuire ordered the unit not to release their drop tanks, a violation of combat doctrine for the situation. Perhaps McGuire felt he could score an easy victory over the lone Oscar and save fuel to resume further combat. The aggressive Oscar continued his concerted attack, closing in on the inexperienced Weaver. McGuire turned to catch the enemy, putting his Lightning on the verge of a stall to help his Wingman. The added stress on the wing tanks caused the P-38 to go into a full stall, snap rolling and inverting at 200 feet and diving into the jungle. At 0708, 7 January 1945, the American WWII Ace Race was over, marked by a huge fireball in the Philippine jungle and several footnotes. (A very detailed account of McGuire's last mission can be found in Volume 2). There were no serious challengers in Europe, as they were either rotated home (Johnson) or made POWs (Gabreski). The Luftwaffe posed no threat and gave the American replacements no opportunity to run up any substantial scores. In the Pacific, the Japanese air forces had expended their front line pilots and fighters, and only the Kamikazes over Okinawa would provide targets, but not in sufficient numbers. David McCampbell flew no further combat. Dick Bong married Marge on 10 February 1945 and was killed testing the P-80 jet fighter on 6 August 1945, the day of the dropping of the atomic bomb on Hiroshima. Thomas McGuire was awarded the Medal of Honor posthumously on 7 March 1945.

Pacific Ace Race Chronology

Victory #	Pilot Name and Rank	A/C	Service	Unit	Date
1-4	**Welch, 2Lt. George**	P-40	USAAC	47PS	12/7/41
5	**Wagner, 1Lt. Boyd**	P-40	USAAC	17PS	12/16/41
5	**O'Hare, Lt. Edward**	F4F	USN	VF-3	2/20/42
5	**Kiser, 1Lt. George**	P-40	USAAC	17PS	2/24/42
6-8	**Kiser, 1Lt. George**	P-40	USAAC	17PS	4/27/42

8	Wagner, Maj. Boyd	P-39	USAAC	5FC	4/30/42
9	Reynolds, 2Lt. Andrew	P-40	USAAC	9FS	7/30/42
9-11	Carl, Capt. Marion	F4F	USMC	VMF-223	8/30/42
12-13	Carl, Capt. Marion	F4F	USMC	VMF-223	9/9/42
13-14	Smith, Maj. John	F4F	USMC	VMF-223	9/11/42
15-19	Smith, Maj. John	F4F	USMC	VMF-223	9/12 to 10/10/42
19	Foss, Capt. Joseph	F4F	USMC	VMF-121	11/7/42
19-26	Foss, Capt. Joseph	F4F	USMC	VMF-121	11/12/42 to 1/15/43
26-28	Bong, Maj. Richard	P-38	USAAF	5FC	4/12/44
29-30	Bong, Maj. Richard	P-38	USAAF	5FC	10/10/44
30	McCampbell, Cdr. David	F6F	USN	VF-15	10/24/44
31-36	Bong, Maj. Richard	P-38	USAAF	5FC	10/24 to 11/11/44
40	Bong. Maj. Richard	P-38	USAAF	5FC	11/11 to 12/17/44

USAAF Victory Chronology PTO

Victory #	Pilot Name and Rank	A/C	Total	Unit	Date
1-4	Welch, 2Lt. George	P-40	16	47PS	12/7/41
5	Wagner, 1Lt. Boyd	P-40	8	17PS	12/16/41
5	Kiser. 1Lt. George	P-40	9	8PS	2/24/42
6-8	Kiser, 1Lt. George	P-40	9	8PS	To 4/27/42
8	Wagner, Maj. Boyd	P-39	8	5FC	4/30/42
9	Reynolds, 2Lt. Andrew	P-40	9.3	9FS	7/30/42
10	Bong, 1Lt. Richard	P-38	40	9FS	4/14/43
11	Lynch, Capt. Thomas	P-38	22	39FS	6/10/43
11	Bong, 1Lt. Richard	P-38	40	5FC	6/12/43
12-15	Bong, 1Lt. Richard	P-38	40	5FC	7/26/43
16	Bong, 1Lt. Richard	P-38	40	5FC	7/28/43
16	Lynch, Capt. Thomas	P-38	22	5FC	9/16/43
17-21	Bong, Capt. Richard	P-38	40	5FC	To 11/5/43
21	Kearby, Col. Neel	P-47	22	5FC	1/9/44
22-25	Bong, Maj. Richard	P-38	40	5FC	To 4/3/44
26-28	Bong, Maj. Richard	P-38	40	5FC	4/12/44
29-30	Bong, Maj. Richard	P-38	40	5FC	10/10/44
35-36	Bong, Maj. Richard	P-38	40	5FC	To 11/11/44
37-38	Bong, Maj. Richard	P-38	40	5FC	12/7/44
39	Bong, Maj. Richard	P-38	40	5FC	12/15/44
40	Bong, Maj. Richard	P-38	40	5FC	12/17/44

Aerial Claims by Theater of Operations

Theater	Victories	Probable	Damaged	Total
CBI	1504	487	787	2778
%	54.1	17.5	28.3	
PTO	13238	1471	1319	16028
%	82.6	9.2	8.2	
ETO	7504	681	2535	10720
%	70.0	6.4	23.6	
MTO	3764	577	1465	5806
%	64.8	9.9	25.2	
Totals	26010	3216	6106	35322
Avg.	73.6	9.1	17.3	100.0

Enemy Aircraft Destroyed by the AAF by Theater in the Air and Ground
Enemy Aircraft Destroyed

Theater/Cause of Loss	Total	1942	1943	1944	1945
ETO		*			*
Total Losses	14,218	7	451	7977	5783
In the Air	7422	7	451	5602	1362
On the Ground	6796	----	----	2375	4421
MTO		**			**
Total Losses	4664	92	1459	2845	268
In the Air	3300	81	1270	1760	189
On the Ground	1364	11	89	1085	79
PTO+		***			***
Total Losses	3556	245	1284	1315	712
In the Air	3113	211	1252	1158	492
On the Ground	443	34	32	157	220
CBI		****			****
Total Losses	1467	52	325	729	361
In the Air	847	52	288	418	89
On the Ground	620	----	37	311	272

* August-December 1942 & January-May 1945
** June-December 1942 & January-May 1945
*** January-December 1942 & January-August 1945
**** April-December 1942 & January-August 1945
+ PTO includes Pacific Ocean Area, Far East AF, and Alaska

After an earlier mediocre tour in the MTO and ETO, the P-38 vindicated itself as an air combat fighter in the Pacific, where combat conditions were more suited to the twin-engine fighter's strengths. It scored more victories in less active combat time (1,700 victories in 108 combat months) than the P-51, P-47, and P-40 combined (1,654 victories in 183 active months).

MIA/KIA/WIA/POW

The large numbers of pilots who were never properly accounted for in fighter combat were included in the category of losses reported as Missing in Action (MIA). While U.S. Intelligence made the distinction between MIAs and definite operational losses called Killed in Action (KIA), the Japanese did not have a category for MIAs, concluding that if a plane did not return, its pilot (and crew) was KIA. The most obvious fate of an aircraft declared MIA was the probability that it succumbed to enemy fire without a friendly pilot witnessing it. World War II Fighter aircraft had become so powerful and complex that they were inherently dangerous to fly, particularly by an inexperienced pilot. Stalls were common in flight and easily managed, but a spin—particularly an inverted spin—a snap roll, or a high-speed stall could be fatal. There was also the danger of running out of fuel or becoming lost, either due to poor navigation or bad weather, which was given a MIA. When neither body remains nor a grave could be positively identified, the deceased was listed as MIA. The American KIA category included aircraft that were seen to crash or aircraft wreckage that was discovered later. After 12 months and a day, the MIA was considered KIA. During the war, 78,750 MIAs were reported and 405,399 were listed as KIA. Pilots who were wounded in action were listed as WIA.

Over the course of the war, 35,933 American aircraft were lost in combat and accidents, and 35,946 more personnel were lost due to non-battle causes, mostly due to operational aircraft accidents. Figures for non-battle deaths by cause were not categorized, but most were due to accidental crashes, which caused some 15,000 deaths in the United States alone. These non-battle deaths excluded personnel who died while interned, POWs, or MIA. In the entire U.S. Army, 15,779 personnel died from diseases, especially in the malarial Pacific jungles, but only a small percentage of these were suffered by Air Force personnel.

Although Japan had signed the 1929 Geneva Convention regarding the treatment of POWs, the Japanese government never ratified it. The Japanese reasoned that ratification contradicted the soldiers' code of Bushido and that the treatment of enemy POWs would be better than they treated their own soldiers. In January 1942, Japan claimed it would abide by the Convention, but seldom did so, beginning with the infamous Bataan Death March. Of the 93,941 American POWs in the ETO, only 1.2% died in captivity, while the Japanese treatment of Allied POWs can be considered criminal at best. Of the 25,600 American POWs captured in Asia, nearly 45% (10,650) died from battle wounds after capture due to lack of treatment and from starvation, disease, or were executed. Some 3,840 died during their transfer to Japan in unmarked transports ("Hell Ships") that were sunk by American submarines. During the war, 90,000 U.S. airmen were taken prisoner by the Germans and 15,000 by the Japanese. Generally, the treatment of U.S. airmen in the ETO was good, as the Luftwaffe rather than the SS was in charge of their imprisonment and Germany was a signee of the Geneva Convention. Of the U.S. airmen imprisoned in Japan, 40.4% died in captivity. Beginning in 1945 and through 1948, the Allies conducted military tribunals, seeking justice against those Japanese officers and enlisted men who deliberately mistreated POWs in the Pacific. (**Note:** Capt. Wilbert Arthur of the 49FG was shot down and became the only 5FC POW to survive captivity. 2Lt. Christopher Bartlett of the 475FG was captured after crashing on Rabaul and was executed.)

The Death and Resurrection of Capt. Richard Suehr

After returning to Leyte in the Philippines from Stateside leave, Capt. Richard Suehr flew his 11th P-38 mission with the 7th Fighter Squadron of the 49th Fighter Group on 1 January 1945. During this bomber escort mission to Clark Field, his Flight was bounced by Japanese fighters, and as Suehr turned into them to fire, his .50s remained silent. After making several passes in which his guns continued to malfunction, Suehr decided to return to base. As he began to gain altitude for the trip home, his Wingman radioed that his Lightning was malfunctioning and he was unable to climb. Suehr radioed that he would descend to fly cover, but as he descended his engines malfunctioned, and his P-38 hit the water and exploded. The impact knocked Suehr unconscious, and when he came to about a half hour later, he found that somehow he had gotten out of the Lightning and inflated his Mae West, but was floating in the middle of the Pacific. He swam for nine hours with a very strong current and reached an island just before nightfall. He was awakened a few hours into his sleep by the engines of a Japanese patrol cruising just offshore. Then, a few hours later that night, a Filipino fishing boat approached the shore, but did not see or hear the American. The next morning the fishermen returned, and Suehr swam out to them and was taken to a Guerilla camp. He then boarded a sailboat to Leyte, and after three days of poor winds and a bombing attack by the Japanese, a U.S. Navy patrol boat was encountered which started him on his return to Leyte. After a few weeks rest, he was assigned as the Group's Assistant Operations Officer at Clark Field, Philippines, and then on Okinawa. When the war ended he was assigned as an Airfield Security Officer in occupied Japan,

Meanwhile, Suehr's Wingman had reported that Suehr had probably been killed in the explosion and after an unsuccessful search he was declared Killed in Action. The Secretary of War sent a telegram to Suehr's wife, Ruth, and their six-month-old son in Pennsylvania, informing of her husband's death (see photo) and of the posthumous award of the Purple Heart. A few days later she received the standard two sentence form letter from Gen. MacArthur, stating:

"In the death of your husband, Capt, Richard Suehr, you have my heartfelt sympathy. His service was characterized by his devotion to our beloved country and in his death we have lost a gallant comrade-in-arms."

Local newspaper obituaries announced Suehr's death. A Requiem Mass was held at Suehr's church and after Taps an Air Force officer presented a flag from the President and the Purple Heart to Ruth.

Through a deplorable series of snafus, news of Suehr's rescue never reached Ruth. Three months later, she received a postcard from her husband, but assumed it had been mailed before the crash. Then, two weeks later, she received another postcard which was postmarked weeks after the accident. Ruth contacted the War Department, which investigated and informed her that her husband was on his way home! This time newspaper headlines announced: "Pittsburgh Airman Comes Back From the Dead after Crash at Sea." Later, the War Department directed Ruth to return the posthumous Purple Heart, which she was more than happy to do! Suehr remained in the postwar Air Force, retiring as a Lt. Colonel in August 1968. Suehr passed away in April 2009 at the age of 93 after celebrating 66 years of marriage with Ruth.

Telegram received by Ruth Suehr, informing her of her husband's death. (AFAA)

Newspaper headline celebrating the return of Capt. Richard Suehr. (AFAA)

3

Victory Markings

American

In addition to names and nose art, victory and mission markings were usually stenciled or applied as stick-on decals and sometimes were hand painted on aircraft. Air Force victories were usually carried on the left side of the fuselage, just below and forward of the cockpit. In the Pacific, AAF kill markings varied widely in design and application. The most common was a red sun on a white flag with radiating rays to the edges, followed by the "meatball"—a plain white flag with a red sun in the center. Some groups used the rising sun naval ensign to differentiate victories over Japanese fighters or bombers. Early in the war plain red circles or aircraft silhouettes were applied as victory markings.

Gallery of AAF Victory Markings

Non-Rising Sun Victory Symbols

1Lt. James Morehead's (8PS) P-40 displayed his seven victories as circles in August 1942. (AAF)

Lt. John O'Neill's (49FG) P-38 *Beautiful Lass* has his eight victories displayed as aircraft in October 1943. (AAF)

Gallery of AAF Victory Markings

Variations on the "Rising Sun" Victory Symbol

1Lt. James Mugavero's **(35FG)** four "Rising Sun" victories, November 1944. (AAF)

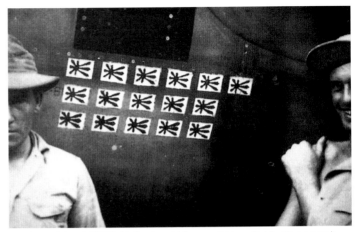

1Lt. Richard Bong's (49FG) 16 victories, which were quickly applied for PR purposes in unusual "Rising Suns" just before he left combat on his first leave in July 1943. (AAF)

Capt. William Shomo (71TRG) in a PR photo session with victory decals after he scored a record seven victories on 11 January 1945. (Shomo)

1Lt. Paul Lipscomb (71TRG), Shomo's Wingman, who shot down three enemy aircraft on 11 January, in the same PR session with different "Rising Sun" decals. (AAF)

Maj. Wallace Jordan's (49FG) six "Rising Sun" victories, October 1944. (AFAA)

Gallery of AAF Victory Markings

Fighter Bomber Success Symbols

Maj. William Dunham (348FG) in December 1944, showing 15 victories, 30 fighter-bomber missions, and the sinking of two enemy ships (see Volume 2: 4 November 1944). (AFAA)

Maj. George Laven (49FG) in April 1945, admiring his destruction of rail cars during fighter-bomber missions over the Philippines and Formosa. (AAF)

Unusual Victory Symbols

1Lt. Louis Curdes (3Cdo) was an eight-plane ace in Europe and the MTO, shooting down seven *Luftwaffe* and one Italian plane. He transferred to the Pacific and shot down a Dinah on 7 February 1945. The U.S. flag indicates an AAF C-47 he shot down to save it (see volume 2; 10 February 1945). (AAF)

Capt. Gerald Johnson (49FG) standing with comedian Joe E. Brown under his scoreboard showing his Australian "victory" flag over a RAAF Wirraway artillery spotter plane whose pilot had survived (see Volume 2: Late November 1943). (AAF)

The Victory Roll

After a particularly successful mission, an exuberant fighter pilot would fly low over his home field before landing, rolling his fighter a number of times to indicate the number of enemy aircraft he destroyed in a forbidden maneuver called the victory roll.

On 25 April 1942, 2Lt. James Morehead, leading a Flight of the 8FS/49FG, had scored three victories to become an ace. When he arrived over Adelaide, he performed three perfect victory rolls, followed by a perfect landing approach which abruptly ended when his P-40 tipped over on its prop. Morehead was unaware that his wing had been hit, destroying his landing gear and ultimately damaging his ego.

Thomas McGuire on the Victory Roll:

"When you are back at home base after a successful combat don't indulge in that last bit of foolishness; don't do a victory roll. You may easily be shot out without your knowing it and the strain imposed on your plane by the victory roll might be enough to break a partially severed control cable or damaged control surface. If that happens you'll never be able to pick up that TS ticket you will have earned by taking a chance at the wrong time. If you really feel so good about a victory then land, check your plane on the ground, and take it up again. It is all right to give the ground crews an idea of just how well you do aerobatics, but don't let the staging expenses for your act run to $125,000 worth of equipment and $25,000 worth of pilot training."

Japanese Victory Symbols

The use of victory symbols by the Japanese Air Forces was fairly prevalent, with one major exception. Unlike the Western Air Forces, the Japanese did not assign pilots to individual aircraft, except for pilots who led units or to high ranking officers. Like a U.S. Navy pilot, a Japanese pilot would fly the aircraft that was most readily available. Thus, an aircraft was credited with the victory, rather than the pilot who made the kill while flying that aircraft. This method of credit was fixed from 1937 through 1944, when the war was going bad and the need for air heroes arose, with photos issued of aces standing with their aircraft adorned with their victory totals. Both the JNAF and JAAF would present their victory markings on the port side of the aircraft, usually under the cockpit, although the JNAF could place them on the rear fuselage or even on the rudder (like the Luftwaffe).

Japanese victory symbols took many forms, but the most common were:
1) Five-Pointed Star appearing from 1937 to 1940
2) U.S. star insignia with arrows into center of star
3) Stylized Bird's Wing or Solid Bird Silhouette
4) Aircraft Outline as a solid silhouette or with a cross arrow or crossed arrows through it
5) Flowers: Cherry Blossom, Chrysanthemum, or Daisy (rarely) as a stenciled outline or solid color, both with veins detailed

Shared or Probable victories were denoted by only one cross or arrow through an aircraft symbol or the lack of veins in the flower symbols.

Sometimes different symbols could appear on the same aircraft, depending on the pilot scoring the victory.

Japanese Victory Markings

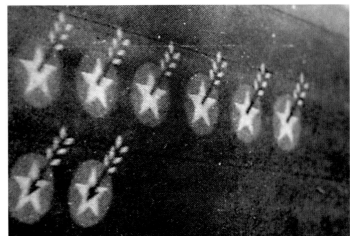

American star insignia with arrows into center of star. (Author's Collection)

Five-Pointed Star appearing from 1937 to 1940. (Author's Collection)

Aircraft Silhouette: Solid or with a cross or crossed arrows through or aircraft ramming. (see lower left on photo) (Author's Collection)

Stylized Bird's Wing or Solid Bird Silhouette. (Author's Collection)

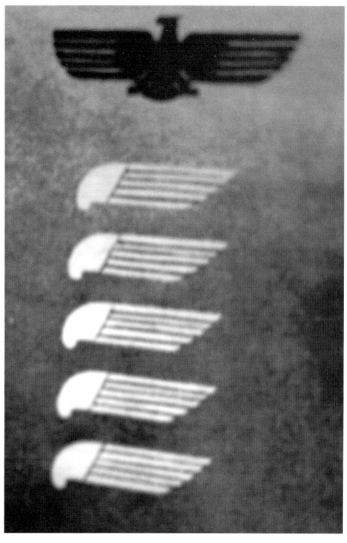

4

5th Fighter Command
Aces in WWII

A

ACE NAME	Rank	FS/FG	Theater	A/C	V.	P.	D.	Notes
Adams, Burnell	Capt	6NFS/-- 80/8	PTO	P-70 P-38	1 6	0 0	0 0	
Adams, Robert	1Lt	80/8	PTO	P-38	5	1	1	KIA 9/2/43
Adkins, Frank	LCol	17P/-- 39/35 313/50	PTO PTO ETO	P-40 P-400 P-51	2 1 2	0 0 0	0 0 0	KIFA 2/23/45
Allen, David	1Lt	7/49 431/475	PTO PTO	P-40 P-38	2 6	0 0	0 0	
Ambort, Ernest	2Lt	9/49	PTO	P-38	5	0	0	
Andrew, Stephen	Maj	7/49 486/352	PTO ETO	P-40 P-47 P-51	1 1 7	0 0 0	1 0 0	POW 7/2/44
Andrews, Stanley	1Lt	39/35	PTO	P-38	6	3	0	
Aschenbrener, Robert	Capt	8/49	PTO	P-40 P-38	3 7	0 0	0 1	

B

ACE NAME	Rank	FS/FG	Theater	A/C	V.	P.	D.	Notes
Baker, Ellis	1Lt	40/35	PTO	P-47 P-51	3 3	0 0	0 0	
Banks, William	Maj	342/348 GHQ	PTO	P-47	9	0	1	
Benz, Walter	Maj	342/348	PTO	P-47	8	1	0	
Blair, Samuel	Capt	341/348	PTO	P-47	7	0	0	
Bong, Richard	Maj	9/49 5FC	PTO	P-38	40	8	7	KIFA 8/6/45 (US)
Brown, Harry	Capt	47/15 9/49 431/475	PTO	P-40 P-38	1 5	0 1	1 0	

C

ACE NAME	Rank	FS/FG	Theater	A/C	V.	P.	D.	Notes
Champlin, Frederick	Capt	431/475	PTO	P-38	9	0	0	

Cloud, Vivian	1Lt	432/475	PTO	P-38	5	1	0	
Condon, Harry	Capt	432/475	PTO	P-38	5	0	0	KIA 1/5/45
Cragg, Edward	Maj	80/8	PTO	P-38	15	4	0	KIA 12/26/43
Curton, Warren	1Lt	9/49	PTO	P-38	5	1	0	
Czernecki, Edward	1Lt	431/475	PTO	P-38	6	1	0	

D

ACE NAME	Rank	FS/FG	Theater	A/C	V.	P.	D.	Notes
Dahl, Perry	Capt	432/475	PTO	P-38	9	0	1	
Damstrom, Fernley	1Lt	7/49	PTO	P-38	8	0	0	KIFA 4/11/45
Davis, George	1Lt	8/49	PTO	P-47	7	0	0	+14 v Korea
Day, Wlliam	1Lt	8/49	PTO	P-40	5	0	0	
Dean, Zack	2Lt	80/8 432/475	PTO	P-38	7	1	0	
Degraffenreid, Edwin	2Lt	80/8	PTO	P-38	6	2	1	
DeHaven, Robert	Capt	7/49	PTO	P-40 P-38	10 4	0 0	0 0	
Della, George	1Lt	341-460/348	PTO	P-47	5	0	0	
Dent, Elliott	Capt	7/49	PTO	P-40 P-38	3 3	0 0	0 0	
Dick, Frederick	Capt	7/49	PTO	P-40 P-38	2 3	1 0	0 0	
Dikovitsky, Michael	1Lt	340/348	PTO	P-47	5	0	0	
Donalson, I.B.	1Lt	21P/24P 9/49	PTO	P-40	5	0	0	
Drier, William	Capt	8/49	PTO	P-38	6	0	0	
Dubisher, Francis	Capt	41/35	PTO	P-400 P-39 P-47	1 3 1	0 0 0	0 0 0	
Dunaway, John	1Lt	36/8	PTO	P-38	7	0	0	
Dunham, William	Maj	342-460/348 GHQ	PTO	P-47 P-51	15 1	0 0	0 0	

E-F

ACE NAME	Rank	FS/FG	Theater	A/C	V.	P.	D.	Notes
Eason, Hoyt	1Lt	39/35	PTO	P-38	6	2	1	KIA 3/3/43
Elliott, Vincent	2Lt	431/475	PTO	P-38	7	0	1	
Everhart, Lee	Capt	35/8	PTO	P-40 P-38	5 1	0 0	0 0	
Fanning, Grover	1Lt	9/49	PTO	P-38	9	2	0	
Felts, Marion	1Lt	8/49	PTO	P-40 P-38	3 2	0 0	0 0	
Fisk, Jack	Capt	433/475	PTO	P-38	7	0	0	
Flack, Nelson	Capt	8/49	PTO	P-40 P-38	2 3	1 0	0 0	

Fleischer, Richard	Cat	340/348	PTO	P-47	6	0	0	
Forster, Joseph	1Lt	432/475	PTO	P-38	9	3	1	
Foulis, William	Capt	341/348	PTO	P-47	6	1	0	

G

ACE NAME	Rank	FS/FG	Theater	A/C	V.	P.	D.	Notes
Gibb, Robert	1Lt	342/348	PTO	P-47	5	0	1	
Giroux, William	Capt	36/8	PTO	P-47 P-38	0 10	3 0	0 0	
Grant, Marvin	1Lt	342/348	PTO	P-47	7	0	0	
Gresham, Billy	1Lt	432/475	PTO	P-38	6	1	0	KIFA 10/2/44
Grosshuesch, Leroy	Capt	39/35	PTO	P-47 P-51	7 1	0 0	0 0	
Gupton, Cheatam	1Lt	9/49	PTO	P-38	5	0	0	

H-I

ACE NAME	Rank	FS/FG	Theater	A/C	V.	P.	D.	Notes
Hagerstrom, James	1Lt	8/49	PTO	P-40	6	0	0	+ 6 v Korea
Homer, Cyril	Capt	80/8	PTO	P-38	15	5	4	
Howard, Robert	1Lt	8/49	PTO	P-40	6	3	2	
Hoyt, Edward	Capt	41/35 465/507	PTO	P-47	5	0	0	
Hunter, Alvaro	Capt	40/35	PTO	P-39 P-40	2 3	0 0	0 0	
Ince, James	1Lt	80/8 432/475	PTO	P-38	6	1	0	

J

ACE NAME	Rank	FS/FG	Theater	A/C	V.	P.	D.	Notes
Jett, Verl	Capt	36/8 431/475	PTO	P-39 P-38	1 6	0 0	0 1	
Johnson, Gerald R.	LCol	9/49	PTO	P-38 P-47	20 2	2 0	0 0	KIFA 10/7/45
Jones, Curren	Capt	39/35	PTO	P-400 P-38	1 4	0 2	0 0	
Jones, John	Capt	80/8	PTO	P-38	8	2	0	
Jordan, Wallace	Maj	9/49	PTO	P-38 P-47	5 1	1 0	0 0	

K

ACE NAME	Rank	FS/FG	Theater	A/C	V.	P.	D.	Notes
Kearby, Neel	Col	--/348	PTO	P-47	22	0	1	KIA 3/5/44
King, Charles	Maj	39/35	PTO	P-38	5	3	4	
Kiser, George	Capt	17P-8/49	PTO	P-40	9	0	0	

Knapp, Robert	Capt	342/348	PTO	P-47	6	1	0	
Kruzel, Joseph	LCol	17P/--	PTO	P-40	3	0	0	
		376/361	ETO	P-47	1.5	0	1	
		HQ		P-51	2	0	0	

L

ACE NAME	Rank	FS/FG	Theater	A/C	V.	P.	D.	Notes
Ladd, Kenneth	Capt	80-86/8	PTO	P-38	12	2	1	KIA 10/14/44
Landers, John	LCol	9/49	PTO	P-40	6	0	0	
		38/78	ETO	P-38	4	0	1	
		--/357		P-51	4.5	0	0	
Lane, John	1Lt	39/35	PTO	P-38	6	2	2	
Lent, Francis	1Lt	431/475	PTO	P-38	11	1	0	KIFA 12/1/44
Lewis, Warren	Maj	431/433/ 475	PTO	P-38	7	5	3	
Loisel, John	Maj	432/475	PTO	P-38	11	0	1	
Lucas, Paul	Capt	432/475	PTO	P-38	6	1	0	
Lutton, Lowell	1Lt	431/475	PTO	P-38	5	0	0	KIA 11/2/43
Lynch, Thomas	LCol	39/35	PTO	P-400	3	0	0	
				P-38	17	1	4	KIA 3/7/44

M-N

ACE NAME	Rank	FS/FG	Theater	A/C	V.	P.	D.	Notes
MacDonald, Charles	LCol	--/475	PTO	P-38	27	2	2.5	
Mahurin, Walker	Maj	63/56	ETO	P-47	19.71	3	1	Ev 3-5/44
		3 Cdo	PTO	P-51		0	0	+ 3 v Korea
Mankin, Jack	1Lt	9/49	PTO	P-38	5	0	0	
		431/475						
Mathre, Milden	2Lt	7/49	PTO	P-38	5	0	0	
McDonough, Wm.	Maj	40/35	PTO	P-39	2	1	0	
		35/8		P-47	3	0	0	KIFA????
McGee, Donald	Capt	36-80/8	PTO	P-39	3	1	0	
		363/357	ETO	P-38	2	0	0	
				P-51	1	0	0	
McGuire, Thomas	Maj	431/475	PTO	P-38	38	3	2	KIA 1/7/45
McKeon, Joseph	Capt	35/8	PTO	P-39	1	0	0	
		433/475	ETO	P-38	4	0	1	POW 10/7/44
		77/20		P-51	1	0	1	
Meuten, Donald	1Lt	8/49	PTO	P-40	6	0	0	KIA 5/7/44
Monk, Franklin	1Lt	431/475	PTO	P-38	5	0	0	
Moore, John	Maj	341/475	PTO	P-47	7	0	0	
Morehead, James	Maj	17/8-49	PTO	P-40	7	0	0	
		71/1	MTO	P-38	1	0	1	
Morriss, Paul	Capt	431/475	PTO	P-38	5	0	0	
Mugavero, James	1Lt	41/35	PTO	P-47	6	0	0	
Murphey, Paul	Capt	80/8	PTO	P-38	6	3	2	

ACE NAME	Rank	FS/FG	Theater	A/C	V.	P.	D.	Notes
Myers, Jennings	1Lt	80/8	PTO	P-38	5	0	0	
Nichols, Frank	Capt	7/49 431/475	PTO	P-40 P-38	4 1	1 0	1 0	

O-P-Q

ACE NAME	Rank	FS/FG	Theater	A/C	V.	P.	D.	Notes
O'Neill, John	1Lt	9/49	PTO	P-38	8	0	0	
O'Neill, Lawrence	1Lt	342/348	PTO	P-47	5	0	0	
Paris, Joel	Capt	7/49	PTO	P-40 P-38	3 6	0 0	0 0	
Pierce, Sammy	1Lt	8/49	PTO	P-40 P-38	3 4	0 1	0 0	
Pietz, John	1Lt	431/475	PTO	P-38	6	0	0	
Pool, Kenneth	1Lt	35/8	PTO	P-40 P-38	2 3	0 0	0 0	
Popek, Edward	Maj	342/348	PTO	P-47 P-51	5 2	0 0	0 0	
Purdy, Jack	1Lt	433/475	PTO	P-38	7	0	1	

R

ACE NAME	Rank	FS/FG	Theater	A/C	V.	P.	D.	Notes
Ray, C.B.	1Lt	80/8	PTO	P-38	5	0	1	
Reynolds, Andy	1Lt	20P/17P 9/49	PTO	P-40	9.33	1	0	
Robbins, Jay	Maj	80/8 GHQ	PTO	P-39 P-38	0 22	2 4	0 4	
Roberts, Daniel	Capt	80/8 432/475	PTO	P-400 P-38	2 12	0 1	1 0	KIA 11/9/43
Roddy, Edward	Capt	342/348	PTO	P-47	8	0	0	
Rowland, Robert	Col	--/348	PTO	P-47	8	0	0	

S

ACE NAME	Rank	FS/FG	Theater	A/C	V.	P.	D.	Notes
Schriber, Louis	Capt	80/8	PTO	P-38	5	6	1	
Shomo, William	Capt	80/71TR	PTO	P-51 F-6	1 7	0 0	0 0	
Smith, Carroll	Maj	418NFS	PTO	P-38 P-61	2 5	2 0	0 0	
Smith, Cornelius	Capt	80/8	PTO	P-38	11	2	1	
Smith, Meryl	LCol	--/475	PTO	P-38	9	0	0	POW 12/7/44
Smith, Richard	1Lt	39/35	PTO	P-38	7	0	1	
Sparks, Kenneth	1Lt	39/35	PTO	P-38	11	2	3	KIFA 3/44 US
Stanch, Paul	Capt	39/35	PTO	P-38	10	1	2	
Stanton, Arlen	Maj	7/49	PTO	P-40	8	0	1	

Strand, William	Capt	40/35	PTO	P-39 P-47	1 6	1 0	0 1	
Suehr, Richard	1Lt	39/35	PTO	P-400 P-38	1 4	0 1	0 1	
Sullivan, Charles	Capt	39/35	PTO	P-400 P-38	1 4	0 1	0 2	Later O'Sullivan
Summer, Elliott	Capt	432/475	PTO	P-38	10	0	1	
Sutcliff, Robert	1Lt	342/475	PTO	P-47	5	1	0	

T-U-V

ACE NAME	Rank	FS/FG	Theater	A/C	V.	P.	D.	Notes
Tilley, John	1Lt	431/475	PTO	P-38	5	0	1	
Troxell, Clifford	Capt	35/8	PTO	P-39 P-38 P-40	2 2 1	1 0 0	0 0 0	
Turner, William	1Lt	20P/17P 41/35 --/32	PTO	P-40 P-400 P-40	2 1 5	0 0 0	0 1 1	
Vaught, Robert	Capt	9/49	PTO	P-40 P-38	2 3	0 0	0 0	

W-X-Y-Z

ACE NAME	Rank	FS/FG	Theater	A/C	V.	P.	D.	Notes
Wagner, Boyd	LCol	--/17P 5FC	PTO	P-40 P-39	5 3	0 0	0 0	
Wandery, Ralph	Capt	9/49	PTO	P-38 P-47	5 1	2 0	0 0	
Welch, George	Capt	47P/15 --/15 8/80	PTO	P-40 P-39 P-38	4 3 9	0 0 1	0 0 0	
Wenige, Arthur	1Lt	9/49 431/475	PTO	P-40 P-38	1 5	1 1	0 0	
West, Richard	Capt	35/8	PTO	P-40 P-38	6 8	3 0	0 0	
White, Robert	Capt	8/49	PTO	P-40	9	1	0	
Wire, Calvin	1Lt	43/475	PTO	P-38	7	2	1	
Wire, Ralph	Capt	9/49 --/51	PTO CBI	P-38 P-38	3 2	3 0	0 0	
Woods, Sidney	LCol	9/49 --/4	PTO ETO	P-38 P-51	2 5	1 0	0 0	POW 4/16/45
Wright, Ellis	Capt	--/49	PTO	P-40	6	0	0	
Yeager, Robert	Capt	40/35	PTO	P-39 P-47	2 3	0 0	0 0	

V=Victories P=Probably Destroyed D=Damaged

5

Top 5th Fighter Command Aces with 10 or More Victories

Richard Bong: 40 Victories

Bong

Richard Ira Bong, the son of Swedish immigrants, was born on 24 September 1920, and grew up on a farm in Poplar, WI, as one of nine children. Bong was the quintessential "All American" boy: doing well in high school, helping on the farm, playing on the school's baseball, basketball, and hockey teams; playing clarinet in the school band; singing in the church choir; and enjoying fishing and hunting. Like many boys of this period, he became interested in aviation at a young age and was an ardent model builder. He enrolled at Superior State Teachers College in 1938, where he joined the Civilian Pilot Training Program, also taking private flying lessons. In 1941, he enlisted in the AAC Aviation Cadet Program and took his Primary Flight Training at Rankin Aeronautical Academy, CA, in June 1941, and completed Basic at Gardner Field, CA. He was sent to Luke Field, near Phoenix, AZ, for Advanced Training in single-engine (fighter) planes, where he mastered the AT-6. On 9 January 1942, Bong earned his Army Air Corps 2nd Lieutenant's commission and his Pilot's Wings. Instead of a combat assignment, his flying talents kept him at Luke to teach gunnery. However, after a few months he got the chance to train in the new P-38 with the 14FG/49FS at Hamilton Field, San Francisco, where he first attracted the attention of Gen. George Kenney, his future mentor and CO of the Fifth Air Force, then Commander of the 4AF. The attention he attracted came on 12 June 1942, when Bong and three other P-38 pilots flew under the Golden Gate Bridge and then flew low along San Francisco's Market Street. Bong was reprimanded by Kenney, who grounded him while the rest of his Group was sent to England in July 1942. Bong then transferred to the 78FG/84FS at Hamilton Field.

On 10 September 1942, 2Lt. Bong was assigned to the 9FS "Flying Knights" of the 49FG, based at Darwin, Australia. While the squadron waited for delivery of the P-38s, Bong and other 9th FS pilots flew detached duty missions with the 39FS/35FG, based at Port Moresby, New Guinea, to gain combat experience. On 27 December 1942, Bong claimed his initial victory, shooting down a Zero and Val over Buna, for which Bong was awarded the Silver Star. On 7 January 1943, Bong shot down two Oscars (with a probable and damaged) over the Huon Gulf and became an ace the next day, when he shot down another Oscar over the Huon Gulf.

In March 1943, Bong returned to the 49FG, based at Schwimmer Field, near Port Moresby. On 3 March, he claimed an Oscar destroyed and one probable over the Huon Gulf, followed three days later by two Zeros destroyed (and a Zero probable and Betty damaged) during the Battle for the Bismarck Sea. On 29 March, he shot down a Dinah over the Bismarck Sea. On 6 April, Bong was promoted to 1st Lieutenant. On 14 April, Bong became a double ace by shooting down a Betty (and another Betty probable claim) over Milne Bay. From mid-June to the end of July, Bong would add six more enemy aircraft to his credit: 12 June, an Oscar (and one damaged) near Bena Bena A/D; 26 July, two Zeros and two Tonys over the Markham Valley, making him a triple ace and winning him the DSC; and then two days later added another Oscar near Rein Bay. He was promoted to Captain on 24 August.

After claiming two Betty probables on 5 September, he shot down a Dinah on 2 October near Cape Hoskins, New Britain, then added two Zeros (and a damaged) on 29 October over Rabaul and became a quadruple ace by shooting down two Zeros over Rabaul on 5 November. He would then go on leave to the U.S. with 21 victories during November and December 1943. Bong met Marge Vattendahl at a Superior State Teachers' College Homecoming and began dating her. After returning to the Southwest Pacific in January 1944, he named his P-38 Marge and decorated the nose with her laminated photo.

When Bong returned from leave, he set his sights on Capt. Eddie Rickenbacker's American record of 26 victories in World War I. He was assigned to 5th Fighter Command HQ and allowed to "freelance" to increase his score. He scored his first victory flying in Marge when he shot down a Tony near Cape Hoskins on 15 February and added two Sally bombers near Tadji A/D on 3 March, followed by two Oscars as a probable and damaged two days later. On 3 April, he shot down an Oscar near Hollandia to come within one victory of the record. On 12 April, Bong would surpass Rickenbacker's record in a big way, with three victories over Oscars over the enemy airdromes at Hollandia. Kenney took him out of action again and promoted him to Major.

During another leave in May 1944, Major Bong traveled the U.S. on a War Bond publicity tour and returned to New Guinea on 10 September. Kenney assigned Bong as HQ "advanced gunnery instructor," and while he was allowed to take part in combat missions, he had orders to "only defend himself and not seek out the enemy." Though assigned to the 5FC HQ Staff and not required to fly combat missions, Bong continued flying from Tacloban, Leyte, during the Philippines Campaign, increasing his official air-to-air victory total by 12 between mid-October and mid-December 1944. During October, he shot down an Irving (Sally?) and Oscar over Borneo on the 10th; an Oscar on the 27th over Biliran Island, PI; and two Oscars (and two Oscars damaged) off the Leyte coast to give him 33 victories. In November, he added three more victories: on the 10th he shot down an Oscar over Ormoc A/D and the next day he shot down two Zeros over Ormoc Bay and was recommended for the Medal of Honor. In December, Bong would conclude his scoring with four victories. On the 7th, he shot down a Tojo and Sally over Ormoc Bay; added an Oscar on the 15th over Panubulon Island; and finished his career by shooting down an Oscar near San Jose, Mindoro. On 12 December, he was awarded the Medal of Honor by MacArthur at Tacloban.

In January 1945, Kenney sent America's Ace of Aces home for good. Bong married Marge and participated in numerous public relations events, particularly promoting the sale of War Bonds. Bong then became a test pilot, assigned to Lockheed's Burbank, CA, plant, where he flew P-80 Shooting Star jet fighters. During an acceptance flight on 6 August 1945, the jet's primary fuel pump malfunctioned during takeoff of P-80. Bong tried to maneuver the stricken jet from a residential area and then bailed out, but was too low for his parachute to deploy. His death was featured prominently in national newspapers, even though it occurred on the same day as the atomic bombing of Hiroshima.

Aerial Victory Credits

Date	Location	Credits
27 Dec 42	Over Dobodura, NG	Val Zero
31 Dec 42	Over Lae, NG	Zero (P)
7 Jan 43	Huon Gulf, NG	2 Oscars Oscar (P) Oscar (D)
8 Jan 43	Huon Gulf, NG	Oscar
3 Mar 43	Huon Gulf, NG	Oscar Oscar (P)
11 Mar 43	Bismarck Sea	2 Zeros Zero (P) Betty (D)
29 Mar 43	Bismarck Sea	Dinah
14 Apr 43	Milne Bay, NG	Betty Betty (P)

12 June 43	Near Bena Bena, NG	Oscar Oscar (D)
26 July 43	Markham Valley, NG	2 Tonys 2 Zeros
28 July 43	Near Rein Bay, NG	Oscar
6 Sept 43	Morobe Area, NG	2 Betty (P)
2 Oct 43	Cape Hoskins, NB	Dinah
29 Oct 43	Rabaul Area, NB	2 Zeros Zero (D)
5 Nov 43	Over Rabaul, NB	2 Zeros
15 Feb 44	Near Cape Hoskins, NB	Tony
3 Mar 44	Traji A/D, NG	2 Sallys
5 Mar 44	Over Dagua A/D, NG	Oscar (P) Oscar (D)
3 April 44	Near Hollandia, NG	Oscar
12 Apr 44	Near Hollandia, NG	3 Oscars
10 Oct 44	Borneo	Sally (Irving?) Oscar
27 Oct 44	Near Biliran Is. NG	Oscar
28 Oct 44	Coast of Leyte, PI	2 Oscars 2 Oscars (D)
10 Nov 44	Near Ormoc A/D, PI	Oscar
11 Nov 44	Ormoc Bay, PI	2 Zeros
7 Dec 44	Ormoc Bay, PI	Sally Tojo
15 Dec 44	Panubulan Island, PI	Oscar
17 Dec 44	San Jose, Mindoro, PI	Oscar

All victories in P-38

Bong often referred to his gunnery skills as "lousy, perhaps the worst in the Army Air Force," and consequently claimed the highest number of probable (8) and damaged (7) enemy aircraft of any 5FC pilot.

Bong's decorations included the Medal of Honor, the Distinguished Service Cross, the Silver Star (with one OLC), the Distinguished Flying Cross (with six OLCs), and the Air Medal (with 14 OLCs).

Aircraft names Marge, after girlfriend/wife.

Thomas McGuire 38 Victories

Thomas Buchanan McGuire, Jr. was born in Ridgewood, NJ, on 1 August 1920, and following his parents' divorce McGuire moved to Sebring, FL, with his mother in the late 1920s. McGuire graduated from Sebring High School and enrolled at Georgia Tech in 1938. Always interested in aviation, McGuire left school after his junior year in July 1941 and enlisted in the U.S. Army Air Corps as an aviation cadet, then was ordered to a contract flying school in Corsicana, TX, where he began Flight School later that year. He earned his Wings and Lieutenant's bars after finishing his flight training at Kelly Field, TX, in early February 1942. While training in Texas, he met his future wife, the trim, attractive Marilynn Geisler, who was given the incompatible nickname "Pudgy."

McGuire was initially assigned to the 313PS/50PG, but wanted to see action and was transferred to the 56PS/54PG on 7 May 1942, serving in Alaska from mid-June to mid-October 1942. He was based at Nome, flying

McGuire

P-39Fs on non-eventful patrols and tests over the Aleutians. McGuire soon began to ask to be transferred, and in late in 1942, he was transferred to Harding Field, LA, where he and Marilynn married in December, shortly before his transfer to in February 1943 to Orange County Airport, to begin transitioning to the P-38 Lightning. He was sent to the South Pacific with the 5th Air Force's 9FS/49FG on 14 March 1943, flying his first mission on 22 April, and was promoted to 1st Lieutenant on 6 June. McGuire remained with the 49FG through July and failed to down any Japanese aircraft. On 20 July, he was transferred to the 431FS, which was part of Kenney's new, all-P-38 475th Fighter Group. Consequently, the 475th was furnished with some of the best pilots and enlisted crews in the Pacific.

The 475th flew its first combat missions in August 1943, over the Owen Stanley Range, flying in support of McArthur's drive up New Guinea's northern coast and attacking the Japanese airdrome at Wewak. On 18 August 1943, McGuire was part of a group flying top cover for bombers bombing Wewak and he shot down two Oscars and one Tony. Three days later, again near Wewak, he downed two more Oscars to finally become an ace after a frustrating year with no opportunities to engage the enemy. Wewak was a fertile hunting ground for the 475th and McGuire, as on 29 August, he shot down a Zero and Tony, and on 28 September he added to two Zeros. He became a double ace over Oro Bay on 15 October, when he shot down a Val (plus two Zero probables).

McGuire's career nearly came to an end on 17 October 1943, when he intercepted Japanese bombers being escorted by Zero fighters over Oro Bay. McGuire dove into the seven enemy fighters and quickly shot down three, but the remaining four Zeros were able to attack McGuire and severely damaged his aircraft. As he exited the doomed aircraft, he became snagged and struggled to free himself, finally deploying his parachute at only 1,000 feet and was rescued. He suffered a wound to his wrist and numerous other injuries, including some broken ribs, and spent six weeks in the hospital before he returned to his unit. For his actions on this day he was awarded a Silver Star and a Purple Heart. He was promoted to Captain on 10 December 1943, but would not make a claim until 16 December, when he damaged a Zero, but finished the year with three Vals downed on 26 December to make him a triple ace with 16 victories.

Over the next five months, McGuire underwent a long victory drought, but was given command of the 431FS on 2 May 1944 and promoted to Major on 23 May. Based at Hollandia, McGuire downed an Oscar near Noemfoer on 16 May and continued to increase his total through the Summer with a Tojo (19 May) and a Sonia and Oscar (on 16 June) to make him a quadruple ace, as well as an Oscar (on 27 July). He spent much of the Summer working with noted Trans-Atlantic aviator Charles Lindbergh.

The famous flyer arrived at the 475th in June 1944 as a civilian contractor to assess and recommend improvements in the range of the P-38. Squadron mates recalled "McGuire ordering Lindbergh around, telling him to run errands as though he were a servant."

McGuire would not score again until 14 October, when he "tacked onto" the 9FS bomber escort to Balikpapan, Borneo, where he shot down an Oscar, Tojo, and Hamp (plus an Oscar probable). Once the Philippines were invaded, McGuire stepped up his scoring at the end of 1944. On 1 November, he downed a Tojo; on 10 November, an Oscar; and on 12 November two Jacks, to give him 28 victories. By December, McGuire became driven to catch Bong, who always seemed to be eight victories ahead.

On 7 December, McGuire flew with Bong, who had 36 victories, and shot down a Sally and Tojo, but McGuire shot down an Oscar and Tojo to remain eight behind. On the 13th, McGuire shot down a Jack, while Bong would shoot down an Oscar on the 15th and 17th for a final total of 40 victories before going home. With Bong gone, McGuire became obsessed with becoming the Ace of Aces. On Christmas Day, he volunteered to lead 15 P-38s to escort B-24s and was attacked by twenty Zeros. McGuire shot down three to give him 34. The following day, he volunteered for a similar mission and McGuire shot down four Zeros, bringing his total to 38. With the Japanese opposition still strong, McGuire expected to break Bong's record. On 7 January 1945, McGuire led a flight of P-38s over Japanese airfields in an attempt to draw them up into battle. At the start of the battle, McGuire had ordered his flight to keep their auxiliary fuel tanks, as they would need them to reach their main objective in the sweep. An Oscar attacked his Wingman from behind and McGuire drew it away, but the Japanese pilot got on McGuire's tail. McGuire rapidly increased his turn rate, which was a very dangerous maneuver at only 300 feet altitude, and caused McGuire's P-38 to stall and snap-roll into the ground, killing him on impact. The order to hold the tanks was against SOP and added extra weight that burdened the fighter, making it less maneuverable and more susceptible to stalls and spins at low speeds. (A detailed description of McGuire's demise can be found in Volume 2: 7 January 1945.)

Aerial Victory Credits

Date	Location	Credits
18 Aug 43	Near Wewak, NG	2 Zeros Tony
21 Aug 43	Near Wewak, NG	2 Zeros TE Fighter (D)
29 Aug 43	Near Wewak, NG	Zero Tony
28 Sept 43	Near Wewak, NG	2 Zeros
15 Oct 43	Oro Bay, NG	Val 2 Zeros (P)
17 Oct 43	Near Buna, NG	3 Zeros
16 Dec 43	Near Aware, NB	Zero (D)
26 Dec 43	Cape Gloucester, NB	3 Vals
17 May 44	Noemfoor, NG	Oscar
19 May 44	Manokwari, NG	Tojo
16 June 44	Near Jefman, NG	Sonia Oscar
27 July 44	Lolobata A/D	Oscar

14 Oct 44	Balikpapan, Borneo	Oscar Hamp Tojo Oscar (P)
1 Nov 44	San Pablo, Leyte, PI	Tojo
10 Nov 44	Ormoc, Leyte, PI	Oscar
12 Nov 44	Northern Cebu Island	2 Jacks
7 Dec 44	Poro Island Near Ormoc Bay	Oscar Tojo
13 Dec 44	Tama A/D, Los Negros	Jack
25 Dec 44	Near Clark/La Paz Fields	3 Zeros
26 Dec 44	Over Clark Field	4 Zeros

All victories in P-38

McGuire finished the war as the second highest scoring American ace with 38 victories, three probables, and two damaged.

McGuire was awarded the Medal of Honor (officially posthumously 7 March 1946), the Distinguished Service Cross, Silver Star with two OLCs, Distinguished Flying Cross with five OLCs, Purple Heart with two OLCs, and the Air Medal with 15 OLCs. In addition, McGuire Air Force Base in his native New Jersey was named in his honor in January 1948.

His P-38s were named Pudgy I through Pudgy V for his svelte wife Marilynn.

Charles MacDonald ("Mac") 27 Victories

MacDonald

Charles Henry MacDonald was born in Dubois, PA, on 23 November 1914. While attending Louisiana State University, he passed the required exams for flight training and after graduation in 1938, he entered the AAC Pilot Training Program at Randolph and Kelly Fields, TX, from 29 June 1938 to 25 May 1939, when he received his Wings and was commissioned a 2Lt. at Kelly Field. His initial assignment was to the 20PG/79PS on 8 June 1939 at Barksdale Field, LA, flying P-36s. He was promoted to 1st Lieutenant on 9 September 1940. He later transferred to the 5PG/70PS on 13 January 1941, then to the 18PG/44PS at Wheeler Field, HI, on 9 February 1941, with the Group's P-36s loaded on the carrier Enterprise. MacDonald had a unique experience for an Army pilot; he had to takeoff from the carrier and land in Hawaii. He was at the Pearl Harbor attack on 7 December 1941 and managed to get airborne, although only after the attack was over. MacDonald was promoted to Captain on 1 March 1942, and to Major on 10 October 1942. MacDonald served in the United States with the 326FG on 13 September 1942, before transferring to the 348FG to command the 340PS at Westover Field, MA. He trained his Squadron in the P-47 from 17 November 1942 to 1 October 1943. In June 1943, MacDonald was stationed in New Guinea with the 348FG, but this combat assignment was uneventful, as he spent several months flying P-47s in escort patrols for transports in the Marilinan area. MacDonald was recruited by Gen. Kenney to join the 475FG, which was the first all-P-38 Lightning-equipped Group in the 5AF, and joined the Group at Dobodura, New Guinea, as the Group Executive Officer. He was promoted to Lt. Colonel on 10 November 1943, and became the Group Commander when George Prentice was rotated home. Three days later, he scored his first two victories (two Vals destroyed and two damaged over Oro Bay), and on 23 and 25 October downed an Oscar and Zeke over Rabaul; he would became an ace on 9 November, when he downed two Zekes near Alexishafen Airdrome. On 21 December, he downed two Vals over Aware and added a Tony (10 January) and a Hamp (18 January) over Wewak to make him a double ace. He was promoted to Colonel on 15 May 1944. He would then score slowly during the Summer of 1944, downing a Zero on 8 June and a Rufe and Val on 1 August. MacDonald would lead the 475FG for 20 months (26 November 1943 to 14 July 1945), except for the period August to November 1944, as punishment for allowing Charles Lindbergh to get into a "dangerous situation." MacDonald returned and would achieve 13 victories in seven weeks over the Philippines, scoring four victories in November (an Oscar on the 10th, two Jacks the next day to become a triple ace, and a Zero on the 28th; all over Ormoc Bay), seven victories in December (three Jacks on the 7th over Ormoc Bay to become a quadruple ace; a Sally on the 13th; and two Jacks and a Zero near Clark Field on the 25th), and a Dinah and Tojo over Clark Field on 1 January to give him 26 victories. MacDonald scored his final victory on 13 February, shooting down a Topsy transport over Indo-China.

MacDonald returned to the United States in July 1945, where he served in various staff and command assignments, including Commander of the 33FG and 23FW, Air Attaché to Sweden, and instructor at the U.S. War College before retiring from the Air Force as a Colonel in July 1961. He moved to Anacortes, WA, where he opened a real estate business and pursued his love of sailing. After his four children finished high school in 1971, he closed the real estate business and he and his wife sailed the Pacific and the Caribbean until her death in 1978. He then settled in Mobile, AL, until he died on 2 March 2002.

Aerial Victory Credits

Date	Location	Credits
15 Oct 43	Oro Bay, NG	2 Vals 1 Vals (D)
23 Oct 43	Over Rabaul	Oscar
25 Oct 43	Vunakanau, Rabaul	Zero
9 Nov 43	Near Alexishafen, NG	2 Zeros Oscar (P)
21 Dec 43	Over Aware, NB	2 Vals
10 Jan 44	Over Wewak, NG	Tony Tony (D)
18 Jan 44	Over Wewak, NG	Hamp
30 Mar 44	Over Hollandia, NG	½ Tony (D)
8 June 44	North of Manokwari, NG	Zero

28 July 44	Near Amahai A/D	Zero
1 Aug 44	Near Koror Island, NG	Rufe Val
10 Nov 44	Ormoc Bay, Leyte, PI	Oscar
11 Nov 44	Ormoc Bay, Leyte, PI	2 Jacks
28 Nov 44	Ormoc Bay, Leyte, PI	Zero
7 Dec 44	Ormoc Bay, Leyte, PI	3 Jacks
13 Dec 44	SW of Negros Island	Sally
25 Dec 44	Over Clark Field, PI	2 Jacks Zero Jack (P)
1 Jan 45	Over Clark Field, PI	Tojo
13 Feb	East of Indo-China	Topsy

All victories in P-38

MacDonald tallied 27 victories, two probables, and 4½ damaged.

Decorations: Distinguished Service Cross with an Oak Leaf Cluster), Silver Star with an OLC, Distinguished Flying Cross with five OLCs, Air Medal with 10 OLCs, and the Legion of Merit

His P-47s and P-38s were named Putt-Putt Maru.

Neel Kearby 22 Victories

Kearby

Neel Earnest Kearby was born on 5 June 1911 in Wichita Falls, TX, and attended high school and North Texas Agricultural College in Arlington, TX, graduating from the University of Texas, Austin, in 1937 with a BA degree. On 25 February, he enlisted as a Flying Cadet at March Field, CA, and trained at Randolph and Kelly Fields, TX, getting his Pilot's Rating in the Reserves and a 2nd Lieutenant commission on 16 February 1938. He transferred to the AAC and was promoted to 1st Lieutenant on 9 September 1940, serving with the 1st, 94th, and 40th Pursuit Squadrons and at Selfridge Field, MI, where he held a succession of assignments, including Flight Commander. He went to the Canal Zone in December 1941 as 14th Pursuit Squadron Commander and was promoted to Captain on 1 February 1942, and to Major on 1 March. He served there flying patrols in P-39 fighters until August 1942, when he returned to the United States and was assigned as Commander of the 348th Fighter Group at Bradley Field, CT, in October, and later at Westover Field,

MA. He and his Group were one of the first to be checked out in the P-47 Thunderbolt and he was immediately impressed with it, convinced that the large and powerful fighter was more than equal to any Axis fighter. He was promoted to Lt. Colonel on 28 November 1942. In late May 1943, the 348th arrived in Australia as the first P-47 Group assigned to the SWPA, where the P-38 Lightning had been the premier Allied fighter for nearly a year.

The 348th was deployed to Port Moresby, New Guinea, but saw no combat until 16 August, after waiting for drop tanks to arrive to be attached to the P-47s to extend their range. Kearby scored his first two victories (a Betty and Oscar) on 4 September, and 11 days later shot down a Dinah. He was promoted to Colonel on 23 September 1943.

On 11 October, Kearby scored six victories (two Zeros, two Tonys, and two Haps) during a fighter sweep over Borum A/D. This made him the first P-47 ace of the Pacific Theater and set an AAC record (at the time) for most victories in a single mission. Gen. George Kenney recommended Kearby for the Medal of Honor, which was presented to him by Gen. Douglas MacArthur on 6 January 1944, the first MOH awarded to an AAC fighter pilot. On 16 October, Kearby would become a double ace with a Zero victory over Wewak. After shooting down two Pete float planes on 19 October, he would become a triple ace by shooting down three Zeros near Wewak on 3 December. He would score two more victories in December (and a damaged) and downed a Sally and Zero on 3 January 1944 for his 18th and 19th victories. On 8 February 1944, he was "kicked upstairs to desk duty" at Fighter Command Headquarters (CO of the 308BW), partly to keep him out of combat and being killed. Kearby expressed his dissatisfaction and Kenney allowed him to fly "restricted combat." Kearby scored a double on 9 January, raising his victory tally to 21 and tying him for the lead with P-38 pilot Richard Bong in the race to beat the all-time high American total of 26 victories scored by World War I ace Capt. Eddie Rickenbacker. On 15 February, Bong scored his 22nd victory, while on 27 February Kearby damaged a Sally. Then, on 3 March, Bong downed two Sallys to give him 24 victories. On the 5th, Kearby led a fighter sweep near Wewak and shot down a Nell bomber for his 22nd victory, but was shot down and killed; his score remained the highest of any P-47 pilot in the Pacific Theater.

Aerial Victory Credits

Date	Location	Credits
4 Sept 43	South of Hopoi, NG	Betty Oscar
14 Sept 43	Near Malahang, NG	Dinah
11 Oct 43	Over Boram A/D, NG	2 Zeros 2 Haps 2 Tonys
16 Oct 43	Over Wewak, NG	Zero
19 Oct 43	Over Wewak, NG	2 Petes
3 Dec 43	Boram A/D, NG	3 Zeros
22 Dec 43	Wewak, NG	Zero
23 Dec 43	Dagua A/D, NG	Tony
3 Jan 44	Near Wewak, NG	Sally Tony
9 Jan 44	Near Wewak, NG	2 Tonys
27 Feb 44	Cape Hoskins, NG	Sally (D)
5 March 44	Over Wewak, NG	Nell

All victories in P-47

Before his death, Kearby had 22 victories and one probable.

His other decorations include two Silver Stars, four Distinguished Flying Crosses, five Air Medals, and a Purple Heart (posthumous).

His P-47s were named Fiery Ginger and Fiery Ginger IV after his wife, Virginia.

Gerald R. Johnson (Jerry and Johnny Eagar) 22 Victories

Johnson

Gerald Richard Johnson was born in the small town of Kenmore, OH, on 23 June 1920. He entered the U.S. Army Aviation Cadet Program in Spring 1941, and was awarded his Pilot's Wings on 31 October 1941 at Luke Field, AZ. On 1 November 1941, he was assigned to the 54PG/57PS/11AF in Alaska from June to October 1942, flying P-39 Airacobras and P-40 Warhawks. Johnson flew 58 combat missions in Alaska in what has been described as "the worst weather in the world." While flying there, he shot down Zeros on 25 September and 1 October 1942, but Squadron records and the 11th Air Force did not document these victories. However, Johnson did not accept this decision and his future aircraft were marked with these two denied victories.

In February 1943, Johnson was transferred from Alaska to the 329FG/332FS, and then in April to Australia and was assigned to the 49FG/9FS/5AF. On 26 July, he got his first verified victories (Oscar and Tony), but the Tony collided into his port tail assembly, tearing it away. Johnson regained control and landed safely at Horanda, but his fighter (#83 Sooner) was scrapped. Johnson was promoted to Captain and CO of the 9FS (the "Flying Knights") in August 1943.

On 15 October 1943, the Japanese sent out a large formation of Zero fighters and Val dive bombers to attack the Allied invasion fleet anchored in Oro Bay and the 49FG P-38s decimated the enemy formations. Johnson downed two Vals and an Oscar to become an ace. On October 17th, the Japanese mounted another strike, this time with a formation of Lily bombers protected by Oscars and Zeros. In late October, Johnson, by demonstrating leadership and flying ability, was promoted to Major. On 10 December, he shot down a Tony while flying a P-47 near Gusap Airstrip to become a double ace with ten victories. He would score his last P-47 victory on 18 January 1944, before being sent home in Spring 1944.

Johnson returned for another tour of duty in the Summer of 1944 and resumed command of the 9FS; he was also named the Deputy Group Commander of the 49FG, which was again flying the favored P-38. During preparations for MacArthur's return to the Philippines, on 14 October, Johnson and the 9FS escorted 5BC heavy bombers over 1,000 miles to the oil fields at Balikpapan, and Johnson would score his first victories in nine months when he downed an Oscar and Tojo. Johnson then became a triple ace on 27 October, when he shot down an Oscar and Val that were attacking Tacloban Airfield during the American invasion of the Philippines.

After two Zero victories over Ormoc Bay on 11 November, Johnson would have his best day of his career on 7 December, with four victories to put him at 21 victories. While leading a formation of P-38s that day, Johnson spotted a large formation of Japanese fighters and ordered an attack. Within minutes, Johnson shot down three Oscars over the tip of Cebu and then a Helen bomber over Ormoc Bay and was promoted to Lieutenant Colonel. During the Spring of 1945, the 49FG flew out of Clark Field and was assigned to provide ground support and had virtually no opportunity to score any aerial victories over the decimated Japanese Air Forces. On 2 April 1945, the 49FG was roving over the China Sea and Johnson scored his 22nd and last victory over a Tojo flying north of Hong Kong. In July 1945, he was promoted to full Colonel and after Japan surrendered Johnson elected to remain in the Air Force and was the CO of Atsugi Air Base in Japan.

On 7 October 1945, Johnson was piloting a B-25 transport aircraft and flew into a typhoon and became completely lost. He ordered everyone to bail out, but one person did not bring a parachute and Johnson gave his parachute away and tried to fly the B-25 back to base safely, but Johnson and his copilot were both killed when the B-25 crashed on its landing approach.

Aerial Victory Credits

Date	Location	Credits
23 July 43	Over Salamaua, NG	Tony (P)
26 July 43	Markham Valley, NG	Oscar & Tony
2 Sept 43	NW Cape Gloucester, New Britain	TE Fighter & TE Fighter (P)
15 Oct 43	NE Oro Bay, NG	2 Vals, Oscar & Val (D)
23 Oct 43	Over Rapopo, Rabaul	Zero
2 Nov 43	Simpson Harbor, Rabaul	2 Zeros
10 Dec 43	North of Gusap, NG	Tony*
18 Jan 44	South of Wewak, NG	Zero*
14 Oct 44	Balikpapan, Borneo	Oscar & Tojo
27 Oct 44	Tacloban area, PI Carigara Bay, PI	Oscar Val
11 Nov 44	Ormoc Bay, PI	2 Zeros
7 Dec 44	South tip of Cebu Ormoc Bay, PI	3 Oscars Helen
2 April 45	North of Hong Kong	Tojo

*While Flying P-47; all other victories in P-38

Johnson finished the war with 22 victories, two probables, and a damaged, and was awarded with two DSCs, six DFCs, the Silver Star, 12 Air Medals, and the Legion of Merit. His named fighters were Sooner #83 (P-38), Jerry #83 (P-38), and Barbara (P-38).

Jay Robbins (Cock) 22 Victories

Robbins

Jay Thorpe Robbins was born on 16 September 1919 in Coolidge, Texas. He graduated from Texas A&M College in 1940 with a ROTC reserve commission. In February 1941, he entered active duty as a 2Lt. in the Infantry, but he later transferred to the AAC and began Flight Training at Corsicana, Rudolph, and Victoria, TX, in July 1942. He completed pilot training at Foster Field, TX, on 3 July 1942. He was sent to the 20FG/55FS at Morris Field, NC, and Drew Field, FL, where he transitioned to fighters. In October, he was assigned to the 8FG in New Guinea flying P-400s.

On Robbins's first mission on 17 January 1943, he damaged two Sally bombers while flying a P-400. On 28 May, Robbins was promoted to 1st Lieutenant. On 21 July, Robbins began his scoring in a big way over Bogadjim, when he shot down three Zeros and claimed another as a probable. It would not be until 4 September when Robbins would score again and he became an ace, scoring in a big way with four Zeros shot down and two more as probables. On 24 October, Robbins became a double ace when he shot down four Hamps (plus one probable), and on 5 November he was promoted to Captain. Robbins would conclude his scoring for 1943 by shooting down two Zeros (plus one probable) to give him 13 victories. The next day, he was named CO of the 80FS; a post he would serve in until 4 October 1944. Under his leadership, and with numerous pilots attaining ace status, the 80FS became the first Squadron in the SWPA to score 200 victories. From 30 March until 17 August, Robbins added eight Japanese fighters to his total during raids against the Japanese strongholds at Rabaul, New Britain, and Hollandia, Dutch New Guinea, as the Allies pushed the Japanese back toward the Philippines. He became a triple ace on 30 March with two Oscars shot down north of Hollandia and a quadruple ace on 16 June with two Zeros downed south of Samate. On 22 May 1944, he was promoted to Major, and in September Robbins became Deputy Commander of the 8FG after Maj. Edward Cragg was MIA. Robbins continued to fly with his old squadron and scored his final victory on 14 November, to give him 22 in 181 combat missions. He returned to the United States in December 1944.

Over the next 30 years in the Air Force, Robbins rose to Lt. General in March 1970 (Lt. Colonel in October 1950, Colonel in April 1953, Brig. General in August 1962, and Maj. General in June 1963), serving as Commander of the 12AF and Vice Commander of Tactical Air Command prior to retiring as Vice Commander of Military Airlift Command in September 1974.

Aerial Victory Credits

Date	Location	Credits
17 Jan 43	Near Ferguson Island, NG	2 Sallys (D)*
21 July 43	Near Bogadjim, NG	3 Zeros Zero (P)
4 Sept 43	Between Lae and Salamaua, NG	4 Zeros 2 Zeros (P)
24 Oct 43	Over Kabanga Bay, Rabaul	4 Hamps Hamp (P)
26 Dec 43	Cape Gloucester, NB	2 Zeros Zero (P)
30 Mar 44	North of Hollandia, NG	2 Oscars Oscar (P)
31 Mar 44	SW of Hollandia, NG	Oscar
12 April 44	Hollandia	2 Tonys 2 Tonys (D)
16 June 44	South of Samate	2 Zeros
17 Aug 44	Haroekoe Strait	Oscar
14 Nov 44	West of Alicante	Oscar

* Flying a P-400 All other victories in P-38

Robbins's totals: 22 Confirmed, six probables, and four damaged

Decorations: Distinguished Service Cross with one Oak Leaf Cluster, Distinguished Service Medal with two OLCs, Silver Star with one OLC, Legion of Merit with two OLCs, Distinguished Flying Cross with three OLCs, and Air Medal with six OLCs.

Aircraft: P-38s Jandina III and IV (after he, Jay and his wife, Ina)

Thomas Lynch 20 Victories

Lynch

Thomas J. Lynch was born in Catasauqua, Pennsylvania, on 9 December 1916. After graduating from the University of Pittsburgh with a Chemical Engineering degree and attending ROTC, he joined the Army Reserves in 1940. On 12 June, he was commissioned as a 2nd Lieutenant and awarded his Pilot's Wings on 7 February 1941 at Maxwell AFB. He was assigned to the 35PG/39PS at Selfridge Field, engaging in maneuvers flying the P-39 Airacobra during the Summer and Fall.

He was shipped to Australia in January 1942, and after arriving at Brisbane, the 39th Squadron underwent an intense training program; it was not until mid-May 1942 that a forward echelon of the Squadron was sent TDY to New Guinea. Lynch achieved three victories over New Guinea flying a P-39: two on May 20th and another on May 26th. On 16 June, he was shot down and wounded and returned to combat after the 39FS was selected to be the first squadron in the SWPA to be equipped with P-38 Lightnings. The 39FS flew top cover over the American beachhead in the Buna-Dobodura area, where Lynch would score his first victories in the Lightning on 27 December, when he shot down two Oscars to become an ace; he would follow with this with two Zero victories four days later. After becoming a double ace, Lynch became 39FS CO on 24 March 1943, when Maj. George Prentice was selected to command the new 475FG. In 1943, Lynch continued to run up his score and was promoted to Major and Commanding Officer of the 35FG. During this time, he had to bail out over water and broke his arm. By October 1943, Lynch had claimed 16 victories and returned home to Pennsylvania to marry his long time love, Rosemary Fullen.

In January 1944, both Lynch and leading SWPA ace Capt. Richard Bong (21 victories) returned to the Southwest Pacific and were assigned to the 5FC. The pair was allowed to freelance and was called "The Flying Circus." During this time Lynch would score his final four victories, and on 28 February was promoted to Lieutenant Colonel.

Aerial Victory Credits

Date	Location	Credits
20 May 42	Wangari, NG	2 Zeros*
26 May 42	Mt. Lawson, NG	Zero*
27 Dec 42	Buna, NG	2 Oscars
31 Dec 42	East of Lae, NG	2 Zeros
7 Jan 43	Huon Gulf, NG	Oscar Oscar (D)
3 Mar 43	East of Lae, NG	Oscar
10 June 43	Near Saidor, NG	TE Bomber
26 July 43	West of Lae, NG	Oscar (P)
20 Aug 43	South of Wewak, NG	TE Fighter TE Fighter
21 Aug 43	Dagua A/D, Wewak	Oscar Zero (D)
4 Sept 43	Huon Gulf, NG	Dive Bomber Oscar (D)
16 Sept 43	NW of Hansa Bay, NG	Dinah
10 Feb 44	Tadji, NG	Lily(?)
3 Mar 44	Tadji, NG	Sally (D) u/i Fighter Tony Sally (D)
5 Mar 44	Over Dagua, NG	Oscar Oscar (D)

*While flying P-400 All other victories in P-38

Lynch had 20 victories, one probable, and five damaged.

Lynch's decorations included the Silver Star, DSC, DFC with three OLCs, ten Air Medals, and two Purple Hearts.

Lynch's aircraft had no known personal markings.

George Welch (Wheaties) 16 Victories

Welch

George Welch was born on 10 October 1918 as George Schwartz, but his father, a senior research chemist for DuPont, changed their name to avoid anti-German sentiment during World War I. He attended St. Andrew's School in 1936, then completed three years of Mechanical Engineering at Purdue before joining the Army Reserves in 1939. Before he was commissioned as a 2nd Lieutenant and awarded his Pilot's Wings on 4 October 1940, he attended Brooks, Kelley, and Randolph Fields and AAC Flight Training Schools at San Antonio, TX, as well as Hamilton Field, Novato, CA. On 24 October 1940, he was assigned to the 55PS/20PG, and on 8 February 1941, he transferred to the Hawaiian Department and was assigned to the 15PG on 21 February, then the 47PS/47PG at Wheeler Field, Oahu, on 1 April 1941, flying the P-40B.

During the attack on Pearl Harbor he shot down two Kates, a Val, and a Zero, and was recommended for the Medal of Honor, but received the first AAC DSC instead, because he took off without permission! After Pearl Harbor, Welch returned to the Continental U.S. to sell War Bonds, after which he was assigned to the 36FS/8FG in New Guinea, flying the P-39. Exactly one year after Pearl Harbor, Welch would shoot down two Vals and a Zero over Buna while flying the P-39.

Welch was transferred to the 80FS/8FG (flying the P-38) and scored nine victories between 21 June and 2 September 1943: on 21 June, he shot down two Zeros (plus a probable) over Lae/Salamaua; on 20 August, he shot down three Tonys over Wewak; and finally, he spectacularly concluded his World War II career by shooting down three Zeros and a Dinah over Wewak on 2 September. Welch flew three combat tours for a total of 348 combat missions with 16 confirmed victories—all achieved in multiples—before he contracted severe Malaria, which sent him back to America.

Welch resigned from the Air Force as a Major in 1944 and became Chief Test Pilot, engineer, and instructor with North American Aviation during the Korean War, where he reportedly downed several enemy MiG-15s while "supervising" his students. However, Welch's victories were in disobedience of direct orders for him not to engage and credits for the kills were thus distributed among his students. Afterward, Welch received some notoriety for reportedly being the first pilot to exceed Mach 1 in the prototype XP-86 Sabre, two weeks before Chuck Yeager's X-1 record flight. Controversy exists as to the actual details of the flight, and if this flight took place, it is generally not recognized as a record because of a lack of verifiable speed measurement and because the Sabre's highest speeds were attained while diving, whereas Yeager's X-1 set the record in level flight. In 1954, Welch died in a crash during a test flight in a North American F-100 Super Sabre. (**Note:** Welch remained in the AAF and then continued in the dangerous test pilot business, despite being the heir to the Welch's Grape Juice fortune.)

Aerial Victory Credits

Date	Location	Credits
7 Dec 41	Pearl Harbor, HI	2 Kates* Val Zero
7 Dec 42	Over Buna, NG	2 Vals** Zero
21 June 43	Over Lae/Salamaua	2 Zeros Zero (P)
20 Aug 43	Over Wewak, NG	3 Tonys
2 Sept 43	Over Wewak	3 Zeros Dinah

* While flying P-40
**While flying P-39 (Remaining victories in P-38)
Welch tallied 16 victories (all in multiples) and 1 probable.
Welch was awarded the DSC, Silver Star, DFC with two OLCs, and two Air Medals.
The only recorded aircraft personal markings was Miss Helen the Flying Jenny.

William Dunham (Bill, Dinghy) 16 Victories

Dunham

William Douglas Dunham was born in Tacoma, WA, on 29 January 1920. He graduated from high school in Nezperce, ID, and attended the University of Idaho at Moscow from 1937 to 1940, joining the Army Reserves. He began as a Flying Cadet on 26 April 1941, and completed the Air Corps Primary and Basic Flying schools at Santa Monica and Moffett Field, CA; graduated from Advanced Flying School at Luke Field, AZ; and received a commission as 2nd Lieutenant and Pilot's rating on 12 December 1941.

Dunham was assigned as a pilot with the 53FG from December 1941 to September 1942 at Tallahassee, FL, and later Howard Field, Canal Zone. He was promoted to 1st Lieutenant on 26 August 1942. He next served as test pilot with the 1st Fighter Command, NY, until November 1942, then as a pilot with the 342FS/348FG at Bradley Field, CT, through December

1942. On 21 January 1943, he was promoted to Captain and deployed with the 342FS to Australia and New Guinea.

Dunham would begin his scoring with four victories in eight days in October 1943. On the 11th, he shot down a Tony east of Boram A/D; on the 16th, he claimed two Zeros over Madang; and on the 19th, he shot down a Pete east of Wewak. On 21 December, he became an ace when he shot down three Vals over Arawe and returned to the U.S. on a three-month leave. When he returned for his second tour in early March 1944, he destroyed a Nell and an Oscar over Wewak on the 5th. He was assigned as CO of the 342FS on 24 May, when Maj. William Banks returned home. He commanded the 342nd until 26 July 1944, when he was named the CO of the newly-formed 460FS of the 348FG. He was promoted to Major on 20 September 1944. Meanwhile, he had to wait until 18 November to become a double ace when he claimed a Zero west of Camotes Island. On 7 December, he had his best career day when he shot down two Zeros and two Oscars in the vicinity of Camotes Island, then shot down a Sally a week later off Talisay to give him 15 victories. On 18 December, he was named Assistant Operations Officer of the 348FG.

In January 1945, Dunham returned to the U.S. and attended a gunnery school at Foster Field, TX, until May 1945. Upon graduation, he immediately returned to the 348FG in the Philippines and continued to serve as Operations Officer, later becoming Deputy Commander. He was promoted to Lt. Colonel on 22 July 1945, and scored his last victory on 1 August 1945, when he downed a Frank during a fighter sweep over Take A/D, Kyushu.

Dunham continued to serve in the new Air Force in various Command positions and was promoted to Colonel on 1 December 1951 and Brigadier General on 1 August 1963; he retired from the Air Force in June 1970 with that rank.

Aerial Victory Credits

Date	Location	Credits
11 Oct 43	East of Boram A/D, NG	Tony
15 Oct 43	South of Madang, NG	2 Haps
19 Oct 43	East of Wewak, NG	Pete
21 Dec 43	Over Arawe	3 Vals
5 Mar 44	Over Wewak	Nell Oscar
18 Nov 44	West of Camote Island, PI	Zero
7 Dec 44	Camote Island area, PI	2 Zeros 2 Oscars
14 Dec 44	Off Talisay, PI	Sally
1 Aug 45	Take A/D, Kyushu, Japan	Frank

All victories flying P-47
Dunham totaled 16 victories.
Dunham's decorations include the Distinguished Service Cross, Silver Star with OLC, Distinguished Flying Cross with three OLCs, Air Medal with six OLCs, and the Legion of Merit.
Dunham's P-47s were named Bonnie and Mrs. Bonnie.

Edward Cragg (Porky) 15 Victories

Edward Cragg was born in Mount Vernon, NY, on 8 September 1918. He spent his boyhood in Greenwich, CT, graduating from high school in 1936, and in September 1937 enrolled in the School of Commerce at New York

Cragg

University, where he was working towards a Bachelor of Science Degree in Accounting. However, in September 1940 he withdrew from the University to join the Army Air Corps.

He enlisted as a Flying Cadet on 30 November 1940, and received his Elementary Training at Albany, GA; his Basic Training at Gunter Field, AL, from February through April 1941; and his Advanced Flying Training at the Air Corps Advanced Flying School, Craig Field, Selma, AL. He was appointed a 2nd Lieutenant, Air Reserve on 11 July 1941, and was ordered to active duty the following day.

Upon graduation from Advanced Flying School, he remained at the School until July 1941, when he was ordered to the Panama Canal Zone for duty as Assistant Squadron Engineering Officer, later becoming Engineering Officer of the 28th Pursuit Squadron in the 37th Pursuit Group, stationed at Albrook Field, where he was promoted to 1st Lieutenant on 5 September 1942. In the Spring of 1942, he was reassigned to what was then designated the 80th Pursuit Squadron, as part of the 8th Pursuit Group, 5th Air Force in the Southwest Pacific Area. Initially, the Squadron flew P-39 Airacobras and Cragg named his fighter Porky; soon he also was given that nickname. He was promoted to Captain on 17 December 1942.

On 8 April 1943, he became CO of the 80FS. Once in command, he gave the Squadron the name "The Headhunters" after the local New Guinean headhunter tribes and also commissioned Crew Chief Yale Saffro, a former Walt Disney artist, to design the 80th's patch, which was the image of the Papuan Headhunter Chief. Soon the Squadron was equipped with the new P-38 Lightning and he named his Porky II.

Cragg scored his first victory near Salamaua on 21 May, when he shot down an Oscar (plus a probable). He was promoted to Major on 6 July 1943, and would become an ace that month. After shooting down two Oscars on the 21st near Bogadjim, two days later, he would shoot down another Oscar, plus a Tony in the same area to become an ace. Then, in a two-week period, Cragg would become a double ace with a Tony and an Oscar on 21 August over Wewak, followed by another Oscar the next day over Wewak, then downing two Zeros between Lae and Salamaua on 4 September. In late October, he would shoot down three Zeros over Rabaul (two on the 24th, the other on the 29th). He shot down a Zero over Wewak on 22 December and became a triple ace on the 26th, when he shot down a Tojo over Borgen Bay, but was reported MIA. He was succeeded in command of the 80FS by ace Maj. Jay Robbins. His body was FOD (Finding of Death) on 16 January 1946.

Aerial Victory Credits

Date	Location	Credits
21 May 43	Near Salamaua, NG	Oscar Oscar (P)
21 July 43	Near Bogadjim, NG	2 Oscars
23 July 43	Over Bogadjim, NG	Oscar Tony
20 Aug 43	Near Wewak, NG	Oscar Tony
21 Aug 43	Near Wewak, NG	Oscar
4 Sept 43	Between Lae and Salamaua	2 Zeros
24 Oct 43	Over Rapopo Strip, Rabaul,	2 Zeros
29 Oct 43	Over Vunakanau, NG	Zero Zero (P)
2 Nov 43	Over Rabaul	Val (P) Zero (P)
22 Dec 43	Over Wewak, NG	Tony
26 Dec 43	Over Borgen Bay, NB	Tojo

All victories in P-38

During his tenure with the 80FS, Cragg compiled an air-to-air combat record of 15 confirmed kills and four probables.

Decorations: Distinguished Service Cross, Silver Star, DFC with four OLCs, Purple Heart with OLC, Air Medal with Silver OLC, and one Bronze OLC (7AMs).

Aircraft personal markings were Porky.

Cyril Homer (Cy, Uncle Cy) 15 Victories

Homer

Cyril Filcher Homer was born on 29 April 1919 in West New Jersey, NJ. He joined the Army Reserves as a 2nd Lieutenant and was Pilot rated on 30 October 1942 at Luke Field, AZ. He was assigned to the 80FS/8FG in February 1943 and claimed a Zero (or Oscar) probable on 21 May 1943 near Salamaua. He would not score his first victory until 21 August, when he shot down two Zeros and a Tony and damaged a twin-engine fighter near Wewak; he was promoted to 1st Lieutenant that month. On 4 September, he shot down a Zero east of

Salamaua and became an ace on 13 September by shooting down an Oscar near Dagua A/D. On 7 November, he took part in the Rabaul bomber escorts and claimed two Zero probables to conclude his scoring for 1943. His three victories in January were tallied over Wewak on the 18th, and an Oscar and an Oscar and Tony (with an Oscar probable) on the 23rd. On 30 March, Homer flew over Hollandia and claimed a Tony (and two others damaged). On 3 April, Homer would have his best day and become a double ace when he shot down two Oscars and two Tonys over Hollandia. He was promoted to Captain that same month. He flew two scoring missions over the Halmaheras airdromes, claiming a Zero probable on 17 June and an Oscar destroyed and another damaged on 27 July. On 4 October, he was assigned as CO of the 80FS. Homer would be credited with his 15th and last victory on 10 November near Palompon, Leyte, and would continue on as the Squadron CO until 9 May 1945. He transferred out of the service on 25 May 1945 and remained in the inactive Reserves until May 1951. Little is known of his post service life, except that he died in August 1975.

DeHaven

Aerial Victory Credits

Date	Location	Credits
21 May 43	Near Salamaua, NG	Zero (P)
21 Aug 43	Over Wewak, NG	2 Zeros Tony TE Fighter (D)
4 Sept 43	Neat Salamaua, NG	Zero
13 Sept 43	Over Dagua A/D, NG	Oscar
7 Nov 43	Rabaul, NB	2 Zeros (P)
18 Jan 44	Near Wewak, NG	Oscar
23 Jan 44	Over Wewak, NG	Tony Oscar Oscar (P)
30 Mar 44	NW of Hollandia, NG	Tony 2 Tonys (D)
3 Apr 44	Over Hollandia	2 Oscars 2 Tonys
17 June 44	Near Jefman A/D	Zero (P)
27 July 44	Lolobata, Halmaheras	Oscar Oscar (D)
10 Nov 44	Near Palompon, Leyte	Oscar

All victories in P-38

Homer totaled 15 victories, five probables, and four damaged.

Homer was awarded the DSC, Silver Star, DFS with two OLCs, and the Air Medal with nine OLCs.

Homer's P-38s were named Cotton Duster and Uncle Cy's Angel.

Robert DeHaven 14 Victories

Robert Marshall DeHaven was born on 13 January 1922 in San Diego, CA. He attended Washington and Lee University, but left to join the AAC in February 1942. He earned his Wings and 2nd Lieutenant Commission at Luke Field, AZ, on 4 January 1943, and was assigned to P-40 training in Florida with the 73FS/318FG. In March 1943, he was sent to Hawaii and then sent to Port Moresby, New Guinea, via Australia in May, where he was assigned to the P-40 equipped 7FS/49FG at Dobodura.

2Lt. DeHaven scored his first victory on 14 July 1943, when he shot down a Val near Salamaua, and as a 2nd Lieutenant continued scoring in October with an Oscar victory over Buna on the 17th and a Zero and Tony off Finschhafen on the 27th. He became an ace on 10 December, when he shot down an Oscar over Alexischafen, and two days later shot down another Oscar near Alexischafen. Between January and May 1944, he continued to fly the P-40, becoming a double ace and the highest scoring 5FC P-40 ace. During this time, he downed a Tony on 2 January; an Oscar near Moem Point, NG, on 23 January; an Oscar on 15 March over Kairiru Island; and a Judy off Biak Island on 7 May.

The 7FS transitioned to P-38s in July-September 1944 for the Philippine invasion. Within seven days, DeHaven would score his last four victories: an Oscar near Biliran Island on 29 October; a Zero destroyed (and Val damaged) near Tacloban A/D on 1 November; a Jack downed near Pors Islands the next day; and his final victory, a Zero over Jaro, Leyte, on 4 November. After leave to the U.S., he rejoined the 49FG at Lingayen as Group Operations Officer, serving into the occupation of Japan.

Following the war, DeHaven joined the Hughes Aircraft Company as an engineering test pilot and personal pilot to Howard Hughes. Eventually he became an executive of the firm and manager of the Flight Test Division for over 30 years.

Aerial Victory Credits

Date	Location	Credits
14 July 43	Near Salamaua, NG	Val*
17 Oct 43	Off Buna, NG	Oscar*
27 Oct 43	Off Finschhafen, NG	Zero*
10 Dec 43	Over Finschhafen, NG	Tony*
12 Dec 43	Near Alexishafen, NG	Tony*
2 Jan 44	? New Guinea	Tony*
23 Jan 44	Near Moem Point, NG	Oscar*
15 Mar 44	Kairiru Island, NG	Oscar*
7 May 44	Near Biak	Judy?*
29 Oct 44	Biliran Island	Oscar

1 Nov 44	Near Tacloban A/D, PI	Zero Val (D)
2 Nov 44	Pors Island, PI	Jack
4 Nov 44	Jaro, Leyte	Zero

*P-40 victories remaining victories in P-38

DeHaven's totals: 14 Confirmed and one Damaged. DeHaven and Ernest Harris of the 8FS/49FG were the top scorers in the P-40 in the Pacific with 10 victories each.

Decorations: Silver Star with one OLC, Distinguished Flying Cross with two OLCs, and the Air Medal with 13 OLCs.

Aircraft Names: An orchid drawing and the name Rita on the P-40 and an orchid shooting drawing on his P-38.

Daniel Roberts 14 Victories

Roberts

Daniel Tipton Roberts was born on 20 September 1918 in Tucumcari, NM. After graduating from New Mexico Highlands University with a degree in music, Roberts taught music until he joined the Army Reserves. He was commissioned as a 2Lt. and received his Wings on 26 September 1941. He was sent to the Pacific in 1942, where he joined the 80FS/8FG flying P-400s, and on 26 August claimed two Zeros and a damaged for his first claims. Capt. Lynch was transferred to the new 475FG to transition to the P-38 with the 432FS and claimed two Vals on 11 April 1943 for his first two Lightning victories. He scored two Zero victories ten days later to become an ace. He was named the CO of the struggling 433FS and soon turned that unit around, and from 17 October to 9 November scored seven more victories to give him 14. He was KIA on 9 November 1943 when he collided with another P-38 (see Volume 1 for details). The mild mannered Roberts was known as the "Quiet Ace," as he neither drank, smoked, nor swore.

Aerial Victory Credits

Date	Location	Credits
26 Aug 42	Buna A/S, NG	2 Zeros* Zero (D)
11 Apr 43	Off Oro Bay	2 Vals
21 Aug 43	Wewak area A/S	2 Haps
7 Sept 43	S. Arawe, CG	Oscar
17 Oct 43	E. Cape Ward Hunt	2 Zeros

23 Oct 43	Near Rabaul	2 Zeros
24 Oct 43	Near Rabaul	Zero
29 Oct 43	Near Rabaul	Zero
2 Nov 43	Near Rabaul	Zero (P)
9 Nov 43	Over Alexishafen	Zero

* P-400 victories; all others in P-38
Robert's totals: 14 victories, one probable, and one damaged
Decorations: DSC, three DFCs, and AM
Aircraft Names: None known

Richard West (Dick) 14 Victories

West

Richard Lee West was born on 12 July 1921 in Trenton, MO. He graduated from Chillicothe Business College, MO, and took a Civil Service position with the Quartermaster's Corps, but soon quit and joined the Army Air Force. He was commissioned as a 2nd Lieutenant and received his Wings on 10 November 1942 at Moore Field, TX. He was assigned to the 81FS/50FG as an Instructor and on 1 September 1942 was transferred to the 8FG/35FG, based in New Guinea.

2Lt. West scored his first victories on 22 September 1943, when he shot down two Zeros and also claimed a probable near Finschhafen while flying the P-40N. 1Lt. West would become an ace on 15 November when he had his best career day, shooting down two Zeros (and a probable) and two Sallys (and a probable) north of Kaiaput, New Guinea. After transitioning to the P-38, he would then score more slowly, claiming a Zero near Jefman, New Guinea, on 16 June 1944 and a Tony over Galela A/D, in the Halmaheras, on 27 July. Capt. West would then score seven victories during the first two weeks of November 1944. He would become a double ace on the 1st, when he shot down two Tojos (and damaged another) off Negros Island. On the 6th, he shot down a Tojo and Oscar over Fabrica A/D, Negros; then an Oscar on the 14th near Alicante A/D, Negros; and concluded his scoring the next day with his 14th victory, an Oscar also over La Carlota A/D, Negros Island. He then rotated home.

Aerial Victory Credits

Date	Location	Credits
22 Sept 43	Near Finschhafen, NG	2 Zeros* Zero (P)
15 Nov 43	North of Kaiaput, NG	2 Zeros* Zero (P) 2 Sallys Sally (P)
16 June 44	Over Jefman, NG	Zero
27 July 44	Galela A/D, Halmaheras	Tony
1 Nov 44	Alicante, Negros	2 Tojos Tojo (D)
6 Nov 44	Fabrica A/D, Negros	2 Oscars
14 Nov 44	Alicante, Negros	Oscar
15 Nov 44	La Carlota A/D, Negros	Oscar

*P-40 victories; all others in P-38
West's totals were six victories and three probables while flying the P-40 and eight victories and a damaged flying the P-38J.
Decorations: Silver Star, DSC, two DFCs, and eight Air Medals.
One of his P-38s was decorated with a Heart Flush.

Kenneth Ladd 12 Victories

Ladd

Kenneth George Ladd was born on 5 March 1920 in Salt Lake City, UT. He joined the Army Reserves and was commissioned as a 2nd Lieutenant, then Pilot rated on 30 October 1942 at Luke Field, AZ. He was assigned to the 80FS of the 8FG in February 1943.

After scoring a Tony probable on 23 July 1943, he claimed his first victory six days later, when he shot down a twin-engine Dinah over Cape Gloucester, New Britain, and was promoted to 1st Lieutenant on 30 July. On 2 September, he would add another Dinah southwest of Madang, followed by a Zero on 15 September over Boram A/D, Wewak. Ladd would score four victories in December: the first near Gasmata A/D on the 13th, then on the 17th during the Cape Gloucester Campaign he shot down a Zero to become an ace. He concluded his scoring for 1943 by shooting down two Vals on the 26th.

Ladd began his 1944 scoring by destroying a Zero over Wewak on 23 January. In March, he claimed Oscars as a probable and a damaged on 30 March north of Hollandia and destroyed another Oscar the next day in the same area. On 3 April, he became a double ace when he shot down another Oscar over Hollandia. He was appointed CO of the 35FS on 1 September. Ladd would score his last victories on 14 October, when he shot down two Oscars during the Balikpapan mission, but was KIA during the mission.

Aerial Victory Credits

Date	Location	Credits
23 July 43	Bogadjim, NG	Tony (P)
29 July 43	Cape Gloucester, NB	Dinah
2 Sept 43	Southwest of Madang	Dinah
15 Sept 43	Near Boram A/D, NG	Zero
13 Dec 43	Near Gasmata, NG	Zero
17 Dec 43	Near Cape Gloucester, NB	Zero
26 Dec 43	Cape Gloucester, NB	2 Vals
23 Jan 44	Over Wewak, NG	Zero
30 Mar 44	North of Hollandia, NG	Oscar (P) Oscar (D)
31 Mar 44	SW of Hollandia, NG	Oscar
3 April 44	Over Hollandia	Oscar
2 Sept 44	Davao, Mindanao, PI	Lily (D)
14 Oct 44	Balikpapan, Borneo	2 Oscars

All P-38 victories
Ladd's totals were 12 victories, two probables, and two damaged. His awards were the Silver Star, DFC with three OLCs, and the Air Medal with seven OLCs.
His P-38s were named X Virgin and Windy City Ruthie.

James Watkins (Duckbutt) 12 Victories

Watkins

James Albert Watkins was born on 26 August 1920 in Clinton, MS. He joined the Army Reserves and served as a Flying Cadet from 10 February to 26 September 1941, when he was commissioned as a 2nd Lieutenant and awarded his Pilot's Wings at Craig Field, AL. He was assigned to the 8PG/36PS, but was transferred to the 49PG on 15 December 1941; he was promoted to 1st Lieutenant on 15 December 1942.

Watkins scored his first victory on 26 December 1942, when he shot down a Zero (and claimed a probable) flying a P-40E for the 9FS over Dobodura. He was promoted to Captain on 16 June 1943 and was near the end of his tour when he scored 10 victories in just nine days in three combats flying the P-38. On 26 July, he shot down four Tonys over the Markham Valley to become an ace. Two days later, he shot down three Oscars over the Cape Raoult area, New Britain. Then, on 2 August, he became a double ace with eleven victories when he shot down three more Oscars near Teliata Point, Saidor.

After his tour, he returned to America and was transferred back to the 49FG in 1945 for another combat tour and shot down a Tojo north of Hong Kong to give him a dozen victories. He was promoted to Major on 4 June 1945 and remained in the postwar Air Force. He was promoted to Lt. Colonel on 19 October 1950; to Colonel on 5 April 1955; and retired from the Air Force in January 1970.

Aerial Victory Credits

Date	Location	Credits
26 Dec 42	Near Dobodura	Zero* Zero (P)
25 July 43	Markham Valley, NG	4 Tonys
28 July 43	Cape Raoult area, NB	3 Oscars
2 Aug 43	Saidor area	3 Oscars
2 April 45	Near Hong Kong	Tojo

*P-40 victories all others in P-38
Watkins's totals were 12 victories and one probable.
Decorations: Two Silver Stars, DFC, DSC with OLC, and three Air Medals.
His P-40 had a Donald Duck™ drawing and his P-38s were named Charlcie Jeanne.

Francis Lent (Fran) 11 Victories

Lent

Francis J. Lent was born on 20 October 1917 in St. Paul, MN, and grew up in Melrose, MN; he managed a grocery store before the war. He joined the Army Air Corps Reserves in 1942 and went to Thunderbird Field, AZ, for Primary Flight Training; he was commissioned a 2nd Lieutenant. He was awarded his Pilots Wings at Luke Field, Phoenix, AZ, graduating on 10 March 1943, along with the famous ace and test pilot Chuck Yeager.

After graduation, 1Lt. Lent was deployed to Glendale, CA, with the 329FG/331FS. On 9 July 1943, he was assigned to the 431FS/475FG ("Satan's Angels") in New Guinea. There he flew the P-38, often as Wingman for Thomas McGuire.

On 1 December 1944, just before going on leave and about to be married, Lent crashed into the ocean off Lae during a test flight of an F-6D, the photo-reconnaissance P-51, and was killed.

Aerial Victory Credits

Date	Location	Credits
18 Aug 43	Over Wewak, New Guinea	Zero
21 Aug 43	Near Wewak, New Guinea	TE Fighter & Zero
15 Oct 43	Oro Bay, New Guinea	Val & 2 Zeros
24 Oct 43	Over Rabaul, New Britain	Tony
2 Nov 43	Over Rabaul, New Britain	Zero & Zero (P)
16 Dec 43	Over Rabaul, New Britain	Betty
11 Mar 44	South of Hollandia, NG	2 Zeros

All victories in P-38
At his death, 1Lt. Lent had been credited with 11 destroyed and one probable.
Lent was awarded two Silver Stars, the Distinguished Flying Cross, and the Air Medal with 6 OLCs.
His P-38s were named T-Rigor Mortis I-III.

John Loisel 11 Victories

Loisel

John Simon Loisel was born in Coeur d'Alene, ID, on 21 May 1920, and moved to Norfolk, NB, in 1922. After graduating from high school, Loisel attended Wayne State Teacher's College, NE, and the University of Nebraska from 1938 to 1941. He then joined the Army Reserves as a Flying Cadet on 10 March and was commissioned as a 2nd Lieutenant and received his Wings on 31 October at Mather Field, CA.

Loisel was initially posted as a Flight Instructor while waiting for assignment. He was then assigned to a unit in the Philippine Islands, but en route by sea the Japanese attacked Pearl Harbor and he was redeployed to the 36FS/8FG, flying P-39s and P-400s based in New Guinea. He was promoted to 1st Lieutenant on 6 April 1943, and by June 1943, he had flown 83 combat missions without an aerial claim. In July, Loisel was selected as part of the cadre for the 432FS of the newly-formed 475FG, the first P-38 Lightning fighter group formed in the Pacific.

On 21 August 1943, Loisel would score his first two victories while escorting 5BC bombers near Wewak. On 22 September, he claimed a Zero near Finschhafen, and on 15 October, he became and ace by downing two more Zeroes near Oro Bay, New Guinea, and three days later was promoted to Captain. In December 1943, during the prelude for the Cape Gloucester landings, he added two more kills: a Zero on the 15th and another Zero on the 21st. Loisel was credited with his eighth victory on 23 January 1944 over a Zero, but would not score again until 3 April, when he shot down an Oscar and Hamp near Hollandia, New Guinea, making him a double ace. On 22 January 1944, he assumed command of the 432FS, which would fly tactical and escort missions supporting MacArthur's return to the Philippines. He was promoted to Major on 27 April.

On 4 August 1944, Loisel returned to the United States, and in January 1945, he returned to the 475FG as Operations Officer. Loisel scored his 11th and final aerial victory on 28 March, when he shot down a Frank near Tre Island, Indochina. On 15 May, he was promoted to Lt. Colonel and on 15 July he became the CO of the 475FG. He relinquished command on 18 April 1946, and returned to the United States as the fourth leading ace in the 475FG.

He remained in the Air Force on return to the U.S. in 1946. He married and re-enrolled at the University of Nebraska to earn his BS degree in physics in 1949. Beginning in May 1947, he served as the CO of the 63FS, and after a staff tour Loisel returned to combat in Korea in May 1953, after having been promoted to Colonel on 1 December 1951. He commanded the 474FBG and flew an additional 22 combat missions. Following the Korean War, Loisel was given various command assignments and in January 1970 he retired. Following his retirement, Loisel attended North Texas State University, obtaining his MS degree in physics in 1972, then taught high school physics until 1985. He died of natural causes on 20 January 2010.

Aerial Victory Credits

Date	Location	Credits
21 Aug 43	Near Dagua, NG	2 Tonys
22 Sept 43	Off Finschhafen, NG	Zero
15 Oct 43	Oro Bay, NG	2 Zeros
13 Dec 43	Over Gasmata, NG	Zero
16 Dec 43	Cape Gloucester, NB	Zero (D)
21 Dec 43	Over Arawe, NB	Zero
23 Jan 44	Brandi Plantation, NG	Zero
3 April 44	Over Hollandia	Oscar Hamp
28 Mar 45	Tre Is. Indo-China	Frank

All P-38 victories
Loisel totaled 11 victories and one damaged
Awards: Silver Star, 4 DFCs, and ?AMs
Aircraft names: P-38 Sooner Kid and Screamin Kid.

Cornelius Smith (Corky) 11 Victories

Smith

Cornelius Marcellus Smith was born on 11 November 1918 in Baltimore, MD. After he graduated from Roanoke College (VA) in 1940 with a BS degree, Smith joined the Army Reserves and served as an Aviation Cadet from 15 December 1941 to 5 September 1942, when he was commissioned as a 2nd Lieutenant and a Pilot rated at Spence Field, GA. In November 1942, he was assigned to the 80F/8FG and sent to New Guinea. On 21 June, he started his scoring career with a bang by downing three Zeros (plus a probable) near Lae. On 15 September, 1st Lieutenant (effective 7 August) Smith claimed another Zero probable, and in October he would become an ace after claiming a Tony on the 16th over Boram A/D, then getting victory #6 (a Zero) over Kabanga Bay, Rabaul, on the 24th. In December 1943, he shot down a Zero on the 22nd off the shore of Wewak and an Oscar on the 26th up the coast from Cape Gloucester, New Britain. On 18 January 1944, he shot down two Zeros over Wewak and was promoted to Captain on 8 February. After a damaged claim on 30 March, he became a double ace when he shot down a Dinah over Hollandia. On 12 April, he claimed his 11th and last victory; an Oscar near Lake Sentani, Hollandia. He finished his combat tour after completing 169 combat missions in May 1944 and remained in the postwar Air Force, being promoted to Major on 27 September 1946; to Lt. Colonel on 1 August 1961; and to full Colonel on 3 November 1964, retiring in November 1968.

Aerial Victory Credits

Date	Location	Credits
21 June 43	Near Lae, NG	3 Zeros Zero (P)
15 Sept 43	Boram A/D, Wewak, NG	Zero (P)
16 Oct 43	Boram A/D	Tony
24 Oct 43	Over Rabaul	Zero
22 Dec 43	Off shore, Wewak	Zero
26 Dec 43	Cape Gloucester, NB	Oscar
18 Jan 44	Near Wewak	2 Zeros
30 Mar 44	North of Hollandia, NG	Oscar (D)
31 Mar 44	Over Hollandia	Dinah
12 April 44	Lake Sentani, Hollandia	Oscar

All P-38 victories
Summer's totals were 11 victories, two probables, and one damaged.
Decorations: Silver Star, DFC with three OLCs, and six Air Medals.
Smith's P-38s were named Corky Jr. and Corky IV.

| 18 July 43 | Salamaua Area, NG | Oscar
Zero (P)
Zero (P) |
| 21 July 43 | Ramu/Madang, NG | Oscar |

All P-38 victories
Sparks's totals were 11 victories, two probables, and three damaged.
Decorations: Silver Star, DFC with three OLCs, and two Air Medals.
Aircraft names: None

Kenneth Sparks 11 Victories

Sparks

Kenneth C. Sparks was born in 1920 in Blackwell, OK. He joined the Army Reserves and was commissioned as a 2nd Lieutenant and awarded his Wings on 24 April 1942. He was assigned to the 39FS/35FG and sent to New Guinea, where the Squadron transitioned to the P-38. The 39FS took part in the air battles over Lae and Buna in December 1942, at which time Sparks shot down a Zero and a Val on the 27th, then two Zeros on the 31st. He would become an ace on 7 January 1943, when he claimed an Oscar and another damaged over the Huon Gulf, after which he would be promoted to 1st Lieutenant. The next day, he shot down two Oscars and damaged another in the Lae area. On 3 March, he damaged a Zero over the Huon Gulf and the next day he shot down a Zero and an Oscar over Lae. On 18 July, he shot down an Oscar and added a Zero probable and damaged over the Salamaua-Lae area to become a double ace. On 21 July, he scored his 11th and last victory in the Ramu Valley/Madang area.

After returning to the States, Capt. Sparks was killed in a flying accident near Muroc, CA, on 5 September 1944 while flying a P-38.

Aerial Victory Credits

Date	Location	Credits
27 Dec 42	Over Buna, NG	Zero Val
31 Dec 42	Near Lae, NG	2 Zeros
7 Jan 43	Huon Gulf, NG	Oscar
8 Jan 43	SE of Lae	2 Oscars Oscar (P)
3 Mar 43	Huon Gulf	Zero (D)
4 Mar 43	Over Lae	Zero Oscar

Robert Aschenbrener (Ash) 10 Victories

Aschenbrener

Robert Wayne Aschenbrener was born on 20 November 1922 in Fifield, WI. He attended Loras College (IA) from 1939 to 1941, but joined the Army Reserves after Pearl Harbor. He was commissioned as a 2nd Lieutenant and Pilot rated on 6 September 1942 at Moore Field, TX. He was assigned to the 49FG in May 1943 as a 1st Lieutenant and flew P-49s with the 8FS, scoring his first victories on 15 November 1943, claiming a Zero and Oscar over Dumpu and Gusap A/Ds. He would not score again until 15 February 1944, when he shot down a Tony over Wewak. After flying 272 combat missions in the P-40, he returned to the U.S. in Summer 1944 and served as a Flight Instructor for three months, then went back to the 49FG for a second tour as a Captain flying the P-38 and serving as Ops Officer of the 8FS. Upon his return, Aschenbrener would score seven victories in less than a month and have his best career day, becoming an ace when he shot down three Tonys and a Zero near Tacloban on 24 November. On 28 November, he shot down a Tony northwest of Ormoc Bay and a Tojo and Zero damaged on 11 December near Balacano, Panay. On 21 December, he would become a double ace by destroying a Zero near Meracano Island. On 25 December, he was shot down by enemy AA fire over Clark Field and parachuted safely and evaded the Japanese; he was returned to the Squadron on 17 January. He continued to fly combat as the CO of the 7FS on 21 February and was promoted to Major on 25 April 1945 and served as 7S CO until 17 May, when he was transferred to New Guinea as an Instructor. After the war he earned a Journalism Degree from the University of Missouri in 1947.

Aerial Victory Credits

Date	Location	Credits
15 Nov 43	Dumpu and Gusap A/Ds	Oscar* Zero
15 Feb 44	Over Wewak, NG	Tony*
24 Nov 44	West of Tacloban, PI	3 Tonys Zero
28 Nov 44	West of Tacloban	Tony
11 Dec 44	Balacano, Panay	Tojo Zero (D)
21 Dec 44	Maracano Island , PI	Zero

*P-40 victories all others in P-38
Aschenbrener's totals were 10 victories and one damaged.
Decorations: DSC, DFC with two OLCs, 10 Air Medals, and a Purple Heart.
Aircraft names: P-40: Naughty Marietta; P-38s: Regina, Maj. R.W. Aschenbrener.

William Giroux (Kenny, Giro) 10 Victories

Giroux

William Kenneth Giroux (pronounced Gir-O) was born in Chicago, IL, on 15 November 1914. He joined the Army Reserves and was commissioned a 2nd Lieutenant and Pilot rated on 6 February 1943 at Luke Field, AZ. He was briefly assigned to the 30FS and the 32FS/37FG in the Panama Canal Zone before transferring to the 5FC in August 1943. He joined the 36FS/8FG on 13 September 1943.

On 7 November 1943, Giroux's ICR describes three Sallys as crashing or on fire north of Nadzab, which may or may not have been his victims, and he was officially credited with a frustrating three probables for his first claims of the war (however, the 36FS historian gave him two victories and a probable for the day). It would not be until 15 March 1944 that Giroux would officially be credited with his first victory, when he shot down a Zero north of Kairiru Island, and then four and a half months later, on 27 July, he got his second victory (an Oscar) over Lolobata A/D. He damaged a Lily on 2 September, but during the first two weeks of November would claim eight victories to make him a double ace. On 2 November, he shot down three Hamps in the Ormoc Bay area to become an ace. He then had another triple two days later, shooting down three Oscars over Alicante

A/D. On 6 November, he shot down a Tony over Fabrica A/D on Los Negros and concluded his scoring by destroying an Oscar, again over Alicante. On 26 December, his P-38 was hit by AA fire over the coast near San Jose and he parachuted into the sea and was rescued, returning to Mindoro. He returned to the U.S. in February 1945.

Aerial Victory Credits

Date	Location	Credits
7 Nov 43	North of Nadzab	3 Sally (P)*
15 Mar 44	North of Kairiru Island	Zero
27 July 44	Near Lolobata A/D	Oscar
2 Sept 44	Davao, Mindanao, PI	Lily (D)
2 Nov 44	Ormoc Bay area	3 Hamps
4 Nov 44	Alicante A/D area	3 Oscars
6 Nov 44	Fabrica A/D, Los Negros	Tony
15 Nov 44	Alicante A/D	Oscar

*While flying the P-47; all others in the P-38
Giroux decorations included: Two Silver Stars, DFC, and an Air Medal with eight OLCs.
Giroux' P-38s were named Whilma I-II/Dead Eye Daisy, Elmer, and a winged G.

Ernest Harris 10 Victories

Harris

Ernest Arnold Harris was born in Morristown, TN, on 26 April 1917. He attended Tusculum College, TN, and the University of Kentucky, then joined the Army Reserves as a Flying Cadet from 16 March to 31 October 1941, when he was commissioned as a 2nd Lieutenant and Pilot rated at Turner Field, GA. He was assigned to the 78PS/18PG at Wheeler Filed, HI, and was present during the attack on Pearl Harbor. He was transferred to the 73PS, then the 6FS, and was promoted to 1st Lieutenant on 7 August 1942. He was transferred to the 8FS/49FG on 3 October 1942 and shipped to New Guinea.

Once in combat flying the P-40, he quickly added to his victory total by downing three Zeros over Markham Bay, New Guinea, on 7 January 1943, followed by another victory over a Zero that he chased between Lae and Malahang on 3 March. After being promoted to Captain on 22 March, he damaged a Zero a week later, then became an ace with another big day. On 11 April, in combat east of Oro Bay, he claimed two Zeros and a Val to give him seven victories. On 14 May, he shot down two Betty bombers northeast of Oro Bay. He would score his last victory to make him a double ace when he shot down a Hap (and also damaged a Betty) over Hopoi, New Guinea, on 21 September. On 10 November 1943, he was promoted to Major and filed a Zero probable on the 15th before being rotated home in December.

After the war, he remained in the new Air Force and was killed in a flying accident in a P-80 on 24 August 1949 near Augsburg, Germany, while serving as Ops Officer of the 36FG.

Aerial Victory Credits

Date	Location	Credits
7 Jan 43	Markham Bay, NG	3 Zeros
3 Mar 43	Lae-Malahang, NG	Zero
28 Mar 43	Oro Bay, NG	Zero (D)
11 Apr 43	Near Oro Bay	2 Zeros Val
14 May 43	Near Oro Bay	2 Bettys
21 Sept 43	Hopoi, NG	Zero Betty (D)
15 Nov 43	Madang, NG	Zero (P)

All victories in P-40
Harris's totals were 10 victories, one probable, and two damaged. Harris and Robert DeHaven of the 7FS/49FG were the top scorers in the P-40 in the Pacific with ten victories.
Decorations: Silver Star, DFC with three OLCs, and four Air Medals.
Aircraft names: Carolina Belle, Miss Kat.

Paul Stanch 10 Victories

Stanch

Paul Martin Stanch was born on 2 June 1918 in Pennsylvania. He joined the Army Reserves and took his flight training starting 29 September 1941, and was commissioned as a 2nd Lieutenant and awarded his Wings on 29 April 1942. In May 1942, he was assigned to the 84PS/78PG, but was transferred to the 39FS/35PG on 21 August 1942, and was sent to Australia and New Guinea. Once in New Guinea, he was promoted to 1st Lieutenant in mid-January 1943 and made his first claim—a Betty damaged over Salamaua—on the 27th. On 3 March, he would score his first victories (two Zeros) east of Lae, and would add an Oscar the next day between Lae and Malahang. On 21 July,

Sparks would become an ace when he shot down an Oscar and Zero (plus a Zero probable) over the Ramu Valley-Malahang area. Two days later, he shot down an Oscar and damaged a Tony in an air battle running from Lae to Salamaua. On 2 September, the newly-promoted Captain shot down a twin-engine fighter south of Wewak, and on the 22nd shot down two Zeros south of Tami Island. He would become a double ace with his last victory (an Oscar) on 23 October, over the St. George Channel.

Stanch remained in the postwar Air Force and was promoted to Major on 15 February 1951; to Lt. Colonel on 4 June 1960; and full Colonel on 15 November 1963, retiring in August 1966.

Aerial Victory Credits

Date	Location	Credits
27 Jan 43	South of Salamaua, NG	Betty (D)
3 Mar 43	East of Lae, NG	2 Zeros
4 Mar 43	Lae-Salamaua	Oscar
21 July 43	Ramu to Madang, NG	Oscar Zero Zero (P)
25 July 43	Lae to Salamaua	Oscar Tony (D)
2 Sept 43	South of Wewak, NG	TE Fighter
22 Sept 43	SE of Tami Is. NG	2 Zeros
23 Oct 43	St. George Channel	Oscar

All P-38 victories
Stanch's totals: 10 victories, one probable, and two damaged.
Decorations: Silver Star, DFC with four OLCs, and five Air Medals.
Aircraft names: None

Elliott Summer 10 Victories

Summer

Elliott Summer was born in Providence, RI, on 22 November 1919. After studying Architecture at Columbia University, he joined the Army Reserves and was commissioned a 2nd Lieutenant and Pilot rated on 4 January 1943 at Luke Field, AZ. He was sent to the 360FG at Glendale, CA, where he took transition training in the P-38 and continued Lightning training with the 329FG before transferring to the 475FG on 23 July 1943 at Amberley Field, Australia. After the Group moved to Dobodura, New Guinea,

2Lt. Summer scored his first victory on 21 August, when he shot down a Zero near Dagua, New Guinea. After his promotion to 1st Lieutenant in October, he shot down two Oscars: one over Oro Bay on the 15th and the other over Rabaul on the 24th. On 16 December, he damaged an Oscar, then became an ace on the 21st when he destroyed two Vals over Arawe. The next day, he concluded his 1943 scoring by shooting down a Zero over Wewak. He did not make another claim until 3 April 1944, when he shot down a Zero while escorting B-25s and A-20s over Hollandia. Seven months later Capt. Summer shot down two Zeros over Tacloban Bay and became a double ace with his last victory: an Oscar over Ormoc Bay on 7 December 1944. After being promoted to Captain in Fall 1944, Summer was named CO of the 432FS on 2 January 1945 and served in this position until the end of July 1945, when he rotated home. Postwar he worked for the FAA and served as a noise abatement administrator.

Aerial Victory Credits

Date	Location	Credits
21 Aug 43	Near Dagua, NG	Zero
15 Oct 43	Oro Bay, NG	Oscar
24 Oct 43	Over Rabaul	Oscar
16 Dec 43	Cape Gloucester, NG	Zero (D)
21 Dec 43	Over Arawe, NB	2 Vals
22 Dec 43	Over Wewak, NG	Zero
3 April 44	Over Hollandia, NG	Zero
12 Nov 44	Tacloban Bay, PI	2 Zeros
7 Dec 44	Over Ormoc Bay, Leyte	Oscar

All P-38 victories
Summer's totals were 10 victories and one damaged.
His decorations were a Silver Star, two DFCs, and 10 Air Medals.
His P-38s were named Blood & Guts, Eileen, and Stiff Motion.

Andrew Reynolds 9.33 Victories

Reynolds

After graduating from the University of Oklahoma with a degree in Chemical Engineering, Andrew Jackson Reynolds joined the Army Reserves in November 1940. After receiving his Wings, he was sent to the Pacific with the 20th and 17th Pursuit Squadrons (Provisional), flying P-40s over Java.

On 6 February 1942, 2Lt. Reynolds shot down a twin-engined bomber misidentified as a Me-110 with two other pilots and it is usually listed as a 1/3 victory (by Olynyck and the 20 PPG history), but some sources (HS **85**) credit him with a whole victory, which would have made him a double ace with ten victories. Reynolds went on to down three Zeros before escaping to Australia from Java. 1Lt. Reynolds served with the 9th FS of the 49th FG from April to the end of August 1942, and was credited with six victories (four Zeros and two Sallys flying P-40s) before leaving combat with 9.33 or 10 victories.

Aces in the Pacific and Europe

John Landers (Whispering John, Firewall, Big Ass)

Maj. Landers ETO (P-38/55FG) (AAF)

Lt.Col. Landers ETO (P-51/78FG) (AAF)

John Landers was unusual, as he scored 14½ victories (six in the Pacific and 8½ over Europe) to make him one of two pilots who were aces in two theaters (along with James Howard, who scored 6.33 with the AVG Flying Tigers and six in the ETO).

John Dave Landers was born in Wilson, OK, on 23 August 1920. He attended Texas A&M and Arkansas State Universities before joining the

1Lt. Landers PTO (P-40/49FG). (AFAA)

Army Reserves. He was commissioned as a 2nd Lieutenant and Pilot rated on 12 December 1941 at Stockton Field, CA, and was assigned to the 9FS/49FG, flying P-40Es over Darwin, Australia. He shot down two Type 97 fighters on 4 April 1942, added a Zero on 14 June, and another on 30 July—all over Darwin. On 26 December, 1st Lieutenant Landers shot down two Zeros over Dobodura, but was shot down, wounded, and returned to the Squadron on 2 January 1943.

After recuperating, he returned to the U.S. as a Flight Instructor and went back to combat as a Major and the CO of the 38FS/55FG, flying P-38s. While with the 55FG, he scored four victories (and a damaged), including three Me-109s on 7 July, making him a double ace. In Fall 1944, he transferred to the 357FG as a Lt. Colonel and Group Executive Officer and completed his second tour with another victory on 18 November 1944 while flying the P-51. He returned to the U.S. in December, but returned to the ETO as CO of the 78FG from late February to late June 1945. While flying the Mustang with that Group, in March he was credited with three and a half victories, and in May he was promoted to full Colonel.

Aerial Victory Credits

Date	Location	Unit	A/C	Credits
	PACIFIC			
4 April 42	Darwin, Australia	49FG	P-40	2 Type 97
14 June 42	Darwin	49FG	P-40	Zero
30 July 42	Darwin	49FG	P-40	Zero
26 Dec 42	Dobodura, NG	49FG	P-40	2 Zeros
	EUROPE			
25 June 44	SW Paris	357FG	P-38	FW 190 Me 109 (D)
7 July 44	Near Bernberg	357FG	P-38	3 Me 109s
18 Nov 44	Violence A/F	357FG	P-51	Me 109
2 Mar 45	Berg A/D	78FG	P-51	2 Me -109s
19 Mar 45	Near Osnabruck	78FG	P-51	Me 109
30 Mar 45	Rendsberg area	78FG	P-51	0.5 Me 262

Top USAAF Night Ace

Carroll Smith

Maj. Carroll Smith, Top Night Fighter Ace (418NFS). (AFAA)

Carroll Smith's night fighting career in the Pacific parallels the evolution of the Air Force's night aircraft and tactics. During his tour with the 418th, he flew the P-70, P-38, and P-61 at night.

In early 1943, air cadets gathered at William's Field, AZ, for night fighter training in the RP-322 and P-70 twin-engine fighters. The RP-322 was a stripped-down early RAF P-38 reject, while the P-70 Nighthawk was a Douglas A-20 conversion. The two represented a makeshift night fighter force made necessary by the slow development of the P-61.

The 418 NFS was activated on 1 April 1943 in Orlando, FL, and assigned to the Air Force School of Applied Tactics. The squadron was shipped to Guadalcanal, then to Milne Bay, New Guinea, in early November, under its leader, Maj. Carroll Smith. The 418th was equipped with a limited number of P-70s, which were supplemented with P-38s, both of which were 6 NFS castoffs. The mixture of P-70s and P-38s required the Squadron to develop new tactics to accommodate the performance of each aircraft. For instance, Japanese bombers could usually out-run and out-climb the P-70! Despite numerous efforts to improve the P-70's performance, the modifications never ameliorated its deficiencies and the aircraft was relegated to low level and intruder missions. The P-38 H and J models were conventional daylight versions without radar or other night fighting aids. The P-38 pilots would patrol over their base and wait for the Japanese to attack and fly into the searchlight beams, a method tried by both the RAF and Luftwaffe ("Wild Sow") with mixed success. This tactic subjected the P-39s to their own AA fire and also to being spotted by enemy bomber gunners. Later, GCI vectored the Lightnings by VHF towards the targets, again without much success. On 13 January 1944, Smith destroyed a Val dive-bomber over Alexishafen in a P-38J to give the 418st its first victory and only one for nine months, as there was little air activity during patrols over the Solomons and New Guinea at that time.

During Fall 1944, the 418th was given some P-61As to replace the P-70s and supplement the P-38s. On 7 October, while on patrol in a P-61A over their base at Morotai, Smith and his radar operator, 2Lt. Philip Porter, were vectored by GCI to a target at 12 miles. With Porter giving directions and Smith flying by instruments, an airborne radar intercept was quickly accomplished on a twin-engine Dinah on a course towards the P-61 base at 8,000 feet. Using his water injection, Smith rapidly closed for a visual contact 2,000 feet ahead. The Jap also saw his attacker and took evasive action by climbing. The P-61 climbed faster and caught the Dinah at 17,500 feet. Smith's first several firing bursts failed to hit or damage the Jap. As the Widow pulled to within 40 yards of the Dinah's port wing, Smith fired a full deflection burst as it flew past, tearing off chunks and setting it on fire. Smith had fired all his ammo in the 20-minute battle.

Back in a P-38, Smith claimed a twin-engine probable on 26 November and a Betty confirmed and probable on 28 November to give him a total of three victories and two probables.

In December 1944, the squadron was stationed at San Jose, Mindoro, Philippines, and received their P-61B versions. Smith nicknamed his aircraft Time's A Wastin and adorned the horizontal stabilizer with the squadron's white crescent moon and star markings. On 29 December, the 418th was assigned shipping convoy escort duty off Mindoro under shipboard GCI, which alerted the P-61s of incoming enemy aircraft at 8,000 feet and 12 to 15 miles out. Using his airborne radar set, Porter guided Smith on a two-mile climbing course to a visual contact on an Irving. After a seven-mile chase through the clouds, Smith was able to make a diving firing run, getting hits on the twin-engine recon bomber's wing root. The burning enemy dove away and crashed into the sea at 1910.

Smith returned to patrolling altitude and Porter soon found another incoming Irving at their altitude. Not having time to maneuver to a more favorable stern attack position because of the Jap's close proximity to the convoy, Smith made a full-throttle head-on attack. He dove to intercept the Irving as it was about to initiate its attack on the convoy. At about 300 yards he fired his 20mm cannons, getting hits on the canopy and fuel tanks and causing it to crash into the sea.

After briefly landing to refuel and rearm, Times A Wastin returned to station on its second patrol. After 30 minutes, GCI vectored Smith and Porter to a single-engine Rufe float plane flying three miles out at sea level. The slow and maneuverable Rufe was a difficult target for the P-61, escaping using low, tight turns. Smith partially lowered his flaps to cut his speed and was then able to put a short, devastating burst of 20mm cannon shells into the fragile Japanese Navy plane.

Two hours later, the Americans were again vectored towards an incoming aircraft, which was identified as a speedy Frank fighter. Utilizing surprise, Porter ranged the P-61 to only 25 yards, where its 20mm shells had deadly effect, disintegrating the Jap for their fourth kill of the night and seventh of the 418th's 20 wartime victories to become aces.

Aerial Victory Credits

Date	Location	A/C	Credits
13 Jan 44	Over Alexishafen	P-38J	Val
7 Oct 44	S Morotai, NEI	P-61A	Dinah
26 Nov 44	SW Morotai, NEI	P-38J	TE (P)
28 Nov 44	W Morotai, NEI	P-38J	Betty (P) Betty
29 Dec 44	NW Mindoro, PI	P-61A	2 Irvings
30 Dec 44	Mindoro, PI NW San Jose, PI	P-61A	Rufe Frank

Aces with the 5th Fighter Command and in Korea

James Hagerstrom

James Philo Hagerstrom was born on 14 January 1921 in Cedar Falls, IA. Hagerstrom entered the Army Reserves and was commissioned as a 2nd Lieutenant and Pilot rated on 26 July 1942 at Luke Field, AZ. He was

1Lt. James Hagerstrom WW II (P-40/49FG). (AAF)

assigned to the 5th Fighter Command and sent to the 8FS/49FG in March 1943, flying P-40Es and Ns. Hagerstrom would score his first victory on 11 April 1943, when he shot down a Zero east of Oro Bay. It would not be until 5 October that 1Lt. Hagerstrom scored his second victory, a Dinah that he chased from Finschhafen to Madang. On 23 January 1944, Hagerstrom would have a career day when he shot down a Tony and three Hamps over Wewak to make him a six-victory ace.

After World War II, he transferred to the new Air Force and was assigned to the 4FIW/334FBS in 1952. The F-86 Sabre equipped unit was sent to Korea, and Major Hagerstrom would shoot down a MiG-15 on 21 November,

Maj. James Hagerstrom Korea (F-86/18FBW). (AFAA)

then claim a MiG probable on 22 December; two days later he damaged three other MiG-15s, followed on Christmas Day by a MiG-15 destroyed while flying with the 335FBS. He transferred to the 18FBW/67FBS, and after destroying another MiG in February 1953, he became a double ace when he shot down a MiG-15 and shared another on 13 March; then two weeks later added two more to become a jet ace with 6½ victories. On 13 April and 16 May, Hagerstrom was credited with a MiG destroyed and one damaged. Hagerstrom remained in the USAF, being promoted to Lt. Colonel in June 1954; to Colonel in April 1954; and retiring in January 1968.

Aerial Victory Credits

Date	Location	Credits
	World War II	6 Victories

14 Apr 43	Finschhafen to Mandang	Zero
5 Oct 43	Over Wewak, NG	Dinah
23 Jan 44	Over Wewak	3 Hamps Tony
	Korea	**8 ½ Victories** **1 Probable** **5 Damaged**
21 Nov 52	Near Youngsi	MiG-15
22 Dec 52	Korea	MiG-15 (P)
24 Dec 52	Korea	3 MiG-15 (D)
25 Dec 52	Near Sinsi-dong	MiG-15
25 Feb 53	Konha-dong	MiG-15
13 Mar 53	Over Womsang-Dong Near Haksong-San	MiG-15 ½ MiG-15
27 Mar 53	Near Sanggyong-dong Near Paksang-ni	MiG-15 MiG-15
13 Apr 53	Near Tangwan-dong	MiG-15 MiG-15 (D)
16 May 53	Near Uiju	MiG-15 MiG-15 (D)

Total: 14½ victories, a probable, and five damaged.
Decorations:
World War II: DSC, DFC, and 5 Air Medals
Korea: Silver Star, 2 DFCs, and 6 Air Medals

George Davis (Curly)

1Lt. George Davis WW II (P-47/348FG). (AAF)

George Andrew Davis was born on 1 December 1920, in Dublin, TX. He served as an Aviation Cadet from 20 March 1942 to 15 February 1943, when he was commissioned as a 2nd Lieutenant and awarded his Wings in Victoria, TX. He was assigned to the 348FG/342FS, flying the P-47, on 30 August 1943, and would score his first victory on the last day of 1943, when he shot down a Val over Arawe. On 2 February 1944, 1Lt. Davis shot down a Tony over Wewak, but would not score again until December. On the 10th, he shot down two Tonys over Negros Island, then a Zero over

Maj. George Davis Korea (F-86/4FIW). (AFAA)

Mindoro on the 20th to become an ace. Davis would conclude his WWII scoring by destroying two Zeros northwest of Clark Field, giving him seven victories. He was promoted to a Captain on 14 November 1944 and transferred out of the 348FG in April 1945, transferring to the Regular Army on 16 February 1946 and then into the new Air Force.

After being promoted to Major on 15 February 1951, he was transferred to the 4th Fighter Interceptor Wing in October 1951 as the CO of its 334FIS, flying F-86E Sabre Jets. After claiming a MiG-15 probable on 4 November 1951, he was credited with two MiG-15s destroyed on 27 November and became a double ace on 30 November, when he shot down three Tu-2s and a MiG-15 to become a jet ace in Korea. On 5 December, he shot down two MiGs to make him a triple ace. Then, on 15 December, Davis would have another big day when he shot down four MiG-15s. On 10 February 1952, he shot down two MiGs, giving him 21 victories. However, during this mission he was shot down in aerial combat south of the Yalu River and was awarded the Medal of Honor posthumously and promoted to Lt. Colonel.

Aerial Victory Credits

Date	Location	Credits
	World War II	**7 Victories**
31 Dec 43	Over Arawe	Val
3 Feb 44	Over Wewak	Tony
10 Dec 44	Over Negros Island	2 Tonys
20 Dec 44	Mindoro	Zero
24 Dec 44	NW of Clark Field	2 Zeros
	Korea	**14 Victories** **1 Probable** **2 Damaged**
4 Nov 51	Near Anju	MiG-15 (P)
27 Nov 51	Near Wong-Ok	2 MiG-15s ½ MiG-15 (D)
30 Nov 51	Near Sahol, Yalu R.	3 Tu-2s 1 Tu-1 (D) 1 MiG-15

5 Dec 51	Near Rinko-Do	MiG-15
	Near Haech'ang	MiG-15
13 Dec 51	Near Yongwon-Ni	MiG-15
	Near Changha-Ri	MiG-15
	Near P'anp'yong-Dong	MiG_15
10 Feb 52	Near Tong Dang-dong	2 MiG-15s

Totals:
World War II: 7 Victories
Korea: 14 Victories, 1 Probable, and 1½ Damaged
No Named Aircraft
Decorations:
World War II: Silver Star, DFC with 1 OLC, and 9 Air Medals
Korea: Medal of Honor, 2 Silver Stars, DFC with OLC, and 1 Air Medal
Note: The other pilots who were World War II and Korean War aces were:
Francis "Gabby" Gabreski: 28 victories ETO/6.5 victories Korea
William Whisner: 14.5 victories ETO/5.5 victories Korea
Vermont Garrison: 7.33 victories ETO/10 victories Korea
John Bolt: 6 victories USMC/6 victories Korea
Harrison Thyng: 5 victories ETO/5 victories Korea

5th Fighter Command Pilots Who Became Aces Later in Other Theaters

George Preddy

1Lt. George Preddy PTO (P-40/49FG). (AAF)

George Earl Preddy was born on 5 February 1919 in Greensboro, NC. He received his Wings on 12 December 1941, and arrived in Australia with the 49FG in March 1942. While flying P-40s, Preddy claimed several bombers as damaged. During the afternoon of 12 July 1942, Capt. Ben Irvin was leading a scheduled 9FS training flight consisting of Lts. Paul Blakely, Leon Howk, George Preddy, John Sauber, and Richard Taylor, during which Preddy, Taylor, and Blakely were to play the role of enemy bombers, while Irvin would lead the attackers, Howk and Sauber, who were joined late by Andrew Reynolds. Reynolds made the first attack, followed by Sauber, who chose Preddy's P-40 as his faux target. Sauber dove on Preddy, but appeared to become disoriented and misjudged his speed and distance; he attempted to evade, but his P-40 went into a violent snap roll and hit the tail of Preddy's P-40. Both fighters dove out of control and the

Maj. George Preddy ETO (P-51/352FG). (AFAA)

flight saw only one parachute open and both P-40s crash. Once he landed, Irvin commandeered an ambulance and he and Lucien Hubbard and William Irving headed toward the downed pilot in the approaching darkness, aided by Lt. Clay Tice, who spotted his position from his P-40. Preddy had crashed through a gum tree that shredded his parachute and dropped him through the branches onto the ground below. When the rescuers arrived, they found Preddy bleeding badly, laying on his parachute with a broken leg and deep, bleeding wounds in his hip and shoulder. Sauber's burnt out fighter was found the next morning with its pilot still in the cockpit. After a protracted hospital stay, Preddy eventually recovered sufficiently to return to the States. After he recuperated, he flew two tours in the ETO assigned to the 352nd Fighter Group of the 8AF, flying P-51D Mustangs. Preddy became the third-ranking American ace in the ETO with 26.83 victories before he was shot down by friendly AA fire on Christmas Day 1944 near Leige, Belgium. Preddy had been pursuing a pair of FW 190s on the deck when a mobile AA unit fired on all three aircraft. The FW 190s escaped, but Preddy's Mustang *Cripes A' Mighty* was hit, but made a belly landing. However, Preddy had been hit by two .50 caliber rounds and was killed.

Frank Adkins

Tennessean Frank Adkins was awarded his Wings on 11 July 1941, and was transferred to the 16PS/51PG, but was sent to the Pacific with the 17PS (P), flying P-40s over Java. He claimed two Zeros (one each on 18 and 21 February) before escaping to Australia to join the 35FS in combat over Northern Australia and New Guinea. On 26 May, 1Lt. Adkins, flying a P-400 over New Guinea, was credited with a Zero, but contracted Dengue Fever and was evacuated. Maj. Adkins became CO of the 313FS/50FG in December 1943 and flew combat in P-47Ds in the ETO. On 26 August 1944, Lt. Colonel Adkins shot down two Me-109s near Elbuef, Germany, to become an ace. Adkins served with that Squadron until mid-September 1944, when he was promoted to Deputy Group CO. He was killed in a flying accident in Texas on 23 February 1945, flying a P-38.

Sidney Woods

Lt.Col. Sidney Woods ETO (P-51/4FG). (AAF)

Maj. Sidney Woods PTO (P-38/49FG). (AFAA)

Texan, Sidney Sterling Woods graduated from the University of Arizona in 1939 and joined the Army Reserves as a 2Lt. in the Cavalry. He served there for two years before transferring to the AAC, winning his wings on 26 September 1941. He was assigned to the 9PS/49FG, flying P-38s. On 11 March 1943, Capt. Woods shot down a Betty over the Bismarck Sea near Oro Bay, and then as a Major he shot down an Oscar and claimed a probable in the Cape Renault area, New Britain. After flying 112 combat missions, Woods completed his tour and returned to the U.S. in August. He transferred to the 479FG at the end of March 1944, where he served another combat tour flying P-51s, before returning to the U.S. He returned to England to serve his third tour with the 4FG on 27 February 1945 as the Group's Deputy CO as a Lt. Colonel. On 22 March, he became an Ace-in-a-Day when he shot down five FW-190s over the German airdromes at Fursterwalde and Eggersdorf. On 16 April, he was shot down by AA fire and taken prisoner, and was repatriated at the end of the war after flying 68 combat missions in the ETO before separating from the Air Force. He served two years during the Korean War as the CO of a training group.

Steven Andrew

Andrew was born in Canada in 1914, but was raised in Dallas. Andrew joined the Army Reserve in May 1935, serving there until March 1941, when he joined the AAC, and at the end of October he was commissioned as a 2Lt. He was assigned to the 7FS/49FG, flying P-40Es. Just after noontime on 27 April 1942, Andrew shot down a Zero and damaged a

Steven Andrew (PTO: P-40/49FG and ETO: P-51/352FG). (AFAA)

bomber in the Darwin area. After completing his combat tour, he joined the 325FG in mid-December 1942, where he flew combat over North Africa in P-40s. After completing this tour, he joined the 352FG/486FS as a Captain in early 1944 and flew combat in the P-51B. In March 1944, he shot down a Me-109; added a Me-109 and FW-190 in April; and completed his scoring with three FW-190s and two Me-109s in May to give him nine victories. On 2 July, his Mustang experienced engine trouble outside of Budapest and he was taken POW until the end of the war.

Joseph Kruzel

Joseph Kruzel (PTO: P-40/49FG and ETO: P-51/352FG). (AAF)

After receiving BS degrees in Chemistry and Education, Pennsylvanian Kruzel joined the Army reserves and received his Wings in December 1940. Following action over the Philippines during the Japanese invasion on 7 December 1941 with the 17PS, the Squadron was moved to the NEI. During February 1942, 1Lt. Kruzel was credited with three victories flying P-40s before his Squadron was evacuated. From March to June 1944, Lt.Col. Kruzel was credited with three and a half more victories flying P-47s (1½ victories) and P-51s (two victories) for the 361FG HQ in the ETO. Kruzel remained in the postwar Air Force and retired as a Maj. General.

Ralph Wire

Ralph Wire (R) (PTO: P-38/49FG and CBI: P-38/50FG). (AFAA)

Phoenix, AZ, native Ralph Wire was Pilot Rated as a 2Lt. in January 1942, and in January 1943 was flying with the 9PS/49FG, flying P-38s. 1Lt. Wire shot down an Oscar in April 1943, and then Capt. Wire added two Zeroes and a Tony and a Betty probable on 6 September, followed by an Oscar probable on 22 September. He completed his tour in November 1943 and returned to the U.S. In November 1944, he was assigned to the 449FS/51FG, flying P-38s in the CBI. On 5 January, he shot down two Oscars off Hainan Island to become an ace. On 2 February, his Lightning suffered engine failure and he was seriously injured when he bailed out; he returned to the U.S. to recover.

Grant Mahony

Grant Mahony (PTO: P-40/24PG and CBI: P-51/23FG). (AAF)

Oregon resident Grant Mahony graduated from the University of California in 1939 and joined the AAC, graduating in March 1940. He served with the 94PS/1PG from May to October, and was transferred to the 4th Composite Group in the Philippines, serving with the 17PS and then the 3PS in January 1941, flying the P-26 and P-35 and then the P-40E. On 8 December 1941, he shot down a Zero over Luzon and evacuated the Philippines for Australia on the 17th. Capt. Mahony was assigned to the 17PS(P), flying the P-40E over Java in February, where he shot down a heavy bomber and two Zeros (plus three probables). On 25 February, he left for India with Gen. Brereton and was assigned to the 51FG, but did not see any combat before leaving to join the 23FG in China in November as the CO of the 76FS. In June 1943, he returned to the U.S. as a Major, and in November he transferred to the newly-formed 1st Air Commando Group, flying the P-51B over Burma. Lt.Col. Mahony damaged an Oscar on 7 March 1944 before becoming an ace when he destroyed an Oscar on 10 April over Imphal. In May, he returned to the U.S., but in December he returned to combat with the 8FG in the Philippines. He was KIA by enemy AA fire over Palawan, Philippines, on 3 January 1945.

Thomas Hayes

Thomas Hayes (PTO: P-40/17PS and ETO: P-51/357FG). (AAF)

After dropping out of the University of Oregon, Hayes joined the Army Reserves and was commissioned and Pilot Rated on 7 February 1941, then was assigned to the 70PS/35PG. He was sent to the Pacific with the 17PS and was shot down and wounded over Java on 19 February 1942. Once he recovered, he was transferred to the 35FG on 21 May 1942 and was credited with two ground victories, which he added to his later ETO score (see photo). He returned to the U.S. in October 1942 and was assigned to the 357FG as a Major flying P-51s. On 2 March 1944, he scored his first aerial victory and ended his scoring as a Lt. Colonel on 14 July 1944 by shooting down a Me-109 to give him 8½ career victories.

5th Fighter Command Aces Scoring
Victories in Three Different Fighters

Clifton Troxell

Clifton Troxell scored victories in three different fighters. (AFAA)

While flying P-39Fs with the 35FS/8FG in May 1942, 2Lt. and then 1Lt. Troxell shot down a Zero on both the 26th and 29th. On 15 September 1943, while flying a P-38G for the 8FG, Capt. Troxell shot down two Zeros near Wewak and would become an ace when shooting down a Zero over Cape Gloucester, New Britain, on 26 December 1943, while flying a P-40N.

George Welch

As described earlier, Welch was credited with four P-40B victories over Pearl Harbor, three P-39D victories over Buna a year later on 7 December 1942, and nine P-38G and H victories.

6

5th Fighter Command Group and Squadron Aces

8th Fighter Group
(453 victories/84 probables, 53 damaged)
Group Aces:
George Welch: 4 (of 16)
Clifton Troxell: 3 (of 5)
Jay Robbins: 1 (of 22)

35th Fighter Squadron
(130 victories/8 probables/11 damaged)
Squadron Aces:
Richard West: 14
William Gardener: 8
Leroy Everhart: 6
Lee Witt: 6
Kenneth Pool: 5
Thomas Lynch: 3 (of 20)
Clifton Troxell: 2 (of 5)
Frank Adkins: 1 (of 5)
Joseph McKeon: 1 (of 6)

36th Fighter Squadron
(94 victories/19 probables/11 damaged)
Squadron Aces:
William Giroux: 10
John Dunaway: 7
Donald McGee: 3 (of 6)
George Welch: 3 (of 16)
Kenneth Ladd: 2 (of 12)
Grover Gholson: 1 (of 5)
Allen Hill: 1 (of 9)
Vernon Jett: 1 (of 7)

80th Fighter Squadron
(213 victories/57 probables/31 damaged)
Squadron Aces:
Jay Robbins: 21 (of 22)
Edward Cragg: 15
Cyril Homer: 15
Cornelius Smith: 11

Kenneth Ladd: 10 (of 12)
Allen Hill: 8 (of 9)
John Jones: 8
Burnell Adams: 6 (of 7)
Edwin DeGraffenreid: 6
Paul Murphey: 6
Robert Adams: 5
George Welch: 5 (of 16)
Jennings Myers: 5
C.B. Ray: 5
Louis Schriber: 5
Daniel Roberts: 4 (of 14)
James Ince: 2 (of 6)
Donald McGee: 2 (of 6)

35th Fighter Group
(387 victories/95 probables/73 damaged)
Group Aces:
William McDonough: 3 (of 5)

39th Fighter Squadron
(186 victories/53 probables/62 damaged)
Squadron Aces:
Thomas Lynch: 12 (of 20)
Kenneth Sparks: 11
Paul Stanch: 10
Leroy Grosshuesch: 8
Richard Smith: 7
Stanley Andrews: 6
Hoyt Eason: 6
Charles Gallup: 6
John Lane: 6
Richard Bong: 5 (of 40)
Curran Jones: 5
Charles King: 5
Richard Suehr: 5
Charles Sullivan: 5

40th Fighter Squadron
(110 victories/49 probables/9 damaged)
Squadron Aces:
William Strand: 7
Ellis Baker: 6
Alvaro Hunter: 5
Robert Yaeger: 5
William McDonald: 2 (of 5)

41st Fighter Squadron
(97 victories/10 probables/2 damaged)
Squadron Aces:
James Mugavero: 6
Francis Dubisher: 5
Edward Hoyt: 4 (of 5)
William Turner: 1 (of 8)

49th Fighter Group
(664 victories/106 probables/61 damaged)
Group Aces:
Gerald Johnson: 11 (of 22)
Ellis Wright: 6
Wallace Jordan: 4 (of 6)
George Laven: 1 (of 4 or 5)
James Watkins: 1 (of 12)

7th Fighter Squadron
(178 victories/19 probables/ 24 damaged)
Squadron Aces:
Robert DeHaven: 14
Joel Paris: 9
Fernley Damstrom: 8
Arland Stanton: 8
Elliott Dent: 6
Frederick Dick: 5
Mildren Mathre: 5
Franklin Nichols: 4 (of 5)
David Allen: 2 (of 8)
William Hennon: 2 (of 7)
Steven Andrew: 1 (of 9)

8th Fighter Squadron
(207 victories/23 probables/17 damaged)
Squadron Aces:
Robert Aschenbrener: 10
Ernest Harris: 10
Robert White: 9
Samuel Pierce: 7
William Drier: 6
James Hagerstrom: 6 (plus 8.5 Korea)
Robert Howard: 6
Donald Meuten: 6
Nial Castle: 5
William Day: 5
Marion Felts: 5
Nelson Flack: 5
James Morehead: 5 (of 8)
George Kiser: 4 (of 9)

9th Fighter Squadron
(254 victories/63 probables/20 damaged)
Squadron Aces:
Richard Bong: 16 (of 40)
Gerald Johnson: 11 (of 22)
James Watkins: 11 (of 12)
Grover Fanning: 9
James O'Neill: 8
John Landers: 6 (8.5 ETO)
Andrew Reynolds: 6 (of 9.33)
Ralph Wandrey: 6
Ernest Ambort: 5
Warren Curton: 5
Cheatum Gupton: 5
Robert Vaught: 5
William Haney: 5 (?)
Ralph Wire: 3 (of 5)
I.B. Donalson: 2 (of 5)
Wallace Jordan: 2 (of 6)
Sidney Woods: 2 (of 7: 5 in the ETO)
Harley Brown: 1 (of 6)
Jack Mankin: 1 (of 5)
Arthur Wenige: 1 (of 6)

58th Fighter Group
(13 victories/0 probables/0 damaged)
No Group Aces

69th Fighter Squadron
(5 victories/0 probables/0 damaged)
No Squadron Aces

310th Fighter Squadron
(2 victories/ 0 probables/ 0 damaged)
No Squadron Aces

311th Fighter Squadron
(6 victories/ 0 probables/ 0 damaged)
No Squadron Aces

201st Fighter Squadron
(0 victories/ 0 probables/ 0 damaged)
No Squadron Aces

348th Fighter Group
(349 victories/21 probables/5 damaged)
Group Aces
Neel Kearby: 12 (of 22)
Robert Rowland: 8
William Banks: 4 (of 9)
William Dunham: 1 (of 16)

340th Fighter Squadron
(76 victories/5 probables/0 damaged)
Squadron Aces:
Meade Brown: 6
Richard Fleischer: 6
Michael Dikovitsky: 5
Myron Hnatio: 5

341st Fighter Squadron
(70 victories/7 probables/2 damaged)
Squadron Aces:
Samuel Blair: 7
John Moore: 7
William Foulis: 6
George Della: 1 (of 5)

342nd Fighter Squadron
(125 victories/9 probables/1 damaged)
Squadron Aces:
William Dunham: 9 (of 16)
Walter Benz: 8
Edward Roddy: 8
George Davis: 7 (plus 14 Korea)
Marvin Grant: 7
Edward Popek: 7
William Banks: 5 (of 9)
Robert Gibb: 5
Robert Knapp: 5
Lawrence O'Neill: 5
Robert Sutcliffe: 5

460th Fighter Squadron
(51 victories/0 probables/1 damaged)
Squadron Aces:
William Dunham: 6 (of 16)
George Della: 4 (of 5)

475th Fighter Group
(552 victories/61 probables/36 damaged)
Group Aces
Charles MacDonald: 27
Merle Smith: 9
John Loisel: 1 (of 11)

431st Fighter Squadron
(221 victories/14 probables/7.5 damaged)
Squadron Aces:
Thomas McGuire: 38
Francis Lent: 11
Frederic Champlin: 9
Kenneth Hart: 8
Vincent Elliott: 7
David Allen: 6 (of 8)
Edward Czarnecki: 6
Verle Jett: 6 (of 7)
John Pietz: 6
Horace Reeves: 6
Marion Kirby: 5
Lowell Lutton: 5
Franklin Monk: 5
Paul Morriss: 5
John Tilley: 5
Arthur Wenige: 5
Harry Brown: 4 (of 6)
Jack Mankin: 4 (of 6)
Warren Lewis: 2 (of 7)
Frank Nichols: 1 (of 5)

432nd Fighter Squadron
(167 victories/21 probables/14 damaged)
Squadron Aces:
John Loisel: 10 (of 11)
Elliott Summer: 10
Perry Dahl: 9
Joseph Forster: 9
Frederick Harris: 8
Zack Dean: 7
Billy Gresham: 6
Paul Lucas: 6
Vivian Cloud: 5
Harold Condon: 5
Arthur Wenige: 5
Grover Gholson: 4 (of 5)
James Ince: 4 (of 6)
Daniel Roberts: 3 (of 14)

433rd Fighter Squadron
(155 victories/23 probables/12 damaged)
Squadron Aces:
Harry Fisk: 7
John Purdy: 7
Daniel Roberts: 7 (of 14)
Calvin Wire: 7
John Smith: 6
Warren Lewis: 5 (of 7)
John McKeon: 4 (of 5)

7

Aircraft of the Aces

5FC P-40 Aces

Ace Name	Rank	Unit (FG)	P-40v	Other V
DeHaven, Robert	Capt	49	10	+4 P-38
Harris, Ernest	Capt	49	10	
Reynolds, Andrew	1Lt	17P/49	9.33	
Kiser, George	Capt	17P/49	9	
White, Robert	Capt	49	9	
Stanton, Arland	Maj	49	8	
Hennon, William	Capt	17P/49	7	
Morehead, James	Maj	17P/49	7	+1 P-38
Turner, William	1Lt	20/17P	7	+1 P-39
Hagerstrom, James	1Lt	49	6	
Howard, Robert	1Lt	49	6	
Landers, John	1Lt	49	6	+4 P-38 +4.5 P-51
Meuten, Donald	1Lt	49	6	
West, Richard	Capt	8	6	+8 P-38
Wright, Ellis	Capt	49	6	
Day, William	1Lt	49	5	
Donalson, I.B.	1Lt	49	5	
Everhart, Lee	Capt	9	5	+1 P-38
Wagner, Boyd	LCol	17P/5FC	5	+3 P-39

5FC P-38 Aces

Ace Name	Rank	Unit FG/ AF	P-38v	Other v
Bong, Richard	Maj	49/5	40	
McGuire, Thomas	Maj	475/5	38	
MacDonald, Charles	LCol	475/5	27	
Robbins, Jay	Maj	8/5	22	
Johnson, Gerald R.	LCol	49/5	20	+2 P-47
Lynch, Thomas	LCol	35/5	17	+3 P-400
Cragg, Edward	Maj	8/5	15	
Homer, Cyril	Capt	8/5	15	
Ladd, Kenneth	Capt	8/5	12	
Roberts, Daniel	Capt	475/5	12	+2 P-400
Lent, Francis	1Lt	475/5	11	
Loisel, John	Maj	475/5	11	
Smith, Cornelius	Capt	8/5	11	
Sparks, Kenneth	1Lt	35/5	11	
Watkins, James	Capt	49/5	11	+1 P-40
Giroux, William	Capt	8/5	10	
Stanch, Paul	Capt	35/5	10	
Summer, Elliott	Capt	475/5	10	
Champlin, Frederick	Capt	475/5	9	
Dahl, Perry	Capt	475/5	9	
Fanning, Grover	1Lt	49/5	9	
Forster, Joseph	1Lt	475/5	9	
Hill, Allen	1Lt	8/5	9	
Smith, Merle	LCol	475/5	9	

Welch, George	Capt	475/5	9	+4 P-40 +3 P-39
Damstrom, Fernley	1Lt	49/5	8	
Harris, Frederick	Capt	475/5	8	
Hart, Kenneth	1Lt	475/5	8	
Jones, John	Capt	8/5	8	
O'Neill, John	1Lt	49/5	8	
West, Richard	Capt	8/5	8	
Aschenbrener, Robert	Capt	49/5	7	
Dean, Zack	2Lt	8-475/5	7	
Dunaway, John	1Lt	8/5	7	
Elliott, Vincent	1Lt	475/5	7	
Fisk, Jack	Capt	475/5	7	
Lewis, Warren	Maj	475/5	7	
Purdy, John	1Lt	475/5	7	
Smith, Richard	1Lt	35/5	7	
Wire, Calvin	1Lt	475/5	7	
Adams, Burnell	Capt	8/80	6	+1 P-70
Allen, David	1Lt	475/5	6	+2 P-400
Andrews, Stanley	1Lt	35/5	6	
Czarnecki, Edward	1Lt	475/5	6	
DeGraffenreid, Edwin	2Lt	8/5	6	
Drier, William	Capt	49/5	6	
Eason, Hoyt	1Lt	35/5	6	
Gallup, Charles	1Lt	35/5	6	
Gresham, Billy	1Lt	475/5	6	
Ince, James	1Lt	8-475/5	6	
Jett, Verle	Capt	475/5	6	

Lane, John	1Lt	35/5	6	
Lucas, Paul	Capt	475/5	6	
Murphey, Paul	Capt	8/5	6	
Paris, Joel	Capt	49/5	6	+3 P-40
Pietz, John	1Lt	475/5	6	
Reeves, Horace	1Lt	475/5	6	
Smith, John C.	2Lt	475/5	6	
Adams, Robert	1Lt	8/5	5	
Ambort, Ernest	2Lt	49/5	5	
Brown, Harry	Capt	475/5	5	+2 P-40
Castle, Nial	2Lt	49/5	5	
Cloud, Vivian	1Lt	475/5	5	
Condon, Henry	1Lt	49/5	5	
Curton, Warren	1Lt	49/5	5	
Gupton, Cheatham	1Lt	49/5	5	
Jordan, Wallace	Maj	49/5	5	+1 P-47
King, Charles	Maj	35/5	5	
Kirby, Marion	1Lt	8-475/5	5	
Lutton, Lowell	1Lt	475/5	5	
Makin, Jack	1Lt	49-475/5	5	
Mathre, Milden	2Lt	49/5	5	
Monk, Franklin	1Lt	475/5	5	
Morriss, Paul	Capt	475/5	5	
Myers, Jennings	1Lt	8/5	5	
Ray, C.B.	1Lt	8/5	5	
Tilley, John	1Lt	475/5	5	
Wandrey, Ralph	Capt	49/5	5	+1 P-47
Wenige, Arthur	1Lt	475/5	5	+1 P-40

5FC P-47 Aces

Ace Name	Rank	Unit	P-47 V	Total V
Kearby, Neel	Col	348	22	22
Dunham, William	LCol	348	16	16
Banks, William	Maj	348	9	9
Benz, Walter	Maj	348	8	8
Grosshuesch, Leroy	Capt	348	8	8
Roddy, Edward	Capt	348	8	8
Rowland, Robert	Col	348	8	8
Blair, Samuel	Capt	348	7	7
Davis, George	1Lt	348	7	7
Grant, Marvin	1Lt	348	7	7
Moore, John	Maj	348	7	7
Brown, Meade	Capt	348	6	6
Fleischer, Richard	Capt	348	6	6
Foulis, William	Capt	348	6	6
Mugavero, James	1Lt	35	6	6
Strand, William	Capt	35	6	6 +1 P-39
Della, George	1Lt	348	5	5
Ditkovitsky, Michael	1Lt	348	5	5
Gibb, Richard	1Lt	348	5	5
Hnatio, Myron	1Lt	348	5	5
Knapp, Robert	Capt	348	5	5
O'Neill, Lawrence	1Lt	348	5	5
Popek, Edward	Maj	348	5	5 + 2 P-51
Sutcliffe, Robert	1Lt	348	5	5

8

Personal Markings of the Aces and Pilots of the 5th Fighter Command

The PR photo of the ace posing under the gaudily decorated nose of his fighter was standard wartime copy. The concept of nose art dates back to the knights of the Middle Ages, who adorned their shields with individual identifying symbols. Sailing vessels that plied the seas bore "figurehead" carvings of voluptuous, scantily-clad females on their prows. Warships throughout history have been given names, such as Horatio Nelson's Victory, John Paul Jones's Bonhomme Richard, the Monitor, and the Merrimac. The Wright brothers named the world's first successful airplane the Flyer. Wiley Post flew the Winnie Mae and Charles Lindbergh crossed the Atlantic in the Spirit of St. Louis. WWII was known as the Golden Age of aircraft art. WWII aircraft art became a morale builder and an extension of the pilot's personality.

The Air Force artists who painted nose art were inspired by Esquire magazine pin-up illustrators: first by George Petty and then, in late 1941, by Alberto Vargas and his Varga Girl (the "S" was dropped, as the magazine trademarked the artist's name). Also during the war, a multitude of pinup pictures and calendars wallpapered billets in every theater. The artwork in the ETO was generally of a much higher quality than those in the Pacific, and the nose art of ETO artists Gil Elvgren and Don Allen were particularly well done. The 49th Fighter Group was considered to have the best nose art of the 5th Fighter Command's Groups in the war. Artistic ground crew personnel became entrepreneurs, sought after by entire squadrons and bases to create or duplicate the pinups. Fighter nose art was often done on the engine cowling (usually the port side), which could be detached and more comfortably done propped up in front of the artist, who could sit in front

The nose art of ETO artists was particularly well done; here **Don Allen** is holding completed nose art on the cowling of a P-47. (AAF)

Nose art was placed on the aircraft's port side, but in some units the starboard could be used by the aircraft's Crew Chief and usually consisted of the ground crew names, as shown on Thomas McGuire's P-38 *Pudgy*. (AAF)

of it. In some units, the starboard could be used by the aircraft's Crew Chief and usually consisted of the ground crew names. This was easier than doing bomber art, which had to be done standing on a ladder. The going rate for aircraft painting and lettering, of course, depended on quality and ranged from $10 up to $35 for an early Allen, and much more once the news photographers posed ace after ace with his fighter. Also, the fighter cowling could be transferred when the fighter was replaced. Soon artists expanded into painting leather A-2 jackets, which are priceless today.

In the more conservative 1940s, a great deal of the nose art and names were considered "X-rated," as much of it had strong pictorial and verbal emphasis on "healthy" females. A survey I took of over 500 WWII personal markings, names, or drawings of American fighter aces showed the following:
• 48% were female names/drawings or references (usually wives, girlfriends, mothers, or a generic female). Of the female drawings, only about a quarter were totally nude, while the remainder were at least partially clothed. Vessels, in general, have always been referred to as females.
• 10% Male names/drawings (usually sons, or the pilot's own name)
• 8% Animal names/drawings or references
• 5% Neutral (cartoon characters, or no clear gender or an animal)
• 29% Miscellaneous (names, often home, state, or city, mottos, aphorisms, or "Jap/Nazi" bashing)

Initially, the tone of the names and art was left to good taste, but it seems that the more remote and distant from Headquarters and civilization, the more bold and indiscreet the nose art became. This is evident when comparing fighter nose art of the ETO in very proper England and that in the "uncivilized and amoral" Pacific islands. As the war went on, there were occasional outcries and movements to eliminate, or at least control personal markings, mostly initiated by civilian visitors to the front, the base clergy, and public relations conscious HQ brass. Photos of aircraft nose art made their way into Stateside publications, also causing a hue and cry among the righteous. In June 1944, Charles Lindbergh accompanied Gen. Paul Wurtsmith to airstrips in New Guinea. In his wartime journals he wrote the following: "The cheapness of the emblems and names painted on the bombers and

fighters nauseates me at times—mostly naked women or "Donald ducks"— names such as 'Fertile Myrtle' under a large and badly painted figure of a reclining nude." In 1943, renowned novelist and champion of the "illustrated literature on aircraft fuselages," John Steinbeck, defended the practice, writing the following to the New York Tribune: "The names must not be changed. There is enough dullness in war as it is." But "boys will be boys," and the markings became increasingly more risqué, especially in the Pacific.

In August 1944, the Air Force issued Regulation (35-22), which stated in part:

1) Policy: The custom of decorating organizational equipment of the Army Air Force with individual characteristic design is authorized by the Secretary of War and is encouraged as a means of increasing morale.
2) Definitions:
   a) "Equipment" as used herein means operating equipment, i.e., airplanes.
   b) "Design" or "Organizational Design" as used herein refers to the markings applied to organizational equipment and does not refer to group or other unit coat of arms, nor to uniform insignia or shoulder or sleeve insignia.

This double speak placated military and civilian protesters, but made no dictates on the type or method of nose art in the field. Generally nothing changed, unless there was to be an official inspection. At that time, indecent female figures had clothing painted over offending areas and particularly offensive verbiage was deleted (all temporarily). There were some interesting names and provocative nude artwork, but many pilots lovingly adorned their second loves with the names of their first loves: their wives or sweethearts.

Gallery of 5th Fighter Command Artwork

Dirty Old Man (**Walter Benz P-47**). (AFAA)

Black Market Babe (**Billy Gresham P-38**). (AFAA)

Black Boy (Nelson Flack P-40). (AFAA)

Empty Saddle (Arland Stanton P-40). (AFAA)

Kathy Veni Vidi Vici (Lawrence O'Neill P-47). (AAF)

Condon Cans (Henry Condon P-38). (AAF)

Eileen-Anne **(Frederick Champlin P-38).** (AFAA)

Josie **(Michael Dikovitsky P-47).** (AFAA)

Little Maggie **(William Drier P-38).** (AFAA)

Top aces Richard Bong (Marge), Thomas McGuire (Pudgy), Neel Kearby (Fiery Ginger), Jay Robbins (Jandina), and Gerald Johnson (Barbara) each named their fighters after their wives. The stories of these aircraft names will be described later. (**Note:** It was very uncommon for Japanese aircraft to exhibit personal markings, as pilots were not assigned personal aircraft. When markings did occur, it was in the form of a pilot's initials placed on the upper portion of the vertical tail. Other exceptional markings took the form of patriotic maxims or symbols of power, such as a lightning bolt.)

Personal Markings of the Top Aces of the 5th Fighter Command

Bong, Richard	Maj	49FG	40	P-38	*Thumper, Marge, Down Beat*
McGuire, Tom	Maj	475FG	38	P-38	*Pudgy I-V*
MacDonald, Charles	Col	475FG	27	P-38	*Putt-Putt Maru*
Robbins, Jay	Maj	8FG	22	P-38	*"J," Jandina*
Johnson, Gerald R.	LCol	49FG	22	P-38	*Jerry, Barbara*
Kearby, Neel	Col	348FG	22	P-47	*Fiery Ginger*
Dunham, William	LCol	348FG	16	P-47 P-51	*Bonnie*
Welch, George	Capt	47PS 8FG	16	P-40 P-39 P-38	NPM *Miss Helen the Flying Jenny* *Snatcher (?)*
Cragg, Edward	Maj	8FG	15	P-38	*Porky*
Homer, Cyril	Capt	8FG	15	P-38	*Cotton Duster,* *Uncle Cy's Angel*

Personal Markings of Other Aces of the 5th Fighter Command

Adams, Robert	1Lt	8	5	P-38	*Princess Pat*
Ambort, Ernest	2Lt	49	5	P-38	*Flying Knight*
Andrews, Stan	1Lt	35	6	P-38	*Lil' Women*
Andrew, Steve	Maj	49	9	P-40 P-47	NPM *Spirit of Los Angeles City College* *
Aschenbrener, R	Maj	49	10	P-40 P-38	*Naughty Marietta* *Maj. R.W. Aschenbrener, Regina*
Banks, William	Maj	348	9	P-47	*Sunshine*
Benz, Walter	Maj	348	8	P-47	*Dirty Old Man*
Blair, Samuel	Capt	348	7	P-47	*Frankie*
Brown, Harry	Capt	475	6	P-40 P-38	*Sylvia* *Florence*
Champlin, Fred	Capt	475	9	P-38	*Buffalo Blitz/We Dood It, Buffalo Blitz Eileen Ann, Eileen*
Condon, Henry	Capt	475	5	P-38	*Condon Cans*
Day, William	1Lt	8	5	P-38	*Jerry*
Della, George	1Lt	348	5	P-47	*Nadine*
Dent, Elliott	Capt	49	6	P-40	*Ann, the B'Ham Special, Grade A*
Dick, Frederick	Capt	49	5	P-40 P-38	NPM *My Marie*
Dikovitsky, Michael	1Lt	348	5	P-47	*Josie/Cleveland Cleaver, Josie II*
Donalson, I.B.	1Lt	49	5	P-40	*Mauree*
Drier, William	Capt	49	6	P-40 P-38	*Sugar, Little Maggie* *My Gal Becky*
Elliott, Vincent	1Lt	475	7	P-38	*Miss Fru-Fru*
Flack, Nelson	Capt	49	5	P-40	*Ana May*
Forster, Joseph	1Lt	475	9	P-38	*Florida Cracker*
Giroux, William	Capt	8	10	P-38	*Whilma, Deadeye Daisy, Elmer, winged G*
Grant, Marvin	1Lt	348	7	P-47	*Sylvia, Racine Belle*
Gresham, William	1Lt	475	6	P-38	*Black Market Babe*
Harris, Ernest	Capt	49	10	P-40	*Miss Kat, Carolina Belle*
House, A.T.	1Lt.	49	5	P-40	*Poopy*
Hart, Kenneth	1Lt	475	8	P-38	*Pee Wee*
Hunter, Alvaro	Capt	35	5	P-39 P-40	*My Baby* *My Baby*
Ince, James	1Lt	475	6	P-38	*Impossible Ince*
Jones, John	Capt	8	8	P-39 P-38	*Panic* *Panic, GI Annie, Little De-Icer*
King, Charles	Maj	35	5	P-38	*King*
Kirby, Marion	1Lt	8,475	5	P-38	*Maiden Head Hunter*
Kiser, George	Capt	24,49	9	P-40	*Lion with Zero Pilot (emblem)*
Ladd, Kenneth	Capt	8	12	P-38	*X Virgin, Windy City Ruthie, Wagon Wheel Drawing*

Lane, John	1Lt	35	6	P-38	*Thumper*
Landers, John	LCol	49	14.5	P-40 P-38 P-51	*Skeeter* *Big Beautiful Doll (ETO)* *Big Beautiful Doll*
Lavan, George	Capt	49	5	P-38	*Itsy Bitsy*
Lent, Francis	1Lt	475	11	P-38	*Trigger Mortis*
Loisel, John	Maj	475	11	P-38	*Sooner Kid*
McGee, Donald	Capt	80	6	P-39 P-38	*Nip's Nenesis*
McKeon, Joseph	Capt	475 20	6	P-38 P-51	*Regina Coeli* *Regina Coeli II-III*
Morehead, James	Maj	49	5	P-40 P-38	*L'Ace* *NPM*
Morriss, Paul	Capt	475	5	P-38	*Hold Something*
Mugavero, James	1Lt	35	6	P-47	*Pat*
Murphey, Paul	Capt	8	6	P-38	*Sweet Sue*
Nichols, Frank	Capt	49/475	5	P-40 P-38	*Nick Nichols Nip Nippers* *NPM*
O'Neill, John	1Lt	49	8	P-38	*Beautiful Lass, Elsie*
O'Neill, Lawrence	Flt/Lt	348	6	P-47	*Cathy, Kathy/Veni, Vedi, Vici*
Paris, Joel	Capt	49	9	P-40 P-38	*Lizzy, Rusty, Sandy,* *Georgia Belle*
Pierce, Sammy	1Lt	49	9	P-40 P-38	*Kay the Strawberry Blond* *Kay the Strawberry Blond/* *Hialeah Wolf*
Pietz, John	1Lt	475	6	P-38	*Vickie* *Pattie P.*
Popek, Edward	Maj	348	7	P-47 P-51	*Little Bess* *The Rollicking Rogue*
Ray, C.B.	Capt.	8	5	P-38	*San Antonio Rose*
Reeves, Horace	1Lt	475	6	P-38	*El Tornado*
Roddy, Edward	Capt	348/35	8	P-47	*Babs*
Rowland, Robert	Col	348	8	P-47	*Miss Mutt/Pride of Lodi, Ohio**
Schriber, Louis	Capt	8	5	P-38	*Screwy Looie*
Smith, Cornelius	Capt	8	11	P-38	*Dottie from Brooklyn*
Smith, Richard	1Lt	35	6	P-38	*Japanese Sandman*
Stanton, Arland	Maj	49	8	P-40	*Empty Saddle, Revenge Side,* *Keystone Katie (or Kathleen)*
Suehr, Richard	1Lt	35	5	P-39 P-38	*NPM* *Regina*
Summer, Elliott	Capt	475	10	P-38	*Blood & Guts, Stiff Action, Eileen*
Sutcliff, Robert	1Lt	348	5	P-47	*Brown Eyes*
Tilley, John	1Lt	475	5	P-38	*Ranooki, MaruBett, Ann*
Troxell, Clifton	Maj	8	5	P-39	*Uncle Dud*
Vaught, Robert	Capt	49	5	P-40 P-38	*Bob's Robin*

Wandrey, Ralph	Capt	49	6	P-47 P-38	Pin up photos on cowling
Watkins, James	Capt	49	12	P-40 P-38	*Duck Butt* *Charlcie Jeanne*
West, Richard	Capt	8	14	P-40 P-38	NPM *Heart flush (emblem)*
White, Robert	Capt.	9			*Kansas City Kittie*
Wire, Calvin	1Lt	475	7	P-38	*Little Eva*
Witt, Lynn	Capt	8	6	P-40 P-38	*Home Sick* *Home Sick*
Woods, Sidney	LCol	49 4	7	P-40 P-38	*Arizona* *Kip*
Wright, Ellis	Maj.	49	6	P-40	*Dottie*

NPM=No Personal Markings   * = Presentation Aircraft

Bong's P-38s and *Marge*

Richard Bong was America's top ace with 40 victories, completing three combat tours flying the P-38 F, G, H, J, and L models. Over the years, there has been confusion among historians and modelers as to the P-38s Bong flew during his career. Bong, like most fighter pilots, did not identify his specific aircraft in his logs or mission ICRs. Veteran pilots were assigned personal aircraft, but often flew other aircraft when theirs were being serviced or repaired. Also, when a pilot was not flying a mission others flew his fighter. As a rookie pilot with the 9FS, Bong scored his first two victories (a Val and Zero) on 27 December 1942 in a P-38F-5 (SN#42-12644) named *Thumper*, which was assigned to six-victory ace Lt. John "Shady" Lane. This Lightning, with #15 on both sides of the nose, was painted in the standard medium green with neutral gray undersides. Many of the 39FS' P-38s exhibited shark mouths on their nacelles, but on 27 December, Lane's Crew Chief had completed a mouth on only one nacelle. Bong then flew an unidentified P-38F-5 (SN#42-12624) from 31 December 1942 to 7 January 1943, and scored two more victories and a probable and damaged. On 8 January, he became an ace when he shot down an Oscar in a P-38F-5 (SN# 42-12653). From 3 March 1943 to 28 July 1943, he scored his next 11 victories while flying one or more P-38G-5 models (except on 11 March, when his log indicated that he scored his seventh and eighth victories plus a probable and damaged in the G-15 variant). The victories in G-5 models are sketchy concerning the specific P-38 he flew on a particular mission, which is not an unusual omission by fighter pilots. However, Bong notes that his Lightnings incurred damage on several missions, but depending on the extent of the damage, there was enough time between missions to repair the damage. His last (#16) victory of his first tour was recorded in P-38F-5 #73, and Bong returned to his home in Poplar, WI. As part of his PR activities, he was to crown Superior State Teacher's College's 1943 Homecoming Queen. While at the Homecoming dance, Bong met a beautiful just-graduated student, Marge Vattendahl. The shy Bong had his sister, Jerry, track her down on campus and she asked Marge to go out on a date with her brother, who, at the time, was 23, a famous fighter pilot, and one of America's most eligible bachelors. During Bong's hectic PR schedule to raise money for War Bonds, the two squeezed in as many bowling and movie dates as possible.

After Bong returned from leave in September 1943, he claimed five victories in the H model P-38 from 6 September to 5 November 1943. The last two victories of the tour were claimed on 5 November, when he shot down two Zeros over Rabaul in P-38H-5 #79. The photo of the P-38 with Bong's 16 victories has its serial number covered by a victory flag and the model number is obscured, but appears to be an H-5. Bong left for home and back to Marge on his second leave with 16 victories.

Bong returned to combat—assigned to the 5th Fighter Command HQ—in February 1944 very much in love, and decided to decorate his personal P-38 with a picture of Marge. This P-38, which Bong is most commonly associated with, was a J-15-LO model (SN#42-103993). Using a small black and white graduation photo of the very pretty Marge, he had intelligence officer Capt. Jim Nichols enlarge it to 20x24 inches and had it tinted. The photo print was glued directly to the nose and heavily varnished to protect it with the name Marge in script and 21 Japanese victory flags. After Bong scored three victories (numbers 22-24) in that aircraft he went on a short leave. It was then used by Lt. Thomas Malone on a weather recon mission on 24 March and was lost when Malone was forced to bail out when the fighter lost its left engine and electrical system. There is a photo of an unidentified P-38J with 25 victory flags which were either applied on 5 March when he shot down an Oscar that was downgraded to a probable or on 3 April when he shot down an Oscar.

Bong broke Eddie Rickenbacker's American victory record of 26 on 12 April, when he downed three Oscars while flying Down Beat ("T" on the nose), a P-38J-15LO (SN# 42-104012) assigned to William Caldwell, who was assigned to the 80FS/8FG. There is some confusion about this aircraft, as Bong had a PR photo done after the historic mission standing in front of another natural metal P-38J-15LO (SN# 42-104380) with 27 victory flags. After breaking Rickenbacker's record, Bong completed his second tour (mid-February to mid-April 1944) and Kenney took him out of action again and promoted him to Major. During this leave in May 1944, Dick and Marge became engaged and Bong toured the U.S. on a War Bond publicity tour. Everyone wanted to meet Marge, who was "the most shot after girl in the South Pacific." Bong later wrote to her, apologizing for exposing her the media frenzy.

Before Bong returned to New Guinea on 10 September, he attended gunnery school and Kenney assigned him as HQ "advanced gunnery instructor." He was allowed to take a limited part in combat missions to oversee his gunnery students. Gen. Kenney had written Bong that he would store his P-38J until he returned, but Bong would score his next two victories flying an unadorned L-1LO (SN# 44-23961) on 10 October, then would score one victory on 27 October and then two more the next day flying a J model to give him 33 victories. On 10 and 11 November, he would score one and two victories, respectively, in a P-38L-1LO (SN#44-23964), and there is a photo showing the 36 victory flags on this aircraft. This fighter was lost on 28 November 1944, when 49FG pilot Capt. John Davis scrambled during dusk interception, but as the fighter just became airborne an engine burst into flames and it crashed, killing Davis instantly. Bong's last four career victories were scored in a P-38L-1 borrowed from arch rival Tom McGuire's 475th Fighter Group. There are no photos showing a Bong P-38 in a combat area with more than 36 victories. By 17 December, Bong had scored his 40th victory and received the Medal of Honor from MacArthur, and in January 1945, Kenney sent America's Ace of Aces home for good.

When he returned home, Ace-of-Aces Dick and beautiful Marge were married in a large wedding in Superior, WI, attended by 1,200 guests. The ceremony was taped and broadcast by the national media, but the large press corps contingent was limited to one photographer to shoot two photos inside the church. The Bongs settled in California, where the famous pilot remained in the limelight, meeting famous movie stars, including Judy Garland, Bing Crosby, and Joan Crawford, among others. Bong went on a PR/War Bond drive after his combat tour flying two (known) specially marked P-38J-20-LO models (SN#s 44-23461 and 44-23491). The first only displayed 40 victory markings without the Marge motif, while the second carried the original Marge photo and stylized Marge lettering. On 8 August 1945, Bong was flying a Shooting Star P-80 jet fighter for Lockheed when it malfunctioned over North Hollywood. He tried to eject after navigating his aircraft to a vacant lot, but he died in the crash. Although

Bong's death occurred on the same day as the dropping of the Hiroshima atomic bomb, his death was featured on the front pages of national dailies.

After Dick's death, the beautiful and well known Marge began a modeling career, working for the largest agency in Hollywood. She met and married Murray Drucker, who published both fashion and dog magazines. They and their two daughters traveled the world on fashion shoots and business for the magazines. Marge became a successful publisher in 1956, when she started the Boxer Review, an award-winning dog magazine which she sold in 2001.

She then returned to Superior after 40 years absence to attend the dedication of the Bong Road Bridge and was asked to speak to the 49th Fighter Group, which was there for a reunion. She was delighted to receive "such a wonderful reception and a welcome back ….that was the beginning of my opening up to the press and the public." Marge Bong Drucker and others, including Bong's family, supported the establishment of the Richard I. Bong WWII Heritage Center. Marge spoke and raised money at various veterans' meetings and the Center opened on 24 September 2002. She also sold her house in Hollywood that she had lived in for more than 50 years and had a new house built on the original Bong homestead in Poplar. She died a year later at 79.

Richard Bong P-38 Gallery

Bong 1: As a rookie pilot, Bong scored his first victories in a P-38F-5 named *Thumper*, which was assigned to Lt. John Lane. (AFAA

Bong 2: Bong's P-38 on 26 July 1943 after he shot four enemy fighters to give him 14 victories. (AAF)

Bong 3: Bong (R) after shooting down two Zeros on 5 November 1943 to give him 21 victories and ready to be sent home on his first furlough. (AFAA)

Bong 4: When Bong returned for his second tour in February 1944, he was in love with Marge Vattendahl. (AAF)

Bong 5: *Marge* with 25 victories after an Oscar victory on 3 April 1944. (AAF)

Bong 6: Bong broke Rickenbacker's record of 26 victories in borrowed P-38 *Down Beat* when *Marge* was lost on 24 March when borrowed for a weather recon mission. The photo shows 27 Rising Suns applied to another P-38 for PR photos. (AAF)

Bong 7: P-38J Bong flew after *Marge* was lost shown at Port Moresby after he had broken the Rickenbacker record. (AFAA)

Bong 8: Bong flew an unmarked P-38 #42 out of Biak as a "gunnery instructor" on his third tour, during which he scored seven victories. (AAF)

Bong 9: The 36-victory total was after 11 November, when Bong shot down three aircraft. This P-38L was lost at the end of November when flown by a 49FG pilot. (AFAA)

Bong 10: When Bong returned home after his third tour, various *Marges* were prepared for PR opportunities. (AFAA)

Bong 11: A P-38 decorated with 40 victory flags for use during his PR tour prior to his death. (AAF)

McGuire's *Pudgy*

Thomas McGuire was a cadet at Randolph Field, San Antonio, during the Winter of 1941, and just after Pearl Harbor he was fixed up on a date by his friends. They all met at a club and he was introduced to a attractive redhead, blue-eyed, Catholic college student named Marilyn Giesler. Her friends explained that she was called "Pudgy" because she had once complained to her friends that she needed to lose weight. McGuire, who had previously been rather shy, and Marilyn found that they had much in common and began dating. On 6 February 1942, McGuire graduated from training and was sent to Key Field, near Meridian, MS, and the romance became long distance, as McGuire began an exhausting fighter training schedule. He phoned her and sent roses, but was unable to see her. In June, he found that he was going to be sent to Alaska to fly P-39s with the 54th Fighter Group and decided to ask her to marry him when he returned and she agreed. Finally, in November, after 10 months apart, he was granted a leave, but due to red tape his travel was restricted and it was not until 4 December that the two were married in the base Chapel at Ft. Sam Houston,

San Antonio. The two lived out of a suitcase at Harding Field, San Antonio, until they were parted when McGuire was assigned to Operational Training in the P-38 at Muroc Field, CA. He was then sent to New Guinea with the 431FS, where he named his Lightning *Pudgy*. He was never to see Marilyn again. On 17 January 1944, Marilyn opened an official U.S. Army letter and thought it was one of a number she had received, telling her of another medal awarded to her husband. Instead, it was a personal letter from Gen. George Kenney, expressing his condolences over "Tommy's" death on 7 January. Kenney had assumed that the telegram notifying her of Tom's death had arrived earlier than his letter. While waiting for the tardy telegram, an Army Officer arrived at Marilyn's home, mysteriously asking her to return Kenney's letter. She refused, but never found the reason for this request. It was not until 51 days after McGuire's death that the official telegram arrived. A few months later, she was informed that her husband would be awarded the Medal of Honor for his combat on 25 December 1945. It was presented to Marilyn on 8 May 1946.

Marilyn married Clem Stankowski; they had a son and remained married for 35 years until his death. A few years later she married Robert Beatty. Marilyn donated McGuire's Medal of Honor and other medals, his famous 500-hour hat (as depicted previously), and Bible to the National Museum of the U.S. Air Force for the Bong and McGuire exhibit.

McGuire's P-38s:		
P-38H-1:	42-66592	Pudgy
P-38H-5:	42-66817	#131
P-38J-15:	??	# 131 Pudgy II
P-38J-15:	??	# 131 Pudgy III
P-38L-1:	??	# 131 Pudgy IV
P-38L-1:	44-24153	# 131 Pudgy V

Thomas McGuire P-38 Gallery

McGuire 1: McGuire and svelte **Marilyn Giesler**, nicknamed "Pudgy", were married in December 1942 and would never see each other again. (Author)

McGuire 2: *Pudgy I* with McGuire (R). (AFAA)

McGuire 3: *Pudgy II* with 12 victories. (AAF)

McGuire 4: *Pudgy III* with 19 victories. (AAF)

McGuire 5: *Pudgy IV* with 22 victories. (AFAA)

McGuire 6: *Pudgy V* with 25 victories. (AAF)

McGuire 7: *Pudgy V* with 37 victories. (AAF)

MacDonald's *Putt Putt Maru*

I can find no reference to MacDonald's reason to give his aircraft the good-humored name *Putt Putt Maru*. Putt putt was the chugging sound made by the engine (*i.e.*, the auxiliary generator of a bomber, which has that name) and the Japanese names for their merchant ships ended in *Maru*. MacDonald's *Putt Putt Marus* also depicted a Hotai—a jolly, plump Buddhist monk who was known for his girth, good nature, and hopes of bringing good fortune. There were five *Putt Putt Marus*:

P-47:	??	#100 Putt Putt Maru
P-38J-15:	42-104024 #100 Putt Putt Maru II	
P-38L-1:	44-24843 #100 Putt Putt Maru III	
P-38L-5:	44-25643 #100 Putt Putt Maru IV	
P-38L-5:	44-25471 #100 Putt Putt Maru V	

Charles MacDonald P-38 Gallery

MacDonald 1: **Original *Putt Putt Maru*.** (AFAA)

MacDonald 2: ***Putt Putt Maru II*** with 10 victories. (AFAA)

MacDonald 3: ***Putt Putt Maru III*** MacDonald (L) with Charles Lindbergh. (AAF)

MacDonald 4: ***Putt Putt Maru IV*** with 24 victories. (AFAA)

MacDonald 5: *Putt Putt Maru V* with MacDonald's final 27-victory total. (AFAA)

Robbins's *Jandina*

The following account was sent to me by Robbins's son Robbie and wife Donna:

"I've read some accounts that thought my mother was Australian, because that's where my parents were married. Ina Louise Priest was born in Vermont and claimed Winchendon, MA, as her hometown. She joined the Army for a year of training at Ft. Devin, MA, after finishing nursing school in Keene, NH. She was due to get out on 12 December 1941. Instead of becoming a civilian, she found herself on the first convoy leaving New York City for the Pacific on New Year's Day 1942. Originally bound for Singapore, the convoy was diverted to Melbourne due to Japanese activity in the area. She became part of the newly-designated 4th U.S. Army General Hospital. It was while there that she later met Jay T. Robbins.

"While flying P-39s with the 80th out of Port Moresby, Dad was grounded after he took his annual physical exam sometime in October 1942. The doctor detected an erratic heart beat (arrhythmia) and wouldn't clear him to fly again until he had an EKG. The nearest EKG was located in Melbourne. My mother claimed that a soldier with measles fell out of bed and she grabbed the first person walking down the hall to help her get him back into bed. That was my parent's first meeting. My father never disputed the story. I think they next saw each other when the 80th moved to Australia to upgrade to the P-38 in early 1943. My mother volunteered to join a field hospital in New Guinea during that Summer. It was located just below the runway at 3 Mile Drone, where Dad was stationed. A month after Dad took command of the Headhunters, they both took some R&R to Melbourne and got married on 22 January 1944. No one knew of their marriage until after the war. The 80th moved to several bases on the north coast of New Guinea. Dad would periodically fly back to Port Moresby to see her before she was reassigned back to Melbourne. My Dad left for the U.S. a month before my mother. After the war ended, my mother told the Army she was married and wished to get out. She was stationed at Ft. Ord, CA, and had enough points to get an early release. In October 1945, she left the Army and joined my father in Santa Rosa, CA. They remained married for 57 years until my father's death in March 2001. Mother died in December 2003."

Robbins flew a P-400 when he damaged two Sallys on 17 January 1943. He then flew a P-38G for his three Zero victories on 21 July 1943 and the P-38H-5 for his next 10 victories in 1943. When he returned from leave in March 1944, he flew the P-38J-15 for his final 12 victories.

Jay Robbins P-38 Gallery

Robbins 1: Jay and Ina Robbins (*Jandina*) in Australia in 1942, where she was a nurse. (Robbins Family)

Robbins 2: *Jandina II* with 13 victories. (AFAA)

Robbins 3: *Jandina III* with 15 victories. (AFAA)

Robbins 4: *Jandina IV* with 26 (of 27 total) victories. (AFAA)

Johnson's *Barbara*

During his first quarter at the University of Oregon in 1939, Johnson and several friends were hiking to the top of a butte when they spotted several girls having lunch in a clearing. Johnson tried to draw the attention of a pretty brunette, but the handsome Johnson, who never had a problem attracting a girl, failed miserably. After a few days, he tracked down and charmed high school senior Barbara Hall and the two began to date. Meanwhile, Johnson entered the Civilian Pilot Training Program and received his pilot's license in 1940. He joined the AAC and was ordered to active duty in March 1941. After Pearl Harbor, Johnson was to be sent to Alaska, flying P-39s for the 57FG, and proposed to Barbara—who was in nursing school—before leaving. After flying P-39s with the 57FG in the Aleutians, Johnson returned to Orlando in October 1942 and was selected for P-38 training. He was soon sent to New Guinea with future aces Wallace Jordan and Thomas McGuire to fly P-38s and would score nine victories. He transitioned to the P-47D in late 1943 and scored two victories in that fighter. By April 1944, Johnson was an 11-victory Major with the 7FS/49FG and was given a 60-day leave to return home for the first time in two years. Jerry and Barbara were married on 1 June, but there was no time for a honeymoon, as Johnson was ordered to attend Command and General Staff School at Leavenworth, KS. Barbara joined him there for two months, and at the end of August the two returned to Oregon for a brief belated honeymoon when Barbara discovered she was pregnant. In early September, Jerry shipped out back to the Pacific, and while Lt.Col. Johnson was scoring 11 more victories for the 49FG, Jerry Jr. was born on 1 June 1945. After flying 262 combat missions, the war finally came to an end. On 7 October, Johnson was flying a B-25 to Kyushu, Japan, with a stop to visit his brother Harold, whose unit, the 348FG, was stationed at Kanoya. As Johnson circled the field, he asked the Controller about the 348th and was told the Group was no longer stationed there. Johnson flew on to Kyushu and ran into a typhoon that damaged the bomber. With 20 minutes of fuel remaining, he ordered the crew to don their parachutes, but two passengers had not brought any along. Johnson and his copilot, 1Lt. James Nolan, gave theirs away and ordered the four passengers to bail out over a beach, with Johnson saying he would return to land on the beach. Johnson and Nolan were never seen again. Harold's unit had been stationed at Kanoya after all, but the new controller did not know that. Despite a stellar life as a pillar of his community, Harold was never able to cope with his part in his brother's death and committed suicide in 1975. Barbara eventually married David Curtis, one of Jerry's high school friends, and the two had four children, but divorced in the mid-1980s.

Gerald Johnson Fighter Gallery

Johnson 1: Jerry and **Barbara Johnson** in 1944, after their marriage during his leave. She would never see him again. (AFAA)

Johnson 2: Johnson's 57FG **P-39** over the Aleutians. (AFAA)

Johnson 3: First P-38 *Sooner* (see faint Sooner UR in photo). (AFAA)

Johnson 4: P-47N with 13 victories. (AAF)

Johnson 6: P-38 *Barbara* without the Wirraway victory. (AAF)

Johnson 5: P-38 *Jerry* showing his Australian Wirraway and two Aleutian victories. (AFAA)

Kearby's *Fiery Ginger*

Very little is known about Kearby's family life, except that *Ginger* was named after his wife Virginia and that they had two children. Joe Stevens's biography on Kearby, *One More Pass before Seeking Cover*, mentions nothing of Kearby's personal life. All Kearby's assigned fighters were P-47D-2s (1943**)** and D-4s (1944).

Neel Kearby P-47 Gallery

Kearby 1: The **Kearbys** (Neel and Virginia [Ginger]) at a dinner with friends, the **William Leverettes**. 11-victory ace Leverette would shoot down seven Ju-87s over North Africa on 9 October 1943, two days before Kearby downed his six Japanese fighters.

Kearby 2: P-47 *Fiery Ginger* with 10 victories.

Kearby 3: P-47 *Fiery Ginger IV*.

Kearby 4: The tail of the original *Fiery Ginger IV* recovered from its New Guinea wreck site and displayed at the NMUSAF at Dayton with a repainted P-47 *Fiery Ginger* in the background.

Gallery of Aces' Aircraft Personal Markings

Lynch 1: P-400 with two victories scored on 20 May 1942.

Lynch 2: Except for this P-400 with the Cobra in the Clouds cartoon on the door, Lynch's aircraft carried no markings.

Lynch 3: Capt. Lynch becomes a double ace on 8 May 1943 in a P-38G.

Lynch 4: Maj. Lynch's P-38H carrying 16 victories in September 1944.

Welch: George Welch and his P-39D *Miss Helen the Flying Jenny* with seven unusual aircraft victory silhouettes on 7 December 1942.

Dunham: William Dunham's P-47D *Bonnie*.

Dunham: *Bonnie* was followed by his P-51K *Mrs. Bonnie* after Dunham got married during leave.

Cragg: Cragg flew P-38s self-named *Porky* to 15 victories before he was KIA on 26 December 1943.

Homer 1: Homer flew *Cotton Duster* for nine victories.

Homer 2: Homer (C) standing with his ground crew under *Uncle Cy's Angel* adorned with his 15 total victories.

DeHaven 1: DeHaven P-40N *Rita*.

DeHaven 2: DeHaven P-40N with Orchid drawing.

DeHaven 3: DeHaven P-38 with Orchid drawing.

Roberts: Daniel Roberts's fighters carried no personal markings and P-38H #197 carried his 14 total victory markings.

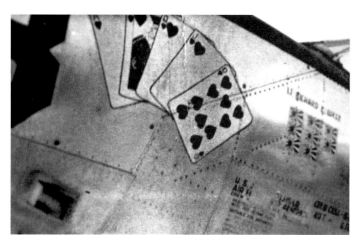

West 1: West's P-38J exhibited a heart flush on the port side.

West 2: The starboard side had a leaping cat on the cowling and *Helen* on the engine nacelle.

Ladd 1: Ladd's P-38G *X-Virgin*.

Ladd 2: *Windy City Ruthie* before she was named (March 1944).

Ladd 3: *Windy City Ruthie* given a name.

Ladd 4: Spinning wagon wheel motif with 10 victories. Ladd scored two victories on the day he was KIA.

Watkins 1: Watkins and his P-40E with Donald Duck rolling up his sleeves.

Watkins 2: P-38H *Charlcie Jeanne* with 11 victories in August 1943.

Watkins 3: P-38L *Charlcie Jeanne* with 12 victories during Watkins's last tour in April 1945.

C. Smith: Smith with his final 11-victory total with his final *Corky IV* (followed *Corky Jr*).

Lent: Lent's P-38J *T Rigor Mortis III* with his final score of 11 victories.

Loisel 2: Loisel's P-38 #100 with mirror-image number.

Loisel 1: Loisel's *Scream'n Kid* with cartoon of a baby in armor.

Aschenbrener 1: Aschenbrener's P-39 *Regina*.

Aschenbrener 2: Aschenbrener's P-40 *Naughty Marietta*, in which he scored two victories.

Aschenbrener 3: *Maj. R.W. Aschenbrener* standing under his P-38J displaying his final 10 victories.

Giroux 1: Giroux standing with a P-39 early in his career.

Giroux 2: Giroux's *Winged G*, in which he claimed three probables.

Giroux 3: Giroux became an ace in *Whilma II* when he shot down three Zeros 2 November 1944.

Giroux 4: Giroux's Dead Eye Daisy (a sitting cat looking at a head hunter) with Elmer (a diving dog) on the engine nacelle.

Harris 1: Harris's P-40 *The Carolina Belle*.

Harris 2: Harris's P-40 *Miss Kat* (with snarling cat head).

Summer 1: Summer's P-38L *Blood & Guts*, showing his 10 victory final total.

Summer 2: Summer's P-38 *Stiff Action*.

9

Japanese Aces and Aerial Victory Claims

In the American Army, Navy, and Marine Air Forces and the British and Commonwealth Air Forces, a pilot who shot down five or more enemy aircraft was unofficially bestowed the enviable and widely publicized title "ace." While the Japanese Air Forces adopted many concepts from the Western Air Forces (especially European), the Japanese culture did not value the Western trait of individuality. Throughout their education, Japanese school children were taught to work and sacrifice for the advantage of the many. During Japanese military training, this group concept continued and punishment for the failing of an individual in a group would be meted out on all, while individual success would be rewarded and recognized as a group accomplishment.

Thus, because Japanese culture discouraged emphasis on the individual, Japanese aces were not given the same attention as Allied aces. However, particularly productive pilots would be rewarded with a promotion, which meant a pay raise for the enlisted and officer pilots. The rewarded pilots then risked being promoted out of their command of flying units. Also, due to the Japanese Air Force's lack of emphasis on individual accomplishment, there was no means to verify or correct victory claims at any level of command. There were no Operations or Intelligence Officers to debrief pilots and to evaluate the mission's combat. After a combat mission, each participating pilot reported the circumstances of his combat, his success, the fate of fellow pilots, etc., to his superior officer, who then summed up the reports of all his pilots, and if possible, reports from friendly ground troops.

During the China War and in the early part of the Pacific War, when Japan was on the offensive, a number of units did record individual victory credits in their mission reports. However, in June 1943, as a means to promote greater teamwork, Navy GHQ issued a directive prohibiting the continuation of this practice and most units followed this new decree.

However, Japanese fighter pilots, being prideful like most young men, did keep personal scores, and would paint victory markings on their fighter aircraft. Japanese pilots flew aircraft on an availability basis, and most, except for high ranking officers, did not have personal aircraft. Thus, the number of victory markings on an aircraft could be misleading, as it was the aircraft and the Group, rather than the pilot, which recorded the victory.

The Japanese had no established rules for determining victories (or probables or damaged) as did the Allies. Many pilots would claim the destruction of an enemy aircraft which was smoking, supposing that it would never make its way back to base. The Japanese did have a few gun

Lt(jg) Tetsuzo Iwamoto. (Author)

cameras, but they were only used for training purposes, and therefore, the claims of Japanese pilots were taken on face value and added to the Group's score. Since there usually were no decorations, promotions, or publicity based solely upon claims, most pilots had no motivation to inflate their totals. Nevertheless, the Group and pilot totals were unintentionally inflated by both the confusion of swirling combat and by a very liberal system of deciding if an enemy aircraft was fatally damaged.

Many of the JAAF's records were lost during the war, as many units were decimated and their records lost or destroyed on the front lines. However, a large percentage of JNAF unit records (70%) are on file in the War History Chamber of the Japan Defense Agency, but the majority of them contain only the combat summary, the names of the participating pilots, and the unit's total victories, not individual victories (as per aviation historian Dan Ford).

Aviation historians have estimated individual Japanese victories from these surviving records, supplemented by contemporary newspaper articles, accounts of the surviving pilots, and many existing pilot diaries and a few pilot log books. Also to be considered was that a Japanese pilot might give his victory to a dead pilot in his unit or to his Commander as a repayment of the giri, or filial obligation, owed to a superior officer.

Postwar Japanese historians, such as Ikuhiko Hata, Yasuho, Izawa, and Henry Sakaida, have recognized the problem of inflated totals and attempt-

Lt.(jg) Hiroyoshi Nishizawa. (Author)

ed to offset them by systematically reducing the totals by percentages. Top scoring Japanese ace in World War II was Lt(jg) Tetsuzo Iwamoto of the JNAF, with an astonishing 202 victories, 26 shared, 22 unconfirmed, and only two damaged. Over his incredible eight-year wartime career he kept a meticulous diary, beginning with 14 victories over China in 1938. Flying out of Rabaul, he claimed 142 victories, including 48 U.S. Navy SBDs and 30 more enemy aircraft destroyed by his aerial bombing. Except for the 20 victories with the 204th Air Group, the units he served with did not keep records of individual totals. Hata and Izawa, in their book Japanese Naval Aces and Fighter Units in World War II, state that "from a conservative point of view, it may perhaps be more appropriate to estimate the number of aircraft (he) downed to be around 80, (which) would be a good estimate."

Another JNAF pilot has also been touted as the top Japanese. Lt.(jg) Hiroyoshi Nishizawa's final victory total has been reported at 147 (which he told his family) and more than 150, according to newspaper articles at the time of his death. However, upon his second evacuation from Rabaul, he personally reported that he had shot down 86 there (plus two F6Fs over the Philippines). However, Hata and Izawa state, "Officially, the estimate would be around 60 to 70 aircraft." In popular literature, Nishizawa is generally credited with being the top Japanese ace, but Hata and Izawa state "it could be that Iwamoto's score even exceeds that of Nishizawa, which would make him the top ace of Japan."

10

Japanese Aces vs.
the 5th Fighter Command

JAAF Aces

Anabuki, M/Sgt. Satoshi

Anabuki. (Author)

Satoshi Anabuki entered the Tokyo Army Aviation School in 1938 and received additional training at Kumagaya and Tachiarai, completing training in March 1941. In July, he was assigned to the 3rd Chutai of the 50th Sentai, stationed in Formosa. On 7 December 1941, Corporal Anabuki participated in attacks on the Philippines and scored his first two aerial combat victories on 9 February 1942. In April 1942, the unit was outfitted with the new Ki-43 Hayabusa fighter and by June he was stationed in Burma. On 24 December 1942, he downed two RAF Hurricanes while fighting with his damaged landing gear extended. In January 1943, he was credited with his first B-24 bomber, then on 8 October, he downed three B-24s and two of their P-38 escorts, with one of the B-24s being rammed by Anabuki, who was injured; this forced a successful crash landing. He received numerous awards and publicity for his actions that day. In February 1944, he returned to Japan, where he served as a flight instructor before being promoted to Master Sergeant and assigned to ferry much needed Ki-84 Frank fighters to the Philippines. It was during these flights that he downed six U.S. Navy F6F Hellcats. He later flew in defense of the homeland, where he downed a B-29 bomber. Master Sergeant Anabuki is credited with 224 missions and 30 victories, although his personal diaries reflect 51 victories. Postwar historians have credited him with 39 victories.

Kajinami, Sgt. Susumu

Kajinami. (Author)

Kajinami was born in Okayama Prefecture in October 1923. He entered the Army in April 1940, and was sent to Kumagaya Flying School in November 1942, receiving combat training with the 246th Sentai, flying Ki-27 Nates. During August 1943, Kajinami was sent to Wewak, flying the Ki-61 Tony for the 2nd Chutai of the 68th Sentai. His first victory there was a P-40 over Hansa Bay, and during his time there he claimed 24 aircraft, including six P-38s, six P-40s, one P-47 of the 5FC, two B-24s, two B-25s, and six USN fighters. Kajinami is officially credited with eight victories and 16 more unofficially. After leaving New Guinea, he ferried aircraft from Japan and Korea. He survived the war.

Kira, WO Katsuaki

Kira was born in Kumamoto Prefecture in 1919. He graduated from Flight School in July 1938 and attended Akeno Fighter School for combat training. He was sent to the 24th Sentai in Manchuria, then took part in the Nomohan battles, where he scored his first victory on 22 June, over a Soviet I-16, then scored eight more victories there. He took part in the initial air battles

Kira. (Author)

over the Philippines at the outbreak of the Pacific War, then was assigned to the defense of the Borneo oil fields. In May 1943, the 24th *Sentai* was re-equipped with Ki-43 Oscars and sent to But Airdrome, New Guinea. Kira defended the Wewak Dromes from 5th Air Force bombers and their P-38 escorts and shot a number of them before succumbing to a P-38 escort after shooting down a B-24; he safely belly landed his severely damaged fighter. The 24th was evacuated from But Airdrome in October 1943 and sent to Manila for almost a year before being sent back to Japan to form the elite 200th *Sentai*, which was comprised of veterans and former instructors and equipped with the new Ki-84 Frank fighter, then rushed to defend the Philippines. Once in the Philippines, the *Sentai* met the P-38s of the 49th Fighter Group around Leyte and Kira scored several victories over Dick Bong's Group. The *Sentai* was withdrawn to Formosa in January 1945 after it had been decimated in the air combat. Kira went on to fight over Okinawa with the 103rd *Sentai* and was one of the few pilots to survive six years of fighting. He is credited with 21 victories.

Noguchi, WO Takashi

Noguchi. (Author)

Noguchi, a native of the Nagasaki Prefecture, joined the Army in 1935, becoming an NCO in the cavalry. After later volunteering for flying training, he graduated in March 1939, then served at Kumagaya and Tachiarai as an instructor until April 1942. He then joined the 3rd *Chutai* of the new 68th *Sentai* at Harbin. Following re-equipment with the Ki-61 Tony at Akeno, the unit moved to Rabaul via Truk, then to Wewak, where it took part in the heavy fighting over New Guinea. Here Noguchi became a very skillful pilot and leader. Before dawn on 15 January 1944, the *Sentai* flew to Nadzab, and Noguchi made two strafing passes, then shot down two of three C-47s. During this time, Noguchi had several close calls: once, following an attack on Rendova and after a dogfight with P-38s, he safely force landed his fighter off the west coast of Bougainville after it had been hit 54 times. On 16 January 1944, during an attack on Saidor, Noguchi was engaged in a dogfight with a P-47 and his fighter was hit; he was wounded in his left arm. As he flew back to Madang he met another P-47, which he claimed to have destroyed, giving him (about) 14 victories. Before reaching Madang, he was forced to ditch into the sea and became unconscious, and was picked up by an USN vessel and spent the remainder of the war as a POW, returning to Japan following the surrender.

Nango, Lt.Col. Shigeo

Namgo. (Author)

Nango was born in Tokyo in 1917, and was the brother of a JNAF ace, Lt.Cdr. Mochifumi Nango, who scored eight victories over China before being KIA in July 1938. He graduated from the Army Flying Military Academy in April 1939, and after fighter training at Akeno was posted to the 33rd *Sentai* in August during the Nomonhan Incident. Nango did not see combat in Manchuria, as he was restricted to training flights. In Spring 1941, he returned to Akeno as an instructor until January 1942, when he was posted to lead the 2nd *Chutai* of the 59th *Sentai* over Java during March, just as the Japanese occupied the Netherlands East Indies. While in Java, the *Sentai* flew their Ki-42 Oscars on convoy patrols and occasional interceptions until June 1943, when they flew two raids on Darwin, Australia. On 12 July, the unit moved to But Airdrome, New Guinea, where Nango was to take part in daily furious fighting for the next six months. Over Tsili Tsili on 15 August, he shot down a C-47 at very close range and his fighter was covered with oil from his victim. Nango thought his fighter had been badly hit and was about to dive into the ground to kill himself when he discovered that he had full control of his aircraft and pulled out. The following day he attacked two Allied aircraft, causing them to collide while attempting to evade their attacker. Due to his skills and the deaths of the 59th's leadership, Nango moved up as the *Sentai*'s Executive Officer. The *Sentai*'s Oscars were greatly inferior to the P-38s and P-47s, and the Japanese suffered heavy losses in the air and to tropical diseases on the ground. Despite fighting at a distinct disadvantage, Nango increased his victory total to 15 (estimated) and was venerated by the JAAF in New Guinea. He was scheduled to return to Japan, but on 23 January 1944, he led a mission to intercept a large formation of 5AF aircraft over Wewak and did not return. He was awarded a posthumous citation and was promoted two ranks to Lt. Colonel. The citation read: "His superb leadership, unprecedented fighting spirit and splendid fighting technique was typical of Army flying unit leaders." He was thought to have shot down 15 aircraft over New Guinea.

Ogura, WO Mitsuo

Ogura. (Author)

Ogura was born in 1914 in Tochigi Prefecture. After joining the Army, he applied for pilot training and graduated in February 1938. After fighter training at Akeno, he became an instructor at Kumagaya until being posted to the 3rd *Chutai* of the 24th *Sentai* in July 1941. At the outbreak of the Pacific War, the *Sentai* operated over the Philippines without claiming any victories. The unit was then sent to Manchuria until July 1942, then fully re-equipped with Ki-43 Oscars and sent to China. Here Ogura claimed a P-40 for his first victory. The unit was then assigned to Palembang, Sumatra, for uneventful air defense until May 1943, when it was sent to New Guinea. On 4 May, the solo Ogura spotted six B-24s over Babo and chased the Liberators for an hour, making repeated attacks with his lightly armed Ki-43 and claiming two destroyed and one damaged. On 12 June, he fought P-38s north of Kainants, claiming two shot down with the expenditure of only 32 bullets, but he was wounded in this action and was to spend a month in hospital. The unit left New Guinea in November 1943, but in May 1944 moved to Sorong, from which they were in range to attack Biak Island. In the face of Allied advances, the *Sentai* withdrew to Celebes, then moved to Fabrica, on Negros Island in the Philippines, in October 1944, to carry out convoy patrols; they met no air opposition. In February 1945, the 24th *Sentai* moved from Makassar to Formosa to operate over Okinawa and remained there until the end of the war, finishing the war with 16 victories.

Onozaki, Capt. Hiroshi

Onozaki was born in 1917 in Tochigi Prefecture and was accepted to the Kumagaya Flying School in February 1936, graduating at the top of his Juvenile Flying Soldier Intake in November 1937. After fighter training at Akeno he was assigned to the 5th *Sentai*, and in November 1939 he was transferred to the 1st *Chutai* of the 59th *Sentai* in China. The *Sentai* then moved to Indochina in December 1941, and on the 7th he strafed aircraft at Kota Bharu Airfield. On 21 December, he claimed a Brewster Buffalo fighter over Kuala Lumpur for his first victory. The 59th moved to Malaya, where Onozaki took part in missions to Singapore, Sumatra, and targets in Java. During these missions, Onozaki became the *Sentai*'s top scorer when he added eight Hurricanes, a Blenheim, and a Dutch trainer to his victory total. In May 1942, he returned to Japan to attend the Army Flying Military Academy and returned to the *Sentai* in November as a 2nd Lieutenant. Twice in January 1943 he and his wingmen shared victories over B-25s over

Onozaki. (Author)

Timor. On 20 June 1943, during the JAAF's attacks on Port Darwin, Australia, Onozaki shot down two Spitfires. After a time in Java, the *Sentai* moved to New Guinea in July. On 15 August, Onozaki claimed a P-38 over Tsili Tsili for his 15th and last victory (including the two shared B-25s). On 18 August, Onozaki barely escaped from a formation of about 20 P-38s over But Airfield. However, he soon contracted amoebic dysentery and luckily was evacuated to Japan before his unit was nearly annihilated. After he recuperated, he served as an instructor at Akeno and later at the 7th Flying Training Unit at Matsumoto, where he served until the end of the war.

Shimizu, WO Kazuo

Shimizu. (Author)

Shimizu was born in 1918 in Setagaya, Tokyo, and initially served with an Army heavy field artillery unit. In 1939, just before his unit was to leave for combat in Nomonhan, he was accepted for pilot training and attended the Kumagaya Flying School, graduating in May 1941. In February 1942, he was assigned to the 59th *Sentai*, where he flew defensive interception and convoy escort missions over Java and Timor. As the Japanese had driven the Allies from the NEI, it was not until early 1943 that he claimed his first victory over Timor. He then flew in the *Sentai*'s two missions over Port Darwin, Australia, before the *Sentai* was based in New Guinea. Soon he contracted dysentery and did not see action until August 1943. Between then and March 1944, he became the *Sentai*'s top scorer. Over Alexishafen on 9 November 1943, he was attacked by six P-40s and shot one down. On 14 February 1944, he dropped the air-to-air *Ta Dan* incendiary/fragmentation bomb on B-25s and was reported to have downed three. The following day he dropped a *Ta Dan* bomb again and claimed two P-47s. In March 1944, his unit returned to Japan, defending Okinawa from April to June and then the Home Island until the end of the war. Shimizu claimed 18 victories, half of them against multi-engined aircraft.

Takamiya, Capt. Keiji

Takamiya. (Author)

Takamiya was born in 1921 in Chiba Prefecture. After graduating from the Army Military Academy, he entered the infantry in July 1941 and six months later he volunteered for pilot training. After attending the Tachiarai and Akeno Flying Schools, he was initially assigned to the 4th *Sentai*, then Wewak, New Guinea, as a replacement to the 2nd *Chutai* of the 78th *Sentai* in July 1942. Soon the inexperienced pilot made his first claim on 21 July 1943, and would become the *Sentai*'s top pilot while flying offensive and defensive sorties. During the night of 1 February 1944, Takamiya's fighter collided with a gasoline truck as he landed at Wewak and he was killed. Since the 78th was subsequently wiped out most records of his claims were lost, but by the end of January he had claimed 17 victories.

Takeuchi, Capt. Shogo

Takeuchi. (Author)

Capt. Shogo Takeuchi is considered the leading JAAF ace over New Guinea. Born in 1918 in Kyoto, he graduated as a Second Lieutenant with the Army Aviation Academy's 52nd Class in September 1939. In the early war, Takeuchi was assigned to the 64th *Sentai*'s 3rd *Chutai*, flying Ki-43 Oscars over Malaya and Singapore, as well as the CBI Theater. During this period, he flew and trained under the *Sentai*'s CO, 18 victory ace Maj. Tateo Kato, and his *Chutai* leader, 32 victory ace Capt. Katsumi Anma, and on 31 January 1942, he shot down three RAF Hurricanes over Singapore to begin his scoring, which would total more than 30 victories in the Theater. Three months later, Takeuchi was transferred to the newly-formed 68th *Sentai* in Manchuria, which soon was training in the Tony, preparing for its transfer to New Guinea. In December 1942, Takeuchi was promoted to Captain and became CO of the 2nd *Chutai*. The 68th was sent to Truk via the aircraft carrier *Taiyo* and then was to fly to Rabaul. However, due to the lack of over water

navigation training and mechanical problems, only two of the 13 Tonys were able to return safely back to Truk. In mid-1943, the 68th *Sentai* arrived at Wewak and soon were in relentless combat, dealing with the Tony's technical problems and increasing Allied opposition during the second half of 1943. The 68th experienced heavy losses, with many of its veteran pilots KIA or grounded due to tropical illness, and also lost numerous aircraft in the air and on the ground, and to serviceability due to a lack of spare parts and mechanics. Nonetheless, Takeuchi continued to lead missions and added steadily to his victory totals. In the beginning of October he was wounded in action, but after 15 days discharged himself from hospital and returned to action still covered in bandages. When the now proclaimed "Hero of Wewak" returned, the 68th had only three pilots ready for combat as U.S. forces landed on Arawe Peninsula, on the southern coast of New Britain. On 21 December 1943, the Japanese reacted quickly, sending a force of light bombers, escorted by Tonys, with one *Chutai* led by Takeuchi. The formation was attacked by a large force of 5FC P-47s, and after shooting down one Thunderbolt, Takeuchi's fighter was damaged while he was attempting to shoot down an American fighter that was attacking 68th *Sentai* CO Maj. Kiyoshi Kimura. Takeuchi was wounded in the battle and he was barely able to nurse his fighter back across the Strait to Hansa Airfield, on New Guinea. As he approached the field his engine seized, and the Tony crashed into the jungle; he was pulled from the wreckage mortally wounded and he died three hours later. It was estimated that Takeuchi flew about 90 combat missions over New Guinea in six months and shot down 16 enemy aircraft and probably destroyed ten more, which could make him the high scoring JAAF ace over New Guinea. These victories were added to the 30+ he had claimed with the 64th *Sentai*. Takeuchi was posthumously promoted to the rank of Major, but a proposed individual citation for Distinguished Service was not presented.

Tarui, Capt. Mitsuyoshi

Tarui. (Author)

Tarui was born in 1915 in Okayama Prefecture. He enrolled in the 1st Juvenile Flying Soldier Program in February 1934 and trained at the Tokorozawa Flying School and in fighter tactics at Akeno. The entire Juvenile Flying School Class was posted to the 1st *Sentai* at Gifu and was dispatched to Manchuria in May 1939, at the beginning of the Nomonhan Campaign; they flew a few sorties without result, but by the end of the fighting Tarui had 28 victories to place him second only to Hiromichi Shinohara. Tarui then attended the Army Flying Military Academy, graduating in July 1941, and returned to the 1st *Sentai* as a Second Lieutenant and flew combat over Malaya, Sumatra, and Java from December 1941 to March 1942. First Lieutenant Tarui was assigned to the 68th *Sentai* in April 1943, based at Wewak, New Guinea, under *Chutai* leader Capt. Shogo Takeuchi. Here he claimed to have shot down at least 10 USAAF aircraft, including the first P-47 to be shot down by Japanese fighters in the area. He was to survive three forced landings due to mechanical failures with the Ki-61 Tony. On

18 August 1944, he was killed by strafing U.S. fighters while retreating on foot from Wewak.

Yamato, Sgt./Maj. Mitsuo

Yamato. (Author)

Born in Hiroshima Prefecture in 1922, at 16, Yamato entered the Tokyo Army Flying School with the 8th Juvenile Flying Soldier Intake. After completion of training there and at the Tachiarai Flying School, he was assigned to teach fighter tactics. In January 1942, he was assigned to the 1st *Chutai* of the 33rd *Sentai* in Manchuria, where he received additional training from senior Juvenile Flying Soldiers before the unit moved to China during the Summer. On 20 August 1943, he claimed his first victory when he shot down a P-40 over Guilin and soon added another P-40 each over Hengyang the next day and then on 1 March 1944, after which the *Sentai* moved to New Guinea. After he downed a B-24, he claimed another over Chungking on the 22nd. The unit was transferred to fly over Indochina and Burma. Here he was shot down by P-47s and bailed out; he was rescued by natives and returned to the *Sentai* a week later. Just as the Allies were about to land at Hollandia, the *Sentai* escaped, flying to Sumatra via the Philippines, where the unit took much needed R&R. In October 1944, the *Sentai* moved to Manila, where it mostly escorted Kamikaze suicide attack units during the Leyte Gulf battle. On 9 November 1944, he claimed an F6F Hellcat destroyed, but in the combat was hit and badly wounded in the right arm. He was able to land safely just before going unconscious and was then evacuated to Japan. He saw no further combat before the war ended and had claimed eight victories.

JNAF Aces

Tainan Kokutai

Tainan Kokutai. (Author)

The Tainan *Kokutai* (Fighter Group) was the most famous of all JNAF fighter units. The unit achieved great success during the early part of the war, especially in the NEI and Eastern New Guinea. This success was realized as all of their pilots were trained in the thorough prewar training programs and most of the unit's original pilots were combat veterans of the Second Sino-Japanese War. The Tainan *Kokutai* was activated on 1 October 1941 at Tainan, Formosa (Taiwan), flying the new A6M Zero and some obsolescent Type 96 Claudes. It was incorporated into the 23rd Naval Air Flotilla and participated in air raids against Iba and Clark Fields in the Philippines, which decimated U.S. air power on the first day of the Pacific War. After the victory in the Philippines, the Tainan *Kokutai* provided air support for the invasion of the Netherlands East Indies, Tarakan, Balikpapan, Banjarmasin, Denpasar, and Bali Island during January and February 1942. The units gained air superiority over the NEI and inflicted heavy losses on the inadequate Allies' air opposition flying inferior aircraft.

In April 1942, the Tainan Kokutai was attached to the 25th Naval Air Flotilla at the new base at Rabaul, but upon arrival, they were deployed to the new Japanese stronghold at Lae, New Guinea. Between April and July 1942, the Group flew 51 missions against the Allied forces at Port Moresby and claimed about 300 (including 45 uncertain) enemy aircraft shot down for the loss of just 20 fighters. However, replacement aircraft were slow in arriving and by August 1942, 55 pilots were available to fly 24 Zeros; because of this pilot surplus, only the most experienced pilots were permitted to fly combat missions. The Kokutai was deadly against poorly escorted 5BC bombers. On 25 May 1942, 14 pilots shared in the destruction of six B-25s attacking Lae, and on 5 August, nine pilots shared five victories over B-17s attacking Buna.

Once Guadalcanal was invaded on 7 August, the Tainan Kokutai was transferred to Rabaul to fly long range bomber escort missions against the American invaders. From August to October 1942, the Kokutai claimed 201 more enemy aircraft shot down (including 37 uncertain) for the loss of 32 invaluable pilots, including Junichi Sasai (killed on 26 August) and Toshio Ota (killed on 21 October). Decimated by the severe fighting in the Guadalcanal battles, the Tainan Kokutai was absorbed into the 251st Kokutai at Rabaul on 1 November 1942 and reconstituted with replacement aircrews. The 20 surviving Tainan pilots were transferred to Japan to form the nucleus of new fighter units. Ten Tainan pilots received posthumous double promotions.

Endo, PO 1c Masuaki

Endo. (Author)

Endo was born in Fukushima-Ken on 20 December 1920. He enlisted in the Navy and graduated from the Enlisted Flight Trainee Class in October 1941. In February 1942, Endo became a member of the Tainan *Kokutai* and arrived with them at Rabaul and Lae in April, where he scored a number of victories. He flew in most of the major combats with the *Kokutai* and was one of very few Tainan *Kokutai* veterans to survive both the Papuan and Guadalcanal Campaigns. On 7 August 1942 over Guadalcanal, as wingman to Lt.(jg) Sasai, he claimed one F4F and two dive bombers. After the intense fighting, he was rotated back to Japan in November 1942. In May 1943, Endo was transferred to the 251st *Kokutai* based at Rabaul, where he was again in daily combat. On 7 June 1943, on a mission to the Russells, Endo's Zero was hit by a 44FG P-40 attacking head-on. Without changing course, Endo rammed the P-40 and was killed, but the P-40 pilot was able to bail out. Endo has been credited with 14 victories.

Honda. (Author)

Honda, Ens. Minoru

Honda was born in Kumamoto Ken in 1923. He graduated from flight training in January 1942 and was assigned to a *Kokutai* attached to the 22nd Air Flotilla HQ, but did not see any combat there. In April, Honda was transferred to the Kanoya Air Group, which was a transient unit in the SWPA. In September 1942, he served eight months at Rabaul, participating in the air battles over New Guinea and the Solomons. He then transferred to Hikotai 407 in October 1943 and flew in the defense of the Philippines, and then in the defense of the Home Islands. Honda scored 17 victories.

Ishikawa. (Author)

Ishikawa, PO 2Cl Seiji

Ishikawa graduated from flight training in January 1940 and served with the Chitose *Kokutai*. He was sent to Rabaul in early 1942, and after a brief stint with the 4th *Kokutai*, was assigned to the Tainan *Kokutai* and was one of Saburo Sakai's wingmen. Ishikawa claimed three P-39s over Lae and fought until November 1942, when he was sent back to Japan in ill health. He served as an instructor until the end of the war. Ishikawa claimed 16 or 17 enemy aircraft destroyed or damaged.

Miyazaki. (Author)

Miyazaki, WO Gitaro

Miyazaki was born in June 1917 in Kochi Prefecture. He entered Flight Training in May 1933; graduated in May 1937; and was posted to the 12th Air Group in China in September 1938. He shot down an I-16 over Hankow on 5 October and returned to Japan in June 1939, where he was assigned to the Yokosuka Air Group, but was sent to China for his second tour there with the 12th Air Group in 1941 and scored another victory. He was sent to the newly-organized Tainan Air Group on Formosa in October 1941. When the Pacific War broke out, WO Miyazaki was the Flight Leader of the 3rd *Chutai* during the attack on the Philippines and moved with the Tainan to the NEI, then to Rabaul in April 1942. Miyazaki flew numerous missions over Port Moresby and achieved 13 victories before being shot down and killed on 24 June 1942 by P-39s and P-400s of the 8th Fighter Group. Miyazaki was honored with the posthumous double promotion to Lt.(jg).

Nishizawa, Lt.(jg) Hiroyoshi

Nishizawa. (Author)

Nishizawa was born in a mountain village in the Nagano Prefecture in 1920. In June 1936, he volunteered to join the Yokaren Flight Reserve Enlistee Training Program and completed his flight training in March 1939. Before the war, he served with the Oita, Omura, and Sakura *Kokutai*, and in October 1941, he was transferred to the Chitose *Kokutai* as a PO 1c, flying the A5M. After moving to Rabaul on 3 February, Nishizawa claimed his first victory of the war, a PBY Catalina (which was downgraded to a damaged after the war). On 10 February, Nishizawa's *Chutai* was transferred to the newly-formed 4th Air Group, and as new Zeros became available, Nishizawa was assigned an A6M2. He scored his first solo victory on 24 March 1942, when he downed a RAAF Spitfire over Port Moresby. On 1 April, Nishizawa *Chutai* was transferred to Lae, New Guinea, and assigned to the Tainan Air Group, where he flew with aces Saburo Sakai and Toshio Ota in a *Chutai* led by ace Junichi Sasai. Nishizawa suffered from Malaria and chronic tropical skin diseases and was considered as aloof and a recluse by his *Chutai* mates, who nicknamed him the "Devil."

Nishizawa would become an ace when he claimed four kills over Moresby in a three-day period from 1–3 May (a P-39 on 1 May, two P-40s on 2 May, and a P-40 the next day). Then, on 7 May, he claimed a P-40 and a P-39 again over Moresby; two P-39s each on 12 and 13 May; and on 17 May, he became an ace-in-a-day when he shot down five P-39s. He continued his hot scoring by downing a P-39 on 20 and 27 May and 1 June; two P-39s on 16 June; and one P-39 on 25 June and 4, 11, and 25 July, which concluded his New Guinea scoring. From 1 May to 25 July, Nishizawa claimed 16 P-39s and four P-40s and shared five victories and five probable victories.

In early August 1942, the Kokutai moved to Rabaul, to immediately begin operations against the U.S. invasion on Guadalcanal. In his first combat there on 7 August, Nishizawa claimed six F4F Wildcats (some historians have confirmed two). Nishizawa would not be credited with another victory until October. The INJ High Command had issued a directive that all victories in the area were to be credited to the unit, rather that the individual. He was assigned to the 253rd Kokutai in September, flying over Rabaul and Vella La Vella, and scored five more victories over four F4Fs and a SBD to give him an estimated 40 to 54 victories.

In mid-November, the Kokutai was recalled to replace its losses and its ten surviving pilots were made instructors. Nishizawa publicly lobbied to return to combat, and in May 1943 he and the 251st Kokutai returned to Rabaul, but recorded no victories and were transferred to the 253rd Air Group on New Britain in September. In November, he was promoted to Warrant Officer and reassigned to training duties in Japan with the Oita Air Group. In February 1944, he joined the 203rd Air Group, operating from the Kurile Islands, away from heavy combat.

In October, the 203rd was transferred to Luzon in anticipation of the Allied Campaign in the Philippines. Nishizawa and four others were detached to a smaller airfield at Mabalacat, Cebu and on 25 October, he led the fighter escort for the first major Kamikaze attack of the war against the U.S. Navy's "Taffy 3" Task Force, defending the landings during the battle for Leyte. While flying this mission, Nishizawa recorded his 86th and 87th victories (both F6F Hellcats) for the final victories of his career. The next day, he volunteered for a Kamikaze mission but was refused, and another pilot flew his Zero, which was crashed into the carrier USS Suwannee. The next day, with his own Zero destroyed, Nishizawa and other pilots of the 2nd Kokutai boarded a Ki-49 transport plane and left Cebu in the morning to ferry replacement Zeros from Clark Field, on Luzon. Over Calapan, on Mindoro Island, the transport was attacked by two F6F Hellcats of VF-14 squadron from the carrier USS Wasp and he was shot down and killed at the age of 24. Upon learning of Nishizawa's death, Adm. Soemu Toyoda, Commander of the Combined Fleet, honored Nishizawa with a mention in all units' bulletins and posthumously promoted him to Lieutenant (jg).

Okano, WO Hiroshi

Okano. (Author)

Okano was born in Ibaraki Prefecture on 27 May 1921. He joined the Navy at Yokosuka in June 1938 and graduated from flight training in May 1941. After graduation, he flew with the Yokosuka and then the Chitose *Kokutai*, which flew air defense over the Marshall Islands, flying the Type 96 Carrier Fighter when the war broke out. In April 1942, Okano joined the 1st *Kokutai*, but still had not been in combat. As part of a 15-plane reinforcement detachment in late May 1942, he was sent to Rabaul and became a member of the Tainan *Kokutai*. Over the next six months, he was part of the furious air battles over New Guinea. On 25 June, he claimed his first victory over Moresby and added six more and a probable over Port Moresby before being transferred to the 201st *Kokutai* in December 1942. Okano flew in defense of the Marshall Islands before returning to Japan in March 1943. In July, the 201st moved to Bun on the carrier *Unyo*. Okano served with the 331st, 202nd, and the Omura *Kokutai*s before joining the elite 343rd *Kokutai*, in which he remained until the end of the war. He was credited with 19 victories and was one of the highest scoring Tainan *Kokutai* pilots to survive the war.

Oki, WO Yoshio

Oki. (Author)

Oki was born on 2 February 1916 in Ibaraki-Ken. He enlisted in the Navy in 1933 and served as a machinist mate before entering flight training in December 1936. He graduated in July 1937 and was assigned to the Yokosuka *Kokutai*. In July 1940, he transferred to the 12th *Kokutai* in China and started his victory total by shooting down four enemy planes over Chunking on 13 September 1940. Oki scored three more victories over China. In July 1942, Oki was transferred to the Tainan *Kokutai*, where he saw heavy combat over New Guinea and the Solomons, scoring a number of victories before returning to Japan in November 1942 and lucky to be one of the few Lae survivors. In May 1943, he returned to Rabaul and served with the 251st *Kokutai*, and was subsequently wounded; then, on 16 June 1943, he was shot down and killed over the Russell Islands in the Solomons. According to group records he had 17 victories.

Ota, WO Toshio

Ota. (Author)

Ota was born near Nagasaki in March 1919. At 16, he enlisted in the Sasebo Naval Barracks in 1935 and graduated as a fighter pilot in September 1939. After serving with the Omura and Yatabe Air Groups, he was posted to the 12th Air Group in June 1941 in China, but saw no air combat. In October 1941, he was transferred to the Tainan *Kokutai* and saw combat in the Philippines, where he scored his first victory on the first day of the war, 8 December. He then served in the NEI, and on 29 January 1942, he was wounded by a gunner on a B-17 over Balikpapan and was out of action for several months. When he returned in April, he joined Sasai's 2nd *Chutai* at Rabaul and was tutored by Sakai. Soon Ota vied with Sasai, Nishizawa, and Sakai to become the Tainan's top scorer. However, on 21 October 1942, after scoring 34 victories, Ota was KIA over Guadalcanal by VMF-212 Wildcat fighters. After his death Ota was posthumously promoted two ranks to WO.

Sakai. (Author)

Sakai, Lt.(jg) Saburo

Sakai was born to a farm family of Samurai descent in Saga, Japan. When he turned 16, he joined the Navy on 31 May 1933 as a Seaman and upon graduation he served as a turret gunner aboard the battleship *Kirishima*. In 1936, he was accepted into the pilot training program and graduated at the top of his class in November 1937 as a carrier pilot (although he was never assigned to carrier duty). In September 1938, Sakai was sent to China, flying an A5M Navy Type 96 fighter with the 12th Air Group.

Sakai and Author. (Author)

While flying combat over central China, he scored his first victory over Hankow on 5 October flying an A5M Claude, and a year later scored his second victory over China. In 1940, he was chosen to fly the new A6M Zero fighters in field tests in combat against the Chinese and scored two victories.

On 8 December 1941, now flying with the Tainan Kokutai, based in Taiwan, he flew one of the unit's Zero fighters against Clark Airfield, in the Philippine Islands, and downed a P-40 and destroyed three aircraft on the ground. On 10 December, he shot down the B-17 Flying Fortress piloted by legendary Capt. Colin Kelly, followed two days later by a P-40 in the air and two enemy aircraft destroyed on the ground. In early 1942, the Kokutai was transferred to Tarakan Island, in Borneo, where he shot down a B-17 and a medium bomber over Balikpapan. The Kokutai fought in the Dutch East Indies and Sakai shot down nine aircraft (two medium bombers, a PBY, three P-36s, two P-40s, and a Dutch F2A Buffalo). His best day was on 19 February 1942, when he shot down three P-36s and a P-40 over Surabaya, Java. Between late January and April 1942, Sakai was grounded due to illness.

In April 1942, PO 1c Sakai rejoined the Tainan Kokutai, now based at Lae, New Guinea. The unit was commanded by Lt.(jg) Junichi Sasai and included aces Hiroyoshi Nishizawa and Toshio Ohta. During his time in New Guinea, Sakai claimed most of his victories during the War (35 individual victories) and participated in 18 shared victories. He became an "ace-in-a-day" on 16 June 1942, when he shot down five P-39s over Moresby.

The Tainan Kokutai was transferred to Rabaul on 3 August, just days before the Americans invaded Guadalcanal. The Tainan Air Group attacked Henderson Field almost daily, and on 7 August, he shot down a F4F Wildcat and two SDB Dauntless dive bombers over Tulagi. Later that month, Sakai encountered SBD dive bombers from the carrier Enterprise over Guadalcanal, but was hit by the rear machine gunner, blowing away his canopy and hitting him in the head. Sakai was blinded in one eye by blood and had to fly inverted to prevent blood from blinding his good eye. He was able to control his damaged fighter, and despite his head wound and partial paralysis, he returned to Rabaul after a nearly five-hour flight without his canopy. He was evacuated to Japan on 12 August and endured a long surgery that required five months recovery.

After he recovered, Sakai instructed fighter pilots. In April 1944, he lobbied his superiors to allow him to fly again, despite the poor vision in his right eye. He was deployed to Iwo Jima, Japan, with the Yokosuka Air Wing and shot down his final two aircraft (two F6Fs), which gave him a total of 64. In August 1944, he was finally promoted to Ensign, 11 years after his enlistment, and in August 1945, just before the war ended, he was promoted to Lieutenant (jg). After the war, Sakai retired from the Japanese Navy at the rank of Lieutenant and became a devout Buddhist.

Sasai, Lt.Cdr. Junichi

Sasai. (Author)

Junichi Sasai was born on 13 February 1918 in Tokyo, the eldest son of retired Navy Captain Kenji Sasai. As a young child he was frail and in poor health, but by his teens his health improved and his athletic and scholastic achievements gained him acceptance to Japan's prestigious Naval Academy at Etajima. Sasai graduated from the Academy in 1939, and in November 1941, he completed flight training and was assigned to the Tainan *Kokutai*. He flew with the *Kokutai* over the Philippines in December 1941, but scored his first aerial victory on 3 February

1942 over Java. In April, the *Kokutai* arrived at Rabaul, then went on to Lae, where Sasai was named the CO of the 2nd *Chutai*. The inexperienced Sasai was tutored in dogfighting by veteran ace Saburo Sakai and soon victories came quickly. In early May, he shot down three 8th Fighter Group P-39s in less than 20 seconds; on 16 June he shot down two P-39s; and on the 25th he shot down another. On 7 August, he became an "ace-in-a-day" when he claimed five enemy planes in the initial air combats over Guadalcanal and became known as the "Richtofen of Rabaul." On 26 August, Sasai's *Chutai* escorted Betty bombers to Henderson Field on Guadalcanal, where they were attacked by 12 USMC F4F Wildcats of VMF-223 led by Maj. John Smith. Marine records show that Sasai was probably shot down by Marine ace Capt. Marion Carl. In a letter to his family before his death, Sasai stated that he had 54 victories and was planning to break Richthofen's record. However, an examination of Tainan records only confirmed 27 victories. After his death he was promoted two ranks posthumously to Lieutenant Commander.

Takatsuka, Ens. Toraichi

Takatsuka. (Author)

Takatsuka was born on 22 February 1914 in Shizuoka-Ken. He graduated from flight school in November 1933 and participated in aerial combat against the Chinese with the 12th *Kokutai*. On 13 September 1940, while flying the new A6M Zero in its theater debut, he shot down three enemy planes during a bomber escort to Chunking. Veteran WO Takatsuka joined the Tainan *Kokutai* and flew over Java and from Rabaul and Lae. On 13 September 1942, he was listed as MIA during combat over Guadalcanal and was later declared KIA and elevated to the rank of Ensign. Tainan *Kokutai* records indicate he had scored 16 victories.

Uehara, PO 2Cl Sadao

Uehara graduated from flight training and was assigned to the Tainan *Kokutai* in October 1941; he flew as Sakai's Wingman over the NEI. On 19 February 1942, Uehara scored his first victory when he shot down a P-40 of the 17PS over Surabaya, Java. When the *Kokutai* moved to Rabaul and Lae, Uehara flew many missions as Sakai's Wingman and then as a Flight Leader in the Papuan and Solomons Campaign, where he scored most of his 22 destroyed or damaged enemy aircraft. When the Tainan *Kokutai* was absorbed into the 251st *Kokutai* in November 1942, Uehara returned to Japan to serve as an instructor. Uehara fought over Luzon, Philippines, in September and October 1944 with the 201st *Kokutai*, but suffered poor health and saw no further combat.

Uto, PO 3Cl Kazushi

Uto. (Author)

Uto was born on 18 August 1922 in Aichi-Ken. He graduated from flight training in October 1941, and in February 1942 he was assigned to the Tainan *Kokutai* and served at Rabaul in April and then at Lae. He became Sakai's Wingman in May, when Sakai's Wingman was KIA. Uto scored his first victory of 19 on 10 April 1942 over Moresby. On the 7 August 1942 mission to Guadalcanal, he had his best when he claimed two victories plus two probables as Sakai's Wingman. On 13 September 1942, on a mission to Guadalcanal, Uto was listed as MIA, along with Sakai's other wingman.

Yamazaki, PO 1Cl Ichirobei

Yamazaki. (Author)

Yamazaki was born 5 May 1920 near Tokyo. He enlisted in the Navy at Yokosuka in 1937 and graduated from flight training in May 1941. He was initially assigned to the Oita Air Group and then to the 4th *Kokutai*, based at Rabaul, in February 1942. In April, he was transferred to the Tainan *Kokutai*, where he saw heavy action over Lae, New Guinea, and Rabaul, then Guadalcanal and the Solomons. In March 1942, he damaged a Hudson, but his aircraft was hit and he was forced down. He was rescued by natives and arrived back at his base via a transport ship, returning to combat over Moresby until he was wounded in May. Returning to combat, Yamazaki claimed two F4F Wildcats on 7 August over Guadalcanal. During an attack over Buna on 26 August, his aircraft was hit and forced down and he was sent back to Japan to recuperate. By May 1943, he had recovered and was posted with the 251st *Kokutai* at Rabaul. On 4 July 1943, he was engaged by USN F4Fs and was shot down and killed over Rendova after scoring 14 victories.

Yoshida, WO Mototsuna

Yoshida. (Author)

Yoshida was born on 1 January 1918 in Okayama-Ken. Yoshida enlisted in the Navy in June 1935 and became a ship's stoker, but was selected for flight training, and in June 1939 he graduated as a fighter pilot. He was sent to China with the 12th *Kokutai* in September 1939. On 14 October, he was wounded during a bombing attack on his air base at Hankow. After recovering, he was sent to southern China, and in July 1940, he became an instructor with the Yokosuka *Kokutai*. In February 1942, Yoshida was posted to the 4th *Kokutai*

and sent to Rabaul where, on 23 February, he attacked a B-17 while flying alone over Rabaul and shot it down. At the end of March 1942 he was wounded again, and after a short recovery he was promoted to Petty Officer First Class in April and transferred to the Tainan *Kokutai*, where he shot down a number of Allied aircraft during raids over Port Moresby. During a mission to Guadalcanal on 7 August 1942, he was shot down by USN F4Fs over Tulagi after scoring 14 victories.

Yoshino, Ens. Satoshi

Yoshina. (Author)

Yoshino was born on 21 February 1918 in Chiba-Ken. At 16, he passed the entrance examination for Naval Preparatory Flight Training and graduated in August 1937. After another flight training course in March 1938, he served with various mainland units before an active duty assignment aboard the carrier Soryu. Yoshino was then assigned to the newly-organized Chitose *Kokutai*, which flew prewar defensive missions over the Marshall Islands in October 1941. Once the war broke out, he was transferred to the 4th *Kokutai* in February 1942 and sent to Rabaul, flying the obsolete Type 96 Claude. On 11 February 1942, his Flight shot down two Australian Lockheed Hudsons over Surumi and three days later added another victory over Surumi. He transitioned to the new Zero and the *Kokutai* moved to Lae, New Guinea, taking part in intense air battles over Moresby and Horn Island. On 11 March, he shot down his first enemy aircraft over New Guinea. After his promotion to Warrant Officer, Yoshino was transferred to the Tainan *Kokutai* and met the P-39s of the 8th Fighter Group. On 9 June 1942, the *Kokutai* encountered eight P-400s of the 39th Fighter Squadron and he was shot down and killed by 5FC ace 1Lt. Curran Jones near Cape Ward Hunt. *Kokutai* records credited Yoshino with 15 victories.

Yoshimura, PO 3c Keisaku

Yoshimura. (Author)

Yoshimura was born on 16 February 1922 in Niigata-Ken. At 17, he joined the Navy in 1939 and graduated in July 1941. Yoshimura joined the Tainan *Kokutai* when it was activated on Formosa in October 1941 and took part in further training. He was detached to the 22nd Air Flotilla and flew in French Indo-China, Malaya, and the NEI before returning to the Tainan *Kokutai*. He arrived at Rabaul at the end of May 1942, then was sent to Lae. On 16 June, his flight encountered an estimated 20 P-39s over Port Moresby and he shot down two. Upon returning to base, he saw a P-39 and shot it down. On 7 August 1942, he claimed five F4F Wildcats over Tulagi to become an "ace-in-a-day." Yoshimura was shot down by USMC F4Fs and killed in action over Guadalcanal on 25 October 1942. He was posthumously elevated to the rank of PO 3c and was credited with nine individual victories, four probable, and one shared. (**Note:** These JNAF and JAAF Ace's biographies were adapted from those written by Ikuhiko Hata, Yasuho Izawa, and Henry Sakaida and from information and photos provided by James Lansdale, noted authority on WWII Japanese combat aviation.)

Note: These Japanese Ace biographies have been excerpted and combined from the works of notable experts on Japanese air combat in World War II, namely Ikuhiko Hata, Yashu Izawa, Henry Sakaida, and James Lansdale.

11

Awards and Decorations

U.S. Awards and Decorations

Acts of notable valor, military achievement in action, wounds received in action, and honorable service over a period of years were recognized by the President, who, through the War Department, awarded appropriate decorations. Units, organizations, and detachments, as well as individual airmen, were cited for outstanding accomplishments. Recommendations for awards were to be made in triplicate to the Air Force HQ. Individual awards were to be worn on the left breast pocket, but when a unit was cited, all members of the unit wore the award on the right breast pocket.

Ace Thomas Lynch displays (L-R) a DSC, Silver Star, DFC, and Purple Heart on his left breast pocket. (AFAA)

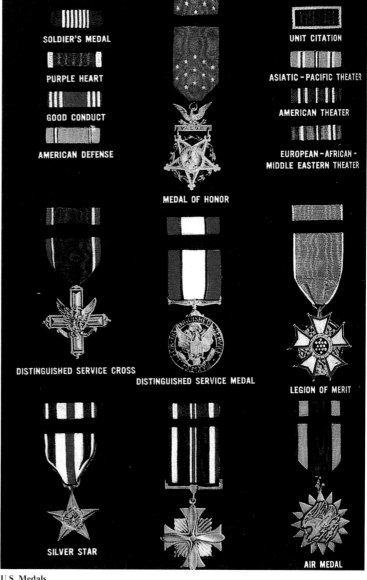

SOLDIER'S MEDAL

PURPLE HEART

GOOD CONDUCT

AMERICAN DEFENSE

MEDAL OF HONOR

UNIT CITATION

ASIATIC-PACIFIC THEATER

AMERICAN THEATER

EUROPEAN-AFRICAN-MIDDLE EASTERN THEATER

DISTINGUISHED SERVICE CROSS

DISTINGUISHED SERVICE MEDAL

LEGION OF MERIT

SILVER STAR

AIR MEDAL

U.S. Medals

**Relative Ranking of Service Awards
(date authorized and date revised):**

ARMY AIR FORCE	Year	NAVY/MARINE CORPS	Year
Medal of Honor	1862 1904 1944	Medal of Honor	1862 1904 1944
Distinguished Service Cross	1918	Navy Cross Marine Corps Brevet Medal	1919
Silver Star	1918 1932	Silver Star	1918 1932
Distinguished Flying Cross	1926	Distinguished Flying Cross	1926
Air Medal	1942	Air Medal	1942
Purple Heart	1782 1932 1942	Purple Heart	1782 1932 1942
Distinguished Service Medal	1918	Distinguished Service Medal	1918
Legion of Merit	1942	Legion of Merit	1942
Bronze Star	1944	Navy & Marine Medal	1942
Distinguished Unit Citation (Later renamed the Presidential Unit Citation)	1942	Distinguished Unit Citation	1942

Medal of Honor

Congressional Medal of Honor (CMH)

The Congressional Medal of Honor was established during the Civil War (1862), with the 1904 design worn in WWII either as a breast medal or hung by the neck ribbon. In 1944, a redesigned neck ribbon version was authorized. The Medal was awarded in the name of Congress, often by the President, to an officer or enlisted man "who in actual conflict with the enemy, distinguished himself conspicuously by gallantry and intrepidity at the risk of his life above and beyond the call of duty," The Citation begins: "The President of the United States of America, in the name of Congress, takes pleasure in presenting the Medal of Honor to…."

Apart from the great honor which the CMH imparted on the recipient, he was entitled to free available military air transport on or off active duty. Enlisted recipients were given $2 a month extra pay, and upon reaching the age of 65, the Medal holder received an extra $10 per month. However, many recipients were awarded their Medal posthumously.

Of the 464 CMH (266 posthumously) awarded in WWII, 17 Fighter pilots (15 in the Pacific Theater and four from the 5FC in bold) received the following medals:

Lt.Col. Harold Bauer (USMC)*
Maj. Richard Bong (AAF)*
Maj. Gregory Boyington (USMC)
Capt. Jefferson DeBlanc (USMC)
Capt. Joseph Foss (USMC)
Maj. Robert Galer (USMC)
1Lt. Robert Hanson (USMC)*
Lt.Col. James Howard (AAF/ETO)
1Lt. Raymond Knight (AAF/ETO)*
Col. Neel Kearby (AAF)*
Cdr. David McCampbell (USN)
Maj. Thomas McGuire (AAF)*
Lt. Edward O'Hare (USN) *
Maj. William Shomo (AAF)
Maj. John Smith (USMC)
1Lt. James Swett (USMC)
1Lt. Ken Walsh (USMC)
*= died in WWII

(**Note:** Maj. George Davis was a 5FC ace who was also an ace over Korea and was posthumously awarded the CMH for combat over Korea.)

Distinguished Service Cross (DSC)

1Lt. George Welch of the 47PS was nominated for the Medal of Honor by Gen. Arnold for his four victories over Pearl Harbor, but received the DSC from FDR. (AAF)

The Distinguished Service Cross (DSC), authorized in 1918, was the Air Force's second highest award for valor "involving extraordinary risk to one's life while in action with the enemy." The first aviator recipient of the DSC in WWII was 1Lt. George Welch of the 47PS (who later became an ace, scoring 12 more victories with the 5FC), who won both the DSC and DFC for his four victories over Pearl Harbor. Welch was nominated for the Medal of Honor by Gen. Arnold, but received the DSC from FDR. During WWII, just over 5,000 DSC awards were made. Lt.Col. John Meyer (ETO Mustang 26-victory ace) and Maj.Gen. James Van Fleet were three-time

recipients. Several fighter aces also received two Distinguished Service Crosses, including 5FC ace Jay Robbins. During WWII, 17 soldiers, including three AAF aviators, received both the Medal of Honor and the Distinguished Service Cross: Richard Bong and Thomas McGuire of the 5FC and 14AF B-24 pilot Horace Carswell. (**Note:** The Navy Cross, established in 1919, was the Navy's second highest decoration awarded to Navy pilots for bravery.)

Silver Star (SS)

The Silver Star was authorized in 1918 and revised in 1932 for acts of distinguished gallantry in combat not warranting the DSC or Navy Cross, and is the third highest decoration "for acts of valor." The Silver Star differs from the Service Crosses, in that it requires a lesser degree of gallantry and could be earned while in a position of great responsibility. Air Force, Navy, and Marine Corps pilots were often considered eligible to receive a Silver Star upon becoming an ace. The Department of Defense does not keep records of Silver Star awards, but research by the Home of Heroes organization estimates that between 100,000 and 150,000 Silver Stars have been awarded since the award was established (about one for every 250 individuals in the services).

Awards for Valor in Air Combat

Two awards were bestowed specifically for valor in air combat: the Distinguished Flying Cross (DFC) and Air Medal. None of these decorations could be issued more than once to any one person. But in the AAF, with each succeeding act to justify the same award a Bronze Oak Leaf Cluster was given. One Silver Oak Leaf was authorized for wear instead of five Bronze Oak Leaf Clusters. In the Navy, a gold star worn on a ribbon attached to the medal marked multiple awards.

Medals (L-R): Silver Star (with Oak Leaf Cluster), Distinguished Flying Cross (with OLC), Air Medal (with OLC), and Purple Heart. (Author)

Distinguished Flying Cross (DFC)

The Distinguished Flying Cross (DFC) was authorized on 2 July 1926, and could be awarded retroactively to 1917. It could be awarded for heroic acts or meritorious achievements in flight, not necessarily in combat. During WWII, the medal's award criteria varied widely, depending on the theater of operations, aerial combat, and the missions completed. The most DFCs awarded to any one pilot were to top ETO ace Col. Francis "Gabby" Gabreski, who received 13.

Air Medal (AM)

The Air Medal was created in 1942—retroactive to 1939—and was awarded for valor and for meritorious achievement. The Air Medal could be awarded for "individual acts or sustained operational activities not warranting the DFC." Capt. Clyde East, F-6 recon pilot for 5TRS, was awarded a record 42 AMs, while Maj. James Hill, five victory P-47 ace of the 365FG, had 39 AMs; both pilots flew in the ETO.

   Note: On 14 August 1943, the criteria for the DFC and AM were changed by Gen. Hap Arnold, prompted by a suggestion by 8AF Maj.Gen. William Kutner. Arnold no longer wanted the awards to be made for undefined "worthy" acts in combat, but more "mechanically" based on the destruction of enemy aircraft or the number of actual combat sorties flown dropping bombs on enemy targets. The destruction of one enemy aircraft was considered equal to ten sorties flown.

E/A Destroyed	Award	Sorties	Award
First	AM	10	AM
Second	OLC*	20	OLC*
Third	2nd OLC*	30	OLC*
Fourth	3rd OLC*	40	OLC*
Fifth	DFC	50	DFC
Tenth	OLC**		
Fifteenth	2nd OLC**		

*Worn on AM Ribbon
**Worn on DFC

Silver Star with **2 Oak Leaf Clusters**. (Author)

Oak Leaf Cluster

An Oak Leaf Cluster consisted of a twig of four oak leaves with three acorns on each stem that was worn to denote the award of second and succeeding awards of decorations (other than the Air Medal). The number of Oak Leaf Clusters typically indicates the number of subsequent awards of the decoration. A Bronze Oak Leaf Cluster was worn to denote award of the second and subsequent awards of the same decoration. A Silver Oak Leaf Cluster was worn in lieu of five bronze Oak Leaf Clusters. Personnel wore Oak Leaf Clusters centered on the service ribbon and suspension ribbon, with the stems of the leaves pointing to the wearer's right.

Bronze Star (BS)

The Bronze Star was created in February 1944 by Executive Order for heroic or meritorious achievement not involving aerial combat and not warranting the Silver Star (when awarded for heroism) or Legion of Merit (when awarded for merit). When awarded for acts of heroism, the medal is awarded with the "V" device. The Navy or Marine Medals, established in 1942, were awarded for heroism in non-combat action only.

Purple Heart (PH)

The Purple Heart was originally established in August 1782 for valor by George Washington, then Commander-in-Chief of the Continental Army. The medal remained inactive after the Revolutionary War, but with the efforts of Gen. Douglas MacArthur it was resurrected on 22 February 1932 (in honor of Washington's 200th birthday), as an award for meritorious service (the first Purple Heart was awarded to MacArthur on this day). Initially, the Purple Heart was exclusively awarded to Army and Army Air Corps personnel and could not be awarded posthumously to the next of kin. On 3 December 1942, the decoration was extended to all services and the Purple Heart, as per regulation, was awarded in the name of the President to any member of the Armed Forces or civilians while serving in any capacity retroactive to 5 April 1917 (the day America entered WWI) that had been wounded, killed, or had died after being wounded. The request for the Purple Heart had to be supported by a medical certificate completed by the Flight Surgeon describing the treatment given. The request for a posthumous award did not require any recommendation, but was automatically awarded by the War Department upon receipt of the notice of death. The Purple Heart receives its name from the purple ribbon from which it is suspended. The profile of George Washington appears inside a black heart framed in a gold heart. On the reverse are the words: "For Military Merit." Oak Leaf clusters are awarded for subsequent wounds. In WWII, 1,076,245 Purple Hearts were awarded.

During 1945, nearly 500,000 Purple Heart medals were manufactured in anticipation of the estimated casualties resulting from the planned Allied invasion of Japan, which military leaders believed would last into 1947. The dropping of the atomic bombs left a large excess supply of the medal, and all American military casualties following the end of WWII, including the Korean and Vietnam Wars, have not exceeded that number. In 2003, there were 120,000 of these Purple Heart medals in stock and combat units in Iraq and Afghanistan are able to keep Purple Hearts on hand for immediate award to wounded soldiers in the field.

Distinguished Unit Citation (DUC) -
Later Presidential Unit Citation (PUC)

The Distinguished Unit Citation was authorized on 26 February 1942, to be awarded in the name of the President for extraordinary heroism in action by a specific group retroactive to 7 December 1941. "The unit must display such gallantry, determination, and esprit de corps in accomplishing its mission under extremely difficult and hazardous conditions so as to set it apart from and above other units participating in the same campaign." The award was deemed equivalent to acts that would warrant the award of the DFC to an individual. The unit was awarded a streamer with the name of the action embroidered in white. The individual emblem consisted of a 1/16 inch wide gold frame with laurel leaves enclosing an ultramarine blue ribbon. Unit members involved in the action were entitled to wear the DUC permanently, but those members who were not involved or joined the unit later were allowed to wear the DUC only while serving with the unit. A unit receiving more than one DUC wore a Bronze OLC on the award.

Meritorious Unit Citation

The Meritorious Unit Citation was created in January 1944 for actions equivalent to the award of the Legion of Merit to an individual. The Meritorious Unit Commendation was awarded to units for exceptionally meritorious conduct in performance of outstanding services for at least six continuous months during a period of military operations against an armed enemy, and although service in a combat zone was not required, the unit's accomplishments had to be "directly related to the larger combat effort." For services performed during WWII, this award was limited to service units and was restricted to services performed between 1 January 1944 and 15 September 1946. Members of units that received the plaque were entitled to wear on their right sleeve a two-inch square of olive drab cloth on which appeared a golden yellow laurel wreath one and five-eighths inches in diameter. However, it appears that this Citation was not awarded to USAAF fighter units.

Ribbons

Campaign ribbons and medals were created for participation in three war theaters: American Campaign, Asiatic-Pacific Campaign, and the European African Mid Eastern Campaign. All three ribbons had colored stripes representing the U.S., while their other colored stripes represented the Axis (e.g. German: black and white; Japan: red and white; and Italy: green, white, and red). The Campaign Medals were hung from ribbons and had engravings depicting combat in the area.

The Good Conduct Ribbon and Medal was authorized on 28 June 1941 by FDR, and was awarded to enlisted men for "efficiency, honor and fidelity for each three year period of service." An eagle is shown with its wings spread while standing on a closed book and Roman sword, encircled by the words: "Efficiency Honor Fidelity." The ribbon is is red with three white pinstripes inside each edge.

Wings

Wings—the symbol of flight—were the coveted reward for aviation qualification by fledgling aviation cadets. The first United States Aviator Badges were issued to members of the Air Service during the First World War. The badges were issued in three degrees: Enlisted, Junior Officer, and Senior Officer. The Army Air Corps also issued a badge for balloon pilots, known as the Aeronaut Badge. During WWII, with the rise of the Army Air Forces, a second series of aviator badges were issued to include a design that continues today. The Army Air Corps Pilot Badge was issued in three degrees, including Pilot, Senior Pilot, and Command Pilot. The AAF Badge was basically the Shield of the U.S. without stars centered in a pair of wings. The Navy and Marine Wings had the starless U.S. Shield centered by a winged fouled anchor.

Lt. Thomas McGuire's **Pilot's Wings**, which were pinned on him by his wife at his graduation at Kelly Field, TX, in February 1942. (Author)

Non-combat Awards

Distinguished Service Medal (DSM)

The Distinguished Service Medal was authorized by Presidential Order on 2 January 1918, and confirmed by Congress on 9 July 1918. The Distinguished Service Medal is the highest non-valorous military and civilian decoration of the United States military, which is issued for "exceptionally meritorious service to the government of the United States in either a senior government service position or as a senior officer of the United States armed forces or other Uniformed services." There is also the President's Award for Distinguished Federal Civilian Service, which is the highest medal that can be awarded to a career government employee. This decoration is distinct from the Distinguished Service Cross (DSC), which is the second highest military decoration that can be awarded to a member of the U.S. Army for extreme gallantry and risk of life in actual combat with an armed enemy force. The Distinguished Service Medal is issued both as a military decoration and civilian award. The Army version of the Distinguished Service Medal is typically referred to simply as the "Distinguished Service Medal," while the other branches of service use the service name as a prefix.

Legion of Merit

The Distinguished Service Cross, authorized in 1918, was the highest medal given for exceptional meritorious service to the government and was almost exclusively awarded to General Officers. The Legion of Merit was established by Congress and approved 20 July 1942 by FDR, and was retroactive to 8 September 1939. The Legion of Merit was awarded to members of the Armed Forces "without degree for exceptionally outstanding conduct in the performance of meritorious service to the United States. The performance must merit recognition by individuals in a key position which was performed in a clearly exceptional manner. The performance of duties normal to the grade branch, specialty or assignment and experience of an individual is not an adequate basis for this award." It was also awarded to foreign personnel in several different degrees unavailable to U.S. citizens. Of the 5,059 DSCs awarded, 762 were awarded to AAF personnel.

5th Fighter Command Medal of Honor Citations

Neel Kearby

Awarded: On 23 January 1944, by Gen. Douglas MacArthur in his office in Brisbane, Australia.

Place and date: Near Wewak, New Guinea, 11 October 1943.

Citation: For conspicuous gallantry and intrepidity above and beyond the call of duty in action with the enemy, Col. Kearby volunteered to lead a flight of 4 fighters to reconnoiter the strongly defended enemy base at Wewak. Having observed enemy installations and reinforcements at 4 airfields, and secured important tactical information, he saw an enemy fighter below him, made a diving attack and shot it down in flames. The small formation then sighted approximately 12 enemy bombers accompanied by 36 fighters. Although his mission had been completed, his fuel was running low, and the numerical odds were 12 to 1, he gave the signal to attack. Diving into the midst of the enemy airplanes he shot down 3 in quick succession. Observing 1 of his comrades with 2 enemy fighters in pursuit, he destroyed both enemy aircraft. The enemy broke off in large numbers to make a multiple attack on his airplane but despite his peril he made one more pass before seeking cloud protection. Coming into the clear, he called his flight together and led them to a friendly base. Col. Kearby brought down 6 enemy aircraft in this action, undertaken with superb daring after his mission was completed.

Richard Bong

Awarded: By Gen. Douglas MacArthur on 12 December 1944 at Tacloban Airfield, Philippines.

Place and date: Over Borneo and Leyte, 10 October to 15 November 1944.

Citation: For conspicuous gallantry and intrepidity in action above and beyond the call of duty in the Southwest Pacific area from 10 October to 15 November 1944. Though assigned to duty as gunnery instructor and neither required nor expected to perform combat duty, Maj. Bong voluntarily and at his own urgent request engaged in repeated combat missions, including unusually hazardous sorties over Balikpapan, Borneo, and in the Leyte area of the Philippines. His aggressiveness and daring resulted in his shooting down 8 enemy airplanes during this period.

William Shomo

Awarded: 7 April 1945 at Lingayen Gulf by Gen. Ennis Whitehead

Place and date: 11 January 1945 over Luzon, Philippines

Citation: Maj. Shomo was lead pilot of a flight of 2 fighter planes charged with an armed photographic and strafing mission against the Aparri and Laoag airdromes. While en route to the objective, he observed an enemy twin engine bomber, protected by 12 fighters, flying about 2,500 feet above him and in the opposite direction Although the odds were 13 to 2, Maj. Shomo immediately ordered an attack. Accompanied by his wingman he closed on the enemy formation in a climbing turn and scored hits on the leading plane of the third element, which exploded in midair. Maj. Shomo then attacked the second element from the left side of the formation and shot another fighter down in flames. When the enemy formed for Counterattack, Maj. Shomo moved to the other side of the formation and hit a third fighter which exploded and fell. Diving below the bomber he put a burst into its underside and it crashed and burned. Pulling up from this pass he encountered a fifth plane firing head-on and destroyed it. He next dived upon the first element and shot down the lead plane; then diving to 300 feet in pursuit of another fighter he caught it with his initial burst and it crashed in flames. During this action his wingman had shot down 3 planes, while the 3 remaining enemy fighters had fled into a cloudbank and escaped. Maj. Shomo's extraordinary gallantry and intrepidity in attacking such a far superior force and destroying 7 enemy aircraft in one action is unparalleled in the southwest Pacific area.

Thomas McGuire

Awarded: Posthumously by the President by General Orders of 7 March 1946. It was presented to his wife Marilyn on 8 May 1946 at City Hall, Paterson, NJ, McGuire's hometown in respect to McGuire's father, who attended the ceremony. Gen. George Kenney hung the Medal around Marilyn's neck while the now reclusive Charles Lindbergh looked on in the background.

Place and date: Over the Philippines on 25 and 26 December 1944, and for his final mission on 7 January 1945.

Citation: For conspicuous gallantry and intrepidity while serving with the 475th Fighter Group, Fifth Air Force, in action over Luzon, Philippine Islands, 25 and 26 December 1944. Voluntarily, Major McGuire led a squadron of 15 P-38's as top cover for heavy bombers striking Mabalacat Airdrome, where his formation was attacked by 20 aggressive Japanese

Maj. McGuire's medals including:

MEDAL OF HONOR

fighters. In the ensuing action he repeatedly flew to the aid of embattled comrades, driving off enemy assaults while himself under attack and at times outnumbered three to 1, and even after his guns jammed, continuing the fight by forcing a hostile plane into his wingman's line of fire. Before he started back to his base he had shot down three Zeros. The next day he again volunteered to lead escort fighters on a mission to strongly defended Clark Field. During the resultant engagement he again exposed himself to attacks so that he might rescue a crippled bomber. In rapid succession he shot down one aircraft, parried the attack of four enemy fighters, one of which he shot down, single-handedly engaged three more Japanese, destroying one, and then shot down still another, his 38th victory in aerial combat. On 7 January 1945, while leading a voluntary fighter sweep over Los Negros Island, he risked an extremely hazardous maneuver at low altitude in an attempt to save a fellow flyer from attack, crashed, and was reported missing in action. With gallant initiative, deep and unselfish concern for the safety of others, and heroic determination to destroy the enemy at all costs, Major McGuire set an inspiring example in keeping with the highest traditions of the military service.

Japanese Awards and Citations

Except for the highest-ranking officers, the only medal awarded to a Japanese soldier was the Order of the Golden Kite (Kinshi-Kunsho/"Messenger of the Gods"), which was awarded for "bravery, leadership or command in battle." It represented a golden kite—the messenger of the Gods that helped the Emperor Jimmu Tenno to defeat enemies in a battle. The medal shows two crossed ancient Samurai shields, dark blue enameled, with two crossed swords enameled yellow with hilts in silver, surmounted by a Golden Kite on a star of eight points of 32 rays enameled in red. During WWII, approximately 1,067,000 Golden Kites were awarded, most of them in its two lower classes. Only 41 of the 1st Class and 201 of the 2nd Class were awarded. Initially, the award came with an annual monetary stipend, but this practice was suspended in 1940. The order consisted of seven classes: enlisted rank soldiers were eligible for the 5th-7th classes; non-commissioned officers were eligible for the 4th-6th classes; junior officers for the 3rd-5th classes; field grade officers for the 2nd-4th classes; and general officers for the 1st-3rd classes. Classes 1-5 were gilded in gold, while Classes 6-8 were gilded in silver.

The Wound Badge was established in August 1938 and was awarded in two classes; the "Koushou" class Badge was awarded for wounds or disability "of a non-combat nature" (such as contracting a disease like Malaria); and the "Senshou" class was awarded for wounds sustained in battle. The recipient also received an award document suitable for framing and a smaller document which was to be inserted in his ID booklet. The document described the circumstances of the award (name, rank, date, award class, why awarded).

The Japanese revered their fallen soldiers and airmen by promoting them one rank posthumously, while "outstanding dead," including all Kamikaze pilots, were promoted two ranks. In 1943, to bolster morale, after more defeats than victories in brutal combat conditions, commanding Japanese Generals and Admirals occasionally awarded citations or a sword on an unsystematic basis to living soldiers who had distinguished themselves in combat.

On 7 December 1944, Imperial Edict established the Bukosho, or Distinguished Service Order, divided into Class Ko and Otsu (Class A and B) for the Japanese Army. The Bukosho was considered the highest award for "extreme bravery" and was considered to be equivalent to the Medal of Honor or Victoria Cross. There was an important difference with the Order of the Golden Kite, as the Bukosho was to be awarded by the Commander in the field, while the Order of the Golden Kite required a lengthy procedure (perhaps two or three years) to be awarded. It is unknown how many were awarded (believed to be about 90), as the list of them was destroyed at the end of the war to prevent its capture. Several Bukosho holders were airmen of the JAAF who flew against the devastating B-29 raids on Japan in the last year of the war.

JAAF ace Capt. Mitsuyoshi Tarui displays a number of medals on his left breast. (Author)

Golden Kite. (Author)

Bukosho. (Author)

Wound Badge. (Author)

12

Pilot Training

USAAF Pilot Training

Introduction

Aerial combat at the outbreak of WWII in 1939 quickly demonstrated that the day of the lone wolf fighter pilot had passed. The transformation of aerial strategy from individual to group coordination and tactics, in which pilots worked together toward an objective, forever altered the pilot's status. The pilot had become only one part of a functioning unit, and although he received the lion's share of the headlines, he was, nonetheless, subordinated to the group and mission. However, the ultimate factor in aerial combat remained the man piloting the aircraft and firing its weapons or delivering its ordnance, and the amount and quality of pilot training was directly proportional to the success of the air force.

Procurement

At Pearl Harbor, the annual manpower goal for the Air Force was 30,000 pilots, but by October 1942, the requirement had risen to 50,000. Prewar experience had shown that of all applicants, only 20% were able to meet the rigid physical and mental standards required, and of these no more than 40 to 50% would graduate. Therefore, to graduate 50,000 pilots annually, 500,000 applicants would be needed to qualify 100,000 entering students. Early in the war, college attendance was required to become a Flying Cadet, but due to the vast, aforementioned manpower requirements, this prerequisite was found too restrictive by Brig.Gen. Carl Spaatz, Air Staff Chief. He felt college requirement placed too much emphasis on formal education and did not utilize the numerous young men who did not have the opportunity for a college education but possessed the native intelligence and background to meet the requirements for flight training.

The Aviation Cadet Examining Board was established to give a two-part (physical and mental) examination. These boards were located in the Post Office or Federal Building of large cities and on most Air Force bases. To be eligible, several general conditions had to be met. The applicant must have reached his 18th birthday, but could not be older than 27. A 17-year-old applicant could, with written parental permission, enlist in the Air Corps Enlisted Reserve. The applicant could be married or single. He had to be a citizen for ten years with proof of place of birth or citizenship (a non-citizen from an Allied nation could request a waiver of the ten year requirement from the Adjutant General). An enlisted man in the Army, with the required

qualifications, could apply for Aviation Cadet Training, and if he was found physically and mentally qualified, he could be transferred in grade (post-1943) to the Air Corps, unassigned. However, in practice this proved difficult, as few Army unit commanders wished to part with the type of man who could qualify for pilot training. Also, prior to 1943, a transferee would lose dependency allowances and often suffered reductions in pay until he was allowed to transfer in grade.

The physical requirements for an Aviation Cadet candidate were the same as those prescribed for appointment and call to active duty as a Reserve Officer in any branch of the Army. However, duty as a flying officer required some special physical standards. Visual acuity, color perception and hearing had to be normal. A flying officer, except for a fighter pilot, had to stand between five feet and six foot four inches and weigh 105 to 200 pounds. A fighter pilot had to measure 5'4" to 5'10" and weigh 114 to 160 pounds. Physical standards were not changed, but the definition of the qualifications was eased by the use of waivers, so that disqualifications decreased from 73% in 1939 to 50% in 1941. Later, when excess manpower was available, the use of waivers was decreased.

The mental test was designed to measure the types of proficiency in comprehension and in problem solving which were typical of those required in training. The examination was of the multiple choice, short answer variety, designed to give a picture of the general field of knowledge possessed by each candidate. It was felt that the test had wide enough latitude that a candidate with above average intelligence but possessing only average academic background could achieve a passing grade.

Pre-Flight Training

Basic Training: Before 1943, Basic Training was considered a weak link in the training program. The lack of experienced personnel to administer the program and the urgency to send recruits on to flight training and specialized schools, along with the lack of facilities contributed to these deficiencies. Reports from combat indicated that graduates lacked sufficient training required for combat survival, particularly marksmanship (increased to 15 hours) and bivouac and survival (increased to 29 hours) and health measures (increased to 20 hours). As the imperative of war subsided, the preflight course was increased from four to five weeks. Of course, the legendary drilling (73 hours), physical training (15 hours), and military procedure (13 hours) were ever present. A period of 18 (usually) to 26 days after the beginning of basic training saw the candidate undergo a series of exhaustive medical, psychological, and mental/psychomotor tests to determine his fitness for advancement into the flight program.

Medical and psychological tests were usually administered during the first five days, while aptitude and psychomotor tests followed in the next five to seven days. An example of these psychomotor (coordination between eyes, hands, and feet) tests was the use of a turret lathe. A turret lathe operates completely opposite the standard lathe. A stylist was held in each hand and held on rotating dime-sized discs, which rotated in opposite directions. This test was not unlike rubbing one's stomach while patting one's head.

The aptitude tests were of a multiple choice type. They were designed to measure speed and accuracy of perception, the ability to read and understand technical information, and measure logic and judgment, along with determining general knowledge in mathematics, general information, and mechanical principles.

In making aircrew assignment, three factors were considered in order of priority: aptitude, individual preference, and quota availability. However, in late 1943, when quotas were progressively smaller, the order of priority shifted to quota availability, aptitude, and individual preference. Candidates eliminated from the program were informed of alternate types of training available to them. Generally, the eliminated was sent to a BTC for reassignment to gunnery or to technical training.

Pre-flight School: The objective of pre-flight training was stated in March 1942 by Brig.Gen. W.W. Welsh, Deputy Chief of Staff Training Command: "Academic preparation will include such subjects as will prepare the trainee for the flight and ground school instruction which he will receive in the Air Corps Flying Schools. Military indoctrination, military customs and regulations and infantry drill. Physical training will fit trainees to absorb future intensive training without undue fatigue or ill effects."

Until early 1942, Pre-flight School was a four-week course, after which a nine-week course was inaugurated. In May 1944, another week was added. There were separate curricula for pilot and non-pilot trainees, with pilot training stressing math, physics, map reading, meteorology, and recognition of the aircraft and shipping. Until 1943, each Pre-flight School exercised

broad latitude in its cadet instruction. This lack of uniformity was shown to be detrimental in later stages of training. A single curriculum was instituted in April 1943.

Because Primary Training—the next stage of the cadet's training—was to be given at Civilian Contract Schools, the purpose of the Pre-flight School was to make certain the cadet would receive military indoctrination. Also, cadets who could not adapt to military regimen could be eliminated in Pre-flight School before too much time and money were invested in their training. In Summer 1943, it was estimated that 80% of cadets who successfully completed Pre-flight School would become pilots.

Pre-flight School was probably the most taxing period of training for a cadet. The two-class system gave upper class students the right to discipline the incoming lower class, so upper class cadets, who five weeks earlier were forced to awake at 4 a.m. to drill in double time, could now require the same of the lower class cadets. Hazing was allowed until May 1943, when public outcry led to its official abolishment. However, in practice, officers unofficially encouraged hazing. The dining room was the favorite area for hazing. Lower classmen had to sit at attention at the dining table on the front two to three inches of their chairs, sometimes with a cracker between their stomach and the table. In the "square meal" ritual, the cadet had to make all eating motions in a square pattern, eyes staring horizontally ahead. Not only did this make finding the plate and food difficult, but also the mouth.

A widespread rumor in pre-flight (and primary) training was that some cadets had been placed in each class to spy on other cadets to report the cadets who were troublemakers and chronic complainers. This accusation cannot be substantiated, but persisted throughout the war.

Despite the Code of Honor, cheating on examinations was widespread and instructors had to proctor the tests. Cadets set a low value on ground school subjects and felt to be eliminated because of failure in a subject such as physics, which was considered to be of no practical value in actual flying, was unfair, and therefore justified cheating.

Weather permitting, full-dress parade and inspection was held every Saturday before open post. Dress parades required absolute stance at attention. Cadets soon learned tricks, such as wetting their white gloves to

Primary School

Classroom: Classrooms had a separate curriculum for pilot and non-pilot trainees, with pilot training stressing math, physics, map reading, meteorology, and recognition of aircraft and shipping. (AAF)

Phys Ed: Pre-flight Training included physical endeavors, such as 15 hours of physical education and 73 hours of drilling. (AAF)

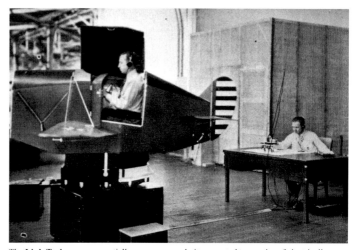

The **Link Trainer** was essentially an opaque cockpit connected to a series of electrically driven pumps and gyroscopes which simulated attitudes of flight. (AAF)

Four AAF standard trainers (top to bottom): Boeing **PT-17** Stearman, Vultee **BT-13** Vibrator, North American **AT-6** Texan, and the Curtiss **P-40** Warhawk. (AAF)

Posed PR photo of cadets surrounded by their **AT-6 Texan** trainers. (AAF)

keep their hands and wrists cool while standing at attention in the heat. Wriggling of the toes kept the circulation moving, but nonetheless, infrequently a cadet would faint and was not allowed to be assisted by other cadets. Cadets were allowed to answer officers in one of three responses: "Yes, Sir," No, Sir," and "No excuse, Sir."

Probably the most impressive ritual was "drumming out." At midnight, the P.A. system would sound with drum rolls, indicating that the entire cadet corps, sometimes numbering several thousand, had five minutes to change into full dress uniform. Late arrivals would incur five tours (a tour was a one-hour march in full dress uniform). Once in formation, cadet officers with swords drawn would inspect the entire cadet corps, "gigging" for the smallest infraction. Then the name of the offending cadet would be read only once, and thereafter he would be referred to by his serial number. To the beating of drums, the details of the offense (usually a breach of honor) was read and the cadet was "drummed out" to the words: "Henceforth, it is decreed, his name shall not be named at (such and such) Field and is to be stricken from the rolls, never to be mentioned or recalled again." These dramatics undoubtedly had great psychological effect on the cadet corps.

Pre-flight School served as a remedial academic and "spit and polish" military phase of a cadet's training. The average day for a Pre-flight School cadet (c.1942) was as follows:
0515: Shave and Shower
0545: Clean room 1515: Free: Study & personal chores
0600: Reveille formation
0615: Back to room 1630: Fall out for parade
0630: Form/march to breakfast
0645: Breakfast 1700: Parade
0715: March back to barracks 1730: March to barracks
0730: Free 1745: Free
0745: March to class 1800: Fall out and march to mess
0800: Classes
1130: Free Time
1145: Fall in & March to lunch
1200: Lunch 1930: Call to Quarters
1230: March back to barracks
1245: Prepare & Fall out for drill
1300: Drill & prepare for athletics
1400: Athletics
1500: Shower/change
1615: Prepare to parade
1645: March to parade
1815: Dinner
1845: March to barracks
1900: Free: Study, visit/socialize
2130: Prepare for bed
2200: Taps

College or Pre-Flight Preparatory Training

During 1942, the AAF had recruited aviation cadets in excess of its immediate needs. These recruits were held in Air Corps Enlisted Reserve (ACER), because Air Force facilities for processing and housing them were inadequate. By the end of 1942, 93,000 men were awaiting classification and instruction. The War Manpower Commission and Selective Service looked upon this large excess of manpower disapprovingly. At this time, America's colleges were financially troubled due to the loss of students to the armed services. The colleges, of course, had the necessary facilities available to feed, house, and instruct cadets. Consequently, Gen. H.H. Arnold recommended to the Secretary of War that these men be called to active duty and be given a

period of remedial training. A directive was issued enrolling 70,000 men in over 150 colleges by April 1943.

An Aviation Cadet Educational Exam (AC 20A) was prepared to be given to pre-aviation cadets to uncover their individual deficiencies. This test determined the number of weeks of college training which was to be given to each man (85% required some additional training, while of these 60% required the entire 20-week curriculum).

Since the program was a personal rather than a true training scheme, the AAF never established a definite educational objective. Academic subjects, including math, physics, English, history, and geography were taught and tested. Failure meant re-examination and tours. The officers of each detachment emphasized military indoctrination, drill, and discipline. Military indoctrination and physical training, rather than academics, were considered the most useful aspect of the college program, as these prepared the student for the regimen of service life and training. Initially, the program was directed to a college level, but as the program progressed, its quality regressed to a high school level.

Many colleges offered a ten-hour flight training program in conjunction with the Civil Aeronautics Administration and civilian contract flying schools. This flying indoctrination, usually in a Cub J-3, was rudimentary at best and was criticized as "riding around." Nonetheless, it certainly was a great morale booster for cadets who had been waiting to fly.

By late 1943, a full quota of men in training, along with a small backlog of inactive recruits, caused the Air Training Command (ATC) to reduce cadet college admission by half. By Spring 1944, a general manpower shortage in the non-flying Army forced the AAF to return to Army Ground Forces and Army Service Forces all personnel recruited from those forces that were not yet in pre-flight training. This order caused the withdrawal of many students and included the Secretary of War to determine the program halted in July 1944, after 254,000 men had been enrolled.

Flight Training

Introduction: In the 1930s, the extent of the Air Corp's training scheme was the 300 pilots it graduated annually from Randolph Field. By the mid-1940s, three regional training centers were established, and in January 1941, the training program was coordinated and supervised by the newly-formed Flying Training Command (FTC), with three regions designated as subcommands: Eastern FTC, Central FTC, and Western FTC. On the outset, FTC was segmented into flight training, ground training, technical training, etc. In mid-1943, the Technical Training Command was merged with the three regional FTCs to form the AAF Training Command.

The key figure in the FTC was a 1907 classmate of Gen. Arnold named Lt. Gen. Barton K. Yount, who was called to Washington from his post as Commandant of the Air Corp's Training Center to head the FTC in January 1942. In his book Global Mission, Gen. Arnold lavishly praised Gen. Yount's immeasurable contribution to AAF training: "He did a grand job. From then on, I knew it would function in accordance with the general directive it had received."

Generally, the four stages of Flight Training were:
1) **Primary:** the student learned to fly a light and stable aircraft of low horsepower
2) **Basic:** the student progressed to a heavier and more complex aircraft containing instruments.
3) **Advanced:** the student learned to fly a trainer whose characteristics were similar to combat aircraft.
4) **Transitional:** the student learned to fly combat aircraft.

Primary Flight Training
In late 1938, with war clouds gathering in Europe, planners at the Office

of the Chief of the Air Corps (OCAC) reported that existing training facilities were inadequate and that expansion was necessary, but without affecting the quality of the training. The course of new construction and expansion would require time and personnel, which were both at a premium. Gen. Arnold hoped to transfer the Primary Training responsibility to free Air Corps resources for later stages of training. In October, Arnold called the operators of the nation's three best Civilian Flying Schools to meet him in Washington. Among those present were Theopholis Lee of the Boeing School of Aeronautics, Oakland, California; Oliver Parks of Park's Air College, East St. Louis, IL; and C.C. Moseley of Curtiss-Wright Technical Institute, Glendale, CA. Gen. Arnold proposed each school establish and expand facilities to train and accommodate Army Flying Cadets. At the time, Arnold did not have any Congressional appropriations nor any official sanctions, but Arnold persuasively assured the school operators that Congress would soon alot the necessary monies. Also, certain laws restricting the number of Army personnel who could be trained in non-military schools had to be redrafted and revised. The War Department and Congress then had to approve the proposed program. Public Law No 18 accomplished this on 3 April 1939, but only by a scant two votes. In May 1939, nine civilian schools were contracted to initiate Primary Training in July.

Early civilian contract Primary Training programs lasted 12 weeks, with new classes beginning every six weeks. But by early 1942, with the pressure of war, the program was reduced to two weeks, with new classes beginning every five weeks. This reduction was at the expense of ground training, which was reduced from 225 hours to 94 hours by transferring this ground study time to pre-flight training. The ground or academic phase of Primary Training was a continuation of pre-flight study with navigation, weather, and aircraft and aero-equipment added. Still later, Primary Training was further reduced to eight weeks, but often cadets were posted for additional training due to the excess number of trainees being processed.

The quality of a Civilian Flying School was directly correlated to the quality of its instructors. When the program was initiated, instructor proficiency levels were high, but as the programs expanded to accommodate more trainees, more instructors were required and were of a lesser quality. Also, the aviation manpower demand of the Navy/Marines, Ferrying Command, airlines, and Selective Service Boards claimed many Civilian Flying School instructors. These groups were asked to voluntarily refrain from taking instructors, which by and large they did, except for the Navy, whose recruiting officers could not resist tempting civilian instructors.

A study by the Training Command found that civilian schools were able to train cadets for about $1.75 per hour less than could military bases. However, the study felt that military schools furnished higher quality trainees and provided better health care and morale. Many cadets who graduated from civilian schools would tend to disagree with the lower morale claim, as civilian schools provided plush accommodations and less military discipline. Training officers in Basic Flight Training often complained that it was difficult to rid the new primary graduates of the "country club" attitude they acquired at the civilian schools.

By May 1943, 56 primary Civilian Contract Schools existed, but by 1944, contract schools were phased out. Of course, by this time the war was being won and many pilots had been graduated. The extra air bases and facilities available to AAFTC could easily handle the diminished number of cadets which were then required. Plainly, the vast numbers of cadets could not have been trained so quickly without the aid of the Civilian Contract Schools.

Primary school flight training consisted of four phases, with the following basic teaching technique used in each phase:
1) Description of each technique by the instructor
2) Demonstration of the technique by the instructor
3) Student execution of the technique under the instructor's direct supervisor
4) Critique of the student's execution of the technique
5) Practice of the technique

Pre-solo Phase: The student was familiarized in fundamental light aircraft handling, usually by observing and feeling from the rear cockpit the instructor's manipulation of the various controls through a linked set of controls. Every day was spent in the air, and after a while the instructor did not touch the controls as the cadet practiced take offs, landings, and spin and stall recovery. One thing most student pilots remember of their first flights was the gosport helmet, which was officially described as: "the instructor's means of verbal communication with the cadet while in flight." However, the gosport was a one-way communications system: instructor to cadet only. A particularly poor execution of a maneuver by a "Dodo," or novice student, often solicited a rather impious tirade from the instructor through the gosport tubes, giving it the nickname "profanity filter." A favorite trick of the cadets was to stuff the instructor's end of the tube with cotton.

Intermediate Phase: The student received pre-solo and precision instruction utilizing elementary aerobatic maneuvers, such as the various eight patterns and Chandelles (climbing turns). Finally, about the third week, the student had gained enough experience and confidence to solo. After the first solo flight, solo practice of take offs, landings, and prescribed flight maneuvers were carried out. The instructor occasionally flew along to further demonstrate elementary maneuvers and spot landings. During this phase, the Link Trainer was utilized. The Link Trainer was essentially an opaque cockpit connected to a series of electrically driven pumps and gyroscopes which simulated attitudes of flight. The student sat in the totally enclosed opaque cockpit and received directions from an instructor for practice in navigation and instrument flying. The student's responses to the instructor's directions were recorded and graphed so that an assessment of his skill and progress could be determined.

Accuracy Phase: The student gained proficiency in landings (*e.g.*, 90° crosswind, spot, short run, etc.). On crosswind landings, each student had to be scored on ten landings, and often it became a race to be first to complete the ten. A favorite method used to accomplish this was to toe the brakes hard, rev up the engine, pull the stick back against the stomach and when the starter waved his flag, snap release the brakes along with some forward stick, causing the light trainer to literally leap into the air. Often in flight, the instructor would suddenly stop the engine in an area with power lines, trees, and other obstructions. The cadet was to find a place to land by gliding and turning. Just at touchdown, the instructor would start the engine and have the student repeat the procedure unexpectedly later. Besides scaring the cadet, the procedure did develop judgment of ground terrain and distance.

Aerobatic Phase: The student in duel and solo practice became accomplished in 180° overhead approaches, pylon and lazy eights, Chandelles, advanced aerobatics, and night flying. Often there were advanced and transitional training fields in the same area, and it was not uncommon for a P-40 or P-39 to bounce an unsuspecting primary cadet in the midst of a Chandelle or Immelmann. The poor cadet, earnestly concentrating on his aerobatic maneuver, would become unnerved at the appearance of such a large aircraft. By the final weeks of Primary Training, the cadet would become pretty cocky about his skills and buzzing pretty country girls and cattle became a favorite activity. The girls were often impressed, but the cows were not, as often the farmers would complain to the base commander that they would stop giving milk. Orders were invariably issued to every class to stop buzzing or be washed out. Buzzing usually stopped, as there always was the threat of an Inspector General's staff officer being present in the area.

Various aircraft were tried in the primary phase, but generally the Stearman PT-17, the Fairchild PT-19, and the Ryan PT-22 and their variants were utilized by virtue of their ease of handling and rugged construction.

Basic Flight Training

Since Basic schools were to make military pilots from Primary School graduates, this phase of training was almost entirely directed by the Air Force. Cadets trained in the "country club" atmosphere of the Primary Civilian Contract Schools had a rude awakening upon graduating to the austere, regimented Basic School surroundings. It was felt that the training officers in Basic Flight Training did as much to "reorient" the newly-arrived cadet.

Basic Ground School stressed the principles of weather, navigation, code, and instrument flying. The chief feature of Basic Ground School development during the war was the decreased emphasis on code, the continued importance of weather, and the increased emphasis on navigation and instrument flying. In this phase, 70 flying hours and 15 hours in the Link Trainer were given. Night flying and instrument flying were stressed. The cadet was introduced to a trainer of greater power, weight, and complexity, with the accent on the mastery of precision and smoothness in flying technique. Instrument training was probably the greatest challenge to most cadets.

The Vultee BT-13 Valiant was the standard basic trainer until 1943, when the North American AT-6 Texan replaced it.

From 1942 to 1944, nine weeks were allotted to basic schooling, but this was to expand to ten weeks as combat studies demonstrated that more time was required for instrument flying. Selection of pilots for single and twin-engine aircraft in the Advanced Schools was the responsibility of the Basic Schools. Students who failed were usually reassigned to various branches of the AAF, such as bombardier or navigator schools if qualified, or else gunnery or mechanical training schools. Later, Basic Schools would assign students to one of five Advanced School categories: **1)** single-engine fighter; **2)** twin-engine fighter; **3)** medium bombardment; **4)** multi-engine heavy bombardment; and **5)** twin-engine standard. The student indicated his first three preferences, while his instructor would recommend the student for three categories.

Advanced Flight Training

Advanced Training was divided into single engine and twin-engine training. These categories themselves were divided into ground and flight schools. Single and twin-engine ground training were similar and included advanced weather instruction, further training in instrument flying, and flight planning, along with the study of aircraft attack and defense. The major differences in the two ground courses were in the aircraft equipment course, as twin-engine aircraft were more complex. Also single engine students received gunnery and armament instruction, which was not required of twin-engine students. Both courses consisted of 60 hours.

Single engine flight training consisted of 70 hours of flying instruction divided into five stages:
1) Transition,
2) Instrument,
3) Navigation,
4) Formation flying, and
5) Aerobatics.

Combat experience had established that increased formation flying training was required. Also gunnery results in combat were unsatisfactory, resulting in 1944 in the separation of gunnery training in Transitional Schools. As single engine school pilots would graduate to become fighter pilots, emphasis was placed on gaining expert control in fast, maneuverable training aircraft.

Transitional Flight Training

As the word "transitional" indicates, the cadet pilot, now awarded his wings and appointed as a flight officer or commissioned as a 2nd Lieutenant, was transposed from training to combat status. The majority of pilots were given transitional training in either Flying Training Command (FTC) or the domestic Air Forces. A few other agencies, whose primary function was not training, but utilized tactical aircraft, also carried out some transitional training, particularly early in the war. Transition procedures conducted by all agencies were generally similar, each having its individual approach to the training program, and therefore, each having its particular difficulties.

Fighter transitional ground and air training attempted to give the pilot total familiarization with instrumentation, controls, engine accessories, flying characteristics, and performance of combat aircraft. Because the pilot's flights were to be necessarily solo, prior intensive ground indoctrination was essential. When possible, an hour's check in a specially modified two-place fighter was completed to demonstrate the student's proficiency in take offs, climbing turns, medium and steep turns, Chandelles, stalls, gliding turns, and landings. In a progressive series of five to eight flights, the student was instructed on what to do, how to do it, and what to look for in aircraft performance and engine operation. At the end of each flight, the student was questioned and tutored upon the various phases of the flight. Gunnery training was initially given in the AT-6, and when proficiency was attained the student was transferred to an obsolete combat fighter, such as the P-39 or P-40. Generally, fighter transition throughout Flying Training Command encountered few problems, with few changes in instructional methods, except to improve on safety.

Twin-engine graduates were sent to separate schools according to the type of combat bomber they were to eventually fly. FTC administered medium and heavy bomber transition, while the Third Air Force conducted light bomber transition as part of Operational Training Units (OTUs). Until late 1942, one year's flying experience was required to enter bomber transitional school, but the demands of war allowed the acceptance of advanced school graduates. However, transitional training was then doubled to ten weeks, with 100 hours of flying. Ground school bomber pilot trainees received more intensive instruction in weather, radio communication, aircraft handling, bombing tactics (e.g., aircraft weight and balance, bombing procedures, and target identification), and leadership/teamwork concepts. Commonly four-engine schools emphasized instrument, formation, and high-altitude flying, while two engine schools emphasized formation flying.

Operational Training

Basically, the AAF copied the RAF operational training system. Certain groups, referred to as "parent groups," with authorized over-strength, were to provide the nuclei of experienced officers for the training of newly-activated groups called Operational Training Units (OTU). Recently graduated students from transitional schools manned the OTUs. Once trained, these new groups would return to the parent group, restoring its over-strength and the cycle would be repeated. A nine-week bomber or twelve-week fighter period was usually needed to complete the formation, organization, and training of a new group before it returned to the parent group. In the operational training scheme of 1943, certain Elements from the parent group were sent to 30 days of instruction at the AAF School of Applied Tactics in Orlando, Florida. This course was divided about equally between academic and practical phases. The academic phase stressed command, intelligence, and operations in connection with the particular function the new group was to execute. Meanwhile, the practical phase consisted of operations and the flying of simulated missions. Upon completion of instruction, these men would be assigned to a newly-formed OTU group to initiate training as instructor officers in the new group.

In mid-1942, Replacement Training Units (RTU) were established to replace crews and crew members lost in combat or returned home after their combat tour was completed. Initially, experienced men or crews were withdrawn from U.S.-based regular units and sent to combat theaters, but this procedure jeopardized OTU training, so the AAF decided to authorize certain units as training units to be maintained at over-strength to fill combat losses. By February 1944, the formation of new combat groups was virtually (90%) completed, therefore phasing out OTU and leaving RTU as the primary operational training organization. The RTU course was shorter than the OTU, with less emphasis on group training as RTU graduates, as individuals or crews, were sent to establish combat units.

The First and Fourth (Domestic) Air Forces were the chief fighter pilot teaching organizations in the operational training phase. Since crew teamwork was not necessary in single place fighter aircraft, training stressed the attainment of individual proficiency and squadron/unit coordination. The basic objectives of operational training to be accomplished were to teach the pilot to have the aircraft become an extension of himself and to aim and fire his armament accurately. Pilots were familiarized in obsolete combat fighter types, such as the P-39 or P-40. After complete familiarization with the mechanical and handling aspects of the aircraft specified, aerobatic, bombing, gunnery, and later rocket exercises were practiced, along with simulated combat. Actual combat experience demonstrated the need in training for increased high-altitude flying, navigation, instrument and night flying, take off and assembly, group landing, and tactical training. The prohibitive losses suffered by Eighth Air Force heavy bombers on unescorted missions over France and the subsequent development of long-range escort fighters necessitated the inclusion of fighter/bomber cooperation into training programs. As the war progressed, the amount of training flying time increased from 40 hours at the end of 1942 to 70 hours at the end of 1944. This increase in training time was due to more emphasis on gunnery, navigation, and instrument and formation flying.

After the pilot had completed operational training, being assimilated into unit (fighters) and crew and unit (bombers), the final phase was modification to meet the requirements of the theater of operations. These alterations were rendered in each theater at a combat replacement center. Here, two purposes were served: first, individual deficiencies were detected and corrected; second, the procedures and problems of the theater of war were learned. After this, the pilot or crew were eased into actual combat operations. In late 1943, the Fighter Training Groups were established—the 495th (26 October) and the 496th (11 December)—to train newly-arrived replacement pilots from the U.S. in operational procedures and gunnery in specific aircraft. Each FTG had two component squadrons; the 495FTG had the 551FS and 552FS, while the 496FTG had the 554FS and 556FS. The 495FTG trained in the P-47C and D and P-38H and J, while the 496FTG trained in P-38s (until August 1944) and the P-51.

In November 1944, pilots coming to combat theatres from training in the U.S. bypassed the 495/496FTGs and went directly to the fighter groups with whom they would fly. Veteran pilots administered these "Clobber Colleges," as they were to be known. The value of this program was soon realized, in that the new arrivals quickly became enthusiastic students, learning the latest combat tactics and the operation and procedures of the group. The new pilots immediately felt they were part of the group and were anxious to fly. The 495/496FTGs continued to furnish conversion and refresher courses and also to train 9AF replacements.

Washout Procedures

A total of almost 132,000 (39%) of all pilot candidates failed to complete the primary, basic, or advanced stages of pilot instruction. A number of factors decided the number of failures. Of course, the individual skill and motivation of the cadet, along with the attitude and quality of the instructor determined the elimination standards, and therefore the rates at a given base and time. Since the judgment of flying skill is subjective rather than an objective measurement, this provides an explanation for the variations in washout rates.

Officially, there was no quota system for washouts, but the training scheme was perceptive to the exigencies of the times and ebb and flow in the attitude of the higher echelons. Whenever large backlogs of pilot trainees occurred and the manpower requirements of combat stabilized, headquarters would accent firm adherence to training standards. Consequently, if because of the above policy the failure rate climbed to exorbitant levels, headquarters would remind the training bases of their manpower wastage.

So, as not to expend manpower needlessly, it is not surprising that 67% of all washouts occurred in primary schools, usually during the first eight hours of dual instruction. During these eight hours, the instructor could usually determine whether the cadet had the "makings" to become a pilot. The major reasons for failure were a lack of coordination, poor judgment, and a general lack of ability. When a cadet received two consecutive "pink slips" from an instructor (in any school: primary, basic, or advanced), he would be sent to "group." Group consisted of two check pilots who would test the student and determine his future. It the two check pilots concurred with the pink slips, then the cadet was washed out. If there was a split decision or two approvals by the check pilots, the student was put on probation and allowed to continue under a more capable instructor.

In primary school, 67% of all eliminations occurred, while 21.8% occurred in basic, 5.5% in advanced, and 5.7% in transitional. More qualified washouts were usually sent to bombardier or navigator school, which actually required more intelligence than pilot training, but of course was not as glamorous. Less qualified washouts were utilized as gunners or mechanics.

Safety and Accidents

Safety was stressed throughout all phases of the training scheme. Very rarely did aircraft mechanical failure cause an accident. Particular idiosyncrasies of an individual aircraft were noted (Form A-1) so that the pilot would be aware of them beforehand. Training accidents were usually attributed to cadet flying inexperience or "pilot error," which in most cases amounted to "fooling around." In some training schools, if a cadet was found guilty of a flying violation he was made to wear the "dumb bell award" around his neck for a number of days determined by the seriousness of the violation and the plausibility of his explanation for it to his instructor.

Primary schools, probably because of more dual flying and closer supervision, had the lowest fatal accident rate at four deaths/100 accidents and 2.6 deaths/100,000 flying hours. Basic school had the highest fatality rate at almost 17 deaths/100 accidents, but only 6.5 deaths/100,000 flying hours. The average for all aviation in the U.S. during a comparable time was 11.5 deaths/100 accidents and 6 deaths/100,000 flying hours. Primary and Advanced schools approximated the U.S. average of 55 accidents/100,000 flying hours with 48 and 55/100,000, respectively. However, Basic schools showed a rate of only 27 accidents/100,000 flying hours. Basically, Primary, Basic, and Advanced schools had fewer accidents than the average rate for all American aviation, which is a tribute to the personnel and aircraft employed in these training programs.

America, because of her vast manufacturing and manpower capabilities, which were protected from enemy attack by the expanse of two oceans, was able to increase pilot quantity without a reduction in quality in her training programs. AAF pilot training was physically and mentally arduous throughout. There were no second chances; the cadet had to succeed or washout. When AAF cadets earned their Wings, they were undoubtedly the world's best.

Japanese Pilot Training in WWII

General

The Japanese Grand Strategy of a quick, decisive war affected their air training programs, which were geared to supply the limited number of pilots that would be required to attain this quickly achieved strategic objective. Therefore, these limited training programs were never able to expand rapidly enough to supply the appetite of the long war of attrition which beset Japan and consumed large numbers of pilots.

Japanese GNP was only about 10% of America's, and once their initial supply of aircraft had been destroyed, their aircraft industry had to compete for resources to manufacture combat aircraft, much less to build training aircraft. America also had a manpower advantage, as at that time, the U.S. had a population of about 150 million, versus Japan's population of about 90 million. However, the American population's average age was much younger, so the actual pool of young men was substantially larger than the analogous Japanese pool. But of course, the number of American pilots would have to be divided between the Pacific and the European Theater of Operations.

For the first few months of the war, America was forced to commit its experienced pilots to stem the Japanese advances in the Pacific. But once the Japanese advance stalled, the Americans calculatingly retained and brought back their best pilots from combat as flight instructors and devoted large quantities of readily available gasoline for the training of new pilots. America's vast industrial capacity allowed it to produce large numbers of training aircraft and to keep increasing numbers of second line combat aircraft in the Continental U.S. for training purposes as more advanced types became available for combat. In training pilots and aviation mechanics, American instructors were able to presume that their students had a head start on the Japanese student. Most young American men of that generation had driven or worked at maintaining an automobile, many had also hunted and fired guns, and then there was that intangible "innate American ingenuity." In contrast, in prewar Japan, there were very few individually owned automobiles and virtually no private firearms.

It required about a year for the USAAF or USN to train a pilot and assign him to an operational unit. Predictably, about a year after Midway, Japanese pilots began to find themselves outnumbered by a seemingly inexhaustible supply of pilots and aircraft. This would be even more troubling for the Japanese, as this period was about the same time the Americans were able to introduce newer aircraft types. Thus, once America began to deliver thousands of newly-trained pilots and new aircraft, the Japanese would have no expectation of fighting them off, even though they began to expand their training programs.

When war broke out, the average Japanese Navy pilot had 700 hours flying time, while Army pilots averaged 500 hours. By the middle of 1943, the Japanese expanded pilot training to as high a level as possible, but the number of flight instructors remained insufficient, as many veteran Japanese pilots, who could lead and further train these rookies, were succumbing to the natural attrition of sustained combat at the Battle of Midway, in the Solomon Islands, or the SWPA. The Japanese had no choice but to continue to shorten the amount of training time due to the exigencies of the war caused by the increasing strength of the Allies and the shortages of gasoline, suitable training aircraft, and experienced training instructors. By late 1944, a new Japanese pilot graduated with just 40-60 hours flying time, while the AAF and USN firmly held to its requirement of at least 200 hours flight time to the end of the war. Furthermore, before entering combat many Japanese student pilots died in flying accidents, particularly when they were assigned fast, unforgiving fighters to fly. While flying accidents and training fatalities were common in the Continental United States, they were much more common in Japan. Relative losses in combat were correspondingly disproportionate, as well-trained rookie American pilots found their Japanese counterparts to be terrified greenhorns and easy victims. So, as the war continued to go badly for the Japanese, the lack of qualified pilot candidates, along with inadequate fuel supplies, training aircraft, and qualified instructors further diminished the quality of pilot training. It is well-documented that

Kamikaze pilots were given only the rudiments of flight training and had to be led to the place of attack due to the utter lack of navigational training.

Thomas McGuire on Japanese pilots:

"Japanese fighter pilots are individuals who do not fly in set patterns, nor attack by Squadron or flight, although lately (mid-1944) a few exceptions have been observed of Japanese imitating standard U.S. four-ship flights escorting their own bombers. The quality of Japanese pilots is unpredictable, although Navy pilots are definitely superior to Army pilots. The variation is entirely between the very able, experienced pilots and very poor pilots, nothing to compare with the more uniform abilities of our own men.

"In the early days of the war, the enemy fighter pilots built up a reputation for skill and aggressiveness, and they had little trouble keeping that reputation as long as they were opposed by ancient models like P-39s and P-40s. With the introduction of the P-38 and P-47 in this theater, and the F4F and F6F in the Solomons, the Japanese learned caution, caution to the point of timidity. Even over their home bases they have shown a distaste for all-out fighting."

JNAF Training

JNAF Training Organization
The Bureau of Training (*Kyoiku Kyoku*) at Naval Air Headquarters was in command of the training of all Naval Air Personnel, while the Combined Air Training Command (*Rengo Koku Sotai*), based at Gifu, was responsible for the actual training.

Combined Air Group
There were six Combined Air Groups (Rengo *Kokutai* - Nos. 11-14, 18 and 19) in this Command, in which all Naval personnel were trained in Training Air Groups (*Kokutai*) under the supervision of the Combined Air Group Headquarters. Each Combined Air Group (CAG) was responsible for training in a particular area. For instance, CAG 11, located in Central Honshu, was responsible for Elementary Flying Training; CAG 12, on Kyushu, and CAG 14, on Formosa, were responsible for Advanced Flying Training; and CAG 13 station in Japan and China trained aircrews in Navigation, Radio, and Gunnery.

Training Air Groups
Training Air Groups (approximately 100) carried out the training of flying and ground personnel. Excluding six in Formosa and those in the Philippines, Korea, China, and Indo-China, all these Air Groups were located in Japan (unlike the JAAF, whose
training units were mainly overseas).

There were five types of Training Air Groups:
1) Pre-flight Training Air Group recruits were drawn from the Navy, civilian sources, or the Youth Air Training Corps, and were trained as pilots or members of air crews. This training, which varied in length in relation to the age of the recruit, ended with the trainees being classified as pilots, navigators, bomb aimers, air gunners, or radio operators. The next year plus of pilot training paralleled Allied training, except with emphasis placed on aerial maneuvers appropriate for dogfights.
2) "Disciplinary Training Air Groups," whose training was similar to the U.S. "boot camp," was for prospective ground personnel.
3) Specialist Training Groups provided elementary and advanced maintenance instruction for personnel other than pilots and aircrews who graduated from Pre-flight Training or for personnel detached from combat units.
4) Elementary Flying Training Groups undertook the training of potential pilot graduates of Pre-flight Training.

5) Advanced Flying Training Groups specialized in fighter, bomber, or reconnaissance training for pilots graduating from Elementary Flying Training Groups.

Initial Individual Training of JNAF Pilots

The initial JNAF pilot training program required more than two years and was harsh and demanding, with corporal punishment being an integral part of training. The majority of Japanese pilots were noncommissioned officers, which was in distinct contrast with the U.S. Army and Navy Air Forces, where most pilots were commissioned officers. In the Japanese Air Forces, there was a large social chasm between officers and enlisted men which ultimately prevented outstanding non-commissioned officers and enlisted men from entering the higher echelons of the air services. Outstanding noncommissioned ace Saburo Sakai, Japan's second leading ace to survive the war, wrote in his memoir *Samurai!* that he and other non-coms were frequently mistreated by their officers. However, ultimately all ranks were dedicated to the Emperor and Japan and to their common cause against the enemy. The Japanese naval pilot training program emphasized quality over quantity, electing to train a very small number of select pilots to a very high level, so the JNAF began the war with a cadre of superbly trained pilots.

Pre-flight Training

The length of the Pre-flight course varied according to the age and educational background of the aircrew candidate. For young 15 to 17-year-old civilian volunteers recently graduated from school, there was a 1½ to 2½ year course (later reduced to three months or less) that was primarily educational and cultural in nature, but included elementary courses in various aspects of the Air Force and flying. These volunteers were trained by the Flight Reserve Enlisted Trainee System (*Hiko Yoka Renshusei*, or *Yokaren*). Military age recruits attended a six- or eight-week Pre-flight "boot camp" designed to improve their physical condition and to introduce them to Air Force routine. Japanese noncommissioned officers drawn from fleet service were trained by the Pilot Trainee System (*Soju Renshusei* or *Soren*). Only a small number of university students were recruited into the Student Aviation Reserve (*Koku Yobi Gakusei*) to become Reserve Ensigns, although this university program expanded rapidly after war broke out, training over 10,000 pilots in 1943. An "aptitude for flying" test was administered at both of these courses, after which recruits were divided into three classes (pilots, navigators, and radio operators) and were posted to other Groups for additional training. Pilot candidates moved on to Elementary Flying Training Air Groups, while those found unqualified for flight duties were consigned to ground duties.

Elementary Flying Training

At this phase, no distinction was made between fighter, bomber, or reconnaissance pilots, all of whom trained together, flying an elementary biplane trainer. Elementary Flying Training continued for four months with 100 hours of flying time, 20 of which were on dual control aircraft, and with instruction emphasizing take off, landings, and flying circuits. Classroom courses emphasized the principles of flying. At the end of this course, trainees were assigned as fighter, bomber, or reconnaissance pilots and posted to Air Groups specializing in these types.

Advanced Flying Training

The pilot candidates spent four months at the Advanced Flying Training Air Groups, flying advanced trainers and obsolete operational aircraft. Flying time for fighter pilots was approximately 100 hours, which included about 10 hours of conversion to combat fighters. Combat tactics, gunnery, navigation, etc., were taught, with the most importance attached to the pilot's actual performance in the air, rather than to his theoretical knowledge (there was no test on theory given to fighter pilots).

Operational Flying Training

Operational Flying Training for pilots who had completed their Advanced Flying Training was conducted in operational units which were often newly formed in Japan. Here, fighter pilots were transitioned to combat aircraft and bomber pilots were assigned their crews—graduates from navigation, radio, and gunnery schools. Operational Training was directed by the Command to which the operational unit was assigned, which was usually an Air Flotilla. Operational training was rigorous, with considerable time given to combat tactics (aerial gunnery and ground support) and formation flying, as well as in carrier landings and night flying. The time spent on Operational Training varied from two to six months, according to operational requirements. After an ideal 12 to 16 months and 250-300 hours of flight training, the JNAF fighter pilot was ready for combat.

Carrier Qualification

During the 1930s, the JNAF included a large land-based contingent, but the best and most qualified students with over 500 hours of flying time from the JNAF training program were selected for carrier duty. By 1938, with the war in China requiring more pilots, the number of hours to carrier qualify was reduced. Once the Pacific War began, pilot training was greatly expanded to fulfill the requirements for both the JAAF and JNAF. As IJN carriers led the advance across the Pacific, more and more carrier pilots were required, especially after the defeat at Midway. Even though carrier qualifications were lowered to 200 hours, the actual training regimen remained comprehensive and disciplined.

Carrier training began with landings on the ground, on which a carrier deck approximately 75 feet by 175 feet was indicated by white flags. Once these simulated ground landings were mastered, the cadet would take off from a land base and make low-speed and low-altitude approaches about 15 feet above a real carrier deck without touching down. The pilot then progressed to touch-and-go landings on a carrier before returning to base. Finally, the pilot would be allowed a full landing with the arrester gear down under the guidance of the Flight Officer, who was ready with a red flag to wave off a wayward landing attempt. Unlike the U.S. and Royal Navies, the IJN did not employ a Landing Signals Officer (LSO) stationed at the end of the flight deck to manually guide aircraft down, but instead used two separate rows of lights to guide the pilot down.

The skill level of carrier pilots remained high throughout 1943, but then deteriorated rapidly, as the loss of veteran pilots and the shortened training programs took their toll. By the time of the Battle of the Philippines Sea, pilots with only 150 total hours of flying time were accepted for carrier qualification with the associated accidents and fatalities.

Expansion of JNAF Training System

None of the Japanese pilots involved in the attack on Pearl Harbor had logged less than 600 hours of flying time, and many Flight Leaders had over 1,500 hours experience. Early in the Pacific War, the JNAF had decided that the training of new pilots was to be continued at a reduced level in order to place all of its experienced pilots, aircraft, and resources in combat, in order to win the "short war." Japan's chronic shortage of gasoline also contributed to this decision, as gasoline stocks had to be diverted for combat, rather than for training. Thus, the JNAF was vulnerable not only to attrition, but was totally unable to compensate for the sudden loss of 300 pilots at Midway. At low prewar training rates, it would have required the JNAF two years to train that many pilots. After the Midway debacle, during the latter part of 1942 and early 1943, continuing battles for Guadalcanal and the SWPA slowly eroded the JNAF's supplies of aircraft, experienced pilots, and mechanics.

As a result of the increasing demands of the war, significant expansion in the JNAF training system occurred in late 1943 and the Spring of 1944.

There was an increase in the number of training groups of all kinds and an increase in the numbers of aircraft used at many of the Elementary and Advanced Flying Training Groups. Personnel for this increased training system were supplied mostly from the graduating classes of University and Higher School that were conscripted in mid-1943. This expansion was very similar to the expansion of the JAAF War Emergency Training Organization, which is described in more depth later.

Japanese Training Gallery

JAAF Training

Japanese Army Air Force training never reached the level of the JNAF and was somewhat less demanding than that of the Navy. The complete training course took two years and cadets graduated with 300 hours flying time. The Army shared the Navy's emphasis on dogfighting and had similar personnel policies.

JAAF Training Organization

At the time of Pearl Harbor, the JAAF training system comprised a number of schools for training in flying and ground services under the Inspectorate General of Aviation Training (*Koku Sokambu*). These schools cooperated with a number of civilian flying training schools in Japan, most of which they absorbed.

The JAAF training organization (Kyodo) consisted of five Schools or Units:

1) Preparatory Schools and Units
Youth Aviation Cadet Schools (*Shonen Hikdhei Gakko*)
Recruits for potential aircrew were teenagers from Middle Schools. No flying was taught. Students graduated to the Elementary Flying Training Schools as Superior Privates and students rejected as aircrew were sent to non-flying Specialist Training.

2) Specialist Technical Training Schools
The Specialist Technical Schools in*cluded a Ground Maintenance School (*Rikugun Koku Seibi Gakko), Technical Schools (*Rikugun Koku Gijutsu Gakko*), and a Signals School (*Rikugun Koku Tsushin Gakko*). All these schools provided courses of instruction for graduates from the Youth Aviation Cadet Schools and the Air Training Units, as well as for personnel on attachment from combat units.

3) Elementary Flying Training Schools
The Elementary Flying Schools (*Hiko Gakko*) received recruits from the Youth Aviation Cadet School and the Air Training Units. The graduates passed onto Advanced Flying Training.

4) Advanced Flying Training Schools
Trainees completing the Elementary Flying courses passed into Advanced Flying Schools (*Hiko Gakko*) for specialist training on fighter, bomber, or reconnaissance aircraft. These schools also provided short courses on other subjects as required for personnel from front line units. New flying units were formed at these schools and on completion of their Advanced Flying courses, trainees were posted to these new units, or to combat units, where they received their operational training.

5) Officer Training Schools
Two schools existed for officers: the Officer Cadet Preparatory School (*Yokashikan Gakko*) and the Air Officer's School (*Koku Shikan Gakko*). At the Officer's School, only Elementary Flying was taught, with officers joining up with other ranks at the Advanced Training stage.

Air Training Units (Koku Kyoikutai)

Air Training Units were set up to primarily supply ground personnel. On completion of this training, recruits passed either to Specialist Schools for further instruction or directly to ground units serving overseas. Secondarily, Air Training Units provided a Pre-flight course for recruits enlisting through the Army as potential aircrew. From here, these recruits entered the Elementary Flying Training Schools with the rank of Corporal.

Operational Training

On completion of their Advanced Flying Training at either the home-based or overseas organizations, aircrews were posted to an operational regiment for operational training which was carried out in operational units mostly in non-combat areas. This training was under the administration of the

Inspectorate-General of Aviation, while the responsibility for the actual training was with the Operations Officer in the Air Brigade and the Intelligence Officer in the Flying Regiment.

The Field Air Replacement Unit (Yasen Hoju Hikotai) under the 3rd Air Army served as an Operational Training Unit for the 3rd and 4th Air Armies. It supplied aircrew and urgently needed ground personnel as replacements for the two Air Armies to the south (not the northern Air Armies), as their greater distance from Japan and their greater combat activity demanded the establishment of this Unit. Training, using operational types of aircraft, was conducted by four units of the Field Air Replacement Unit: a Fighter Unit, a Light Bomber Unit, a Medium Bomber Unit, and a Reconnaissance Unit.

Individual Training of JAAF Recruits

Preparatory Training

The length of this introductory training program varied with the age of the schoolboy recruits and personnel transferred from other branches of the Army. Schoolboy recruits, not of military age, took a 12-month cultural course in academic subjects, including science, mathematics, and history. Military-aged recruits received two months of recruit training of a general nature designed to provide an introduction to air force routine and engender a spirit of devotion to that service. Physical training was an important part of the curriculum. Not all graduates of these courses were intended to be pilots, as at the end of training the trainees were divided into pilots, radio operators, navigators, and maintenance crews, with the pilots being posted to Elementary Flying Training and the remainder being sent to Specialist Schools.

Elementary Flying Training

Elementary Flying Training required eight months, with the first six months having all future pilots train all together, regardless of the aircraft type they may eventually fly. During this period, flying time totaled 20 hours duo and 70 hours solo, all in a biplane trainer. At the conclusion of the first six months of the course, recruits were separated into fighter, bomber, and recce classes. During the last two months of Elementary the pilots transitioned (30 hours) to the type of aircraft they would use at the Advanced Training Schools.

Advanced Flying Training

At an Advanced Flying Training School, pilots spent four months flying 120 hours (the flying time of bomber pilots was somewhat longer) flying advanced trainers, obsolescent operational types, and front line combat aircraft. They were instructed in formation flying, combat tactics, aerial gunnery, and night flying.

Operational Training

After Advanced Flying Training, pilots were posted to an operational combat unit to receive further instruction in combat tactics and become familiar with local fighting conditions. Although six months was the declared training time, pilots often participated in combat operations long before that time, especially in areas where the Allies were particularly active. Newly-graduated JAAF pilots were found to be particularly deficient in over water and night flying capabilities, which were important in the far flung areas of the new Japanese Empire.

JAAF War Emergency Training Organization Mid-1942

The early war training system was inadequate for the growing requirements of the war and in May 1942, it was supplemented by a second system providing additional facilities for Advanced Flying Training, which eventually provided about triple the number of replacement personnel supplied by the previous system, which was maintained as a "home" organization. The new organization was primarily used to develop training facilities overseas, although it was directed from Japan.

The supplementary organization set up to meet the war emergency was under the 1ˢᵗ Air Army, which was also formed in May 1942. There were two Flying Divisions under the 1ˢᵗ Air Army: one was an operational Flying Division, with its own battle order; while the second was a Flying Training Division known as the 51ˢᵗ Kyoiku Hikoshidan, located at Gifu.

A number of administrative Flying Training Brigades (Hikodan) were formed under the Flying Training Division to direct the activities of 18 Flying Training Regiments (Hikorentai). These provided flying training overseas similar to that given at the Advanced Schools of the "home" organization.

The Air Training Units were transferred to this organization and remained in Japan. Later, an Air Training Brigade (Koku Kyoikudan) was formed to direct their activities. Graduates from these ground units and from the Flying Training Regiments transferred to overseas operational units.

Late 1943 and Mid-1944

Two important changes in the War Emergency Training Organization occurred in late 1943 and mid-1944.

In the Fall of 1943, the War Emergency Organization was expanded and to increase the number of pilots, conscription was applied to students of universities and higher schools who previously were exempt from compulsory service, causing the closure of 4,000 of these schools. This large influx of new recruits was too great for the two existing training organizations to manage, and consequently, in the Spring of 1944, Elementary Flying Training establishments were considerably enlarged and the Advanced Flying Training Regiments (Kyoiku Hikorentai) were increased in number from 18 to approximately 50. At the same time, they were renamed Flying Training Units (Kyidiku Hikotai). Other training units (Rensei Hikotai) were also formed to conduct Specialist Advanced Flying Training and all, except five, were located overseas, being divided—in the second half of 1944—almost equally between Manchuria, Korea, Formosa, Philippines, Malaya, Java, and China. Their activities were directed in each area by Flying Training Brigades, which were in turn subordinated for operations to the Air Army in whose area they were located and which was responsible for the training in that area.

The other change in the War Emergency Training Organization occurred in the Summer of 1944, when the Training Schools located in Japan were raised to Divisional status (Kyodo). The 1944 Kyodo organization had three functions: the formation of new units, the training of units withdrawn from active service for re-equipping, and the supply of replacement personnel to serving units. There were two sources supplying personnel (air and ground) for flying units:

1) The home-based system of schools directly under the Inspectorate-General of Aviation Training supplied about a quarter of the required number.
2) The system of training units, almost entirely overseas, controlled by the Directorate-General of Aviation Training through the 1ˢᵗ Air Army and the 51ˢᵗ Flying Training Division provided about three-quarters of the flying personnel required

13

USAAF and JAAF/JNAF Ranks

USAAF Ranks

Commissioned Officers	Enlisted Ranks
General of the Air Force (Gen. HH Arnold)	Warrant Officer
General	Flight Officer
Lt. General	Master Sergeant
Maj. General	First Sergeant
Brig. General	Technical Sergeant
Colonel	Staff Sergeant
Lt. Colonel	Technician 3rd Grade*
Major	Sergeant
Captain	Technician 4th Grade*
1st Lieutenant	Corporal
2nd Lieutenant	Technician 5th Grade*
	Private 1st Class

* On 8 January 1942, the War Department created and replaced the existing specialist ranks with these Technician ranks (T/3, T/4, and T/5). A T/5 was properly addressed as "Corporal," while T/4s and T/3s were referred to as "Sergeants." Although they wore chevrons similar to Corporals and Sergeants, Technicians had no command authority or duties and could not issue orders to regular Sergeants, Corporals, or Privates.

Officer Rank/Insignia

Rank	Insignia
General	★★★★
Lt. General	★★★
Maj. General	★★
Brig. General	★
Colonel	(eagle)
Lt. Colonel	(oak leaf) (Silver)
Major	(oak leaf) (Gold)
Captain	(double bars)
1st Lieutenant	(bar) (Silver)
2nd Lieutenant	(bar) (Gold)
Warrant Officer (chief)	(bar) (Brown)
Warrant Officer (j.g.)	(bar) (Brown)
Flight Officer	(bar) (Blue)

Enlisted Rank/Insignia

Rank	Sleeve Insignia
Private (7th grade)	no chevrons
Private first class (6th grade)	
Corporal (5th grade)	
Sergeant (4th grade)	
Staff Sergeant (3rd grade)	
Technical Sergeant (2nd grade)	
Master Sergeant, First Sergeant (1st grade)	

Officer Pay Rates

Rank USN	Rank AAF USMC	$ Annual Base	$ Monthly Base	$ Monthly Long.	$ RSA Dep.	$ RSA WO	$ RA Dep.	$ RA WO
Capt	Col	4000	333.33	16.67	42	21	120	105
Cdr	Lt.Col	3500	291.67	14.58	63	21	120	105
Lt.Cdr	Maj	3000	250.00	12.50	63	21	105	90
Lt	Capt	2400	200.00	10.00	42	21	90	75
Lt(jg)	1Lt	2000	166.67	8.32	42	21	75	60
Ens	2Lt/FO	1800	150.00	7.50	42	21	60	45

Long.=Longevity RSA=Ration Subsistence Allowance RA=Rental
Allowance Dep.=Dependents WO=Without dependents

Typical Flying Officer Pay Scales

Rank USN	Capt	Cdr	Lt.Cdr	Lt	Lt(jg)	Ens
Rank AAF/ USMC	Col	Lt.Col	Maj	Capt	1Lt	2Lt/FO
Typical years of service	12	9	6	>3	>3	>3
Monthly base $	333.33	291.67	250.00	200.00	166.67	150.00
Longevity $ (1)	66.67	43.74	25.00	10.00	8.33	7.50
Ration subsistence $	42.00	63.00	63.00	42.00	42.00	42.00
Rental allowance $	120.00	120.00	105.00	90.00	75.00	60.00

Flight pay $ (2)	200.00	167.70	137.50	105.00	87.50	78.75
Overseas pay $ (3)	53.33	45.94	38.75	30.50	25.42	22.88
Monthly pay $	815.33	732.05	619.05	477.50	404.92	361.13
Annual pay $	9784	8785	7431	5730	4859	4334

(1) 5% for every 3 years of service
(2) 50% of the sum of base pay + longevity pay
(3) 10% of the sum of base pay + flight pay

Dependent pay:
1) $22/month was deducted from pay, but the government contributed the remainder.
2) A wife with no children received $50/month.
3) A mother with one child received $80/month, plus $20/month for each additional child.
Death Allowance: Six months pay, including longevity and flight pay, but not rental or other subsistence allowances.
Allotments: Personnel could specify portions of their pay to be deducted and sent to designated payees to insure regular payments (e.g., to relatives, insurance premiums, etc.) even if they were POW or MIA.

Japanese Air Forces Ranks

Japanese Army Air Force Ranks (JNAF Equivalent)

Japanese	English	JNAF
(JAAF)	Equivalent	Equivalent
Tai-sho	General	Admiral
Chu-jo	Lt. General	Vice Admiral
Sho-sho	Maj. General	Rear Admiral
Tai-sa	Colonel	Captain
Chu-sa	Lt. Colonel	Commander
Sho-sa	Major	Lt. Commander
Tai-i / Dai-i	Captain	Lieutenant
Chu-i	1st Lieutenant	Lieutenant(jg)
Sho-i	2nd Lieutenant	Ensign
Jun-i	Warrant Officer	Warrant Officer
Socho	Master Sergeant	Chief Petty Officer
Gunso	Sergeant	Petty Officer
Gocho	Corporal	Petty Officer
Heicho	Private	Seaman

Japanese Naval Ranks

Commissioned Ranks

Admiral	Tai-sho	Adm
Rear Admiral	Sho-sho	RAdm
Vice Admiral	Chu-jo	VAdm
Captain	Tai-sa	Capt
Commander	Chu-sa	Cdr
Lt. Commander	Sho-sa	LtCdr
Lieutenant	Tai-i	Lt
Lieutenant (jg)	Chu-i	Lt(jg)
Ensign	Sho-i	Ens

Enlisted Ranks (Post June 1941)

Flight Warrant Officer	Hiko Heiocho	WO
Flight Chief Petty Officer	Joto Hiko Heiso*	CPO
Flight Petty Officer 1st Class	Itto Hiko Heiso	PO1c
Flight Petty Officer 2nd Class	Nito Hiko Heiso	PO2c
Flight Petty Officer 3rd Class	Santo Hiko Heiso+	PO3c
Flight Leading Seaman	Hiko Heicho*	LdgSea
Flight Superior Seaman	Joto Hikohei*	SupSea
Flight Seaman 1st Class	Itto Hikohei	Sea1c

* Rank established November 1942
+ Rank abolished November 1942

14

Rotation and Replacement Policy

USAAF Rotation and Replacement Policy

During the first year of the war, one of the most urgent problems faced by Gen. Kenney and the men in his command was the question of replacements. Pilots and crews who flew combat missions in conditions characterized by poor weather and living conditions did so without a set rotation goal, as the inconsistent replacement policy gave the men no choice but to fly until they burned out, no matter how many combat hours they had flown, or were killed.

Many pilots had been in continual combat for as many as ten months, while ground crews and service and depot personnel were being worn down by 12 to 18 hours of daily hard labor. Flight Surgeons reported that 45 to 60% of the pilots in some units were suffering from combat fatigue, owing to almost continual combat operations, poor living conditions without suitable food or recreational facilities, and the lack of promotions. The signs of combat fatigue were irritability, short temper, and general apathy. Fifteen pilots of the 8FS of the 49FG had served for a year in the combat zone and the squadron combat status report stated that their "ability, aggressiveness, and morale were becoming very low." The absence of a definite policy of rotation gave these war-weary veterans little hope of relief.

Even though the need of a personnel rotation policy was recognized, it was difficult to establish a satisfactory balance between the demands of the theater for replacements and the realities of the quantity and quality of the training program supplying replacements. It was a question of whether it was more prudent to keep exhausted veterans in the theater or to replace them with untrained and vulnerable newcomers. In October and November 1942, after its extended operations in the Philippines, the NEI, and Australia, the 19th Bombardment Group (H) was the only combat group in the SWPA to be replaced as a unit since the beginning of the war. Even so, the news of the return of the 19BG to the United States and the initial arrival of some replacements did give hope to those veterans who had been in combat for lengthy periods that they would be rotated home. In reality, it was impossible to depend on the regular arrival of trained replacements in large enough numbers. The arrival of replacements created a new problem, as frequently high-ranking officers and enlisted men arriving directly from the States had no combat experience and required extensive instruction from veterans of lesser rank. These veterans had not been promoted during their long months in combat, while their "students" had received undeserved stateside promotions. The veterans found this to be an intolerable situation. Kenney championed the cause of his veterans by constantly urging that no high-ranking officers should be sent to his theater unless specifically requested, and that he should be authorized to promote his deserving men regardless of the table of organization. When a Major and ten First Lieutenants arrived from Hawaii, Kenney sent them back, urging that only Second Lieutenants were to be sent in the future. Kenney was allowed to fill 200 vacancies for First Lieutenants above the Technical Order of the Fifth Air Force and was promised that consideration would be given to a similar provision for the promotion of First Lieutenants and Captains. Nonetheless, the promotion and rotation problems remained unsolved in early January 1943.

Kenney Sets 300 Combat Hours to Rotate Home

Unlike MacArthur, who never considered sparing his troops from combat, Kenney went out of his way to protect his aircrews, believing that they could only be kept proficient with high morale in combat if tour limits were conscientiously maintained. In practice, this meant that a fighter pilot in the 5AF could typically expect to be eligible for rotation after about 300 hours in combat or about 15 months on tour, unless he accepted a position of advanced responsibility, such as Operations Officer or Squadron Commander. Once Kenney set the 300 combat hours flown requirement for rotation home, the men did have some hope, though still unrealistic, of going home. However, the rotation situation was much better for aircrews than for ground crews, who were informed that "personnel can be returned only under the most exceptional circumstances….and little hope is held out for an early improvement."

Points System to Rotate Home

After Luzon was secured in June 1944, MacArthur approved the new "points rotation system" for a general rotation back home for all FEAF personnel. In the previous rotation system, the men with most time in the theater were scheduled to be sent home on an intermittent basis. If adverse combat conditions prevented releasing troops for rotation, they could be trapped in that place for the duration. The points system, called the Advanced Service Rating Score (ASRS), had been previously set up in the ETO and awarded points as follows:

1 point for each month service

5 Points for first and each award received: DSC, LM, SS, DFC, SM, BS, AM, and PH

5 Campaign Stars worn on theater ribbons
12 points for each child under 18 up to a limit of 3 children.

The ASRS was adopted in the Pacific, so once a man serving in the Pacific accumulated at least 85 points under the new system, he would automatically be rotated home. After the implementation of the new policy, units were sending dozens of men home, while before then the average was no more than four or five a month.

Upon arriving back in the U.S., the rotating officer or enlisted man would report to a Reception Station, and from there would have a 21-day leave. After leave, they were to report to one of four Personnel Distribution

Lt.Col. John Loisel had the longest combat deployment of any American fighter pilot in the Pacific. (AAF)

Command Stations (Miami and Atlantic City on the East Coast and Santa Ana and Santa Monica in California) for two weeks. Although AAF policy could send returned veterans back overseas on a second tour, it was only if absolutely necessary.

From the Distribution Center, enlisted men eligible for Officer Candidate School (OCS) would proceed there (but only a few were accepted in 1945). Enlisted men volunteering for a second tour were sent to a refresher course and given the opportunity to upgrade their duty status. These enlisted volunteers would usually remain in the U.S. for six months before being redeployed overseas, but most remained in the U.S. in their combat capacity (i.e., as mechanics or Crew Chiefs), or were assigned to administrative duties. Many enlisted ground crew had already served two years or more overseas—some from the beginning of the war—and had no intention of returning.

Officers were also sent to a refresher course from the Distribution Center. Pilots were often trained to become instructors or reassigned to other flying duties, or to administrative or technical postings. Pilots volunteering for a second tour were often given additional training (Richard Bong received additional gunnery training) and were usually returned to their previous combat duty and combat unit. Many pilots who served from the beginning of the war had already spent too many months in combat and eagerly returned home. However, the top aces, like Thomas Lynch, returned to combat and were subsequently KIA.

Demobilization at the End of the War
When the war in Europe ended in May 1945, the manpower requirements in the ETO were reduced to Occupation duties in Germany. With many new troops being trained in the States, there would be replacements readily available for what was projected to be a protracted war in the Pacific. When the atomic bomb unexpectedly and officially ended the Pacific war in September 1945, there was a large backlog of troops waiting to invade Japan. In response, the number of required ASRS points was reduced to 80, and as of 1 October 1945, the critical score was further reduced from 80 to 70; by 1 November, it was lowered again for enlisted men with ASRS scores between 50 and 59, inclusive, and two years of active service. There were a succession of critical score reductions, and soon the backlog disappeared and separation bases were being inactivated, so that by March 1946, all enlisted men with two years of service would have enough points required for separation. Demobilization reduced AAF strength from 218 groups to 109 between the Japanese surrender and the following Christmas,

AAF Rotation Procedure. (AAF)

and the rate continued sharply downward through the first half of 1946. By the end of June 1946, the nominal strength of the AAF had been cut in half again to 54 groups, a figure that alarmed many career airmen, who would prove to be right when the Korean War broke out four years later.

Before the war, 2Lt. John Loisel was posted to a unit in the Philippine Islands, but en route the Japanese attacked Pearl Harbor. Over the next four years, he would score 11 victories with the 432FS/475FG and as a Lt. Colonel he would assume command of the 475FG on 14 July 1945. On 18 April 1946, Loisel returned to the United States after the longest combat deployment of any fighter pilot in the Pacific (301 operational missions and 852.5 combat hours).

Japanese Rotation Policy

The Japanese leaders assumed that every soldier would do his duty and death would be an honor. There was no policy of relieving units or individual pilots. Exhausted units were reassigned, and if one was decimated, its remnants were sent to Japan for rebuilding or for refurbishing other units. Generally, Japanese pilots served until they were killed, wounded, or evacuated due to disease. However, some enlightened air commanders created pretexts to reassign pilots when their performance inevitably began to deteriorate. Vital Japanese ground crews and mechanics were abandoned as the Allies advanced.

PART 2:
Units of the Combatants

1

Units of the
5th Fighter Command

5th Fighter Command Chain of Command

The Fifth Air Force and its subordinate commands followed conventional AAC organizational configuration, which was deemed to be the easiest method of administration and supply. Initially, this method was not completely suitable for operations, because it was unable to maintain the chain of command as units rapidly moved to forward areas that were not readily accessible. This problem was resolved by differentiating between "operational control" and "assignment" of units. Basically, assignment carried the "responsibility of administration and for nonexpendable supplies for units," whereas operational control referred to "the control of units in combat, with the responsibility of tactical direction and furnishing of expendable supplies." Operational control of a unit was generally the responsibility of the senior air command conducting operations in the immediate area of the unit and significantly reduced communications and staff orders. Operational control varied with the tactical situation and could be redesignated on a daily basis, if necessary. Administrative channels, however, remained standard, regardless of the location of units. It should be pointed out that these numerous changes in tactical responsibility were detrimental to maintaining any large-scale coordination between subordinate commands, but it was also largely responsible for the ability to maintain flexibility in the deployment of forces needed for operational efficiency in the theater.

3rd Air Commando Group

- Constituted as 3rd Air Commando Group on 25 April 1944
- Activated on 1 May 1944
- Moved to the Philippines late in 1944
- Assigned to Fifth Air Force for operations with P-51, C-47, and L-5 aircraft
- Attacked Japanese airfields and installations in the Philippines, supported ground forces on Luzon
- Provided escort for missions to Formosa and the China coast, made raids on airfields and railways on Formosa, and furnished cover for convoys
- Transported personnel, dropped supplies to ground troops and guerrilla forces, evacuated casualties from front-line strips, adjusted artillery fire, and flew courier and mail routes
- Moved to the Ryukyus in August 1945
- Flew some patrols over Japan, made local liaison flights, and hauled cargo from the Philippines to Okinawa
- Moved to Japan in October 1945
- Inactivated on 25 March 1946
- Disbanded on 8 October 1948

5TH AF TACTICAL UNIT HISTORY

UNIT	1942				1943												1944												1945						
	S	O	N	D	J	F	M	A	M	J	J	A	S	O	N	D	J	F	M	A	M	J	J	A	S	O	N	D	J	F	M	A	M	J	J	A
FIGHTER GROUPS (3 SQ)																																			
35TH																																			
49TH																																			
8TH																																			
348TH																																			
475TH																																			
58TH																																			

Squadrons
3rd Fighter: 1944-1946
4th Fighter: 1944-1946
157th/159th/160th Liaison: 1944-1946
318th Troop Carrier: 1944-1946

Bases
Drew Field, FL, 1 May1944;
Lakeland, FL, 5 May 1944;
Alachua, FL, c. 20 August 1944;
Drew Field, FL, 6-24 October 1944;
Leyte, December 1944;
Mangaldan, Luzon, c. 26 January 1945;
Laoag, Luzon, April 1945;
Ie Shima, Okinawa August 1945;
Chitose, Japan, c. 27 October 1945.

Commanders
Maj. Klem Kalberer, May 1944;
Col. Arvid Olson, June 1944;
Lt.Col. Walker Mahurin, September 1945;
Lt.Col. Charles Terhune, 20 October 1945-.

Campaigns
Air Offensive, Japan;
China Defensive;
Western Pacific;
Leyte;
Luzon;
China Offensive

Decorations
Philippine Presidential Unit Citation

Insignia
None

8th Fighter Group
- Authorized on the inactive list as 8th Pursuit Group on 24 March 1923
- Activated on 1 April 1931
- Redesignated as 8th Pursuit Group (Fighter) in 1939 and 8th Pursuit Group (Interceptor) in 1941
- Trained, took part in maneuvers and reviews, and tested planes and equipment, using PB-2, P-6, P-12, P-35, P-36, P-39, and P-40 aircraft prior to WWII
- In December 1941, became part of the defense force for the New York metropolitan area. Moved to the Asiatic-Pacific Theater early in 1942
- Redesignated as 8th Fighter Group in May 1942
- Became part of 5th AF
- Equipped first with P-39s, added P-38s and P-40s in 1943, and used P-38s thereafter
- Established headquarters in Australia in March 1942, but sent detachments to New Guinea for operations
- Moved to New Guinea in September 1942 and served in combat until malaria forced the organization to withdraw to Australia in February 1943
- Resumed operations in April 1943 and served in the theater through the rest of the war. Covered Allied landings, escorted bombers, and attacked enemy airfields in New Guinea. Supported operations of the U.S. Marines at Cape Gloucester, Feb-Mar 1944

- Flew long-range escort and attack missions to Borneo, Ceram, Halmahera, and the southern Philippines;
- Provided cover for convoys, attacked enemy shipping, and won a DUC for strafing a strong Japanese naval force off Mindoro (26 December 1944)
- Covered landings at Lingayen
- Supported ground forces on Luzon
- Escorted bombers to targets on the Asiatic mainland and on Formosa
- During the last days of the war, attacked airfields and railways in Japan
- Remained in the theater after V-J Day, being based in Japan for duty with Far East Air Forces

Bases
Langley Field, VA, 1 April 1931;
Mitchel Field, NY, c. 5 November 1940-26 January 1942;
Brisbane, Australia, 6 March 1942;
Townsville, Australia, 29 July 1942;
Milne Bay, New Guinea, 18 September 1942;
Mareeba, Australia, February 1943;
Port Moresby, New Guinea, 16 May 1943;
Finschhafen, New Guinea, 23 December 1943;
Cape Gloucester, New Britain, c. 20 February1944;
Nadzab, New Guinea, 14 March 1944;
Owi, Schouten Islands, 17 June 1944;
Morotai, 19 September 1944;
San Jose, Mindoro, 20 December 1944;
Ie Shima, 6 August 1945

Commanders
Unknown: 1931-1932;
Maj. Byron Jones, 25 June 1932;
Capt. Albert Guidera, 31 March 1934;
Lt. Col. Adlai Gilkeson, 1 July 1935;
Lt. Col. William Kepner, 7 July 1938;
Lt. Col. Edward Morris, 1 February 1940;
Lt.Col. Frederic Smith, 17 January 1941;
Lt.Col. William Wise, 22 May 1942;
Lt. Col. Leonard Storm, 8 March 1943;
Lt. Col. Philip Greasley, 1 April 1943;
Lt.Col. Emmett S Davis, 18 January 1944;
Lt.Col. Philip Greasley, 28 June 1944;
Col Earl Dunham, 8 August 1944;
Lt.Col. Emmett Davis, 16 June 1945;

Squadrons

33rd Fighter Squadron (1932-1941)
35th Fighter Squadron (Black Panthers) (1932-)
Aircraft Flown: P-39, P-40, P-38
COs:
Capt. W.H. Wise: 23 April 1941
1Lt. G.B. Greene: January 1942
Capt. N.C. Morris: 2 October 1942
Capt. E.S. Davis: 7 March 1943
Maj. H.M. McClelland: 19 January 1944
Capt. L.B. Everhart: 3 October 1944 (KIA)
Capt. L.E. Witt: 13 October 1944
Capt. D.M. Leighton: May 1945 to VJ-Day

36th Fighter Squadron (Flying Fiends) (1931, 1932-)
Aircraft Flown: P-39, P-47, P-38
COs:
Lt. Hillary: 1941
Capt. J.K. McNay: 24 May 1942
Capt. R.L. Harringer: 21 November 1942
Capt. R.C. Smith: 22 December 1943
Capt. W.R. Danson: 31 December 1943 (KIA)
Capt. D.J. Campbell: 15 March 1944
Capt. K.G. Ladd: 1 September 1944 (KIA)
Capt. T.R. Huff: 15 October 1944
Capt. A.E. Hill: 16 November 1944
Capt. H.B. Grahan: 30 June to VJ-Day

80th Fighter Squadron (Headhunters) (1942-1945)
Aircraft Flown: P-400, P-39, P-38
COs:
1Lt. P.H. Greasley: 10 June 1942
Capt. I.C. Conner: 28 December 1942
Capt. C. Falletta: 4 April 1943
Capt. E. Cragg: 8 April 1943 (KIA)
Capt. J.T. Robbins: 27 December 1943
Capt. C.F. Homer: 4 October 1944
Maj. J.P. Johnson: 9 May 1945 (MIA)
Capt. R.G. Hochuli: 31 May 1945 (MIA)
Maj. J.R. Breeden: 22 August 1945 to VJ-Day

Campaigns World War II
East Indies;
Air offensive, Japan;
China Defensive;
Papua; New Guinea;
Bismarck Archipelago;
Western Pacific;
Leyte;
Luzon;
Southern Philippines.

Decorations
Distinguished Unit Citations:
Papua: September 1942-23 January 1943;
Philippine Islands: 26 December 1944.

Insignia
Shield: Azure, a chevron nebule or Crest: On a wreath of the colors (or and azure) three *fleur-de-lis* or in front of a propeller fesswise azure
Motto: Attaquez et Conquerez (Attack and Conquer). (Approved 6 September 1934)

35th Fighter Group
• Constituted as 35th Pursuit Group (Interceptor) on 22 December 1939
• Activated on 1 February 1940
• Trained with P-35, P-36, P-39, and P-40 aircraft
• Two squadrons (21st and 34th) moved to the Philippines in November 1941
• Headquarters and another Squadron (70th) sailed for Manila on 5 December, but because of the Japanese attack on Pearl Harbor they returned to the U.S., where the squadron flew some patrols
• Headquarters and the 70th Squadron sailed for Australia on 12 January 1942. Three days later, all the combat squadrons were relieved and three others, still in the U.S., were assigned

• Headquarters reached Australia in February 1942 and moved on to India
• Meanwhile, the squadrons had moved from the U.S. to Australia and were training for combat with P-39s
• Headquarters was transferred back to Australia, without personnel and equipment, in May 1942
• Redesignated as the 35th Fighter Group
• Served in combat with the Fifth Air Force, operating successively from bases in Australia, New Guinea, Owi, Morotai, and the Philippines
• First used P-38s and P-39s; equipped with P-47s late in 1943 and with P-51s in March 1945
• Helped halt the Japanese advance in Papua
• Took part in the Allied offensive that recovered the rest of New Guinea, flying protective patrols over Port Moresby, escorting bombers and transports, attacking Japanese airfields and supply lines, and providing cover for Allied landings
• In 1944, began long-range missions against enemy airfields and installations in the southern Philippines, Halmahera, and Borneo, preparatory to the U.S. invasion of the Philippines
• Beginning in January 1945, operated in support of ground forces on Luzon
• Also escorted bombers and completed some fighter sweeps to Formosa and China
• Bombed and strafed railways and airfields in Kyushu and Korea after moving to Okinawa during June 1945
• Moved to Japan in October 1945 as part of Far East Air Forces

Bases
Moffett Field, CA, 1 February 1940;
Hamilton Field, CA, 10 September 1940-5 December 1941 and 9 December 1941-12 January 1942;
Brisbane, Australia, 1 February 1942;
New Delhi, India, March 1942;
Sydney, Australia, 4 May 1942;
Port Moresby, New Guinea, 22 July 1942;
Tsili Tsili, New Guinea, 15 August 1943;
Nadzab, New Guinea, 5 October 1943;
Gusap, New Guinea, 7 February 1944;
Owi, Schouten Islands, 22 July 1944;
Morotai, 27 September 1944;
Mangaldan, Luzon, c. 20 January 1945;
Lingayen, Luzon, c. 10 April 1945;
Clark Field, Luzon, 19 April 1945;
Okinawa, 28 June 1945;
Irumagawa, Japan, October 1945.

Commanders
Maj. O.R. Strickland, 1940;
Col. George Tourtellot, 1940-unknown
Col. Richard Legg, 12 March 1942;
Lt.Col. Malcolm Moore, 26 July 1943;
Lt.Col. Edwin Doss 23 October 1943;
Lt.Col. Furlo Wagner, 12 February 1944;
Col. Edwin Doss, 4 May 1944;
Col. Harney Estes, 27 July 1945.

Squadrons

18th Fighter Squadron: (1940)
20th Fighter Squadron: (1940)
21st Fighter Squadron: (1940-1942)
34th Fighter Squadron: (1940-1942)
39th Fighter Squadron: (Flying Cobras) (1942-)
Aircraft Flown: P-400, P-39, P-38, P-51
COs:
1Lt. M. McNickle: 5 March 1941
Lt. F.R. Royal: 19 January 1942
Lt. D.J, Green: 25 March 1942
Maj. J.W. Berry: 4 April 1942
Lt. S.L. David: 4 August 1942 (acting)
Lt. F.R. Royal: 17 August 1942
Maj. G.W. Prentice: 18 September 1942
Maj. T.W. Lynch: 24 March 1943
Maj. C.W. King: 20 September 1943
Maj. H.L. Denton: 18 December 1943
Maj. R.T. Cella: 29 June 1944
Capt. L.V. Grosshuesch: 7 November 1944
Maj. B. Wedmann: July 1945
Capt. L.V. Grosshuesch: August 1945 to VJ-Day

40th Fighter Squadron: (Red Devils) (1942-)
Aircraft Flown: P-39, P-40, P-51
COs:
1Lt. S.M. Smith: 20 January 1942
Capt. R.I. Eugenes: 15 May 1942
Capt. H.J. Scandrett: 8 October 1942
Capt. M.A. Moore: 21 November 1942
Capt. T.H. Windburn: 25 April 1943
Capt. J.E. Lamphere: 10 November 1943
Capt. J.F. Herbert: 12 February 1944
Capt. J.M. Davis: 4 March 1944
Capt. R.R. Yaeger: 21 April 1944
Capt. J.R. Young: 5 May 1944
Capt. A.J. Hunter: 8 November 1944
Capt. D.L. Cherry: 8 December 1944
Capt. C.E. Dannacher: 2 June 1945 to VJ-Day

41st Fighter Squadron: (1942-)
Aircraft Flown: P-40, P-38, P-47
COs:
1Lt. G. Contello: ? (KIFA)
Capt. J.A. Wilson: 8 June 1942
Capt. E.A. Doss: 12 September 1942
Capt. A.W. Schinz: 19 October 1942 (acting)
Capt. E.A. Doss: 27 October 1942
Capt. F.W. Wagner: 6 November 1942
? F.E. Thompson: ?
Capt. F.E. Dubischer: ?
1Lt. D.V. Parsons: 15 March 1944
Capt. R.L. Dorothy: 1 December 1944
Capt. M.H. Beamer: ? 1945 to VJ-Day

42nd Fighter Squadron: (1942)
70th Fighter Squadron: (1941-1942)
Campaigns:
East Indies;
Air offensive, Japan;
China Defensive;
Papua;
New Guinea;
Bismarck Archipelago;
Western Pacific;
Leyte;
Luzon;
Ryukyus;
China Offensive.

Decorations
Distinguished Unit Citation:
Papua, 23 Jul 1942-23 Jan 1943.
Philippine Presidential Unit Citation

Insignia
Shield: Azure, a dexter cubit arm or grasping a dagger point to base gules
Motto: Attack to Defend (Approved 21 February 1941.)

49th Fighter Group
• Constituted as 49th Pursuit Group (Interceptor) on 20 November 1940
• Activated on 15 January 1941
• Trained with P-35s
• Moved to Australia, January-February 1942
• Became part of 5th Air Force
• Redesignated as the 49th Fighter Group in May 1942
• Received P-40s in Australia and, after training for a short time, provided air defense for the Northern Territory, being awarded a DUC for engaging the enemy in frequent and intense aerial combat while operating with limited materiel and facilities, March-August 1942
• Moved to New Guinea in October 1942 to help stall the Japanese drive southward from Buna to Port Moresby
• Engaged primarily in air defense of Port Moresby; also escorted bombers and transports and attacked enemy installations, supply lines, and troop concentrations in support of Allied ground forces
• Participated in the Allied offensive that pushed the Japanese back along the Buna trail
• Took part in the Battle of the Bismarck Sea (March 1943) and fought for control of the approaches to Huon Gulf
• Supported ground forces during the campaign in which the Allies eventually recovered New Guinea
• Covered landings on Noemfoor and had a part in the conquest of Biak
• After having used P-38, P-40, and P-47 aircraft, was equipped completely in September 1944 with P-38s, which were used to fly long-range escort and attack missions to Mindanao, Halmahera, Ceram, and Borneo
• Arrived in the Philippines in October 1944, shortly after the assault landings on Leyte
• Engaged enemy fighters, attacked shipping in Ormoc Bay, supported ground forces, and covered the Allied invasion of Luzon
• For intensive operations against the Japanese on Leyte, the Group was awarded a DUC
• Other missions from the Philippines included strikes against industry and transportation on Formosa and against shipping along the China coast
• Moved to Okinawa in August 1945 and to Japan in September

Bases:
Selfridge Field, MI, 15 January 1941;
Morrison Field, FL, 25 May 1941-January 1942;
Melbourne, Australia, 2 February1942;
Bankstown, Australia, 16 February 1942;
Darwin, Australia, c. 16 April 1942;
Port Moresby, New Guinea, 9 October 1942;
Dobodura, New Guinea, March 1943;
Gusap, New Guinea, 20 November 1943;
Finschhafen, New Guinea, 19 April 1944;
Hollandia, New Guinea, c. 17 May 1944;
Biak, 3 January 1944;
Tacloban, Leyte, 24 October 1944;
San Jose, Mindoro, c. 30 December 1944;
Lingayen, Luzon, c. 25 February 1945;
Okinawa, 16 August 1945;
Atsugi, Japan, 15 September 1945.

Commanders
Maj. Glenn Davasher, 16 January 1941;
Maj. John Egan, 10 February 1941;
Maj. George McCoy, 2 May 1941;
Col. Paul Wurtsmith, 11 December 1941;
Col. Donald Hutchinson, 11 November 1942;
Lt.Col Robert L Morrissey, 30 January 1943;
Col. James C Selman, July 1943;
Lt.Col. David Campbell, 25 January 1944;
Lt.Col. Furlo Wagner, 3 June 1944;
Col. George Walker, 19 July 1944;
Lt.Col. Gerald Johnson, 10 March 1945;
Lt.Col. Clay Tlce, 16 July 1945;
Lt. Col. Wallace Jordan, 4 February 1946.

Squadrons:

7th Fighter Squadron: (Screamin' Demons) (1941-)
Aircraft Flown: P-40, P-38
COs:
1Lt. R.L. Morrissey: 24 December 1941
?
?
Capt. Arland Stanton: ?
Capt. E.A. Peck: 2 September 1944
Capt. R.W. Aschenbrener: 21 February 1945
Maj. C.M. Isaccson: 17 May 1945
Maj. J.A. Watson: July 1945 to VJ-Day

8th Fighter Squadron: (Black Sheep) (1941-)
Aircraft Flown: P-40, P-38
COs:
Capt. R.D. Van Auken: 1941
Capt. A.W. Strauss: 1 April 1942
Maj. M.F. Sims: 17 April 1942
?
?
Maj. R.V. McHale: ?
Capt. C.E. Peterson: 22 May 1944
Capt. W.C. Drier: 27 August 1944
Capt. M.H. Vinzant: 22 May 1945 to VJ-Day

9th Fighter Squadron: (Flying Knights) (1941-)
Aircraft Flown: P-40, P-38, P-47
COs:
1Lt. T.J. Barrett: 16 January 1941
Capt. V.F. Pixey: 8 May 1941
Capt. J.C. Selman: 30 November 1941
Capt. B.S. Irvin: 28 August 1942
Maj. J.C. Peaslee: 1 November 1942
Maj. S.S. Woods: 22 May 1943
Maj. G.R. Johnson: 27 August 1943
Maj. W.R. Jordan: 29 January 1944
Maj. R.M. McComsay: 13 October 1944
Maj. W.R. Jordan: 31 October 1944
Capt. W.F. Williams: 1 January 1945
Capt. J.R. Petrovich: 25 January 1945 to VJ-Day

Campaigns
East Indies;
Air Offensive, Japan;
China Defensive;
Papua;
New Guinea;
Bismarck Archipelago;
Western Pacific;
Leyte;
Luzon;
China Offensive.

Decorations
Distinguished Unit Citations:
Australia, 14 March-25 August 1942,
Papua, October 1942-23 January 1943;
Philippine Islands, 27 October-7 December 1944.

Insignia
Shield: A gyronny of three gules, or and azure, a bolt of lightning, bend sinisterwise argent, in chief, a knight's helmet, winged of the last, in dexter chief, five stars (Southern Cross) argent, two on gules, and three on azure, in sinister base a covered wagon, trees and road scene, all proper
Motto: Tutor Et Ultor: Protect and Avenge

58th Fighter Group
• Constituted as 58th Pursuit Group (Interceptor) on 20 November 1940
• Activated on 15 January 1941
• Redesignated as the 58th Fighter Group in May 1942
• Used P-35, P-36, P-39, and P-40 fighters while serving as a replacement training unit for pilots until 1943. Prepared for combat with P-47s
• Moved to New Guinea, via Australia, October-December 1943
• Assigned to 5th Air Force
• Began operations in February 1944, flying protective patrols over U.S. bases and escorting on raids over New Guinea, attacked Japanese airfields and installations, and escorted convoys to the Admiralty Islands
• Moved to Noemfoor in August 1944, and until November bombed and strafed enemy airfields and installations on Ceram, Halmahera, and the Kai Islands
• After moving to the Philippines in November 1944, conducted fighter sweeps against enemy airfields, supported ground forces, and flew patrols over convoy and transport routes
• Received a DUC for strafing a Japanese naval force off Mindoro on 26 December 1944 to prevent destruction of the American base on that island

• Moved to Okinawa in July 1945 and attacked railways, airfields, and installations in Korea and Kyushu before V-J Day
• Remained in the theater after the war as part of Far East Air Forces
• Inactivated on 27 January 1946

Bases
Selfridge Field, MI, 15 January 1941;
Baton Rouge, LA, 5 October 1941;
Dale Mabry Field, FL, 4 March 1942;
Richmond AAB, VA, 16 October 1942;
Philadelphia Municipal Airport, PA, 24 October 1942;
Bradley Field, CT, c. 3 March 1943;
Green Field, RI, 28 April 1943;
Grenier Field, NH, 16 September-22 October 1943;
Sydney, Australia, 19 November 1943;
Brisbane, Australia, 21 November 1943;
Dobodura, New Guinea, 28 December 1943;
Saidor, New Guinea, c. 3 April 1944;
Noemfoor, 30 August 1944;
San Roque, Leyte, 18 November 1944;
San Jose, Mindoro, c. 30 December 1944;
Mangaldan, Luzon, 5 April 1945;
Porac, Luzon, 18 April 1945;
Okinawa, 10 July 1945;
Japan, 26 October 1945

Commanders
Capt. John Sterling: 15 January 1941-unknown;
Maj. Louis Chick: unknown;
Col. Gwen Atkinson: 8 December 1942;
Lt.Col. Edward Roddy: 12 March 1945-unknown.

Squadrons

67th Fighter Squadron: (1941-1942)
68th Fighter Squadron: (1941-1942)
69th Fighter Squadron: (1941-1946)
Aircraft Flown: P-47
COs:
Capt. J.C. Kilburn: 16 January 1941
1Lt. W.W. Korges: 8 April 1941
Capt. W.G. Ayers: 19 June 1942
Maj. I. McCall: 27 June 1942
Capt. H.J. Whiteman: 23 September 1942
Capt. C.W. Stuke: 12 December 1942
1Lt. M.M. Self: 2 February 1943
Capt. G.V. Bosenbark: 6 April 1945 (acting)
Maj. T.H. Winburn: April 1945 (ill)
Maj. S.O. Andrews: 20 May 1945 to VJ-Day

310th Fighter Squadron: (1942-1946)
Aircraft Flown: P-47
COs:
Maj. J.D. Mayden: 9 February 1942
Maj. L.W. Chick: ?
1Lt. H.M. Odren: 24 October 1942
1Lt. H.A. Tuman: 1 November 1942

Capt. J.T. Klemovitch: 10 December 1942
Capt. R.R. Bonebrake: March 1943
Maj. J.C. McClure: 1 July 1943
Maj. H.A. Tuman: 27 April 1944 to VJ-Day

311th Fighter Squadron: (1942-1946)
Aircraft Flown: P-47
COs:
Maj. C.L. Tinker: 26 September 1942
Maj. H.C. Whiteman: February 1943
Capt. H.A. Tuman: March 1943 (injured)
Maj. I.O. Carter: May 1943
Maj. H.M. Odren: 13 February 1944
Maj. J.T. Klemovitch: 18 February 1945
Maj. S.O. Benner: 27 May 1945 to VJ-Day

201st Fighter Squadron (Mexican): (1945)
Aircraft Flown: P-47
COs:
Capt. R.G. Andrade

Campaigns
American Theater;
Air Offensive, Japan;
New Guinea;
Bismarck Archipelago;
Western Pacific;
Leyte;
Luzon;
China Offensive.

Decorations
Distinguished Unit Citations:
Philippines, 26 December 1944

Insignia
Shield: Azure, on clouds in base a representation of the Greek mythological goddess Artemis with quiver and bow, in her chariot drawn by the two deer
Motto: Non Revertar Inultus: I Will Not Return Unavenged

348th Fighter Group
• Constituted as 348th Fighter Group on 24 September 1942
• Activated on 30 September 1942
• Prepared for combat with P-47s
• Moved to the Southwest Pacific, May-June 1943
• Assigned to 5th Air Force
• Operated from New Guinea and Noemfoor until November 1944
• Flew patrol and reconnaissance missions and escorted bombers to targets in New Guinea and New Britain
• Covered Allied landings and supporting ground forces on New Britain, 16-31 December 1943, (awarded a DUC)
• In 1944, began to attack airfields, installations, and shipping in western New Guinea, Ceram, and Halmahera to aid in neutralizing those areas preparatory to the U.S. invasion of the Philippines
• After moving to the Philippines in November 1944, provided cover for convoys, flew patrols, escorted bombers, attacked enemy airfields, and supported ground forces
• Attacked shipping along the China coast and escorted bombers to Formosa and the Asiatic mainland

- Moved to the Ryukyus in July 1945 and completed some escort and attack missions to Kyushu before the war ended
- Moved to Japan in October 1945 as part of Far East Air Forces
- Inactivated on 10 May 1946

Bases

Mitchel Field, NY, 30 September 1942;
Bradley Field, CT, 4 October 1942;
Westover Field, MA, 29 October 1942;
Providence, RI, c. 3 January 1943;
Westover Field, MA, 28 April-9 May 1943;
Port Moresby, New Guinea, 23 June 1943;
Finschhafen, New Guinea, 16 December 1943;
Saidor, New Guinea, 29 March 1944;
Wakde, 22 May 1944;
Noemfoor, 26 August 1944;
Leyte, 16 November 1944;
San Marcelino, Luzon, 4 February 1945;
Floridablanca, Luzon, 15 May 1945;
Ie Shima, Okinawa, 9 July 1945,
Itami, Japan, October 1945-.

Commanders

Col. Neel Kearby: October 1942;
Col. Robert Rowland: 17 November 1943;
Lt.Col. William Banks: 8 June 1945;
Maj. Walter Benz: 26 November 1945-unknown.

Squadrons

340th Fighter Squadron: (1942-1946)
Aircraft Flown: P-47
COs:
Lt. L.V. Sutter: 30 September 1942
Lt. L.H. Stevens: 27 October 1942
Capt. F. Oksala: 6 November 1942
Capt. C.H. MacDonald: 17 November 1942
Maj. H.B. Carpenter: 1 October 1943
Capt. M.R. Wiecks: 30 April 1944
Capt. M.M. Brown: ? 1944
Capt. C.W. Brown: August 1945 to VJ-Day

341st Fighter Squadron: (1942-1946)
Aircraft Flown: P-47
COs:
Maj. D.A. Campbell: 15 November 1942
Maj. J.T. Moore: 15 November 1943
Maj. S.V. Blair: 18 July 1944
Capt. M.M. Zeine: 6 October 1942
Maj. G.M. Barnes: March 1945
Maj. P. Meyer: August 1945 to VJ-Day

342nd Fighter Squadron: (1942-1946)
Aircraft Flown: P-47
COs:
Lt. W.T. Shorts: 10 October 1942
Capt. W.W. Banks: 2 November 1942
Maj. R.K. Gallagher: 26 November 1942
Maj. W.M. Banks: 18 November 1943
Maj. W.D. Dunham: 24 May 1944

Maj. W.G. Benz: 26 July 1944
Maj. E.S. Popek: March 1945 to VJ-Day

460th Fighter Squadron: (1944-1946)
Aircraft Flown: P-47
COs:
Maj. W.D. Dunham: 16 July 1944
Capt. W.O. Carter: 18 December 1944
Capt. R.C. Frost: 30 December 1944
1Lt. D.R. Searles: 22 January 1945
Maj. C.C. Albright: 19 May 1945 to VJ-Day

Campaigns

Air Offensive, Japan;
China Defensive;
New Guinea;
Bismarck Archipelago;
Western Pacific;
Leyte;
Luzon;
China Offensive.

Decorations

Distinguished Unit Citations:
New Britain, 16-31 December 1943;
Philippine Islands, 24 December 1944.
Philippine Presidential Unit Citation.

Insignia

Shield: Azure, within a bordure dimidiated, gules, hand gauntleted in armour proper, encircled with wreath of laurel, vert, grasping a torch argent, flamant proper
Motto: None until August 1951

475th Fighter Group

Activated in Australia on 14 May 1943 by special authority granted to Fifth Air Force Prior to constitution as 475th Fighter Group on 15 May 1943

- Equipped with P-38s and trained to provide long range escort for bombers during daylight raids on Japanese airfields and strongholds in the Netherlands Indies and the Bismarck Archipelago
- Moved to New Guinea and began operations in August 1943
- Missions in August 1943, when the group not only protected B-25s that were engaged in strafing attacks on airdromes at Wewak, but also destroyed a number of enemy fighter planes that attacked the formation
- Intercepted and destroyed enemy aircraft sent against American shipping in Oro Bay during mid-October 1943
- Covered landings in New Guinea, New Britain, and the Schouten Islands
- After moving to Biak in July 1944, flew escort missions and fighter sweeps to the southern Philippines, Celebes, Halmahera, and Borneo
- Moved to the Philippines in October 1944 and bombed and strafed enemy airfields and installations, escorting bombers and engaging in aerial combat during the first stages of the Allied campaign to recover the Philippines, October-December 1944
- The group flew many missions to support ground forces on Luzon during the first part of 1945
- Also flew escort missions to China and attacked railways on Formosa. Began moving to Ie Shima in August, but the war ended before the movement was completed
- Moved to Korea in September 1945 for occupation duty as part of Far East Air Forces

Bases

Amberley Field, Australia, 14 May 1943;
Dobodura, New Guinea, 14 August 1943;
Nadzab, New Guinea, 24 March 1944;
Hollandia, New Guinea, 15 May 1944;
Biak, c. 14 July 1944;
Dulag, Leyte, 28 October 1944;
San Jose, Mindoro, 5 February 1945;
Clark Field, Luzon, 28 February 1945;
Lingayen, Luzon, c. 20 April 1945;
Ie Shima, Okinawa, 8 August 1945;
Kimpo, Korea, c. 23 September 1945.

Commanders

Lt.Col. George Prentice, 21 May 1943;
Col. Charles MacDonald, 26 November 1943;
Lt.Col. Meryl Smith, August 1944;
Col. Charles MacDonald, 13 October 1944;
Lt.Col. John Loisel, 15 July 1945.

Squadrons

431st Fighter Squadron: (1943-1949)
Aircraft Flown: P-38
COs:
Maj. F.A. Nichols: 1 July 1943
Maj. V.E. Jett: 20 November 1943
Maj. T.B. McGuire: 28 April 1944 (KIA)
Capt. R.F. Cline: 23 December 1944
Maj. J. Vogel: 23 June 1945
Maj. E. Weaver: 16 July 1945 to VJ-Day

432nd Fighter Squadron: (1943-1949)
Aircraft Flown: P-38
COs:
Maj. F.D. Thomkins: June 1943
Capt. J.C. Ince: 16 January 1944 (acting)
Maj. J.S. Loisel: 22 January 1944
Capt. H.L. Condon: 4 August 1944 (KIA)
Capt. E. Summer: 2 June 1945
Maj. D. Duttack: 5 July 1945
Capt. E. Summer: 17 July 1945 (acting)
Maj. D. Duttack: 28 July 1945 to VJ-Day

433rd Fighter Squadron: (1943-1949)
Aircraft Flown: P-38
COs:
Maj. M.L. Low: 3 May 1943
Capt. D.T. Roberts: 3 October 1943 (KIA)
Maj. W.R. Lewis: 9 November 1943
Capt. C.P.M. Wilson: August 1944
Capt. C.C. Wire: December 1944
Maj. J. Wilson: May 1945
Capt. W.F. Haning: July 1945 to VJ-Day

Campaigns

China Defensive;
New Guinea;
Bismarck Archipelago;
Western Pacific;
Leyte;
Luzon;
China Offensive.

Decorations

Distinguished Unit Citations:
New Guinea, 18 and 21 August 1943;
New Guinea, 15 and 17 October 1943;
Philippine Islands 25 October-25 December 1944.
Philippine Presidential Unit Citation.

Insignia

Shield: Azure over crossbow or, string argent, bow striped red and silver; a lightning bolt gules, highlighted of the third, surmounting the stock; a pair of wings argent, issuing from the end of the stock; between four seven-pointed stars and one five-pointed star, spattered over the field; all within a diminutive border per pale argent and gules
Motto: None until November 1956

5th Fighter Command Unit Victory Statistics

USAAF Top Squadrons

Total V.	FS	FG	AF	Aces #
295	353	354	9	18
254	**9**	**49**	**5**	**12**
230	62	56	8	18
221.5	62	56	8	11
221	**431**	**475**	**5**	**16**
213	**80**	**8**	**5**	**15**
212	317	325	12/15	15
211.5	364	357	8	17
207	**8**	**49**	**5**	**13**
201	96	82	12/15	13
200.7	334	4	8	11

USAAF Top Groups

Total V.	FG	AF	Aces #
667	**49**	**5**	**34**
664.5	56	8	41
637	354	9	39
595.5	357	8	41
583	31	12/15	32
555.2	4	8	32
553	82	12/15	26
552	**475**	**5**	**34**
540	325	12/15	26
519	23	14	29

2

Japanese Air Forces Flying Units

General

Japan did not have an independent Air Force, as the Japanese Army Air Force (JAAF) was an integral part of the Army, while the Japanese Naval Air Force (JNAF) was organized independently as an integral part of the Navy. The Emperor, through Imperial Headquarters, controlled the Japanese Army Air Force through three organizations: the Army General Staff, War Ministry, and the Inspector General of Aviation. The Japanese Navy Air Force was also controlled by the Emperor through Imperial Headquarters via three organizations: the Navy General Staff, Navy Ministry, and Naval Aviation Headquarters.

Flying Units of the Japanese Army Air Force (JAAF)

Before WWI, the basic unit of the Army Air Service was the Air Battalion (*Koku Daitai*), consisting of two Squadrons (*Chutai*) with nine aircraft each, plus three reserve aircraft and three for use by the Headquarters for a total of 27 aircraft per Air Battalion. The officer commanding the *Chutai* was the *Chutaicho*, who was usually a Captain. The Commander's aircraft frequently had distinguishing tail markings, often partly or totally scarlet, red, orange, or yellow.

In the reorganization of 1927, the Air Regiment (Hiko Rentai) was created, each consisting of two Battalions, with each Battalion consisting of up to four Squadrons. Each Air Regiment was a mixed purpose unit, consisting of an assortment of fighter and reconnaissance squadrons.

With the start of the Second Sino-Japanese War in 1937, operational conditions there favored the employment of many small units, resulting in the creation of many independent Air Battalions (Dokuritsu Hiko Daitai) or even Independent Squadrons (Dokuritsu Hiko Chutai), each with its own distinctive markings.

In August 1938, a complete reorganization of the Army Air Service resulted in the creation of the Air Combat Group (Hiko Sentai), which replaced all of the former Air Battalions and Air Regiments. Each Air Combat Group was a single-role unit, typically consisting of three Squadrons divided into three Flights (Shotai) of three aircraft each. Together with reserve aircraft and the Headquarters Flight, an Air Combat Group generally had 45 fighters, or up to 30 bombers or reconnaissance aircraft. Two or more Air Combat Groups formed an Air Division (Hikodan) which, together with Base and Support Units and a number of Independent Squadrons, formed an Air Corps (Hiko Shudan). The flying units of the JAAF were organized similarly to those of the Allied air forces.

Air Armies

The JAAF began the war with no Command higher than an Air Division (*Hikoshidan*). It was not until 1942, when Japan reached the maximum expansion of its Empire and these captured territories had to be defended that Air Armies

JAAF Organization Chart

were formed. In Summer 1942, the JAAF was organized into its first three Air Armies, called *Kokugun*. In early 1943, the Fourth Air Army was established in New Guinea and the Solomons, while the Fifth Air Army was formed in Nanking in late 1943. The Sixth Air Army was formed to cover Taiwan and Okinawa in late 1944.

The Air Armies

1st Air Army: HQ Tokyo, basing in the Kanto Plain covering the Japanese Home Islands, Taiwan, Korea, Chishima (Kurile Islands), and Karafuto (Sakhalin Island)

2nd Air Army: HQ Hsinking, covering Manchukuo (Manchuria)

3rd Air Army: HQ Singapore, covering Southeast Asia

4th Air Army: HQ Rabaul, covering the Solomon Islands, New Guinea, and the Celebes

5th Air Army: HQ Nanking, covering Japanese-occupied portions of southern and eastern China.

6th Air Army: HQ Kyushu, covering Taiwan and Okinawa

The Air Armies in Japan and Manchuria were different from those located in active combat theaters. They were to be available for the "defense of the Empire" and were also to form a reserve air force which was trained or in training, from which the Air Armies in China and the South Pacific could be reinforced.

Air Army Headquarters were responsible for and were to cooperate with the local Area Army Headquarters for the direction of air operations, training, and to ensure the flow of equipment, supplies, and personnel to wherever they were needed.

Air Divisions

The Air Division (Hikoshidan) was the largest Air Army tactical organization and implemented operational and administrative control over subordinate air units in its command. The uniform distribution of Air Divisions in their respective Air Division territories did not continue for long, as two Air Divisions from Manchuria transferred to the Philippines in Summer 1944 in anticipation of the Allied invasion.

Air Brigades (Wings)

The Air Brigade (*Hikodan*), subordinate to the Air Division, was formed to conduct the tactical employment of Army flying units. Three or four Fighter Regiments and a Reconnaissance Squadron were assigned to an Air Brigade Headquarters. Also, there was a Mixed Medium Bomber Air Brigade or a Mixed Light Bomber Air Brigade, both comprised of one or two Bomber Regiments protected by one or two Fighter Regiments. There were usually two Air Brigades attached to a single Air Division. The Air Brigade was a highly mobile, operational organization with a small Headquarters staff which was mainly concerned with tactical issues. Operations of the Air Brigade included close support of ground forces, fighter bombing, interception of enemy aircraft, protection of ports, airfields, and other strategic targets, and attacks on enemy airfields and shipping.

Flying Regiments, Squadrons, and Flights

Most JAAF air operations were carried out by a Flying Regiment (*Hikosentai*) with a strength of 27, 37, 42, or 49 aircraft, depending on the type of aircraft operated and the location. Flying Regiments were identified by numbers 1 to 98 (with a few in the 100s and 200s). There were five types of Flying Regiments assigned according to their equipment and function:

Type of Regiment	Type of Aircraft	# of A/C	# Personnel
Fighter (1 Engine)	Oscar, Tojo, Tony, Frank	42 or 49	400
Fighter (2 Engines)	Nick	42 or 49	425
Light Bomber	Lily	27 or 42	460
Medium Bomber	Sally, Helen, Peggy	27 or 37	600
Reconnaissance	Sonia, Dinah	18 or 27	360

Fighter Regiments

Fighter Regiments made up approximately 50% of JAAF, and most were equipped with single-engine fighters. The usual strength of each Air Brigade was three or four Fighter Regiments (*Hikosentais*). A Fighter Regiment would have approximately 400 officers and men. The Regiment CO commanded a Headquarters Platoon of 50 men. The *Hikosentai*, or simply *Sentai*, was the basic operational unit of the JAAF, composed of three or more Squadrons called *Chutais*. *Sentais* were equipped with between 27 and 49 aircraft, with each Squadron comprising roughly 16 aircraft and a similar number of pilots, plus a Maintenance and Repair Unit composed of approximately 100 men. Of the 16 pilots, only three or four were commissioned officers. The Flight (*Shotai*) was the smallest flying unit, usually consisting of three aircraft. However, as the war evolved, it was found that the odd man in a three-fighter flight usually became separated in combat and would be shot down. The Japanese attempted to adopt the Allied two-element Finger Four formation and added a fighter to the *Shotai*.

Bomber Regiments

Light and Medium Bomber Regiments were similarly organized to Fighter Regiments, with a Headquarters Platoon and three Squadrons of nine of 12 aircraft in each Squadron and a Maintenance and Repair Unit.

Reconnaissance Regiments

Reconnaissance Regiments were generally assigned to the Headquarters responsible for planning their operations (e.g., Air Brigades, Air Divisions, or an Air Army). The Reconnaissance Regiments usually consisted of two Squadrons of 18 aircraft (sometimes three Squadrons of 27 aircraft).

Other Units of the JAAF

Independent Air Units or Air Companies (*Dokuritsu Hikotai* or *Hikochutai*) Independent Air Units were attached either to Air Armies or to the Headquarters of an Air Division and were detailed for duties such as long range reconnaissance, meteorological flights, army cooperation, and antisubmarine patrol.

Direct-Cooperation Air Units (Chokkyo Hikotai)

The Direct-Cooperation Air Unit operated either in support of ground forces or as a liaison.

Air Intelligence Regiment or Unit (Koku Joho Rentai or Tai)

These Air Intelligence organizations were attached to an Air Division, with detachments in forward areas engaged in collecting, evaluating, and disseminating intelligence, as well as reporting on weather.

JAAF Unit Designations and Equivalents

Japanese	English Translation	Equivalent
Hentai	Air Section	Flight
Hiko Chutai	Air Company	Squadron
Hiko Sentai	Air Regiment	Group
Hikodan	Air Brigade	Wing or Division
Hiko Shidan	Air Division	Numbered Air Force
Kokugun	Air Army	Theater or Allied Air Force

In April 1944, another reorganization of the Japanese Army Air Service occurred. Maintenance and Ground Service Units—formerly a separate command—were merged into the Air Combat Group (Hikosentai). The flying Squadrons of the Air Combat Group were redesignated as Attack Units (Kogekitai) and the Ground Units were designated Maintenance Units (Seibutai). Other changes in the concluding period of the war were the formation of "Special Attack Units" and "Air-Shaking Units," which were transitory units with their own names (often taken from Japanese mythology or history) and markings. These units were part of existing Squadrons, but were specifically designated and trained with the mission of air-to-air

ramming of Allied bombers using fighters with their armaments removed and their airframes reinforced. In the final phase of the war, the Special Attack Units evolved into dedicated suicide units for Kamikaze missions. Approximately 170 of these units were created (57 by the Instructor Air Division). These units were equipped with 12 aircraft each and eventually these suicide units comprised about 2,000 aircraft.

The final JAAF reorganization took place during preparation for Operation Ketsu-Go (the defense of the Home Islands in 1945), when all the Air Armies were combined under a centralized command.

JAAF Air Strength
In 1940, the Japanese Army Air Service consisted of the following: 33,000 personnel; more than 1,600 aircraft (including 1,375 first line combat aircraft) organized into 86 Squadrons; 36 fighters; 28 light bombers; and 22 medium bombers.

In mid-Summer 1944, JAAF strength was about 2,000 front line aircraft organized into 75 Flying Regiments grouped into 25 Air Brigades, making up 10 Air Divisions in five Air Armies. Japan's total military strength in August 1945 was 6,095,000, including 676,863 in the Army Air Service.

Flying Units of the Japanese Naval Air Force (JNAF)
The Imperial Japanese Naval Air Force was controlled by the Navy Staff of the Imperial Japanese Navy and the Navy Ministry. The flying units of the JNAF (*Dai-Nippon Teikoku Kaigun Koukuutai*) were organized much like their Allied counterparts: the Royal Navy's Fleet Air Arm (FAA) and the U.S. Navy's Naval Aviation branch. The Imperial Japanese Navy Aviation Bureau (*Kaigun Koku Hombu*) of the Ministry of the Navy of Japan was responsible for development and training.

Air Fleet and Base Air Forces
Air Fleets were Air Flotillas grouped together, commanded by Rear Admirals of the Air Fleet HQ. Base Forces (*Konkyochitai*) were formed as a system of Pacific naval bases to defend the Empire.

Air Flotillas
Air Flotillas were usually composed of three or four Air Groups (and rarely from six to ten), the number depending on its location and expected operational requirements. Each Air Group in an Air Flotilla was equipped with aircraft of one type, so that one could provide fighters, another reconnaissance, another dive bomber, etc., thus forming a mixed tactical force with great flexibility and strength. About two-thirds of Air Flotillas were land-based and only 5% were carrier-based, while 10-15% were attached to surface fleets and 15-20% were assigned in Japan.

Air Group (Kokutai)
The working component of the JNAF was the Air Group (*Kokutai*; later called *Koku Sentai*) as an equivalent to the JAAF *Hiko Sentai*. There were about 90 Air Groups within the JNAF and depending on the size of the unit, these controlled between 36-64 (or more) aircraft. Air Groups

---

Imperial Japanese Army Air Force Deployment:
Kokugan = Air Army
Hikoshidan = Air Division
Hikodan = Air Brigade or Regiment
Sentai = Btn?
Hikotai = Air Btn?
Chutai = Squadron

1st Kokugan	Home Islands and Manchuria		
	1st Hikoshidan: 17,18,19, 20 Hikodans		
2nd Kokugan	Manchukuo		
	2nd Hikoshidan: 2, 6, 7, 8 Hikodans		
	4th Hikoshidan: 4, 9, 10, 13 Hikodans		
	15th & 28th Doritsu Hikotai (4 independent Chutais)		
	2nd Sentai (strategic recon)		
3rd Kokugan	Southern Front and China:		
	Burma:	4th Hikodan + 83rd Hikotai (3 sentai), including:	
		• 64th Sentai in Ki.43 II	
		• 13th Sentai in Ki.45 Toryu	
		• 77th Sentai in Ki.61?	
	Malaya:	7th Hikodan (3 Sentai + 3 transport Chutai)	
	Java:	3 Sentai + 1 Chutai of 3rd Hikodan	
	Sumatra:	2 Sentai of the 12th Hikodan	
	Indochina:	2 Sentai (1 ftr, 1 bombr?) and 2 transport Chutai	
	Phillipines:	3 Sentai	
	China:	3rd Hikoshidan w/8 Sentai (includes 25th, 33rd, 54th and 62nd)	
	New Guinea/ Rabaul	(Dec) 6th Hikoshidan (110 a/c, mostly Ki.43 & Ki.48). Later transferred to the 4th Kokugan	
4th Kokugan (Aug-43)	NewGuinea	**6th Hikoshidan**	**7th Hikoshidan**
		1st Sentai (Ki.43-II-Ko) Wewak	14th Hikodan Hollandia
		11th Sentai (Ki.43-II-Ko)	
		13th Sentai (Ki.43-II-Ko) Wewak?	
		24th Sentai (Ki.43-II-Ko) Wewak?	
		59th Sentai (Ki.43-II-Ko) But	
		68th Sentai (Ki.61-I) Wewak	
		77th Sentai (Ki.61-I)	
		78th Sentai (Ki.43-II-Ko + Ki.61) Wewak	
		244th Sentai (ftr)	
		248th Sentai (ftr)	
	(Oct-44)	Philippines	237 aircraft / 83 Sentai (fighters, including 24th Sentai (withdrawn from New Guinea Oct-43) 200th Sentai (with Ki.84 new unit in Oct-44)

JAAF Deployment 1

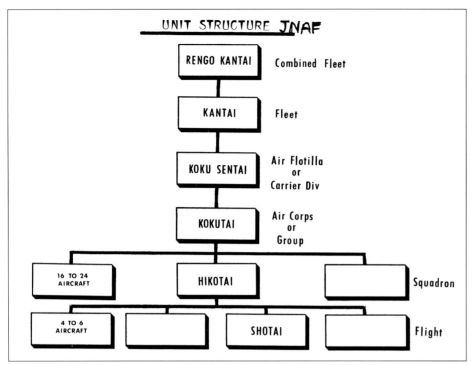

UNIT STRUCTURE JNAF

RENGO KANTAI — Combined Fleet

KANTAI — Fleet

KOKU SENTAI — Air Flotilla or Carrier Div

KOKUTAI — Air Corps or Group

16 TO 24 AIRCRAFT — HIKOTAI — Squadron

4 TO 6 AIRCRAFT — SHOTAI — Flight

JAAF Deployment 2

Air Group Identification

Naval Air Groups 101 to 199: Night Fighter Groups, Reconnaissance Aircraft Groups.
Naval Air Groups 201 to 299: Carrier-borne Fighter Groups.
Naval Air Groups 301 to 399: Fighter Interceptor Groups.
Naval Air Groups 401 to 499: Floatplane Groups.
Naval Air Groups 501 to 599: Carrier-borne Dive Bomber Groups and Carrier-borne Torpedo Bomber Groups.
Naval Air Groups 601 to 699: Carrier Air Groups, Submarine-launched Floatplane Groups.
Naval Air Groups 701 to 799: Land-based Bomber Groups, Land-based Torpedo Bomber Groups.
Naval Air Groups 801 to 899: Flying Boat Groups.
Naval Air Groups 901 to 999: Maritime Patrol Aircraft (Maritime Escort) Groups.
Naval Air Groups 1001 to 1099: Military Airlift Groups.

Unattached Air Groups

There were 40-50 Air Groups not attached to Air Flotillas or Carrier Divisions that acted as a "Coastal Command" for Japanese Homeland waters. They were equipped with torpedo bombers, float planes, fighters, or a mixture of the three. They were to provide escort for convoys, anti-submarine patrols, intercept enemy reconnaissance aircraft, and be the main naval and air forces to engage a major enemy attack on Japan.

tended to have a principal base and send detachments to other areas that required aerial support. Each Air Group was comprised of a flying unit and a corresponding ground component which was adequate in strength to administer an airfield or carrier. An Air Group varied in size depending on its aircraft complement. For instance, a medium bomber Air Group could have 84 bombers and 2,000 personnel and would be capable of operating independently for long periods if its supplies and replacements were assured.

Air Attack Force

The Air Attack Force consisted of the flying units of the Air Groups in the Air Flotilla that were grouped into this flexible fighting force. The composition of the Air Attack Force varied according to the operation, which may require a fighter *Hikotai* or another operation which may require a bomber *Hikotai*, or perhaps a combination of fighter and bomber *Hikotai*.

Carrier Division (CarDivs)

Each Carrier Division included one Air Flotilla, which was to execute a variety of tasks carried out by an assortment of aircraft. All CarDivs were placed under the Third Fleet, which combined with the Second Fleet (Battleships), while the First Mobile Fleet was the main Navy striking force.

Naval Air Group Identification

Air Groups were either identified by names or numbers. Named Groups were associated with a particular air command or base: Yokosuka, Chitose (201st), Tainan (251st), 6th (204th). With a few exceptions, such as the Tainan Air Group, most units that went overseas discontinued their names and were given number designations, such as the Kanoya Air Group, which became the 253rd Air Group. Air Groups with numbers between 200 and 399 were fighter units and float plane units were numbered between 400 and 499, while those in the 600 to 699 range controlled a mix of aircraft. Carriers were too small to accommodate entire Air Groups, so the units on board took their names from the carrier they were deployed to, such as the Akaga Fighter Squadron.

Daitai/Hikotai (Squadrons)

Before early 1944, there was only one *Daitai* of 18 to 27 aircraft for each major aircraft type in the Air Group. In early 1944, the Air Groups were reorganized with two or three numbered *Hikotai* which could operate the same type of aircraft. Each Naval Air Group consisted of several Squadrons (*Hikotai*) of nine, 12, or 16 aircraft. This was the main IJN Air Service combat unit and was equivalent to a *Chutai* in the JAAF. There were usually four Flights/Sections (*Shotai*) in each *Hikotai*, and each Section had three or four aircraft; by mid-1944, it was common for a *Shotai* to have four instead of three aircraft.

Unlike many of their Allied opposite numbers, the majority of Japanese pilots were not officers, but enlisted men and non-commissioned officers. While a Squadron could be commanded by a Lieutenant (jg), it could also be commanded by a Warrant Officer, or even an experienced Chief Petty Officer. The smallest operational unit in the Squadron was the Flight (*Shotai*), which consisted of between three and four aircraft, and four flights usually comprised the Squadron. Initially, a Flight consisted of three aircraft, but in 1943, Lt. Zenjiro Miyano was the first to effectively duplicate and refine the American four-fighter Flight (Finger Four) formation. Positions one and three were flown by veterans, while positions two and four were flown by rookies. This method gave the new pilot a better survival rate while learning valuable combat skills from his leader. By 1944, the three-fighter Flight had been generally abandoned, as it was found that the third man in the Flight often became separated or shot down.

4th Kokugan in New Guinea

Jun 43 = replacements of about 60 a/c per month

	6th Hikoshidan	7th Hikoshidan
Fighters	180	
Bombers	108	
Recon	36	
	250 operational at the Wewak complex	84 total

6th Hikoshidan in New Guinea:

Makes up bulk of 4th Air Army in New Guinea

Oct-43			Feb-44	
Fighters	248th Sentai	30/32 Ki.43-I (some II)	63rd, 33rd, 77th Sentai arrive with
	13th Sentai	~15 Ki.43	Ki.43-II
	59th Sentai	~25 Ki.43	59th Sentai leaves
	68th Sentai	10/12 Ki.61	
Assault	26th Sentai	27 Ki.51	
LR	10th Sentai	7/10 Ki.46-I	
Recon	76th Dokuritsu Chutai +another independent sqdn		
SR Recon	1 SR recond sqdn	~3 Ki.51	
Bomber	208th Sentai	10-15 Ki.48	
	7th Sentai	9 Ki.49	
	9th Sentai	6-8 Ki.49	
	14th Sentai (withdrawn mid-Nov-43)	9 Ki.21-II	

Japanese Air Strength in the Philippines: Oct-44

The Philippines had suffered strong carrier raids in Sep-44. Just before the Invasion of Leyte, Japanese air strength in the central Pacific was (approximately)

Area	Unit	Aircraft	Fighters	Types
Philippines 19 airfields on Luzon, 5-8 near Leyte, 20 more on Negros, Oebu, Mindanoa	5th Base Air Force: 4th Kokugan	203 237	115 83	mostly A6M including Ki.43, Ki.45, Ki.61, Ki.84
Formosa to southern Kyushu 11 naval air fields, 2 Seaplane bases	6th Base Air Force (added 11-14 Oct)	737 +688	223 +~60	Includes 83 bombers from T-buntai, 172 carrier aircraft.

11th Air Fleet Approximate Strengths

Plus Feb 42 – Feb-44 replacement rate was about 50 IJN a/c per month – 40 ftrs/10 bombers – but op losses took some of these before they fly across the Pacific

Jan-July 43	Oct-43
150-200 a/c at Rabaul 50-100 at Lae and Gasmata Attacks from Bettys nearly ceased due to losses over Guadalcanal	240 a/c at Rabaul Most Zeros, with many tactical (carrier) bombers. At June, say 230 fighters and 75 tactical bombers down Solomons, but by Oct, many were gone.
+ 75-100 IJA at Rabaul	50a/c at Gasmata

Chutai (Division)

Pre-1944 there were nine aircraft per Chutai and after the reorganization there were eight.

Shotai (Flights/Sections)

Each Shotai had three aircraft pre-early 1944 and four afterward to fly the Finger Four type formation.

Buntai (Element/Pair)

After the establishment of the Finger Four formation during early 1944, there were two *Buntai* in each *Shotai*.

Eleventh Air Fleet and Land-based Air Fleets

Land-based aircraft provided the majority of Japan's naval aviation until the beginning of WWII, so the JNAF also maintained a shore-based system of Naval Air Fleets (*Koku Kantai*) and Area Air Fleets (*Homen Kantai*) containing mostly twin-engine bombers and seaplanes.

JNAF Air Strength

JNAF Aircraft strength in 1941 comprised 3,089 combat aircraft of all types and 370 trainers. There were 1,830 first line aircraft, including: 660 fighters (including 350 Zeros); 330 Carrier-based strike aircraft; 240 land-based twin-engine bombers; and 520 seaplanes (including fighters and reconnaissance) and flying boats.

In mid-Summer 1944, the JNAF had about 2,700 front line aircraft organized into 25 named Air Groups and 65 numbered Air Groups. The named Air Groups (with one or two exceptions) were in the Empire, and were to form a defensive screen for the Home Islands, while the numbered Air Groups (about 45) were organized into 11 Air Flotillas which were organized into seven Air Fleets. Five of the numbered Air Groups belonged to the Carrier Divisions and nine were attached to surface fleets. Portions of four Air Groups were attached to Base Forces. From 16 December 1941 to 20 March 1945, IJN aviation casualties killed were 14,242 aircrew and 1,579 officers.

PART 3:
Aircraft of the Combatants

1
Fifth Fighter Command Aircraft

Bell P-39 Airacobra

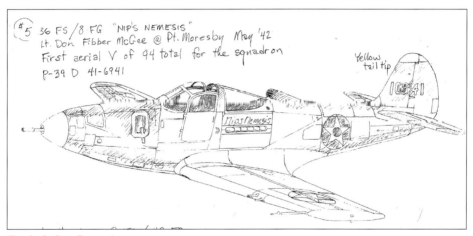

#5 36 FS/8 FG "NIP'S NEMESIS"
Lt. Don Fibber McGee @ Pt. Moresby May '42
First aerial V of 94 total for the squadron
P-39 D 41-6941

Yellow tail tip

(Drawing by Steve Ferguson)

After less than three years in business, the Bell Aircraft Company presented its XP-39 on 6 April 1938 as a high-altitude bomber interceptor that could remain beyond the enemy bomber's defensive fire and lob 37mm cannon shells at it. The aircraft was a departure from the conventional fighter configuration, as Bell designer Robert J. Woods mounted the 1,150hp Allison V-1710 engine below and behind the cockpit, amidships near the center of gravity. This engine placement allowed a smaller nose arrangement, provided improved handling and maneuverability, and permitted the placement of the armament in its most advantageous position, at the centerline of the fighter. However, the disadvantage of this engine placement was that connection of the propeller to the engine was via a shaft coupled to a gearbox located in the nose. Also, engine air cooling was provided through scoops located on the sides of the fuselage (later on the wing leading edge). Other unique features were that it was the first AAC single-engine fighter to employ a tricycle landing gear and automobile-type cockpit doors.

The P-39 prototypes were very small for an American fighter and had high wing loading, which gave them relatively high speeds at all altitudes and good agility; it was theoretically considered one of the most advanced aircraft in the world. The first test flights were performed using a supercharged engine giving the prototype a performance of nearly 400mph at 20,000 feet, but these tests revealed that some modifications were required. The evaluation lot of 13 YP-39s for service testing was contracted at the end of April 1938, but these fighters were ordered without superchargers, which would be a decision that would change the combat potential of the P-39. On 10 August 1939, the AAC placed an order for 80 Bell P-45 Airacobras (this identification was changed to the P-39C).

The C models were equipped with modifications that added to the fighter's weight and denigrated performance. These modifications and the lack of a supercharger resulted in a lower rated engine that drove a heavier gross weight fighter, causing its performance to decline to less than 370mph at only 13,500 feet. P-39 development continued because the impressive armament of two .30 caliber and two .50 caliber machine guns and a 37mm cannon placed in the centerline, which was in the engineless nose. Only 20 Cs were produced, while the remaining 60 were converted to the D model. But by the time it came into inventory in early 1941, much of the P-39's early potential had disappeared and the operational P-39D showed little similarity to the prototype.

The P-39D differed from the P-39C primarily in having even heavier armament: four wing-mounted .30 caliber machine guns with 1,000 rounds per gun (rpg), two fuselage-mounted .50 caliber machine guns with 200rpg, plus the 37mm cannon (with increased ammunition capacity of 30 rounds). Bulletproof windshield panels were included and some armor protection for the pilot was provided, adding 245 pounds to the weight of the aircraft. Self-sealing fuel tanks were introduced which reduced internal fuel capacity from 141.5 gallons to 100 gallons. This internal fuel could be supplemented by a 72-gallon drop tank carried under the fuselage. In place of the drop tank, a 300 or 600-pound bomb could be carried. A different Curtiss Electric propeller was mounted, the fuselage length was increased, and a very small dorsal fin was added just forward of the rudder. These modifications caused the climb and altitude performance to diminish, as the maximum speed at 15,000 feet fell to 360mph. With the high altitude performance now considered to be mediocre, the AAC relegated the heavily-armed fighter for use in a low altitude ground support role. The initial batch of Ds was contracted by the French, but was assumed by the British Purchasing Commission in 1940 after France fell to the Germans. The first P-39s designated as the P-400, which was equipped with a 20mm cannon, arrived in England in July 1941 and became operational in October with the RAF. Without superchargers, these aircraft were limited to ground support duties and the RAF withdrew them from service, with the remainder turned over to the AAC for training purposes. Once America entered the war, these P-400s were pressed into combat. A additional 863 Ds were built and used in a ground support role, as the V-1710-35 engine performed best under 10,000 feet.

The D through M models differed mainly in engine power rating and armament: E (three test models), F (229 produced), G (1,800 to K, L, M, and N), J (25), K (210), L (250), M (240), N (2,095), and Q (4,905). There were no H, I, O, or P models. The N and Q were similarly powered, with the Q being somewhat faster and armed with .50s instead of .30s. Production of the P-39Q finally terminated in August 1944, with most delivered to the Soviet Union. Some 4,758 N and Q models were sent to Russia under Lend-Lease, with only a few serving with American units. These aircraft performed well on the Eastern Front in a ground support role for the Soviets between 1942-45. A total of 9,558 Airacobras were produced and would give rise to the P-63 Kingcobra (1,725 As and 1,227 Cs built), but the much improved P-63s did not see U.S. service.

As the months went by, ground support became increasingly important in New Guinea, and the P-39 proved well suited to that task. In time, the 37mm cannon proved more reliable and the Airacobra was a good aircraft for attacking the multitude of small ships and barges that the Japanese became increasingly dependent upon for supplies. The Airacobra reached its maximum usage by the AAF in early 1944, with over 2,100 in service, but after this they were quickly replaced by P-38s, P-47s, and P-51s. By April 1944, the last 5FC P-39 squadrons in the SWPA (the 82nd and 110th Tactical Reconnaissance Squadrons) had transitioned to the P-51. Thereafter, P-39Qs were flown at training bases in the United States until the end of the war.

Bell P-39D Airacobra Specifications

Engine	1,350hp Allison V-1710-63 Inline
Weight	(Empty/Loaded/Maximum): 5,968lbs-7,600lbs-8,052lbs
Length	30.2 feet
Wing Span	34 feet
Wing Area	213 square feet
Wing Loading	(Empty/Loaded/Maximum): 28.0lbs/sqft-35.6lbs/sqft-37.8lbs/sqft

Armament	4x.30 caliber Browning MG and 2x.50 caliber Browning MG or 4x.30 caliber Browning MG and 1x37mm M4 cannon
Bomb Load	1 bomb up to 500lbs
Maximum Speed	320mph
Full Flaps Speed	115mph
Climb	1,000 to 5,000 feet: 52 seconds 5,000 to 10,000 feet: 84 seconds 10,000 to 15,000 feet: 84 seconds
Maximum Diving Speed	490 mph

P-39 Described

Cockpit

The cockpit of the P-39 was unusual, in that it was small and had a two automobile-type door entrance and exit doors with roll-down laminated glass windows. The cockpit was designed for pilots under five feet eight inches tall (160 pounds; later 200 pounds) wearing a parachute. The cockpit was entered on the starboard side with the engine running and a hand hold was provided for the pilot to pull himself up onto the wing, but there was no other assistance until the door was reached. Entry into the cockpit was also difficult, as the roof was low and did not open, and pilots said that three hands would have been helpful; two to get into the cockpit and one to hold the door open. While exiting the aircraft on the ground was not particularly difficult, an emergency bail out in the air exposed the pilot to hitting the tailplane. Early models had problems with smoke and fumes from the nose-mounted machine guns and cannon entering the cockpit. The gun charging handles were placed too low and required too much force to operate, and the pilots had to lean over to use them, diverting them from looking around outside. Visibility was considered good, but visibility forward was interrupted by the metal top of the bulletproof windscreen and the metal frame of the cockpit top. The canopy was a precursor of the full-blown canopy. The metal bucket seat was not adjustable and the seat belt was attached to the seat by a roller mechanism. A relief tube was located under the right side of the seat, the first aid kit on the left hand cabin door, a signal light on the right hand door, and a flashlight on the left hand wall. Two constant flow heating and cooling ducts were located on the cockpit floor behind the pilot and the temperature was controlled by two butterfly flaps operated from handles at the right of the seat.

Pilot Protection

P-39 pilot armor protection consisted of:
1) Cockpit forward fume-tight bulkhead 0.625 inch armor plate
2) Lower windshield non-magnetic 7mm armor plate
3) Windshield armored 1.5 inch glass located from the gunsight mount to the top of the windshield frame.
4) Aft armored 2.5 inch glass located in the curve of the fuselage just aft of the pilot, allowing the pilot view to the rear.
5) Two pieces of aft 0.25 inch armor plate bolted to the bulkhead just aft of the pilot.

Armament

A 37mm cannon—or a 20 mm cannon on export models—was located on the aircraft centerline, with the barrel projecting through the reduction gearbox and propeller hub. Two .50 caliber M-2 machine guns were located

P-39Q Cockpit (NMUSAF)

P-39 Armament 1: P-39 Nose Armament: 37mm on the P-39 (shown) or 20mm on the P-400. (AAF)

in the forward fuselage just ahead of the pilot and were synchronized to fire through the propeller arc. Wing armament of two .30 caliber machine guns on each side was found on all early models through the N model. Q model wing gun installation was usually replaced with a single external underwing pod-mounted .50 caliber machine gun on each side, but on some types all wing armament was removed.

Cannon and wing guns were manually charged by pulling charging handles in the cockpit. The 37mm cannon was loaded on the ground by pulling the charging handle and the loading handle once, which put a live round into the chamber. If the guns jammed in the air, both handles were pulled once more. The cockpit handles were connected to the gun by direct mechanical linkage. The .30 caliber wing gun charging system comprised of mechanical linkage and cables running from the wing leading edge section, then aft to the gun breeches. The .50 caliber fuselage guns projected aft into the cockpit, making the gun charging levers directly accessible to the pilot. These guns were charged by pulling the operating handles completely rearward. The .50 caliber nose guns in later Airacobra models were equipped with impulse-type synchronizer and flame-suppressor blast tubes. Exhaust louvers were located in the gun compartment cowl to evacuate fumes. In the late models, .50 caliber guns were installed in wing pods and were manually charged from the outside before takeoff.

All guns were fired electrically by solenoids actuated by two firing switches on the control stick. The machine guns were fired by a trigger on the stick forward section and the cannon was fired by a button on top. Toggle

switches would fire selected machine guns. If a gun jammed the others would continue to operate.

The 30-round 37mm cannon magazine was an oval section endless belt type installed around the front machine gun barrels and an ejection compartment was provided for the links and cases. Each .50 caliber nose gun had a separate 200-round ammunition case with expended links and cases deposited into ejection chutes leading into a triangular space in the outer fuselage.

Models with two .30 caliber wing guns had an ammunition box located outboard of the guns between front and rear spars. The box capacity was 1,000 rounds, 700 rounds of which was considered alternate load. Wing gun ejection chutes dropped the links inboard, while the cases dropped directly down. Four small doors on each lower wing surface ejected their contents outside. The .50 caliber guns under the wings of late models were provided with 300 rounds of ammunition per gun.

A 500 or 600 pound bomb could be carried under the fuselage as an alternate to a fuel drop tank. A Type-B Bomb Shackle was installed on the lower surface of the wing center section and included a Spring-loaded hook device which released the bomb automatically when the bomb release handle in the cockpit (located at the left side of the instrument panel) was pulled up and aft. The bomb was armed by an armed/safe lever in the cockpit.

Engine, Propeller, and Fuel Tanks
The placement of the 1,100-1,300hp Allison V-1710 liquid-cooled 12-cylinder engine was the most unusual of any American fighter. The Allison was placed aft of the cockpit, just behind the pilot, and connected to the propeller by reduction gear assembly by a 10-foot connecting shaft. This arrangement gave the fighter its notorious center of gravity and stability problems. The thought of this high-speed shaft running forward between their legs made some pilots uncomfortable. The rear-mounted engine was considered more vulnerable than the standard front mount, as there were more attacks from the rear and protecting the engine with armor was too weight excessive.

The P-39 was equipped with either three blade, 10.33 foot Curtiss electric or 10.42 to 11.63 foot Aeroproducts hydraulic propellers, which were constant-speed, governor-controlled. Some later models spun four blade Aeroproducts props. Both had an aerodynamic spinner supported by a hub.

The fuel tanks were two internal 60-gallon tanks consisting of six leak-proof bags built integrally into each outer wing panel, providing a total of 120 gallons. The 60-gallon wing tank included a 20 gallon reserve. Later

N and Q models had a reduced 87 to 110 gallon capacity. A jettisonable auxiliary 75 to 175 gallon tank could be carried on the centerline bomb rack.

Flying the P-39

The P-39 was thought to have the best ground handling characteristics of all AAF fighters by pilots who flew it and other fighters. Its tricycle gear gave it good taxiing visibility and the pilot did not have to weave while taxiing like tail-dragging fighters (P-47s and P-51s). However, on the forward strips in the Pacific, the small main wheel tires of the P-39 and P-400 had a tendency to sink into the soft ground. The nose gear was also considered too fragile, and there are reports of numerous gears fracturing at the oleo strut. As with all single-engine AAF fighters, the P-39 propeller torque caused the fighter to swing left and the trim tabs had to be set for takeoff while taxiing: the elevator tab to keep the nose slightly up and the rudder tab for right rudder. Taxi and idle time were critical, as the engines rapidly overheated, so this short taxiing/overheating time required P-39 units either take off first or last when coordinating with units consisting of other aircraft. But on longer range missions, because of the P-39's fuel limitations, its Squadrons were usually assigned to start engines last and take off last.

The P-39 was one of a few U.S. aircraft that was difficult to takeoff. On takeoff, the pilot had to avoid the tendency to shove the stick forward (as with flying tail draggers), which could collapse the nose gear and/or catch the prop. Once lined up for takeoff, the pilot left the flaps up or lowered no more than a quarter, kept the stick neutral, and eased the power on. He used the rudder to keep the plane lined up on the runway while not over-steering. The brakes, operated by pedals above the rudder bar, were released, and as the fighter sped along the runway, the nose wheel was raised a bit early to decrease tire wear. Any left torque was corrected by using right rudder and right brake. At about 100mph IAS, the P-39 was airborne, the front gear rotated up, and the main gear retracted.

Once in the air, the P-39 was very unstable, as the wings were located directly under the engine and the center of gravity, and at low speeds the small fighter pitched around. However, trimming was good, and once a pilot learned to cope with this instability it could be beneficial in bringing the nose and guns around quickly to pull an extra 5° of lead on an enemy before opening fire. A pilot flying the P-39 was able to perform most combat maneuvers, but snap rolls were not recommended and outside loops and intentional spins were forbidden. The fighter featured very sensitive controls, but care had to be taken not to jerk the stick, which could send the fighter into a sudden spin. Stick and rudder forces were light, quick, and responsive, while the fabric-covered ailerons were light in normal flight, but became much heavier in high-speed dives. Thus, the sensitive controls did not have to be moved much through turns and too much movement could lead to a high-speed stall and a snap roll. For this reason, the P-39 gained the reputation of being difficult to fly and maneuvers had to be concentrated on. Once all the nose ammunition had been expended, the aft center of gravity became even more exaggerated and stability deteriorated. The fighter's roll rate was poor compared to other AAF fighters. The Airacobra could be dived to 475 mph IAS. Before diving, the pilot had to trim the fighter nose heavy to decrease the severity of the pullout. During the dive left rudder had to be applied, as the fighter tended to yaw right. Another liability which gave the P-39 its "tricky to fly" reputation was that dangerous stalls developed without warning of aircraft or control buffeting, and there were many stall-spin "incidents" reported. Often the slightest sudden movement of the very sensitive controls would initiate a high-speed stall with a downward pitch, together with yawing and rolling. A stall recovery could be made by quickly using only down elevator to keep the nose down. If a pilot could not get out of the stall a flat spin would result, especially if all the ammunition had

been fired. The Bell P-39 Pilot's Manual stated: "If the recovery technique is not closely followed the aircraft might not recover from the spin," and as Airacobra pilots related it would "tumble and spin and soon auger in."

On the landing approach, the P-39 gear could be extended at 200mph and the flaps dropped and power on idle in a very steep glide path with the nose high. A speed of 130mph had to be maintained to maintain enough elevator control to level out. Care had to be taken not to apply too much rudder or allow the airspeed to become too low, which would cause a sudden snap roll that could be fatal for an inexperienced pilot. It was recommended that the nose be held up as long as possible for the lowest possible touchdown speed and shortest run. A speed of 110mph was required to make a power-on approach. With the nose still high, the main gear touched first at 95 to 100mph, with the nose gear following without pilot action. There was no predisposition to bounce or ground loop. Braking was to be intermittent to prevent overheating or locking.

Once in combat in the Pacific, one of the P-39's most serious faults was a severe lack of range to cover the long distances required in the Theater. The P-39 was a small aircraft, and the engine occupied the area that would normally contain the fuel tank; the small wings allowed little space for fuel, especially when fitted with self-sealing tanks. Its range on internal tanks was less than two hours, while when fitted with a small drop tank, its range was increased another hour. The Allison engine was considered fragile and servicing difficulties were encountered. Rearming required an excessive amount of time.

Flying the P-39 was a love-hate affair, as once mastered, skilled pilots considered it more than adequate to fly and good in general performance, but also many pilots never were able to master the aircraft and detested it. Flying the P-39/P-400 Airacobra

by Richard Suehr: One P-400 victory 39 FS (5 total)

Suehr

(**Note:** During the early 1980s, I was an editor for the American Fighter Aces Association's Aces Album, and during writing the Aces' biographies I got to meet and interview numerous aces. As part of these interviews, I asked a number of Aces to write about their impressions flying various aircraft.)

The P-39/P-400 was a small, beautiful streamlined fighter with many modern features for its time, such as the tricycle landing gear, air-cooled inline engine located behind the cockpit, and the heaviest armament on any American fighter of the time.

We entered the cockpit over the right wing through a door that was similar to an automobile door, complete with roll-down windows (editor's **note:** they were manufactured by the Hudson Motor Car Co.). The throttle quadrant was on the left side of the cockpit, so the real obstacle was to crawl over it. The sturdy cockpit was spacious for a small 5'5" pilot like me. It was very comfortable, with everything right at my elbows or fingertips. The instruments were easy to see or read. But the gun sight above the panel could rearrange a pilot's face in a crash landing. The visibility was excellent in all directions because the canopy was almost a full bubble and the aircraft stood on a tricycle gear. Our radio system was a state-of-the-art four channel VHF, but it tended to be crowded.

The 1150hp Allison engine was located behind the cockpit and was coupled by a long drive shaft passing under the cockpit to a reduction gearbox that connected it to the prop. When starting the engine, all these gears and linkages made a racket and shook the plane until enough revs were reached to smooth things out. The engine and linkages were generally reliable, but were low-altitude rated and condemned the P-39 to low-level combat and ground support duties. As was usual, the combat versions of a fighter become overweight from the prototype versions and thus become underpowered—this was certainly the case with the P-39.

The tricycle landing gear gave the P-39 very good ground handling characteristics during taxiing, take off, and landing. We tried not to waste too much time on the ground because of the Allison's tendency to overheat. We also had to watch our fuel consumption, which was somewhat more than two hours. We were later equipped with a 75-gallon belly tank which helped extend our range by about an hour. The Airacobra had a high rate of climb from takeoff, but at 12-13,000 feet the plane almost stopped dead in the air. It took forever to climb from there to 20-25,000 feet, where the Japs usually flew. We were hurting when and if we reached this altitude and would have had trouble catching a Jap fighter, or even a Betty bomber! A turbo supercharger would have been a great help. We had no maneuverability up there and our main hope was to make one surprise run at them and dive for our lives. The P-39 did have beautiful dive characteristics, as it could dive away from the pursuing Jap like a brick! Our best bet in combat was to lure the Jap below 12,000 feet, where we were more maneuverable and had some chance. The plane was good in a shallow climb, but had no ability to pull straight up to gain altitude advantage. But even at these favorable altitudes, the quick, maneuverable Japanese aircraft often overmatched us. Fortunately, our small fighter was ruggedly built, with armor plate surrounding the cockpit and bulletproof glass fore and aft of the canopy. The fuel tanks were self-sealing.

The Airacobra was a stable gun platform and was the most heavily armed American fighter of the time. It was equipped with a 37mm cannon which fired through the propeller hub, two nose mounted, propeller synchronized .50 caliber machine guns, and four wing-mounted .30 caliber machine guns. The 39th FS flew a mixed bag of P-39Ds and P-400s (which were RAF rejects). The only difference between the two were the 37mm cannon in the P-39 and the 20mm cannon in the P-400, along with slight engine variations and a different, non-interchangeable oxygen system. The 37mm fired about 30 shells, and its looping trajectory took some time to master. When it worked, it could put some good-sized holes in the sides of Japanese ships and barges. It was useless in aerial combat.

The P-39's performance was discouraging to pilots engaging in aerial combat, but its ruggedness and firepower made it a great ground support weapon. Sitting on the ground and in pictures, the P-39 looked to be a great fighter, but its performance in the air never matched its great looks. The fondest memories I have about the aircraft are of the people I flew with and who supported us on the ground.

The P-39 in Combat in the Pacific

May 1942: P-39 vs. Zero: A First Combat Analysis

The reactions of the P-39 pilots after their first engagement with the enemy in May 1942 were remarkably similar. Most of the pilots remembered their first and last shot vividly, but few could accurately recall what occurred in the interim. Psychologically, the effects of this initial combat were consistent: "a deep feeling of the seriousness of fighter combat, and a keen anticipation for the next combat mission." Additionally, all AAC pilots had a thorough respect and appreciation of the flying qualities of the Zero fighters and their teamwork was described as excellent.

The pilots were already aware that the P-39, like the P-40, could not perform effectively above 18,000 feet, and that its rate of climb was slow; this became very apparent in combat. American pilots discovered that when they tried to turn with the Zero, the enemy fighter quickly got on their tails, as the nimble Zero certainly had a maneuverability advantage over virtually every other fighter in the war. The P-39 could equal the Zero's speed at sea level, so it could run from a Zero, hoping that another Airacobra would come to the rescue. Apparently flying in a three-ship stagger formation, the second plane kept a distance of about 100 yards behind the leader, while the third plane stayed the same distance behind the second. The flights were ragged, with all planes except the leader weaving loosely. The Japanese followed very definite tactics in their attacks on a single P-39. All Zeros except one (which attacked from the rear) placed themselves on either side, even with and slightly above the P-39 in an attempt to "box" the plane. First one Zero and then another would get into position behind the P-39, firing intermittent bursts for about 10 seconds, then zooming up to either side to be replaced by the most forward plane on that side. While the P-39 was "roughly slipping and skidding violently" in evasive tactics, the firing was inaccurate, especially at long range.

The pilots made some observations about their aircraft. The performance of the P-39 against enemy aircraft was described as "excellent and as approximately 10% better than the P-40 in every respect except maneuverability." As all the P-39s shot down were hit in the engine and coolant systems, the main weakness of the P-39 was thought to be in the lack of rear armor plate protection for the rear-mounted engine. The combats also revealed that the hydraulic propellers threw oil on the windshields, causing poor forward visibility. Immediate attempts to stop this oil leakage by the installation of a new type of gasket were only partially successful. Other instances of malfunctions were found in the landing gear, nose gear, and radio equipment. Other criticisms concerned the wing-mounted .30 caliber guns, which often jammed or stopped completely, especially in a turn. The 20mm nose cannon often only fired once or twice and had a low rate of fire, as well as a large trajectory which prevented it from being used in conjunction with the machine guns. The .50 caliber nose-mounted machine gun was dependable, but had a weak firing mechanism. The pilots were led to believe that the 37mm cannon was to be an "extremely desirable weapon," but stoppages in combat were frequent and it was difficult to reload and recharge during combat because of the high loading and charging forces. Thus, the American pilots in the SWPA went into combat knowing that their aircraft were inferior at high altitudes and thus used their aircraft to best advantage at lower altitudes. But the bottom line was that the P-39 could not out-climb, outmaneuver, or match armament with the Zero, but it was generally as fast and could usually dive away; however, it was unable to climb to the altitude of high-flying Japanese bombers.

The Combat Diary of the 39FS included these comments on the P-39 from its pilots. Lt. Atkins: "Could have done better with a truck. It's more maneuverable and will go higher." Lt. Wahl stated: "Could have done damn good with an altitude ship." When Pearl Harbor hero and then seven-victory ace George Welch was asked what he like about the P-39, he replied: "Well, it's got 1,200 pounds of Allison armor plate." Also, many pilots requested a P-400 over a P-39 because it had a 20mm cannon which was far more reliable than the 37mm, which constantly jammed.

Despite all of its faults, the P-39 was a modern fighter, and like all U.S. fighters, it was well built and could dive very well and, importantly, was available in large numbers at the start of the war. The D and the repossessed P-400 saw combat in AAC service during the months after Pearl Harbor, but were found to be completely inadequate in aerial combat and did yeoman duty in ground support, particularly in North Africa and the South Pacific.

The first P-39D Airacobras entered service with the AAC in February 1941, with the 31st Pursuit Group based at Selfridge Field, MI. At the time

of Pearl Harbor, the AAC had five Pursuit Groups equipped with the P-39, including the 8th Pursuit Group. At the time of Pearl Harbor, the P-39, along with the P-40 and a very few P-38s, was virtually the only modern fighter available, and those P-39s already in service were deployed at U.S. bases, but were quickly deployed to bases in Australia, Alaska, Hawaii, Panama, and New Guinea.

On 30 April 1942, 13 P-39s from the 35th and 36th Pursuit Squadrons flew their first combat mission under Lt.Col. Boyd Wagner, and for the next year and a half, the P-39 and P-40 were the primary front line fighters of AAC units in the Pacific and played a major part in the initial Allied aerial effort to deter the rapid Japanese advance.

Curtiss P-40 Warhawk

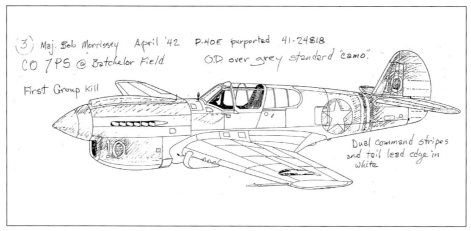

(Drawing by Steve Ferguson)

The P-40 was America's first mass-produced single-seat fighter and operated with the AAC/AAF and other Allied Air Forces in every theater during the war. During the first half of the war it, and the P-39, made up more than half of AAC fighter strength. Although not a particularly outstanding fighter aircraft, it was on hand at the time when the P-47, P-38, and P-51 were in the early stages of their development and production. During this time, the P-40 gained a reputation for dependability and ruggedness and was able to hold its own against enemy fighters, but only when using tried and proven tactics.

The AAC's 1930s concept of bombardment aviation had taken precedence over pursuit aviation, which restricted American fighter development. Donovan Berlin and the Curtiss design team developed the P-36 (Hawk 75A) in 1934, and when that design was unable to compete with its contemporaries, the design was improved and the P-40 was the direct descendant.

The P-40 had the prerequisites of a modern fighter (a low-wing cantilevered monoplane with stressed skin over a semi-monocoque airframe), and although the P-40's long, low fuselage gave it the look of a fighter, its airframe was not innovative in any way. The prototype XP-40, designated the Hawk 81A, was a converted P-36 airframe with an Allison 1,160hp V-1710-19 liquid-cooled engine. But the P-40 was built for ruggedness, handling capability, and low-altitude performance.

After the prototype first flew on 14 October 1938, an order for 524 P-40s (there were no P-40As) was placed on 27 April 1939 (the largest aviation American aircraft contract awarded to that time). The first production model flew on 4 April 1940. This initial order was later reduced to 200 to allow Curtiss to build 192 for the French, but these in turn were diverted to the RAF, who named it the Tomahawk I. Because this fighter was only armed

with two .30 caliber machine guns and had no protective armor or self-sealing tanks, the British sent them to the Middle East. After the 200th production aircraft, two additional wing-mounted .30 caliber were added, along with some protective armament and self-sealing tanks, and this modification was designated the P-40B. The RAF took delivery of 110 as the Tomahawk II, while the AAC took delivery of 131. Later, 100 of the RAF order were diverted to supply the American Volunteer Group in China.

The P-40C added two more wing guns to the two .50s in the cowling and four .30s in the wing. The AAC received 193 and the RAF 930 as the Tomahawk IIB. The 1,040hp V-1710-33 was mounted in the P-40, P-40B, and P-40C, which were essentially similar, except for armament and some internal differences.

Allison introduced a new engine, the 1,150hp V-1710-39, which had originally been proposed for the experimental Curtiss XP-46 fighter. The AAC had decided not to interrupt the P-40 production lines for a new XP-46 fighter and decided instead to adapt the new engine to the existing P-40 on 10 June 1940. The new project was designated the P-40D, and was considered sufficiently different from previous P-40 versions that Curtiss allocated a new company designation, the Model 87. The P-40D introduced a new shorter nose design that gave it a completely different nose geometry that was retained by all subsequent P-40s. The D's overall length was reduced by six inches, the cross section of the fuselage was reduced, and the undercarriage was shortened, while the radiator was increased in size and moved forward. About 175 pounds of armor were added. The fuselage guns were deleted and two .50 caliber machine guns with new hydraulic chargers were installed in each wing, while provisions in the wings for two 20mm cannon were added, but these were never actually used. Shackles were added under the fuselage to accommodate a 51-gallon auxiliary fuel tank or a 500-pound bomb. Wing rack attachment points were provided for six 20-pound bombs. Gross weight of the D model was increased to 8,670 pounds, and consequently, the climb rate and ceiling continued to remain poor. Only 22 Ds were delivered to the AAC and 560 to the RAF as the Kittyhawk I.

The P-40E (Kittyhawk IA) was the first large-scale P-40 production model; of the 2,320 built, 820 went to the AAC and 1,500 to the RAF. The P-40E was similar in most respects to the P-40D, except for a slightly more powerful engine and an extra .50 caliber gun in each wing, bringing the total to six. It was faster at altitude, but climb and its maneuverability continued to be mediocre. The P-40E was the variant that bore the brunt of air-to-air combat in the crucial period of early to mid-1942. They were flown by the first U.S. squadrons to replace the AVG in China (the AVG was already transitioning to this type from the P-40B/C), by the Australians at Milne Bay, and by the RAF/Commonwealth in North Africa as the Kittyhawk IA.

The P-40F was powered by the Packard license-built 1,300hp Rolls Royce Merlin V-1650 engine instead of the Allison. The 12 cylinder V liquid-cooled engine gave the F Model a maximum speed of 364mph at 20,000 feet and significantly increased the rate of climb. Maximum range was 700 miles at 20,000 feet (clean), 875 miles (one 43 Imp gal drop tank), and 1,500 miles (141.5 Imp gal drop tank), while the service ceiling was 34,400 feet. Its fuselage was elongated by two feet two inches (to 33 feet 4 inches) in order to improve directional stability, and this longer fuselage was retained in all later P-40 versions. Weights were 6,590 pounds empty, 8,500 pounds normal loaded, and 9,350 pounds maximum. Armament consisted of six .50 inch machine guns in the wings. Of the 1,311 built, 100 were delivered to the Soviet Union and 307 others to the Free French (FAFL), but the RAF Kittyhawk II order was canceled. The 904 P-40Fs were the first P-40s to be designated the Warhawk. But the U.S. Army designation "Warhawk," although used in the popular media, was not used by American pilots, who referred to the fighter only as the "P-40" (I noticed this in my interviews and asked why, but no one could give an answer).

There were 1,300 P-40Ks (increased fin area) produced, 700 P-40Ls (similar to the P-40F, but with only four guns), and 4,219 P-40Ns (four guns and F and L characteristics, along with the 1,360hp V-1710-81 engine).

By mid-1943, the performance of the Warhawk continued to lag behind that of other AAF types, such as the P-38, P-47, and P-51, which were beginning to come into service. The P-40N was introduced at this time in an effort to improve the capabilities of the basic P-40 design and thus avoid interrupting Curtiss production lines by having the company introduce an entirely new fighter type. The first 1,500 of this new Warhawk model were to have been delivered as P-40Ps powered by Merlin engines, but shortages of the Packard-built Merlin which were to power the new P-51 Mustang caused the P-40P order to be cancelled and the P-40N to be powered by the 1,200hp Allison V-1710-81. A new lightweight structure was introduced, two of the six wing-mounted guns were removed, smaller and lighter undercarriage wheels were installed, head armor for the pilot was reintroduced, and aluminum radiators and oil coolers were installed. The resulting reduction in the weight, along with the installation of the V-1710-81 engine, made the P-40N the fastest P-40 model. Even though by 1943 standards the Warhawk was quickly becoming obsolete, the P-40N became the most widely produced version, with 5,220 being built before production finally ceased. Many of the P-40Ns were shipped to Allied air forces under Lend-Lease and comprised the majority of the 1,097 P-40s sent to the USSR and 456 as the Kittyhawk IV in RAF service. Most of their operational flying took place in the Pacific in fighter bomber or escort roles, with most of them flown by RAF, RAAF, and RNZAF pilots. In AAF service, the P-40N was relegated largely to training roles, as later types, such as the P-51 Mustang or the P-47 Thunderbolt, became increasingly available in quantity.

The P-40R was the conversion of 300+ P-40F and L models from Merlin to Allison engines to be used as advanced trainers. Production of the P-40 ceased in December 1944, when the 13,738th model rolled off the production lines; they were used in all theaters of the war and by the air forces of 28 nations.

Curtiss P-40E Warhawk Specifications

Performance-wise, the P-40E was inferior to many early war fighters, as it accelerated and climbed poorly, was a poor vertical performer, could be out-turned, and was out-rolled at the high and low ends of its speed range. However, it had one of the best roll rates from 275 to 375mph and handled well at 300 to 400mph, which made it a good diving attack aircraft if it could climb to altitude and was not attacked from above.

Engine	1,150hp Allison V-1710-39 Inline
Weight	(Empty/Loaded/Maximum): 6,550lbs-7,400lbs-8,720lbs
Length	33.33 feet
Wing Span	37.33 feet
Wing Area	236 square feet
Wing Loading	(Empty/Loaded/Maximum): 27.8lbs/sqft-31.4lbs/sqft-36.9/sqft
Armament	2x.50 caliber Browning MG (nose) and 4x.50 caliber Browning MG (wings)
Bomb Load	1x500lb bomb
Maximum Speed	363mph
Full Flaps Speed	115mph
Climb	1,000 to 5,000 feet: 70 seconds 5,000 to 10,000 feet: 106 seconds 10,000 to 15,000 fee: 118 seconds
Maximum Diving Speed	495mph

P-40 Described

Cockpit

The cockpit was considered "roomy" for even a large pilot and had seat and rudder pedal adjustments. Entry was via the port wing root using a hand hold along a rather steep walkway which would benefit from a non-slip surface. The E-models had more room than earlier versions and there was ample seat adjustment for height. Pilots felt that the control column was set too far away, which made it difficult to get full forward movement. The layout of the instruments was satisfactory, with the flying instruments above and to the left of the engine instruments of the panel and conveniently grouped. Cockpit heating was considered adequate for its moderate operating altitudes, but ventilation was considered "almost" adequate to inadequate, especially at low altitudes in the tropical Pacific climates (pilots often flew with their canopies opened). Heating was from the radiator via ducts to the cockpit and controlled by a mixing lever. There was a space between two layered windshields, through which warm air was passed to prevent icing and fogging. There was no cooling system. Cockpit noise was tolerable with the cockpit closed. The instruments could be easily seen and read, and control layout was generally good for the period. Forward taxiing visibility was nil, but visibility in the air was good forward and to the side, while rearward vision (except in late P-40Ns) was aided by concave cutouts

P-40E Cockpit (NMUSAF)

Armament: Beginning with the P-40D and in subsequent models, the fuselage guns were eliminated and the armament consisted of six wing-mounted .50 caliber machine guns. (AAF)

The P-40B/C had the same gun installation as the P-40, with two fuselage guns carrying 760 rounds. The wing armament was increased to two .30 caliber machine guns in each wing supplied by 980 rounds. The C could carry a 500-pound bomb on its centerline.

Beginning with the P-40D and in subsequent models, the fuselage guns were eliminated and the armament consisted of six wing-mounted .50 caliber machine guns supplied by 1,410 rounds carried in wing trays. The K, M, and N models did not have gun chargers, so if a gun did jam in the air, it could not be made operable.

Engine, Propellers, and Fuel Tanks
The P-40 was powered by either the Allison V-1710 liquid-cooled 12 cylinder V-inline engine or later a Packard Rolls Royce Merlin V-1650-1 liquid-cooled 12 cylinder V-online engine (in the P-40F and L). All Allison engines used an integral single-stage, single-speed supercharger, while the Merlin P-40 superchargers were single-stage two-speed. The fighter spun a constant-speed 11-foot Curtiss electric three-blade propeller.

There were three internal protected fuel tanks: two in the wings inboard and one in the fuselage. The 50.5 gallon (capacity varied with the model) main wing tank was installed straddling the fighter's lateral centerline near the central wing spar, and the 35 gallon reserve tank was also installed on the lateral centerline on the wing spars. The 62.3 gallon fuselage tank was installed behind the cockpit. The standard 52 gallon external fuel tank was installed on the fighter centerline and was unprotected.

Flying the P-40
Being a tail-dragger with a long nose, forward visibility of the Warhawk on the ground was non-existent (worse than the Mustang but better than the Thunderbolt), but visibility to the forward quarters and sides was generally considered good. Like other tail-draggers, the pilot taxied in S-turns, swinging side-to-side using the forward quarter to view ahead. The pilot applied the brakes to turn without worry of overheating. The tail wheel was not lockable, thus the fighter was limited to 30-40° turns when the tail wheel was not in full swivel. During taxiing, the engine caused torque swings which were offset by braking and rudder once the taxi speed was high enough.

Before takeoff, the rudder trim tab was set nose right. The flaps were not usually lowered during operational takeoffs, but could be used if set less than halfway down. Cockpit checks were completed and the fighter was run up with the brakes on. The P-40 was possibly the most demanding U.S. fighter to keep straight on takeoff. The brakes were released as the takeoff

covered by transparent panels in the structure aft of the cockpit. The rearview mirror mounted above the windscreen was considered useless. No production P-40s ever received the bubble canopy. The seat could be moved by a release handle, but on the N model, the seat could only be adjusted on the ground by moving bolts. All models had a relief tube.

Pilot Protection
The P-40 was renown for its rugged structure and there are numerous reports of Warhawks staggering home with various machine gun and cannon hits; only a hit on the coolant system would stop it. But the P-40's cooling system was considered much less vulnerable than that of the P-51, as it was concentrated in the nose, rather than aft. P-40 pilot armor protection consisted of:
• P-40B/C: A steel plate was placed forward of the cockpit and two steel plates were placed aft of the pilot.
• the P-40E-M: Two armor plates were placed, one forward and the other aft of the pilot (with differences in weight and thickness) and bulletproof windshield glass.

Armament
The initial P-40s were armed with two .50 caliber machine guns mounted in the forward fuselage supplied by 400 rounds. The ammunition boxes and ejection chutes were located in the same bay just below the guns. A .30 caliber machine gun was installed in each wing and was supplied by 500 rounds.

run was begun. To counteract the powerful torque that caused the fighter to turn left, hard right rudder needed to be initially applied. But even with an even application of power, the aircraft tended to swing left and resolved right rudder pressure was necessary, as the left swing decreased almost proportionally as speed built up. It was claimed that a veteran P-40 pilot could be recognized by his "brawny right leg." If the tail was forced up too firmly in the initial takeoff phase, the pilot could lose control of the steerable tail wheel before rudder control was achieved. The tail was to be raised slightly after sufficient speed was acquired. In addition to the torque swing, when the tail came up, the left wing had to be brought up using judicious right stick, as too much would increase the tendency to swing left. The P-40 was not to be taken off three-point.

Takeoff speed was 90 to 105 mph IAS using MILITARY power, depending on the model and aircraft weight. Lift off was achieved by allowing the aircraft to "fly itself off using some smooth aft stick." Once in the air, the pilot "cleaned up the fighter." The flaps, if used, were to be retracted quickly, but a rule was not to retract them under five feet altitude. Landing gear came up more slowly, most often one leg at a time. Climbing power was set, with the optimum climbing speed being 150 160 mph IAS, then slightly as altitude was increased. In a climb right rudder pressure increased. A right climbing turn required extra rudder pressure, while a left climbing turn needed only modest pressure.

In every P-40 model, every power and speed change caused an immediate trim change, which the pilot had to either counteract or trim out; this was more than in other U.S. fighters at the time and a characteristic of flying the Curtiss. As was typical of many single-engine fighters, the vertical tail fin was offset slightly to counter propeller slipstream effects at cruising speed. In a dive, as speed increased, more left rudder trim had to be progressively applied and a pilot had to practically stand on the left rudder pedal to keep the ball centered. Although directional trim tab power existed to zero out pedal force, left rudder trim could not be rolled in fast enough with high dive acceleration. Slowing down in a climb, only a small amount right rudder trim was needed. On the P-40E, lowering the landing gear made the aircraft slightly nose heavy; there was no appreciable trim change with flap positioning. The elevator trim system could control the minor effects of lowering the gear or dropping an external fuel tank, as well as longitudinal variations due to speed and power changes.

The ailerons were light and responsive at all speeds up to maximum level speed. They were effective in level flight and during climbs and glides, but deteriorated close to stall speeds. Aileron control became heavier with an increase in speed, and at speeds above 400mph serious problems were encountered; at 460mph the plane became immovable. There was little change of lateral trim with speed, thus the aileron trim was used infrequently. Elevator control was considered moderate and effective throughout the speed range, becoming heavier with increased speed. The elevator trim was effective and gave adequate trim for all flight conditions. The rudder was the heaviest of the three controls, especially with increased speed. It became light at landing speeds and near a stall. The heavy rudder control was offset by very good aileron control.

The P-40's ability to dive without flutter or vibration, gaining speed at a high rate, was one of the aircraft's chief assets. Because dive acceleration was rapid during the initial pullout, stick force tended to be heavy and elevator trim tab was very sensitive and not to be used to assist pullout unless "absolutely necessary." A very significant dive characteristic of the P-40 was its tendency for strong right yaw and right wing heaviness that increased with increased speed. Immediate trim tab action was required to counteract both turning and rolling forces in dives. Pilots had to keep hard left rudder pressure to avoid skidding. Generally, P-40s would not experience compressibility because dives were not started high enough or continued long enough. The major design changes in the P-40E led to significant

deficiencies in directional stability and control. To minimize production line impact, the initial solution (used in late P-40Es and some P-40Fs and Ks) was to add a dorsal fillet, a zero-offset fin, a rudder trim tab only, and delete the balance tab. The short fuselage P-40s had greater rudder and elevator loads, thus requiring more rudder and elevator pressures. Later, the P-40F, with a longer fuselage, was introduced, reducing the nastiest directional problems. When pulling out of a dive in the P-40, stick forces grew very heavy, with profound effort necessary to bring the nose up at diving speeds approaching 400mph IAS. Controls solidified approximately linearly with increased airspeed, and elevator and rudder forces were high in high-speed dive pullouts. Pilots were to pull out of a dive "firmly and smoothly," as pulling out of a dive too abruptly could trigger a high-speed stall and cause the fighter to snap over and start a spin.

The P-40 was designed to perform most all fighter maneuvers, but with limitations due to its directional stability and control problems. Prohibited maneuvers were outside loops, sustained inverted flight, spins of over three turns (no spins with baggage or external stores), inverted spins, and no barrel or slow rolls over 140 to 180mph. Generally, P-40s were very maneuverable, especially below 15,000 feet, and early intelligence credited them as being more maneuverable and able to turn inside the P-39, and definitely the P-38 and P-47. Continuous rudder trim control and a higher propeller rpm setting were recommended in a turn. Before the P-40 reached stall in a turn, it gave plenty of warning by shuddering violently, and a tight turn could be made even under shuddering conditions by using smooth coordinated controls. Like other U.S. fighters, the P-40's **Wing Loading:** was too high for close-in maneuvering with Japanese fighters. P-40s were especially proficient in rolling at a high rate. There was good rudder control of unfavorable yaw during roll and sideslip situations with the rudder pedal forces about average. The aileron forces were also about average and effective through the flight speed range. Elevator forces tended to be a bit heavy.

The Warhawk was directionally and longitudinally stable under all flight conditions. With the flaps and gear up, there was little warning of an impending stall, except for the high position of the nose and a tendency to yaw right. P-40 stall characteristics were considered good, with the warning being the usual shutter occurring a few miles above the stall speed (84mph loaded and 90mph clean); however, there was some variation among different models and different aircraft. The stall was gentle, and at the break the nose dropped straight down. During a stall there was little drop of the wing, but when badly mishandled the fighter would tend to snap roll over on its back and enter a spin. With proper handling there was no tendency to spin from a stall. The pilot recovered from a stall by pushing the stick forward. A high-speed stall, such as in a tight turn, gave less warning and was more intense, and could easily snap into a dangerous spin. High-speed stall recovery procedure was the same (release stick back pressure at the first shudder), but had to be made immediately. Spin characteristics varied among P-40 models. A P-40C was almost impossible to spin. However, the P-40F could go into a violent spin from which it was very easy to recover if there was enough altitude, as the spinning fighter would recover in two or three turns, with each turn losing about 1,000 feet and full recovery taking about 2,000 feet after the aircraft stopped turning. The recovery procedure was to throttle back and apply opposite rudder, push the stick forward, and not use ailerons against the spin, as that covered the rudder.

The P-40 accelerated and climbed poorly and had poor vertical performance; it could be out-turned in the high and low ends of its speed range. However, it did have one of the best roll rates from 250mph to 375mph and handled well at speeds of 300-400mph. Thus, at high speeds, the P-40E had quite good defense due to its excellent roll rate, but it needed to keep diving to reach these speeds. In comparison to the P39D, the P40E was heavier and both had similar Wing Loading:s. Both used slightly different variants of the same engine, but the Airacobra had almost 200hp extra; the P40E's engine had a turbo-supercharger, while the P39D did not. Concerning acceleration, climb, and diving performance, the P39D had the edge, although the P40E handled better in most situations. In maneuvering both fighters were nearly equal, but the P-39D's extra horsepower gave it better vertical maneuverability. Both fighters had to get above their targets and against better turning opponents had to maintain speed and remain above their opponents until diving on them. This was difficult, as their low horsepower-to-weight ratio made gaining altitude difficult. On the defensive, the only alternative for each was to dive away.

Another P-40 trait was its unfavorable landing characteristics, especially involving crosswinds. The P-40 was considered by many of its pilots as the most difficult of any AAF fighter to land, as was attested by the many ground loops. The narrow landing gear, particularly when landing the short fuselage P-40s, was the main cause of the ground loops. During a P-40 approach, the maximum gear down speed was 170mph and the maximum flap down speed 140mph, while an approach glide was established at 110 to 115mph. Landing speed varied with the model and loading. The throttle was cut and the landing was made three point. Generally, the P-40 handled well if the approach speed was correct, with all controls being effective and showing no tendency to float or sink too fast. Visibility in the landing pattern was adequate because the approach was made in a turn and the pilot could see the runway until he lined up and the nose came up into the three point set down position. In the run out on the ground, the P-40 could be very sensitive, particularly in a crosswind, and had to be very carefully handled until a low speed was reached. Fortunately, the brakes were effective. For crosswind landings, the practice was to come in a little fast with no more than 30° of flap with a wing dipped into the wind and to land on the main gear wheels first. The nose tended to swing into the crosswind and the pilot made corrections with the rudder and brakes.

Flying the P-40 Warhawk (PTO)
by Richard West: 6 victory P-40 ace 8FG (14 total victories)

I flew the P-40N for six months for the 35th Fighter Squadron of the 8th Fighter Group in late 1943, over New Guinea. Luckily, on my first encounter with the Japanese on 22 September, I was able to shoot down two Hamp fighters and claim a probable near Finschhafen. I did not see another Jap until 15 November, when I shot down two Zekes and two Sallys and got a probable of each.

We were flying the P-40N-5, which was the most improved P-40 model of the time. But these improvements over the M and N series only included a new radio, better seat, and the addition of external bomb racks. Along with rust and corrosion due to the high New Guinea humidity, my pre-flight checks often showed a number of fluid leaks of various kinds: fuel, hydraulic, coolant, etc., streaking the aircraft.

The cockpit was fairly roomy, but the controls, pedals, and instrument panel could be too far forward for a small pilot, who would require a cushion; I had no problem, being 5'10"/175 pounds. For the novice pilot, ground handling and taking off in the P-40 was difficult, because it was equipped with a number of late 1930s systems that required four hands to even start the engine. I never had any problems with the P-40 on the ground. Its long cowling and tail-down mode made ground handling difficult. To taxi, you had to make S-turns and look through the side panels to navigate. Because of the tropic heat we left the canopy open and hung our heads out the side to taxi, but we then stuck our noses into the exhaust smells and had to hold our breath. The Allison heated up very quickly, and it was not long before the coolant gauge went into the red, so a quick takeoff was necessary or you were forced to shut down. The brakes were effective in turning, but as a novice you had to watch not to apply them too hard and nose over. The tail wheel was effective but stiff. On the takeoff run, you steered with the

West

brakes at first until the tail lifted off the ground, then the rudder was used. The Allison's great torque pulled the left wing down and to keep the wings level, right stick and hard right foot were required. A major weakness of the aircraft was its agonizingly slow climb to altitude. To gain speed in the climb ASAP it was necessary to use full military power, which in the Allison was about five minutes.

Once in the air, the P-40's foibles on takeoff disappeared and it was normal in all flight characteristics and was easy to fly after some practice. But in green hands it was demanding and unforgiving. The fuel mixture settings were straightforward and a fuel low warning light flashed a reminder to change tanks. As the fuel was used, the CG moved forward and added stability, making the fighter a better gun platform. Trim required some manual dexterity and vigilance. A slight buffeting warned of a stall. Once in a spin, the aircraft would come out of it by itself if the controls were released. To get out of a spin quickly, you had to cut the throttle, kick the rudder the opposite direction of the spin, and pull the stick forward. The aircraft did not have enough range or altitude capacity. A supercharger would have made it a dandy fighter. It was reasonably maneuverable due to its extremely responsive ailerons and being easy to roll. The main asset the P-40 had going for it was that it was a great diver and picked up speed quickly in a dive. However, in a dive the normally light ailerons got heavy and you had to stand on the rudder to keep the diving fighter flying straight.

Like the Flying Tigers, we used our diving advantage to initiate and leave combat at our choice. The more nimble Japanese fighters could easily best us in a dogfight but could not catch us in a dive.

The pipper gun sight was ok, although you had to duck down in your seat to see the pipper. It was supplemented with a cowl-mounted ring and bead sight. The sight was used both to shoot and drop bombs. It would fog up to a point of uselessness going from 15,000 feet to deck. This fogging happened in my first combat, but I managed to get two Japs mainly by luck and also by flying up their asses. I always felt that a good combat pilot needed to combine good flying and good shooting. I had grown up hunting, so shooting was a given for me. I habitually tried to approach the Jap as close as possible, although I was always scared of Japanese tail gunners. It was important to go over enemy aircraft recognition charts. Once you got within 20-30 yards the effect of six .50 caliber machine guns was awesome.

The P-40 landed like a rock and the air speed indicator needed to be monitored at all times. When the carburetor scoop came up it blocked the view of the runway. Once on the ground, it was necessary to taxi quickly to your destination before the engine overheated. If you overheated, you could either shut down or face into the wind to get more air into the radiator.

The P-40 was not as bad as a lot of people would have you think, especially the later models. A good fighter jock could do the job against the Japs anytime.

P-40 in Combat in the Pacific

The P-40 models used in the SWPA generated 350 horsepower, which was more than the Zero's radial engine, but the P-40 was much heavier, which gave it a much poorer power-to-weight ratio than the Zero. However, the P-40 was designed to maximize different qualities than the Zero. The Zero's designers gave it a huge wing and tail for lift and maneuverability. Curtiss attempted to maximize the P-40's speed in both a straight line and a dive by designing it two feet longer than the Zero, shortening its wing by two feet (decreasing its wing area), and setting its wing much farther aft. Consequently, while the P-40 was much less maneuverable than the Zero, it was its equal in speed and significantly faster in a dive.

The Allison was very reliable for an inline engine and gave good performance up to 15,000 feet. Nevertheless, all P-40 models were underpowered in view of their weights, and the Allison engine, unless turbocharged, did not perform well at high altitudes. The few turbochargers available were set aside for bombers and more advanced fighters, like the P-38 and P-47. Poor performance at high altitudes prevented the P-40 from engaging high-flying bombers and reconnaissance aircraft. The Zero, like the P-40, was also optimized for fighting at moderate altitudes, but performed somewhat better than the early-model P-40s at higher altitudes, providing it with yet another advantage.

While the Zero had generally superior performance compared to the P-40, the Warhawk was better armed and much more rugged if hit by the lightly-armed Zero. The early-model P-40s deployed in the Philippines and the East Indies were armed with two .50 caliber and four .30 caliber machine guns, but later model P-40s over New Guinea carried six .50 caliber machine guns, more pilot armor, and much better self-sealing fuel tanks. The number of rounds carried per gun was low and a pilot could exhaust his ammunition in not much more than ten seconds of continuous firing; like all early war fighters, the P-40 was subject to gun jams.

During the war, the Allies demonstrated a remarkable ability to modify their air tactics. Gen. Claire Chennault (CO of the AVG Flying Tigers in China), after some trial and error, was the first to use the P-40 effectively. Later in March-April 1942, Australian squadrons based at Port Moresby improved Chennault's tactics, and by the time the AAF deployed their first P-40 squadrons to New Guinea, the basis of an effective air doctrine had been established: good group tactics and maintaining speed. If the Japanese had altitude advantage, which was often the case early in the war, a P-40 pilot was to turn into the attacker and exchange fire in a head-to-head pass. The more heavily-armed and rugged P-40 had the likelihood of success, and after he completed the pass the Warhawk pilot could out-dive the Zero for safety, or if the P-40 pilot had equal or greater altitude and if his flight was still together, he was to gain a small amount of altitude and make another firing pass. A veteran P-40 pilot could hold his own against a Zero at medium and low altitudes with an even better chance for success than pilots flying more advanced fighters at the same altitudes. Although the P-40 had many shortcomings, it was relatively nimble for an American fighter at medium and low altitudes. Because the P-40 had a slight speed advantage over the Zero and could dive much better, it could take advantage of the Zero's poor high-speed handling. The Zero had large wings and ailerons, which allowed it to perform extraordinary maneuvers if its speed was 200mph or less. However, above that speed its large ailerons had much more difficulty moving against the increased air pressure. Because the designers of the Army Oscar fighter enhanced the design of the Zero, this predilection of the aileron movement in that agile fighter was even more obvious. The wings and ailerons of the P-40 were smaller, offering far less drag at high speeds. While the P-40 did not have a very tight turning radius, it did have a very good ability to change direction, particularly at high speeds (roll rate). At slow speeds, a Zero flown by a skilled pilot could easily gain position, while at high speeds a P-40 pilot had a brief advantage. It was imperative for the P-40 pilot to know when he no longer had this momentary edge, as a maneuver of any kind cost a pilot either speed or altitude. Nevertheless, the P-40 pilot always had the standard opportunity to break off combat by using the P-40's superior diving speed.

The Japanese considered the P-40 a worthy opponent, as it was relatively fast, maneuverable, and had good armament and pilot and aircraft protection. However, the Japanese did not chose to engage the P-38 or P-47, which had outstanding high altitude performance compared to their fighters. Thus, the Japanese were forced to seek out combat at lower altitudes, which was the bailiwick of the Warhawk.

In a turning fight with a Zero, the P-40 pilot could outrun it by dropping the nose to keep airspeed up. At low speed, the Zero could out-roll the P-40 because of its big ailerons. If the P-40's speed was over 275mph, it could out-roll the Zero, as its large ailerons did not have the strength to make high-speed rolls and became very heavy. A Zero could out-climb the P-40 at very low speeds (e.g., 90mph), but the P-40, flying at 250mph or more, could out-climb the Zero. The P-40 pilot was always in control of the combat, as he had the overriding advantage of being able to break off the fight at his discretion, since he could out-dive and outrun the enemy, who could not leave the combat because the P-40 was faster. In many conditions, a P-40 could out-turn a P-38, which some pilots did not realize until they transitioned between the two aircraft.

In pursuit of an enemy aircraft that was in any turn, even a gentle turn, and with the P-40 approaching at a 1 to 15° angle from its tail, the P-40's long nose hindered accurate aiming. The P-40 pilot had to pull his fighter's nose in front of the enemy to be able to lead it without really seeing it.

Lockheed P-38 Lightning

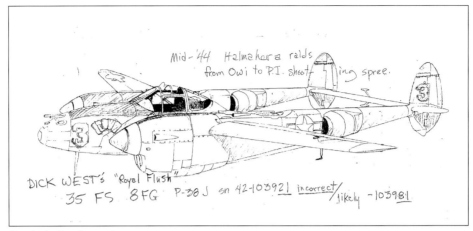

Mid-'44 Halmahera raids from Owi to P.I. shooting spree.

DICK WEST's "Royal Flush" 35 FS 8 FG P-38 J sn 42-103921 incorrect/ likely -103981

(Drawing by Steve Ferguson)

Although it had problems that diminished its effectiveness in the ETO and MTO, the P-38 was one of few weapons appearing in modern warfare that was better suited to its time and place than was the Lightning in the Pacific. The Lightnings of the 5th and 13th Fighter Commands decimated the JNAF and JNAF in New Guinea and the Solomons.

The P-38's design was initiated in 1937, at a time when interest worldwide in twin-engine single-seat fighter design was being revived. However, it would be the only twin-engine design from that time to see mass production and extensive service in WWII. In 1936, the AAC issued specifications for a twin-engine interceptor capable of high-speed flight at both sea level and 20,000 feet (maximum 360mph), and it had to climb to 20,000 feet in six minutes. At that time, the available aircraft engines would make these specifications very difficult to fulfill. Lockheed designers H.L. Hibbard and Clarence "Kelly" Johnson, however, proposed an inspired solution which was a radical departure from conventional American fighter development.

Lockheed's unique solution was a twin-engine prototype with twin booms attaching the engines and twin tails. The pilot was seated in a small copula-type cockpit attached to the wing bridging between the two engines. The design had double the power of the Allison engines without doubling the size of the fighter, but nonetheless, it was the largest, heaviest, and fastest American fighter of the time, with exceptional maneuverability at high speed provided by the twin tails. Other divergence from the conventional included its tricycle landing gear and imposing firepower, which was provided by four .50 caliber machine guns and a 20mm cannon.

The Lockheed Model 22 was the winner of the AAC competition, and in June 1937 one XP-38 prototype was ordered to be powered by the new Allison V-1710 engine developed by Norman Golman. The Model 22 was first flown by Lt. Ben Kelsey on 27 January 1939. The prototype crashed two weeks later, but despite the crash, the Army Air Corps was so impressed by its performance that it ordered 13 YP-38s. The first YP-38 flew on 16 September 1940 with the more powerful 1,150hp Allison V-1710 engines and the replacement of two of the four .50s by .30s and the 20mm cannon by the 37mm.

P-38 D and E

Like the P-39 Airacobra, the P-38 prototype performed very well, but as the XP-38 transformed into a fighter with the concomitant changes in armament, pilot protection, self-sealing fuel tanks, avionics, and other prerequisites of an operational fighter, its performance decreased significantly. The production version of 35 P-38Ds (there were no As, Bs, or Cs) had the original XP-38 gun arrangement, the addition of pilot armor, self-sealing

fuel tanks, and minor airframe modifications. It was followed by 210 P-38Es that reverted back to the 20mm cannon and carried twice the ammunition. The name Lightning was given by the RAF, which had ordered three Lightning Is. By 1941, the Allison engine that appeared to be adequate in 1938 had become critically underpowered and endangered this promising design. The British canceled a large contract for 524 P-38s after finding them to be virtually ineffective above 15,000 feet. The P-38 design was salvaged by the addition of turbo-superchargers to the 1,225 horsepower Allison engines.

Early in the war, Lockheed issued a critical internal report that exposed many of the Lightning's problems to be due to serious management errors. The company's chief designers were among the finest in the aviation industry, but the P-38's unorthodox design required a large and skilled team. The company report estimated that mass production of the P-38 was delayed at least nine months due to poor management and basic design failures. The Lockheed report also disclosed that many of its best personnel were transferred to work on more profitable export models like the Hudson, while their replacements on the P-38 contract were inexperienced and had to be continually supervised in even the most basic matters. If Lockheed management had concentrated itself and its best personnel on the P-38 project, by early 1942 P-38Fs, instead of P-40s and P-39s, could have met Japanese Zeros over Darwin and New Guinea.

P-38F and G

The unwanted Lightning I's were repossessed by the AAC, which converted them to the F and G standard. An increase in engine power was the major improvement in the F and G models and enabled them to carry external fuel tanks and/or weapons on under-wing racks for the first time. A production run of 527 P-38Fs and 1,082 P-38Gs, with deliveries occurring during 1942, supplied P-38s for deployment in the ETO, North Africa, and the PTO, where operational P-38s weighed well over twice as much as a Zero and, if fully loaded, nearly as much as a Betty bomber!

The P-38F was used in the ETO during the early stages of the war and proved to be inferior in climb and acceleration when compared to the Me 109. Its diving performance was good if the pilot did not exceed 375mph and its roll rate was good at less than 300mph. Its high speed handling at speeds over 375mph was particularly poor, and its roll rate at this speed was non-existent due to excessive stick forces (solved by the addition of power-assisted ailerons in the J-model). The turbulence and lift problems at these speeds negated the elevators (dive flaps in the P-38L solved this problem). The tail flutter problem in early models was solved, but the compression and the high-speed turbulence that destroyed lift were not solved until well into the J-model. The Luftwaffe quickly found that they could escape by Split-s'ing (which the P-38 could not follow due to its slow rolling deficiency) and then diving away (which the P-38 could not follow due to its compressibility problem). The F-model was a very poor vertical fighter, and any fighter with adequate vertical maneuvering capability could follow the P-38 and match any of its evasive vertical turns. The only real advantages the F-model had were its heavy nose-mounted armament, as armament changed significantly from the early models. The original armament consisted of a 23mm cannon and four .50 caliber machine guns to a 37mm cannon and two .30 caliber and two .50 caliber machine guns, then finally to a 20mm cannon and four .50 caliber machine guns. The P-38F had good horizontal turn rate and by using this turning advantage the P-38 pilot hoped to have a chance in a turning combat.

Engine	2x1,350hp Allison Y-1710-49 Inline
Weight	(Empty/Loaded/Maximum): DO DO
Length	37.8 feet
Wing Span	52 feet
Wing Area	327.5 square feet
Wing Loading	(Empty/Loaded/Maximum): DO DO
Armament	4x.50 caliber Browning MG and 1x20 mm Hispano-Suiza cannon
Bomb Load	2x100lb, 2x500lb, or 2x1,000lb
Maximum Speed	320mph
Full Flaps Speed	110mph
Climb	1,000 to 5,000 feet: 62 seconds 5,000 to 10,000 feet: 103 seconds 10,000 to 15,000 feet: 107 seconds
Maximum Diving Speed	490 mph

P-38J

Through all the modifications leading from the XP-38 to the P-38H, the 2,970 P-38Js were the only Lightnings to undergo major external changes. The P-38J version, which first began to appear in August 1943, introduced some appreciable differences in the geometry of the engine nacelles which make this and later versions easily distinguishable from earlier versions of the Lightning. Other external changes were the introduction of chin air cooler intakes under the prop spinners, a flat panel replaced the curved windscreen, and the radiators located in the booms were enlarged.

Compared to the P-38F, the J-model had better vertical performance, was able to attain a higher speed before control problems occurred, had a slightly improved roll rate, faster acceleration, and comparable rate of turn. Unfortunately, the P38's main weakness (high speed control) was not solved until later versions of the P38J and P38L, as the later P-38J production block introduced power-boosted, hydraulically-actuated ailerons and dive flaps, making it easier for the pilot to maneuver the fighter at high airspeeds. This boosting system was one of the first employments of powered controls to any fighter and required only 17% of the previous stick forces. The hydraulic aileron booster system greatly improved the roll rate and thus increased the effectiveness of the P-38 in combat, giving it one of the highest roll rates of any fighter. More powerful engines and improved propellers helped speed and climb, making it the fastest of the P-38s, with a top speed of 420mph. Its increased internal fuel capacity, along with external tanks, gave it an in air endurance of 12 hours.

Engine	2x1,425 hp Allison V-1710-89 Inline
Weight	(Empty/Loaded/Maximum): 12,780lbs-17,400lbs-21,700lbs
Length	37.8 feet
Wing Span	52 feet
Wing Area	327.5 square feet
Wing Loading	(Empty/Loaded/Maximum): 39.1lbs/sqft-53.1lbs/sqft-66.0lbs/sqft
Armament	4x.50 caliber Browning MG and 1x20 mm Hispano-Suiza cannon
Bomb Load	6 rockets, 6 rockets with 2x500lb, or 2x1,000lb
Maximum Speed	340mph
Full Flaps Speed	130mph
Climb	1,000 to 5,000 feet: 47 seconds 5,000 to 10,000 feet: 69 seconds 10,000 to 15,000 feet: 69 seconds
Maximum Diving Speed	495 mph

P-38L

The P-38L was the final production version and numerically was the most prolific of all the Lightning models, with Lockheed producing 3,810 P-38Ls and Consolidated-Vultee (Nashville) having orders for 2,000 more, but building only 113 more before the order was canceled at the end of the war. The P-38L was powered by 1,475hp Allison V-1710-111/113 engines with a war emergency rating of 1,600hp at 28,700 feet and a military rating of 1,475hp at 30,000 feet.

The L-model demonstrated Lockheed's ability to continually improve its design from model to model, so that the L seemed to be an entirely different design based on performance figures. The addition of hydraulic ailerons and dive flaps in the J models had solved the major remaining problem, the locking of controls at high speed. Another improvement of the propeller increased speed and climb. While the F could not dive at speeds higher than 375mph without losing control, the L could dive at speeds in excess of 500mph with minimal degradation of control. It has to be stated the P-38L was "the Jack of all trades and the master of most." It was among the best fighters regarding speed, diving ability, high altitude performance, and roll—especially above 275mph—excellent climb rate, and gunnery installations with surplus ammunition. The L's (as in all Lightnings) only weakness was its large size, which made it a good target, but its excellent roll rate enabled it to roll away when approached.

With no torque, it was easy to fly and vertical maneuvers were easy. The only control problem was the aileron-induced yaw, which occurred during a rapid roll when one of the ailerons created more drag than the other and the wide placement of the ailerons caused a brief yaw that could disrupt a gunnery run. Previous models did not have this problem, because the force of the wind on the ailerons at speed prevented them from being employed enough to make a significant difference. The L did not climb and turn well simultaneously and a spiraling climb by a good climbing enemy fighter could gain an offensive advantage on the Lightning, or at least be able to escape it. While in a sustained turning combat, the L could turn with the Zero but not beat it, and it would be inadvisable for the Lightning pilot to try, as if the Zero pilot had higher remaining power, he could quickly gain 20-30° on the P-38 and get into firing position. The P-38 pilot could escape by employing full flaps and fly to the edge of a stall, hoping the Zero pilot followed into the stall, as it was not advantageous for the Zero pilot to use flaps.

Engine	2x1,475 hp Allison V-1710-111/113 Inline
Weight	(Empty/Loaded/Maximum): 12,800lbs-17,500lbs-21,600lbs
Length	37.8 feet
Wing Span	52 feet
Wing Area	327.5 square feet
Wing Loading	(Empty/Loaded/Maximum): 39.1lbs/sqft-53.4lbs/sqft-66.0lbs/sqft
Armament	4x.50 caliber Browning MG and 1x20 mm Hispano-Suiza cannon
Bomb Load	10 rockets, 10 rockets with 2x500lb, or 2x1,000lb
Maximum Speed	340mph
Full Flaps Speed	120mph
Climb	1,000 to 5,000 feet: 47 seconds 5,000 to 10,000 feet: 71 seconds 10,000 to 15,000 feet: 72 seconds
Maximum Diving Speed	510mph

A total of 9,923 Lightnings were produced. Like most mass produced fighter aircraft, the P-38 was converted to perform other duties. The 75 two-seat radar-equipped M model night fighters were converted from P-38Ls. The P-38 F-4s or F-5s were the most numerous photo recon aircraft of WWII, with approximately 1,400 being converted from the P-38E, F, G, H, J, and L models.

P-38J Cockpit (NMUSAF)

P-38 Described

Cockpit
The P-38 cockpit was roomy and comfortable, but taller pilots thought the canopy top was too low. The seat was adjustable only in height. Because the P-38 was a twin-engine fighter, it had many more controls and displays than single-engine fighters (an assortment of 21 dials and 69 controls). The cockpit layout was considered to be poor and the worst of all AAF fighters, with the landing gear and flap controls worst of all. As described previously, ground taxi visibility was very good due to the tricycle gear arrangement. In-flight visibility was excellent in the forward and downward directions, but very poor to the side and particularly poor to the lower rear quarters. During the cold European Winters, in particular, it had the reputation as a cold aircraft, since cockpit heating and defrosting were wholly insufficient. In the SWPA the cold was of little concern, but frosting over of the window areas could be a concern despite heat outlets blowing air on the windshield. Heat was supplied by a removable flexible tube and an outlet on the floor. Ventilating air entered from a port on the left. There was no cooling system.

Pilot Protection
Pilot protection consisted of self-sealing fuel tanks, bulletproof glass, and armor plate. The armor plate protection was small pieces of face-hardened steel that were attached separately to facilitate replacement. The pilot was protected by armor plate mounted on the aft bulkhead of the gun compartment, two pieces of armor plate lining the bottom and back of the seat, and a single piece mounted behind the seat. Additional armor plate (or circular deflectors) were installed on the inboard sides of the turbo-superchargers to protect the pilot from broken turbo blades.

The P-38 was vulnerable to ground and small arms fire. The P-38 was never equipped with fire extinguishers. It was claimed that with two engines, a pilot could return to base on the good engine, but conversely, there was twice the chance of having an engine hit. Often a damaged engine caught fire and the pilot had to bail out. There was a saying that "the P-38 was designed with two engines so that you could return to base on one." Liquid-cooled engines were inherently more vulnerable and a hit in a P-38 cooling system disabled the engine very quickly, as the cooling systems spread out over two-thirds of each P-38 boom.

Armament
The P-38's machine gun and cannon installation in the nose made it a formidable gun platform, spewing accurate concentrated firepower and having the same pattern at all firing ranges. Japanese pilots did not wish to engage a P-38's firepower head-on or pull up in front of a P-38. The Lightning was armed with four .50 caliber machine guns and a 20mm cannon in the gondola nose ahead of the pilot. Each machine gun was supplied with 500 rounds and the cannon with 150 rounds, with the spent casings ejected through chutes below the ammunition compartment. The only undesirable aspect (in early models) was that if one gun stopped firing, the pilot was

P-38 Armament: The P-38's four .50 caliber machine guns and 20mm cannon installation in the nose made it a formidable gun platform. (AAF)

unable to determine which one and had to charge them using a single gun charge lever on the upper right section of the instrument panel. From the J model on guns were charged on the ground and could not be recharged in the air.

On later models, streamlined bomb supports were attached to the underside of the wing center section on each side. Bombs weighing 100 to 2,000 pounds could be carried. The P-38L was equipped to carry 10 2.76-inch HVAR rockets: five under each wing on zero-length launchers.

Engine, Propellers, and Fuel Tanks

The Lightning was powered by two 1,200 to 1,500 horsepower turbo-supercharged Allison V-1710 liquid cooled twelve cylinder V-type inline engines. The propeller was an 11.5-foot Curtiss three blade, electric, constant speed, selective pitch full feathering type. The port prop rotated counterclockwise (viewed from aft) and the right clockwise. At low and medium altitudes the Allisons were very satisfactory, but at high altitudes they had problems, which were a major reason the P-38 was removed from 8th Air Force bomber escort missions over Europe and transferred to tactical missions in the 9th Air Force and to eager-to-get-them Generals MacArthur and Kenney in the SWPA.

The two main 90-gallon, self-sealing fuel tanks were installed in the wing center inboard of the booms between the main wing beam and aft shear beam. The two 60-gallon self-sealing reserve tanks were located in the wing center sections between the main wing beam and forward shear beam for a normal capacity of 300 gallons. On later models (some Js and all Ls) another 55-gallon self-sealing tank was a added in each outboard wing panel leading edge section to give these models a 410-gallon total capacity. A 300-gallon drop tank could be carried under each wing center section to give late models a fuel capacity of 1,010 gallons. Smaller 75 and 150-gallon auxiliary tanks could also be carried. The drop tank release switch was located on the left side of the cockpit.

Flying the P-38

The P-38's ground handling characteristics were considered good. The fighter could be turned sharply, and unlike tail draggers, full braking could be used because of the tricycle landing gear. Differential engine power could be used to save the brakes when turning. Taxiing visibility was good, as the pilot could easily see forward and both wingtips because the P-38's attitude was level due to the tricycle gear. The cockpit roll-up side windows could be rolled down for taxiing in hot weather, but had to be closed before takeoff, or tail buffeting would result. Because of the two opposite rotating

propellers there was no torque to pull the fighter to one side, so the P-38 was easy to steer on the ground.

Takeoff procedure was to keep the flaps retracted or set them in half down position, hold the aircraft with the brakes on, and run up the manifold pressure and rpm until the turbos cut in. With the brakes on and power increasing the nose would drop and compress the nose strut, and the entire aircraft would shake and vibrate until the brakes were released. Once the brakes were released, the specified manifold pressure was reached as the roll started. The control column was eased back at 70mph, and lift off would occur at 90 to 100mph. The single engine control speed was 120 to 125mph (i.e., the speed at which rudder and aileron power were sufficient to continue under control if an engine failed). At speeds under 120mph, an engine failure would put the fighter into a half roll and an inverted crash, so the pilot had to keep the plane on the ground until it was over 120mph and then pull it into the air and retract the gear. Upon normal takeoff, the gear was quickly retracted and best climbing speed was established.

The P-38's trim was good to fair, but once properly trimmed it was easy to fly. No adjustment of rudder or elevator trim was required with power or speed changes. Once trimmed for straight and level flight, the P-38 could be flown "hands off." Pilots claimed that if the fighter was put off attitude (within limits) it would slowly sway and oscillate, then finally return to straight and level flight because its center of lift was above its center of gravity, while other fighters had a lower center of lift and would drop off on one wing.

The P-38 accelerated rapidly in a dive due to its weight and streamlined design. At high speeds compressibility became a problem, with the fighter buffeting and vibrating severely. Compressibility could be stopped by reducing speed, but it was not remedied until some P-38J and all P-38L models were introduced with a dive recovery flap system. The flaps were located under the wings on each side just outboard of the booms and when extended lessened the lift loss in compressibility and also added drag, which together with higher allowable dive speed permitted dives at steeper angles. Flaps were extended just before or after starting a dive. If the P-38 was already in compressibility buffet, the flaps were extended and buffeting would momentarily increase, but then diminish. The P-38 was generally rated last among AAF fighters for stability and control in a dive.

The P-38 was stable, and there were no restrictions on maneuvers except dives at speeds at compressibility. Since the Lightning lost altitude so quickly, the pilot had to pay attention when attempting maneuvers requiring a downward recovery and were cautioned not to attempt maneuvers below 10,000 feet. The Lightning was excellent for precision maneuvers such as floops and aileron rolls, and was particularly suited for vertical maneuvers, with its great ability to change vertical direction, and had excellent zoom climb characteristics. Being a large heavy fighter, the P-38 was not suited for quick snap maneuvers and had an especially slow initial response in roll which could be disconcerting when being attacked by an enemy. Power boosted ailerons, introduced at the same time as dive recovery flaps, improved roll characteristics at high speeds, but did nothing to improve them at low and moderate speeds, where maximum roll performance was dependent only on full aileron deflection instead of pilot effort. Early model P-38s could not roll into a dive quickly enough to catch an enemy diving down and away in their favorite Split-S evasive maneuver. Once rolled into a turn, however, the P-38 could then turn very tightly for a large fighter, particularly at low altitudes, and was able to stay with most single-seat fighters. An 8° maneuver flap was fitted to the P-38's Fowler flap system which when deployed provided substantial improvement in turning capability without stalling. If the P-38 stalled in a very tight turn, it would just mush outward and forward stick pressure would get it out of the stall with little loss of altitude. During a panic break when being attacked from the rear, the Lightning pilot could pull his fighter into such a tight turn that the aircraft would buffet, but still have excellent aileron control.

The cockpit control column had considerable travel, but the P-38 was considered fairly heavy on the controls, especially on the ailerons before power boost was installed. After this installation, most pilots rated aileron control force characteristics and effectiveness as very good at high speeds but poorly at low speeds. Elevator control for maneuvering was considered to be very effective. Rudder force and effectiveness characteristics were good.

Approach and landing a P-38 was usually easy due to no torque—thus no constant adjusting of the rudder trim—the wide tread main gear and tricycle nose wheel configuration, and the effective braking system. The approach was made with gear down and flaps set to the MANEUVER position at 120mph; on the final approach leg, the flaps were lowered full down, reducing the speed to 110mph and flaring to about 80mph. Touch down was with the main wheels first and the tail slightly low to keep the nose wheel off the ground. Single-engine landing was similar to a two-engine landing, but once committed to land the pilot could not go around again.

P-38 stall characteristics were very good. When approaching the stall speed, the wing center section stalled first and began a conspicuous shaking of the fighter. The fighter mushed forward, but if carrying tanks or bombs would have one wing drop; there was no tendency to spin. The nose then dropped slightly and as speed increased, the wing would come back up. The result was the same for a high-speed stall.

Pilots were prohibited from deliberate spinning because a spin tended to flatten out after two or three turns, forcing back the control column, and engine power had to be applied to return it forward. Before the spin flattened out, recovery could be made without using engine power by applying full opposite rudder and easing the control column forward.

Flying the P-38 Lightning (PTO)
by Jay Robbins: 22 victories 8FG (4th ranked P-38 ace)

Robbins

Pre-Flight Procedure
The walk around and pre-flight procedure for the P-38 was relatively simple and easy to perform in the SWPA. Climatic conditions were such that extremely adverse weather conditions were uncommon. However, getting onto the wing via a ladder and into the cockpit was not always easy at night or when high temperatures made the metal very hot.

Cockpit
The cockpit was roomy compared to other fighters I had flown (P-400 and P-39). The seat could easily be adjusted to accommodate pilots of different heights. The seat and rudder pedals were easily adjusted to suit a pilot of my height (6'1"). Very small pilots needed to use cushions to reach the rudder pedals. Cockpit temperature control was no problem in the SWPA because of the climate and flight operating procedures in this theater. We did not operate at high altitudes so we had no need for heating. I understand that in the ETO cockpit heating was a problem. The oxygen system was adequate in early models of the P-38 (the F and G), but it was considerably improved in later models (J and on). The instrument layout was fairly simple, with instrument groupings being easy to learn. Instrument flying *per se* was not difficult, although we tried to maintain VFR whenever possible to simplify formation flying. In fast, the P-38 was very good under instrument conditions due to its inherent stability and lack of torque. Control layout left little to be desired and was better than most aircraft I have ever flown. Visibility was exceptionally good both on the ground and in the air for all phases of operation. As with all fighter aircraft, visibility to the rear and low was limited. Communications were adequate and any limitations were not peculiar to the P-38. We originally had low frequency radios which had the advantage of range but whose clarity was, at times, not very good. When the VHF radios were introduced, the range was sacrificed but clarity improved dramatically.

Engine
The two Allison engines were very good in all models, but the later version Allisons were considerably improved. Aborts for engine problems were not excessive, considering the operating environment in New Guinea and on up the ladder of recaptured islands, where maintenance facilities were meager at best. Although I made several one-engine landings, most were combat related. I considered the liquid-cooled Allisons reliable and rugged, although loss of coolant due to enemy action was not uncommon. Radial engines probably enjoyed an advantage in this respect. Having two engines in the SWPA was a distinct plus, since most of our operational flying was either over vast expanses of water or over dense jungles. The confidence factor alone for the pilot was immeasurable. The fact that we had the ability to return to base on a single engine, in case one engine was lost for whatever reason, tended to make the pilots more aggressive in combat.

Climbing to Altitude
The P-38 could take off and climb to altitude better than most other fighters. Performance in this phase was not too important, except in attaining safe airspeed as soon as possible. As Squadron leader, I normally operated at reduced power at squadron join-up and only increased power to desired climb parameters when all aircraft were in proper formation.

Cruise
I have no significant comments in this regard. Our cruise procedures were dictated by a number of operating factors and not necessarily by the aircraft's capabilities. Mainly, we wanted to conserve fuel. We wanted to avoid adverse weather conditions and early detection by the enemy that would use additional fuel and jeopardize mission accomplishment. During bomber escort, we reduced power as much as we could in order to be able to weave back and forth over the bombers until they reached the target.

Combat
The extremely long range of the P-38 was one, if not the most important, combat characteristic it possessed. This feature enabled us to escort bombers to Japanese targets at ranges even the Japanese thought impossible. In later models of the aircraft, combat missions in excess of seven hours were not

uncommon. Earlier in the war, the normal mission time was three to four hours. This was dictated in some measure by the strategic situation and a number of aircraft we had available in the SWPA in the early days of 1942-43. With the prospect of replacement personnel aircraft questionable, it was paramount that we preserve the limited resources we had on hand. Understandably, priority for equipping the Air Force went to the European Theater, with build up in the Pacific taking place later. As our fighter and bomber forces grew and we took the offensive, we operated at longer ranges and struck more diverse targets. The combat range of the P-38 improved significantly after technical representatives, particularly Charles Lindbergh, visited all groups in the theater. Lindbergh's "very high manifold pressure/low rpm" technique was not well received at first, but was eventually adopted with considerable success. It allowed us to hit deep targets and utilizing large external tanks, special missions of eleven hours or more were possible.

The concentration of four .50 caliber machine guns and a 20mm cannon in the nose was a highly desirable feature for several reasons. This concentration of firepower insured a shoot down if you were in range and squarely on target. A burst of three to five seconds would bring down most Jap fighters. The concentration of armament in the nose eliminated the need for figuring convergent fire that was common for fighters with guns in the wings. We had a variety of gunfights depending on the aircraft model. The F and G models had the old 70-mil fixed ring sight (circle and dot). Later models were equipped with the computing sight. I preferred the old fixed sight, because that was what I learned on and had confidence in. I had a natural tendency for high angle deflection shooting, since I had done considerable bird shooting as a boy with my father.

Bombing and strafing were relatively simple because of the lack of propeller torque and negative trim problems. Only slight trim was necessary, even when air speed varied greatly. The Lightning was also an excellent dive-bombing platform. I never used rockets in combat.

Maneuverability was limited in the early models but improved later with the addition of dive and maneuvering flaps. The distinct advantage the P-38 had over most Jap fighters was in high-speed climbs and shallow dives, which enabled us to engage or disengage almost at will. Even with maneuvering flaps, we did not try to get into a turning engagement with most Jap fighters. In the early P-38 models, we had to avoid high vertical dives at relatively low altitudes because the aircraft tended to tuck under. We were made well aware of this tendency and knew how to avoid it.

I considered the Lightning to be fairly rugged. Armor plating and self-sealing fuel tanks enabled the aircraft to take a lot of punishment and continue to operate, even with one engine. On one mission I had one engine shot out, took 189 bullets and cannon hits, and was still able to return home.

Landing
The P-38 was simple to land and directional control was good. Single-engine landings only required that you maintain adequate airspeed and avoid turning into the dead engine. In early models, emergency extension of the landing gear was a problem. It took 125 to 150 strokes on a manual pump to lower and lock the gear, and it always seemed to happen after a long and tiring mission when you were very low on fuel. Later models had an emergency electrical pump to extend the gear.

Bailout and Ditching
I never had to bail out, but we were all well aware of the dangers of hitting the horizontal stabilizer during bailout. I never had to ditch in the water, but did belly in once without difficulty. Although the aircraft was badly damaged, I sustained no injuries. I had turned off all electrical switches prior to impact to prevent the aircraft from catching fire. The cockpit remained basically intact, although the nose section was badly broken.

Overall Impressions
I always had great confidence in the Lightning and my ability to use it effectively in any combat situation. Compared to most Jap fighters, the P-38 was a superstar in nearly every respect, except in turning, and we learned early on not to get into a turning contest.

P-38 Tactics (PTO)
by Wallace Jordan: 6 Victories/49FG

Jordan

Six victory ace and leader/tactician Maj. Wallace Jordan of the 9FS/49FG had flown P-39s with the 54R in the Aleutians with fellow 22-victory ace and tactician Gerald Johnson. Jordan transitioned to P-38s in the U.S. and was stationed at Dobodura. Jordan wrote this opinion on combat in the P-38 late in the war:

"Primarily, one principle which underlies the successful application of all the following fighter-to-fighter combat tactics with the Japanese is the neutralization of the excellent maneuverability of his airplane. In my experience, maneuverability is the only quality in which the enemy excels, and when allowed, he will use it to its fullest extent. The neutralization is effected simply by fighting in a manner that does not allow him to use his maneuverability.

"Individual Defensive Tactics
"First, do not attempt to dogfight. If you do, your chances are minimized by allowing the enemy to use maneuverability.

"When enemy contact is imminent (i.e., over a target), maintain an IAS of at least 250mph. From this speed, increased settings will quickly give you the necessary high speed when needed.

"Upon being attacked, several things can be done according to the type of attack. If seriously outnumbered and attacked from above, establish a shallow dive at War Emergency setting until out of danger. If attacked from below, use a high-speed shallow climb. The enemy climbs more vertically and cannot stay with you in this type of climb.

"If attacked by a single enemy, allow him to commit himself in his pass—turn sharply in and under at the critical moment. A great many times you will be able to get a short head-on shot in this situation. Maintain this turn through the shortest possible period. Get out far enough to regain altitude and return offensively.

"Recently, with the use of the dive flaps and aileron boost on the L-series P-38, the following defensive maneuver has been very successful. Split-S roll 180° while going straight down and pull out. This maneuver was used by a pilot in the squadron at 3,000ft. Low, it should be used only as a last resort, since it allows the enemy to use his maneuverability if he so desires and is good enough to follow. High, it can be used to better advantage, since you will be able to hold straight down after the 180° straight down roll, building up excessive speed to where the attacker cannot stay with you. This maneuver and the normal Split-S should not be used unless absolutely necessary, because the consequent loss of altitude is to your general disadvantage.

"At any time, your best individual defensive action is to rejoin another friendly airplane and use the teamwork of the two-ship Element for your mutual protection.

"Individual Offensive Tactics

"When individually attacking an enemy fighter, use the speed necessary to prevent over-running, come from sun or cloud cover, and do not fire until minimum range is reached, unless the enemy aircraft starts evasive action before that time. With premature firing your ammunition is wasted by your tracers, prompting the enemy to evasive action that you cannot possibly follow. The best pass, if you can get set for it, is to come in directly behind and slightly low. From this position, you can close to minimum range, pull up to level altitude with the enemy, and destroy him before he realizes you are there.

"The majority of Japanese pilots dislike the head-on pass and will not press it to minimum. If one does, your superior firepower will give you a distinct advantage.

"If attacking superior numbers, pick the most vulnerable target, make a straight pass with plenty of speed, and keep on going. In this instance, if you turn more than 45°, you will usually be immediately and seriously on the defensive.

"The evasive maneuvers favored by the enemy are the Split-S, Immelmanns, tight loops, steep diving turns, and Chandelles. I have seen the double Immelmann used occasionally. The enemy does this difficult maneuver with amazing ease. Most of these turns will be made to the left. Usually, they are executed so quickly and the radii of the turns is so short that you cannot follow. Bide your time, keep altitude, and make another pass. If you try to follow, the tight loop or a reversal from any of the enemy's tight turns can easily put him on your tail.

"If you anticipate fighting the Japanese, be especially proficient in deflection shooting, because the majority of your shots fired in anger will be that type.

"Squadron Defensive Tactics

"The squadron formation, both offensive end defensive, is based upon, and expands from, the two-ship Element. The flights are four-ship, consisting of two two-ship Elements. Within the flight, the Wingman of the flight leader and the Element fly wide, almost abreast on opposite sides of the flight leader. The Wingman crosses under and the second Element over. As much of the time as possible the second Element is flown high, with the first Element between the second and the sun. This makes for easier handling of attacks from the sun. Close checking upon Element leaders is sometimes necessary to see that this is done, since some may thoughtlessly fly the more comfortable sunward side.

The squadron formation, if each flight is considered as a single airplane, looks relatively the same as a flight when viewed from above. There is an average depth, stepped up from the lead flight, of 1,000ft. These positions afford maximum visibility, flexibility, and ease to hold. From them, maximum firepower can quickly be brought to bear on an attack from any direction. We insist upon close show formation around home base before and after missions. This increases alertness of the pilots for all formation flying.

"In instances where it is impossible to get away otherwise, flights or Elements who are outnumbered and cannot fire-out of ammunition, etc., can usually force the enemy to break off by making bluff passes. This has been done successfully a number of times. Recently, Lt. Helterline (2Lt. Frederick), out of ammunition, made bluff passes on three enemy fighters which were attacking an airplane with only a single operable engine. They broke off and the single engine returned safely.

"Upon completion of a fight, squadron formation must be resumed as quickly as possible in order to conserve gas and to protect any cripples.

"Squadron Offensive Tactics

"When we are offensive to start, we strive to maintain the flight formation but do not insist upon it, since keeping a flight together in the general melee of a fight is very difficult. We do, however, insist that the Wingman stay in and keep the two-ship Element intact. There will be a few instances where even this will not be possible. If a break up of two-ship Elements occurs, the singles must rejoin another friendly fighter as soon as possible, and where possible, Elements rejoin to form flights.

"When an enemy formation is sighted, the squadron or flight leader immediately calls in the clock position of enemy aircraft, and if they are higher, attains an altitude necessary to attack. At this time, the flights must space themselves far enough to avoid following the leader's flight too closely, thus having time to pick a good target, make an effective pass, and avoid collisions with enemy or friendly aircraft.

"Once the initial pass has been made and the enemy formation has been dispersed, it is the job of the various two-ship Elements to mop up the remaining Japanese aircraft. Pilots must be indoctrinated to restrain their eagerness to shoot where several are trying to get in a pass. If they all press in at once, none will get a shot and collisions will be imminent. If two or more are attacking (this applies especially where there are several trying to get one aircraft), the formation should spread very wide and allow one man to attack. If this is done, the enemy's evasive move will usually carry him within range of another member of the formation.

"Another aspect of this case is concerned with hot guns and the resultant swirling of rounds there from. After any amount of sustained shooting, your guns need at least ten minutes of cooling. If they are not given this cooling the rounds will swirl, go in every direction, and you will hit nothing. When the swirl is observed, pull off and allow someone else to take over the attack until your guns have returned to normal. Actually, your guns will not get the chance to overheat if you coordinate properly with the rest of the flight or Element, because the target's evasive actions will change his attacker frequently. Recently, we had an enemy aircraft get away from a flight of six P-38s simply because all members, thinking of their own personal score of course, shot at once, got in each other's way, and in the end could not hit anything with overheated guns.

"Intelligence Officers must continually brief pilots as to enemy order of battle, types likely to be encountered, and all information concerning them—mainly speeds—because they are necessary to compute lead in the oft-encountered deflection shot.

"Long Reach

"All the foregoing information applies fundamentally to the tactics of long reach. The differences will occur in the formation to and from the target. We use 1,600rpm and the necessary manifold pressure setting to maintain 185mph IAS, which is the computed most efficient airspeed for minimum fuel consumption where the airplane carries two external tanks. The speed without external tanks is 175mph. These figures were given to us by Charles Lindbergh, and since we have no other source of information, we have taken them to be correct. Actually, we have never had to cut the LAS back that far on return. Without external tanks, 24 inches and 1,600rpm will give an IAS of 200mph at 10,000 feet.

"In order to reduce drag, the external tanks are burned out separately and dropped when empty. Most airplanes will give two hours, or slightly better, with a climb included. If the mission is not over 800 miles, the second tank will last to the target plus 15 minutes. The last 15 minutes are at high settings, since you are over the target, so we assume that we could probably reach 900 miles on the external wing tanks.

"The accomplishment of long radius of action (over 300 miles) is based upon the following use of eight-ship section—which I will explain in the next paragraph—no interception en route, an advanced rendezvous point, and good weather. An advance fighter sweep is not essential, but is preferable.

"On a mission where the radius is over 800 miles, we split the squadron and go on course as eight-ship sections, which take off and go on course immediately. The leader will make a turn of no more than 180° after take off, assembling loosely and going on course without waiting for the second eight. A squadron assembly over the field, and maintenance of it to the rendezvous, will result in the use of too much fuel. Obviously, this condition prevails only where one strip suitable to take off one aeroplane at a time is available—for example, Morotai during the Borneo missions. With proper on-the-ball assembly a full squadron can perform the mission, but would have a very small fighting and weather reserve.

"At low settings, the changes in speed of the airplane are very sluggish. Increase of manifold pressure at the excessively low rpm has very little effect upon increasing the speed of the airplane. However, increase of rpm to the necessary amount has the desired effect. For this reason, all pilots use rpm to maintain formation on the longer missions.

"The type of formation flown is identical to normal combat type, except that it is flown much more loosely. This prevents jockeying of settings and consequent use of extra fuel. The formation is not so loosely flown that aircraft are outside supporting distance of one another.

"These are fighter tactics as we know and use them. Having only recently become a full P-38 group, our squadron tactics may change somewhat to accommodate operations where the group flies as a unit. However, we do not anticipate any important fundamental change."

Kenney on the P-38

"I wanted the P-38 in the Pacific because of the long distances, but not only for long distances. You look down from the cockpit and you can see schools of sharks swimming around. They never look healthy to a man flying over them. Say we were going into a combat and you go in with a P-51, a 100% warplane: give it a status of 100 for combat. The pilot starts out with a rating of 100. But by the time he gets four or five hundred miles out over the ocean his morale has been going down steadily by looking at that water down there, and my guess was that he would arrive at combat about a 50 percent efficient pilot. So the total score of pilot and plane is 150. Now the P-38 is not a bad combat airplane, I'd give it a rating of 75 as compared to the P-51, easily, maybe more than that, but give it 75. But the pilot arrives there 100%; he is just as good as when he took off because he knows one of those big fans can bring him home. He has two engines. So his score, his fighting score, is 175 against the other's 150. And you could hang gasoline on them. We put two 300-gallon tanks on those wings. One time we took off, flew 1,200 nautical miles, and fought over the target for forty minutes and then came home. Now some of them ran out of gas taxiing back on the runway, but still they all got back; we did not lose a single airplane because of fuel."

The P-38 in Combat in the Pacific

The Lightning was suited for combat in the Pacific, as it possessed a performance clearly superior to that of any of its American fighter rivals. It seemed that every strong point possessed by the P-38 corresponded to a weakness of Japanese aircraft.

It possessed a range significantly better than that of the P-39s, P-40s, and P-47s available in 1942 and 1943 in the Southwest Pacific, and its twin engines offered an additional safety factor when operating over long stretches of water and jungle. The Lightnings proved to be extremely rugged, sustaining heavy battle damage and remained flying. Missions of nine, ten, or even twelve hours became routine, and many damaged Lightnings were able to arrive back at base on only one engine. The P-38's unique configuration allowed Lockheed designers to mount four .50 caliber machine guns and a 20mm cannon in the nose ahead of the pilot, who could virtually point the fighter at his target and have a reasonable chance of scoring a hit with this tremendous firepower.

During late 1942 and 1943, Kenney demanded more Lightnings, but a lower priority had been given to the Pacific Theatre by Washington; once the initial Japanese thrusts at Guadalcanal and New Guinea had been checked, his requests for more Lightnings were mostly unheeded. It was not until August 1943, that the first all-Lightning Fighter Group of the Fifth Air Force, the 475FG, began combat operations. Later in the year, the continuing shortage of P-38s forced both the 35th and 49th Fighter Groups to convert their single P-38 squadron to fly P-47Ds, thus leaving the Fifth Air Force at the end of 1943 with only four P-38 squadrons, versus eight squadrons with P-47s and three with P-40s. At that time, the Eighth Air Force in England had 27 squadrons of P-47s and six squadrons of P-38s, which were found to be inadequate in that theater and were being phased out in anticipation of the arrival of the long-range P-51. In the Summer of 1944, the Fifth and Thirteenth Air Forces had been reorganized into the Far East Air Force in preparation for the invasion of the Philippines. By that time, the shortage of P-38s had been alleviated somewhat and there were five Fighter Groups fully equipped with P-38s: the 8th, 49th, and 475th of the 5FC and the 18th and 347th of the 13FC. By this time, the Japanese had lost the majority of its veteran pilots and the vaunted Zero and even newer fighter aircraft were found to be inferior, especially when flown by under-trained and inexperienced pilots.

The large and heavy Lightning was not an agile fighter, but considering its size, it had a reasonably good turning radius and a respectable overall rate of roll. In combat, regarding speed and maneuverability at medium and low altitudes, the Lightning was inferior to its agile Japanese opponents, but by the use of appropriate tactics P-38 Squadrons in New Guinea and the Solomons achieved outstanding victory totals. The P-38 could not out-turn a Zero at low or medium altitudes and dogfighting at these altitudes was usually fatal. However, the P-38 had a far higher top speed, rate of climb, and operational ceiling, and was much better armed; when utilizing these unique characteristics to best effect, the results were devastating.

The P-38 could achieve approximately 400mph and was an excellent performer above 20,000 feet. The Lightning pilot's principal offensive tactic was to remain at high altitudes and dive on enemy formations, unleashing its concentrated firepower, then using its notable climbing rate to zoom back up out of danger.

The early Lightnings in the ETO had problems with cockpit temperature regulation, which were often too cold at high altitude because the distance of the engines from the cockpit prevented easy heat transfer. In the Pacific, Lightning pilots were often too hot in the tropical sun, as the canopy could not be fully opened without causing severe buffeting.

The P-38 was one of the first aircraft fast enough to experience "compressibility" ("shock stall") problems during high altitude, high-speed dives. Basically, in a sustained dive from high altitude, speed quickly built to the condition where the airflow over portions of the aircraft (such as the upper wing surface) reached supersonic speeds (the airplane was not breaking the sound barrier but the airflow in certain places was). A shock wave formed that destroyed the lift over that part of the wing and also caused the air flowing off the wing to affect the tail in an abnormal way by increasing lift at the tail. The loss of lift from the wings, together with increased lift from the tail, caused the nose to drop. The increased dive angle caused the speed to increase even more and the pilot's instinctive response was to pull back on the yoke, which should cause the elevators to increase the down force at the tail and bring the nose up to pull out of the dive. However, as the pilot tried to pull back on the stick, the up force on the tail increased and no matter how firmly he pulled, the aerodynamic force on the tail pushed even more. The controls "seemed to be set in concrete" and the fighter was totally out of the pilot's control.

The P-38 was not alone in experiencing compressibility in dives from very high altitudes where the air is thin. The big, radial-engine P-47 and F4U fighters would dive uncontrollably toward the ground until they reached the thicker air at lower altitudes. The speed of sound increases as the altitude gets lower and the increased drag of the thick air on the Thunderbolt's and Corsair's large frontal engine surfaces would limit further increases in speed. So, when the speed of sound increased as these fighters got lower, the shock waves started to dissipate (the airflow over the wings began to Fall back below the increased speed of sound), and as the increased drag started to affect the airplane, the speed of the airflow also decreased and the shock waves dissipated more. Finally, the pilot would begin to regain some control but continue to pull the stick as firmly as he could and would finally go into a zooming climb. However, the P-38's exceptionally clean, streamlined design had a drag so low that the thicker lower air did not have enough effect for the pilot to regain control in time, often ending in a fatal crash. The problem was further exaggerated by a tail flutter set up by these excessive speeds, which often caused the tail to be shed. Test pilots put the P-38 through a stressful series of test dives at progressively steeper angles before the diving boundaries and solution were found. The compressibility problem was solved by changing the geometry of the underside of the wing in a dive so as to keep lift within bounds of the top of the wing. In February 1943, quick-acting dive flaps that extended downward 35° in 1.5 seconds were tested and then installed outboard of the engine nacelles. The flaps did not act as a speed brake, but affected the center of pressure distribution so that the wing would not lose its lift.

Aerodynamic buffeting was another early problem which was difficult to distinguish from compressibility, as both were reported by test pilots as "tail shake." Buffeting—shudder at high speeds—was caused by disturbances of the airflow forward of the tail due to the straight connection of the wing root to the fuselage pod. Leading edge wing slots and combinations of filleting between the wing, cockpit, and engine nacelles were tried as remedies. After 15 wind tunnel tests to properly position the fillets, the buffeting problem was solved.

The two propellers rotated in opposite directions, eliminating the direction-changing torque found in single-engine fighters and making the P-38

unusually stable during normal flight. But its distinctive outwardly rotating (at the tops of the propeller arcs) counter-rotating propellers did cause problems. Losing one of two engines in any twin-engine non-centerline thrust aircraft on takeoff created sudden drag, yawing the nose toward the dead engine and rolling the wing tip down on the side of the dead engine. Standard training in flying twin-engine aircraft when losing an engine on takeoff would be to push the remaining engine to full throttle; if a pilot did that in the P-38, regardless of which engine had failed, the resulting engine torque and asymmetric propeller loading (p-factor force) produced a sudden uncontrollable yawing roll and the aircraft would roll over and crash into the ground. Ultimately, procedures were taught to allow a pilot to manage the situation by reducing power on the functioning engine, feathering the prop on the dead engine, then increasing power gradually until the fighter was in stable flight. Single-engine takeoffs were possible, though not with full fuel and ammunition loading. The twin-engine design had a small disadvantage while rolling because the ailerons had to move not only the wing, but also the weight of an engine, so inertia made its initial rate of roll slow. This impaired the P-38 in Europe more than in the Pacific. At high speeds, like other American fighters, the P-38 could turn inside a Zero, particularly at high altitudes. Because of its great power, the Lightning had an excellent rate of climb and could out-dive the Zero.

The P-38's range (approximately 400 miles) was superior to other U.S. fighters, but for combat over the long distances in the Pacific it was still less than desirable. However, because the P-38 had so much power it could carry a sizeable external load, including a large drop tank that gave it excellent range or bombs and later rockets.

Yet the P-38's configuration presented several disadvantages. With two engines instead of one, maintenance was more difficult, especially in the hot, rainy tropic climate of the SWPA. A P-40 Squadron was allotted 24 aircraft (although it was unusual for all to be serviceable for a mission), while a P-38 Squadron was allotted 20 aircraft due to the additional burden placed on the ground crew.

Perhaps the major problem with the twin engines occurred during takeoff, as the engines were most prone to shutdown at that time. If one of the counter-rotating props shut down on takeoff, the pilot was confronted with extreme torque and low power that could be handled only by an experienced pilot. Also, Lockheed boasted that the P-38 could be flown back to base on one engine, which was true again for an experienced pilot, but the 8th Air Force grounded the P-38 in the ETO for a time because of excessive single-engine fatalities.

The Lightning's larger size made it a bigger target, which did not matter greatly during air combat, but became important later in the war, during its increased ground attack role. Having two engines doubled the chance that an enemy round from the ground could start a catastrophic engine fire. Early model P-38s had only one generator, and if it failed the other engine would continue to operate, but all electrical systems failed, causing an emergency situation.

The foremost lesson learned by wise Lightning pilots was to accept the fighter's failings and concentrate on its strengths, which often required time. The fighter's outstanding speed and firepower lured novice pilots into overconfidence during their first combats and they would be tempted to dogfight the Zero. If they survived their initial errors, they learned to adopt established combat tactics, using the advantage of their excellent high-altitude speed and performance and their superior diving speed. They would dive from high altitude into Zero formations, firing their heavy machine guns and cannon, then zoom away in a climb that no Zero pilot could hope to catch. By using these tactics, P-38 pilots rarely found themselves in a situation in which they were forced to engage in a close-in maneuvering dogfight.

The P-38 could not turn with the Japanese fighters and its pilots had to keep their speed up and always try to get an altitude advantage. If not, they would dive to keep airspeed always above 350mph so that an enemy pilot could not close. If the P-38 pilot had the altitude advantage over an enemy formation, he and his Wingman would dive and take their shots, and if the Zero maneuvered away, they would pass through the enemy formation, climb, and dive and attack again. The enemy fighter could not match the Lightning's dives, climbs, and high-altitude performance and the American pilot would never allow the enemy pilot to fight on their terms in a low-altitude, turning dogfight.

Republic P-47 Thunderbolt

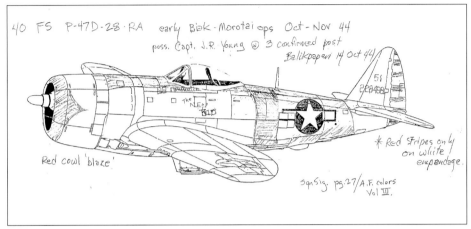

(Drawing by Steve Ferguson)

In June 1940, the AAC issued requirements for a new fighter based on advantageous characteristics found during air combat in the early war in Europe. The original XP-47 design was to be a high-altitude interceptor armed with a .50 caliber and a .30 caliber machine gun and powered by an Allison V-1710 engine like that already equipping the P-40 and P-39. In 1939, Republic Aviation designer Alexander Kartveli created the lightweight XP-47, but before manufacture could begin he recognized that this design would not meet the requirement; fortunately, Republic built the heavyweight XP-47B instead. Like the smaller fighters equipping the Luftwaffe and RAF, the Thunderbolt used the proven characteristics that determined a good fighter: speed, high-altitude performance, diving ability, firepower, ruggedness, and pilot protection. The Republic design, at 11,500 pounds, was by far the largest and heaviest single-seat fighter at that time. The huge fighter was powered by the potent new turbo-supercharged 2,000hp Pratt & Whitney R-2800 Radial engine, which gave it high speeds, especially in a dive. It was heavily armed by eight .50 caliber machine guns with a huge supply of ammunition and had the most complete armor package of any fighter. Although no fighter could dive like the Thunderbolt, Republic relinquished all maneuverability and a great deal of climbing ability. In a dive, the P-47 gained speed to outrun any opponent, and when the pilot leveled out, the fighter's weight and inertia kept it flying quickly for a relatively long time. But then the Thunderbolt pilot had the job of climbing back to altitude, as he did not want to be caught "low and slow" in his huge target.

P-47 Bs and Cs

Orders for 171 P-47Bs and 602 Cs were placed in September 1940. The B and C models basically differed only in the slightly longer fuselage of the C, which gave it better maneuverability. Although the XP-47B was first flown on 6 May 1941 by test pilot Lowry Brabham, it was another year and a half of testing and redesign before the huge fighter came off the Farmingdale production lines and became combat ready as the P-47D, now called the Thunderbolt.

P-47D

The D was the first Thunderbolt model to go into large-scale production, beginning with the first AAF order for 850 on 14 October 1941, which would be followed by thousands more. In its original version, the P-47D differed very little from the P-47C-5-RE that preceded it. The P-47D had some changes in the turbosupercharger, additional cowl flaps were added to improve engine cooling airflow, and more pilot armor protection, but generally, early P-47Ds could only be distinguished from Cs by their serial numbers. As demand and orders for the Thunderbolt increased, Republic built a new factory at Evansville, IN, to manufacture 1,050 P-47Ds ordered on 31 January 1942. The first Evansville-built P-47D came off the assembly line in September and could only be distinguished from Farmingdale-built P-47Ds by their serial numbers.

The D was the most numerous P-47, with 12,602 built by Republic in four runs and 354 by Curtiss as the P-47G. Variations in the D included external provisions for fuel tanks or bombs and water injection. All early Thunderbolts were powered by the R-2800-21 engine. Water injection capability was added to this engine beginning with the D-4-RA (Farmington) and D-5-RE (Evansville) production blocks. Provision was made for the mounting of a 15 gallon tank carrying a water-alcohol mixture to the bulkhead just aft of the engine. A line from this tank was plumbed directly into the fuel intake. When injected into the combustion chamber, the water checked a dangerous rise in cylinder head temperature while manifold pressure was boosted. For brief moments, a 15% increase in engine power could be obtained, giving a maximum war emergency power of 2,300hp. However, the major modification (8,179 models) was the introduction of the bubble canopy that replaced the cockpit, blending into the fuselage spine that ran back to the tail and gave the fighter its "razorback" nickname. The weight saved allowed extra fuel to be carried, but necessitated a dorsal fin fairing to be added to restore stability. Shackles for a belly tank or a 500 pound bomb were added to P-47D-5-RE (D-11-RA) and later blocks. Underwing pylons were introduced on the D-15-RE and D-15-RA production blocks, which permitted a drop tank or a bomb to be carried underneath each wing, in addition to the stores carried on the fuselage shackles. Fuel changes had to be made to incorporate plumbing for the underwing tanks. Bomb selection increased to two 1,000 pound or three 500 pound bombs, with maximum bomb load being 2,500 pounds. Alternatively, a 108-gallon drop tank could be carried underneath each wing, adding 150 miles to the P-47's range. The underwing pylons had a negative affect on performance and their air resistance took 45mph off the maximum speed, but a later redesigned, more streamlined pylon decreased the loss of speed to about 15mph. The Ds entered AAF service in November 1942 and became operational in Europe with the 8AF in April 1943 and in the Pacific with the 348FG in June.

P-47D Thunderbolt Specifications

Engine	2,000hp
Weight	(Empty/Loaded/Maximum): 11,000lbs-14,600lbs-20,700lbs
Length	36.1 feet
Wing Span	40.75 feet
Wing Area	332 square feet
Wing Loading	(Empty/Loaded/Maximum): 33.0lbs/sqft-43.9lbs/sqft-62.3/sqft
Armament	8x.50caliber Browning MG
Bomb Load	2x1,000lb bomb 10xRockets and 3x500lb bomb 10xRockets and 2x1,000lb bombs
Maximum Speed	340mph
Full Flaps Speed	115mph
Climb	1,000 to 5,000 feet: 66 seconds 5,000 to 10,000 feet: 94 seconds 10,000 to 15,000 feet: 94 seconds
Maximum Diving Speed	510 mph

P-47M

The next major model was the M (the superseding E-Ls were various experimental models), which was a D airframe fitted with a 2,800hp R-2800-57 engine driving a larger CH-5 turbosupercharger. This model (160 built) was an improvisation to counter the German V-1 "Buzz Bomb" and had a speed of 470mph and needed to be fitted with air brakes to allow them to decelerate after attacking their highly explosive targets.

P-47N

The P-47N version of the Thunderbolt was the last version to be manufactured in quantity. It was a specialized long-range version built specifically for service in the Pacific Theatre, as the air war there required fighter ranges even greater than did operations over Germany from the UK. In mid-1944, to increase long range performance, a new "wet wing" of slightly larger span and area was installed on the third YP-47M prototype and this aircraft was redesignated the XP-47N. For the first time in the Thunderbolt series, fuel was carried in the wings when a 93-gallon tank was installed in each wing. When maximum fuel was carried in external tanks, the total fuel load of the XP-47N was an imposing 1,266 gallons, giving the fighter a potential range of 2,350 miles. However, the increased fuel load increased the gross weight of the aircraft, and in order to deal with the increased gross weight, the undercarriage of the XP-47N had to be strengthened, which further increased the weight to over 20,000 pounds. The new wing also incorporated

larger ailerons and squared-off wingtips which enhanced this Thunderbolt's roll rate and improved its maneuverability. The AAF was so confident in the Thunderbolt design that they ordered 1,900 P-47Ns on 20 June 1944, even before the first XP-47N had flown on 22 July. Performance of the P-47N-5-RE included a maximum speed of 397mph at 10,000 feet, 448mph at 25,000 feet, and 460mph at 30,000 feet, as well as an initial climb rate of 2,770 feet per minute at 5,000 feet and 2,550fpm at 20,000 feet. Armament included six or eight .50 caliber machine guns with 500rpg and two 1,000 pound or three 500 pound bombs or ten 5-inch rockets, which made it a superlative fighter bomber.

The P-47N was destined to be the last version of the Thunderbolt to be manufactured. A total of 1,667 P-47Ns was produced by the Farmingdale plant between December 1944 and December 1945, when the Thunderbolt line finally closed down (149 more P-47Ns were built by the Evansville factory). P-47 production ended in December 1945, with 15,680 being built and two-thirds surviving the war and operating with many postwar air forces.

The P-47 Described

Cockpit

The P-47 had a sizeable, comfortable, and well laid out cockpit, but there was not enough leg room for large pilots despite adjustable pedals and seat, so they had to sit with their knees bent. The seat was a metal bucket type which could be adjusted for height by lifting a lock release handle at the right of the seat and raising or lowering it. A relief tube was located under the seat and a first aid kit was provided in the cockpit. The cockpit layout received very mixed reviews, with high scores for comfort, but its control layout had some controls that were difficult to see and identify and were poorly arranged. The cockpit of the "razorback" P-47s was not particularly good. Although there was ample space for the pilot to move his head, the view forward was poor because of the fighter's long nose. Forward quarter and side visibility was only fair and limited rear quarter visibility was enhanced by cut outs aft of the cockpit. The later electrically operated bubble canopy provided excellent visibility (except over the nose), but became very hot in the tropical conditions in the South Pacific.

Pilot Protection

The P-47D was the best armored and least vulnerable of all AAF fighters due to its armor, very rugged airframe, and an air cooled radial engine that was without the problems of leaking coolant and freezing up from battle damage. Tales of severely damaged P-47s making their way back to base are legion. Armor consisted of a face-hardened steel armor plate running from the top of the main fuel tank to the bottom of the windshield, a bullet-resistant glass panel behind the forward windshield (the built-in flat forward panel was found in later bubble canopy models), and a large face-hardened steel armor plate behind the pilot at the rear of the cockpit. If the P-47D had an Achilles, it was its lack of a self-sealing oil tank and unarmored supercharger.

Armament

Performance of the eight .50 caliber machine guns on the P-47 was generally considered good, and the guns were reliable and the installation good. Four .50 caliber machine guns, their ammunition, and supporting equipment were installed in each wing panel. The guns were located side by side in a staggered arrangement. A large access panel in the top of the wing was provided for gun installation and removal, and ejection chutes were located beneath each gun position. Ammunition boxes were carried in the wing section outboard of the guns. Maximum ammunition storage capacity per gun was 425 rounds. The fire rate was such that 300 rounds was equivalent

P-47D Cockpit (NMUSAF)

P-47 Armament: The eight .50 caliber machine guns, combined with its bomb and rocket carrying capacity, made it arguably the best AAF fighter-bomber. (AAF)

to about 20 seconds of fire. No round counting indicators were provided. If one gun jammed the others would continue to fire.

Early models could carry only a single bomb weighing up to 500 pounds on a centerline bomb rack. Many C and D aircraft were updated to carry bombs (up to 1,000 pounds each side) on wing racks mounted in large pylons. Beginning with the P-47D-35RA, provision was made in production for a maximum of 10 five-inch High Velocity Aircraft Rockets (HVARS) under the wings (without bombs or drop tanks).

Engine, Propeller, Fuel Tanks

The Thunderbolt was powered by the 2,000 to 2,300hp Pratt & Whitney Wasp air-cooled 18 cylinder two row radial engine. Early model P-47s used the 12 foot 2 inch Curtiss Electric hollow four blade propeller. Late D model P-47s onward used the 13 foot Curtiss Electric or the 13 foot Hamilton-Standard Hydromatic two-blade propeller.

Prior to the bubble canopy P-47s, the main fuel tank was a 205 gallon, L-shaped self-sealing unit located in the fuselage forward of and partly under the cockpit. On later D-models and the M-model, the main tank was increased to 270 gallons by adding space above the tank. The other internal fuel tank was a 100 gallon self-sealing tank installed aft of the main tank and under the rear end of the cockpit. Early model P-47s were equipped with a large external "slipper-type" 200-gallon, jettisonable fuel tank. Later

models (D-25 and G) carried various external tanks on bomb shackles on the fuselage center line and/or on pylons under the wings. The belly tanks were commonly 75 or 110 gallon, while the wing-mounted were 150 or 300 gallon. The P-47N used in the Pacific had the same 370 gallon internal fuel capacity, but with the new wing two 93 gallon internal wing tanks were added to give a total of 556 gallons of internal fuel. The N-model had the same external fuel capacity as the D models.

Flying the P-47

The tail dragging P-47 with its huge R-2800 radial engine up front had nonexistent forward visibility and the fighter had to be taxied using the usual, but wider S-turns so the pilot could look forward through forward quarter side windows. The lockable tail wheel was unlocked for free castoring during taxiing and S-turning. Directional control was achieved by a combination of engine power application and differential braking as required. The brakes were very good, and the aircraft was easy to taxi assisted by the wide tread main landing gear; however, the fully castoring tail wheel required riding the downwind brake. There was no tendency for the plane to nose over with a sudden application of power.

For takeoff, the pilot turned the fighter to head down the runway and moved forward to line up the tail wheel, which was then locked to prevent a swing developing on the takeoff run. Five degrees of right rudder trim was applied to provide control of the initial torque swing when MILITARY power was employed for the takeoff run; it also allowed pedal forces to be trimmed out during climb out. Flaps could be left full up or be set halfway down to shorten the takeoff distance. The takeoff could be made with or without the turbosupercharger, but its use resulted in a shorter run that was normally very long compared to other fighters. During takeoff, the aircraft had satisfactory handling qualities, with good rudder control of torque swing, and was very stable due to the wide tread landing gear. The gear was retracted as soon as the aircraft left the ground. Later models, from the P-47D-25 onward, with a propeller change to the wide "paddle" blades improved takeoff performance capability, but only somewhat, as they were heavier, which countered the improvement in propeller thrust. P-47s were continually loaded with more and more fuel and ordnance and takeoff performance on forward airstrips, as well as weight limits on tires, became critical. In the Pacific, the P-47D-25 used the 2,535hp WAR EMERGENCY power setting to better advantage for takeoff on the short airstrips.

The P-47 had a "mediocre to poor" rate of climb, often being compared to that of a "brick." The best climbing speed of the P-47 was 140 to 155mph. For long climbs in the tropical Pacific, cowl flaps were opened and climb speed was increased to cool the engine. In later models, the paddle blade propeller was specifically designed to improve climb performance and it and water injection greatly improved the climb rate.

There were some variations in trimming between models, but generally longitudinal and lateral trim was satisfactory on the P-47 and tabs were very responsive. There was very little trim change with gear retraction and initial acceleration, but dropping the flaps made the fighter slightly nose heavy. Longitudinal trim changes with power and speed changes were small and elevator tab power was sufficient to trim stick forces to zero at all speeds and all normal center of gravity locations. For all flight conditions, the power of the aileron trim tab was adequate and the rudder tab could trim pedal forces to zero at all speeds above 120mph, but the rudder trim force change with changing power or speed was much too high.

While the P-47 climbed like a brick, its most outstanding capability was its ability to dive—also like a brick—so what it lacked in climb it made up in dive. Its turbosupercharger allowed it to start a dive from very high altitude. The recommended maximum dive speed limit was 500mph and 400mph at 25,000 feet, and no dive was to be started below 12,000 feet.

Early P-47B versions went into compressibility in high-altitude dives, causing the fighter to nose down ("tuck under"), the stick to become immovable, and chopping the throttle to be ineffective. The P-47 also had the proclivity to reverse controls in a high-speed dive, particularly in the thin air of high altitudes, and aileron forces became high at speeds over 350mph. If very high indicated airspeeds were reached, the elevator tab had to be used for recovery. However, using much nose up trim could be dangerous, as the collective effect of this trim and heavy pull up force by the pilot could cause a G excess as the fighter entered the denser air of lower altitudes and a tail structural failure could result. Dive recovery flaps, hinged under each wing, were installed on late P-47 models to assist in recovering (not preventing) compressibility and were quite effective.

The consensus was that the P-47 had "fair to poor" maneuverability, but this improved with an increase in altitude. The Thunderbolt pilot was permitted most customary acrobatic maneuvers, but not outside loops, snap rolls, intentional spins of more than half a turn, whip stalls, sustained inverted flight, and violent maneuvers and high-speed dives with belly or wing tanks. Slow rolls were permitted up to 313mph. Aileron performance was rated as particularly poor. The new paddle blade propeller caused initial directional instability and control problems. The rule of thumb to safely and effectively fly the P-47 was simple coordinated flying and not to use full rudder force. The stall warning (in the P-47D-30 115mph clean and 100mph loaded) was a mild buffet about four to five mph above stall speed, decreasing aileron effectiveness, and increased elevator stick force. Recovery from a stall was by standard procedures. Spin characteristics were normal and the Thunderbolt would never spin on its own, but had to be forced into a spin by use of rudder and elevator. The spin recovery procedure was full opposite rudder, neutral elevator, and ailerons set against the spin, with all control movements rapid but smooth. This procedure would usually provide spin recovery in a half turn.

During landing, the P-47 was known for its fast approach speed that was compensated for by its ease of "settling in" on touchdown. Maximum allowable gear down speed was 250mph and 195mph for flaps down. Touchdown speeds for the C and D versions varied from 92 to 105mph, depending on weight. Once on the ground, the wide landing gear track and excellent brakes contributed greatly to the good landing qualities of the fighter.

Flying the P-47 Thunderbolt (PTO) by Walter (Jim) Benz: 8 victories 348 FG (Fourth highest P-47 ace PTO)

Benz

Although I spent all of my nearly 30 years in the Air Force associated with fighter flying activities and loved to fly, I was never very interested in how the aircraft was put together or what made it go. I just got in and went. I flew 330 combat missions, flying 806 combat hours in the P-47 and later flew the F-80 and F-86 in Korea.

In May 1943, my 348th Fighter Group was the first unit to use the P-47 in the Pacific Theater and the fighter proved itself to be very effective in combat against Japanese aircraft and later in the air-to-ground role.

The cockpit was large and comfortable, but at the low altitudes we flew at over New Guinea it was just plain hot! Pacific versions did not have a pressurized cockpit, and above 35,000 feet I frequently got very uncomfortable pains in my joints. The instrument and control layouts were very good. For a good bit of our time in New Guinea, our radios were original issue. They had a hard-to-see dial and were difficult to crank in and tune to desired frequencies. After these were replaced by the push button VHF sets the radio problems were solved.

The radial Pratt & Whitney was a rugged, reliable, and almost indestructible engine. It could take a great deal of combat damage and still bring you home. P&W fuel consumption was something else and a major concern in the Pacific, where there were long distances over water to the target. Some 25-30 gallons could be used just to warm up and take off. In cruising we used about 100 gallons per hour, and in a dog fight we could use 275 gallons per hour or more. When we learned the Charles Lindbergh method of cruise control, we greatly extended our range. We had 305 internal gallons, to which 75-150 gallon belly auxiliary tanks were first added. Later, the addition of two larger wing tanks further increased our range. The P-47 had an adequate, but not great rate of climb, and with the turbo super charger you could get it up to 39,000 feet and a little more, but this altitude was seldom necessary. The top speed depended on its load configuration, which often was staggering. Clean, we could do 350mph at 5,000 feet and 425 at 30,000 feet. Most of the time we were loaded down with external fuel tanks, bombs, rockets, napalm, etc., which greatly affected the fighter's speed and performance until they were jettisoned.

The P-47 was equipped with eight .50 caliber machine guns, probably making it the best armed fighter in WWII. We had a good gunsight and an adequate amount of ammunition. With this heavy firepower, using a combination of tracer, ball, and AP ammo, we could blast any Japanese aircraft out of the sky.

The Thunderbolt was a versatile fighter, successfully performing all the missions assigned to it: air-to-air fighter, bomber escort, and fighter bomber. Against Japanese fighters we were not as maneuverable and could not climb with them, but we had the great advantage of speed in a dive and could stay with them in a turn. In the P-47's ground support/fighter bomber role, it was an outstanding and reliable aircraft. The main reason for this was that it was so rugged and could withstand a lot of battle damage. We used it very effectively as a dive bomber and skip bomber against Japanese shipping. Against enemy airfields and personnel we used rockets, napalm, and machine guns with devastating effect. In the Philippines we saw lots of action, particularly low-level bombing and strafing, in which the Japanese threw up considerable AA and ground fire. In these missions we were thankful we were flying our tough old Thunderbolts.

P-47 Tactics
by Maj. Edward Roddy, an eight-victory ace flying
P-47s with the 342FS/348FG.

(Roddy wrote this opinion on the P-47 late in the war):

Roddy

"It has been several months since I have had contact with airborne enemy aircraft. However, I will endeavor to convey in this letter the tactics which I used then, and which I intend to use again soon. To make this letter as clear and concise as possible, and to keep from repeating myself, I will devote paragraph two to a few of the conceded practices upon entering aerial combat.

"A text could be written on the approach to combat, but the high spots are to see the enemy first, then make sure that you are not being baited, and decide upon a plan of attack and put it into action right away. After dropping wing tanks and advancing the throttle, all combat is commenced on a full tank of gas at a minimum indicated airspeed of 250mph. My own personal point of view on how to fight the Japanese with minimum risk to my flight and myself, while administering maximum destruction to the enemy, is as follows.

Defensive Tactics
When on the defensive, wingmen, flights, Elements, or however the case may be are well up in line abreast, with a little more than normal spacing laterally. Whether leading a squadron or smaller unit, there are only three situations which force me to take the defensive.

1) When the enemy fighters are above
2) Men the enemy fighters are of superior numbers at level flight
3) When the enemy fighters are firing before their presence is know

"Any situation other than those mentioned above, whether with fighters or bombers, puts me strictly on the offensive. Naturally, the prime objective when these situations arise is to reverse the set-up and get on the offensive as soon as possible. The methods for doing this are explained below.

"When the enemy fighters are above, make them commit themselves before you expose the evasive tactics you are going to use. After the enemy has committed himself, turn into him, and if possible, fire a head-on burst. After passing him, keep right on going, as this will put the greatest amount of distance between yourself and the enemy in the shortest period of time. Then work for altitude and prepare for offensive tactics. When the enemy fighters are of superior number at level flight, the best defense is an aggressive offense. Make a head-on pass if possible and go right through them, climbing at high speed as soon as you cease firing, striving again for altitude and a better set-up for going on the offensive.

"When the enemy fighters are firing before their presence is known, immediate violent evasive action is called for, diving, if necessary, to get out of their range. Then strive to get the advantage on them by use of the tactics mentioned above.

Offensive Tactics
Enemy bombers in this theatre are vulnerable to nose attack, being lightly armed forward compared to aft. So if the situation and time permit, these attacks should be favored and pressed home to point blank range. Aim for the leader and concentrate your fire on his most vulnerable parts: the engines and wing roots. Since the enemy bombers are going in the opposite direction, the heavy caliber tail guns will be in effective range for only a few seconds, and a violent turn in that period does not give them a chance to even swing their guns in the general direction of their attackers.

"Since the enemy bomber formations are usually flat Vs, a stern approach should be started with a 2,000 or 3,000-foot shallow dive out of range to put yourself at the same altitude with a 100mph advantage in speed. Then approach level with about 30 to 40° deflection, concentrating on the nearest aeroplane of the V and using him to block out the guns on the other ships of the formation. Stay on him until the deflection decreases to about 10°, breaking sharply away to the same side on which your pass originated. Coordinated attacks from any side are very effective in this case, as one aeroplane does not bear the brunt of the entire defensive fire.

"The target afforded by an enemy fighter is very small, so the most effective passes are of 15° or less deflection from head-on or astern. Press these attacks home until you have to veer off to keep from ramming him. Do not reef the aeroplane into a turn or the indicated airspeed will drop off rapidly. Make your pass, fly out a short distance, turn around, and come back for another pass. These deflections may seem to be very small, but I believe the majority of pilots, including myself, are not expert deflection shots.

In my estimation, newly-assigned pilots should concentrate on the following points:
1) Building up a technique for spotting Bogies.
2) Fuel-saving tactics for long range missions.
3) Building up faith in instruments, especially compasses.
4) Homing procedures for lost aircraft.
5) Radio silence and air discipline.
6) Jungle kit essentials, and escape procedures.

Leadership and Control of the Unit

Generally speaking, it is relatively easy to keep a squadron together if the mission is to patrol a convoy, escort bombers, or cover a landing. In these cases, the fighters have a central reference point, and usually stick pretty closely to the center of activities. Against fighters, however, the squadron usually breaks down into the basic two-ship Elements, and against Japanese bombers the four-ship flight remains intact. The radio is no longer a means of controlling the flight once the fight is started, and prearranged tactics and rendezvous points have to be utilized. The scarcity of enemy aeroplanes results in the over-eagerness of everyone on the flight, and there is often a mad scramble to see who will get to the enemy first, with all precaution thrown to the four winds. Were it not for the superiority of our equipment, our casualties would run much higher."

P-47 Thunderbolt in Combat in the Pacific

By Spring 1943, the Allied Air Forces had slowly put the Japanese on the defensive, but the aircraft sent to Australia and New Guinea during 1942 were becoming war weary and the future offensive operations would require fighters with greater range than the P-39 and P-40 could provide; furthermore, the quantity of P-38s headed for the theater was going to be limited for the immediate future. Thus, Kenney was in critical need of more fighters that could outperform the Japanese and went to Washington to press his case with Hap Arnold and President Roosevelt. He was promised more P-38s, but not in the numbers he hoped, and instead he was offered the 348th Fighter Group equipped with new Republic P-47D Thunderbolts, which he willingly accepted.

Many 5AF officers, including Col. Paul Wurtsmith, CO of the 5th Fighter Command, openly complained at the prospect of receiving the Thunderbolt. Prewar, the P-47 and P-38 had been intended to be the American equivalent to modern European fighters, but the development of both fighters was more difficult than expected and their initial debut in the ETO was disappointing. With the promising P-51 Mustang in the pipeline and the P-47 still unproven in the theater, Arnold was agreeable to part with some for operations in the Pacific.

The distinguishing feature of the P-47 was its size, since it was nearly twice that of the P-40. The large fighter was given the nickname and unanimously known by their pilots and ground crews as the "Jug." There was an anecdote that when the first P-47s arrived in Australia, an amazed RAAF ground crewman asked a P-47 pilot, "Where is the rest of the crew?" Even when powered with the formidable Pratt and Whitney R-2800 radial engine, the P-47 had a poor rate of climb and was ungainly while flying low and slow. Although it carried much more fuel than a P-40, its weight and poor fuel economy meant the early P-47's range did not exceed even the P-40's! The Fifth Air Force was experienced in performing field modifications at its northern Australian depots and Kenney's engineers quickly developed a 200 gallon drop tank for the P-47 by contracting with Ford of Australia for fabrication construction. These tanks gave the P-47 a range that surpassed that of the P-40, but never equaled that of the P-38.

When pilots first flew the Thunderbolt, they found its weight and size gave it poor climb, zoom, and turning capabilities, mushing in during high-speed turns and stalling and snapping into a spin at any speed. To offset these shortcomings, they found that the Thunderbolt had outstanding high-altitude performance; the ability to out-dive any opponent, thus enabling it to break off combat at will; the extraordinary ability to absorb damage; and very heavy armament installation of eight .50 machine guns. Soon the Thunderbolt was transformed into a powerful, versatile fighter after only a few field modifications, and when flown by the 348th Fighter Group's well-trained pilots using sound tactical doctrine.

The P-47 with a turbo-supercharged Pratt and Whitney engine did little to increase its climbing ability, but its high-altitude performance was greatly increased with its maximum power output and performance at 27,000 feet. The P-47 was considered the best high-altitude fighter used by the Americans during the war, especially in the ETO. If there had been more high-flying Tonys in the Pacific, the P-47 would have enhanced its reputation in that theater. As the war developed, the extremely dangerous ground support role became an ever greater responsibility of heavily armed fighter bombers, and in this task the Thunderbolt had no equals in Europe and the Pacific.

For a very brief period in early 1944, a majority of 5th Fighter Command Squadrons flew P-47s. The reason appears to be that in late 1943, the Eighth Air Force, suffering severe losses of unescorted B-17s over Germany (especially during the disastrous Schweinfurt/Regansburg mission), decided that it needed long range fighter escorts immediately. With the slow introduction of the superlative Merlin-powered Mustang, P-47s were paired with longer-range P-38s, causing a brief shortage of Lightnings. The 9th Fighter Squadron of the 49th Fighter Group was very reluctantly assigned P-47s to replace their worn out Lightnings. This decision reverberated inside the 5FC, but a rebellion was averted when Lockheed increased Lightning production and the Eighth Air Force finally appreciated the Mustang's long-range escort capabilities, so this problem solved itself in a few months. Although several squadrons flew P-47s until the end of the war or until re-equipped with Mustangs, most 5FC squadrons received Kenney's preferred Lightning.

North American P-51 Mustang

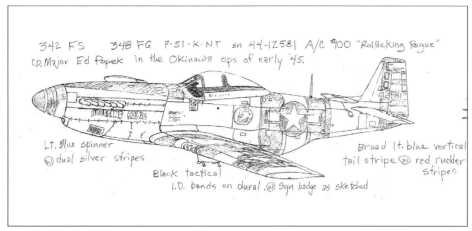

342 FS   348 FG   P-51-K-NT   sn 44-12581 A/C #100 "Rollicking Rogue"
Co. Major Ed Popek in the Okinawa ops of early '45.

Lt. blue spinner
w/ dual silver stripes.

Black tactical
I.D. bands on dural .w/ Sqn badge as sketched

Broad lt. blue vertical
tail stripe w/ red rudder
stripes

(Drawing by Steve Ferguson)

The first Merlin-powered Mustangs were the P-51B and C; the Rolls Royce engines licensed to Packard. The P-51D was the first major design change which would give the Mustang its classic lines. The D carried six .50 machine guns instead of four, moved the wing slightly forward, and provided rocket launchers. The D was the most numerous P-51 model, with 7,956 being produced.

P-51 Specifications

Engine	1,590 hp Packard V-1,650-7 (Rolls Royce Merlin)
Weight	(Empty/Loaded/Maximum): 7,125lbs-10,100lbs-11.600lbs
Length	32.25 feet
Wing Span	37 feet
Wing Area	233.3 square feet
Wing Loading	(Empty/Loaded/Maximum): 30.6lbs/sqft-43.3lbs/sqft-49.7lbs/sqft
Armament	2x.50 caliber Browning MG (nose) and 4x.50 caliber Browning MG (wings)
Bomb Load	10xRockets 2x1,000lb bombs 6xRockets and 2x1,000lb bombs
Maximum Speed	360mph
Full Flaps Speed	145mph
Climb	1,000 to 5,000 feet: 49seconds 5,000 to 10,000 feet: 74 seconds 10,000 to 15,000 feet: 77 seconds
Maximum Diving Speed	515 mph

P-51 Described

Cockpit
The Mustang cockpit was small for an AAF fighter, having less room than the P-40, and was considered overall as fair to good. P-51D cockpit arrangements were improved on the P-51B, with the seat and pedal modified to be adjusted to accommodate pilots of different sizes.

The P-51D had a seat with vertical adjustment; pins could snap into any of nine holes. The pilot's parachute was used as a seat cushion and the kapok-filled seat back could be used as a life preserver. A first aid kit was located on the right side of the seat. A data case with a drop message bag was carried at the left of the seat. An arm rest was located on the left longeron aft of the engine control quadrant. A relief tube was stowed on the floor to the left of the seat.

In the P-51D, warm air was routed to the cockpit from a scoop aft of the coolant radiator. The warm air passed through a flexible duct to a point behind the pilot's seat; from there, a duct led to the hot air outlet valve at the right side of the cockpit. Air from the forward side of the radiator air scoop was used to cool the cockpit. Hot and cold air control handles and knobs were on the floor near the stick. Some of the hot air was directed to the windshield.

Three different cockpit canopies were employed on various P-51 models. The original canopy, called the "birdcage," was used on Allison Mustangs and Merlin B and C models. Visibility from the birdcage was notably poor forward because of the low pilot position and heavy framing. The second canopy was the bulged, frameless sliding "Malcombe" hood designed in England and fitted to most British Mustangs. A few made their way to America and were fitted to AAF Mustangs, and were lauded for their excellent visibility. The third Mustang cockpit canopy was the frameless full bubble introduced into the P-51D. The bubble afforded excellent visibility and was rated the best "all around visibility" of U.S. fighters. Some pilots in the Pacific complained the bubble-canopied P-51D cockpit became very warm in low and moderate altitude tropical flying conditions.

Pilot Protection
The Allison P-51s incorporated an armor-plated firewall as basic integral equipment to protect the pilot from the front, along with a forward windshield section made up of bullet-resistant glass. Provision was made, as overload equipment, for armor plate behind the pilot seat to protect his head and back. All armor was sufficient to counter .30 caliber fire from any angle and .50 caliber fire from oblique angles. On the P-51B, a combination steel

P-51D Cockpit (NMUSAF)

P-51 Armament: The P-51D was armed with six .50 caliber machine guns in two different combinations. (AAF)

armor plate firewall was installed forward. Rear protection was provided by two steel plates aft of the cockpit. The windshield was a bulletproof five-ply piece of laminated glass. All internal fuel tanks were self-sealing. The armor complement of the P-51D and P-51K was similar to that of the P-51B.

Armament
The P-51D was armed with six .50 caliber machine guns in two different combinations: the six-gun combination: 500 rounds (400 in later models) for each inboard gun and 270 rounds for each center and outboard gun; or the four gun combination: the center gun could be removed, allowing the inboard guns to be supplied with 500 rounds (400 in later models) and the outboard wings to carry 500 rounds. Ammunition containers were mounted in each wing and the empty cases were ejected through the bottom of the wings. The guns were charged on the ground.

External removable bomb racks, one on each wing, could carry 100, 250, or 500 pound bombs. Late model P-51s were equipped to carry ten zero rail rocket launchers attached to two under wing pads.

Engine, Propeller, and Fuel Tanks
The engine for the earlier Allison models (the P-51, P-51A, and A-36A) was a 1,200 horsepower, liquid-cooled, 12-cylinder, V-type inline Allison V-1710. Later models (the P-51B/C and P-51D/K) used a Packard-built

1,500hp, liquid-cooled, 12-cylinder, V-type inline Rolls Royce V-1650 Merlin engine. The early-model P-51s used the 10.75 foot Curtiss Electric, solid three blade, constant speed, variable pitch propeller. The later Merlin P-51s were equipped with the 11.2 foot Hamilton Standard or the Hydromatic four blade, automatic constant speed variable pitch propellers.

The Allison P-51s had two protected 90-gallon internal fuel tanks located inboard between the main and rear wing spars. The port tank included a 31-gallon (of the 90 gallons) as a reserve. The external tanks were the slipper-type of 75 or 150 gallons on the bomb racks of both wings. The Merlin P-51s had two protected 92 gallon fuel tanks in the inboard wings and 110-gallon metal or 108-gallon pressed paper external wing tanks.

Flying the P-51 Merlin Mustang
The Merlin Mustangs were considered good ground handling fighters, as they had a wide gear, good brakes, and a tail wheel lock. The view ahead was very poor, and S-turns were required on taxiing due to the tail dragger configuration. The toe brakes were used as required for turning. Before taxi, the rudder trim tab was set nose right and the elevator tab set slightly up in preparation for takeoff. The tail wheel lock was on the stick, and when the stick was pushed forward in neutral rudder it unlocked the wheel for turning.

Takeoff was with locked tail wheels and either no flaps for a normal takeoff or for the shortest run with flaps down 10 to 20°. The tail was held down until rudder control was attained, then raised slowly. Elevator power was adequate to raise the tail at about half the takeoff speed. With flaps down, the aircraft was taken off in three point attitude. The powerful Merlin Mustangs produced great torque, which had to be carefully offset with strong right rudder during takeoff.

On the climb out, the gear was retracted and flaps, if used, were pulled up gradually. Best climb out speed of 160 to 170mph was reached quickly. Mustangs were known for their ease to trim. Gear retraction and power or flap setting changes required only small trim variations. Directional trim increased with speed and power changes. The changes in tab settings for climbing and diving were negligible. Tab controls were sensitive and had to be used carefully.

Merlin-powered P-51Bs and Cs were much heavier and were fitted with four blade propellers to take advantage of their more powerful engines, especially for high altitude operation. This new propeller greatly decreased the fighter's directional stability, which became serious at high speeds, and if the pilot did not apply enough opposite rudder, the fighter was apt to increase the slip or skid by itself and ultimately go into a nasty snap roll or spin. Early P-51Ds continued to be directionally unstable, and as a remedy the horizontal tail structure was strengthened, a dorsal fin was added to increase directional stability, and a rudder anti-balance tab was installed to keep pedal forces acting correctly. These tail changes were made separately in the field and incorporated simultaneously on the production line.

The maximum permissible dive speed for a P-51D was 505mph below 9,000 feet and 300mph at 35,000 feet; if these diving limits were exceeded compressibility would be experienced. In a dive, compressibility effects were instability, uncontrollable rolling or pitching, stiffness of controls, or combinations of these, along with vibration. Nose-heaviness (tuck-under) was noticeable and became more severe with increased speed. Dive recovery procedure was to reduce power and pull up as gradually as possible, depending on aircraft altitude.

The maneuvering qualities of the Merlin P-51B/C and D/K models were not as good as those of the lighter Allison versions, which had exceptional maneuvering qualities. The Allison Mustangs were permitted all normal acrobatics and were positively stable under all flight conditions. It seems as though as the P-51 was modified it became a less good fighter. In the Merlin P-51s fitted with the aft fuselage fuel tank, which was added to increase range, longitudinal stability was lost with the tank more than half full, as the center of gravity was moved aft. This instability was particularly dangerous in a dive pullout at high speeds, where the great acceleration could cause the wings to fail. The addition of a weight on the elevator made the fighter at least marginally stable. Turns at speeds above 250mph and above four Gs were especially dangerous and a pilot not equipped with an anti-G suit could black out, at least partially.

The Merlin P-51B/Cs and D/Ks had internally sealed and balanced ailerons which tended to keep stick forces light. Generally, the roll rate performance of these ailerons at high speeds equaled or was slightly improved over the earlier P-51, but low speed performance was substantially increased. Even after the horizontal tails of P-51B/C airplanes were strengthened to withstand the very high speed snap maneuvers resulting from the directional instability mentioned earlier, slow rolls were prohibited. Once the dorsal fin and reverse boost rudder tab were integrated, the slow roll restriction was canceled.

Approach characteristics of the Merlin Mustangs were similar to those of the Allison models; a typical approach speed was 120mph with touchdown at 90. Although the manual mandated continuous back pressure on the stick to obtain a tail low attitude for touchdown, combat pilots landing in flights often made tail up level landings for better vision for as long as possible. Because of its wide landing gear and locked tail wheel, the Mustang's landing characteristics were good.

Stalls were characterized in a clean aircraft by mild tail buffeting and light ailerons; there was no warning with a dirty aircraft. Stall recovery was by the release of back pressure on the stick and application of rudder opposite from the dropping wing, but this reaction had to be done quickly, as control was possible for only a short time before the fighter began to roll violently.

Pilots were prohibited from intentionally spinning their Merlin Mustangs, as the maneuver was very dangerous. When a spin was started, the aircraft snapped a half turn in the spin direction with the nose dropping to near vertical. At the end of one turn to or above the horizon the spin slowed down, occasionally coming to a complete stop. The aircraft then snapped a half turn, with the nose dropping to 50 to 60° below the horizon and continued as during the first turn, with some rudder buffet noticeable. The spin recovery procedure was to close the throttle and apply flight controls as in a power off spin recovery. When controls were applied for recovery, the nose dropped to near vertical position and the spin sped up, then stopped in one to one and a quarter turns. About 1,000 feet of altitude was lost for every spin turn. Recovery necessitated as many as five or six turns after the rudder was applied and 9,000 to 10,000 feet of total altitude could be lost.

P-51 Mustang in Combat in the Pacific

Because of the higher priority of the war in Europe, the P-51D Mustang did not arrive in the Pacific until late in 1944. But by the time the P-51 made its appearance in the Pacific, almost all Japanese aerial resistance had disappeared and the fighter's air-to-air combat attributes proven over Europe were unneeded. Above 300mph and at virtually any altitude, the P-51 was arguably the best and most forgiving fighter of the war.

Pacific Mustangs were mostly supplied to the Seventh Fighter Command. However, Philippine-based 5th Fighter Command Mustangs mostly flew uncontested bomber escort missions and were usually relegated to the ground attack role for which it was unsuited, with its vulnerable liquid-cooled engine and only six .50 caliber machine guns. As Japanese resistance on Luzon came to an end, the Philippine based Mustangs were used to bomb and strafe Japanese forces based on Formosa.

Northrop P-61 Black Widow

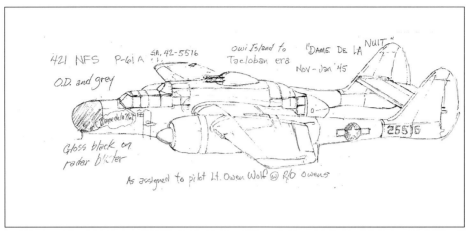

(Drawing by Steve Ferguson)

In less than two years after its founding, Northrop Aircraft designers John Northrop and Walter Cerny were able to offer a design proposal for an AAF design specification for a large radar-carrying, long range, high performance dedicated night fighter. Northrop was awarded a contract for two XP-61 prototypes, which were twin-boomed, cantilever mid-wing fighters powered by two Pratt & Whitney R-2800 radial engines and armed with four fixed ventral 20mm cannons and a dorsal GE turret with four .50 caliber machine guns. The test fighters were painted black and consequently given the name "Black Widow." It had a crew of three: the pilot, the radar operator in the nose, and the observer/gunner situated above the pilot. Weighing 25,000 pounds, it was as large as a medium bomber, but had the speed and maneuverability of a fighter. The twin engines were housed in twin nacelles that tapered back towards the vertical tailplanes, which were connected by a horizontal tailplane with control flaps. The aileron surfaces were very small and were mounted at the wing tip to give the necessary roll for a turn. A small set of retractable spoilers positioned forward of the flaps acted as ailerons, enabling the P-61 to quickly reverse direction. The first of 200 P-61As were delivered in November 1943. The first 37 had dorsal turrets and the remainder were delivered without them, as they caused buffeting (so the observer/gunner position was deleted). The turret buffeting problem was solved and all P-61s from 201 onward had the dorsal turret. Throughout its operational life, the P-61 maintained its original appearance, with little external change. The Pratt & Whitney R-2800 engines were minimally upgraded in the A and B models, and the supercharged P-61C models increased the maximum speed from 370 to 430mph. The first operational P-61s were delivered in the Pacific in early 1944 and in the ETO in May 1944. The P-61 was a successful night fighter design, but it entered service too late to have any serious effect on the outcome of the air war, as neither the Luftwaffe nor Japanese were able to mount any night attacks. Of the 706 Black Widows produced, there were 200 P-61As, 450 P-61Bs, and 517 P-61Cs, of which only 41 were produced before the contract for the remaining 476 was terminated as the Pacific war ended. The P-61 was the forerunner for postwar all-weather fighters and remained in front line service until the early 1950s.

P-61 Specifications

Engines	Two Pratt & Whitney R-2800s of 2,100 hp each
Weight	(Empty/Loaded/Maximum): 23,450 lbs/35,855 lbs/36,200 lbs
Length	49.6 feet
Height	14.7 feet
Wing Span	66 feet
Wing Area	664 square feet
Wing Loading	45 lb/sqft
Armament	Four .50 caliber machine guns in upper turret and four ventral 20 mm cannons
Bomb Load	6,400 pounds of bombs
Maximum speed	425mph
Cruising Speed	275mph
Climb	2,090 ft/min
Range	1,200 miles
Ceiling	46,200 feet

P-61 Described

Cockpit

The P-61 cockpit was comfortable, but gave poor visibility; its arrangement was considered poor, being cluttered, with the instrument panel placed too far away. The P-61A pilot's seat was mounted on tracks and rollers and could be moved to the right of center on its track for easier entrance and exit. A track adjustment lever was located below the seat. The P-61B pilot's seat was bolted to the floor. Pilot seats in both cases could be adjusted vertically by a local control lever. Another lever allowed the seat pan to be tilted up or down, and in addition, the complete seat could be tilted back to facilitate entrance and exit. The gunner's seat was mounted on a fore-aft track; however, it was normally not necessary to move it in flight. The seat could be rotated through 360° and could be locked in forward or aft facing

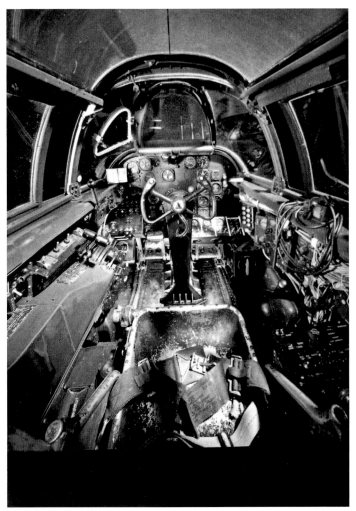

P-61C Cockpit (NMUSAF)

P-61 Armament: With four .50 caliber machine guns and four 20mm cannons, the P-61 had fearsome firepower. (AAF)

position. The radio operator's seat was mounted on a post assembly held in the seat base by a locking pin. It could be locked in either the gun firing (aft) or the radio operating (forward) position. All seats had a metal pan, padded back, and a seat belt; relief tubes were provided at the three crew positions and hand fire extinguishers were installed. The heating and ventilation system for the P-61A consisted of four fuel-air mixture heaters, a manifold to provide heat to the 20mm cannon and the turret section, and three crew ventilators. For ventilation, a manually operated louver-type ventilator opening into the airstream was provided at each crew station. The P-61Bs were equipped with two fuel-air type surface combustion heaters. The forward heater received fuel from the right engine and provided heat for the forward compartments. The aft heater received fuel from the left engine and provided heat for the radio operator and the guns.

Pilot and Crew Protection
Bullet resistant glass formed the forward windshield panels for both the pilot and the gunner. There was armor and deflector plates scattered throughout the crew pod: armor plates were located at the forward bulkhead behind the nose radar, ahead of the gunner below his windshield, ahead of the turret ammunition containers and cannon ammunition containers, and behind the radio operator. The two radial air-cooled engines were less vulnerable to enemy fire than liquid-cooled engines.

Armament
Early A models were equipped with four fixed 20mm cannon in the fuselage belly and a dorsal gun turret outfitted with four .50 caliber machine guns that was to swivel and cover the full 360° of azimuth, as well as a sizeable range of elevation. The dorsal turret was deleted because of air turbulence buffeting, but after extensive revisions and testing the problem was solved and the turret was reinstalled on later B models. The four .50 calibers and four 20mm cannons gave the P-61 fearsome firepower. Either two or four bombs weighing from 100 to 1,600 pounds could be mounted on the wing racks and used alternately for fuel drop tanks, depending on the aircraft mission.

Engine, Propellers, and Fuel Tanks
The Black Widow A and B models were powered by two 2,000hp Pratt and Whitney R-2800 Double Wasp, air-cooled, 18 cylinder, two-row, radial engines. The propellers were Curtiss Electric four blade constant speed, collective pitch, and full-feathering. The internal fuel system provided a total of 646 gallons carried in four self-sealing tanks, two on a side. The two 118-gallon inboard tanks were located in the inboard wing sections between the fuselage and nacelles and between spars. The outboard 205 gallon nacelle tanks were placed over the nacelles between spars. The right side wing fuel tank was designated the reserve. Late P-61A and early P-61B aircraft had provisions for installation of two external pressurized auxiliary droppable tanks under the outer wing panels. These tanks could be either 165 gallons or 310 gallons each.

Flying the P-61
The tricycle landing gear of the P-61 facilitated the ground handling of this large twin-engine aircraft which needed a lot of room to operate. During taxiing, the P-61 needed to be in motion in order to castor the nose wheel. The aircraft would turn better at lower speeds, but the pilot had to be careful not to allow the inside wheel to stop rolling in the turn. Changing directions during taxiing was done by combined or separate use of differential engine power, rudder use, and differential braking, being careful to avoid excessive brake use. The P-61A taxied with flaps up (the brakes lost effectiveness when flaps were operated), aileron and rudder tabs left at zero or neutral setting, and the elevator tab was set according to aircraft weight.

When the aircraft was lined up takeoff, the pilot ran up the engines, released the brakes, and the roll started. The flaps were either left up or set one-third down, depending on the load and runway length. Flaps down would decrease takeoff roll distance. Takeoff speed was 100 to 110mph. After leaving the ground, the pilot raised the gear, reduced the power to climb setting, and set the airspeed to about 160mph for the best rate of climb. The P-61 trimmed very easily. Before diving, the aircraft was trimmed for level flight at 275mph and no further trimming was necessary to recover from the dive. After trimming, the aircraft was pushed over into the dive to a maximum limit speed of 420 or 430mph, after which buffeting and tuck-under would begin to occur. Dive acceleration, control forces, and recovery characteristics were considered only fair to good. The pilot had to be careful in high-speed dives and pullouts when carrying external loads. For a large fighter with the size and weight of a medium bomber, the maneuverability of the P-61 was considered fair to mostly poor. Permitted maneuvers included half rolls, normal inside loops, Immelmanns, chandelles, slow rolls, and barrel rolls; well-coordinated barrel rolls could be done with relative ease, but slow rolls were somewhat more difficult. Prohibited maneuvers were outside loops, only momentary inverted flight, spins, and snap rolls, along with very high-speed slow rolls and Immelmanns. The P-61's rolling ability was poor, but lateral control forces with the small ailerons and the spoilers were light, even up to high speed. While the spoiler-type ailerons operated easily at high speeds, they were considered only fair to good at low and high speeds. The P-61, with its small conventional ailerons and spoilers, came closest to having full-span flaps than any other U.S. fighter. The P-61B was very stable about all axes and its elevator and rudder force requirements and surface effectiveness were good. The P-61 had outstanding stall and spin characteristics. The Widow had gentle stall characteristics either using two engines or only single-engine power and gave sufficient stall warning in the form of a strong tail buffet. Controls remained effective up to and into the stall, and no control deflections were required to prevent roll in a normal two-engine stall. Recovery was basic, with no tendency for a wing to drop, and the nose would drop slightly, then rise again. Stall speeds on the P-61B ranged from about 110 to 115mph clean and power off to a loaded power on of 70 to 80mph, depending largely on aircraft landing weight. The aircraft would recover from a spin up in the half turn mark almost instantly when pressure was reduced on either rudder or elevator controls and could be made without great difficulty after two and a half turns by reversal of rudder and elevator. If there was no definite indication of regaining control in a fully-developed spin below 5,000 feet, the crew was to bail out.

The P-61B's approach and landing characteristics were very good—a particularly important attribute for a night fighter. Maximum flaps and gear down speed was 170mph. The landing gear was lowered during the downwind leg of the approach and the flaps were to be lowered in two stages. At the halfway point of the approach base leg, flaps were lowered half way and on the final leg, lowered fully. Landing speed was 100 to 110mph power on and 115mph power off.

Flying the P-61 Black Widow (PTO)
by Carroll Smith: 7 Victories (5 P-61) 418 NFS
(Top American Night Fighter Ace)

"The heavy, box-like P-61 looked more like a bomber than a fighter, but indeed, it was one and more. The P-61 was hindered by problems getting into production, and thus its late start prevented it from becoming one of the best fighters of the war.

"Our pre-flight procedure was a normal walk-around, checking for general safety, such as tires, the gun load, landing gear, fuel (we drained off a bit of fuel for water residue), and so forth. One thing we did not have to check, though our missions were night flights, were the lights, as to use them was

Smith

inviting trouble. The cockpit was entered through the nose wheel well and it was about as comfortable as any other WWII aircraft. The Lucite canopy hatches were always checked, as they were unreliable. We always checked our instrument panel lights, as they were vital in our night operations. Everything had to be usable by feel, for we used a very minimum of light to better retain our night vision. The instrument panel layout was good for the time. The tricycle landing gear made the fighter good to taxi, take off, and land. The main gear was the same as the B-25, but was reversed in its trunions. Our communications consisted of two SCR-522 four-channel VHF sets for air-to-air and air-to-ground communications. They functioned reasonably well, although we had some problems with mountain interference. We had tail warning radar set and a SCR-695 IFF (Identification Friend or Foe) transponder, which was known as "parrot" since it squawked.

I can't say enough about the Pratt & Whitney 2800 radial engine. It was simply a great engine and probably one of the most rugged, efficient, and reliable aircraft engines ever built. It kept running when by all rights it shouldn't have and was an excellent confidence builder. Our aircraft had four internal fuel tanks: two in the engine nacelles (205 gallons each) and two in the inner wing (118 gallons each). This fuel load gave us about 3 ½ hours of normal cruising, but our endurance could be stretched out quite a bit through judicious flying. One time I extended my flight to 5¼ hours and had 60 gallons left. This was possible by using only 1500rpm or less and a very lean mixture (this did not seem to damage the engines). The next series were equipped with four wing-mounted drop tanks which extended their range significantly.

The P-61 had four 20mm cannons in the belly and four .50 caliber machines guns in the remote dorsal turret, which was installed in the early models. We discarded this turret and saved 1,100 pounds, dropped a crew member, and greatly reduced drag. The loss of this turret was more than compensated by the increase in performance and the remaining four 20mm with their 600 rounds gave us enough firepower. Our gun sight was adequate, as most of our work was done at close range. We were ordered to identify any aircraft we shot at, so we had to be at quite close range.

The P-61's climb rate was very good for the time and it could out-climb most of the Japanese aircraft we were up against. The P-1 was the most maneuverable I ever flew, and I flew 58 types in my career. You could stall one at 500 feet and not worry. I could turn with any aircraft when climbing, diving, or in level flight. The unique spoiler aileron system Northrop used was very effective in combat. The aircraft had no bad characteristics and was a pleasure to fly. The Widow was tough; we were shot up but not shot down. I do not know of a P-61 that was shot down by an enemy fighter. Our main concern was anti-aircraft fire, sometimes from our own nervous ground troops! I am familiar with only one bailout from the Widow. Hit by AA, the pilot slowed the aircraft down, walked out on the wing, and stepped off with no problems. No problems, at least until he got to the ground, where had to demonstrate his .45 pistol to some unfriendly natives. The P-61 was simple to land, with no bad habits. We rarely used landing lights for safety reasons, and if we did, it was only for a few seconds.

As I said, I flew 58 aircraft types during my career and I consider the P-61 my favorite. It made me an ace and got me home safely.

Effectiveness of 5th Fighter Command

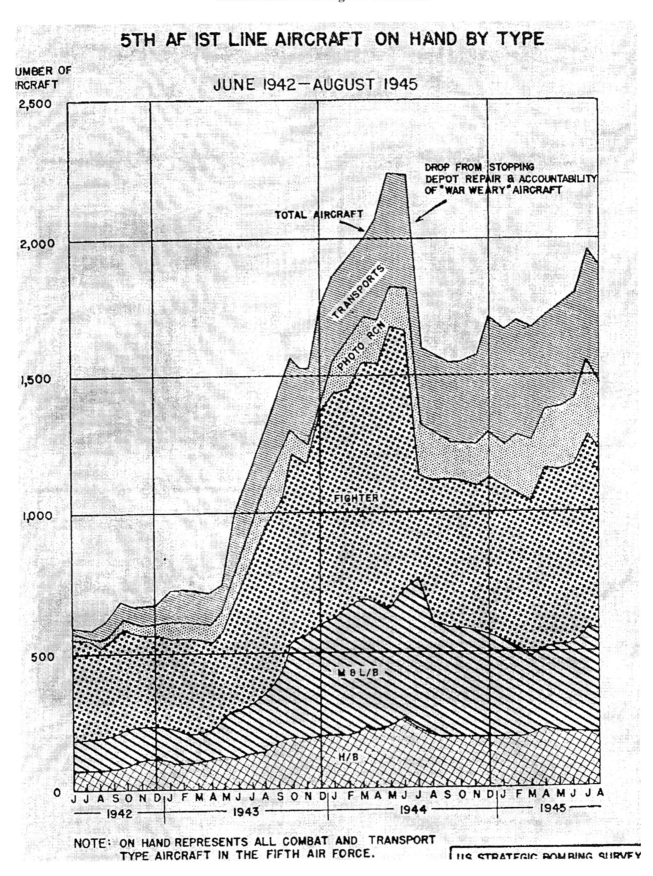

NOTE: ON HAND REPRESENTS ALL COMBAT AND TRANSPORT TYPE AIRCRAFT IN THE FIFTH AIR FORCE.

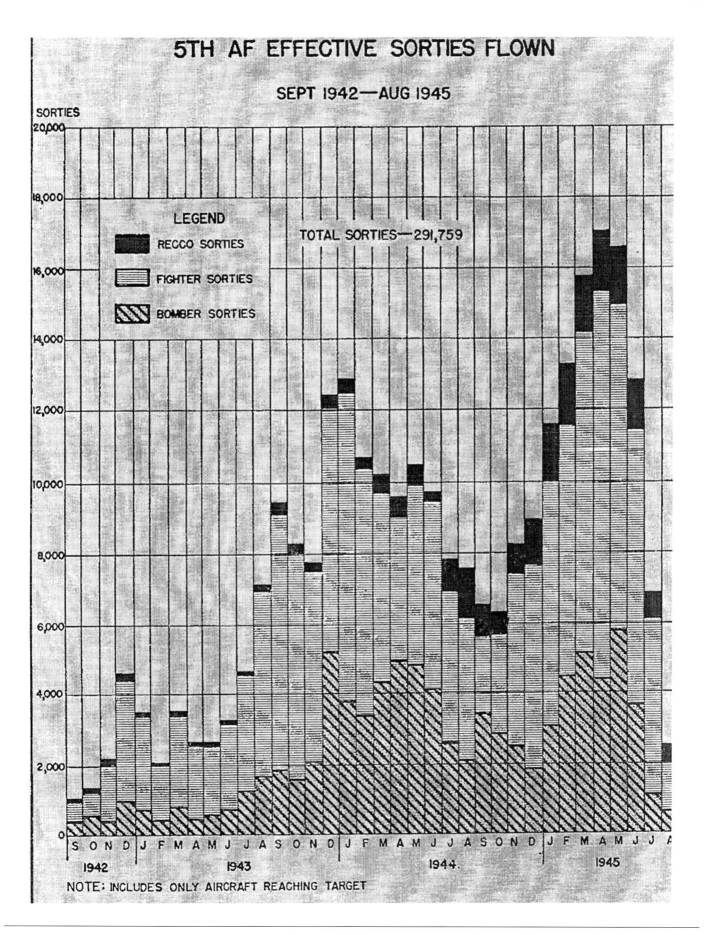

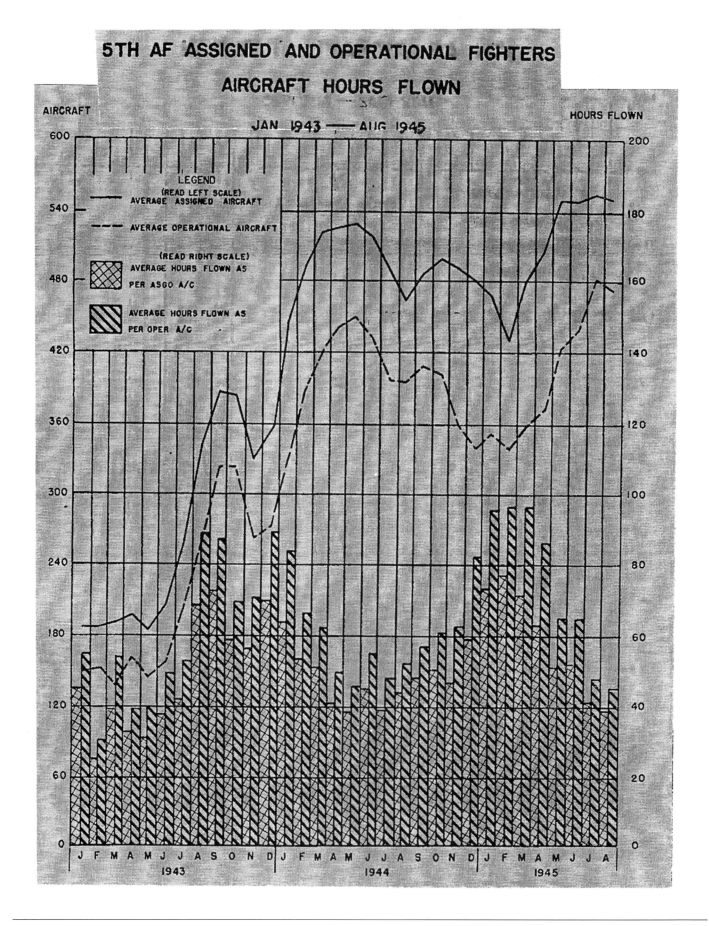

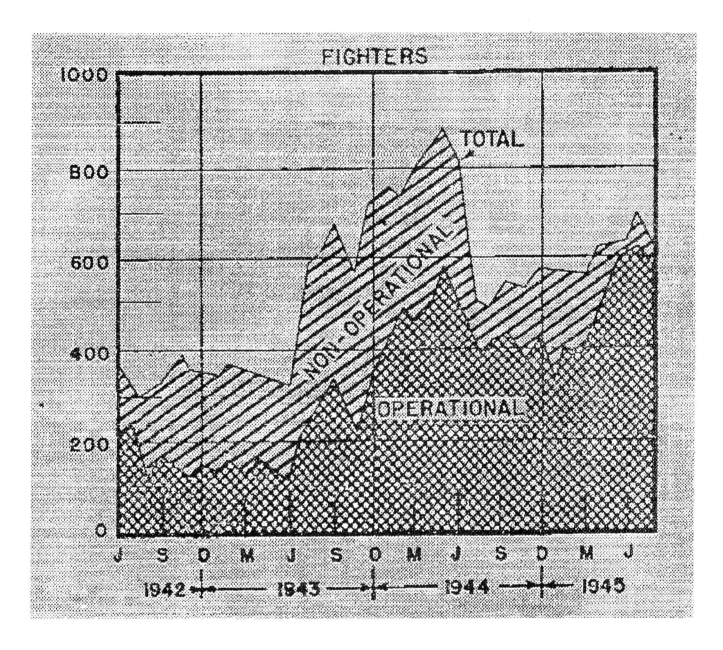

Fighter Comparisons

The Joint Fighter Conference, held between 16-20 October 1944 at NAS Patuxent, MD, was attended by representatives of U.S. fighter manufacturers, company and NACA test pilots, and by combat pilots of the three services. These representatives discussed the operational and technical capabilities of various U.S. fighters, then ranked the current operational fighters: the P-38, P-39, P-40, P-47, P-51, P-61, P-63, F4U, F6F, and FM-2 (other aircraft evaluated were the U.S. YP-59, F7F, F8F, and XF2G; the RAF Firefly, Seafire, and Mosquito; and the Zeke 52). The following discussion takes into consideration only AAF fighters, and if some are not listed in various categories, they were not mentioned as best/worst.

The factors considered and aircraft ranked in order were:

Performance

Climb:
Early War Fighters: P-38G, P-39D, P-47C, P-51, P-40E
Late War Fighters: P-63A, P-38J/L, P-47D, P-39N/Q, P-51D, P-40N

Acceleration (Level Flight):
Early AAF Fighters: P-38F, P-47D, P-51, P-40E
Late AAF Fighters: P-38L, P-47M, P-51D, P-39Q, P-63A, P-40N
Roll rate: P-40, P-63, P-51, P-47, P-38, P-39, P-61
Turning: P-63A, P-61B, P-51D, P-38L, P-47D

Dive
Initial Dive: P-38G, P-51D, P-47D, P-39D, P-40E
Dive Finish: P-47D, P-51D, P-63A, P-40E, P-39Q, P-38J/L, P-61A
Stability: P-61B, P-39L, P-47B, P-51D, P-38L

Stall Characteristics: P-61B, P-38L, P-51D
Range (No external tanks): P-61D, P-38J, P-47D, P-61B, P-40E/F, P-39D, P-63A

Cockpit

Engine Control Arrangement: P-51D, P-47D, P-63A, P-61B, P-38L
Gear and Flap Control Arrangement: P-51D, P-63A, P-47D, P-61B
Canopy: P-47D, P-51D
All Around Visibility: P-51D, P-47D, P-63A
Most Comfortable: P-47D, P-61B, P-51D
Best Cockpit: P-51D, P-47D, P-63

Controls

Ailerons
At High Speed (350 mph): P-51D, P-38L, P-47D, P-61B
At Low Speeds (100 mph): P-47D, P-51D, P-38L, P-61B
Elevator: P-51D, P-47D, P-61B, P-38L, P-63A
Rudder: P-38L, P-51D, P-47D, P-61B, P-63A

Armor Protection: P-47D, P-51D

Armament: P-38*, P-61*, P-47*, P-51, P-40, P-39 (* 3 way tie)

Best Fighters
Above 25,000 Feet: P-47D, P-51D, P-38L
Below 25,000 Feet: P-51D
Fighter Bomber: P-47D, P-51D, P-38L
Strafer: P-47D, P-51D, P-39L, P-63A

Another comparison not included in the Joint Fighter Conference was the number of victories and aces in each fighter in the Pacific:

Fighter	Victories	Aces
P-38 Lightning	1,700	90
P-40 Warhawk	706	28
P-47 Thunderbolt	697	32
P-51 Mustang	296	5
P-39 Airacobra	243	1
P-61 Black Widow	63	1

The USN/USMC totals by comparison were:

Fighter	Victories	Aces
F6F Hellcat	5,156	306
F4U Corsair	2.140	93
F6F Wildcat	1,008	62

The F6F has often been hailed as the best fighter in the Pacific with much credence, as the 12,275 Hellcats produced by Grumman excelled in their fighter, fighter bomber, bomber support, and night fighter roles. The Joint Fighter Conference considered it to be the best of all American fighters in the Pacific.

P-40/P-38/P-51: An Appraisal
by John Landers: 14½ victories/Two theater ace: P-40 (6v.)/P-38 (4v.)/P-51 (4 ½ v.)

Landers

"Comparing these aircraft is difficult, because I flew them in different combat situations, in different theaters, and during various phases of the war.

"I had just graduated with Class 41-I when I was sent to Australia to join the 49th Fighter Group. I delivered a P-40 to Darwin in early April 1942, and I think this flight gave me a grand total of 10 hours in the aircraft. The next afternoon, the squadron was scrambled and I was thrown into my first combat. Luckily, I was able to shoot down two Japanese bombers, even though my P-40 was having engine problems and I was left alone to be shot up by Zeros. In the Pacific, the Japanese were on the offensive and most of my flying was defensive over Darwin and Port Moresby. The Warhawk was a good fighter, but it had to be used right, as it was no match for the Zero in a dogfight. As General Chennault had shown with the Flying Tigers in China, you had to get the altitude advantage, dive, shoot, and get out. Its strong points were its diving speed, six .50 caliber machine guns, and its ruggedness. After my last two victories the day after Christmas 1942, my P-40 was hit by a bunch of Zeros. The fighter held together and I was able to bail out into the jungle and walk out.

After my Pacific tour, I was able to spend a lot of time in the States as an instructor training P-38 pilots. I finally got back into combat as CO of the 38th Fighter Squadron of the 55th Fighter Group in mid-1944. In the Winter of 1943, the P-38 had its share of problems as a high-altitude escort. At the time I joined the 55th, the 8th and 9th Air Forces were in the process of gaining air superiority over the Luftwaffe and knocking out tactical targets in preparation for D-Day. Our role was to seek out German fighters both in the air and on the ground and destroy transportation targets. The P-38 was better suited for these missions, as they were conducted at lower altitudes at which the Lightning was more efficient. The P-38 was very good in the fighter bomber role, being a stable gun platform and having tremendous punch with its guns and ability to carry a large payload. Also, at lower altitudes we were able to hold our own against the German fighters.

Headquarters had long decided to gradually phase out the P-38 in favor of the Mustang by the Fall of 1944. I was assigned as acting CO of the 357th Fighter Group, which flew Mustangs. I scored my first Mustang victory over a Me-109 in November to end my second tour. I then joined the 78th Fighter Group, which flew Mustangs as their CO in early January 1945, and we continued to attack the Germans on the ground, harassing their transportation and communication systems, along with their airdromes.

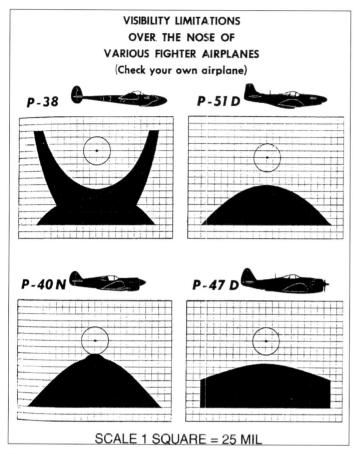

The P-51 was the best all-around fighter I flew in the war. It could do everything well, at high or low altitudes and at the longest ranges of any fighter of WWII. The Merlin engine was vulnerable to ground fire, but I was able to score 17 strafing victories in two missions in April 1945. In the air at this time we had it pretty much our way, as the Luftwaffe was low on fuel and experienced pilots. It was a time of easy pickings for the Mustangs, which roamed everywhere over Germany.

U.S. National Insignia and AAF Markings

National Insignia

The Type 1 National Insignia design was implemented on 1 January 1921, and was changed five times until the final version, in use today, was adopted in early 1947.

The Type 1 National Insignia consisted of an Insignia Blue (shade 47) circle 50 inches in diameter, with an Insignia White (shade 46) five point star inside, and an Insignia Red (shade 45) circle was contained within the star and placed on the top and under surfaces of both wings, centered 92 inches from the wing tip. However, this placement had to be changed on wings with ailerons and tapered wings. An identical insignia, only measuring 45 inches in diameter, was applied to the sides of aircraft fuselage aft of the

wings. A Technical Order issued in February 1941 required removal of the insignia from the starboard upper wing surface and the port underwing surfaces, leaving only two Insignias on opposite wings to be painted in flat paint.

In wartime, the instant recognition of aircraft (friend or foe) was imperative. The insignia of many other air forces was based on a circular field and immediate recognition was often difficult and positive recognition was not accomplished until the range was quite close. The red circular center of the U.S. National Insignia could be confused with red Japanese "Meatball" insignia. Thus, after 20 years, the Type 1 Insignia design was revised as the Type 2 on 18 August 1942, by the deletion of the red disk within the star and a 20-inch minimum diameter with five-inch diameter step increases in disk/star size.

Various insignia designs were tested, and on 29 June 1943, there was another change ordered for the National Insignia. The addition of rectangular white bars to each side of the circular blue field was ordered, as aerial observation testing showed a clear improvement in rapid identification. The length of the white bar was made equal to one-half of the star diameter and equal in width to one-fourth of the star diameter, extending outward on each side, the top edges continuous with the top edge of the horizontal star points. A red border one-sixteenth of the star diameter was added as a complete surround. This new design was designated as the Type 3 (AN-I-9a).

Once the Type 3 Insignia was introduced, aircraft with National Insignias on all four wing surfaces had white rectangles added with a red surround. These additional underwing National Insignias and the painting of the fin were suspended on replacement aircraft reaching the theater, but these markings continued on older aircraft for many months and were finally painted over by the end of 1943, at which time the next National Insignia style appeared.

Although the Type 3 design was more easily recognized from Axis German, Italian, and Japanese insignia at a far greater distance than the Type 2 and 2A, both the 5AF and 13AF found that at longer ranges, the red border tended to fade from view and rejected this marking. On 2 August, these units advised Washington that the red surround would be added and after negotiation, the Chief of Air Staff agreed to standardize a Pacific version of the insignia: a white star tangent to a blue circle with white side bars but no surround.

Thus, in August 1943, it was directed that a Type 4 (AN-I-9b) insignia be adopted. The red surround was to be replaced by extending the blue field to replace the red, while the proportions of the insignia were to remain the same as for the Type 3. The blue that over-painted the red often faded into the red, leaving a purplish border. The unbordered insignia could be seen in the Pacific until the end of the war. On Navy or Marine aircraft painted black or midnight blue, the insignia was limited to the star and adjacent white bars. Navy gray was an authorized substitute for white on upper wing insignia.

The final insignia change became effective in early 1947, with the addition of horizontal red bars equal in width to one-twelfth the star diameter, located horizontally across the centers of the white rectangular bars of the Type 4 insignia.

USAAF Markings Gallery

Red and white rudder stripes were discontinued in August 1940, while the Type 1 Insignia design was revised as the Type 2 in August 1942. (AAF)

Once the Type 3 Insignia was introduced in June 1943, aircraft with National Insignias on all four wing surfaces had white rectangles added with a red surround. (AAF)

In October 1942, the "US ARMY" marking was to be removed from all aircraft. (AAF)

In May 1941, all propeller blades were to be painted black, but this was modified in August 1941, when the tips of the prop blades were to be painted yellow. (AAF)

Rudder Markings

As per specifications of 1 November 1926, rudder stripes were standard concurrently with the Type-1 National Insignia. Rudders were to be painted with 13 alternate horizontal stripes of equal width: seven in Insignia Red and six in Insignia White, with one vertical Insignia Blue stripe forward of 13 horizontal stripes. The width proportions were 1/3 vertical to 2/3 horizontal stripe. Rudder stripes were discontinued in August 1940.

Propeller Markings

A technical order issued in May 1941 stipulated that all propeller blades be painted black, but this was modified on 28 August 1941, when it was ordered that the tips of the prop blades be painted yellow.

Each propeller blade had a blade drawing number and an angle setting if required, stamped with a rubber stamp or painted with the aid of a stencil on the camber side of the blade approximately between the 18-inch and 24-inch stations and approximately on the mid-chord position, using letters and numerals ½-inch high. The markings were to be applied parallel to the longitudinal center line of the blade in such a way as to be read from the trailing edge. In no instance should such markings be indented or cut into the metal. The serial number with military prefix made up the blade drawing number, preceded by the letter R if the blade had been repaired. On unpainted blades, black ink was used for marking. On blades painted black, white ink was used. Black Matthews Vulcan Ink or its equivalent and White Matthews Ink number 550 (or its equivalent) were found best for this purpose. After the ink dried, the lettering was to be covered with a coating of stencil varnish

or clear lacquer, except on unpainted anodized blades. In addition to the above ink marking, the manufacturer's identification decal was affixed midway out on the camber side of each blade so as to be read from the trailing edge.

To determine the manufacturer of a propeller on a photograph: if the manufacturer's logo decal is round on the blade it is either a Curtiss or Aero Products, and if it is oval lengthwise on the blade it is a Hamilton-Standard.

"US ARMY"

In a Technical Order of 15 October 1926, it became mandatory that the words "US ARMY" be painted in 24 by 18-inch letters under the wings and four-inch letters on the sides of the fuselage. The letters were to be either black or white, depending on which ever contrasted against the aircraft's background color. The letters "US" were painted under the right wing and "ARMY" under the left, positioned in line with the National Insignia. In October 1942, the "US ARMY" marking was to be removed from all aircraft.

2

Japanese Aircraft

Japanese Aircraft by Designations

During the opening months of the war, Japanese aircraft were fairly well known and described in Allied Intelligence Recognition Manuals, but these Manuals were not in wide distribution and used descriptions rather than designations to describe Japanese aircraft. For example, the Mitsubishi Type Zero Carrier Based Fighter quickly became well known as the "Zero," or "Navy Zero," or "Navy Naught." Later, when the Mark II (later Model 32) version to the Zero arrived, it was identified as the "Square Wing" or "Mark II Zero." Many British and American publications referred to the Zero as the "Mitsubishi" or "Nagoya" Zero, as Nagoya was the site of the Mitsubishi factory. The new JAAF Nakajima Ki-43 (later Oscar) was unknown to the Allies at the beginning of the war and often was identified as a Zero. The JNAF Mitsubishi A5M (later Claude) was identified in reports as the Navy Type 96; sometimes with the addition of Single Engine/Single Place Navy Fighter. By and large, the Allies had no standardized system to identify Japanese aircraft until mid-1942.

In Summer 1942, Australian Air Commodore J.E. Hewitt, Allied Director of Air Intelligence (SWPA), assigned U.S. Army officer Capt. Frank McCoy of the Technical Air Intelligence Unit (TAIU) to devise a system of nomenclature to help identify the expanding number of Japanese aircraft for intelligence and communication purposes (but was A6M2 or Ki-32 any more difficult than Me 109 or FW 190?). The basic guideline for naming was:

1) Fighters and reconnaissance seaplanes were given men's Christian names or first names (Zeke, Frank)
2) Bombers, dive bombers, torpedo bombers, flying boats, and reconnaissance aircraft other than seaplanes received women's Christian names or first names (Betty, Kate)
3) Transport aircraft were given girls' names beginning with T (Tess, Tabby)
4) The names of trees were used for trainers (Willow, Oak)
5) Gliders were named after birds. (Gander, Buzzard)

Since McCoy was from Tennessee and had a hillbilly name, his first selections were names like Zeke, Nate, Rufe, and Jake. Once hillbilly names were expended, TAIU personnel used the names of wives and family. McCoy's wife, Louise, and daughter, June, were honored. McCoy used his first name, Frank, then those of his two assistants, Francis (T/Sgt. Williams) and Joe (Corp. Gratten). The Val was one of the first Japanese aircraft to be code named and was named after an Australian friend of McCoy's Supervisor who made the specific request. The Betty, with its large gun blisters, was named after a voluptuous Pennsylvania woman. The Sally was named after the wife of McCoy's earlier CO, Gen. Fay Upthegrove.

The Zero was named because it was the Mitsubishi Navy Type 0, but was replaced by the name Zeke; however, Zero remains the most well known today. The Model 32 Zeke was originally named the Hap after Air Force Chief Gen. Henry "Hap" Arnold, but during a Headquarters intelligence briefing Arnold heard of all the Haps being destroyed in the Pacific and became furious. Very soon the Hap was redesignated as the Hamp. The Tojo first appeared in the CBI and was given that name there after Japanese Prime Minister Tojo. When it appeared in the SWPA it was named John, but this name was soon dropped for Tojo. When the K-61 single-engine fighter appeared in the SWPA, it was thought to closely resemble the Italian Macchi MC 202 and was given the Italian type name Tony. But since it also looked like the Messerschmitt Bf 109 from a distance, a number of early ICRs reported Bf 109s. The George was named by Flt./Sgt. George Remington of the RAAF, who was attached to the TAIU.

In September 1942, McCoy's unit published a high quality booklet entitled "Intelligence Information Memorandum No.12: Japanese Air Services and Japanese Aircraft," which was widely distributed without authorization in quantity by Gen. Kenney throughout the SWPA and also to Washington, D.C., London, and New Zealand on 4 November. The British Air Ministry was the first to reply to the Memorandum, saying that the suggested names were "appreciated," but that "operational requirements necessitate abbreviations but consider essential that official style of designations be adhered to except for purely local purposes." The AM stated that designations would be given after captured documents identified enemy aircraft by service (Navy or Army), followed by Type Number, followed by duty, and the manufacturer's name when known.

At MacArthur's General HQ, Maj.Gen. Stephen Chamberlain sent a note to MacArthur's Chief of Staff, Maj.Gen. Richard Sutherland, reviewing Memorandum No.12 and stating that it "appeared that the Air Force has established a list of identifying names (replacing serial numbers)" and that the list of names was to be accepted "as universal." He went on to write that "improper channels" were used to disseminate Memorandum No.12 outside the SWPA, and that unless Kenney had approved it, the Air Force had "erred in sending this data." Chamberlain continued, "I doubt we should attempt to impose our own system upon others" and that "it would be much better to refer to Japanese aircraft by types rather than some identifying name. Code names could be very much overdone." He (G-3) recommended that the AAF reconsider Memorandum No.12 and withdraw it, but suggested that the matter be taken up with Gen. Kenney. On 11 November Sutherland—as described in Volume 1—always the political animal and not wanting to rankle rising 5ᵗʰ Fighter Command star Kenney, withdrew HQ's (his) objection to the Memorandum. Kenney then pursued getting Memorandum No.12 received officially, but it had been distributed throughout the SWPA

and was considered "official" by most Intelligence Officers. As pilots, aircrews, and Intelligence Officers familiar with the old nomenclature were replaced by new personnel, the use of the Memorandum No.12 code names became more common, and by 1945 they were used almost universally.

USAAF Code Names for Major Japanese Aircraft

Code Name	Service	Manufacturer	Designation	Description
Ann	Army	Mitsubishi	Ki-30 Type 97	2 place SE light bomber
Betty	Navy	Mitsubishi	G4M	7 place TE bomber
Claude	Navy	Mitsubishi	A5M Type 96	1 place SE carrier fighter
Dinah	Army	Mitsubishi	Ki-46	2 place TE night/recon fighter
Emily	Navy	Kawanishi	H8K	9 place TE recon flying boat
Frances	Navy	Kugisho	P1Y	2-3 place TE bomber/night
Frank	Army	Nakajima	Ki-84 Type 4	1 place SE fighter/FB
George	Navy	Kawanishi	N1K2-J	1 place SE fighter
Grace	Navy	Aichi	B7A	2 place carrier torpedo/DB
Helen	Army	Nakajima	Ki-49	8 place TE heavy bomber
Irving	Navy	Nakajima	J1N1	2-3 place SE recon/night
Jack	Navy	Mitsubishi	J2M3	1 place SE fighter (land)
Jake	Navy	Aichi	E13A	2 place SE float recon
Jill	Navy	Nakajima	B6N	2 place SE carrier bomber
Kate	Navy	Nakajima	B5N	3 place SE carrier bomber
Lily	Army	Kawasaki	Ki-48 Type 99	4 place TE light bomber
Nate	Army	Nakajima	Ki-27 Type 97	1 place SE fighter/FB
Nell	Navy	Mitsubishi	G3M	5 place TE bomber
Nick	Army	Kawasaki	Ki-45 Type 2	2 place TE FB/night fighter
Oscar	Army	Nakajima	Ki-43 Type 2	1 place SE fighter
Peggy	Both	Mitsubishi	Ki-67 Type 4	6-8 place TE bomber
Pete	Army	Kawasaki	Ki-10 Type 95	2 place SE observation
Rufe	Navy	Nakajima	A6M2-N Type 1	2 place SE float fighter
Sally *	Army	Mitsubishi	Ki-21 Type 97	5 place TE bomber
Sonia	Army	Mitsubishi	Ki-51 Type 97	2 place SE light bomber
Tabby	Navy	Showa (DC-3)	L2D	3-5 place TE transport
Tess	Army	Douglas	DC-2	3-5 place TE transport
Tojo	Army	Nakajima	Ki-44 Type 2	1 place SE fighter
Tony	Army	Kawasaki	Ki-61 Type 3	1 place SE fighter
Val	Navy	Aichi	D3A Type 99	2 place SE carrier DB
Zeke **	Navy	Mitsubishi	A6M Type 0	1 place SE carrier fighter

*also Jane
** also Zero, Hap, Hamp
SE=Single Engine and TE=Twin Engine

U.S. Codenames for Foreign Aircraft in Japanese Service (Suspected)
At the beginning of the war, due to confusion and lack of information, many code names were assigned to non-existent or not used foreign aircraft, especially German designs.

Luftwaffe	Code
Bf 109	Mike
Bf 110	Doc
FW 190	Fred
FW 200	Trudy
Ju 52	Trixie
Ju 87	Irene
Ju 88	Janice
He 111	Bess
He 112	Jerry
Italian	**Code**
Fiat BR 20	Ruth
American	**Code**
Seversky A8V	Dick
Lockheed 14	Thelma
Vultee VG 11	Millie

This codename system was considered easier than a type system using the manufacturer and a number, such as for identifying Luftwaffe aircraft: He-111 (Heinkel), Ju-88 (Junkers), or Me-109 (Messerschmitt, really Bf-109 for Bayerische Flugzeugwerke). However, Luftwaffe aircraft and their manufacturers were known to the Allies, while Japanese aircraft and their manufacturers were not. JAAF Kitai number (Ki Number System) designations (i.e., Ki-61) and JNAF model types (i.e., A6M2) were not used, as the Allies were not aware of them until late in the war. These systems are described next. The Allied codename system had as many faults as an official designation system, as pilots often misidentified enemy aircraft, such as when a JAAF Tony was identified as something as incongruous as a Me 109 when it first appeared! Of all the Japanese aircraft, the Zero probably had the most codenames. The A6M3-32 variant was initially called Hap, but after objections from "Hap" Arnold, the name was changed to Hamp. The Zeke had variously been called the Zeke 21, 22, 32, and 52, while the Nakajima A6M2-N (float plane version of the Zero) was called Rufe. In my research on individual pilots' Individual Combat Reports for a single combat, I found that pilots would variously identify a Mitsubishi A5M2 as a Zero or Zeke, or even an Oscar. While composing his original, Frank McCoy gave a non-existent Mitsubishi Type Zero Medium Bomber. Despite its faults, the Allies considered the adoption of the codename system the most practical means of identifying Japanese aircraft and it remains in use in today's literature, while designations such as the Ki-43-I and Ki-43-II variants (Oscars) are postwar innovations.

Japanese Aircraft Designations

JNAF Aircraft Designations
At the beginning of World War II, the Japanese Navy Air Force used three different systems to designate their aircraft:
1) Experimental Shi numbers,
2) Type and Model Numbering System,

3) Type, Series Number, and Manufacturer (called the "Short designation"), which was more or less similar to that used by the U.S. Navy from 1922 until 1962.

Later during the war, two new systems were added: popular names and the Service Airplane Development Program (SADP) system.

Experimental Shi Numbers
Every new design—actual or projected—from 1931 onward received an experimental or Shi number derived from the current year of the Japanese Imperial reign, which for Emperor Hirohito began in 1926 and was called *Showa*. Added to the Shi number was the purpose of the new design (i.e., carrier fighter, carrier bomber, etc.), to differentiate between different designs. Thus, the A6M Zero was designed to meet a 1937 specification called the 12-Shi Carrier Fighter, that year being the twelfth year of *Showa*, and upon entering production the fighter was given a Type number. The Aichi B7A1 Ryusei, which entered service as the Navy Carrier Attack Bomber Ryusei in 1944, began life in 1941 as the Aichi Navy Experimental 16-Shi Carrier Attack Bomber.

Type and Model Numbering System
The earliest designation system in use during WWII was the Type Number System, which was originally introduced in 1921. In this system, each Naval aircraft was given a Type Number based on the year it entered service, followed by a short description of the aircraft's purpose. From 1921 to 1928, the year code was based on the year of reign of the current Japanese Emperor. From 1921-26 this was the Emperor Yoshihito, whose reign was known as the Taisho Era, and so aircraft from those years were Types Taisho 10 to Taisho 15. Emperor Hirohito became the Emperor in 1926, and aircraft accepted in 1927 and 1928 became Types *Showa* 2 and *Showa* 3. After 1928, the Japanese Navy used the Japanese Army system, in using the last digits of the calendar year. Thus, the Aichi dive bomber, which entered production in 1939 (2599 in the Japanese system), was the Type 99 Carrier Bomber. Only a single digit was used when the year ended in 00, as with the Type 0 Carrier Fighter (thus the name "Zero"), which entered production in 1940, or the Japanese year 2600.

Different models of the same aircraft were originally given a single digit model number with dash numbers for subtypes (Model 1 for the first version, Model 1-1 for the first subtype). By the late 1930s, model numbers had evolved to two digits, beginning with 11 for the first version, indicating the first airframe version and the first power plant configuration. Thus, the Type 0 Carrier Fighter Model 11 was the original production Zero, while the Model 21 was the next production version, with the addition of folding wing tips (hence the "2" for airframe modification in 21). The Type 0 Carrier Fighter Model 52 was the Zero after five major airframe and two engine configurations.

Finally, sub-types of a model were given a final letter, taken from a series of Japanese characters called the Ten Stems (or Celestial or Heavenly Stems), which are part of the Japanese Zodiac. The full sequence runs ko-otsu-hei-tei-bo-ki-kou-shin-jin-ki, and was originally used during the Chinese Shang Dynasty as part of a dating system. In English translations, they are normally replaced by the ABCs (ko=a, otsu=b, hei=c, etc.), as with the Navy Type 0 Carrier Fighter Model 52c.

Short Designation by Type, Series Number, and Manufacturer
In the late 1920s, the IJN introduced an aircraft designation system basically similar to that used by the U.S. Navy from 1922 until 1962. Each new design was given a "short designation" consisting of a set of Roman letters and numbers. The first letter (sometimes two) indicated the basic type or purpose of the aircraft, as specified in the following table:

A	Carrier fighter
B	Carrier attack (torpedo or level) bomber
C	Carrier reconnaissance
D	Carrier (dive) bomber
E	Reconnaissance seaplane
F	Observation seaplane
G	Land-based bomber
H	Flying-boat
J	Land-based fighter
K	Trainer
L	Transport
M	Special-purpose seaplane
N	Fighter seaplane
P	Bomber
Q	Patrol
R	Land-based reconnaissance
S	Night fighter

A Series Number followed the Type Letter, indicating the number of major sub-types produced by that manufacturer. Unlike USN practice, the digit 1 was not ignored in this system and was included. Thus, the designation G4M designated the fourth attack bomber (**G4**) designed or produced by Mitsubishi.

The Manufacturer's Code letter followed the Type Number and the Series number:

A	Aichi
D	Showa
K	Kawanishi
M	Mitsubishi
N	Nakajima
P	Nihon
S	Sabeso
Si	Showa
V	Seversky
W	Kyushu, Watanabe
Y	Yokosuka

The first Type Letter(s) and the Series Number remained the same during the service life of each aircraft, however, minor to moderate changes in the design (usually reflected in a new Type Model number) were indicated by adding a second subtype number after the manufacturer's letter. Further minor changes were indicated by adding letters after the subtype number as in the Type/Model scheme above. The A6M2 was thus the second major version of the Zero. This was sometimes followed by a third lower case letter used to distinguish between minor versions of a particular model. In this system, the A6M2c would hence be the fourth sub-version of the second model of the Mitsubishi produced sixth-generation carrier-based fighter.

In a few cases, when the designed role of an aircraft changed, the new use was indicated by adding a dash and a second type letter to the end of the existing short designation, so the H6K4 was the sixth flying boat (H6) designed by Kawanishi (K), fourth version of that design (4). When this aircraft was equipped primarily as a troop or supply transport (L), its designation was then H6K4-L.

Popular Names

In July 1943, popular names were given to JNAF aircraft in place of type numbers. These popular names were mostly used on late war designs and some which came into service. These names were chosen based on the aircraft's primary role, as listed below:

Aircraft	Popular Name Derivative
Fighters	Meteorological phenomena
Carrier Fighters	Wind names ending in pu or fu
Seaplane Fighters	Same as Carrier Fighters
Interceptor Fighters	Lightning names ending in den
Night Fighters	Light names ending in ko
Attack	Mountain names
Bombers	Star (sei) or constellation (zan) names
Patrol	Sea or ocean names
Reconnaissance	Cloud names
Training	Tree or plant names
Transports	Sky names
Miscellaneous	Landscape or flower names

Representative JNAF Popular Names:

Popular Name	Aircraft .
Shoki/Devil Queller	Nakajima Ki44 Type 2 (Tojo) Fighter
Seiran/Mountain Haze	Aichi M6A Float Fighter
Shiden/Magnificent Lightning	Kawanishi N1K1-J (George) Interceptor Fighter
Raiden /Thunderbolt	Mitsubishi J2M (Jack) Interceptor Fighter
Reppu/Hurricane	Mitsubishi A7M (Sam) Carrier Fighter (Design)
Kyofu/Mighty Wind	Kawanishi N1K1 (Rex) Floatplane
Gekko /Moonlight	Nakajima J1N1-S (Irving) Night Fighter
Renzan/Mountain Range	Nakajima G8N1 (Rita) Attack Bomber
Tenzan/Heavenly Mountain	Nakajima B6N (Jill) Attack Bomber
Suisei/Comet	Yokosuka D4Y (Judy) Bomber
Ginga/Milky Way	Yokosuka P1Y (Frances) Bomber
Momiji/Maple	Kyushu K9W1 Type 2 (Cypress) Trainer
Manazuru/Crane	Kokusai Ku7 (Buzzard) Glider
Tokai/Eastern Sea	Kyushu Q1W1 (Lorna) Patrol

Ohka/Cherry Blossom	Yokosuka MXY7 Ohka (Baka) Kamikaze
Kikka/Orange Blossom	Nakajima Me-262 Copy

Service Airplane Development Program (SADP) Systems

The SADP was initiated in 1939 as a research program by the IJN's Bureau of Aeronautics. Each design considered was to be coded with its manufacturer's letter under the existing short designation system, plus a two digit number (i.e., 10, 20, 30, etc.). However, this system was not common and few records of SADP designations survived the war.

Japanese Army Aircraft Designations

The Japanese Army Air Force used three overlapping aircraft designation systems: the Type number, based on the year the aircraft was accepted; the *Kitai*, or airframe number, allocated while a project was under development; and a series of popular names adopted just after the start of the Pacific War. A fourth name system was adopted by the Allies, in which each aircraft was given an easy-to-remember code name.

Type Numbers

From 1927, new Army aircraft were given a Type Number based on the last digits of the Japanese year that the type was accepted into service. Up to the year 2599 (1939 in the West), the last two digits formed the type number. In year 2600 (1940), the number 100 was used, and from year 2601 (1941) only the last digit of the year was used. Thus, the Army Type 97 Heavy Bomber and Army Type 97 Fighter were both accepted in 2597 (1937) and can be differentiated by the functional description attached to each. New versions of an existing type were indicated by adding a Model number and letter (i.e., Army Type 3 Fighter Model 2A).

The Type Number was supplemented by a short description of the type's function, which before the introduction of the Kitai System was the only method to distinguish between different types of aircraft accepted from the same manufacturer in a particular year, so in 1928 this included the Kawasaki Army Type 88 Reconnaissance and Type 88 Light Bomber types. All later versions of the same aircraft retained the same Type Number, regardless of when they entered service, which applied to versions that were produced for different purposes (i.e., the Tachikawa Ki-54 Army Type 1 Advanced Trainer, which was also produced as an Operations Trainer, Transport, and Patrol Bomber). Major models of the same aircraft were distinguished by a Model number, with versions of the basic model getting a Kaizo (modification) symbol (i.e., the first version of the Mitsubishi Ki-67 to enter service was thus the Army Type 4 Heavy Bomber Model 1A, followed by the Model 1B, while a more advanced version planned for 1946 would have been the Model 2). From 1932, the model numbers used in the Type system matched the model designations used in the Kitai system.

Kitai Numbers (Ki Number System)

The Type Number System required relatively long descriptive function names to completely identify an aircraft. The *Kitai* or Ki Number System was adopted in 1932, and assigned a number to each aircraft planned or projected to be built. Some existing aircraft were also given Ki numbers. Initially, the numbers were assigned sequentially, but in 1944, new Ki numbers were scrambled.

New versions of an existing design had Roman numbers (I, II, III, etc.) added to the Ki number and sub-variants had lower case letters (a, b, c, etc.), as used in some JNAF systems. Occasionally, the model and variant numbers and letters were replaced by a Kaizo (KAI), or modification code.

Using the Kawasaki Hien with a Kitai Number of 61 and Allied code name Tony as an example: the project and prototypes were called Ki-61.

The first two production versions were Ki-61-Ia and Ki-61-Ib. The next two versions carried KAI modification codes as Ki-61-I KAIc and KAId. Finally, the prototype of a second model was Ki-61-II and the first production of this new model was Ki-61-II KAIa. This last example (the Ki-61-II version), the Ki-61-II KAIa, was called the Army Type 3 Fighter Model 2A in the Type Number System.

A few foreign designed or built aircraft actually entered Japanese service, and these were given an alphabetical type rather than a numeric one, based on the country of origin. For example, the Italian Fiat BR 20 was designated as the Type I Heavy Bomber or the manufacturer's name, as with the U.S. Lockheed Model 14 designated as the Type LO Transport.

Representative Ki Numbers

No.	Ki	Type	Allied Code
1	Mitsubishi Ki-1	Army Type 93 Heavy Bomber	None
10	Kawasaki Ki-10	Army Type 95 Fighter	Perry
15	Mitsubishi Ki-15	Army Type 97 Command Reconnaissance Plane	Babs
17	Tachikawa Ki-17	Army Type 95-3 Primary Trainer	Cedar
21	Mitsubishi Ki-21	Army Type 97 Heavy Bomber	Sally
27	Nakajima Ki-27	Army Type 97 Fighter	Nate
30	Mitsubishi Ki-30	Army Type 97 Light Bomber	Ann
32	Kawasaki Ki-32	Army Type 98 Single-engined Light Bomber	Mary
34	Nakajima Ki-34	Army Type 97 Transport	Thora
36	Tachikawa Ki-36	Army Type 98 Direct Co-operation Plane	Ida
43	Nakajima Ki-43	Army Type 1 Fighter	Oscar
44	Nakajima Ki-44	Army Type 2 Single-seat Fighter	Tojo
45	Kawasaki Ki-45	Army Type 2 Two-seat Fighter	Nick
46	Mitsubishi Ki-46	Army Type 100 Command Reconnaissance Plane	Dinah
48	Kawasaki Ki-48	Army Type 99 Twin-engined Light Bomber	Lily
49	Nakajima Ki-49	Army Type 100 Heavy Bomber	Helen
51	Mitsubishi Ki-51	Army Type 99 Assault Plane	Sonia
54	Tachikawa Ki-54	Army Type 1 Transport, Trainer, and Patrol Bomber	Hickory
55	Tachikawa Ki-55	Army Type 99 Advanced Trainer	Ida

56	Kawasaki Ki-56	Army Type 1 Freight Transport	**Thalia**
57	Mitsubishi Ki-57	Army Type 100 Transport	**Topsy**
59	Kokusai Ki-59	Army Type 1 Transport	**Theresa**
61	Kawasaki Ki-61	Army Type 3 Fighter	**Tony**
70	Tachikawa Ki-70	Army Experimental Recon Bomber	**Clara**
73	Mitsubishi Ki-73	Army Experimental Fighter	**Steve**
74	Tachikawa Ki-74	Army Experimental Recon Bomber	**Pat, Patsy**
76	Kokusai Ki-76	Army Type 3 Command Liaison Plane	**Stella**
84	Nakajima Ki-84	Army Type 4 Fighter	**Frank**
201	Nakajima Ki-201	Army Me 262 Jet Fighter Design*	**None**

*Last assigned Ki Number

TAIU Australia

Popular Names

The *Kitai* and Type number systems remained in use until the end of the war, but soon after the start of the Pacific War, the Japanese Army realized that it needed shorter, easier to remember, and more dramatic names for use in public relations statements. Unlike the JNAF, however, the Army chose names randomly, with most coming from flying beasts or birds or weather, without any clear pattern. For instance, the Ki-61 Tony fighter was Hien (Swallow), the Ki-43 Oscar fighter was Hayabusa (Peregrine Falcon), the Ki-67 Peggy bomber was Hiryu (Flying Dragon), and the Ki-84 was the Hayate (Gale)

Name (Japanese/English)	Ki	Type
Hayabusa (Peregrine Falcon)	Nakajima Ki-43	Army Type 1 Fighter
Shoki (Demon)	Nakajima Ki-44	Army Type 2 One-seat Fighter
Toryu (Dragon Killer)	Kawasaki Ki-45	Army Type 2 Two-seat Fighter
Donryu (Storm Dragon)	Nakajima Ki-49	Army Type 100 Heavy Bomber
Hien (Swallow)	Kawasaki Ki-61	Army Type 3 Fighter
Hiryu (Flying Dragon)	Mitsubishi Ki-67	Army Type 4 Heavy Bomber
Hayate (Gale)	Nakajima Ki-84	Army Type 4 Fighter

Technical Air Intelligence Unit (TAIU) and Center (TAIC)

After Pearl Harbor, the Allies realized how little was known of Japanese aircraft and the Technical Air Intelligence Unit Southwest Pacific was created. In addition to its well-known creation of code names, the TAIU was responsible for gathering wrecked and captured Japanese aircraft and

TAIC Manual Cover

equipment to build an information base. TAIU HQ was established at Eagle Farms, near Brisbane, Australia, where, at first, bits and pieces of Japanese aircraft were brought to study, photograph, and measure to make drawings and determine performance. The task was made more difficult, as the Japanese labels and plates had to be translated. After the Allies went on the offensive, wrecked but mostly complete enemy aircraft were captured and brought to Eagle Farms for study. As the war further expanded, TAIU units were formed in other theaters, and in June 1944, the Technical Air Intelligence Center was established at Anacostia NAS, near Washington, D.C., to consolidate information. However, field units remained in the war zones to collect aircraft and equipment. The captured Japanese airfields at Hollandia and in the Philippines yielded a bonanza of specimens. Anacostia rebuilt enemy aircraft into airworthy condition and performed flight evaluations. In December 1944, TAIC published *Japanese Performance & Characteristics Manual No. 1*. The Manual provided detailed information of Japanese aircraft, such as range, speed, climb, performance characteristics, engines, dimensions, fields of fire and attack, vulnerability, exhaust flame patterns, and armament. Line drawing views, graphs, charts, and pictures of the actual aircraft on the ground and in the air were provided, along with separate sections for engines, armament, and radio with supporting pictures and charts. The Manual was designed to be expanded and revised with a metal clip binding. Pages from this Manual are used to illustrate the salient characteristics of various Japanese aircraft met by the 5th Fighter Command.

Japanese Warplanes
Japanese Navy Air Force Aircraft

Zero (Zeke/Hap/Hamp)/Mitsubishi A6M

Zero

The legendary Mitsubishi A6M Zero-Sen was the symbol of Japanese air power and represented the beginning of a new era in naval aviation, in which it was the first shipboard fighter capable of surpassing land-based aircraft and was to bear the brunt of almost every air combat in the Pacific until the end of the war.

On 19 May 1937, the Imperial Navy submitted specifications for a new fighter to supersede the Mitsubishi A5M, Navy Type 96 Carrier Fighter (Claude), which had just become operational and was found to be deficient. The new carrier-borne fighter was to be fast, climb quickly, be as maneuverable as the Claude, have great range, and was to be armed with cannons to destroy bombers. The Navy ordered two prototypes, and designs were submitted by Nakajima and Mitsubishi. Nakajima decided to abandon their proposal and Mitsubishi, led by its gifted engineer/designer Jiro Horikoshi, was awarded the contract, which promised to be difficult to fill. The Mitsubishi A6M1 prototype was an all-metal, low-wing monoplane with retractable gear and was powered by a 780hp Mitsubishi Zuisei 13 engine. Because even the best Japanese aircraft engines of the time could generate no more than 800hp, Horikoshi's design philosophy necessitated making the Zero as light and aerodynamic as possible and to make it fuel efficient, with a range of more than 1,100 miles (an external fuel tank extended the range to 1,900 miles). A sophisticated one-piece wing was fabricated of lightweight aluminum and was an integral part of the fuselage. This design decreased the wing's weight and made the Zero easy to disassemble and maintain, which was an advantage for a carrier-based aircraft. The length and width of the large wing gave the light fighter great lift from a carrier deck, while the long fuselage and a very large tail gave the Zero exceptional stability. During testing, the two-blade variable pitch propeller was replaced with a three-blade variable pitch propeller. The Zero was impressively armed with two 20mm cannons and two 7.7mm (.30 caliber) machine guns. Zero pilots had excellent visibility from the large cockpit, which was covered by a full bubble canopy. Mitsubishi met or exceeded all specifications except

for maximum speed, and the fighter's characteristics made it one of the few WWII fighters that was mostly without idiosyncrasies and relatively easy to fly and land.

Despite being a world military power, Japan was a poor country; in relative economic development, Japan was closer to Italy than to Germany and much less so than America. Therefore, Horikoshi worked under austere economic limitations and his Zero design suited Japanese military doctrine, as well as its economic restraints. The Zero was less expensive to manufacture, as the raw materials required were less than for a larger, more sophisticated American fighter; its fuel consumption was less; and equipment not directly related to performance was deleted. However, the Zero's relatively sophisticated design made it demanding for the Japanese to manufacture, as it was labor intensive and required parts and labor from many small workshops.

The Navy had approved the production of the first batch of A6M2s, and while flight testing the A6M1, a new engine (the 925hp Nakajima NK1C Sakae 12) was accepted and was installed in the third A6M2 prototype. The initial trials were completed in July 1940, and the Navy assigned 15 A6M2s to combat trials in China, where they destroyed 99 outdated Chinese aircraft for the loss of only two. The aircraft was accepted for production in July 1940 as Navy Type 0 Carrier Fighter Model 11, and in September 1941, were prepared for the impending war with the Allies. Modifications were introduced during production and the modified aircraft was designated Navy Type 0 Carrier Fighter Model 21. The A6M2 Model 21 was used at Pearl Harbor and the Japanese Navy had 328 A6M2s in first line units at that time.

It took a while before Mitsubishi was able to produce Zeros in large quantities, as between March 1939 and March 1942, only 837 were manufactured. From April 1942 to March 1943, when the JNAF urgently needed aircraft, only 1,689 were produced. Finally, during April 1943-March 1944, Nakajima greatly added to the Mitsubishi totals when 3,432 Zeros were manufactured, while between April 1944 and March 1945 a production peak of 3,487 aircraft was attained. More Zeros were produced than any other Japanese combat aircraft with original manufacturer and a name synonymous with the Zero (Mitsubishi), building 3,879, but with Nakajima building many more at 6,215. Together with the 844 trainer and float plane variants produced by Sasebo, Hitachi, and Nakajima, a total of 10,938 Zero fighters were produced.

Mitsubishi A6M Reisen Series Zero

The A6M series of carrier-based fighters were designed solely for maneuverability with high-speed handling, high-altitude performance, robustness, and pilot protection being secondary. And being extremely maneuverable, they were the best dogfighters in the world, but handled poorly in a dive and its pilot was to pursue an enemy only in a dive if he could get a quick, certain victory. If the Zero was bounced its pilot was to break off immediately.

Zero Variants

Model 11
Model 21 ...Model 41
Model 32
Model 22 ...Model 22 Kou
Model 52 ...Model 52 Kou ... Model 52 Otsu.. Model 52Hei... Model 62
Model 53 ...Model 63
Model 54 ...Model 64

A6M1, Type 0 Prototypes

The first A6M1 prototype was completed in March 1939, powered by the 580kW (780hp) Mitsubishi Zuisei 13 engine with a two-blade propeller. It first flew on 1 April, and passed testing in a remarkably short period of time. By September, it had already been accepted for Navy testing as the A6M1 Type 0 Carrier Fighter, with the only important change being a modification to a three-bladed propeller to alleviate a vibration problem.

A6M2 Type 0 Model 11

While the first two prototypes were being tested, the third was fitted with the 700kW (940hp) Nakajima Sakae 12 engine. Because Mitsubishi had its own Kinsei engine the company was disinclined to use the Sakae. Nevertheless, when the first A6M2 was completed in January 1940, the Sakae's extra power was found to increase the the Zero's performance considerably beyond the original specifications. This new version was so promising that the Navy sent 15 to China in July 1940, before testing was completed. In combat against pesky Polikarpov I-16s and I-153s they were eminently successful, and the Navy immediately ordered the A6M2 into production as the Type 0 Carrier Fighter, Model 11.

A6M2 Reisen Model 21

After the delivery of only 65 fighters by November 1940, changes were incorporated on the production lines, particularly folding wing tips to allow the Model 21 to fly from aircraft carriers. The Model 21 would become one of the most produced versions early in the war, as when the lines switched to updated models, 740 Model 21s had been completed by Mitsubishi and another 800 by Nakajima. Two other versions of the Model 21 were built in small numbers: the Nakajima-built A6M2-N "Rufe" float plane (based on the Model 11 with a slightly modified tail) and the A6M2-K two-seat trainer, of which a total of 508 were built by Hitachi and the Sasebo Naval Air Arsenal.

The A6M2 had all the same problems of the A6M, but also had difficulties with its Type 99 20mm cannon. The cannon was fed by a meager 50-round drum, which meant that the pilot was never to fire the cannon unless he

was relatively sure of getting a hit with this relatively small amount of ammunition. Meanwhile, the backup 7.7mm machine guns were inadequate for combat. The Zero pilot needed constant situational awareness, because one hit on his fragile fighter could cause critical damage. The Zero was particularly vulnerable when chasing an American fighter, as the AAF's Leader/Wingman Element strategy could mean the enemy Wingman was in a position to attack. The A6M2 did not have the slow speed roll capability of the later A6M3 and A6M5, and its pilot had to begin his defensive maneuvers earlier. During a head-on attack, the Japanese pilot was to start a barrel roll and reverse direction just before the enemy got into range and watch the 7-9 o'clock for the enemy to overshoot.

Engine	940hp Nakajima Sakae Radial
Weight	(Empty/Loaded/Maximum): 3,704 lbs-5,313 lbs-6,164 lbs
Length	29.75 feet
Wing Span	39.3 feet
Wing Area	241.5 square feet
Wing Loading	(Empty/Loaded/Maximum): 15.3 sqft-22.0 sqft-25.5 sqft
Armament	2 x 7.7 mm Type 94 MG and 2x20 mm Type 99 Cannon
Bomb Load	2 x 100 pounds
Maximum Speed	275mph
Full Flaps Speed	95mph
Climb	• 1,000 to 5,000 feet: 62 seconds • 5,000 to 10,000 feet: 92 seconds • 10,000 to 15,000 feet: 98 seconds
Maximum Diving Speed	460 mph

A6M3

The A6M3 was the best maneuvering of the A6Ms. The A6M2 could eventually outrun it, but the A6M3 could out-roll it by a large margin and at all speeds. It had a better horse power to weight ratio and was better at higher altitude and had better high-speed handling. The A6M3 was considered somewhat better than the Army's Ki-43 Oscar, except in turns. It was most agile at low speeds and therefore most able to defend self at low speeds.

A6M3 Type 0 Model 32

In late 1941, Nakajima introduced the Sakae 21 engine, which used a two-speed supercharger for better altitude performance and increased power to 1,130hp. The new engine was slightly heavier and somewhat longer due to the larger supercharger, which moved the Zero's center of gravity too far forward on the existing airframe. To correct the CG, the engine mountings were reduced by eight inches, moving the engine aft towards the cockpit. However, the size of the main fuel tank (located to the rear of the engine) was reduced from 137 to 120 gallons. The wings also included larger ammunition boxes, allowing for 100 rounds for each of the 20mm cannon. The only other major changes were to the wings, which were simplified by removing the Model 21's folding tips, changing its appearance sufficiently to cause its codename to be changed to Hap, which was quickly changed to Hamp in deference to Hap Arnold, but soon it was realized that the Hamp was simply a new model of the Zeke. The changes in the wing had much greater effects on performance than expected, as their smaller size produced a better roll and their lower drag allowed the diving speed to be increased to 420mph. However, maneuverability was reduced and range declined due to both decreased lift and the smaller fuel tank. This shorter range proved a significant limitation during the Solomons Campaign of 1942. The first Model 32 deliveries began in April 1942, but it remained on the lines only for a short time, with 343 being built.

Engine	1,130hp Nakajima Sakae Radial
Weight	(Empty/Loaded/Maximum): 3,984 lbs-5,313 lbs-6,474 lbs
Length	29.75 feet
Wing Span	36.2 feet
Wing Area	232 square feet
Wing Loading	(Empty/Loaded/Maximum): 17.1 sqft-24.1 sqft-27.5 sqft
Armament	2 x 7.7 mm Type 97 MG and 2 x 20 mm Type 99 Cannon
Bomb Load	2 x100 pounds
Maximum Speed	295mph
Full Flaps Speed	105mph
Climb	• 1,000 to 5,000 feet: 52 seconds • 5,000 to 10,000 feet: 75 seconds • 10,000 to 15,000 feet: 86 seconds
Maximum Diving Speed	480 mph

A6M3 Type 0 Model 22 (A6M5a)

To correct the Model 32 deficiencies, a new version incorporating the Model 21's folding wings, new in-wing fuel tanks, and attachments for a 90-gallon drop tank under each wing were introduced. The internal fuel was increased to 137 gallons, which regained all of the lost range. As the airframe was the Model 32 and the engine remained the same, this version received the Navy designation Model 22, while Mitsubishi called it the A6M3a. The A6M5a was a compromise of the standard Zero, with added weight in the form of pilot armor and a heavier skin, better armament, and more ammunition, and fuel tanks that were self-sealing and contained fire control mechanisms. With the added weight this Zero was the worst performing of all, except in roll rate and diving ability. When attacked by a P-38, the Zero pilot was to increase his speed and go into an instantaneous turn, which would leave the P-38 far behind. The new Type 99 cannons were high velocity, which meant that the machine guns had a similar trajectory and enabled the Zero pilot to take more accurate long-range shots, especially with the increased ammunition loading. Since the cannon continued to have a relatively low ammunition loading, the pilot was to first take tracking shots with his machine guns. The new model began production in December, and 560 were ultimately manufactured. This company constructed some for evaluation armed with 30mm Type 5 Cannon under the denomination A6M3b (model 22b). A few late-production A6M3 Model 22s had a wing similar to the later shortened, rounded tip wing fitted to the A6M5 Model 52. These were probably a transition model; at least one was photographed at Rabaul East in mid-1943.

Engine	1,130hp Nakajima Sakae 21 Radial
Weight	(Empty/Loaded/Maximum): 4,136 lbs-6,025 lbs-7,174 lbs
Length	29.9 feet
Wing Span	36.2 feet
Wing Area	232 square feet
Wing Loading	(Empty/Loaded/Maximum): 18.1 sqft-26.3 sqft-28.5 sqft
Armament	2 x 7.7 mm Type 97 MG and 2x20 mm Type 99 Cannon
Bomb Load	2 x 100 pounds
Maximum Speed	295mph
Full Flaps Speed	105mph
Climb	• 1,000 to 5,000 feet: 53 seconds • 5,000 to 10,000 feet: 79 seconds • 10,000 to 15,000 feet: 90 seconds
Maximum Diving Speed	480 mph

A6M4 Type 0 Model 41

The A6M4 consisted of two A6M2s equipped with an experimental turbo-supercharged Sakae engine designed for high-altitude use. The design, modification, and testing of these two prototypes was undertaken by the First Naval Air Technical Arsenal at Yokosuka during 1943. The turbo-supercharger and its ducting suffered due to suitable alloys and consequently further development was cancelled.

A6M5 Type 0 Model 52

The Model 52 was considered the most effective Zero variant. It was developed to combat the more powerful and well-armed F6F Hellcat and F4U Corsair. The variant was an unexceptional update of the A6M3 Model 22, with non-folding wing tips and thicker wing skinning to permit faster diving speeds, along with an improved exhaust system and an improved roll rate of the clipped-wing A6M3 now built in.

A6M5a Model 52a "Kou"

The Kou was equipped with a Type 99-II cannon with belt feed of the Mk 4 instead of the drum feed Mk 3 (100rpg), allowing a larger ammunition supply increase (125 rpg).

A6M5b Model 52b "Otsu"

The Otsu had an armor glass windscreen, a fuel tank fire extinguisher, and a 13.2mm/.51 inch Type 3 Browning-derived gun (2,700 feet/second muzzle velocity and a range of 2,950 feet) with 240 rounds replacing the 7.7mm (.303 inch) Type 97 gun in the left forward fuselage. The larger weapon required an enlarged cowling opening, creating a distinctive asymmetric appearance to the top of the cowling.

A6M5c Model 52c "Hei"

The Hei had thicker armored windshield glass and armor plate behind the pilot's seat. The wing skinning was further thickened in localized areas to allow for a further increase in dive speed. This version also had a modified armament array of three 13.2mm (.51 inch) guns (one in the forward fuselage and one in each wing with a rate of fire of 800rpm), twin 20mm Type 99-II guns, and an additional fuel tank with a capacity of 97 gallons often replaced by a 550-pound bomb.

Other A6M5 variants were the A6M5d-S night fighter modified for night combat, armed with one 20mm Type 99 cannon (that was inclined back to the pilot's cockpit) and the A6M5-K Zero-Reisen (Model l22) tandem trainer version, also manufactured by Mitsubishi.

A6M6c Type 0 Model 53c

This was similar to the A6M5c, but with self-sealing wing tanks and a Nakajima Sakae 31a engine featuring water-methanol engine boost.

A6M7 Type 0 Model 62

The Model 62 was similar to the A6M6, but was intended for attack or the Kamikaze role.

A6M8 Type 0 Model 64

The Model 64 was similar to the A6M6, but was powered by the 1,560hp Mitsubishi Kinsei 62 engine that was 60% more powerful than the out-of-production Sakae. This resulted in an extensively modified cowling and nose, with the larger cowling causing the deletion of the fuselage mounted machine gun, but armament was otherwise unchanged from the Model 52 Hei. In addition, the Model 64 was modified to carry two 40 gallon drop tanks on either wing and a 550 pound bomb on the underside of the fuselage. Only two prototypes of the ambitious 6,300 production program were completed in April 1945.

The Zero in Combat

The Zero's psychological impact upon its appearance into the war was so influential that all contemporary fighters were judged by the standards it set. It had great acceleration and was dangerous to dogfight at low speeds and low altitudes, and in any turning combat where radius of turn or maneuverability was essential. The Zero had almost total command of the Pacific skies until the middle of 1942. When an intact Zero was captured in Alaska and returned to the U.S. for evaluation, its major shortcomings were determined, which were the result of design trade-offs and economics and could be exploited in combat. Because the fighter was built lightly for economics, it had speed but an under-powered engine, poor diving qualities, poor pilot armor protection, and no self-sealing fuel tanks. An engine CO_2 fire extinguisher was present, but was only effective for taxiing or stationary fires while on the ground. The lift generated by its large wing area, along with its light weight, was maximized at lower altitudes. The Zero began to lose its exceptional maneuverability when flying above 15,000 feet, and as it approached its maximum ceiling of 32,000 feet, it lost almost all maneuverability. High altitude performance was greater on aircraft with the high power and the low drag associated with smaller wings (i.e., high wing loading, where most of the engine's power was used to keep the wing in the air). One of the Zero's assets was its excellent cockpit visibility. During the early war, this high altitude deficiency was not significant, because American fighters were also underpowered and ineffective at high altitude. When second generation U.S. fighters appeared in early 1943, Zero pilots were confronted with a dilemma: they could either defer the altitude advantage or fight at high altitudes, where the American fighters had superior performance. Either option favored the Americans.

The Battle of Midway in June 1942 was the turning point in the Pacific war, not only because of the devastating losses incurred by the Japanese, but from that point improved new Allied aircraft flown by highly-trained pilots achieved superiority over Zeroes, whose design would basically remain the same as first conceived in 1937. Into early 1943, Zeros were in short supply, and while there were sufficient numbers to maintain unit strength, there were not enough to establish many new units. Even by mid-1943, when Zero production increased and other new aircraft, such as the Tony, were coming off the production lines in numbers, many new Allied

units arrived in the Pacific equipped with new second generation fighters that gave the Allies a quantitative and qualitative superiority that would continue to increase throughout the war. The myth and reality of the Zero steadily declined and its lowest point was reached when it was selected to lead the Navy's Kamikaze force.

Koga's Zero

Koga's (Akutan) Zero

On 4 June 1942, a Zero piloted by FPO Tadayoshi Koga was hit by ground fire over Dutch Harbor, Alaska, and crashed upside down but virtually intact in a bog. The Zero was salvaged and shipped to North Island San Diego and repaired, and was flown in September and October in simulated dogfights against first line U.S. fighters to determine tactics to be used against it. A report stated:

"The Zero had superior maneuverability only at the lower speeds used in dogfighting, with short turning radius and excellent aileron control at very low speeds. However, immediately apparent was the fact that the ailerons froze up at speeds above two hundred knots, so that rolling maneuvers at those speeds were slow and required much force on the control stick. It rolled to the left much easier than to the right. Also, its engine would cut out under negative acceleration (as when nosing into a dive) due to its float-type carburetor.

"We now had an answer for our pilots, who were unable to escape a pursuing Zero. We told them to go into a vertical power dive, using negative acceleration if possible to open the range quickly and gain advantageous speed while the Zero's engine was stopped. At about two hundred knots, we instructed them to roll hard right before the Zero pilot could get his sights lined up."

Lt.Cdr. Eddie Sanders flew 24 test flights in the Akutan Zero between 20 September and 15 October 1942 and reported:

"These flights covered performance tests such as we do on planes undergoing Navy tests. The very first flight exposed weaknesses of the Zero which our pilots could exploit with proper tactics... immediately apparent was the fact that the ailerons froze up at speeds above 200 knots, so that rolling maneuvers at those speeds were slow and required much force on the control stick. It rolled to the left much easier than to the right. Also, its engine cut out under negative acceleration due to its float-type carburetor. We now had the answer for our pilots, who were being outmaneuvered and unable to escape a pursuing Zero: go into a vertical power dive, using negative acceleration if possible to open the range while the Zero's engine was stopped by the acceleration. At about 200 knots, roll hard right before the Zero pilot could get his sights lined up."

Jack/Mitsubishi J2M

Jack

The Mitsubishi J2M Raiden Thunderbolt was designed by Jiro Horikoshi, celebrated designer of the Zero, to a 1939 requirement as primarily a local defense fighter. The JNAF's emphasis upon speed and climb rate, rather than its traditional desire for range and maneuverability, prompted Horikoshi to adopt a squat single-engine design with long radial engine cowling, laminar-flow wings, and curved windscreen. The first flight of the prototype J2M1 occurred on 20 March 1942, and in all, production totaled only 621 aircraft in six variants from J2M1 through J2M6.

The J2M design was conventional, with the cockpit placed in the middle of the stubby fuselage, a single vertical fin at rear, and round, low-mounted rounded wings just forward and under the cockpit. The fighter was powered by the 1,800hp Mitsubishi MK4R-A Kasei 23a, 14-cylinder 2-row radial, which had the problems that limited the range of the fighter and delayed full scale production by a year or more. Being an interceptor, the J2M design featured a potent armament array consisting of four 20mm Type 99-2 cannons in the wings. Fuel drop tanks could be added to increase range, but with the concomitant loss of performance.

Jacks in Combat

After its introduction in December 1942, the Jack helped to provide air superiority in the early years of the war. However, JNAF pilots soon criticized the fighter for numerous shortcomings, but modifications to rectify them were delayed due to Mitsubishi's preoccupation with A6M Zero production. Production of the modified J2M2 fighters occurred slowly, and they entered service with the 381st *Kokutai* late in 1943 and were followed by the J2M3 version with a stronger wing stressed to mount four 20mm cannon. This heavier armament reduced the performance of the Jack to such a degree that it no longer met the original demands, and the J2M4 model endeavored to restore the performance by adding a turbocharger. The final production variant (J2M**5**) was powered by a 1,820hp Mitsubishi Kasei 26a radial.

Some J2Ms fought on in the Battle of the Philippine Sea and in the Philippines, but were mostly relegated to Homeland defense to unsuccessfully combat high-flying B-29 Superfortresses during daylight raids. However, near the end of the war, when the USAAF began nighttime bombing, the Jacks were withdrawn from combat.

General Characteristics

Length	32.7 feet
Wingspan	35.4 feet
Height	13 feet
Wing Area	216 square feet
Empty Weight	6,259 pounds
Loaded Weight	7,676 pounds
Powerplant	1 × One 1,820 hp Mitsubishi MK4R-A Kasei 23a 14-cylinder two-row radial engine

Performance

Maximum speed	382mph
Range	348 miles
Service Ceiling	36,910 feet
Rate of Climb	3,838 feet/minute
Wing Loading	35 lb/square feet
Power/Mass	0.24 hp/lb

Armament

Guns	4 × 20 mm Type 99-2 cannons in the wings, two in each wing, inboard guns having 190 rpg, outboard guns 210 rpg.
Ordinance	2 × 132 pound bombs or 2 × 53 U.S. gallon drop tanks

JACK 11
FIELDS OF FIRE

FORWARD GUNS
"A", AND "B"
¾-front view from above

EXHAUST FLAME PATTERNS

REAR VIEW

VULNERABILITY

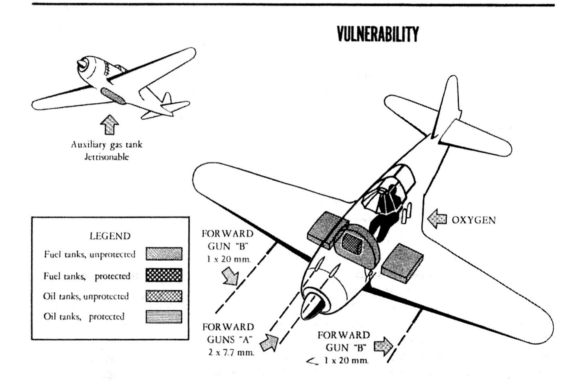

Auxiliary gas tank
Jettisonable

LEGEND

Fuel tanks, unprotected
Fuel tanks, protected
Oil tanks, unprotected
Oil tanks, protected

FORWARD
GUN "B"
1 x 20 mm.

FORWARD
GUNS "A"
2 x 7.7 mm.

FORWARD
GUN "B"
1 x 20 mm.

OXYGEN

ARMAMENT

	No.	Size	Rds. Gun.	Type		No.	Size	Rds. Gun	Type
Forward	4	20 mm	100	Fixed	Tail				
or	2	7.7mm	550	Fixed					
Top and	2	20 mm	100	Fixed	Wing				
Side									
Bottom									

DATE December 1944

TACTICAL DATA

JACK is more powerful and heavily armed than previous Japanese fighters. Probably less maneuverable than ZEKE but superior in diving and climbing at high speeds.

No armor or fuel protection have been indicated.

RESTRICTED

Irving/Nakajima J1N1

TAIC Irving

The JNAF Nakajima J1N1 Gekko was a twin-engine aircraft used for reconnaissance, night fighting, and later for Kamikaze missions. It was given the codename "Irving" since the earlier reconnaissance version, the J1N1-C, was mistaken for a fighter.

In mid-1938, the JNAF requested a twin-engine fighter design to serve as an escort for the Mitsubishi G3M Nell, which had a range of 2,730 miles. The operating range of the standard Navy fighter (the Mitsubishi A5M Claude) was only 750 miles, which was inadequate when compared with the G3M's. Moreover, at the time, the potential of the Zero fighter, then still under development, remained to be evaluated, stressing the need for a long-range escort fighter.

In March 1939, Mitsubishi and Nakajima began the development of project 13-Shi. The prototype left the factory in March 1941, equipped with two 1,130hp Nakajima Sakae 21/22, 14-cylinder radial engines. There was a crew of three, and the aircraft was armed with a 20mm Type 99 cannon and six 7.7mm (.303 in) Type 97 machine guns. Four of these machine guns were mounted in a powered turret, the weight of which reduced the performance of the aircraft considerably, so its intended use as an escort fighter had to be abandoned. Instead, production was authorized for a lighter reconnaissance variant (the J1N1-C), also known by the Navy designation Navy Type 2 Reconnaissance Plane.

The JNAF also placed orders with Nakajima for the newly-designated J1N1-S night fighter design. This model was christened the Model 11 Gekko ("Moonlight"). It required only two crew and had a twin 20mm pair of Type 99 Model 1 cannon firing at a 30° upward angle and a second pair firing downward at a forward 30° angle placed in the fuselage behind the cabin, similar to the German Schräge Musik configuration. Early versions had nose searchlights in place of radar, while later variants without nose antennae or searchlight added a 20mm cannon to the nose. It had protected fuel tanks and armor plate behind the pilot, while leading edge wing slots gave it good maneuverability at slows speeds and good stall characteristics.

Irving in Combat

The J1N1-S was used against B-29 Superfortresses over Japan, though the lack of good radar and insufficient high-altitude performance handicapped it, since usually only one pass could be made against the higher-speed B-29s. Many Irvings were shot down or destroyed on the ground. A number were relegated to kamikaze attacks, using 550 pound bombs attached to the wings.

General Characteristics

Crew	two
Length	41.9 feet
Wingspan	55.8 feet
Height	14.9 feet
Wing Area	430 square feet
Empty Weight	10,648 pounds
Loaded Weight	15,422 pounds
Max Takeoff Weight	8,005 pounds
Powerplant	2 × Nakajima Sakae, 1,130 hp each

Performance

Maximum speed	317mph
Range	2,361 miles
Service Ceiling	30,570 feet
Rate of Climb	1,712 feet/minute
Wing Loading	36 lb/sqft
Power/Mass	0.15 hp/lb

Armament

Guns	• 4 × 20 mm Type 99 cannon, two upward- and two downward-firing • 3 × 20 mm Type 99 cannon, all three upward firing in later models

IRVING 11

FIELDS OF FIRE

FORWARD GUNS "A", AND
"B" AND TOP GUN "C"
¾-rear view from above
Reconnaissance
Version

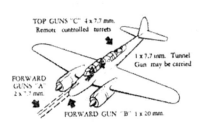

TOP GUNS "C" 4 x 7.7 mm.
Remote controlled turrets

1 x 7.7 mm. Tunnel
Gun may be carried

FORWARD
GUNS "A"
2 x 7.7 mm.

FORWARD GUN "B" 1 x 20 mm.

Reconnaissance Version
¾-front view from above

Fuel and Oil tanks and oxygen cylinders
are same on both versions

ARMOR PLATE

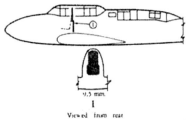

9.5 mm.
I
Viewed from rear

EXHAUST FLAME PATTERNS

REAR VIEW

VULNERABILITY

Jettisonable
Fuel tanks

BOTTOM FORWARD
GUNS "C" 2 x 20 mm.

Fixed at 30° angle

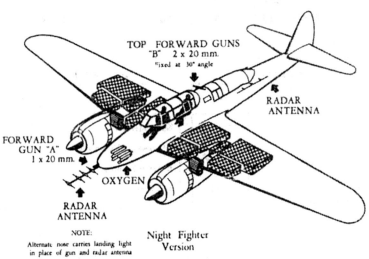

TOP FORWARD GUNS
"B" 2 x 20 mm.
Fixed at 30° angle

RADAR
ANTENNA

FORWARD
GUN "A"
1 x 20 mm.

OXYGEN

RADAR
ANTENNA

NOTE:
Alternate nose carries landing light
in place of gun and radar antenna

Night Fighter
Version

		LEGEND		
Fuel tanks, unprotected		Oil tanks, unprotected		
Fuel tanks, protected		Oil tanks, protected		

ARMAMENT

	No.	Size	Rds. Gun.	Type		No.	Size	Rds. Gun	Type
Forward	1	20 mm (Not always found)	100	Fixed	Tail				
Top	2	20 mm	100	Fixed	Wing				
Side									
Bottom	2	20 mm	100	Fixed					

DATE December 1944

TACTICAL DATA

The top and bottom 20 mm guns are mounted to face forward at a fixed angle of 30° from the longitudinal axis of the fuselage.

Armor plate is installed to protect the pilot's back and head.

Armament has varied considerably in recce versions.

Nell/Mitsubishi G3M

Nell

The Mitsubishi G3M Type 96 Land-based Attack Bomber, (Rikko, Nell) had its origins in 1933, in an Imperial Japanese Navy specification tendered to Mitsubishi requesting a heavy bomber with an unprecedented range which would be required by Japan's future territorial ambitions. The requirement for speed was also unprecedented, as the bomber would need to not only cover long distances, but necessarily have exceptional speed to strike distant targets with a minimal attack time. The requirement for bomb load was again unprecedented, and was necessary to accommodate the 1,764-pound aerial torpedo for use against the armored Allied battleships cruising the vast Pacific. Thus, the G3M was the epitome of Japanese military aircraft design in the brief interlude leading to the Pacific War, with powerful offensive armament of bombs and torpedoes and range and speed emphasized over protection and defensive capabilities.

To maintain the speed and high-altitude performance of the G3M with a heavy payload, it was originally designed without any defensive weaponry, but purely as a bomber craft, with its high-altitude performance being regarded as sufficient to evade enemy AA and its high speed in combination with the planned high performance Zero as an escort considered sufficient to counter enemy fighters. The G3M benefited from a broad developmental program which saw the construction of 21 prototypes and preproduction aircraft, with three different engines placed in the prototypes. Even after the modified final prototype, which did include three defensive machine gun emplacements, the G3M retained its lightweight structure and lacked any form of defensive armor or self-sealing fuel tanks, as these were considered to impede speed and altitude. This characteristic in Japanese aircraft design would manifest itself again in its successor, the G4M Betty.

Nell in Combat

The G3M first saw combat during terror bombings of Chinese cities in August-November 1937. When the Pacific War began in December 1941, although the G3M was considered to be obsolete, a number were deployed from Formosa in the Battle of the Philippines, some bombed Singapore from bases in Indo-China, and Wake Island was also attacked by Nells. On 19 February 1942, AAC P-40s intercepted Nells during the infamous Japanese attack on Darwin.

Later, the Nakajima Company redesigned the G3M into the improved G3M3 (Model 23), with more powerful engines and increased fuel capacity. This version was only manufactured by Nakajima, being the most rapidly produced in wartime. This version entered service in 1941, and was maintained in service for two years; it was later used in 1943 alongside the

G3M2s for long-range maritime reconnaissance with radar due to its excellent long-range performance. From 1943, the majority of Nells served as glider tugs, aircrew and paratroop trainers, and for transporting high-ranking officers and VIPs between metropolitan islands, occupied territories, and combat fronts until the end of the war.

General Characteristics

Crew	7
Length	54 feet
Wingspan	82 feet
Height	12 feet
Wing Area	807 square feet
Empty Weight	10,923 pounds
Loaded Weight	17,600 pounds
Powerplant	2 × Mitsubishi Ha-45 Kinsei radial engine, 1,075 hp each

Performance

Maximum speed	233 mph
Cruise Speed	174 mph
Range	2,730 miles
Service Ceiling	30,200 feet
Rate of Climb	1180 feet/minute

Armament

Guns	• 1 × 20 mm Type 99 cannon in rear dorsal turret • 4 × 7.7 (.303 inch) Type 92 machine gun in cockpit, left and right side positions, and in retractable forward dorsal turret.
Bombs	1,764 pounds of bombs or 1 × aerial torpedo

NELL 23

FIELDS OF FIRE

TOP GUN "A"
1 x 7.7 mm.
¾-rear view from above

TOP REAR GUN "B"
1 x 20 mm.
¾-rear view from above

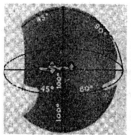

SIDE GUN "C"
1 x 7.7 mm.
Side view from above

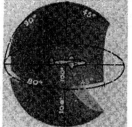

SIDE GUN "D"
1 x 7.7 mm.
Side view from above

NOTE:
1 x 7.7 mm. FORWARD GUN, aft
of pilot and co-pilot, may be fired
from port, st'b'd. or bottom positions.

EXHAUST FLAME PATTERNS

REAR VIEW

VULNERABILITY

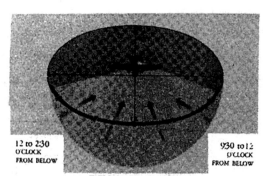

12 to 2:30
O'CLOCK
FROM BELOW

9:30 to 12
O'CLOCK
FROM BELOW

FIELDS OF ATTACK
Do not attack from above

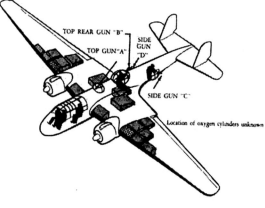

TOP REAR GUN "B"
TOP GUN "A"
SIDE GUN "D"
SIDE GUN "C"
Location of oxygen cylinders unknown

	LEGEND		
Fuel tanks, unprotected		Oil tanks, unprotected	
Fuel tanks, protected		Oil tanks, protected	

ARMAMENT

	No.	Size	Rds. Gun	Type		No.	Size	Rds. Gun	Type
Forward	1	7.7 mm	300	Flex.	Tail				
Top Forward	1	7.7 mm	300	Flex.	Wing				
Top Aft	1	20 mm	60	Turret					
Side	2	7.7 mm	300	Flex.					
Bottom									

DATE December 1944

TACTICAL DATA

NELL has no armor protec-
tion for pilot, crew or engines. Unprotected fuel tanks
are another source of weakness.

Forward 7.7 mm may be
shifted to forward lateral or
ventral positions.

TAIC Nell

Betty/Mitsubishi G4M

Betty

In July 1937, Mitsubishi's new twin-engine, land-based G3M Nell attack bomber first saw combat in China, but was immediately found to be deficient and virtually defenseless, and the Imperial Navy issued a specification to Mitsubishi to replace the G3Ms. However, the requirements were unparalleled, with a maximum speed of 247mph and an altitude of 9,845 feet, a range of 2,933 miles without a torpedo or equivalent weight in bombs, or at least 2,300 miles loaded with a torpedo or the same weight in bombs.

The Mitsubishi head designer, Kiro Honjo, developed the G4M with a streamlined but somewhat rotund fuselage, which provided room for a bomb bay within the wing center section and permitted the seven to nine-man crew to move around inside. Three to four gunners manned defensive gun positions, which the Nell lacked. The G4M mounted 7.7mm (.30 caliber) guns in the nose, atop the mid-fuselage behind the cockpit, and on both sides of the fuselage behind the wing, while the tail contained a 20mm cannon. Although the G4M was well armed, Honjo forfeited crew security for great range by excluding armor plate protection and utilized wing fuel tanks that were not self-sealing; while lighter in weight, they were subject to explosion if punctured during combat.

The first G4M prototype first flew on 23 October 1939, but while the initial test results were impressive, the Navy deferred the bomber in favor of the G6M1 variant, which was the "escort fighter" version of the Betty. The G6M1s were produced by reconverting the first 30 mass-produced Bettys by adding a turret with two 20mm cannon in the bomb bay. These Bettys were intended to protect the numerous older Nells, which experienced heavy losses over China. These escort Bettys were too slow for their proposed function and were relegated to training.

After the G6M1 was abandoned, the first production G4M (2,414 built) was available in April 1941, and the JNAF now had a competent bomber that would prove its worth in early combat. The sinking of the British warships HMS Repulse and the HMS Prince of Wales was the highlight of the bomber's first year of combat. However, any dominance that the G4M may have had in the early war was soon lost, as newer, better, and more numerous AAF and USN fighters were encountered. After 1943, Mitsubishi introduced many Betty variants and sub-variants to fulfill new requirements and to purge the various weaknesses in the basic design, mainly installing different engines and armament packages. The G4M2 was almost a complete redesign, but it did not overcome the bomber's vulnerability to enemy

fighter firepower and Mitsubishi attempted to reduce the bomber's penchant to catch on fire. A new version, called the G4M Model 34, was designed with the wing changed to a single spar configuration and self-sealing fuel tanks were installed, but with a capacity about one-third less than earlier models. Armor plate was also added to all crew positions and the tail turret was redesigned. As a result of these modifications the fuselage was shortened, shifting the center of gravity forward, and to rebalance the bomber, dihedral was added to the horizontal stabilizer.

Betty in Combat

The Zero, with its very long range ability, was unable to escort a Betty formation to its maximum range, and without fighter escorts, even the relatively well-armed Bettys were virtually defenseless. As a result, the Betty's long range was, in effect, irrelevant. It would have been far more practical for the JNAF to initially relinquish the Betty's long range and speed for structural integrity, self-sealing fuel tanks, and crew armor. What Japan needed was the counterpart of a B-25, which was nearly as fast as the Betty, carried a comparable bomb load, and was extremely rugged. Although the Mitchell's range was less than half the Betty's, a Japanese version of the B-25 would nevertheless still have had a range greater than the Zero's. B-25 missions generally had fighter escorts, but a solitary B-25's firepower and ruggedness gave it a very good chance of surviving an interceptor attack.

Both Allied fighter pilots and JNAF Betty pilots gave the Betty mocking nicknames, referring to its as "the flying Zippo," "the flying cigar," and "Hamaki" (Japanese for Cigar) because of their tendency to explode or catch on fire from any slight damage to the wings containing the fuel tanks after being hit by aerial or ground fire.

In view of Japan's technology, the Betty, like the Zero, was an advanced aircraft, but due to poor production techniques the bomber's construction was substandard, its equipment inferior, and it was difficult to maintain. Since a multi-engine bomber is more complicated to manufacture than a fighter, between January 1941 and January 1944, only 1,200 Bettys were manufactured. While another 1,100 were finally produced by Mitsubishi in the last year of the war, the supply of Japan's best bomber was always insufficient. In fact, the Betty was an inferior bomber design and would be very poorly matched for the type of war that developed in the Pacific. The

Japanese were never able to develop their equivalent of the devastating American B-25 and B-26 medium bombers, which were well suited for the Pacific War. Near the end of the war, the Betty was relegated as a common Kamikaze carrying and launching platform for carrying the Ohka Kamikaze rocket aircraft.

On the many occasions that the Betty was used for low-altitude torpedo attacks, its performance advantages were negated and it was easily shot down by AA fire or even by small arms. Also, the Betty's relatively large size made it an easy gunnery target and the conventional approach path required for a torpedo run made it an easy interception by enemy fighter planes.

When the Betty was used for medium to high-altitude bombing against stationary land targets, such as airfields, supply depots, or enemy positions, the Betty was much less vulnerable. Using its long range and high speed, the G4M could appear from any direction and then retreat before fighters could intercept them. The Betty's 20mm cannon in the tail turret was much heavier armament than commonly installed in bombers, which made dead astern attacks very dangerous for attacking enemy fighters. But with so little other opposing fire power, the attacks most likely to succeed were those from head-on or high from the side, so the attacking Allied pilot was able to take his time in choosing his attack. The wing fuel tanks were easily ignited, while the oxygen bottles located near the cockpit were easily exploded if hit.

Performance

Maximum speed	265 mph
Cruise Speed	196 mph
Stall Speed	75 mph
Range	2,664 miles
Service Ceiling	27,890 feet
Rate of Climb	1,800 feet/minute

Armament

Guns	1 × 20 mm Type 99 cannon (tail turret), 4× 7.7 mm Type 92 machine gun (nose turret × 1, waist positions × 2, top turret × 1)
Bombs	1 ×1,892 pound Type 91 Kai-3 (improved model **3**) aerial torpedo or 1 × 1,764 pound bomb or 4 × 551 pound bombs

General Characteristics

Crew	7 (pilot, copilot, navigator/bombardier/nose gunner, captain/top turret gunner, radio operator/waist gunner, engine mechanic/waist gunner, tail gunner)
Length	65.7 feet
Wingspan	81.6 feet
Height	16.1 feet (in a horizontal position)
Wing Area	840.9 square feet
Airfoil	Mitsubishi type
Empty Weight	14,860 pounds
Loaded Weight	20,944 pounds
Max Takeoff Weight	28,350 pounds
Powerplant	2 × Mitsubishi MK4A-11 Kasei (Fire star) 14 cylinder radial engines, 1,530 hp each
Propellers	4-blade Hamilton Standard licensed Sumitomo constant speed variable-pitch

BETTY 22

FIELDS OF FIRE

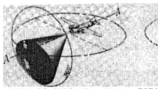

FORWARD GUN "A" 1 x 7.7 mm.
¾-front view from above
Nose rotates mechanically thru 360°
about axis "A"—"A". Gun is ball and
socket mounted, off center, in nose.

FORWARD GUN "B" 1 x 7.7 mm.
¾-front view from above
This gun is interchangeable from
port to st'b'd. side of nose. Ball and
socket mount

TOP GUN "C" 1 x 20 mm.
¾-rear view from above
Powered turret

SIDE GUN "D" 1 x 7.7 mm.
Approx. side view from above.
Post and sliding bar mount.
Field of fire for SIDE GUN "E" similar

TAIL GUN "F" 1 x 20 mm.
¾-rear view from above

FIRE FREE FIELDS

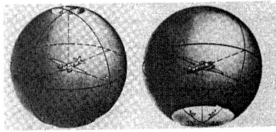

¾-front view from above.   ¼-front view from below.

EXHAUST FLAME PATTERNS

REAR VIEW

ARMOR PLATE

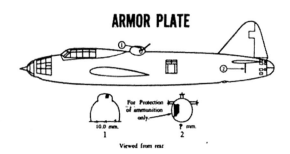

Viewed from rear

VULNERABILITY

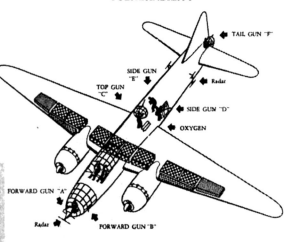

LEGEND			
Fuel tanks, unprotected		Oil tanks, unprotected	
Fuel tanks, protected		Oil tanks, protected	

ARMAMENT

	No.	Size	Rds. Gun	Type		No.	Size	Rds. Gun	Type
Forward	2	7.7 mm	300-776	Flex.	Tail	1	20 mm	90-360	Flex.
or	1	13 mm		Flex.					
Top	1	20 mm	90	Power Turret	Wing				
Side	2	7.7 mm	300-776	Flex.					
or	2	20 mm	90						
Bottom									

TACTICAL DATA

This is the first example
of a power operated dorsal
turret in use by the J.A.F.
Late reports indicate some
sort of leak-proofing of the
fuel tanks is in use.
Armor plate used around
turret.

DATE December 1944

Kate/Nakajima B5N2

Kate

Beginning in 1936, the JNAF operated the B4Y1 (Type 96) Jean biplane torpedo bomber, which was similar to its contemporary, the British Fairey Swordfish. With the introduction of the Mitsubishi A5M Zero carrier fighter, the JNAF wanted a monoplane "carrier attack bomber" (torpedo bomber) with corresponding performance. In 1935, the JNAF issued a specification requiring a single-engined monoplane with a crew of three; a maximum speed of 207mph at 6,560 feet; an endurance of four hours or a maximum of seven hours at 155mph; an armament of one 1,764 pound torpedo; a single rearward-firing 7.7mm machine gun for protection; and a wingspan of less than 52.5 feet, with provision for hydraulic wing folding to reduce the span to no more than 24.6 feet.

Nakajima chief designer Katsuji Nakamura produced the Type K, a very clean low-wing monoplane with a hydraulically retractable undercarriage. The fuselage, when compared to the large folding wing, looked unusually small, but had to be kept relatively short at 33.8 feet to fit on the Navy's standard carrier elevators. Other Nakamura enhancements were Fowler flaps and the Nakajima Hikari 2, nine-cylinder radial engine that powered a variable-pitch propeller. The B5N1 prototype first flew in January 1937, and although its 230mph far surpassed the requirement, hydraulic problems needed to be resolved and there were worries that the many technical innovations would make it very difficult to maintain in the field. Nakajima simplified the second prototype and also had the newer Hikari 3 engine with a constant-speed propeller installed, along with wing fuel tanks with increased capacity. The second prototype easily prevailed over Mitsubishi's B5M1, and it went into production in November 1937 as the Navy Type 97 Carrier Attack Bomber Model 11 (B5N1 Model 11).

In Spring 1938, carrier qualification trials were conducted at the same time it was flying its initial combat missions over China as a single-engined level bomber. While no major modifications were necessary for the China operations, the JNAF was aware that the opposition there was mediocre at best, and in 1939, Nakajima developed an improved variant of the B5N1 as the B5N2 Model 12 (or Type 97 Carrier Attack Bomber Model 12), which first flew in December 1939. Externally, it was similar to the B5N1, but was re-engined with the more reliable Nakajima Sakae 11 14-cylinder radial, which was especially important, as the B5N2 would fly most of its missions long distances over water. During its career 1,149 B5Ns were built: 669 by the parent company Nakajima between 1936 and 1941; 200 by Aichi in 1942-43; and 280 by the Naval Air Arsenal in 1942-43.

Kate in Combat

In the late 1930s, the Nakajima B5N2 was considered the best dive bomber in the world; an accolade that continued into the first year of the war and helped expand the Japanese Empire to its greatest extent. By the start of the Pacific War, the B5N2 had completely replaced the B5N1 in all front-line land-based and carrier-based units. The Kate was exceptionally stable, with an extremely low wing loading and the ability to carry an impressive ordnance load, including the superlative Japanese aerial torpedo. The Kate was relatively fast and was a good aircraft when flown by the outstanding

pilots of the early war. The highlight of the B5N2's career was the Pearl Harbor attack, when combined with high-level bombers they sank five battleships and heavily damaged three more. The Kate would play a major role in sinking the USN carriers *Lexington*, *Yorktown*, and *Hornet* in the carrier battles of 1942, but not without very heavy losses to themselves. Unlike the later Val, the Kate was defenseless, as it was substantially slower with a lesser rate of climb and diving ability. It also had no pilot armor or self-sealing fuel tanks. Its only advantage was its ability to turn extremely fast and tight, as like the Val, it could turn with the Zero. But since the Kate had no forward-firing guns, this one advantage was worthless. Kate formations required the protection of escorting Zeros and Oscars.

Later Kate units flew operations from land bases, where it performed an important part in the Solomons, Marianas, and Philippines air campaigns. Its last carrier-based engagement was the Battle of the Philippine Sea in June 1944, where its unsatisfactory performance and poor crew and fuel-tank protection were the major factor in its heavy losses. By the end of 1944, the Kate was relegated to training units and because of its excellent long range ability, it served in a second-line role for maritime reconnaissance and anti-submarine patrols in areas where Allied fighters were unlikely to be encountered.

General Characteristics

Crew	3 (1 pilot, 1 commander, and 1 rear gunner/radio operator)
Length	33.8 feet
Wingspan	50.9 feet
Height	12.1 feet
Wing Area	406 square feet
Empty Weight	5,024 pounds
Loaded Weight	8,380 pounds
Max Takeoff Weight	9,040 pounds
Powerplant	1 × Nakajima Sakae 11 14 cylinder radial engine, 1,000 hp

Performance

Maximum speed	235 mph
Range	1,237 miles
Service Ceiling	27,100 feet
Rate of Climb	1,283 feet/minute
Wing Loading	21 lb/sqft
Power/Mass	0.12 hp/lb

Armament

Guns	1 × 7.7 mm Type 92 Ru machine gun (Lewis-type) in rear dorsal position, fed by hand loaded drum magazines of 97 rounds. A number of B5N1s were equipped with 2 × 7.7 Type 97 machine guns in the wings.
Bombs	1 × 1,760 pound type 91 torpedo or 1x 1,760 pound bomb or 2 × 550 pound bombs or 6 × 293 pound bombs

KATE 12

FIELDS OF FIRE

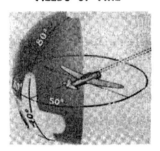

TOP GUN "B" AND
FORWARD GUNS "A"
¾-rear view from above

EXHAUST FLAME PATTERNS

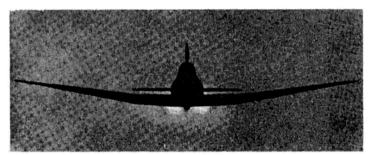

REAR VIEW

VULNERABILITY

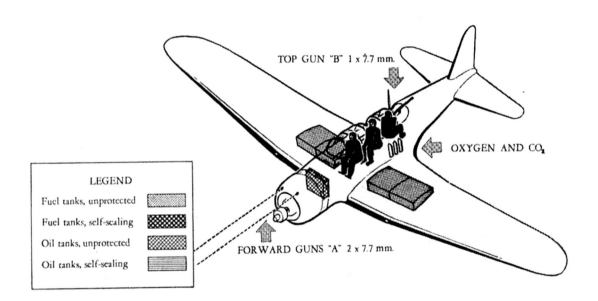

TOP GUN "B" 1 x 7.7 mm.

OXYGEN AND CO_2

FORWARD GUNS "A" 2 x 7.7 mm.

LEGEND

Fuel tanks, unprotected
Fuel tanks, self-sealing
Oil tanks, unprotected
Oil tanks, self-sealing

ARMAMENT

	No.	Size	Rds. Gun	Type		No.	Size	Rds. Gun	Type
Forward	2	7.7mm	600	Fixed	Tail				
Top Rear Cockpit Side	1	7.7mm	300	Flex.	Wing				
Bottom									

TACTICAL DATA

KATE is vulnerable to attack because of its low speed and unprotected crew and fuel tanks.

Radar is carried.

DATE December 1944

RESTRICTED

Val/Aichi D3A1

Val

In mid-1936, the JNAF issued a design specification for a carrier-based monoplane dive bomber to replace the Aichi D1A carrier-based Susie biplane. Aichi, Nakajima, and Mitsubishi submitted designs and the JNAF contracted Aichi and Nakajima each to submit two prototypes. The Aichi design was basically all-metal with a circular-section fuselage, low-mounted elliptical wings, a standard tail unit, and non-retractable landing gear with large speed fairings. As the Val flew so slowly anyhow, the drag of this fixed landing gear did not create a significant problem and was used for the sake of simplicity. The power plant was the nine-cylinder 730hp Hikari 1 radial that had powered the D1A2. Flight tests confirmed that the Val was underpowered, so the second prototype was powered by the 840hp Mitsubishi Kinsei 3 radial engine, and this and other modifications proved the Val to be superior to Nakajima's D3N1JNAF dive bomber contender. In December 1939, the Aichi prototype was ordered into production under the designation Navy Type 99 Carrier Bomber Model 11 (Aichi D3A1). Production aircraft differed from the second prototype, as power was again increased with the introduction of a 1,000hp Mitsubishi Kinsei 43 engine on early D3A1 production models. The D3A1 completed carrier trials and entered operational service with the JNAF in China and Indo-China. A total of 1,495 D3As of different versions was built.

Val in Combat

Beginning with the Pearl Harbor attack, the D3A1 participated in all major Japanese carrier operations during the first ten months of the war and was Japan's primary dive bomber, as its well-trained crews had exceptional success. The Val had extremely good turning capability, being able to turn with the Zero. If a Val could survive an initial snap fighter attack, it could outrun early first generation AAC fighters, and with its 50 seconds of continuous firepower, it was able to shoot one down with an effective rear gunner, or if the pursuing fighter overran and got into range of the Val's forward guns. The lack of pilot armor and self-sealing fuel tanks made the Val very vulnerable, and after only several hits it would catch fire and explode. Its bomb load of 1 x 500lb and 2 x 100lb bombs was inadequate to do much damage and the Val had to be deployed in large numbers to be effective. If a formation of Vals attacked a target defended by AA, it would have to drop its bombs above 5,000 feet, instead of the more accurate 3,000 feet, due to the Val's acute vulnerability when hit.

Like the Kate and Zero, the early war Val benefited from its excellent pilots more than from any intrinsic qualities. Both the Val and Kate were poorly armed and extremely vulnerable to fighter attack. The JNAF lost large numbers of Vals and veteran pilots during the Battle of Santa Cruz, and the Val's success changed in late 1943 with the loss of skilled pilots; its bombing accuracy fell under 10% and the Val ceased to be a threat.

When the Yokosuka D4Y Suisei Judy came into inventory, the Vals were transferred to land-based units or operated from carriers which were too small to effectively accommodate the fast-landing Judy. When U.S. forces recaptured the Philippines in 1944, land-based D3A2s joined in the air combat, but were found to be entirely obsolete and suffered heavy losses. By then, many D3A1s and D3A2s were flown by training units in Japan. During the last year of the war, the D3A2s were returned to combat as Kamikazes. The Aichi D3A was the first Japanese aircraft to bomb American targets in WWII and before the war was over, it had sunk more Allied military ships than any other.

General Characteristics

Crew	Two (pilot and gunner)
Length	33.4 feet
Wingspan	47.1 feet
Height	12.7 feet
Wing Area	375.6 square feet
Empty Weight	5,309 pounds (D3A1) & 5,666 pounds (D3A2)
Max Takeoff Weight	8,047 pounds (D3A1) & 9,100 pounds (D3A2)
Powerplant	• D3A1: 1 × Mitsubishi Kinsei 44, 1,070 hp • D3A2: 1 × Mitsubishi Kinsei 54, 1,300 hp

Performance

Maximum speed	242mph (D3A1) and 267mph (D3A2)
Range	915 miles (D3A1) and 840 miles (D3A2)
Service Ceiling	30,500 feet (D3A1) and 34,450 feet (D3A2)

Armament

Guns	• 2 × fixed, forward-firing 7.7mm (0.303 inch) Type 97 machine guns • 1 × flexible, rearward-firing 7.7mm (0.303 inch) Type 92 machine gun • 1 × 551 pound or 2 × 132 pound bombs

VAL 22

FIELDS OF FIRE

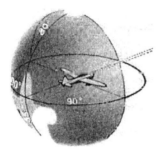

TOP GUN "B" AND
FORWARD GUNS "A"
¾-rear view from above

EXHAUST FLAME PATTERNS

REAR VIEW

VULNERABILITY

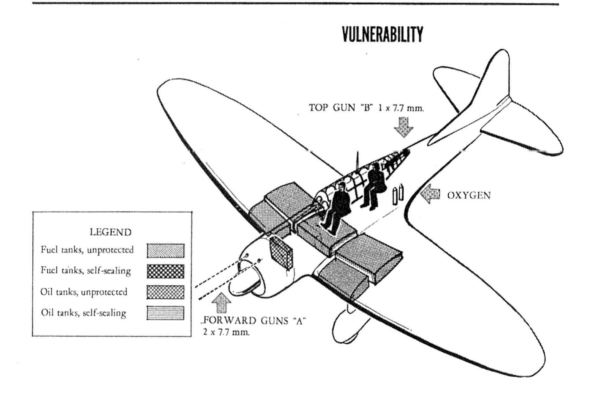

TOP GUN "B" 1 x 7.7 mm.

OXYGEN

FORWARD GUNS "A"
2 x 7.7 mm.

LEGEND

Fuel tanks, unprotected	
Fuel tanks, self-sealing	
Oil tanks, unprotected	
Oil tanks, self-sealing	

ARMAMENT

	No.	Size	Rds. Gun	Type		No.	Size	Rds. Gun	Type
Forward	2	7.7 mm	791	Fixed	Tail				
Top Rear Cockpit Side	1	7.7 mm	1000	Flex.	Wing				
Bottom									

DATE December 1944

TACTICAL DATA

Up to the present time, neither fuel tank protection nor armor plate has been found on VAL.

RESTRICTED

Jill/Nakajima B6N

Jill

In 1939, the JNAF issued a specification for a modern carrier-based torpedo bomber to supersede the Nakajima B5N Kate. The specifications required a maximum speed of 288mph, a cruising speed of 230mph, and a range of 1,000 nautical miles (empty). To meet the requirement, Nakajima designers decided to base their design on an airframe very similar to that of the successful B5N Kate, differing primarily in its vertical tail surfaces. Although the JNAF had specified a Mitsubishi Kasei radial engine, Nakajima chose to install its own 1,870hp Nakajima NK7A Mamoru 11 radial engine, which powered a four-bladed Hamilton-type licensed propeller. The first of two prototypes was flown in Spring 1941, but initial flight tests uncovered a number of problems which were worked out; but at the end of 1942, final carrier flight testing revealed further problems. After extended flight testing, integrating a number of modifications, it was not until February 1943 that the Jill was ordered into production as the Navy Carrier Attack Bomber Tenzan (Heavenly Mountain) Model 11, with the Nakajima company designation B6N1. However, after only 135 production NK7As had been delivered, Nakajima was ordered to terminate manufacture of its Mamoru engine and install the more reliable 1,850hp Mitsubishi MK4T Kasei 25 engine; fortunately, the adaptation of the B6N airframe to accept this engine presented no major difficulties. Later models differed from the B6N2 only by having a rear firing machine gun of 13mm (.50 caliber) instead of the 7.7mm (.30 caliber) used on the B6N2.

Jill in Combat

The B6N1's combat debut was during the Battle of the Philippine Sea, where they were outnumbered and outclassed and were unable to have any effect, taking heavy losses. Improvements were made, but when a new model was available in mid-1944, the Imperial Fleet had lost most of its large carriers and experienced pilots. From this point, most B6N2 operations therefore took place from land bases, but failed to achieve any major successes and were rarely met by fighters of the 5FC. They were used extensively in the Battle of Okinawa, where they were also used for Kamikaze missions for the first time.

General Characteristics

Crew	3
Length	35.6 feet
Wingspan	48.9 feet
Height	12.6 feet
Wing Area	400 square feet
Empty Weight	6,636 pounds
Loaded Weight	11,460 pounds
Max Takeoff Weight	12,460 pounds
Powerplant	1xMitsubishi Kasei 25 14-cylinder air-cooled radial engine (1,850 hp) (take off power)

Performance

Maximum speed	299mph at 16,075 feet
Cruise Speed	207mph at 13,125 feet
Range	1,892 miles
Service Ceiling	• 29,660 feet • Climb to 16,400 feet: 10 minutes 24 seconds

Armament

Guns	1x7.7mm (.303 inch) Type 92 machine gun in rear cockpit and 1x7.7mm (.303 inch) Type 92 firing through ventral tunnel
Bombs	1 torpedo or 1,760 pounds of bombs

JILL 12

FIELDS OF FIRE

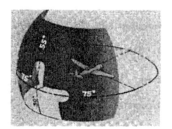

TOP GUN "A"
¾-rear view from above
Provisional field of fire

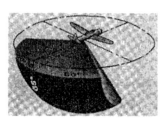

BOTTOM GUN "B"
¾-rear view from above

EXHAUST FLAME PATTERNS

REAR VIEW
Flame Patterns vary

VULNERABILITY

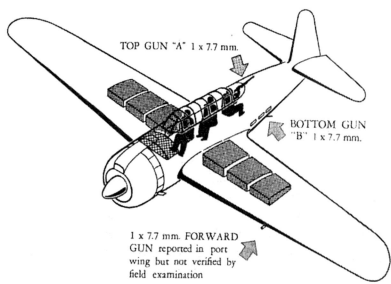

TOP GUN "A" 1 x 7.7 mm.

BOTTOM GUN "B" 1 x 7.7 mm.

1 x 7.7 mm. FORWARD GUN reported in port wing but not verified by field examination

Location of oxygen cylinders unknown

LEGEND

Fuel tanks, unprotected	
Fuel tanks, self-sealing	
Oil tanks, unprotected	
Oil tanks, self-sealing	

ARMAMENT

	No.	Size	Rds. Gun	Type		No.	Size	Rds. Gun	Type
Forward Left Wing	1	7.7 mm	400	Fixed	Tail				
Top Rear Cockpit	1	7.7 mm	700	Flex.	Wing				
Bottom	1	7.7 mm	700	Flex.					

DATE December 1944

TACTICAL DATA

Ineffective fuel tank protection and light armament, together with no evidence of armor indicates that JILL has no decided advantage over KATE except in speed and climb.

There is evidence of radar being installed on JILL.

Japanese Army Air Force Aircraft
Oscar/Nakajima Ki-43

Oscar

In December 1937, the Imperial Japanese Army issued a specification to Nakajima for an advanced successor to the company's popular Ki-27 Nate. The specification called for a top speed of 311mph, a climb rate of 16,400 feet in five minutes, and a range of 500 miles, with maneuverability to be at least equal that of the nimble Ki-27. Nakajima designer Hideo Itokawa had the first of three prototypes completed for its initial flight during January 1939. The prototype was a cantilever low-wing monoplane with an enclosed cockpit, retractable landing gear and tail wheel, and was powered by Nakajima's new supercharged 975hp Ha-25 Sakae radial engine. Service tests of the prototype showed that it met the specifications, but was only slightly faster than the Ki-27, and its maneuverability was so poor that, at one point, it seemed unlikely that the Army would accept it. However, 10 pre-production aircraft were ordered and modifications were made to improve maneuverability, with the most important modification being the introduction of the unique Fowler-type maneuvering flaps, which significantly enhanced its performance in tight turns. The problems were corrected and the type was ordered into production as the Army Type 1 Fighter Model 1A Hayabusa (Peregrine Falcon), Nakajima designation Ki-43-1a (later Oscar in the AAF code name system).

The first production model was armed with two 7.7mm (.30 caliber) machine guns and could carry two 33-pound bombs on external racks, but two sub-variants differed in armaments: the Ki-43-Ib armed with one 7.7mm (.30 caliber) and one 12.7mm (.50 caliber) machine gun and the Ki-43-Ic armed with two 12.7mm machine guns. Production began in March 1941, and when the K-43 arrived in operational units it was the most maneuverable fighter in the JAAF inventory by a wide margin. It had substantial success in the early stages of the Pacific War, but with the introduction of more effective Allied fighters the shortcomings of these first Oscars became obvious, initiating the order of five Ki-43-II prototypes for evaluation. The IIs introduced the more powerful Nakajima Ha-115 engine, some pilot armor protection, and an early type of self-sealing fuel tanks. After satisfactory flight tests, the JAAF ordered the manufacture of the Ki-43-IIa, which had reduced wing span, a modified canopy, the same machine gun armament as the Ki-43-Ic, and two underwing racks, each capable of carrying a 551 pound (250kg) bomb. Late series Oscars were generally similar, except for some equipment and armament alterations. Production totaled 5,919, with 3,239 built by Nakajima, 2,631 built by Tachikawa, and 49 aircraft built by the Army Air Arsenal at Tachikawa.

The Oscar in Combat
Like the Zero, the radial-engined Ki-43 was light and easy to fly. It became renowned for its combat actions in East Asia, the NEI, and New Guinea in the early war, with its pilots easily outmaneuvering any of its mostly obsolete adversaries. However, it did not have armor or self-sealing tanks, and its armament was mediocre until the last version produced in 1944. The nimble

Ki-43s were difficult targets, but after only a few hits they burned easily or disintegrated. As the war continued, the Oscars experienced high loss rates in combat due to the same failings as other Japanese fighters: its light pilot armor, ineffective self-sealing fuel tanks, and inadequate armament of two machine guns against the more heavily armored Allied aircraft.

In spite of its shortcomings, Ki-43 pilots shot down more Allied aircraft than any other JAAF fighter. By the end of the war, most Oscar units received Ki-84 Hayate Frank fighters, but a few flew the Hayabusa until the end of the war. The Ki-43 also served in an air defense role over Formosa, Okinawa, and the Japanese Home Islands, and like most Japanese fighters, many Oscars were expended in Kamikaze attacks.

General Characteristics

Length	29.3 feet
Wingspan	35.6 feet
Height	10.8 feet
Wing Area	230.4 square feet
Empty Weight	4,211 pounds
Loaded Weight	5,710 pounds
Max Takeoff Weight	6,450 pounds
Powerplant	1 × Nakajima Ha-115 fourteen cylinder air-cooled radial engine, 1,150hp

Performance

Maximum speed	329mph at 13,125 feet
Cruise Speed	273mph
Range	1,095 miles
Ferry range	1,990 miles
Service Ceiling	36,750 feet
Wing Loading	24.8 lb/sqft

Armament

Guns	2 × fixed, forward-firing 12.7 mm (.50 inch) Ho-103 machine guns in the cowl with 250rpg
Bombs	2,551 pounds of bombs

OSCAR 2

FIELDS OF FIRE

FORWARD GUNS "A"
¾-front view from above

EXHAUST FLAME PATTERNS

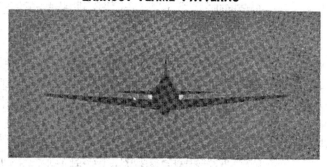

REAR VIEW

VULNERABILITY

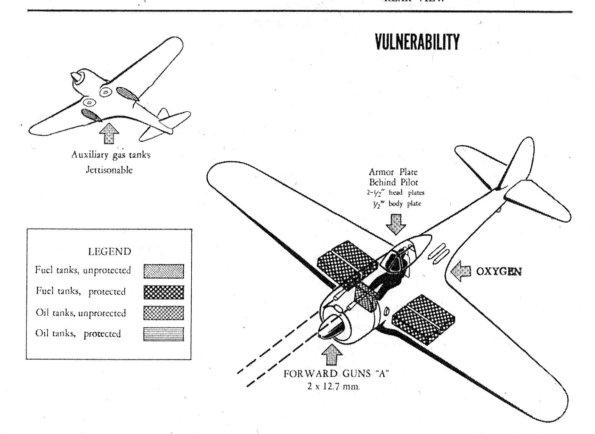

Auxiliary gas tanks
Jettisonable

LEGEND
Fuel tanks, unprotected
Fuel tanks, protected
Oil tanks, unprotected
Oil tanks, protected

Armor Plate
Behind Pilot
2-½" head plates
½" body plate

OXYGEN

FORWARD GUNS "A"
2 x 12.7 mm.

ARMAMENT

	No.	Size	Rds. Gun	Type		No.	Size	Rds. Gun	Type
Forward	2	12.7 mm	250	Fixed	Tail				
		or							
Top	2	20 mm	150	Fixed	Wing				
Side									
Bottom									

TACTICAL DATA

12 mm armor plate behind pilot.

Fuel tanks are equipped with protective rubber coating.

OSCAR 2 has a diving speed restriction of 372 mph.

DATE March 1945

RESTRICTED

Tony/Kawasaki Ki-61

Tony

When the JAAF realized that their Oscar was not competitive with more contemporary designs and that no modifications could be made to revamp it, they began to develop entirely new fighter types. The first was the Kawasaki Ki-61 Hien ("Swallow"), code-named Tony, the only inline engine Japanese fighter built in sizeable numbers during the war.

Throughout much of the interwar years, the JAAF procured most of its aircraft from Kawasaki until later, when Nakajima became a dominant factor in the Japanese aircraft industry. Meanwhile, Kawasaki officials had cultivated a good relationship with Germany and in early 1940, received Me (Bf) 109 blueprints, two airframes, and a production license for the Daimler Benz 601A engine that powered the Me-109. Takeo Doi—who had worked under German aircraft designer Richard Vogt between 1923 and 1933—Shin Owada were Kawasaki's head designers on the Ki-61 project. The German influence in the Ki-61 design can be seen in its nose design, the placement of the cockpit, its small tail section, and the scoop under the fuselage. An improved DB 601A engine was adapted to the Japanese industrial scheme by Kawasaki as the Ha-40 engine.

For their new fighter, the Kawasaki design team added aerodynamic modifications: the wing was increased in size and length to improve maneuverability and the fuselage was narrowed to improve speed. The engine was placed well ahead of the cockpit, which was placed in the center-forward position of the upper fuselage. It had low-mounted monoplane-type wings with rounded ends, as were the horizontal and vertical tail surfaces of the empennage. The landing gear was widened tire-to-tire to allow the fighter's use from primitive forward airfields. It had self-sealing fuel tanks, heavier armor and armament, and could be fitted with two 53 gallon drop tanks. Since design work on the Ki-61 had proceeded in parallel with the unsuccessful Ki-60 program since December 1940, the Ki-61 also incorporated some refinements from the Ki-60. The 1,275hp Kawasaki Ha-40 V-12 piston engine gave the Ki-61 a performance of 367mph top speed, a 32,000 foot ceiling limit, and an imposing 1,100-mile operational range and a fast diving speed. The prototype built first flew a few weeks after Pearl Harbor, but despite having blueprints of a proven aircraft, developmental problems slowed the start of production until August 1942.

Initial production consisted of two variants: the Ki-61-1a armed with 12.7mm (.50 caliber) machine guns in the fuselage and 7.7mm guns in the wings; and the Ki-61-1b armed with 12.7mm machine guns in both the fuselage and wings. However, despite this heavy armament, the Ki-61 did not have the firepower to easily down the rugged and well-armed American bombers, but the Kawasaki designers had foreseen this problem. The Japanese Ho-5 20mm cannon was unavailable, but the Japanese obtained 800 Mauser MG-151 20mm cannons from Germany in August 1943 and modified 388 Ki-61-I airframes to carry these German weapons in place of the two 12.7mm wing guns. Once the Ho-5 cannon became available, Kawasaki designers then reversed the arrangement of the guns, putting the 20mm guns in the forward fuselage and the 12.7mm guns in the wings.

The Kawasaki production lines encountered many problems, as a very high percentage of Tonys failed inspection and had to be transferred to the large JAAF repair depot at Kagamigahara, in Japan. At a time when the JAAF was facing a debacle in New Guinea and desperately needed more fighters, monthly production averaged scarcely 50 fighters from April to October 1943, which was not nearly enough to maintain air parity in New Guinea, much less to replace Oscars there with this more advanced fighter. To exacerbate the situation, many Tonys were lost due to accidents, poor navigation, mechanical problems, etc., while being ferried to New Guinea. Once the remaining Tonys did arrive in the theater, many were afflicted with mechanical problems from the wear and tear of the long ferry trip and the few trained Tony mechanics who followed lacked spare parts and had a severe shortage of tools and repair equipment to refurbish them. The Tony was beset with chronic engine cooling and hydraulic system problems that could not be handled by inexperienced ground crews in the field. The nearest Tony supply depot was 1,000 miles away in the Indies, while an engine change required that the fighter be shipped to Clark Field, near Manila. It was not until November 1943 that production reached 100 per month, but by that time the JAAF was beginning to collapse in New Guinea. Kawasaki continued to improve the Tony, and late in the war it did become one of the most effective fighters to defend the Japanese Home Islands against bomber attack. Yet when the Tony was needed it was a failure, in that it appeared in limited quantity and Japan had to keep the obsolete Zero and Oscar in production until the end of the war, as they were easily available in numbers. Over 3,000 Ki-61s in various forms were produced during the war.

Ki-61 Tony in Combat

In early 1943, after their defeat at Guadalcanal and their first major defeat in New Guinea at Buna (which was to presage further moves by MacArthur in the SWPA), the Japanese Army became anxious over prospects in the South Pacific. It began stripping units from Manchuria and China to assemble a major force in New Guinea. The Navy was being beleaguered at its mega base at Rabaul and the Army transferred air units, including the 200 operational Tonys, there to defend the upper Solomons. Soon the Army and Navy agreed to divide the Pacific Theater: New Guinea was to be under JAAF control, while the JNAF would continue to defend the Solomons and Rabaul. In Spring 1943, the Army began building an airbase complex near Wewak, in New Guinea, and over this area the JAAF confronted American and Australian aircraft in some of the war's largest and most fiercely contested air battles.

Once its teething problems were solved, the Tony proved to be superior to the Zero, and when it appeared over New Guinea in mid-1943, it proved to be a match for American fighters. When the first K-61s appeared in the SWPA, they were thought to closely resemble the Italian Macchi MC 202, so it was given the Italian type name Tony. But since it also looked like the Messerschmitt Bf 109 from a distance, a number of early ICRs reported meeting Bf 109s. It was relatively fast, had respectable high-altitude performance, and could dive faster than a P-39 and almost as fast as a P-40. An Allied fighter pilot could no longer escape with a high-speed dive. The Tony was fitted with pilot armor and self-sealing fuel tanks that, although unreliable, were much better than none at all. Although the Tony's maximum range of 650 miles was far less than the Zero's, this did not matter at this stage of the war, as the Japanese required fighters to defend their bases in their shrinking empire. Armed with only four 12.7mm machine guns, the Tony was inadequately armed to be an interceptor, but could hold its own in fighter-to-fighter combat against the P-39 or P-40; when it faced second generation American fighters, such as the P-47, P-38, or F4U, it was somewhat deficient in most performance categories, but a good pilot could make the Tony a dangerous opponent. When 5th Air Force Commander Gen. George Kenney found his P-40 Warhawks were completely outclassed by the Tony he became aware of the need for more P-38 Lightnings.

The Tony was not an altitude fighter, but was faster than the Zero in level flight and was extremely fast in a dive. A successful evasive tactic against a diving Tony was to make a diving turn to the right, because at high speeds the Tony handled very poorly to the right. If pursued by a Tony from the rear and on the level, a very high-speed, shallow climb kept the Allied pilot out of range and eventually he would be able to pull away.

General Characteristics

Length	29.3 feet
Wingspan	39.3 feet
Height	12.1 feet
Wing Area	215.3 square feet
Internal Fuel Capacity	• 121 Imp gallons • External fuel capacity: 44 Imp gallons drop tanks
Empty Weight	5,800 pounds
Loaded Weight	7,650 pounds
Powerplant	1 × Kawasaki Ha-40 liquid-cooled inverted V12 engine, 1,175 hp

Performance

Maximum speed	360mph at 5,000 feet
Range	360 miles
Service Ceiling	38,100 feet
Rate of Climb	2,983 feet/minute
Wing Loading	35.5 lb/sqft
Power/Mass	0.15 hp/lb
Time to Altitude	7.0 minutes (16,405 feet)

Armament

Guns	• 2 × 20 mm Ho-5 cannon, 120rpg each • 2 × 12.7 mm (0.50 inch) Ho-103 machine guns, 250rpg each • 2 × 551 pound bombs

TONY 1
FIELDS OF FIRE

FORWARD GUNS
"A", AND "B"
¾-front view from above

EXHAUST FLAME PATTERNS

REAR VIEW

VULNERABILITY

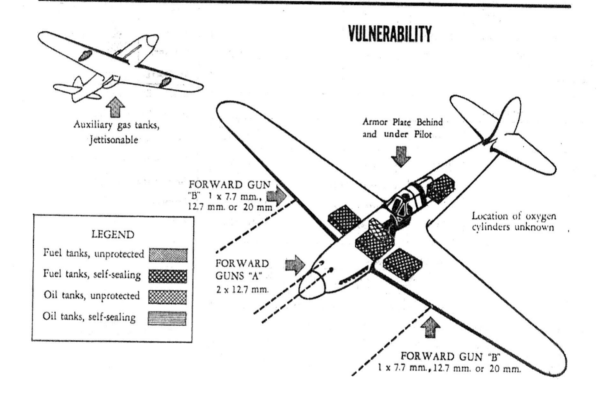

Auxiliary gas tanks,
Jettisonable

Armor Plate Behind
and under Pilot

FORWARD GUN
"B" 1 x 7.7 mm.,
12.7 mm. or 20 mm

Location of oxygen
cylinders unknown

FORWARD
GUNS "A"
2 x 12.7 mm.

FORWARD GUN "B"
1 x 7.7 mm., 12.7 mm. or 20 mm.

LEGEND

Fuel tanks, unprotected

Fuel tanks, self-sealing

Oil tanks, unprotected

Oil tanks, self-sealing

ARMAMENT

	No.	Size	Rds. Gun	Type		No.	Size	Rds. Gun	Type
Forward	2	12.7 mm		Fixed	Tail				
Top					Wing	2	12.7 mm		Fixed
Side					or	2	20 mm		Fixed
Bottom									

DATE December 1944

TACTICAL DATA

Armor plate is used to
protect the radiator.

Tojo/Nakajima Ki-44

Tojo

Only three weeks after Pearl Harbor, the JAAF requested Nakajima begin the design of a fighter to replace their newly-introduced Oscar with the basic requirement being for a general purpose interceptor that would be superior to those that were currently under development in America and England. The new design was to have speed and rate of climb as its principal performance objective, as compared to the traditional maneuverability that distinguished Japanese fighter aircraft. To accomplish the speed and climb goal, the company's designers chose the 14-cylinder 1,250hp Nakajima Ha-141 engine. It was not the best selection due to its large cross section, but Nakajima was able to mount this engine into a much smaller fuselage with a narrow cross section. The JAAF specifications required maneuverability, so a pair of like Fowler-type combat flaps like those on the Ki-43 allowed a maximum speed of 370mph at 13,000 feet, to be achieved in five minutes. To meet specifications the wing area was relatively small, yielding a high wing loading and a comparatively high landing speed when compared to the Ki-43 and Ki-27, which had a low wing loading. The Tojo's armament was comprised of a pair of 7.7mm (.30 caliber) and a pair of 12.7mm (.50 caliber) machine guns. In addition, the new fighter was to be provided with armor protection for the pilot and was to have self-sealing fuel tanks installed.

The first Ki-44 prototype flew in August 1940, and the initial flight testing was generally satisfactory, but problems arose, such as a high landing speed and the large radial engine created poor forward visibility during taxiing. The Tojo was less maneuverable than the Oscar and it required careful limitations by the pilot during maneuvering. Nonetheless, during further comprehensive service trials, the Ki-44 exhibited enough positive characteristics to enter production and it was ordered under the designation Army Type 2 Single Seat Fighter Model 1A Shoki (Demon), company designation Ki-44-Ia, which carried the same armament as the prototypes. A total of only 40 Ki-44-I aircraft were produced, including small numbers of the Ki-44-Ib armed with four 12.7mm (.50 caliber) machine guns and the similar Ki-44-Ic, with some minor refinements. A more powerful Nakajima Ha-109 engine was installed in later models, but the increased power did not eliminate other causes for its pilot dissatisfaction. Also, the higher wing loading in these later versions made the Tojo even more difficult to handle during high-speed maneuvers. However, when flown by skilled veteran pilots, which at that time were becoming a rare breed, it could match Allied fighters in climbs and dives. Inferior pilot training during the latter part of the war repeatedly made the novice pilots easy targets.

Tojo in Combat
After a successful combat introduction during the invasion of Malaya, the Tojo was ordered into production and saw combat over China throughout its service career, as well as the defense of the Philippines and the Homeland. At one point, Tojos equipped 12 JAAF *Sentais* before their partial replacement

with Ki-84 Franks near the end of the war. Nakajima manufactured a total of 1,225 Ki-44s of all versions, including prototypes.

General Characteristics

Length	29 feet
Wingspan	31.1 feet
Height	10.2 feet
Wing Area	161 square feet
Empty Weight	4,641 pounds
Loaded Weight	6,094 pounds
Max Takeoff Weight	6,602 pounds
Powerplant	1 × Nakajima Ha-109 Army Type 2 fourteen cylinder air-cooled radial engine, 1,519hp

Performance

Maximum speed	376mph
Cruise Speed	249mph
Stall Speed	93mph
Range	1,060 miles
Service Ceiling	36,750 feet
Rate of Climb	3,940 feet/minute
Wing Loading	41 lb/sqft
Power/Mass	0.13hp/lb

Armament

Guns	4 × 12.7mm (.50 caliber) Ho-103 machine guns, two synchronized cowl-mounted (about 657rpm rate each), and one in each wing (900rpm rate of fire each), 760 rounds total.

TOJO 2
FIELDS OF FIRE

FORWARD GUNS
"A", AND "B"
¾-front view from above

EXHAUST FLAME PATTERNS

REAR VIEW

VULNERABILITY

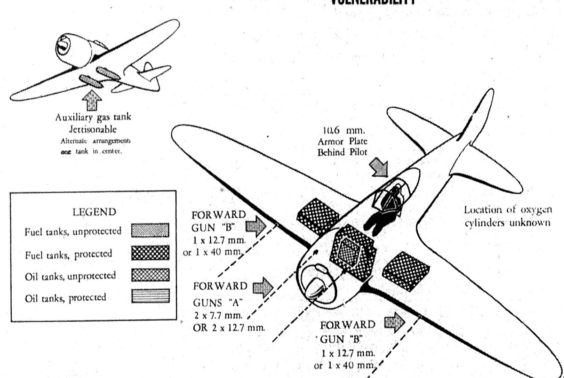

Auxiliary gas tank
Jettisonable
Alternate arrangement
one tank in center.

10.6 mm.
Armor Plate
Behind Pilot

Location of oxygen
cylinders unknown

LEGEND

Fuel tanks, unprotected
Fuel tanks, protected
Oil tanks, unprotected
Oil tanks, protected

FORWARD
GUN "B"
1 x 12.7 mm.
or 1 x 40 mm.

FORWARD
GUNS "A"
2 x 7.7 mm.
OR 2 x 12.7 mm.

FORWARD
GUN "B"
1 x 12.7 mm.
or 1 x 40 mm.

ARMAMENT

	No.	Size	Rds. Gun	Type		No.	Size	Rds. Gun	Type
Forward Cowl	2	7.7 mm or	500	Fixed	Tail				
Top	2	12.7 mm	250	Fixed	Wing	2	12.7 mm or	250	Fixed
Side						2	40 mm	10(?)	Fixed
Bottom									

DATE   March 1945

TACTICAL DATA

TOJO is restricted against snap rolls, spins, stalls and inverted flight at high speeds. This plane is equipped with armor plate behind the pilot and self sealing fuel tanks ineffective against .50 calibre fire.

RESTRICTED

Frank/Nakajima Ki-84

Frank

The JAAF Nakajima Ki-84 Hayate (Frank) was arguably one of the best Japanese fighters of the war, especially when flown by experienced pilots, which were uncommon at the time of its introduction. Before going to their drawing boards, Nakajima designers took into account pilot observations and combat reports, and established that their new fighter design was to have sturdiness, heavy firepower, diving ability, acceleration, and especially speed. The Frank had all these qualities, and even had reasonable maneuverability. Like all late-war Japanese fighter projects, it was designed with a slender and aerodynamic fuselage and a cockpit with superb visibility. The powerful and proven 1,800hp Nakajima Ha-45 radial engine produced a top speed of nearly 400mph, a service ceiling of 35,000 feet, and an operational range of just over 1,000 miles. The basic armament of early models included two 12.7mm machine guns in the upper forward part of the nose and two 20mm cannons in the wings. A 550-pound bomb could be carried under each wing.

The Frank was somewhat light for its size, weighing 8,000 pounds, and could not maintain its diving speed above 350mph. To compensate, the 1,800hp Ha-45 engine could rapidly accelerate the fighter to 300mph, and using this acceleration, a Frank pilot could zoom climb into combat after spotting the enemy. The Frank dove rather well, using full elevator up to 550mph, but the ailerons tended to lock at 350mph, so being in trim was vital.

The Frank's design was optimized for speed, so it did not turn well, and its maneuverability was not equal to other Japanese fighters. An aircraft with low wing loading turns extremely well, but the extra wing area adds to the drag and slows the aircraft. Nakajima used the same solution for the Frank as it did for the Oscar; extendable flaps which increased the wing loading (area) at low speeds to turn. During high-speed turns the flaps were very effective, but although they decreased the fighter's speed quickly, they were the means to making the Frank Japan's most formidable fighter.

The Frank in Combat

The Ki-84 was found to be the equal of even the most advanced Allied fighters that opposed it, and on occasion could be their superior, especially when flown by the infrequent veteran pilot. It was well armed and armored, fast, and very maneuverable. Although it was usually outnumbered, it nonetheless often was able to hold its own in the air battles over the Philippines, Okinawa, and the Japanese Home Islands.

The Frank was easy to fly, and pilots with only minimal training could fly it with relative ease. However, it did have poor control traits which could be easily overcome by a veteran pilot, but which could be fatal to the novice pilot. Taxiing and ground handling were considered to be especially poor. On takeoff, once the tail came up, continual pressure had to be maintained on the starboard rudder pedal to counteract a tendency to swing to port caused by the high engine torque. In flight, the controls were sluggish compared to those of the Oscar and the elevators tended to be heavy at all speeds. The ailerons were excellent up to about 300mph, after which they became rather heavy. The rudder was mushy at low speeds for near neutral angles. Because of its ineffective supercharger, the Frank functioned best a low altitudes and its performance dropped off with altitude. The Frank was considered by many as the best "vertical" fighter in the Pacific, as with its low power to weight ratio it could zoom up 6,000 feet and its low wing loading allowed the Frank pilot to get his fighter's nose around after his pursuers had stalled out.

General Characteristics

Length	32.7 feet
Wingspan	36.9 feet
Height	11.1 feet
Wing Area	226 square feet
Empty Weight	5,875 pounds
Loaded Weight	7,972 pounds
Max Takeoff Weight	8,594 pounds
Powerplant	1 × Nakajima Ha-45-21 Homare 18 cylinder radial engine, 1,990 hp

Performance

Never Exceed Speed	496mph
Maximum Speed	390 mph at 20,013 feet
Range	1,339 miles
Service Ceiling	34,450 feet
Rate of Climb	3,790 feet/minute
Wing Loading	35 lb/sqft
Power/Mass	0.25 hp/lb

Armament

Guns	• 2 × 12.7mm Ho-103 machine guns in nose, 350 rounds/gun • 2 × 20mm Ho-5 cannon in wings, 150 shells/cannon • 2 × 220 pound bombs • 2× 551 pound bombs • 2 × 53 U.S. gallon drop tanks

FRANK 1

FIELDS OF FIRE

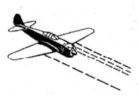

FORWARD GUNS "A", AND "B"
¾-front view from above

EXHAUST FLAME PATTERNS

REAR VIEW

VULNERABILITY

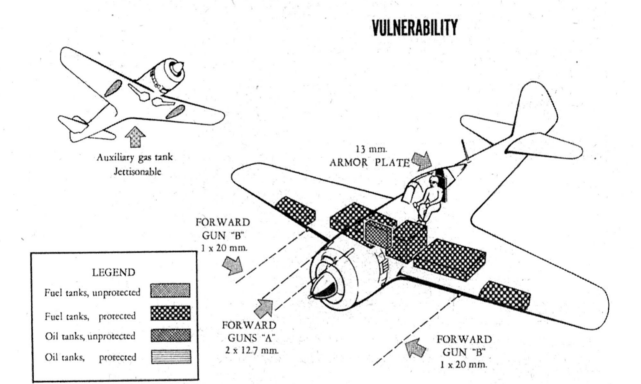

Auxiliary gas tank
Jettisonable

FORWARD
GUN "B"
1 x 20 mm.

13 mm.
ARMOR PLATE

FORWARD
GUNS "A"
2 x 12.7 mm.

FORWARD
GUN "B"
1 x 20 mm.

LEGEND

Fuel tanks, unprotected

Fuel tanks, protected

Oil tanks, unprotected

Oil tanks, protected

ARMAMENT

	No.	Size	Rds. Gun	Type		No.	Size	Rds. Gun	Type
Forward Cowl	2	12.7 mm	350	Fixed	Tail				
Top					Wing	2	20 mm	150	Fixed
Side									
Bottom									

DATE   March 1945

TACTICAL DATA

Documents state that FRANK has a bullet-proof windshield 65 mm thick. Armor plate is provided for pilot's back and head.

RESTRICTED

TAIC Frank

Lily/Kawasaki Ki-48

Lily

During the 1937 Sino-Japanese War, the Japanese were so impressed by the Russian-built SB-2 light bomber's performance during hit-and-run attacks that Kawasaki received an order from the JAAF in December 1937 to develop a high-speed bomber powered by two Nakajima Ha-25 radial engines. The Ki-48 was to be capable of 300mph at 9,840 feet; be able to reach 16,400 feet within 10 minutes; carry a bomb load of 882 pounds; and have a defensive armament of three or four flexible 7.7mm machine guns. Design work began in January 1938, headed by Dr. Takeo Doi, who was working on the similar, higher-priority Ki-45, which caused the Ki-48 prototype to be delayed until July 1939. But during the delay Kawasaki had the advantage of the experience of designing the Ki-45 twin-engined heavy fighter, so most technical problems were solved; however the aircraft had a number of defects. The prototype had a mid-mounted cantilever wing to allow an internal bomb bay carrying a normal 800 pound bomb load. The crew of four consisted of the pilot, a bombardier/nose gunner with a 7.7mm machine gun, a radio-operator/gunner manning the dorsal 7.7mm machine gun, and a navigator/gunner with a ventral 7.7mm gun.

During the prototype's flight trials, it easily met all performance requirements and in very late 1939, quantity production of the new light bomber was begun under the designation Army Type 99 Twin-Engined Light Bomber Model 1A (or Ki-48-Ia), and the first production Ki-48-Ia was completed in July 1940.

Lily in Combat

By Fall 1940, the Ki-48 was deployed to North China, where it performed satisfactorily against minimal Chinese opposition. When the Pacific War began, the Ki-48 was the most important JAAF light bomber outside the Chinese front. Ki-48-equipped *Sentais* were deployed against Commonwealth forces in Malaya and Burma, and against the Americans in the Philippines before being transferred to the Dutch East Indies, and later to New Guinea. However, when engaged by more modern Allied fighters, the previous performance advantage it had over China waned and it was now too inferior to evade Allied fighters. Also, its defensive armament was totally inadequate, its bomb load too small, and like other Japanese aircraft, it lacked any crew or fuel tank protection. To limit their combat losses, the early model Lilys were transferred for night attacks whenever possible, which reduced their effectiveness even more, but did save some crews for a while.

The Ki-48-II, an improved Lily model, was being developed when the war began, but differed little from its predecessor, except for improved engines and some fuel tank and crew armor protection. Although the maximum bomb load of the Ki-48-II was double that of the Ki-48-I, it was nonetheless much less than that of the A-20 Havoc standard Allied light bomber. Although the speed of the Ki-48-II was superior to that of the -I, it still was not fast enough to outrun the improved Allied fighters. But the Lily's fatal flaw continued to be its totally inadequate defensive armament,

which had not been improved since the prototype. The Lily was an easy victim in the air and large numbers were also destroyed on the ground in New Guinea, despite efforts to disperse and camouflage the planes on jungle airstrips.

All models continued in service until the Battle of Okinawa during April 1945, when many were converted into kamikaze aircraft armed with a 1,760-pound bomb. That all models continued in service until 1945 reveals that many Ki-48s survived more often than not, due to the use of small ship formations of three to ten bombers escorted by large numbers of fighters (Oscars) that engaged and allowed the Lilys to avoid interception. Production ended in October 1944 with 1,977 being built, but the Lily continued in service because by then, the Japanese needed any flyable aircraft, particularly later for Kamikaze units.

General Characteristics

Crew	Four
Length	41.8 feet
Wingspan	57.3 feet
Height	12.4 feet
Wing Area	430.6 square feet
Empty Weight	10,031 pounds
Loaded Weight	14,350 pounds
Max Takeoff Weight	14,881 pounds
Powerplant	2 × Nakajima Ha.115 radial engines, 1,130 hp each

Performance

Maximum speed	314mph at 18,375 feet
Range	1,491 miles
Service Ceiling	33,135 feet

Armament

Guns	• 3 × 7.7mm (0.303 inch) Type 89 machine guns, in nose, dorsal and ventral positions • 1,764 pounds of bombs

LILY 2

FIELDS OF FIRE

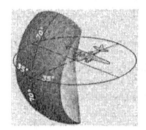

FORWARD GUN "A" 1 x 7.9 mm.
¾-front view from above

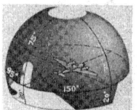

TOP GUN "C" 1 x 12.7 mm.
¾-rear view from above
Manually operated turret

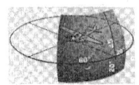

FORWARD GUN "B" 1 x 7.9 mm.
¾-front view from above
This gun is interchangeable from
port to st'b'd. side of nose.

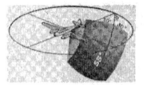

BOTTOM GUN "D"
1 x 7.9 mm. or 2 x 7.7 mm.
¾-rear view from below.

EXHAUST FLAME PATTERNS

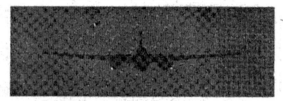

REAR VIEW

ARMOR PLATE

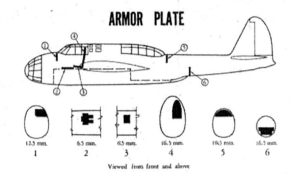

Viewed from front and above

VULNERABILITY

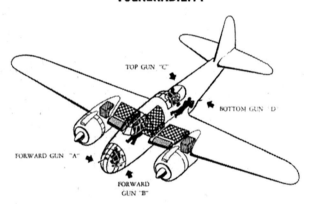

TOP GUN "C"

BOTTOM GUN "D"

FORWARD GUN "A"

FORWARD GUN "B"

LEGEND			
Fuel tanks, unprotected		Oil tanks, unprotected	
Fuel tanks, protected		Oil tanks, protected	

FIRE FREE FIELDS

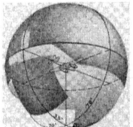

¾-front view from above.

¾-rear view from below.

ARMAMENT

	No.	Size	Rds. Gun	Type		No.	Size	Rds. Gun	Type
Forward	1	7.9 mm	525	Flex.	Tail				
Top	1	12.7mm	700	Hand Turret	Wing				
Side Aux. Nose	1	7.9 mm		Flex.					
Bottom	1	7.9 mm	525	Flex.					

DATE March 1945

TACTICAL DATA

LILY is heavily armored. In addition to pilot protection, plates are installed aft for the gunner.

Fuel tank protection is installed.

RESTRICTED

Sally/Mitsubishi Ki-21

Sally

In 1936, the JAAF issued a requirement for a new twin-engine heavy bomber to replace both the Ki-20 and Ki-1. The ambitious design parameters mandated a crew of at least four, top speed of 250mph, endurance of at least five hours, and a bomb load of 1,650 pounds. Both Mitsubishi and Nakajima built two prototypes each, with another proposal from Kawasaki being rejected. In November 1937, the Mitsubishi Ki-21 met the JAAF requirements and won a production order over the Nakajima Ki-19 prototype. The Ki-21 was a cantilever, all-metal, mid-wing monoplane incorporating retractable tail wheel and landing gear, a ventral bomb bay, and two radial engines. The cockpit was just forward of the wing root and the nose was a glass greenhouse type with more small windows positioned to look more downward than upward. Armament on early models consisted of a few 7.7mm machine guns and a dorsal turret was installed just aft of the wings with a single vertical tail surface on the empennage. The first of the production aircraft began to enter service in Summer 1938, but when used operationally in China later that year, they were soon found to be vulnerable due to their lack of self-sealing fuel tanks and defensive armament. The armament would be upgraded to several more machine guns in later models, including a heavy caliber 12.7mm (.50 caliber) gun in the later Ki-21-II model series. Improved versions were developed to overcome shortcomings: the Ki-21-Ib introduced modified horizontal tail surfaces, larger area trailing-edge flaps, an enlarged bomb bay, and armament increased to a total of five 7.7mm (.30 caliber) machine guns. The generally similar Ki-21-Ic differed in having increased fuel capacity and the addition of one more 7.7mm (.30 caliber) gun. Several improved versions followed before the production of the type ended in September 1944, with a total of 2,064 Sallys built (1,713 by Mitsubishi and 351 by Nakajima). It was succeeded in production by the newer Nakajima Ki-49 Donryu Helen, which would prove to be a disappointment.

Sally in Combat

The Ki-21-Ia played an important role in the opening period of the war, being used in combat in China in autumn 1938, initially with great success, but not in great numbers, as production delays prevented the JAAF from re-equipping its *Sentais* until the end of 1939. However, by late 1941, improvements in Chinese Air Force fighter quality and quantities caused Ki-21-Ia losses to increase, so that they were relegated to training or second-line duties.

Front line JAAF units from mid-1940 were equipped with the Ki-21-IIa, which became the main version flown by most heavy bomber squadrons at the beginning of the Pacific War and played a major role in many early campaigns. For operations over the Philippines, the JAAF sent Sallys from Taiwan to attack American targets, while fighter-escorted Sallys based in Indochina attacked British and Australian targets in Thailand and Malaya. However, beginning with operations over Burma in early 1942, Sally crews found themselves facing Allied fighter aircraft (P-40s and Hurricanes) of

better quality and in greater quantity, and Ki-21 losses began to increase sharply.

Further revisions of defensive armament were made with the Ki-21-IIb, replacing the dorsal gun position with a manually operated gun turret containing one 12.7mm (0.50 in) machine gun. Despite its shortcomings, the Ki-21 remained in service until the end of the war, being utilized as freight and troop transport, a bomber crew and paratrooper trainer, for liaison and communications, special commando and secret missions, and Kamikaze operations.

General Characteristics

Crew	5-7
Length	52.5 feet
Wingspan	73.9 feet
Height	15.9 feet
Wing Area	752.12 square feet
Empty Weight	13,354 pounds
Loaded Weight	23,320 pounds
Powerplant	2 × Mitsubishi Army Type 100 (Ha-101) 14 cylinder radial engine, 1,500 hp each
Propellers	three blade metal variable-pitch propellers propeller

Performance

Maximum speed	300mph at 15,400 feet
Cruise Speed	236mph
Range	1,680 miles
Service Ceiling	32,800 feet
Rate of Climb	13.3 minutes to 19,680 feet

Armament

Guns	• 4 × 7.7mm (.303 inch) flexible Type 89 machine guns in nose, ventral, beam, and tail positions • 1 × 12.7mm (.50 inch) Type 1 Heavy Machine Gun in dorsal turret
Bombs	2,200 pounds of bombs

SALLY 2

FIELDS OF FIRE

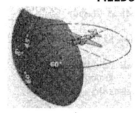

FORWARD GUN "A" 1 x 7.9 mm.
¾-front view from above
Alternate, 1 x 7.7 mm.

TOP GUN "B" 1 x 12.7 mm.
¾-rear view from above
Manually operated turret

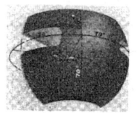

SIDE GUN "C" 1 x 7.9 mm.
Approx. side view from below.
Field of fire for SIDE GUN "D" similar
Alternate, 1 x 7.7 mm.

BOTTOM GUN "E" 1 x 7.9 mm.
¾-rear view from below.
Alternate, 1 or 2 x 7.7 mm.

TAIL GUN "F" 1 x 7.7 mm.
¾-rear view from above
Remote controlled by turret gunner.

FIRE FREE FIELDS

¾-front view from above   ¾-rear view from below.

EXHAUST FLAME PATTERNS

REAR VIEW

ARMOR PLATE

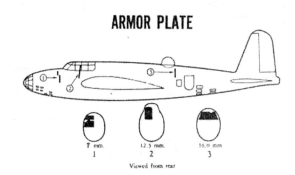

7 mm.   12.5 mm.   16.9 mm
1   2   3

Viewed from rear

VULNERABILITY

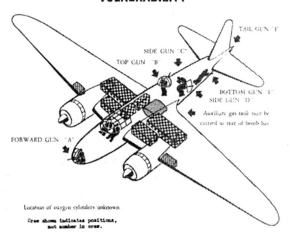

Location of oxygen cylinders unknown

**Crew shown indicates positions,
not number in crew.**

LEGEND			
Fuel tanks, unprotected		Oil tanks, unprotected	
Fuel tanks, protected		Oil tanks, protected	

ARMAMENT

	No.	Size	Rds. Gun	Type		No.	Size	Rds. Gun	Type
Forward	1	7.9 mm	600	Flex.	Tail	1	7.7 mm	600	Flex.
Top	1	12.7mm	600	Turret	Wing				
Side	2	7.9 mm	600	Flex.					
Bottom	1	7.9 mm	600	Flex.					

DATE December 1944

TACTICAL DATA

Fuel tanks have partial leak protection with rubber laminated covering. Armor plates are found around the dorsal turret.

Top turret is bicycle pedal operated in traverse.

RESTRICTED

Helen/ Nakajima Ki-49

Helen

The Nakajima Ki-49 Donryu Helen was designed as a replacement for the Mitsubishi Ki-21 Sally, which was just entering service in the Spring of 1938. The JAAF benefited from service trials of the Ki-21 and realized that no matter how advanced it may have been at the time of its introduction, their new Ki-21 would be unable to operate without fighter escorts. Consequently, the JAAF specified that its replacement rely on speed and heavy defensive armament to enable it to operate independently. It was to have a maximum speed of 311mph (vs 261mph for the K-21), a range of 1,864 miles, a bomb load of 2,205 pounds, and heavy (for the time) defensive armament, including one flexible 20mm cannon in the dorsal position and several flexible 7.7mm machine guns, including the first ever bona fide tail turret fitted to a JAAF bomber, and unexpectedly, the specification called for crew armor and self-sealing fuel tanks.

The prototype first flew in August 1939, and the development program continued through nine more prototypes and pre-production models; in March 1941, the Donryu went into production as the Army Type 100 Heavy Bomber Model 1. The Ki-49 design emerged as a very serviceable heavy bomber design, although the term "heavy bomber" was hyperbole, as production Ki-49s could barely carry over 2,000 pounds of internal ordnance. The aircraft's design did not depart from previous Japanese twin-engine bomber designs that featured a slender fuselage with clean lines, a mid-fuselage monoplane wing assembly, a single vertical tail, and various gun positions. The defensive armament consisted of a nose-mounted 7.7mm machine gun; a 7.7mm machine gun in a tail gun position; two 7.7mm machine guns, one each in beam positions; a 7.7 mm machine gun in a ventral position; and a 20mm cannon in a flexible dorsal mounting.

Helen in Combat
The Helen became operational in Fall 1941, first seeing service in China, and on 19 February 1942, the Donryu made its combat debut during the devastating bombing of Darwin, Australia; afterward, it was frequently encountered over New Guinea and New Britain. Like the prototype, these early Helens were armed with five 7.7mm (.30 caliber) machine guns and one 20mm cannon. Soon combat experience in China and New Guinea showed the Helen to be underpowered, with a concomitant decrease in bomb capacity and speed. Thus, in Spring 1942, a new version was produced with more powerful Ha-109 engines designated as the production Army Type 100 Heavy Bomber Model 2, or Ki-49-IIa. This Model 2 also introduced improved armor and self-sealing fuel tanks and was followed by the Ki-49-IIb, in which 12.7mm machine guns replaced three of the 7.7mm guns.

In spite of these improvements, Ki-49 losses continued to mount with the increase in quantity and quality enemy fighter opposition, and in the face of its increasing vulnerability while performing its intended role, the Ki-49 was used in other roles towards the end of the war, including anti-submarine patrol, troop transport and, ultimately, as Kamikazes. After 819

bombers had been completed, production ended in December 1944. The Ki-49-II never totally replaced the Ki-21-II in service. It was the best-protected and best-armed JAAF twin-engined bomber until the Mitsubishi Ki-67 Hiryu was introduced in October 1944. When the 5th Fighter Command returned to the Philippines in October 1944, many Helens were thrown into combat and suffered huge losses until December, when most of the survivors were expended in suicide attacks against the U.S. landing force at Mindoro. Many more were also used as Kamikazes over Okinawa. Because the Ki-49 was a disappointment to the JAAF, the type saw very limited production of just over 800 and appeared in a few variants, then was quickly written off as an equal to the successful Ki-21 instead of its replacement.

General Characteristics

Crew	7-8
Length	54.1 feet
Wingspan	67 feet
Height	14 feet
Wing Area	743.3 square feet
Empty Weight	14,396 pounds
Loaded Weight	23,545 pounds
Max Takeoff Weight	25,133 pounds
Powerplant	2 × Nakajima Ha-109 14 cylinder radial engine, 1,500 hp each

Performance

Maximum speed	306mph
Cruise Speed	217mph
Range	1,833 miles
Service Ceiling	30,510 feet
Wing Loading	7.8 lb/sqft

Armament

Guns	1× 20mm Type 99 cannon, 5 × 7.7mm (.30 inch) Type 89 machine guns.
Bombs	2,205 pound bomb load

HELEN 2

FIELDS OF FIRE

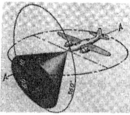

FORWARD GUN "A" 1 x 12.7 mm.
¾-front view from above
Turret can be rotated manually thru
360° about axis "A"-"A"
Alternate nose gun 1 x 7.7 mm.

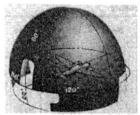

TOP GUN "B" 1 x 20 mm.
¾-rear view from above

SIDE GUN "C" 1 x 7.9 mm.
Approx. side view from above
Field of fire for SIDE GUN "D" similar

BOTTOM GUN "E" 1 x 7.9 mm.
¾-rear view from above

TAIL GUN "F" 1 x 12.7 mm.
¾-rear view from above

FIRE FREE FIELDS

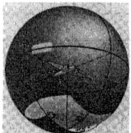

¾-front view from above

¾-front view from below

EXHAUST FLAME PATTERNS

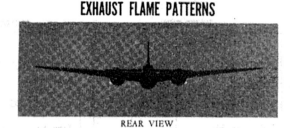

REAR VIEW

ARMOR PLATE

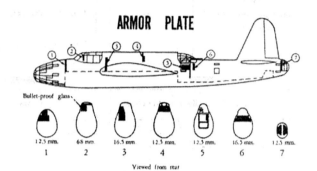

Bullet-proof glass

1	2	3	4	5	6	7
12.5 mm.	68 mm.	16.5 mm.	12.5 mm.	12.5 mm.	16.5 mm.	12.5 mm.

Viewed from rear

VULNERABILITY

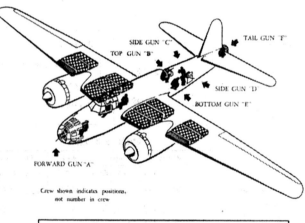

SIDE GUN "C"   TAIL GUN "F"
TOP GUN "B"
SIDE GUN "D"
BOTTOM GUN "E"
FORWARD GUN "A"

Crew shown indicates positions,
not number in crew

LEGEND

Fuel tanks, unprotected	Oil tanks, unprotected
Fuel tanks, protected	Oil tanks, protected

ARMAMENT

	No.	Size	Rds. Gun	Type		No.	Size	Rds. Gun	Type
Forward	1	12.7mm		Flex.	Tail	1	12.7 mm		Flex.
Top	1	20 mm		Flex.	Wing				
Side	2	7.9 mm		Flex.					
Bottom	1	7.9 mm		Flex.					

DATE December 1944

TACTICAL DATA

Bullet proof glass and armor plate for the pilot plus armor for the tail gunner and the dorsal turret gunner offer ample protection in HELEN. Fuel tanks are leak-proofed with thin laminated rubber and kapok.

Nick/Kawasaki Ki-45

Nick

In the mid-1930s, the European powers were rapidly developing twin-engine heavy fighters, such as the Messerschmitt Bf 110. In 1937, the JAAF requested Kawasaki to develop a two-seat, twin-engine fighter to be used for long-range operations over the Pacific. The result was the Ki-38, which was developed only to the mock up stage, but by December, the Army ordered a working prototype as the Ki-45, which first flew in January 1939. The aircraft was a cantilever mid-wing monoplane with a slender fuselage, providing enclosed accommodation for two in tandem and retractable tail wheel landing gear.

The Ki-45 Toryu ("Dragon Slayer") was given JAAF designation "Type 2 Two-Seat Fighter." Results from the test flights, however, did not meet the Army's requirements, as the Ha-20 Otsu engine was underpowered and prone to failures and the aircraft suffered from stalls. In October 1940, the JAAF ordered Kawasaki to continue development and the proven 1,080hp Mitsubishi Ha-102 engine was installed, but it was not until September 1941 that the Ki-45 KAIa entered production. Armament of this initial series version comprised one forward-firing 20mm cannon, two 12.7mm machine guns in the nose, and a 7.92mm machine gun on a flexible mount in the rear cockpit; there was also provision to carry two drop tanks or two 550 pound bombs on underwing racks. The type entered service in August 1942, but did not see its first combat until October 1942. A new version, the KAIb, was developed specifically for the ground-attack/anti-shipping role. Standard armament comprised one 20mm cannon in the nose, a forward-firing 37mm cannon in the fuselage, and one rear-firing 7.92mm machine gun, plus the underwing provision for drop tanks or bombs. Some 1,675 Ki-45s of all versions were produced during the war.

Nick in Combat

The Ki-45 was initially used as a long-range bomber—like the Bf-110—but were no match for single-engine fighters, such as the AVG's P-40s. Soon it was evident the Ki-45 could not stand up against fighters in aerial combat and they were subsequently deployed in several theaters in the roles of interception, ground and ship attack, and fleet defense. Its greatest strength turned out to be as an anti-bomber interceptor, as was the circumstance of the Bf 110 in Europe. For that time in the war, the Ki-45 KAIa was heavily armed and proved effective against B-24 Liberators that were being extensively for night operations. In 1944, this new anti-heavy bomber capability led to the development of the JAAF's only night fighter, the Ki-45 KAIc, which proved to be one of the most successful Japanese night fighters, with 477 being produced. In New Guinea, the JAAF also used the aircraft in an anti-ship role, where the Ki-45 KAId was heavily armed with one 37mm and two 20mm cannons and could carry two 550 pound bombs

under the wings. After serving as a night fighter over New Guinea and the Philippines, it was later used for the night defense of Tokyo and in the Manchuria, Burma, Singapore, and Sumatra operations. Ki-45 Toryus remained in service until the end of the Pacific war.

General Characteristics

Crew	Two
Length	36.1 feet
Wingspan	49.3 feet
Height	12.2 feet
Wing Area	344 square feet
Empty Weight	8,820 pounds
Loaded Weight	12,125 pounds
Powerplant	2 × Mitsubishi Ha-102 14 cylinder radial engines, 1,050 hp each

Performance

Maximum speed	336mph
Range	1,243 miles
Service Ceiling	32,800 feet
Rate of Climb	2,300 feet/minute
Wing Loading	35 lb/sqft
Power/Mass	.16 hp/lb

Armament

Guns	KAIa: 1 × 20 mm, 2 × 12.7 mm 2 × 7.92 mm KAIb: 1 × 37 mm, 2 × 12.7 mm , 1 × 7.92 mm KAIc: 1 × 37 mm, 1 × 20 mm, 1 × 7.92 mm KAId: 1 × 37 mm, 2 × 20 mm
Experimental	1 × 40 mm

NICK 1

FIELDS OF FIRE

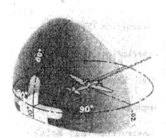

FORWARD GUNS "A"
AND TOP GUN "B"
¾-rear view from above

EXHAUST FLAME PATTERNS

REAR VIEW

BOTTOM FORWARD GUN "C"

1 x 37 mm.

Loaded manually by rear gunner.

¾-front view from below

VULNERABILITY

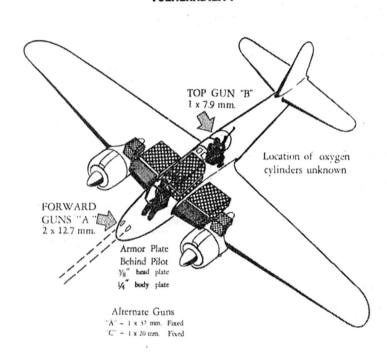

TOP GUN "B"
1 x 7.9 mm.

Location of oxygen
cylinders unknown

FORWARD
GUNS "A"
2 x 12.7 mm.

Armor Plate
Behind Pilot
⅛" head plate
¼" body plate

Alternate Guns
"A" – 1 x 37 mm. Fixed
"C" – 1 x 20 mm. Fixed

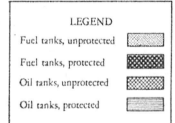

LEGEND

Fuel tanks, unprotected	
Fuel tanks, protected	
Oil tanks, unprotected	
Oil tanks, protected	

ARMAMENT

	No.	Size		Rds. Gun	Type		No.	Size	Rds. Gun	Type
Forward or	2	12.7	mm		Fixed	Tail				
	1	37	mm		Fixed					
Top	1	7.9	mm		Flex.	Wing				
Side										
Bottom	1	20	mm	Slung under fuselage firing forward.						

DATE December 1944

TACTICAL DATA

NICK carries armor plate for the back of the pilot's seat. Rear gunner is unprotected. Some reports mention the use of phosphorus air-to air bombs by NICK.

Latest information indicates 20 mm slung under fuselage with 37 mm or 2 x 12.7 in nose.

RESTRICTED

TAIC Nick

Dinah/Mitsubishi Ki-46

Dinah

On 12 December 1937, Mitsubishi received a specification issued by the JAAF to develop a long-range strategic reconnaissance aircraft to replace the Mitsubishi Ki-15 Babs. The only requirement of the specification was a six-hour flight time and sufficient speed (375mph) to evade interception by any contemporary fighter. Ki-46 designer Tomio Kubo had a very difficult assignment, as Japan did not have a high power liquid-cooled engine associated with high-speed aircraft. Tomio selected the Mitsubishi Ha-26 radial engine and placed it in a new cowling design that reduced drag and improved the pilot's sideways view from the cockpit. The Ki-46 was a twin-engined, low-winged monoplane with a small diameter oval fuselage which housed a two-man crew of a pilot and observer, who were placed in individual cockpits separated by a large fuel tank. Additional fuel tanks were located in the thin wings both inboard and outboard of the engines. The Dinah was considered one of the most aerodynamically perfect aircraft of its time, often favorably compared to the DeHavilland Mosquito.

The Ki-46 prototype first flew in November 1939, and tests showed that it was underpowered, with a speed 37mph slower than required, but otherwise the tests were successful. Because it was still faster than the JAAF's latest fighter (the Ki-43 Oscar), as well as the Navy's new A6M2 Zero, an initial production batch was ordered as the Army Type 100 Command Reconnaissance Plane Model 1 (Ki-41-I). In March 1941, Mitsubishi replaced the engines, increased fuel capacity, and reduced empty weight, which increased performance in the Ki-46-II; it was then ordered into production, with deliveries starting in July 1941. By the Spring of 1941, the Army had at least 386 Ki-46s on order, but they were only being delivered at the rate of four a month. Mitsubishi was ordered to discontinue production of some older aircraft and transfer its resources to manufacturing the Dinah, and by November 1941, deliveries reached ten aircraft a month. Monthly production would continue to increase to a peak of 75 aircraft delivered in March 1944. Mitsubishi factories manufactured 1,742 Dinahs of all versions (34 Ki-46-I, 1,093 Ki-46-IIs, 613 Ki-46-IIIs, and four Ki-46-Ivs) during 1941-44.

Dinah in Combat

Initially, the Dinah was almost untouchable, although its rate of climb was not as fast as expected and the controls were sluggish and sometimes unresponsive; these problems were not particularly important, as the Ki-46 was expected to use its speed and altitude performance to avoid combat. But when improved Allied fighters—such as the AAF P-38 Lightning and USN F6F Hellcat—arrived, the JAAF realized the Dinah could be caught, and in July 1942, Mitsubishi was requested to produce an improved version (the Ki-46-III), which was available in December 1942. This model had more powerful, fuel-injected Mitsubishi Ha-112 engines giving a top speed of 391mph and a redesigned nose with a fuel tank ahead of the pilot, as

well as a new, smoothly-faired canopy. The single defensive rear-firing machine gun of the earlier aircraft was also omitted, as the aircraft was designed to avoid combat with its superior speed and altitude capability.

Early in the SWPA war, the Ki-46 was based in Timor, in the Dutch East Indies, and was able to fly recon flights over northern Australia, where the obsolescent fighters based there lacked the speed and rate of climb to reach the Ki-46. Allied radar may have made the difference, but that was not available early in 1942. The Ki-46 would see service in nearly every Theater in the Pacific, operating in small recon units.

General Characteristics

Crew	2 (pilot and observer)
Length	36 feet
Wingspan	48.2 feet
Height	12.8 feet
Wing Area	344 square feet
Empty Weight	7,194 pounds
Loaded Weight	11,133 pounds
Max Takeoff Weight	12,787 pounds
Powerplant	2 x Mitsubishi Ha-102 Army Type 1 14 cylinder radial engines, 1,080 hp (take off) each.

Performance

Maximum speed	375mph at 19,000 feet
Cruise Speed	249mph
Range	1,537 miles
Service Ceiling	35,200 feet
Wing Loading	2.3 lb/sqft Climb to 26,250 feet: 18 minutes

Armament

Guns	1x rearward-firing 7.7mm (.303 inch) Type 89 machine gun

DINAH 3

FIELDS OF FIRE

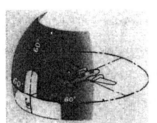

TOP GUN "A" 1 x 7.7 mm.
OR 2 x 7.7 mm.
¾-rear view from above.

EXHAUST FLAME PATTERNS

REAR VIEW

VULNERABLITY

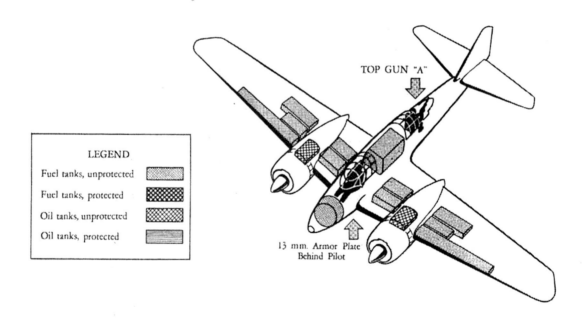

TOP GUN "A"

13 mm. Armor Plate
Behind Pilot

LEGEND

Fuel tanks, unprotected
Fuel tanks, protected
Oil tanks, unprotected
Oil tanks, protected

ARMAMENT

	No.	Size	Rds. Gun	Type		No.	Size	Rds. Gun	Type
Forward					Tail				
Top					Wing				
Rear	1	7.7 mm		Flex.					
Cockpit									
Bottom									

DATE December 1944

TACTICAL DATA

Maximum armament recovered has been 1 x 7.7 mm top rear free gun. One report indicated 2 x 7.7 free guns. Has used grenade discharge device.

RESTRICTED

TAIC Dinah

**Other Japanese Aircraft
Encountered by the 5th Fighter Command**

Nate/Nakajima Ki-27

Nate

In mid-1935, the JAAF requested the Kawasaki, Mitsubishi, and Nakajima companies to design and construct prototypes of an advanced fighter. Nakajima's submission, designed by Hideo Itokawa and Yasushi Koyama, was a single-seat all-metal (except for fabric covered control surfaces) monoplane fighter which was based on the company's Type PE private venture. It had a cantilevered low-wing, a conventional tail, fixed landing gear and tail skid, and was powered by a 650hp Nakajima Ha-1a radial engine. The Ki-27 prototype was first flown in July 1936, and three months later, incorporating minor modifications, was tested against the Kawasaki and Mitsubishi designs; while the Kawasaki Ki-28 was the fastest of the three contenders, Nakajima's Ki-27 was by far the most maneuverable and ten pre-production examples were ordered for further service evaluation. Following further testing in 1937, the type was ordered into production as the Army Type 97 Fighter Model A Nakajima Ki-27a.

The Nate in Combat
The Ki-27 flew combat over northern China in March 1938, where it established air superiority until the faster Russian Polikarov I-16 biplane fighters arrived. At the beginning of the Pacific War, the Ki-27s were included in the invasion of the Philippines, Burma, Malaya, and the Netherlands East Indies. Once more modern Japanese fighters became available, they were transferred back to Japan for home air defense until 1943, when they became used increasingly as advanced trainers. As with many Japanese aircraft, their final use was as Kamikazes. A total of 3,999 Nates would be built by Nakajima (2,020) and Mansyu Hikoki Seizo (1,379) before production ceased at the end of 1942.

General Characteristics

Length	24.7 feet
Wingspan	37.1 feet
Height	10.7 feet
Wing Area	199.8 square feet
Empty Weight	2,588 pounds
Loaded Weight	3,523 pounds
Max Takeoff Weight	3,946 pounds
Powerplant	1 × Nakajima Ha-1 Otsu air-cooled radial engine, 650 hp

Performance

Maximum speed	275mph
Cruise Speed	218mph
Range	390 miles
Service Ceiling	32,940 feet
Rate of Climb	3,010 feet/minute
Wing Loading	18 lb/ft²
Power/Mass	0.18 hp/lb

Armament

Guns	2 × 7.7 mm Type 89 machine guns, 500 rounds/gun or 1 x 12.7 machine gun and 1 x 7.7 machine gun on later models
Bombs	220 pounds

Sonia/ Mitsubishi Ki-51

Sonia

In December 1937, the JAAF issued a specification for a ground attack aircraft stressing maneuverability, crew protection, and the capability of operating from emergency airfields located near the combat area. The specifications required a maximum speed of no less than 260mph, a bomb load of at least 440 pounds carried externally, and defensive armament consisting of three machine guns: two fixed and one on a moveable mounting. In Summer 1939, Mitsubishi produced two prototypes which were developed from their Ki-30, a light bomber under the designation Mitsubishi Ki-51. It was similar externally to the Ki-30, but the new design was generally smaller, with the monoplane wing relocated from a mid to low-wing configuration, and was powered by the Mitsubishi 940hp Ha-26-II radial engine. Originally, the JAAF planned to produce two versions of the Ki-51: the Army Type 99 Assault Plane and the Ki-51a Army Type 99 Tactical Reconnaissance Plane, carrying cameras in the rear cockpit. Instead, the Army decided to give every Ki-51 the capability to carry cameras and the aircraft could easily be exchanged between roles in the field. The two prototypes were tested during Summer 1939, and were modified, then ordered into production. The Ki-51 began a production run that totaled 2,385 aircraft—built by Mitsubishi (1,472) and by the First Army Air Arsenal at Tachikawa (913)—before production ended in July 1945.

Sonia in Combat
The Ki-51 was initially used in a close support role in China and in every theatre where the Japanese Army fought during the war; it was deployed against the Allies until the end of the Pacific War. Although the Ki-51 lacked speed, it was maneuverable and unusually well protected for a Japanese aircraft of the Second War. It was also easy to maintain and could operate from small airfields close to the front line. In major combat areas, the comparatively slow Sonias were easy prey for Allied fighters, but in secondary theatres, where an ability to operate from rough and short fields was important, the Ki-51 gave crucial and frequent close support. In the closing stages of the war they were used in Kamikaze attacks.

General Characteristics

Crew	Two
Length	30.2 feet
Wingspan	39.7 feet
Height	9 feet
Wing Area	259 square feet
Empty Weight	4,129 pounds
Loaded Weight	6,169 pounds
Max Takeoff Weight	6,415 pounds
Powerplant	1 × Mitsubishi Ha-26-II 14 cylinder air cooled radial engine, 950 hp

Performance

Maximum speed	263mph
Range	660miles
Service Ceiling	27,130 feet
Wing Loading	23.8 lb/sqft
Power/Mass	0.15 hp/lb
Climb to16,400ft	9 minutes 55 seconds

Armament

Guns	• 2x fixed, forward-firing 7.7 mm (.303 inch) Type 89 machine guns (replaced with 2x12.7 mm (.50 inch) Ho-103 machine guns in later models • 1x7.7 mm (.303 inch) Te-4 Machine gun rearward-firing machine gun.
Bombs	441pound bombs (normal operations); 551 pound for suicide operations

George/Kawanishi N1K1-J

George

The JNAF Kawanishi N1K1-J Shiden George is also often considered as one of the best Japanese fighters. When flown by veteran pilots, it was actually superior to most of the carrier-based U.S. Navy fighters that opposed it, including the later model F4U Corsairs. 5th Fighter Command fighters had relatively little contact with the George, which surely would have been a problem for the P-38, as it held its own against the later model P-51 Mustangs. Unfortunately for the Japanese, the George was unavailable until too late and in inadequate numbers to affect the outcome of the war.

The N1K2-J George had an unusual developmental history. In December 1941, Kawanishi designers proposed the conversion of the N1K1 Rex Seaplane fighter into a land-based fighter. Initially only a few changes were considered, other than the replacement of the floats with retractable land undercarriage. However, they decided to replace the 14 cylinder Kasei engine with an 18 cylinder Nakajima Homare 11 air-cooled radial.

The land-based fighter made its initial flight on 27 December 1942, and since it was a private project, it had no military designation and was identified as the Model X-1 Experimental Land-based fighter by Kawanishi. It was armed with two 7.7mm Type 97 machine guns in the fuselage and two 20mm Type 99 Model 2 cannon housed in underwing gondolas. Since the Homare 11 engine had been accepted for production before the completion of its final testing, it was beleaguered with teething problems. By July 1943, four prototypes had been delivered, but their performance was disappointing, with the maximum speed being only 357mph, which was 46mph less than expectations. However, it was faster than the Mitsubishi A6M5 Reisen Zero and was more maneuverable and longer ranged than the faster Mitsubishi J2M2 Raiden Jack. After additional modifications and testing during 1943, quantity production was ordered by the JNAF as the Navy Interceptor Fighter Shiden Model 11. By the end of 1943, 70 had been manufactured and the N1K1-J entered service with land-based squadrons of the JNAF early in 1944. Armament consisted of two 7.7mm machine guns in the fuselage and four 20mm cannon in the wings (two in the wing, two in underwing gondolas). The 520 N1K1-J production aircraft built by the Naruo plant and 468 N1K1-J production aircraft built by the Himeji plant, along with the prototypes, brought the total production of the Shiden to 1,007. Production of the N1K1-J was phased out at the Naruo plant in December 1944 to manufacture the improved N1K2-J. Production of the N1K1-J at the Himeji plant was halted by the damage caused by B-29 raids.

George in Combat

Georges were first engaged over the Philippines and Formosa, where they quickly established themselves as one of the most dangerous Japanese fighters yet to be engaged in combat. Following the Fall of the Philippines,

the Shiden was encountered in large numbers during the invasion of Okinawa and were based at Shikoku, Japan, in defense of the Home Islands during the Spring of 1945.

The George proved to a well-balanced design, with adequate firepower and protection, good speed, and surprising maneuverability, which was partly due to automatic combat flaps. The George had a relatively poor rate of climb and poor high altitude performance, and thus was unable to successfully intercept the high-flying B-29s over the homeland. The fighter was too powerful and difficult for the poorly-trained pilots available at the time it was ready for combat. Its sophisticated Homare engine pushed the limits of Japanese industry and was quite unreliable; its maintenance was a problem. Aircraft operational availability was frequently limited by insufficient maintenance crews and logistics problems, especially spare parts. The fighter was plagued by chronic undercarriage malfunctions and inadequate wheel brakes that were so poor that many pilots chose to land their Georges on the grass alongside the runway in order to shorten the landing run.

General Characteristics

Length	30.8 feet
Wingspan	39.3 feet 4 in
Height	13 feet
Wing Area	253 square feet
Empty Weight	5,855 pounds
Loaded Weight	8,820 pounds
Max Takeoff Weight	10,710 pounds
Powerplant	1 × Nakajima Homare NK9H radial engine, 1,990 hp

Performance

Maximum speed	369mph
Range	1,066 miles; 1,488 miles ferry
Service Ceiling	35,500 feet
Rate of Climb	4,000 feet/minute (high octane fuel)
Wing Loading	34 lb/sqft
Power/Mass	0.226 hp/lb

Armament

Guns	• 4 × 20 mm Type 99 Model 2 Mk 4 cannon in wings. 200 rounds per gun (up from 100 rounds per gun internally and 70 rounds per gun in underwing boots for the early N1K1-J). The 20 ×101 mm round had an effective range 3,280 ft and a muzzle velocity of 2,297 ft/s. The 128 g shell had 6-8% HE. Rate of fire was about 500 rounds/min per gun. The guns were synchronized to converge at 656 feet. • 2 × 551 pound bombs • 2 × 105 gallon drop tanks

Judy/Yokosuka D4Y

Judy

The JNAF Yokosuka D4Y Suisei ("Comet") Judy dive bomber was one of the fastest dive bombers in the war, but developmental delays stalled its entry into service, while its predecessor, the tougher but slower Aichi D3A Val, remained in service for years. Despite its limited use, the speed and range of the D4Y made it valuable as a reconnaissance aircraft, as well as on Kamikaze missions, but it was only rarely encountered by the 5FC. Lacking armor and self-sealing fuel tanks, the Judys did not fare well against American fighters; however, they did cause extensive damage to USN shipping, including the carrier USS *Franklin*, which was severely damaged and nearly sunk by a lone D4Y.

In 1938, the Yokosuka Naval Air Technical Arsenal began development of the D4Y as a carrier-based dive bomber to replace the Aichi D3A Val. Its design was greatly influenced by a Heinkel He 118 dive bomber provided by the Germans. It was a single-engine, all-metal low-wing monoplane, with a slim fuselage that enabled it to attain high speeds in both horizontal flight and in dives, while its low wing loading gave it excellent maneuverability; all giving the Judy superior performance to contemporary dive bombers, such as the SB2C Helldiver. It had a wide-track retractable undercarriage and wing-mounted dive brakes. Its crew of two (pilot and a navigator/radio-operator/gunner) were seated under a long, glazed canopy which provided good all-round visibility. The aircraft was powered by an Aichi Atsuta liquid-cooled inverted V-12 inline engine—a licensed copy of the German DB 601 rated at 1,200hp—which drove a three blade propeller. As usual, in order to ensure that its aircraft could out-range the enemy, the JNAF minimized the Judy's weight by not installing self-sealing fuel tanks or armor, making the D4Y extremely vulnerable and with a tendency to catch fire when hit.

Bombs were fit under the wings and in an internal bomb bay, unusual in a single-engine aircraft. It carried one 1,100 pound bomb and only 70 pound bombs were carried externally. The aircraft was armed with two 7.7mm (.303 inch) machine guns in the nose and one 7.92mm (.312 inch) Type 1 machine gun in the rear of the cockpit. The 7.92mm was carried because of its higher rate of fire, but later, it was replaced by a 13mm (.51 inch) Type 2 machine gun. This light gun armament was typical for a Japanese carrier-based bomber.

The first D4Y1 prototype made its first flight in December 1940, but structural problems appeared that precluded its use as a dive bomber and the initial production aircraft were used as reconnaissance aircraft (the D4Y1-C), taking advantage of its high speed and long range while not over-stressing the airframe. Small scale production of the D4Y1-C continued until March 1943, when the aircraft's structural problems were finally solved and the increasing losses sustained by the D3A Val resulted in production switching to the D4Y1 dive bomber version. Although the Judy was able to operate successfully from the large and fast fleet carriers that were the nucleus of the Combined Fleet at the start of the war, it had difficulties operating from the smaller and slower carriers such as the Hiyo Class, which formed a large portion of Japan's carrier fleet after the carrier losses in the Battle of Midway. Catapult equipment was therefore fitted, giving rise to the D4Y-1 Kai (or improved) model. Ultimately, 2,038 of all variants were produced, mostly by Aichi.

Judy in Combat

During the Battle of the Marianas "Turkey Shoot," 400 Japanese aircraft were shot down in a single day, many being all the available D4Ys. The Judy was relegated to land operations, where both the liquid-cooled engine D4Y2 and the radial engine D4Y3 fought against the USN fleet, scoring some successes. An unseen D4Y bombed and sank the *Princeton* on 24 October 1944 and D4Ys hit other carriers as well, in both conventional attacks and Kamikaze actions, damaging the carriers *Enterprise, Yorktown, Franklin, Wasp, and Bunker Hill.*

General Characteristics

Crew	two (pilot & gunner/radio operator)
Length	33.5 feet
Wingspan	37.8 feet
Height	12.3 feet
Wing Area	254 square feet
Empty Weight	5,379 pounds
Loaded Weight	9,370 pounds
Powerplant	1xAichi Atsuta AE1P 32 liquid-cooled inverted V12 piston engine, 1,400hp

Performance

Maximum speed	342mph
Range	910 miles
Service Ceiling	35,105 feet
Rate of Climb	2,700 feet/minute
Wing Loading	37 lb/sqft
Power/Mass	0.15 hp/lb

Armament

Guns	• 2 x forward-firing 7.7 mm machine guns • 1 x rearward-firing 7.92 mm machine gun • 1,020 pounds of bombs (design), 1,764 pounds of bombs (Kamikaze)

Transports

Both the JNAF and the JAAF did not anticipate the necessity for large numbers of transport aircraft. While the Germans managed with the old but very serviceable Ju-52, Japanese companies were licensed before the war to manufacture the outstanding U.S. DC-3 (C-47), and also had several twin-engine aircraft that could easily have been converted into ample transport aircraft. In view of the ineffectiveness of most of Japan's multi-engine bombers, the Japanese would have been better off producing fewer Helens and Lilys and more transports escorted by fighters to supply their beleaguered and cut off forces.

Japanese Aircraft Markings

Hinomaru National Marking

The Japanese red national identification emblem *Hinomaru* (literally "sun's red disc") was also called the "meatball" or "rising sun" by the Allies. The JNAF and JAAF showed no significant differences in their application of the *Hinomaru*, and it was generally applied in six positions: being applied above and below the outer sections of both wings (either overlapping the control surfaces or not) and on either side of the fuselage behind the wings (it was discontinued on JAAF aircraft between 1937 and 1942, after which it reappeared for recognition purposes). On biplanes, *Hinomaru* wing markings appeared only on the top of the upper wing and the bottom of the lower wing. On lighter colored aircraft it usually was not outlined by a standard 75mm white circle, but as darker colored camouflage was applied it was outlined in the white circle. Since the *Hinomaru* varied in size, the width of the red circle appeared to be thinner on large *Hinomarus* (as painted on the Betty or Helen bombers) and thinner on the smaller ones. The *Hinomaru* was painted a variety of bright reds which faded to rust orange and Allied pilots were advised to look out for enemy aircraft with bright red *Hinomaru*, as this denoted a new replacement aircraft which was often flown by easier to shoot down rookie pilots. Toward the end of the war, JAAF Home Defense Units painted a white square or wide white stripe around the wing and fuselage *Hinomaru*.

Hinomaru Gallery

Plain red *Hinomaru* on light-colored aircraft. (Author)

JAAF Home Defense Units painted a white square or wide white stripe around the wing and fuselage *Hinomaru*. (Author)

JAAF Home Defense Units painted a white square or wide white stripe around the wing and fuselage *Hinomaru*. (Author)

Sentai Tail Markings

Very distinctive and unusual markings were carried on a JAAF aircraft's vertical tail to identify its *Sentai* and even its *Chutai* sub-unit. These markings were often very striking highly stylized versions of the *Sentai's* number or a *Kanji* (Japanese) character denoting some aspect of the traditions of a unit. Within each *Sentai*, each *Chutai* was assigned a color and the *Sentai's* tail marking was placed on the *Chutai* aircraft in the color.

Very distinctive and unusual markings were carried on a JAAF aircraft's vertical tail to identify its *Sentai*. (Author)

AVG pilots examine the colorful tail markings of the 77th *Sentai*. (Author)

3

Aircraft Vulnerability

The two major causes for aircraft lost or damaged in combat are air-to-air combat (enemy aircraft fire) and ground-to-air (anti-aircraft fire).

The primary factors affecting loss and damage to an aircraft are:
1) Aircraft susceptibility to enemy action by type and make
2) Characteristics of enemy opposition
3) Mission and combat conditions/theater of operations
(**Note:** In this case, a lost aircraft is defined as one that fails to return to base, while a damaged aircraft is one that does return to base after being hit.)

   In 1950, the "Think Tank" at the Rand Corporation of Santa Monica, California, conducted an extensive investigation of aircraft vulnerability titled RM 402: Aircraft Vulnerability in WW II for Air Force and Navy Aircraft in WW II using the above determinates.

Vulnerability by Aircraft Type

USAAF
Three principal fighter types were studied: the P-47, P-38, and P-51. The P-47 mounted the air-cooled Pratt & Whitney engine; the P-38 was powered by twin Allison liquid-cooled engines; and the Mustang initially had an Allison engine, but later became a great fighter when it converted to the liquid-cooled Packard Rolls Royce. The engines of the P-38 and P-51 were liquid-cooled and caught fire when damaged, while the air-cooled Pratt & Whitney of the P-47 was less vulnerable to damage. The ruggedness of the P-47 airframe and engine during the war is legend. When hit by gunfire, approximately eight of ten P-47s returned to base, as compared to seven of ten P-38s and six of ten P-51s.

   If a fighter was able to continue flying after it had been damaged, distance to base became a major factor. Holed oil or coolant systems would allow about 10 to 20 minutes flying time. If friendly territory were within this time span, the damaged aircraft could probably return to base. The P-51 had the longest range of the three and was used as a long-range bomber escort. This assignment contributed to the Mustang's higher loss rate when hit far from base. The P-47, because of its lesser fuel capacity, was assigned shorter missions that would tend to reduce its loss rate. Contrary to the belief that the second engine of the P-38 increased its chances to return

safely, the study found less than 10% of damaged P-38s returned to base on one engine. A rough measure of the degree of exposure to enemy action is the number of claims versus enemy aircraft. While the loss rate for the P-51 was three times that of the P-47 per 1,000 sorties, its claim rate was approximately four times that of the P-47. In contrast, the P-38 loss rate was about the same as the P-51, but its claim rate was lower than both the P-51 and P-47. In the latter stages of the war, after Luftwaffe and JNAF/JAAF fighter opposition was decimated, anti-aircraft fire became the major cause for damage and loss for Allied aircraft, but much more so by the heavy and accurate German Flak concentrations in the ETO. With no air opposition, the Air Force concentrated on ground support and strafing sorties against targets that were protected by AA and small arms fire. An interesting finding was that bombers hit by enemy aircraft fire were about ten times more likely to be lost than those hit by AA fire, whereas fighters hit by enemy aircraft fire were only two times as likely to be lost as those hit by AA fire. Almost all AA fire causing bombers (B-24s) to be lost was of large caliber (75mm to 120mm)/large fragmentation type fired to the high altitudes at which these bombers operated. However, for fighter and medium bomber strafers, most of the hits from AA weapons were small caliber, consisting of armor-piercing, incendiary, and cannon shells, along with small arms fire. Comparing hits from enemy aerial machine guns and cannon showed the following: hits from .50 caliber were about 2.4 times as lethal as .30 caliber, while 20mm cannon hits were 5.4 times more lethal as .30 caliber and 2.2 times as .50 caliber.

Vulnerability to Enemy Anti-Aircraft

(A/C lost/A/C hit)

A/C	%	A/C	%
P-51	29%	F4U	26%
P-38	25%	F6F	25%
P-47	10%	F4F	22%

F4F includes FM-2

Vulnerability to Enemy Aircraft

(A/C lost/A/C hit)

A/C	%	A/C	%
P-38	49%	F4U	46%
P-51	46%	F6F	36%
P-47	37%	F4F	25%

F4F includes FM-2

USAAF Fighter Aircraft Losses by Theater and Type of Loss

Theater & Type of Loss	Total	1941*	1942	1943	1944	1945**
All Theaters						
Total Losses	19,568	310	1085	3240	9400	5551
1st Line Losses	17,839	211	1035	3219	8800	4574
2nd Line Losses	1747	99	50	21	600	977
ETO						
Total Losses	7421	----	68	301	4897	2155
1st Line Losses	7124	----	68	301	4758	1997
2nd Line Losses	297	----	----	----	139	158
MTO						
T Total Losses	5107	----	138	1689	2231	1049
1st Line Losses	4572	----	138	1678	2150	606
2nd Line Losses	535	----	----	11	81	443
PTO ***						
Total Losses	5414	310	809	1000	1545	1750
1st Line Losses	4664	211	765	990	1226	1472
2nd Line Losses	750	99	44	10	319	278
CBI						
Total Losses	1644	----	70	250	727	597
1st Line Losses	1479	----	64	250	666	499
2nd Line Losses	165	----	6	----	61	98

1st Line Losses are combat losses
2nd Line Losses are accidental losses
* December 1941
** January through August 1945
***PTO includes Pacific Ocean Area, Far East AF, XX AF, Alaska, and miscellaneous areas

USAAF Fighter Combat Losses by Theater and Cause

Fighter Combat Losses Theater/Cause of Loss	Total	1942	1943	1944	1945
ETO		*			*
Total Losses	5324	10	178	3765	1371
Enemy Aircraft	1691	10	161	1293	227
Anti-aircraft Fire	2449	----	1	1611	837
Other Causes	1184	----	16	861	307
MTO		**			**
Total Losses	3157	54	1088	1571	444
Enemy Aircraft	1357	46	816	441	24
Anti-aircraft Fire	822	8	115	493	206
Other Causes	1008	----	157	637	214
PTO +		***			***
Total Losses	1695	199	310	513	673
Enemy Aircraft	636	192	244	141	59
Anti-aircraft Fire	300	1	9	100	190
Other Causes	759	6	57	272	424
CBI		****			
Total Losses	774	24	146	371	233
Enemy Aircraft	295	20	94	157	24
Anti-aircraft Fire	208	----	10	86	112
Other Causes	271	4	42	128	97

* August-December 1942 & January-May 1945
** June-December 1942 & January-May 1945
***January-December 1942 & January-August 1945
**** April-December 1942 & January-August 1945
+ PTO includes Pacific Ocean Area, Far East AF, XX AF, Alaska, and Miscellaneous Areas

Japanese Aircraft Vulnerability

While many of the Japanese aircraft claimed by American pilots were bombers and reconnaissance aircraft, probably three-quarters were fighters. Even though the Zero or Oscar was a forgiving fighter to fly, they were extremely dangerous to fly in combat, especially when flown by inexperienced, ill-trained pilots, who appeared in increasing numbers as the war progressed. These enemy fighters were easily destroyed when surprised by another fighter, were extremely vulnerable in the ground attack role, and were susceptible to bomber turret fire. The aircraft designers of the other combatant nations designed strong airframes with heavier, solid components held together with more welds and rivets. There was little redundancy in Japanese fighter airframe construction and there were several areas vulnerable to damage that would disable or collapse the airframe. Because the Zero or Oscar's airframes were so lightly built, a fast, abrupt maneuver at near-maximum speed could cause structural damage, and more significantly made it extremely vulnerable to battle damage. To save weight, the Zero/Oscar's cockpit was not armored and the fuel tanks were not self-sealing nor armored, and if hit, a fire or explosion would destroy the fighter. Structural failure could also easily start a fire, so it was impossible to determine whether a Zero/Oscar's fuel tanks were hit or if the catastrophic fire was caused by a collapsing airframe. Although the Zero/Oscar was developed into several models, the last were little improved over the first to appear over Pearl Harbor/China. American P-38s and P-47s, and even the venerable P-40 improved greatly, as they were modified throughout the war. (**Note:** TAIC Vulnerability drawings are included with each Japanese aircraft type.)

External Vulnerability Factors for All Aircraft

Navigation and Terrain

Early in the war both sides, but particularly the Allies, flew over terrain using maps drafted by the British, Dutch, and Australians decades before the war. While the general location of the major islands was perceptible, as was the coast of New Guinea, any area inland was generally unknown territory. Obviously, this geographical ambiguity, combined with unpredictable weather, made the planning and execution of operations exceedingly difficult until navigation aids were more developed.

New Guinea or islands in the Solomons had many large and small mountains which often could be shrouded in clouds. New Guinea had particularly large mountain ranges, most notably the Owen Stanleys, which traversed the spine of the island, reaching over 12,000 feet, while most of the SWPA islands were volcanic, with peaks ranging from 1,500 feet to nearly 10,000 feet on Bougainville.

Weather

With only a basic knowledge of aerial navigation, their ignorance of the terrain, and poor communications, the airmen in the South Pacific were further exposed to the hazards posed by poor weather. Fortunately, the weather in the South Pacific was not particularly severe when compared with many other theaters, though pilots in the South Pacific had to deal with flying over vast expanses of water in intense heat through huge cloud formations and unpredictable and rapidly forming weather patterns that in practice did claim hundreds of lives, and nearly every pilot in the Pacific could claim at least one harrowing weather or navigational experience.

Although Allied weathermen in the Pacific were given good instruments, there were not enough weather data collecting bases to correlate the gathered weather information. Also, much of the developing weather could be over enemy-controlled territory or over the vast stretches of unoccupied ocean, making aerial weather recon risky and/or incomplete. Hydrogen weather balloons were regularly released to measure wind velocity at several altitudes ranging from 2,000 to nearly 40,000 feet, and also to closely monitor barometric pressure, seeking the rapid fluctuations that indicated a potential storm. Special weather reconnaissance flights were also dispatched each predawn and climbed to a specified ceiling, then descended in large circles at 500 feet a minute. Instruments would measure the temperature and pressure to determine any changes in the weather pattern. In New Guinea, several Bomb Groups began sending one aircraft ahead of the others to radio back weather conditions in code every 30 minutes. This practical measure undoubtedly helped some formations avoid unexpected weather fronts, but ultimately, there was no bona fide solution to the problem, considering the available technology and terrain.

Bad weather exposed pilots and crews to two deadly threats. First, poor visibility could cause an aircraft to become lost and then run out of fuel over some of the world's most inhospitable geography. Often, long range missions were dispatched that required pilots to burn most of their fuel, leaving them with little margin for error on their return. Secondly, even if a pilot was on course and had sufficient fuel, there was the ever present threat of rapidly moving storms, which could either directly destroy the aircraft or cause it to crash into the ground or into another aircraft due to the reduced visibility or disorientation. The "Perfect Storm" occurred over New Guinea on 16 April 1944, a mission the Fifth Air Force called "Black Sunday," which is described at length on that date in volume 2.

Pilots flying from Moresby to the New Guinea north coast (e.g., Dobodura) flew through the "Gap," a pass between peaks in the Owen Stanleys that were 12,000 feet or higher. That distance for an aircraft was relatively short and countless aircraft made the flight safely, despite the almost daily cloud buildup. Nonetheless, scores of aircraft trying to fly through the Gap were listed among the many "operational losses" that made up the majority of Allied losses in New Guinea.

The Japanese flew over the same hazardous terrain as the Allies, but were flying much less rugged aircraft equipped with inferior communications. Although during most of the war the Japanese had the advantage of defending directly over their own bases, they did initiate a large number of missions over long distances, especially the sustained long range air offensive from Rabaul to Guadalcanal, and to a lesser extent to Port Moresby. Although an accurate percentage will never be known, postwar investigations determined that perhaps more than half the Japanese aircraft lost in the theater were the victims of accidents or simply disappeared. The weather could be a far more dangerous enemy.

4

Fighter Armament and Equipment

As maximum aircraft speeds increased and manufacturing materials became stronger, designers realized that more destructive gun power was needed to overcome heavier armor and ever-shrinking windows for shot opportunities. Research centered on creating better, faster, and more powerful guns, and WWII became the "Golden Age" of gun combat.

World War II Fighters as Gun Platforms

WWII fighters were gun platforms, and whether they mounted machine guns or cannons, their firing range was limited to a maximum of 1,000 yards; in reality, the killing zone was much shorter. In air combat, both the gun and its target were moving very quickly. From the early Ring and Bead sights, WWII fighters evolved to electric gun sights that could compensate for the position of the pilot's head in the cockpit and would inform the pilot where the bullets were going to hit if the aircraft was on a true course, as well as the approximate range of the enemy.

In most fighters, the main armament was mounted on the wings and each gun was separated by a foot or more. If fired directly ahead, the bullets from only one or two guns would hit the target, lacking punch. To compensate, all guns were adjusted so that bullets would strike a convergence point in the distance (the boresight point); normally about 250 yards for the .50 caliber machine gun, but varied on pilot preference. The maximum impact was at a particular boresight range, but inside and outside that range caused misses. The Lightning pilot did not have to worry about a boresight point, as he always had maximum fire of the four .50s and the 20mm firing in a parallel stream in front of him and could hit a target at a somewhat greater range than any other AAF fighter.

A narrow cone of fire was extremely effective, but only if it hit the target, whereas a broader cone of fire increased the poor marksman's chances of hitting a target, albeit less effectively. In combat studies, it was found that a high percentage of kills were made at very close range and inside the convergence point, where the problem of convergence did not matter as much. The kinetic energy from a round of ammunition became greater as the range decreased. Thus, even if the convergence point was set at 300 yards, an enemy aircraft inside the zone was actually at great risk because more area contained bullets, and it did not require many rounds to do serious or fatal damage to a lightly protected Japanese aircraft. In 1943, some units in the Pacific discontinued the use of armor-piercing rounds because they felt that standard lead shot, which had a tendency to splatter when it hit, was more likely to strike a structural failure point or fuel tank than an armor-piercing round, which might make a clean hole through the light Japanese fuselage. Both combatants always used incendiary rounds as part of the ammunition composition because of the devastating effect of fire on an aircraft.

Thomas McGuire on Gunnery:

"New pilots have had gunnery drummed into them in schools, but it is not until they get into combat that they find out that a high degree of skill is necessary. Using the 70-mil sight, an enemy bomber will fill the sight at three hundred yards; a fighter will fill half the sight. Unless they fill the sight to that extent, hold your fire; it doesn't count beyond 300 yards. On the other hand, the closer you get the better. Your chances of scoring hits and the destructiveness of your fire will increase in proportion. Go in close and then, when you think you're too close, go in closer. The majority of pilots with good scores believe in closing to minimum range, were there is no chance of missing and where firepower has its maximum effect. When you do close in, don't fire all the way. Use several bursts of one to three seconds duration. Long bursts cause jamming and overheating of the guns. You are aiming at a target, not spraying the general area. If you take a shot in deflection, pull your sight through the enemy's line of flight. Misses are due more to shooting over or under than to improper lead. Above all, keep your flying smooth when you fire. The smoother the pilot the better his gunnery, for one smooth burst is more likely to bear results than a number of nervous, jerky bursts. Try taking a deep breath just before you press the button, or develop any psychological trick which will keep you steady through that brief moment when you have drawn a bead and are ready to let fly."

5th Fighter Command Armament and Aircraft Equipment

Machine Guns

Browning .30 Caliber Aircraft Machine Gun M2

The .30 Caliber Aircraft Machine Gun M2 was completed at a time when a post-WWI peacetime America lost interest in the military and withheld funding for machine gun projects. By the time of Pearl Harbor, the .30, known as the BAMG (Browning Automatic Machine Gun), was America's first line machine gun in both single and twin flexible mounts and as fixed wing or nose guns. The fixed M2 weighed 21.5 pounds, while the flexible

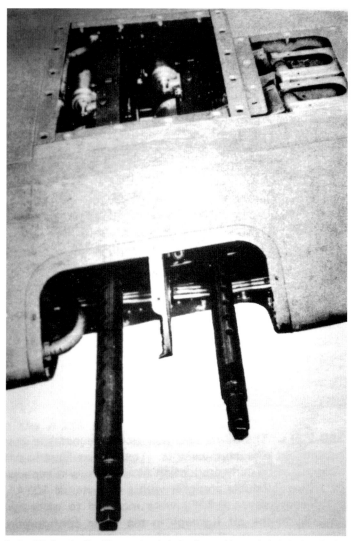

By Pearl Harbor, the .30 caliber was America's first line machine gun in both single and twin flexible mounts and as fixed wing or nose guns. Wing guns on a P-39D are shown. (AAF)

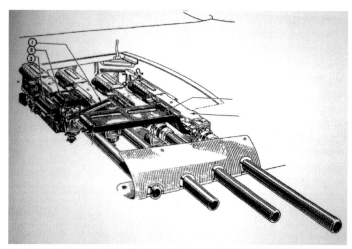

American air forces adopted the .50 caliber M2 Browning Machine Gun as its standard fighter weapon during WWII (P-47 wing mount shown). (AAF)

Informative photo showing armorers preparing their charge for combat. (AAF)

M2 gun weighed 23 pounds, with the recoiling parts weighing 6.56 pounds and the barrel weighing 3.81 pounds in both versions. Both types were 39.7 inches long with 23.9 inch barrels with four grooves.

Early in the war, the .30 caliber machine gun was used on a flexible mount in situations where the .50 caliber gun was too unwieldy. Soon after America entered combat, it was found that this rifle caliber machine gun was inadequate against fast, armored German aircraft and armored vehicles that were appearing on the battlefields. The .30 caliber aircraft gun was discontinued, except for its installation on several Navy and AAC aircraft (P-39s and early P-40s) for use against the more lightly armored Japanese aircraft in the Pacific. The .30 caliber aircraft machine gun served an important function throughout the war in its employment as the standard equipment for training range practice because of its smaller rounds.

Browning .50 Caliber M2 Machine Gun
The American air services adopted the .50 caliber derived from the .50 caliber ground service heavy machine gun as its standard fighter weapon during WWII. It was a recoil-operated, air-cooled, belt-fed gun that weighed 64.5 pounds and was 57 inches long (barrel 36 inches). Its rate of automatic fire averaged 700 to 750 rounds per minute, depending on attachments, such as a flash suppressor or muzzle booster. Its muzzle velocity was 2,700

to 2,850 feet per second. Its extreme range (extent of forward travel) was 20,000 to 21,500 feet, and its effective range (round able to penetrate airframe or engine to cause damage) was 3,400 to 3,500 feet. All of the above performance figures varied in the field due to internal (e.g., age and condition of the mechanism and barrel, age of the ammunition, feed and type) and external (e.g., temperature) conditions. Gun jams were a problem, especially early in the war. It was unusual when all six machine guns functioned flawlessly, and often at least one of them failed, which was why pilots fired in short bursts.

The M2 could be mounted in the engine, nose, or wing. When engine-mounted, it was synchronized to fire through the propeller by a mechanical trigger motor attached to the gun receiver, causing the gun to fire semi-automatically. When the gun was wing-mounted or nose-mounted (as in the P-38), firing was attained through a remote control solenoid attached to the receiver, causing it to fire automatically. To assure that a fighter's gunfire would exact the maximum damage to an enemy aircraft, the guns were harmonized so that their fire would converge at the optimum combat range. Harmonization range was often the personal preference of the individual pilot, but it is well known that most aces preferred very short ranges.

Pilots often felt that by firing all their guns they were slowing down their fighter, but the speed loss was actually a very inconsequential fraction of a mile per hour. The perceived speed loss was due to the vibration of the six or eight guns recoiling. A 14,000 pound P-47 traveling at 300mph (440 feet/second) had a forward kinetic energy of 47 million foot pounds. All eight .50s firing at the same time would have a reverse kinetic energy of only 100,000 pounds, so the net effect of the guns was insignificant.

Though the .50 caliber bullet lacked the punch of a 20mm cannon shell, the concentrated firepower from six or eight machine guns had a devastating effect. There were four basic types of .50 caliber ammunition: armor piercing (distinguished by a painted black tip), tracer (red tip), incendiary (blue), and armor piercing incendiary (silver). The bullet weighed about 1.75 ounces and was about 5.5 inches long. Between 267 and 500 rounds of ammunition could be stowed per gun (rpg). The P-47 carried eight guns with 425 rpg, the P-38 four machine guns with 500 rpg (plus a 20mm cannon), the F6F and F4U mounted six guns with 400 rpg, while the P-51 carried four guns supplied with 400 rpg.

37mm cannon installation on the P-39. (AAF)

The Browning .30 and .50 Caliber Machine Guns Compared
The operation and care of the two guns was similar, and the only differences "which must be known to use, clean, and adjust the gun" were specified on just a single page in the *Gunner's Information Manual*.

Differences in Performance and Construction

Gun	.50 Caliber	.30 Caliber
Weight (pounds)	62	21.25
Length Overall (inches)	57.09	39.72
Barrel Length (inches)	36	23.9
Barrel Weight (pounds)	9.75	3.75
Rate of Fire (rounds/minute)	750-850	1,330
Muzzle Velocity (feet/second)	2,900	2,715
Chamber Pressure (psi)	50,000 to 52,000	48,000 to 50,000
Maximum Range (yards)	7,200	3,400
Lands and Grooves (number)	8/8	4/4
Feed	Right	Right or Left

Cannon
The U.S. dabbled with cannon armament in early fighters. The P-39 Airacobra was equipped with a 30-round Oldsmobile 37mm T-9 or M-4 cannon. Because of its inherent inaccuracy and low rate of fire the cannon was abandoned in favor of the .50 caliber machine gun. The P-38 effectively used the Hispano-Suiza 20mm cannon in conjunction with four .50 caliber machine guns all firing a concentrated, accurate burst from the central nose position. Late in the war, several other fighter bombers were fitted with 20mm cannon, as was the P-61 night fighter. Because no Axis fighter could withstand the pounding of multiple .50s and Axis bombers were of the medium bomber classification and also susceptible to .50 fire, cannon placement in American fighters was reserved for special purposes. The P-38 Lightning and P-39 Airacobra were the only 5FC fighters to mount cannons in combat.

Differences in AAF Cannon Performance and Construction

Gun	20mm*	37 mm+
Weight (pounds)	102	135
Length Overall (inches)	93.7	213
Barrel Length (inches)	67.5	65
Barrel Weight (pounds)	47.5	55
Muzzle Velocity (feet/second)	2,850	2,000
Projectile Weight (pounds)	0.20	1.1
Rate of Fire (rounds/minute)	600-700	60
Duration of Fire (seconds)	13.4	11.8
Weight of Fire (Pounds/second)	3.2	1.65

*Hispano-Suiza
+M4

20mm cannon installation on the P-38. (AAF)

Lockheed P-38 Lightning

The definitive P-38 armament configuration featured four .50 caliber machine guns with 500rpg and a Hispano 20mm cannon with 150 rounds replacing the unreliable Oldsmobile 37mm gun mounted on the YP-38 and P-38D production versions (there were no P-38Bs or Cs). While the machine guns had been arranged symmetrically in the nose in earlier variants, they were staggered above the 20mm cannon on the P-38E and later versions, with the .50 muzzles protruding from the nose in relative lengths of roughly 1:4:6:2. This was done to ensure a straight ammunition belt feed into the weapons, as the earlier arrangement led to jamming. The rate of fire was about 650rpm at a muzzle velocity of about 2,887fps and an effective range

of approximately 1,200 yards. Continuous fire was 15 seconds with an ammo belt composition of two AP, two tracer, and two HE. There was a separate thumb-operated cannon trigger located on the front of the wheel/yoke and a .50 caliber gun trigger located on the forward side of the wheel; however, this arrangement could vary.

Bell P-39 (P-400) Airacobra

The British elected to install the Hispano 20mm cannon in place of the 37mm cannon in the P-39C export version, which the British dubbed the Airacobra I. When America entered the war, 179 of these fighters were diverted from the RAF and over 100 were sent to Australia as the redesignated P-400 mounting the 20mm cannon firing 60 rounds through the propeller hub. Additional armament was two synchronized .50s installed in the cowling and a pair of .30s in each wing. The Hispano was intensely disliked by American pilots over Guadalcanal and New Guinea because of its constant jamming problems, low rate of fire, and dissimilar trajectory to the machine guns.

The original Bell design had called for a 25mm cannon, but an updated French Hotchkiss was the only contemporary 25mm cannon, which was secret and not available for export. The Madsen 23mm cannon was then contemplated, but its low rate of fire and erratic feeding mechanism led to its rejection. The only option was the installation of the 37mm T9 long-recoil cannon which had been previously installed in the Bell FM-1 Airacuda. The armament of the 1940 P-39 was to be the heaviest carried by an American production fighter to that time, replacing the standard two rifle caliber .30 machine guns that armed pursuit aircraft. However, the weapon had a low rate of fire and low velocity, and although Bell considered it an interim solution, it would remain operational throughout the war in the production P-39C through Q models and the P-63 King Cobra.

AAF Ammunition

Types of Ammunition

Type	Use	Color of Tip	How It Works
Ball	Against personnel and light material targets	Unpainted; plain metal	The outer jacket point contains a lead and antimony filler that covers the tip of the underlying steel core. When the projectile hits a target, the soft outer jacket and filler smears, giving the steel core a grip. The core then penetrates the surface instead of being turned aside.
Armor-Piercing	Against armored aircraft and vehicles, concrete shelters and other bullet-resisting targets	Black	The projectile is the same as the ball cartridge, except that the core is made of very hard tungsten-chrome steel to give it greater penetrating power.
Armor-Piercing Incendiary	Used to set fire to armor-plated and inflammable targets.	Aluminum or Medium Blue	Similar to the armor-piercing projectile, except that there is incendiary compound behind the steel core.
Armor-Piercing Incendiary-Tracer	Used to set fire to armor-plated and inflammable targets	Red	Similar to the API except it contained a tracer materiel
Incendiary	Used to set fire to explosive or very inflammable targets	Light blue	In front of the jacket is an incendiary composition that is sealed by plugs of an alloy that easily melts. As the bullet goes through the barrel, the heat melts the plugs and the incendiary composition is set on fire as it meets the air.
Tracer	For observing fire, it makes a streak of light easily seen at night and usually is visible in daylight	Red	Inside the outer metal jacket is a slug of lead and antimony. Behind it is a pocket of tracer composition that is set afire by the propelling charge as the projectile leaves the cartridge case.
Dummy	Training	Unpainted (hole in side of case)	Has no priming or propelling charge.

Ammunition Feeds

Box

Ultimately, ammunition had to be stored in the aircraft and then be fed into a gun. The method of supplying cartridges to the breech was a fundamental and critical design consideration. The most uncomplicated method was the box magazine, in which a strong Spring located at the end of the box containing the cartridges forced the cartridges into the gun mechanism. The box could be mounted to the side or bottom of the gun, but a top-mounting was favored on larger guns, as gravity could facilitate feeding. The disadvantage with the box feed mechanism was that it was restricted to a limited number of cartridges; otherwise, the feed boxes would become too long and unwieldy.

Drum

The drum (sometimes called a "pan") contained rounds arranged in a circle, pointing inwards, that were fed into the gun by a circular Spring. Some drums contained more than one layer of rounds. These drums were propelled by a Spring or rotated by the gun as it fired. In the drum magazine, the rounds were parallel to each other in a coil array and were moved by a Spring that was wound tight when the drum was loaded. Drums often had unwieldy shapes for installation and were commonly used with machine guns on a flexible mount on which the gun could move freely.

Belt

Generally, the drum- and box-fed magazines had a limited capacity of rounds, with a maximum of 100. The belt was a better alternative, as a larger number of rounds could be linked to a belt that could be stored in a box or tray with a practical shape. The belt was pulled through the mechanism by the action of the gun as it fired; each cartridge was pushed or pulled out of the belt and into the chamber. Early belts were fabric, but by the beginning of the war metal disintegrating-link belts were standard. However, for a short period during 1943, some fabric belts were issued for U.S. .50 caliber machine guns due to a production shortage of disintegrating links. The disintegrating belt, after the removal of the round, broke into links that could be collected or dumped overboard. The belt could be as long as the feeding mechanism could pull. However, the belt feed mechanism was more complicated than that of a drum, especially for the heavier cannon rounds. For this reason most cannon had drums. During WWII, there was an ongoing controversy over the different types of projectiles that were to be used in a belt. There was no one answer and different air forces preferred different combinations, depending on the type of gun employed and the mission.

The Machine Gun vs. Cannon Controversy

One of the most difficult problems faced by prewar fighter designers was choosing between cannons and machine guns for the main armament array. Since WWI, the rifle-caliber machine gun (.30 caliber/7.7mm) had been the standard weapon arming fighters, but by the late 1930s, large-caliber machine guns (.50 caliber/13mm) and small-caliber cannons (typically 20mm/80 caliber) were available for aircraft use.

The difference between a machine gun and cannon was that a machine gun fired a solid slug, while a cannon fired rounds called shells that could be solid, but were often hollow and filled with detonation or incendiary material. The solid machine gun round did its damage through kinetic energy, which is the function of projectile weight times its velocity squared. The .50 caliber slug weighed about 1.6 ounces, while the 20mm projectile weighed 4.6 ounces and the 37mm projectile weighed almost 17.6 ounces. The machine gun had a somewhat higher muzzle velocity (the speed at which the projectile leaves the barrel). Thus, the machine gun round's

Ammunition Expended in the PTO by Fighters

(Machine Gun & Cannon in 1,000s of Rounds)

(August 1942 to May 1945)

Total*	1942	1943	1944	1945	Total
Machine Guns:					
.30 cal.	3	46	282	42	373
.50 cal.	38	647	5,727	4,552	10,964
Cannon:					
20 mm	----	----	8	26	34
37 mm	----	1	1	----	2
75 mm	----	----	----	6	6
Fighters					
Machine Guns:					
.30 cal.	----	9	61	1	71
.50 cal.	6	28	2,526	2,870	5,430
Cannon:					
20 mm	----	----	8	26	34
37 mm	----	1	1	----	2

* By Fighters and Bombers

Ammunition Expended by FEAF Fighters

(Machine Gun & Cannon in 1,000s of Rounds)

(1942 to August 1945)

Total*	1942	1943	1944	1945	Total
Machine Guns:					
.30 cal.	326	2,345	2,116	5	4,792
.50 cal.	982	11,186	39,481	52,183	103,832
Cannon:					
20 mm	13	133	344	725	1,215
37 mm	----	1,690	----	106	1,796
75 mm	----	124	----	16	
Fighters					
Machine Guns:					
.30 cal.	169	466	806	----	1,441
.50 cal.	628	2,453	10,675	18,884	32,640
Cannons:					
20 mm	13	128	343	725	1,209
37 mm	----	1,690	----	106	1,796

* By Fighters and Bombers

kinetic energy was higher, as its higher muzzle velocity was squared. It also had a higher rate of fire than the cannon, which meant it could fire more rounds per minute, or more correctly, per second, to do damage. The muzzle velocity affected the round's kinetic energy and the flight time to the target. The shorter time to the target gave the target less time to maneuver. Guns with higher muzzle velocities were more likely to hit a target, could be fired at longer ranges, and would cause more damage.

A cannon shell, depending on its design, would explode on contact or penetrate and then explode, or set a fire. A solid machine gun slug would penetrate and depend on its kinetic energy to cause damage. The aircraft cannon was a more deadly weapon due to their heavier explosive shells. But they were heavier than a machine gun, often weighing more each than two machine guns depending on the caliber (a 37mm cannon weighed 135 pounds and a 20mm cannon weighed 118 pounds, vs. a .50 caliber machine gun that weighed 52 pounds and a .30 caliber machine gun that weighed 24 pounds). Therefore, the equal weight of two machine guns could fire many more rounds per second than cannon. Also, cannon shells weighed more and were larger than machine gun rounds, so a cannon-equipped fighter could carry far fewer rounds than a machine gun-equipped fighter: the 37mm gun (P-39) could carry 30 rounds per gun (rpg), the 20mm (P-38) 150 rpg, the .50 caliber (P-47 or P-51) between 400-450rpg, and the .30 caliber (P-39) 1,000 rpg. Fewer cannon shells meant a shorter firing time at a lower rate of fire. The 30 rounds of 37mm shells fired by a P-39 had a duration of fire of 11.8 seconds, while its four-.30 caliber machine guns with 1,000rpg fired for 67 seconds per gun. The P-38's 20mm cannon fired 150 rounds at 11.2 rounds per second in 13.4 seconds. The .50 caliber machine gun fired 12 rounds per second for duration of 35 seconds (425 rounds). A cannon shell caused more damage per hit, but there were less potential hits when compared to the higher rate of fire and more rounds found in machine gun equipped fighters. Many British and Luftwaffe fighters carried a combination of machine guns and cannon, with the machine guns being used to find range and attain hits and the cannon to deliver the lethal blow. The RAF replaced its Browning .303 caliber machine guns with the Hispano-Suiza 20mm cannon, as one 20mm shell did much more damage than four .303 hits, which were ineffective against armor plate and self-sealing fuel tanks. The 20mm cannon, with its explosive shell, would leave a large hole upon impact. The American fighter aircraft .30 caliber machine gun was replaced with the .50 caliber. Both projectiles left small, clean entrance holes in the metal fuselage surface, but after they hit, they would be deflected and begin to tumble end over end. The larger .50 caliber slug would cause a substantially larger exit or secondary hole than the .30 caliber.

Aircraft Guns and Cannon of World War II

Weight of Fire (lbs/sec)

GUN	USA	UK	Germany	USSR	JAAF	JNAF
LMG	0.42	0.46	0.40	0.79	0.35	0.42
HMG	1.34	1.34	1.15	1.85	1.26	1.52
20 mm	2.87	2.87	2.82	2.82	3.09	2.31
30 mm	-----	-----	-----	6.88	5.18	5.78

LMG = Light Machine Gun **HMG** = Heavy Machine Gun

In summary, only a few hits from a cannon could easily destroy a fighter, and even a heavy bomber. Again, there was a trade off, as cannon ammunition was heavy and sizeable, and thus aircraft armed with cannons could carry only a relatively few rounds. Since the rate of fire was also less than that of machine guns, it was more difficult to hit an enemy with cannon because there were fewer shells in the air, but a single hit was much more damaging. Fighters mounting rifle-caliber machine guns carried hundreds of rounds

per gun, fired them more quickly and, because the guns were lighter, more guns could be mounted on an aircraft.

These calculations led the major European combatants and the Japanese to mount a combination of machine guns and cannons on their fighters. This mixed armament array had many advocates in both the AAC and the USN. After experimenting extensively with cannons and a cannon/machine gun combination for all their major fighters, the Americans decided that heavy machine guns were their choice (with the notable exception of the P-38 Lightning). The main reason for the American decision was because they envisaged fighters as being designed to shoot down other fighters. Unlike Germany, the United States never had to be concerned about powerfully armed and armored heavy bombers and no Japanese aircraft would be able to take a solid hit from a heavy machine gun.

The standard armament on most U.S. fighters was six .50 caliber machine guns (eight on the P-47). While this array put less weight of fire in the air during a sustained burst and forfeited the additional advantage of an exploding shell, it did put more bullets in the air than did a mixed cannon/machine gun configuration. The destructive power of the .50 caliber armor-piercing round, at most angles, penetrated any pilot armor and could damage an engine block. If it hit an enemy aircraft from any rear angle, it penetrated through the aircraft or embedded into an essential area, such as the engine and cockpit. Also, when accounting for the larger number of rounds fired there was a better chance of hitting the enemy, and because .50 caliber rounds weighed less than cannon rounds, it was possible to carry far more of them, decreasing the possibility of running out of ammunition.

Comparison of U.S. and Japanese Aircraft Guns

Gun Type	Caliber	Rate of Fire	Wt of Fire	Effect
.30	.30	20	0.48	20
Ho-103	12.7 mm	15	1.10	45
.50 M2	.50	13	1.24	60
Type 99-1	20 mm	8	2.26	108
Type 99-2	20 mm	8	2.26	120
Ho-5	20 mm	14	2.44	154
Hispano-Suiza	20 mm	12.5	3.59	250
37 mm M4	37 mm	2.5	3.35	160

Rate of Fire = Rounds per second
Weight of Fire = Pounds per second
Effect = Destructive Effect is an approximate rating of an aircraft gun's firepower conceived by Anthony Williams. It is calculated by multiplying the projectile weight, muzzle velocity, rate of fire, and a multiplier for the average percentage of incendiary or high explosive material contained in the projectile (e.g., 5% content multiplier is x 1.5; 10% is x 2; 15% is x 2.5, etc.)

Thus, the American fighter carrying six or eight .50 caliber machine guns possessed enough concentrated firepower to cope with Axis fighters, especially against the fragile Japanese fighters in the Pacific, particularly when using the API round. Also, the major Axis bombers (German He-111, Do-17, and Japanese Betty, Lily, or Helen) were usually of medium bomber size and not well armed or armored. Hence, the .50 caliber machine guns mounted in the superior P-51, P-47, P-38, or F4U and F6F gave the American fighter pilot a good chance of achieving a high probability shot, firing out the most number of rounds in the shortest amount of time. (For a more

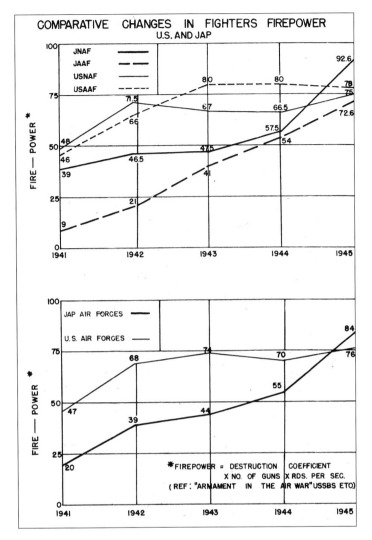

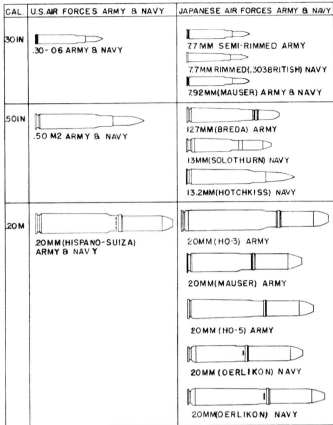

Mark 8 Gunsight (Author's Collection)

extensive look at the machine gun/cannon controversy refer to my book U.S. Aerial Armament in World War II: Volume I: Guns, Ammunition, and Gunsights)

Gunsights

The simple ring and bead gun sight of the interwar years was no longer sufficient with the increasing performance and combat ranges seen in the newer monoplane fighters of the mid-1930s. The N-series (3, 6, 8, and 9) of reflector sights was developed, but was basically a refined ring and bead sight. The image of the ring(s) and bead was superimposed onto a special glass in front of the pilot's eyes in such a way that they were only visible if the pilot were looking along the longitudinal axis of the fighter (convergence of the guns). The pilot had only to track the target and get it into the center of the sight. The sight was accurate when closing on an enemy at the same speed and course, but deflection shooting ("lead shooting" e.g., bird hunting) continued to be the province of the gifted pilot.

The N-2, N3A, L3-B, N-9, and MK VIII optical sights succeeded the ring and bead type sights, with the latter two eventually becoming the standard. They were characterized by a center dot or "pipper" surrounded by 50-mil and 100-mil radii rings which aided in the calculation of deflection. The retile image of this sight, although it was only a few inches from the pilot's eye, was made to look as if it were at a distance in front of the fighter. There was no need to readjust focus and the sight could be viewed with

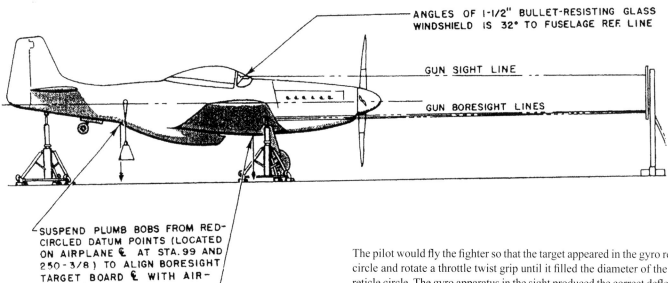

Harmonization (AAF)

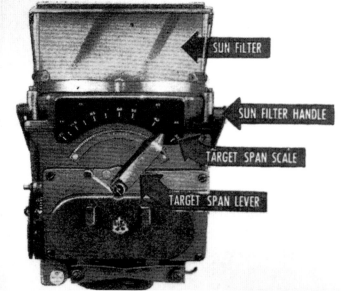

Gunsight K-14: K-14 Gunsight (AAF)

both eyes open; the pilot could move his head without changing the alignment of the target. The pilot would superimpose the reticle on the target and fire.

The AAF K-14 series and Navy Mark 18 were introduced in July 1944, and were a development of the British gyroscopic Mk IIC and Mk IID sights. It was originally developed for bomber turrets, but engineers adapted it as the standard U.S. fighter gunsight. The new sight provided much improved deflection shooting by the average pilot, as it computed the correct lead angle for a target crossing speed at ranges of 200 to 800 yards. The K-14 was based on the reflector sight, but was combined with a gyroscope. Below the reflecting glass was a panel with a control calibrated to the wingspan of the intended victim. The pilot dialed in the enemy's wingspan (pre-marked on the controls as Me-109, Zero, etc.) and the sighting reticle on the reflector glass then adjusted itself to the size of the enemy wingspan.

The pilot would fly the fighter so that the target appeared in the gyro reticle circle and rotate a throttle twist grip until it filled the diameter of the gyro reticle circle. The gyro apparatus in the sight produced the correct deflection for the range and rate of turn corresponding to the target size. The pilot would frame the target with the twist grip as the range changed, then track the target for at least one second and then fire. Initially, this sight was not well received because of its size and apparent intricacy, but soon earned the nickname "No Miss Um." It allowed shooting at twice the previous maximum range and more importantly, greatly improved deflection shooting, while the N-9/MK VIII sights were a combination of guesswork and individual ability. The K-14 made even 90° deflection shooting as easy as from dead astern. Though the new sight required some additional manual coordination, it greatly increased the number of kills at long range (500+ yards) and at large deflection angles (45+°).

Harmonization, commonly called bore sighting, is the aligning the path of the rounds fired from all guns. It was accomplished by one of two methods. One was to converge the four, six, or eight machine guns to a point 250 to 300 yards ahead of the fighter. At a three mil setting, the convergence pattern at 300 yards was about three feet in diameter, which is difficult for the average pilot/marksman and resulted in excessive dispersion at most ranges. A remedy to gain wider bullet dispersion was to boresight each gun at different ranges: generally 250, 300, and 350 yards for outboard, middle, and inboard guns, respectively. Called "pattern harmonization," it was innately less damaging than a tighter cone of fire, but the greater dispersion of bullets made the probability of obtaining a hit more likely for the average pilot. Against Japanese aircraft, which lacked pilot armor protection and self-sealing fuel tanks, a few hits could be lethal.

Japanese Armament and Aircraft Equipment

Armament

The French and British Air Missions to Japan after WWI allowed the JNAF and JAAF to purchase the machine guns of the Western Allies. Thus, in the inter-war years, the Japanese showed very little originality in their aircraft armament, except in modifying foreign designs, such as those of Great Britain, the United States, Switzerland, and Germany.

At the start of the Pacific War, several license-built modified, synchronized (through the propeller arc) WWI-style rifle caliber machine guns were in use by both the JNAF and JAAF, along with several original designs. During the war, some progress was made in developing larger caliber machine guns and cannon. JAAF guns of 11mm or less were referred to a "machine guns," while those of 11mm plus were called "machine cannon." The JNAF only used the term "machine gun" to describe any automatic gun of any size used on an aircraft.

Japanese aircraft armament showed a far reaching failure to standardize on any one particular weapon for each caliber size. The JNAF and JAAF carried out multiple separate developmental projects that produced an unparalleled variety of aircraft weapons requiring various types of ammunition. For example, the Japanese air forces required a .50 caliber aircraft machine gun and the Japanese decided to adopt the tried-and-true American Browning. However, the JNAF and JAAF had each deployed their own developmental and engineering staffs to develop the .50 caliber machine gun in separate projects. With this duplicate effort, there was the opportunity to combine the best of each into a standardized production version, but instead, each service insisted on adhering to specific, but minor, design variations and each began to manufacture its own .50 caliber machine gun. The result was that both Browning actions were not quite identical to allow for interchangeability. To make matters worse, each service adopted a different cartridge design: the JNAF a .51 cartridge and the JAAF a .50.

Major Japanese Aircraft Guns

Model	Caliber (mm.)	Weight, pounds	Length, inches	Type of operation	Rate of fire rpm	Type of feed	Quantity rounds	Remarks
Army Type 89 Navy Type 97	7.7	27	40.75	Recoil	700- 900	Belt	70	Vickers type
Navy Type 92	7.7	13.6	38.6	Gas	600	Drum	97	Lewis Copy
Army Type 98 Navy Type 1	7.92	15.5	42.5	Recoil	1000-1100	Saddle drum	75	Flexible. Copy of German MG 15/MG17
Navy Type 99	20	57.5	55	Recoil	450	Drum Belt	60-200	Oerlikon Copy
Army Type 100 (Ho-103)	13	50.2	49.9	Recoil	400- 900	Belt	350	Browning Model 1921 Copy
Army Type 2 (Ho-5)	20	81	55.1	Recoil	750-850	Belt	120	Hispano-Suiza Browning Type

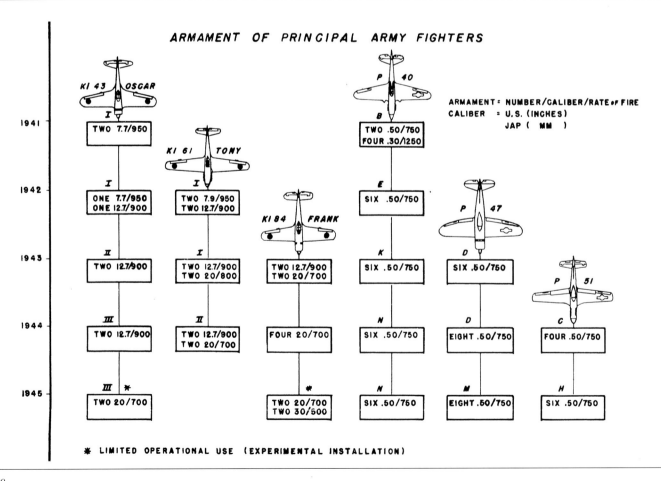

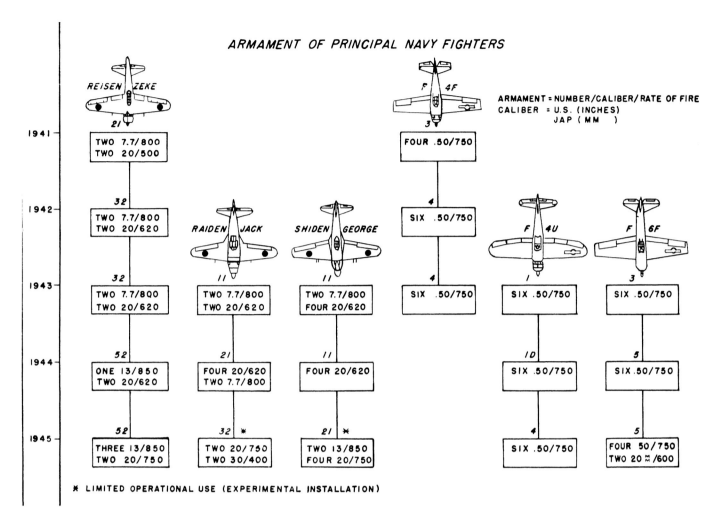

ARMAMENT OF PRINCIPAL NAVY FIGHTERS

ARMAMENT = NUMBER/CALIBER/RATE OF FIRE
CALIBER = U.S. (INCHES)
JAP (MM)

* LIMITED OPERATIONAL USE (EXPERIMENTAL INSTALLATION)

The Zero mounted two rifle caliber (7.7mm/.303 caliber) machine guns (Army Type 89/Navy Type 97 Lewis-derived) and two 20mm (Navy Type 99 Oerlikon-derived) cannons, but both had significant drawbacks. The rifle caliber machine gun fired rapidly, but the bullet's weight was inadequate to cause lethal damage to the heavily-built American fighters and bombers unless the Japanese pilot was a marksman or very lucky. A rifle caliber machine gun round, unlike a .50 caliber round, could not penetrate pilot armor at most angles and would pierce much smaller holes in fuel tanks, and probably not do fatal damage to an engine block. Furthermore, while the range of a light machine gun was about 600 yards, in combat, it had to be fired at least 300 yards or closer to be effective. Cannons and heavy machine guns hypothetically offered longer range, but considering contemporary gunsights, most kills were made much inside their effective range. Outstanding marksmen, which Japan possessed early in the war, used the Zero's maneuverability to fire a long burst at very close range with light machine guns, then fired their cannons. The Japanese attempted to copy the Browning .50 caliber (12.7mm) machine gun, and while successful, it did not synchronize well as a fixed mount, where it lost its high rate of fire and was relegated to flexible use. The JAAF's primary fighter in the early war was the Oscar, which was even more lightly armed than the Zero, mounting two fixed forward-firing 12.7mm (.50 inch) Ho-103 machine guns in the cowl with 250rpg.

The ballistic qualities of Japanese light machine guns and cannons were poor. Despite their theoretical range, it was crucial for the Japanese pilot to get as close as possible with light machine guns, especially during a stern attack, when the bullet lost impact as the target moved farther away.

Theoretically, cannons should have compensated for this problem, but actually, the Japanese 20mm cannon was a mediocre weapon with a low rate of fire and poor muzzle velocity. The JAAF Type 2 20mm (Ho-**5**) cannon was potentially the best 20mm aircraft cannon of the war, but suffered due to manufacture with inferior materials and by relatively unskilled labor. Additionally, to reduce drag on early Zero models, the cannon barrels were made as short as possible, which further decreased the cannon's ballistic properties. Thus, it was much more difficult for a Japanese pilot to hit a target with the slow-firing 20mm cannon, which were fed by only 60 rounds, than with the faster-firing light machine guns supplied by many more rounds. Mitsubishi and other Japanese designers, aware of the relative invulnerability of Allied medium and heavy bombers to machine guns, began to develop new fighters with multiple cannons. However, Mitsubishi did not dramatically improve the Zero's armaments throughout the war and it remained a fighter with mediocre armament and very poor defensive qualities.

Second generation Japanese fighters were armed with heavy machine guns (12.7mm/.50 caliber) and cannon to cope with the rugged Allied fighters and to shoot down Allied bombers menacing Japanese bases and shipping:

Tony: 2× 20 mm Ho-5 cannon (120 rpg each gun) and 2× 12.7 mm Ho-103 machine guns (250 rpg each gun)

Tojo: 4× 12.7 mm Ho-103 machine guns, two synchronized cowl mounted and one in each wing (760 rounds total).

Jack: 4 × 20 mm Type 99 cannons, two in each wing, (inboard guns having 190 rpg, outboard guns 210 rpg).

Frank: 2× 12.7 mm Ho-103 machine guns in nose (350 rounds/gun) and 2× 20 mm Ho-5 cannon in wings (150 shells/cannon)

George: 4× 20 mm Type 99 Model 2 Mk 4 cannon in wings (200 rpg)

Gunsights

Japanese gunsights ranged from the basic Fixed Ring and Bead sights to the Telescopic to the Reflector sights, and near the end of the war to an experimental Gyroscopic Computing Lead sight. The most important and most used gunsights were the JNAF Type 98 Reflector, which was a copy of the early German Revi gunsights(from a purchased He-112 fighter). The Type 98 was used on the Zero, Jack, George II, Rufe, Judy, and Irving. The JAAF Type 100 Reflector sight was developed by the Japanese and was installed on the Oscar, Tony, Tojo, Nick, and early Frank fighters. These gunsights were considered adequate, but did not reach the technological standards or quality of Allied gunsights.

Thomas McGuire on Japanese Gunnery: "It is a seeming contradiction to say that Japanese gunnery is good, but results don't show it. The discrepancy lies in the poor quality of the guns and the lack of convergence, factors which reduce the theoretical firepower and which have saved many of our pilots from being hit when the Japanese gunner had his lead and timing absolutely right. Don't underestimate Japanese gunnery!"

13mm (.50 cal.) **Ho-103** machine gun mounted in Ki-61 Tony. (AAF)

JAAF **Type 89 Telescope Sight** mounted on a Ki-43 Oscar. (Author)

40mm **Ho-301 cannon** mounted on a Ki-44 Tojo captured at Clark Field 1 February 1945. (AAF)

JNAF **Type 98 Gunsight**, which was commonly used on the A6M Zero. (Author/NMUSAF)

5

Pilot Protection and Safety Equipment

AAF Pilot Protection and Safety Equipment

Armor

Theoretically, the ideal means to protect the pilot would be to armor the entire aircraft so that there would be no vulnerable areas. Of course, this aircraft would probably be so heavy that it would be unable to get off the ground. So aircraft designers attempted to find a compromise between the "maximum protection/minimum weight" formulas in their designs. The ever-increasing speeds of the fighter during the war meant that the 400mph+ fighter flew so fast as compared to rate of fire of machine guns and cannon that bullet holes were four inches or more apart. So, unless the pilot or a vital area of the fighter was hit, the wide dispersal of bullet strikes gave the aircraft a protection to hits. Aircraft speed not only dispersed the hits, but also brought about changes in the angles the bullets struck a rapidly moving aircraft. Knowing the angles from which enemy attack was most probable, designers were able to strategically locate the armor plate. Stopping and deflecting the bullet were two ways to protect a pilot. To stop bullets, a heavy armored plate was placed behind the propeller hub, in front of the cockpit (to stop bullets from the front not stopped by the engine and hub plate), and a heavy armor bulkhead was placed behind the pilot's seat to stop bullets hitting from the rear. When ground strafing became more prevalent a floor plate was fitted. To save weight, these bulkheads were placed as close to the pilot as possible so he could hide directly behind them, and thus they could be made smaller than if they were placed further away. This armor plate was a nickel-alloy steel known as X-7440, and was either face-hardened or homogeneous. Face-hardened, as its name indicates, had the front face of the plate hardened, while the homogeneous was uniformly hard throughout. The face-hardened plate was preferred, as when a bullet struck it only a small coin-size piece fell off the plate, while the homogeneous plate tended to shatter. Also, in plate thicker than 3/8 of an inch, face-hardened was lighter and had a higher ballistic limit (e.g., bullet resistance). Face-hardened was less adaptable to mass production methods, however, and required complex heat treatment and therefore cost more.

Another method of protecting the pilot while reducing weight was to fit the fighter with aluminum alloy deflector plates to protect the cockpit and engine. The engine was protected by curved aluminum plates on top and under the cowling to protect the engine and pilot from bullets from a head-on attack. Deflector plates were placed at the left and right sides of the cockpit to deflect bullets fired at angles from the rear. All armor needed to be accessible and was bolted for easy removal and repair in case of hits.

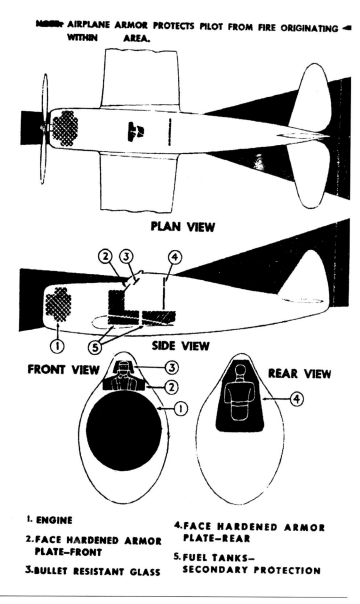

AIRPLANE ARMOR PROTECTS PILOT FROM FIRE ORIGINATING WITHIN AREA.

PLAN VIEW

SIDE VIEW

FRONT VIEW

REAR VIEW

1. ENGINE

2. FACE HARDENED ARMOR PLATE–FRONT

3. BULLET RESISTANT GLASS

4. FACE HARDENED ARMOR PLATE–REAR

5. FUEL TANKS– SECONDARY PROTECTION

Bullet-Proof Windscreens

Windscreens presented a particular problem, because laminated glass needed to be very thick and thus was heavy because of its low ballistic limit; a one square foot piece 1.5 inches thick weighed 30 pounds. This thickness stopped the penetration of a .30 caliber bullet, while twice that thickness was required to stop a .50 caliber bullet (0.5 inch of armor plate could do the same). Armored glass was manufactured by taking sections of highly polished glass and sandwiching them between sheets of transparent plastic, then bonding them under very high heat and pressure. Because laminated glass does not resist bullets at right angles, it was set at deflection angles as close as possible to the pilot's eyes. Armored glass stopped a bullet by breaking it up and absorbing the pieces between the layers of glass. At the point of impact the glass powdered, starred, and cracked three inches around impact.

Crazed **Bullet-Resistant Glass** installed on a P-47. (AAF)

Self-sealing Fuel Tanks

Self-sealing fuel tanks (cells) were fabricated of hard, thick-formed rubber in two layers with a gel-like substance sandwiched between the inner and outer layers of rubber. The gel expanded when it contacted gasoline, so when a bullet penetrated the tank, gasoline leaked into the gel, which expanded to close the hole. When the damaged aircraft returned to base, the hole could be easily repaired by placing a piece of rubber in the hole.

All fuel cells were constructed of three parts (lining, sealant, and outer retaining covering), all of which consisted of seven plies. The inner, two-ply liner was the oil (gasoline) resistant layer that acted as the container. It was made of Buna-N, a synthetic rubber first derived from acetylene by the Germans in the city of Buna in 1934. This liner had oil resistant and excellent adhesive qualities and was backed by rayon or nylon fabric. The sealant layer was made of three plies sealed with compound rubber. Two of the sealant plies were made from Buna-S, which was a synthetic rubber with good mechanical and bonding properties, could blend with natural rubber, and most important, swelled when it came in contact with aromatic fuels. The third sealant ply was a cord fabric impregnated with natural and Buna-S rubbers, whose cords ran lengthwise down the cell. The two-ply outer retainer gave the fuel cell its strength and support and increased the efficiency of the mechanism that restored the punctured area to its original shape. One outer covering ply was a cord fabric similar to the third sealant ply, but applied at a 45° angle to the cell. The outer sealant ply was similar to the third and sixth plies, except that it was impregnated with Buna-N instead of Buna-S.

Self-sealing fuel tanks (cells) were fabricated of hard, thick-formed rubber in two layers with a gel-like substance sandwiched between the inner and outer layers. (AAF)

Parachutes

The standard U.S. fighter parachute was the Type S-1 or AN6510 seat type with cushion. The ripcord handle was located on the left side. It had snap fasteners for the three-point harness release: one on the chest and one on each leg strap. The Type S-1 had a 24-foot nylon canopy, while the S-2, with a 28-foot nylon canopy, was designed for pilots weighing over 180 pounds. The harness was constructed of flexible or nylon webbing. The primary element was the main lift web, which passed from the connector links at the hips in slings around each leg connecting to the shoulder straps, which were secured by a fastener across the chest and criss-crossed the back. The rip cord assembly was a 31-inch metal cord which attached to a "D" ring. The S-1 was replaced by the AN6510 (S-**5**) and the S-2 by the AN6511 (S-6) in 1943, and were almost identical to their predecessors except for minor differences in cushions, chest straps, and fasteners. The B-7 was standardized in October 1940, and featured the standard 24-foot canopy with a three-point harness release and a waistband to hold it close to the body. In June 1942, the B-7 was standardized for Army/Navy use as the AN6512 (the AN designated ArmyNavy). P-38 and P-47 pilots wore the S-1 or AN6510 with the C-type dinghy backpack while P-51 pilots wore the B-8 backpack parachute and the dinghy pack as the cushion. The pilots carried a sheafed ankle knife to cut away the heavy parachute/dinghy pack in case it was necessary, such as in a ditching.

AN 6510/S-1 Parachute (AAF)

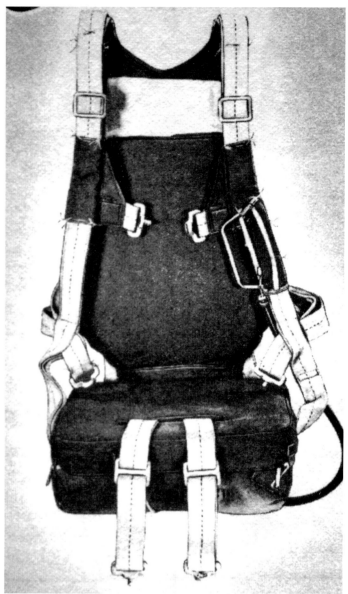

AN 6512/B-7 Parachute (AAF)

One Man Dinghy

The AN6520-1 one man parachute type pneumatic life raft was widely used by Army and Navy fighter pilots. The raft fit into a parachute pack, which was stowed on the pilot's seat or fastened to his parachute harness by snap rings. Its weight with accessories was 16 pounds and inflated dimensions were 66x40x12 inches. The accessory pack contained a CO_2 cylinder, sail, sea anchor, bailing cup, pair of hand paddles, can of drinking water, first aid kit, repair kit, bullet hole plugs, three cotton cord, and a can of sea marker.

Life Vests

The B-3 and B-4 life vest was dubbed the "Mae West" by the British after the buxom 1930s Hollywood star. It was constructed from rubber and bright yellow canvas and worn over all flight clothing. Two small CO_2 cylinders inflated each of the two inflatable bladders in the chest compartments and were supplemented by mouth tube to each bladder. The vest weighed about four pounds. In early 1944, the B-4 was designated AN6519-1.

Oxygen Equipment

Two main kinds of oxygen systems were used by pilots and crews in WWII who flew at high altitudes: Continuous Flow and Diluter Demand.

Continuous Flow Oxygen System

In a continuous flow system, oxygen was provided to the user continuously. Oxygen flowed from the time the system was started whether or not the user was exhaling or inhaling. A rebreather bag or reservoir bag below the oxygen mask collected oxygen during exhalation and allowed a higher aspiratory flow rate during the inhalation cycle, which reduced the amount of air dilution and as a result allowed a higher flow rate during the inhalation cycle. Ambient air was added to the supplied oxygen during inhalation after the reservoir bag oxygen supply was depleted. The exhaled air was released into the cabin.

All oxygen readings for the continuous flow oxygen system were provided by an oxygen flow indicator portion and oxygen pressure gauge portion of an oxygen regulator. The oxygen flow indicator portion indicated the altitude at which sufficient oxygen flow was present at the oxygen mask. The oxygen

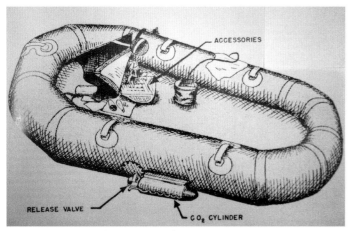

AN6520-1 **One man** Parachute type Pneumatic **Life Raft**. (AAF)

Life Raft Rations (AAF)

Mae West Deflated

Mae West Inflated

The **AN6519 B-4 Life Vest** was dubbed the "Mae West". (AAF)

flow indicator had graduations of 5,000 feet from 0 to 35,000 feet. The oxygen pressure gauge portion indicated in 50 pounds per square inch graduations from 0 to 500psi.

It soon became apparent that the Continuous Flow System would not be adequate for long combat missions, as the face masks would freeze at low temperatures, oxygen was wasted at low altitudes, and at high altitudes, with high pilot activity, there needed to be an insured adequate supply. But it would be months—early Spring 1943—before aircraft would be equipped with the new Demand Oxygen System.

Diluter Demand Oxygen System

In a Diluter Demand System, as the altitude increased (ambient pressure, and therefore, the partial pressure of ambient oxygen decreased) the oxygen flow increased, so that the partial pressure of oxygen was roughly constant.

The Diluter Demand Oxygen System supplied oxygen from cylinders to a regulator outlet. The components for the Diluter Demand Oxygen System were a large shatterproof oxygen cylinder, a regulator, an oxygen flow indicator, and an oxygen pressure gauge. All readings for the Diluter Demand Oxygen System were provided by an oxygen flow indicator and

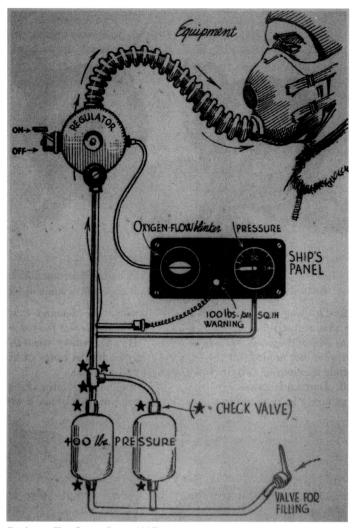

Continuous Flow Oxygen System (AAF)

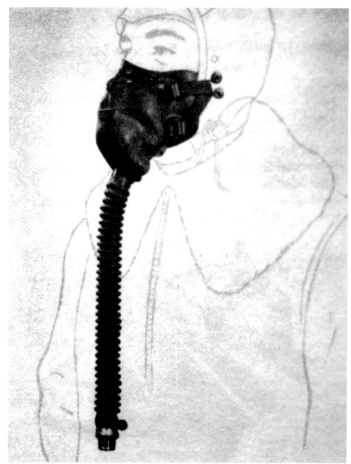

Type 10 Demand Oxygen Mask (AAF)

an oxygen pressure gauge. The oxygen flow indicator indicated oxygen flow by means of a blinker activated by the breathing of the user. The indicator did not function unless the mask was in use and oxygen was being delivered to it.

The Diluter Demand regulators were essentially diaphragm operated flow valves, which were opened by suction (inspiration) and closed automatically when the suction stopped. The regulator delivered a mixture of oxygen and air containing an increasing proportion of oxygen as the altitude of the airplane increased. At approximately 34,000 feet, 100% oxygen was supplied and could be used up to 40,000 feet. A red knob on the regulator could be used for emergency 100% oxygen and also to exhaust the system.

The oxygen flow indicator provided a visual indication of the operation of the regulator unit by blinking at each inspiration of the crewman wearing the oxygen mask. The flow indicator was located adjacent to the regulator outlet and was connected to the regulator by tubing. Oxygen pressure was indicated by a pressure gauge. A filler valve was installed in the system for the purpose of recharging the aircraft oxygen system and had a check valve to prevent the escape of oxygen from the filler line. The necessary connecting tubing used in the low pressure diluter demand oxygen system was mounted on cushioned clips to reduce vibration and chafing.

Oxygen Masks

Type 9
The Type 9 Demand Oxygen Mask was the first demand-type oxygen mask and was standardized in December 1941. It was produced on a limited basis and replaced by the improved and superior Type 10 mask. This mask was difficult to attach and fit, as it came in only two sizes.

Type 10 (A10A)
The Type 10 Demand Oxygen Mask was similar to the A9 and was standardized in April 1942; it was identifiable by its distinctive nose strap that crossed the top of the mask and ran between the wearer's eyes. This mask was considered uncomfortable and frequently slid down over the pilot's face during diving pullouts; it was also subject to freezing. The Type A10A mask deleted the nose strap, modified the shape of the mask, and used a two-point harness that snapped to the helmet. Though replaced by the Type 14, it was not declared obsolete until March 1946.

Type 14 (A14A)
The Type 14 Demand Oxygen Mask was standardized in July 1943, and was considered one of the best oxygen masks of the war, as it utilized all the experience gained from previous masks. It consisted of a medium green rubber face piece, corrugated oxygen delivery tube and attaching straps, and an integral microphone pocket. It operated on the intermittent flow principal, in which oxygen was only furnished when the pilot inhaled. The slight suction caused during each inhalation operated the demand regulator, causing it to open and supply oxygen to the mask. When the pilot exhaled,

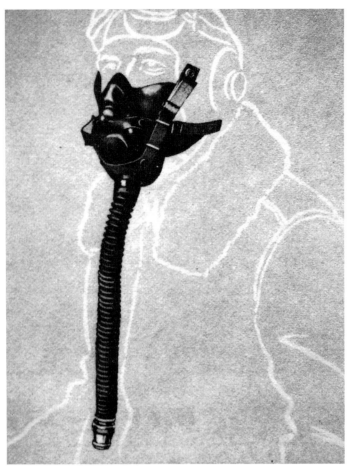

Type 14 Demand Oxygen Mask (AAF)

P-47 Razor Back: Turtleback area just aft of the canopy. Bubble canopy: One on each leading edge section of the wing ahead of the forward spar and just outboard of the fuselage
P-51: Allison Mustangs: Two cylinders in the fuselage aft of the cockpit.
Rolls Royce Mustangs: Two Type D-2 low pressure cylinders and two Type F-2 cylinders in the aft fuselage.

Drop Tanks

Of the developments which affected the course of the air war, the jettisonable auxiliary fuel tank was one of the most significant. The "belly" or "drop" tank gave the fighter extended range, allowing it to provide continuous escort to bomber formations or reach deeper into enemy territory on fighter bomber missions. For example, during 1942, it became evident that the P-47 did not have sufficient range for bomber escort duties and various wing-mounted tanks were tried, ranging from two 75 gallon steel tanks to two 108 gallon metal or composition paper tanks to two 150 gallon steel tanks. Single fuselage centerline 108 gallon paper or steel, 150 gallon steel, and/or 200 gallon paper or steel tanks were used. The P-51, which had very good range without tanks, used two wing-mounted 108 gallon paper tanks as more or less the standard drop tank. The P-38 generally used two 165 gallon steel tanks.

200-gallon **Drop Tank** being filled on a F-5 Photo P-38. (AAF)

the demand regulator automatically shut off and the exhalation flowed out of the mask through the flutter valve. The A14 was modified to the A14A to reduce icing, which was not as big a problem in the tropics as it was in the ETO.

Oxygen Mask Use

1) Oxygen masks were to be carried on all flights where the altitude could exceed 10,600 feet.
2) Oxygen use was to start at 7,000 to 10,000 feet on all daytime flights where altitude at any time could exceed 12,000 feet.
3) Oxygen was to be used on all daytime flights at 8,000 feet or above when the duration of the flight could exceed four hours.
4) Oxygen was to be used from the ground up on all night flights during which altitude could reach 16,000 feet.

An outlet tube extended outward from the bottom of each regulator and the hose from the oxygen mask slipped over this tube. A low pressure rubber tube connected the mask to the regulator. When oxygen was not being drawn from a regulator, the valve was to be completely closed to prevent leakage. The small valve at the bottom of the re-breather bag was used for draining off any water collecting in the bag. A weak solution of creosol was used to clean and sterilize the mask parts.

Oxygen Cylinder Placement in AAF Fighter Aircraft

P-39: Armament compartment in the fuselage forward section with additional tanks in the leading edge of the wing
P-40: Fuselage aft of the pilot
P-38: Three bottles: two in the port boom and the other in the starboard

The auxiliary tank was attached behind the center of gravity or in tandem under each wing, which affected handling characteristics. To remedy this situation, after using the main wing tank for takeoff the pilot switched to the fuselage tank and used it until there were about 30 gallons remaining. He then switched to and alternated between the external drop tanks, changing from one to another about every three quarters of an hour to an hour, and when they were empty he jettisoned them. He then had the 30 gallons of fuselage fuel and a large amount of wing tank fuel left for combat and to return to base. But if a drop tank did not deliver fuel to the engine or did not release the sortie needed to be aborted, not only for the troubled fighter, but also for another pilot assigned to escort him back to base.

The lighter plastic impregnated (laminated) paper tanks were preferred to steel tanks by ground crews because they were easier to manhandle and by pilots because they had less effect on flight characteristics. However, paper tanks could not store fuel for an extended period of time, though they worked quite well for the time it took to fly a single mission. These tanks were cheaper, lighter in weight, and were useless to the enemy if recovered after being dropped, as not only did they break apart, but they did not provide the enemy with any reusable materials that could be scavenged for their own war effort. However, fighters could not land with the tanks in place because of the hazard of rupture and explosion. Fighters recalled from a mission or that had not jettisoned them for some reason were required to drop paper tanks into a safe designated "dump" area near their respective fields, resulting in substantial losses of aviation fuel.

Aircraft Fuels

American fighter aircraft operated on 100 Octane, 130 grade aircraft engine fuel (AN-VV-F-781). The Octane scale—the rating of a fuel—was developed by Dr. Russell Marker of the Ethyl Corp. in 1933. It is a mathematical grade assigned to a fuel in direct proportion to its ability to withstand pre-ignition (premature firing) and detonation (how much the fuel can be compressed before it spontaneously ignites). Two reference fuels were chosen: iso-octane and normal heptane. Used in a test engine, these fuels respond identically under identical conditions. To rate a new fuel it is compared to these preference fuels. If it matches the anti-knock ability of iso-octane it is rated as 100 grade fuel. If its performance is less, normal heptane is added to the iso-octane. Thus, if a fuel matches in performance a mixture of 87% iso-octane and 13% normal heptane it is rated as 87 grade fuel.

A "high-performance" aircraft engine has a higher compression ratio (the ratio between the volume of a combustion chamber and cylinder, when the piston is at the bottom of its stroke and the volume when the piston is at the top of its stroke) and requires higher octane fuel. The advantage of a high compression ratio is that it gives the engine a higher horsepower rating for a given engine weight (e.g., "high performance"), but is more expensive.

During WWI, it was discovered that tetraethyl lead (TEL) could be added to gasoline to appreciably enhance its Octane Rating above the octane/heptane combination. Thus, less expensive grades of gasoline could be made usable for aircraft by adding TEL, which was known as AvGas (which years later was banned, as it added toxic lead to the atmosphere). 100 AvGas is the gasoline's performance rating, not the percentage of actual Octane of the gasoline. The addition of lead increases the compression level of the gasoline but does not add more Octane.

Japanese Pilot Protection and Safety Equipment

Armor

The Japanese did not consider aircraft armor until 1939, when they found that the Russian bombers used by the Chinese had armor sheet installed. However, the requirements for armor installation did not become pressing until the beginning of the Pacific War, when they captured a B-17 and began a systematic study of U.S. aircraft armor. Nickel, chrome, and manganese steel alloys were developed with optimum sheet thickness of 16mm being adopted as standard, as it could stop U.S. armor-piercing and high explosive ammunition. Generally, basic pilot back and seat armor were added to most new fighters and over time armor was also added to protect vulnerable equipment. When installed, Japanese fighter armor weighed between 88 and 110 pounds and was generally mounted behind the pilot. Bomber armor weighed up to 265 pounds and was distributed between the pilot, copilot, and gunner. Despite the development of this armor, some new aircraft types were designed without either armor or bullet-proof glass. Provisions were made for the armor to be detachable at the pilot's or unit's discretion, and since the weight of the armor decreased aircraft performance, many pilots had it removed.

Japanese aircraft have long been considered as being poorly constructed of inferior materials and thus structurally weaker than their rugged Allied counterparts. In their effort to lighten their aircraft structure, the Japanese did not do so at the expense of safety or structural integrity and there was not much difference in Japanese and American aircraft construction techniques and materials. In fact, Japanese aluminum alloy skin had basically the same

properties as American aluminum alloys. Zero wing spars were constructed of Extra Super Duraluminum (ESD), which the Americans could not match during the war. The postwar U.S. Strategic Bombing Survey (USBBS) stated that so as long as the Japanese aircraft industry had materials available, its construction standards generally equaled those of the Allies. However, because of their lighter construction, Japanese aircraft were more vulnerable to the impact of .50 caliber bullets.

Oxygen Equipment

Generally, the Japanese reserved oxygen systems for high-flying medium bomber crews (most Japanese bombers were actually medium bombers). The design of Japanese oxygen systems were based on early European systems, and while their parts were generally considered good, the basic principles used were not considered to be very good. The Japanese used the low pressure system because of the vulnerability of the high pressure system. The Japanese oxygen system usually consisted of the following parts: oxygen bottle(s), pressure reducing regulator, pressure gauges, automatic regulator, and masks or tubes. There were two types of bottles: a forged cylinder and a drawn and welded bottle, with neither being protected by either armor or wire wrappings to prevent shattering. The well-designed automatic regulator's oxygen flow was shut off until 10,000 feet was reached, at which altitude an aneroid moved the metering needle, allowing oxygen to pass through the outlet. As the war progressed, rubber became scarce and rubber sealed masks gave way to triangular aluminum frames sealed by leather or felt.

Parachutes

Contrary to popular belief, Japanese pilots and crew were equipped with parachutes. The Japanese used a quickly attachable seat type parachute for their fighter pilots and other smaller aircraft, and another type parachute for their bomber and transport crews. The material in the canopy and shrouds

Well-equipped Japanese fighter pilot on display at the NMUSAF. (NMUSAF/Author)

was a good quality silk and was held in the pack by a series of hook-ended bungee cords. The Type 97 harness and pack were made of good quality cotton, but the harness was not as strong as the American type. The Type 97 harness was preferred, as it could be easily detached (and reattached) and left in the aircraft while the pilot was on standby on the ground. In general, except for the advantageous four silk shrouds, this type parachute was considered inferior to those made in the United States. However, being able to parachute from a stricken aircraft during long-range missions to attack American bases was a moot point, as the Japanese had no organized system of Air-Sea Rescue (an estimated 540 Allied airmen were rescued by PBY Catalina Flying Boats protected by fighters). After the Japanese went on the defensive, protecting their air bases, many Japanese pilots were able to bail out over friendly territory.

Fuel Tank Protection
The JNAF had investigated self-sealing fuel tanks in the late 1930s, and sent a team to England during the Battle of Britain to gather information which was used to begin experiments in April 1941 at their Naval Ordnance Depot. The JAAF showed somewhat more interest in fuel tank protection, covering the fuel tanks of their Type 97 Heavy Bombers with a thin rubber sheet and thin fabric covering before the Allies did so on their bombers, then later added this rubber sheet on their Type K-27 fighters. While the JAAF applied this makeshift protection to its fuel tanks into 1943, the JNAF continued its research to find a truly effective self-sealing tank. By March 1943, the Navy Ordnance Depot finally felt it had developed an adequate "leak-absorbing" tank, but it was composed of a sponge rubber of which there were no large-scale production facilities. Thus, the Depot left future self-sealing research to aircraft manufacturers, who proceeded very slowly. The JAAF continued its research and developed a "leak-proof" tank which was adopted by many JNAF aircraft. The JNAF, unlike the JAAF, was reluctant to reduce the size and capacity of the rubber-sheaved core aluminum

tank and also did not pursue the manufacturing technology involved in the development of an all rubber self-sealing fuel tank.

After foregoing fuel tank protection during the early war, the Japanese later introduced three main types of fuel tank protection toward the end of the war:
• "Leak absorbing" was the first generation of tank and was the least effective, consisting of four layers of natural rubber joined together and totaling 0.125 inch in thickness, then covered by kapok matting, which in turn was covered by a silvered fabric resembling balloon silk.
• "Leak-proofing" was the next generation, appearing in late 1943, and was composed mostly of heavy crude rubber in two layers about a 0.5 inch thick over an aluminum tank.
• "Self-sealing" tanks were introduced in 1945, and were considered nearly equivalent to Allied self-sealing tanks. They were .125 inch thick and comprised of six rubber layers reinforced by an inner silken mesh and an outer galvanized iron mesh. The self-sealing properties were considered to be fair, with only the outer surface effective. The tanks proved to be too bulky and heavy for the light fighter airframes, but were used in their bomber types. Persistent leaking was a major problem for Japanese self-sealing tanks.

The increased usage of incendiary ammunition by the Allies and the ineffectiveness of their self-sealing tanks caused the Japanese to abandon further self-sealing tank development as too complicated, especially in view of an increasing shortage of rubber.

Fuels
The Japanese fuels were considered good, although some contained a rather high amount of aromatics. As the supplies of oil became reduced in October 1944, the Japanese looked to adapt their aircraft to use alcohol from potatoes and sugar as a substitute fuel. The Japanese intended to convert all aircraft to alcohol, but by the end of the war only training aircraft had been converted.

PART 4:
Air Tactics and Combat

In volumes 1 and 2, the Individual Combat Reports (ICRs) written by pilots after a mission would relate their aerial duels, often describing how the Squadron, Flights, Elements, and individual pilots would use established tactics to gain the advantage on or escape from their Japanese opponents, who would in turn use similar tactics for similar purposes. The next chapters will try to explain the deadly aerial chess match from the basic physics of flight in relation to the aircraft and pilot, then continue by describing the general tenets of air combat and then the specific tactics used by the 5th Fighter Command and the JNAF and JAAF. I wish to thank Steve Ferguson for his drawings of these principals and tactics, which prove that a picture is worth a thousand words.

Goal of Air Combat
Fighters and bombers exist for only one reason: to destroy enemy aircraft and targets on the ground. During and after WWI, aircraft and weapons evolved to accomplish this purpose rapidly and effectively. Even before WWII, it became evident that the outcome of all future wars would be mainly determined by which side could achieve and maintain air superiority. The goal of each combatant was to ensure that friendly aircraft could freely patrol the skies over vital areas while denying that same freedom to the enemy. Whoever controlled the skies had a definite advantage, as that power could conduct strategic bombing attacks, support and supply front line forces, conduct reconnaissance, and slow or contain enemy advances.

Once airpower established itself as a major instrument of war, WWII became a testing ground for aerial combat equipment and technique. The monoplane fighters built in the 1930s and 1940s were faster, stronger, and more intimidating than the biplanes of the past and required the development of new combat techniques. Many of the methods of air combat developed by combat pilots were based on experience rather than theory, and many of their time-tested techniques continue in use today and are taught in combat aviation schools around the world.

Combat can either be offensive or defensive, thoroughly planned or spontaneous, and most importantly, victorious or fatal. Much of success in the air is due to training, but just as often depended upon a pilot's natural ability and instincts. An outstanding combat pilot had a good understanding of the basics, but also possessed an inherent aptitude for air combat.

Air combat has several discrete phases which do not necessarily occur linearly, but in reality, combat is most often a constantly changing combination of the five:
1) Detecting the enemy
2) Positioning for an attack
3) Maneuvering during combat
4) Firing guns
5) Defending during an attack
   Part 4 will discuss and tie all these phases together.

1

Physics of Flight

Flight is possible because man has created the technology to oppose the natural forces that keep all objects on the ground. Four forces affect an aircraft: two assist flight (thrust and lift) and two resist flight (gravity and drag), and when an aircraft is flying straight and level these forces are balanced, or in equilibrium.

Lift

Lift is the key aerodynamic force, as it opposes weight. As the wings cut through the air in front of the aircraft, air flows both over and under the surface of the wing and lift is created. It is this force that pushes an aircraft up into the air. The wing is designed so that the top surface is longer (front to rear) than the bottom surface (front to rear) in any given cross section. Air moving over the wing must travel the longer distance on the top of the

wing in the same amount of time as the shorter distance on the bottom. Therefore, the air is moving faster along the top of the wing, which creates a difference in air pressure above and below, an occurrence called the Bernoulli Effect. The pressure pushing up is greater than the downward pressure and lift is created. When the aircraft is banking lift occurs in a slightly sideways direction. When the aircraft is inverted, lift actually pulls it downward toward the ground. Several factors determine how much lift is created. First, consider the angle at which the wing hits the air—called the angle of attack—which is independent of the aircraft's flight path vector. The steeper this angle, the more lift occurs.

At angles steeper than 30° or so, however, airflow is disrupted (i.e., airflow is separated from the wing's upper surface), resulting in a rapid decrease in lift called a stall. During a stall, no lift is created and the aircraft

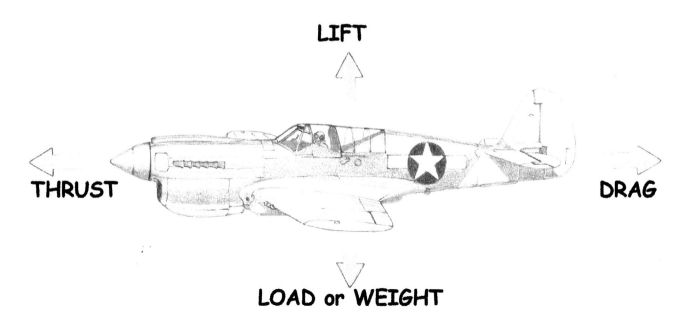

BASIC FORCES

LIFT

THRUST

DRAG

LOAD or WEIGHT

Falls into a dive and can recover lift only after regaining airspeed. An aircraft always stalls at the same angle (called the stalling or critical angle of attack), no matter the airspeed, flight attitude, or weight.

Thrust

Thrust is the forward acting force created by the engines that opposes drag. As propeller blades push air past the airplane it moves forward. During straight and level unaccelerated flight, lift and drag are equal. Thrust is increased by using the throttle to increase power; thrust exceeds drag and the aircraft accelerates. This acceleration is accompanied by an increase in drag until thrust again equals drag and the aircraft is flying at a higher speed.

Drag

Drag opposes the direction of flight and thrust. Drag mainly occurs because of simple "skin friction" (parasitic drag), as the aircraft's surface deflects or interferes with the smooth flow of air over these surfaces (i.e., air molecules "stick" to the aircraft surface). Some drag does not involve air resistance and is actually a secondary result of lift. Because lift angles backward slightly, it has both an upward, vertical force and a horizontal, rearward force. The rearward component is drag, called induced drag. Another type of drag is generated at speeds near Mach 1, when a pressure differential begins building up between the front and rear surface of the airfoil. The pressure in front of the wing is greater than the pressure behind the wing, which creates a net force that opposes thrust. In the aircraft of WWI, this last type of drag occurred only during prolonged, high-speed dives.

Gravity and G-Forces

Gravity is actually a force of acceleration on an object. The Earth exerts this natural force on all objects. As it is a constant force, it always acts in the same downward direction. Thrust creates lift to counteract gravity. In order for an aircraft to take off, enough lift must be created to overcome the force of gravity pushing down on the aircraft.

Related to gravity are G-forces, which are artificially created forces that are measured in units equivalent to the force of gravity. A "G" is a measurement of force that is equal to the force of gravity pushing down on a stationary object on the earth's surface. Gravitational force actually refers to an object's weight (Force equals Mass times Acceleration, or F=MA). An aircraft flying level at low altitudes experiences 1G. Extra G-forces in any direction can be artificially created by sudden changes in velocity or in the direction of motion.

G-forces can be either positive or negative. Positive Gs make a person feel heavier, because they act in a relatively downward direction (e.g., they push a person back into his seat and primarily occur during sharp turns or steep climbs). Negative Gs make a person feel lighter, because they are pulling in a relatively upward direction. When a person is in a steep dive, Gs pull him out of his seat. The direction of G-forces is always relative to the position of the aircraft; if flying inverted, upward Gs actually pull in a downward direction.

Apparent weight refers to how heavy something seems considering the current direction and magnitude of G-forces acting on it. In level flight, 1G is acting on the aircraft and the pilot and both weigh the same as they do when stationary. If the pilot makes a steep climb, the positive G-force temporarily acts on both the pilot and the aircraft, making them in essence heavier throughout the climb. Any sudden increase or decrease in acceleration brings about a change in apparent weight of an object.

Human bodies can endure approximately nine or 10 positive Gs or two to three negative Gs for several seconds at a time. Exceeding positive G limits for longer than that causes blood to collect in the lower part of the body and torso, causing the brain and retinas to receive less blood, and therefore less oxygen. Eventually vision turns gray, followed by tunnel vision and pilot blackout. Excessive negative Gs have a similar effect, except that blood pools in the brain and upper torso, causing the small capillaries in the eyes to swell, creating a red-out effect.

Center of Gravity (CG)

The center of gravity is the position which is determined by the distribution of weight in the aircraft, either by engineering design or by the pilot. The CG position affects the longitudinal stability of the aircraft; if the CG is too far forward then the aircraft will be nose heavy, while if the CG is too far aft then the aircraft will be tail heavy. All aircraft have forward and aft limits for the position of the CG and the distance between these limits is called the CG range.

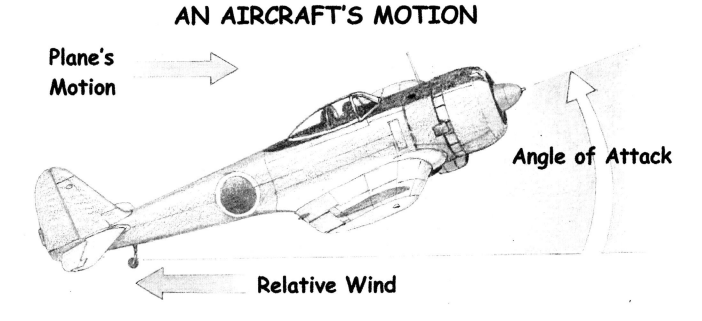

AN AIRCRAFT'S MOTION

Plane's Motion

Angle of Attack

Relative Wind

2

Control Surfaces and Vectors
(Axes) of Movement

Three Axes of Movement

All flight maneuvers make use of one or more vectors of movement: pitch, yaw, and roll. Before any discussion of aerial maneuvers, these three axes of movement (movement vectors) need to be defined.

Yaw is the side-to-side rotation of the aircraft's nose around a vertical axis through the center of the aircraft and allows the airplane to move left or right while in flight about a vertical axis line drawn from wing tip to wing tip. It changes the direction of horizontal flight but does not affect altitude. The rudder works to control the yaw of the airplane. The pilot moves the rudder left and right with left and right pedals. Pressing the right rudder pedal moves the rudder to the right, and this yaws the aircraft to the right. Used together, the rudder and the ailerons are used to turn the plane.

Pitch is the up or down movement of the aircraft's nose and is flown around a horizontal axis extending from one wing tip to the other. The pilot applies pitch by pulling back on the stick to angle the aircraft's elevators up, causing the nose to rise. Lowering the elevators makes the plane nose go down and allows the plane to go down.

Roll is the rising or dipping of the aircraft's wing about a horizontal axis stretching from the nose to the tail of the aircraft. The aircraft maintains its current direction of flight, but the wings rotate around an imaginary line drawn from the nose through the tail. Roll occurs when the pilot moves the stick left or right, causing the one aileron on one wing to angle down and the other to angle up. This increases the lift under one wing tip, while decreasing lift under the other, thus creating roll.

Aircraft Control Surfaces

The three axes of movement are initiated by the aircraft's control surfaces: the rudder, elevators, and ailerons and combinations of these three controls enable an airplane to maneuver. All aircraft control surfaces utilize the principle of lift but they apply lift forces in different directions. These forces can act either independently or in combination with one another to produce various maneuvers. Each maneuver is the net resultant force of all individual forces. A Resultant Force is the average force that results when two forces are combined. For example, a pure vertical force and a pure horizontal force create an angled force.

Elevators

Elevators are flat, hinged surfaces on the tailplane (the horizontal part of the tail assembly). While the entire tailplane surface helps stabilize the aircraft during flight, the elevators apply pitch by angling the trailing (rear) edge of the tailplane up or down. To generate pitch, the pilot gently pulls the stick back or pushes it forward while taking care not to perform pitch maneuvers too quickly. If the angle of attack (angle that the air meets the wing) becomes too steep, the flow of air around the wings can become disrupted. Air no longer flows smoothly over the wing; instead, it buffets in several different directions and disrupts the air pressure around the wing's surface, producing a stall.

Rudders

The rudder is the vertical component of the tail assembly. The rear half of the vertical tail section is hinged, allowing it to angle left or right. When rudder is applied, the aircraft's nose was redirected either left or right. Applying left rudder yaws the nose to the left, while applying right rudder turns the nose to the right. Note that applying rudder also produces a very slight rolling movement which can be negated by pushing the stick in the opposite direction.

Ailerons

Ailerons are thin, hinged surfaces on the outer trailing edge of each wing. They angle in opposite directions to move the wings up and down or roll the aircraft about its nose/tail axis. When applying left or right stick, the aileron on one wing angles down and the other angles up. This rolls one wing up and forces the other wing down, effectively rolling the airplane. When left stick is applied, the left aileron raises and the right one drops and the aircraft rolls to the left. The opposite occurs if the stick is pushed in the opposite direction.

Flaps

Similar to ailerons, flaps are thin, hinged surfaces on the trailing edge of the wing. However, they are located nearer to the wing root than ailerons and operate in tandem. (e.g., if one flap is lowered or raised so is the other). A raised flap conforms to the wing's natural shape, while a lowered flap alters the airflow around the wing, effectively changing the wing's aerodynamic shape and increasing the amount of available lift. Extending the flaps during takeoff gains additional lift, but they are then retracted during flight to maximize airspeed. While flaps increase an aircraft's angle of attack, they also increase drag. In an emergency, flaps can be used while chopping the throttle to quickly reduce airspeed. Flaps can only be extended at low to medium speeds. If the aircraft is flying too fast, air flows too quickly over the flaps and causes drag. In high-speed dives, flaps and other control surfaces may become unusable until the aircraft slows down.

Compressibility

Compressibility is a condition that causes an aircraft's control surfaces to become inoperable. It occurs at very high speeds, such as those achieved during a long, steep dive. Air that flows around the airfoil surface separates into two directions at some point in front of each wing, called the point of impact. At higher speeds, this point moves further and further in front of the wing and creates pressure disturbances on and around the wing. As an aircraft's speed approaches Mach 1 (The Mach number is the aircraft's speed divided by the speed of sound for the current altitude and temperature), the speed of the air flowing over the wings reaches the speed of sound before the aircraft does. (**Note:** air flows faster over the top of the wing and

is actually traveling faster than the aircraft at any given point in time.) The pressure waves generated by the movement of wings through the air have been likened to ripples on a pond as they radiate outward and "warn" the yet-undisturbed air molecules in the path of the approaching wing. As the aircraft's speed approaches Mach 1, these pressure waves pile up in front of the wing and at some point, the wing is traveling so fast that the waves no longer radiate ahead of the wing. This creates shock waves and causes the aircraft to buffet. Aileron and elevator controls mounted on the wing and tail surfaces freeze up due to excessive pressure, or act in directions opposite than normal. Compressibility occurs only at very high speeds. The only remedy in prop aircraft was to chop the throttle and attempt to pull out before it was too late, as not reacting quickly enough could cause the control surfaces to freeze, causing a crash.

BASIC AERODYNAMICS

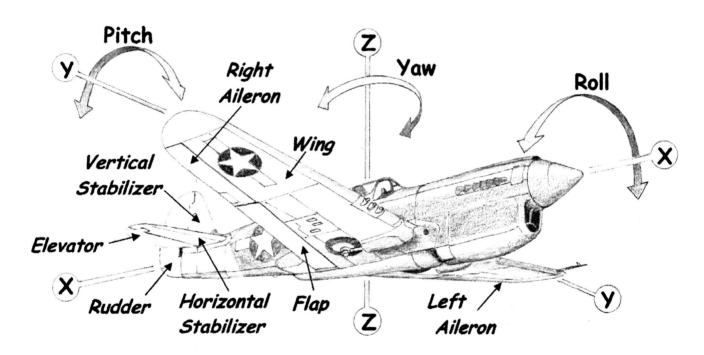

3

Basic Flight Applications

This chapter covers the basics of flight, from takeoff, climbing, turning, diving, and descending to landing and procedures to recover from common flight mishaps, such as stalls and spins.

Takeoff

Taking off from an airfield was a fairly uncomplicated procedure. The pilot first lowered the flaps to change the aerodynamic shape of the wing, then applied full throttle. Once enough forward airspeed and lift were generated, the tail wheel (if the aircraft had one) lifted off the runway. The pilot then gently pulled back on the stick to lift the nose up approximately 10°, being careful not to climb too steeply by keeping the pitch steady. If the airspeed began to Fall, the pilot needed to reduce the pitch angle to avoid stalling (decrease in lift).

Climbing

After take off, the pilot's first step was to reduce drag in order to build up speed by retracting the landing gear. The throttle was to be maintained on its full setting and the nose pitched slightly upward until it was at about a 20° angle. If airspeed was decreasing or if the stall warning appeared, the pilot was to drop the nose down until level flight was attained, then was to resume climbing at a more moderate angle. If there were no aircraft approaching, the pilot continued to climb steadily until he reached his assigned altitude. Once he was ready to level out, he decreased the throttle until he slowed down to the desired cruising speed. While cruising, the pilot would make slight adjustments to the throttle, setting until he was flying at a constant speed and altitude.

Descending/Diving

There are two methods to reduce altitude. First is to reduce the throttle setting, which creates less lift and consequently gradually decreases altitude, but gains some airspeed while descending due to gravity. The second method was to pitch the nose downward, causing a dive which quickly bled off altitude and gained airspeed. The dive was often used to attack lower-flying aircraft, or as a recovery procedure following a stall. The pilot needed to be careful of protracted or extremely steep dives at low altitude, as the aircraft's controls could freeze due to compressibility.

Banked Turns

Turning is also known as banking, or the combining of pitch and roll maneuvers to alter the heading. A banked turn was made by pulling the stick back to either left or right. The pilot could also apply rudder in the intended direction of the turn to make the turn more quickly. If the pilot entered a banked turn without adjusting the throttle, altitude or airspeed, or both, could be lost by the time the turn was finished. This happened for two reasons. First, the angle of attack (angle of the wings as they meet the airflow) was changed, creating drag that slowed the aircraft. Second, lift acted nearly perpendicular to the aircraft's wings. If the wings were angled, so was the lift vector. This yielded less pure vertical force and would cause a loss of altitude.

Landing

Landing appears to be a straightforward procedure: directing the aircraft's nose in the general direction of the airfield, bleeding off some speed and altitude, lowering the landing gear, and settling down. But landing requires a steady hand and a series of smooth of changes in throttle and pitch. In preparation to touchdown, the pilot needed a distance of at least three miles from the airfield, flying level at about 500 feet, and the throttle set to about three-quarter speed. The gear was extended and the flaps lowered (flaps down gave more lift and slowed the aircraft down without going into a stall). The pilot then gently pitched down to start his descent, striving for an optimal airspeed. Once the aircraft reached the edge of the runway, at between 20 and 30 feet, the pilot pulled the stick back firmly to raise the nose up past the horizon, then chopped the throttle to zero as the main wheels touched down.

Stalls

A stall is the loss of lift commonly encountered in propeller-powered aircraft, especially during steep climbs in which gravity reduced airspeed. Stalls occur because the aircraft's airspeed drops below that required to maintain lift. Without lift, the aircraft descends toward the ground with its control surfaces useless. Stalls most commonly occur during tight turns, steep climbs, loops, or during takeoffs and landings. To resolve a stall situation, the pilot should allow the aircraft to Fall while trying to keep the nose directed toward the ground (most aircraft nose down automatically) and making certain that the throttle was set at 100%. Eventually, this procedure gains enough airspeed to restore airflow over the control surfaces and allows the pilot to regain control of the aircraft. Note that climbing steeply is not the same thing as pitching up too quickly. The former type of stall is caused by lack of airspeed, while the second type is due to disrupted airflow around the wing.

Spins

A spin is a special type of stall that occurs when one wing loses lift but the other does not. Usually, a spin occurs during a hard turn with the nose pitched too steeply. Lift is lost on one wing and it begins to drop toward the ground. Meanwhile, the opposing wing continues producing lift and rises. If the rudder is engaged, it rotates the aircraft about its yaw axis and the result is a spinning corkscrew motion.

All aircraft have a critical angle of attack or a maximum angle at which the wings can still provide lift. If the nose is moved up drastically at high speeds, the angle of attack may be surpassed and causes a stall or spin. There are three types of spins. The most common spin is the upright spin, which is a slight nose down and yawing motion in the same direction. The inverted spin has the aircraft spinning upside down with yaw and roll occurring in opposite directions. The third most uncommon but most deadly type of spin is the flat spin, during which the aircraft simply yaws about its vertical axis with a pitch attitude about level with the horizon.

To recover from a spin, the pilot had to neutralize the aircraft's rotating motion by centering the stick and applying the rudder in the opposite direction of the spin, then direct the plane downward and when the spinning stopped, the pilot leveled out. Hopefully, he would have enough altitude to recover and break out of the spin.

The STALL

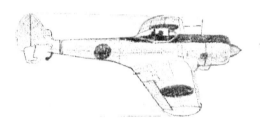

The approach at level......

Shallow climb at reduced power......

STALL

The nose drops fully "*below the horizon*" while the stick holds your descent level.

The SPIN

-A-

A. Straight and level with
ample altitude, idle the throttle.

-B-

B. Stall signals the pilot to apply both
aileron and rudder in the same
direction, right or left; SPIN begins.

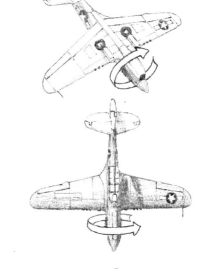

C. Return of rudder and aileron to
neutral plus up-elevator with a smooth
throttle advance pulls your plane out of
its descent and back to level.

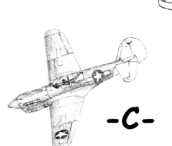

-C-

4

Two Fundamental Tenets of Air Combat

Positional Advantage

Surprise is the pilot's supreme advantage, as if the enemy was caught unaware, a pilot could carefully maneuver into a good firing position. When reading through pilot ICRs, the most successful attacks were those that caught the enemy off guard, and of these, most were made from the rear quarters. Whether or not the pilot had been detected, being behind an enemy aircraft gave the attacker a huge positional advantage. The venerable trick of hiding in the sun would work until the development of radar at the end of the war. Taking advantage of a position in the sun was always desirable, because the sun's glare blinded the pilot being attacked, but since the sun's position seldom was compatible with the mission it could not be relied on. Using clouds to conceal an approach (or make an escape) was useful; of course, the disadvantage of cloud cover was that the potential attacker may become the victim of an enemy attack from the clouds above.

For self preservation, it was imperative that a pilot spot the enemy as soon as possible, and pilots were trained to scan the skies continuously. Inevitably, long missions and/or sustained combat meant that pilots became tired and found it difficult to stay alert. Except during periods of approaching weather fronts, only scattered clouds appeared in the tropical South Pacific skies, which were unusually clear, providing visual contact at great range.

Often the pilot would have difficulty looking to the rear or to parts of the sky that could be obscured by his own aircraft structure, especially downward under the wings, so the pilot had to constantly alter his flight path, usually by weaving left to right, to have a full view of his surroundings. To check his left rear, he looked over his left shoulder or rear view mirror by weaving left and to check his right rear by weaving right. He could pitch slightly upward or downward or roll slightly left or right to check above and below. To scan the lower hemisphere of his view he could even momentarily invert his aircraft. Since it was more difficult to scan all 360° while flying alone, it was important for the wingman to keep close and for each pilot of the Element to constantly cover the others' blind spots until it was time to break formation to the enter combat.

Approaching enemy aircraft first appeared as dark dots or "glints" of light in the distance that certain pilots would pick up sooner than others. Generally, if they were in formation they were bombers, while Japanese fighters flew in apparently undisciplined "gaggles." Once spotted, if the distance was large enough, it was frequently possible for one side or the other to break away if they were in a positional disadvantage, especially when at a lower altitude or at a great numerical inequality. What constituted an advantageous tactical position previous to combat depended to large degree upon the mission and aircraft type. However, during an escort mission, it would be difficult for the escorting fighters to avoid combat regardless of conditions, as they had been assigned to protect the bombers.

Once opposing aircraft came into firing range two occurrences almost always resulted: the larger formations broke up and the combat either ended quickly or continued at a progressively lower altitude. Air combat often progressed from high altitude to low and from order to disorder, ending with aircraft scattered across the sky at low altitudes and often alone. The ideal result of the first or second pass by fast U.S. fighters was to break up the Japanese formation, making individuals and pairs vulnerable to attack by the American Element of two aircraft.

Altitude is Energy

Altitude takes advantage of the fundamental rules of energy. Potential energy (stored in the form of altitude) can easily be converted into kinetic energy (airspeed) by diving. Whichever pilot has the most speed holds the initiative. He can choose to press the attack or break it off if the situation is unfavorable. However, air combat most often progressed from high altitude to low and from order to disorder, ending with aircraft scattered across the sky at low altitudes and often alone.

Of all the tactical advantages altitude was the most important, because Japanese fighters could maneuver quicker and at a slower speed than their American opponents. Any maneuver, no matter how minor, decreases either speed or altitude. A pilot can exchange altitude for speed by diving, while climbing causes the opposite to occur. When the elevators on the tail move upward the nose rises. When the angle of the wing relative to its flight path changes (the angle of attack) more lift occurs. Drag, however, is also increased, slowing the aircraft down. In a climb, therefore, due to the result of the twin forces of drag and lift, the aircraft rises due to lift, but also slows due to drag. When a pilot turns or banks, the lift generated by the wings is no longer parallel to the ground; however, the force of gravity remains parallel. When banking, the tighter the bank, the more the wing drops and the higher the apparent weight (gravity); consequently, more lift is required. The pilot accomplishes this by raising the aircraft's nose, thereby increasing the angle of attack and thus lift. The result, however, is that the aircraft slows down. During a hard defensive turn or break, the pilot rolled the wings until they were perpendicular to the ground and pulled back firmly on the stick, causing an abrupt high-speed turn that while losing the enemy, also bled off speed at a very high rate. Thus, during maneuvers speed and altitude are exchanged.

5

Air Combat Maneuvers

The Basics

Classic air combat maneuvers are established moves perfected over decades, and calculated to gain the pilot the most maneuverability for the least loss of energy. The most important component in air combat maneuver is energy, which is a dynamic combination of airspeed and altitude. Airspeed is a measure of an aircraft's immediate capability to maneuver, while altitude is a measure of an aircraft's potential ability to gain speed quickly by diving. Together, they are the fighter's current energy status. Maneuvering exchanges energy for position.

Energy

As discussed previously, energy is classified into two types. Energy that is currently in use is called kinetic energy and is determined by the aircraft's mass and current speed. In a climb more kinetic energy is used. Potential energy is stored energy in the form of altitude. In a dive, altitude (potential energy) is converted into speed (usable energy). In terms of the aircraft, energy is the amount of current or stored directional force the aircraft has available. Energy is commonly used as a combat term, referring to the amount of mechanical energy an aircraft has versus the enemy's aircraft. In the air, energy relates directly to maneuverability.
The Choice: "Energy Fight or Turning Fight"
Before entering combat, it was essential for the pilot to decide what type of fight he wanted to pursue. The terms "energy fight" and "turning fight" were two different approaches to combat based on which combatant had more current speed and/or the faster fighter.

In an energy fight, an aircraft climbed and accelerated as the pilot attempted to outmaneuver his opponent by using his speed advantage. He would make a series of slashing and quick hit-and-run attacks interspersed by climbs, dives, and rapid breakaways.

In a turning fight, a pilot flying an aircraft with superior turning capabilities attempted to out-fly the opposing pilot by using short, quick turns. This was the traditional aerial dogfighting combat depicted in Hollywood movies, with two opposing pilots zooming through the skies, struggling to gain positional advantage. Each turn diminished valuable airspeed and eventually one pilot either became the victor or disengaged. Either type of fight could succeed in the correct situation, but not unless the pilot took advantage of the optimum flight characteristics of his fighter.

Turn Rate and Turn Radius

All aircraft have two basic turn-related performance qualities: turn rate and turn radius. The first is how fast an aircraft is able to turn in degrees per second, while the second indicates the size of the arc of the turn. Generally, faster airspeeds convert into faster turn rates but produce large, relaxed turn radii, while the opposite is true, as slower airspeeds produce slower turn rates but tighter turn radii.

When an aircraft with a quick roll rate pursues an aircraft with a tighter turn radius, rolling away during a turn can help increase closure. As the pursued fighter begins his tight turn, the pursuer rolled away from the direction of the turn and its pilot then threw the stick forward to swing under or over the target and then push the nose toward the completion point of his turn.

Offensive Air Combat Maneuvers

Once the element of surprise disappeared, air combat became a battle of individual skill and stamina. Before committing to combat, the pilot had to consider his fighter's strengths and weaknesses compared to the enemy's aircraft. Because of their slower top speeds and short-range weapons, WWII fighters, unlike modern radar and missile-equipped fighters, were not capable of combat beyond visual range. Close-in combat tested a pilot's skills to their limits.

It has been stated that air combat is "perhaps the only contest where it's both honorable and desirable to shoot someone in the back." The goal of air combat maneuver is to get on the enemy's tail because:
1) The enemy fighter's guns will not be directed at the attacker. (Enemy bomber tail guns and some dorsal turret guns were the obvious exception)
2) Firing from astern is basically uncomplicated, as there is little or no necessity to lead the target.
3) The tail position attack is the best from which to adjust to a target's evasive moves.

Aileron Roll

The Aileron Roll caused by the sideways movement of the stick is one of the first maneuvers taught in basic aerobatics courses, as it is a basic component of every air combat maneuver. The fledgling pilot maneuvers his aircraft in a complete 360° revolution about its longitudinal axis. When

AILERON ROLL

A. Pick a visual marker on the horizon and slightly elevate the nose. Push the stick fully right or left and hold the nose steady on the marker.

B. Hold the roll-over until the stick is re-centered as level flight returns.

Well executed aileron rolls held at half and quarter-roll positions are the essential first elements of performing more complex aerobatics.

BARREL ROLL

A. Raise the nose & push the stick into a roll, right or left.

B. Pull the stick back as you roll fully inverted.

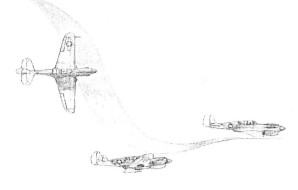

C. The nose will draw a complete circle on the horizon as you regain level flight.

executed correctly, the aircraft leaves the maneuver on the same heading as it entered with no noticeable change in altitude. The Aileron Roll is commonly executed through the application of full aileron in one direction, starting the maneuver by trading altitude for airspeed (diving), then pitching the aircraft up significantly (20 or 30°), which minimizes altitude loss and ensures that the aircraft will have sufficient control to complete the maneuver. Further complicating the maneuver is the requirement to apply enough rudder to avoid departing from coordinated flight and possibly entering a stall. The Aileron Roll was commonly used in aerial combat training, and while use of the pure aileron roll in air combat was not frequent, the Immelmann Turn, Barrel Roll, and Split-S all depended on the Aileron Roll.

Barrel Roll Attack

The term "Barrel Roll" is commonly used incorrectly to refer to any roll by an airplane—such as an Aileron Roll or to a Spiral Roll—in which the aircraft's nose remained directed generally along the flight path. The maneuver is begun by raising the nose and then pulling gently back on the stick to maintain the roll. Sideways pressure is to be continued on the stick during the inverted roll, then centered upon returning to level flight. During the maneuver the stick is basically in the left or right hand corner of the cockpit. The fighter's nose follows a circle on the horizon and does not rotate around a point as in the Aileron Roll. A perfect Barrel Roll would be maintained at the same altitude with no loss. The Barrel Roll Attack is a climbing turn designed to prevent overshooting and to reacquire an evading, lower-energy target.

Loops

The Loop Over (commonly the "Loop") is a method to complete a vertical circle and end up in the same position as when the maneuver was begun. When flying a Loop, enough airspeed is required so as not to stall at the top of the loop, because as the fighter climbed airspeed is lost so the stick has to be pulled back slowly. Once inverted, the pilot has to ease back on the stick and add a little back pressure as he starts down on the back side of the loop, then reduces the throttle in the dive. The pilot has to watch his left wing tip to determine where in the loop he is with the wing drawing a circle on the horizon. The loop is most effective against very slow targets, such as heavy bombers, or against fighters that are just taking off from an airfield. Loops are rarely symmetrical in practice and frequently resemble a lowercase "e."

The Loop Under is essentially a reverse Loop Over, but is more useful in combat, as airspeed is gained early in the maneuver. While high airspeed is required in the Loop Over, less airspeed is required in the Loop Under, especially so as not to hit the ground! Enough altitude and few negative Gs are also to be maintained. The stick is to be pulled back smoothly in a half Aileron Roll to get inverted and the subsequent gain in airspeed will aid in getting into the other side of the Loop. When the climb is begun, back pressure is to be maintained, and during the loss of airspeed once inverted the pilot needs to push the stick forward slightly to end the loop. The maneuver is completed with another half Aileron Roll to bring the fighter back to its original direction and altitude.

LOOP (Over)

B. Fully inverted, throttle back and keep a light touch of pressure on the stick as you start back down.

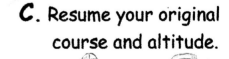

C. Resume your original course and altitude.

A. From the level, advance throttle and pull the stick straight back.

LOOP (Under)

More complicated than a Loop-Over, this downward **LOOP** is a combat essential that immediately converts LOAD to high acceleration against a lower target. An attacker then employs his speed upward to regain his altitude advantage.

A. With plenty of altitude, execute a half-aileron roll to fully invert and smoothly pull back on the stick.

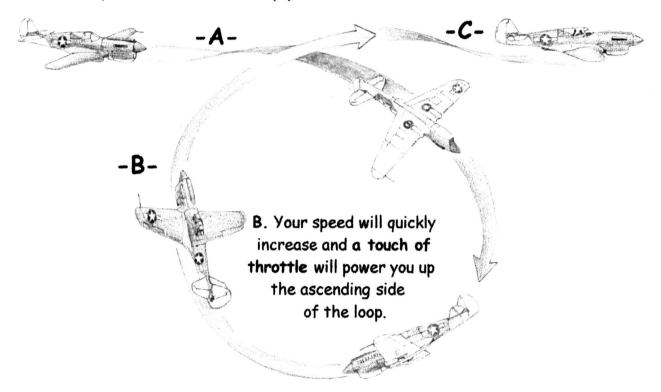

B. Your speed will quickly increase and a **touch of throttle** will power you up the ascending side of the loop.

C. Ease the stick forward to end the LOOP and from this inverted position, **employ another half-roll** to regain your original position.

Lead Turn

The Lead Turn is a first move to gain the advantage on an opponent by out-turning him. When closing on a target, the attacker begins turning into the enemy aircraft to get a snap shot, then follows through with the turn to get on the enemy's tail (his six o'clock or "6"). The pilot then eases off on the throttle to maintain a tight turn. When in the tightest possible turn, full throttle is to be applied while keeping the stick back as far as possible without stalling. Timing is essential, as care has to be taken not to begin the Lead Turn too soon, since it could put the attacker in front of the target and then they become the target. The Lead Turn is only to be attempted if the attacker is certain that his fighter could turn with or out-turn the target, or if the target's speed is so high that it could not turn tightly.

Lag Turn

The Lag Turn is the opposite of the Lead Turn, as it is used by a pilot after passing a turning target to reposition himself behind the target. The Lag Turn is used if the attacker is flying faster than the target or is unable to out-turn the enemy plane. The pilot turns into the enemy but not too tightly, allowing his fighter to drift widely. As the attacker loses momentum, he is to tighten his turn and continue to increase throttle. It is important to keep the enemy constantly in sight in the turn. Airspeed is then decreased to just above stalling to maintain the tightest turn possible, pulling all the way back on the stick to get behind the enemy. Full throttle is to be applied to remain above stalling and the stick held back. During the Lag Turn, the enemy fighter could outdistance the attacker who is losing speed in the

LEAD TURN

If you foil an attack with a break turn, your opponent may well fall victim to a well timed **Lead Turn**.

A. If your attacker tightens his turn to re-acquire you as a

-B-

target, **advance throttle and ease forward** while turning inside his decelerating turn.
He will be in view ahead of you and a bit higher.

-A-

B. Your firing pass should present   itself as your speeds equal out.....throttle up and pull into a shot from dead astern.
Keep you stick back and **DON'T STALL**.

turn. The Lag Turn is a difficult maneuver, leaving little margin for error, and even when skillfully performed, it allows only a small window to fire on the enemy.

Head-on Pass

A successful head-on attack is to be made at a zero degree deflection angle, flying straight at the enemy aircraft and firing when in range and continuing to fire, waiting until the last possible moment to break away. The high rate of closure could lead to mid-air collisions. More courageous pilots would fly through an enemy formation, while more conservative pilots would break downward to gain speed to escape any pursuit.

Successful pilots looked for the opportunity to make a head-on attack, which is often the final phase of a defensive maneuver. If a Japanese fighter had been in the six o'clock position but was out of firing range, American pilots would use their superior speed to gain distance, then quickly turn around and head directly at the enemy and fire in less than two seconds. The area exposed on the target was small, only presenting the profile of the engine and cockpit. Most often, the Japanese pilots would choose to quickly break away and the U.S. fighter would speed past before squeezing off a shot. Sometimes the Japanese pilot would accept what was a one-sided battle, particularly when facing the devastating concentrated centered fire from a P-38, and perish in often spectacular fashion, as did hundreds of fragile Japanese aircraft during the war.

Yo Yo Attack

The High Yo Yo attack is possibly the most difficult maneuver for new pilots to understand and employ. The attacker makes a high-speed pass (or was carrying too much speed) on a slower target that attempts to evade with a break turn. The attacker converts his speed into altitude by pulling his fighter into a vertical climb, rolling his fighter so that his fighter flies

in the direction the target tried to escape. The attacker, by pulling back on the stick as he rolls, directed his vertical momentum toward the target, allowing him to dive onto the target's tail. The attacker needs to be aware that the target is continuing his turn. This maneuver enables a fighter with a wider turning radius to cut into the breaking target and fire.

In the Low Yo Yo, the attacker flies slower than the target and closes on the target by diving to convert altitude into airspeed to cut inside the target's turn. The Low Yo Yo uses the same principle as the High Yo Yo, but in the opposite way. With the High Yo Yo, the attacker converts speed to altitude in order to reduce his closure rate, while in the Low Yo Yo, the attacker converts altitude to speed to increase his rate of closure. This maneuver is useful when close to stalling and there is the need to gain speed. The attacker drops his nose into the target's breaking turn, gaining speed in a diving turn, then pulls his nose up into the target at full throttle and turns as tightly as possible. Extra lead on the target is desirable, as when the target pulls up it would be into the attacker's fire.

Roll Away

The Roll Away maneuver achieves the same basic purpose as the High Yo-Yo, which is to improve the attacker's offensive position and prevents the attacker from overshooting the target. The Roll Away causes the attacking fighter to climb, thus decreasing closing speed similar to the High Yo Yo, except after the climb, the attacker dives off to the outside of the target's turn, then approaches from behind the target.

Chandelle

The Chandelle (French for candle) is used to engage an enemy attacking from the rear. It is one of the less extreme combat maneuvers, but is not a tactic to be used in close quarters; it is a good preparatory move if an enemy is spotted behind and the defending pilot wants to turn to face him. The

LAG TURN

If your opponent is more maneuverable than you, an
option is to LAG, or delay your turn as your opponent
bleeds off speed in his tighter turn.

-C-

A. Reduce throttle and drift in a
wider turn. A separation will ensue,
so **keep your target in view.**

-B-   **-A-**

B. A brief chance opens up when your opponent's slower turn has
reached critical speed loss, even though his is well ahead of you.
C. **Lay on the throttle** and **tighten your turn** from your wider
flight path until you negate the separation. **Hold your stick back**
to nullify a stall and close in at dead astern.

HEAD-ON
PASS

A. Before you commit to your
HEAD-ON pass, check for
enemy escorts who may well
be **above your own flight.**

B. Accelerate well ahead of
the target and break hard
into the enemy's flight path.
Pick a single target.....
not the entire formation.

C. Timing is critical, because your gunfire trajectory **will last only seconds**
at your high rate of closure. **Keep your target centered.** The least
deflection lessens the number of your rounds that hit the mark.

HIGH YO-YO

Conversely to the Low Yo-Yo, if you have the speed and the altitude edge, but your target ~~~~ broke out of your firing pass, a **HIGH YO-YO** could put you back in firing position.

A. Convert your speed into a climbing aileron turn as your adversary continues his escape turn below.

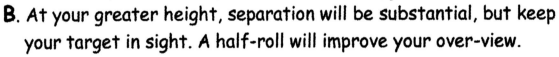

B. At your greater height, separation will be substantial, but keep your target in sight. A half-roll will improve your over-view.

C. With your target re-acquired, your task is to execute a diving firing pass on a fully alerted opponent. Advance throttle in your descent and close in....**you won't get a third chance.**

LOW YO-YO

When your **break turn** is successful, a well flown **LOW YO-YO** can quickly put you in firing position.

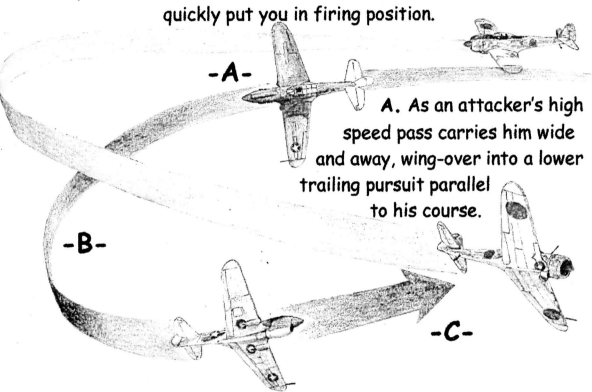

A. As an attacker's high speed pass carries him wide and away, wing-over into a lower trailing pursuit parallel to his course.

B. As you separate in the initial turn, drop the nose and throttle downward adding THRUST to your pursuit.

C. Raise your nose at optimal range and throttle forward into your opponent's *deep-6*.

ROLL AWAY PASS

Methods increase in difficulty as a more aggressive pilot modifies his
High Yo-yo gunnery pass into the **ROLL AWAY** pass.

A. As before, your opponent
assault and you pull upward
rolls into your higher speed
to cut your speed.

B. This go'round, you opt
direct of your quarry
to **ROLL AWAY in the opposite**
and go inverted through a Split-S
to better observe his lower
flight path.

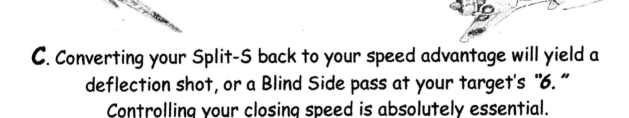

C. Converting your Split-S back to your speed advantage will yield a
deflection shot, or a Blind Side pass at your target's *"6."*
Controlling your closing speed is absolutely essential.

Chandelle is a wide, precision control 180° sweeping wide-radius reversing turn that includes a constant variation of altitude in all three axes. At the midpoint (top) of the roll, the aircraft is flying inverted, with the nose pointing at a 90°angle (sideways) to the general path of flight. The aircraft is not to lose altitude during the last part of the maneuver or during the recovery, when engine power could be used to re-establish normal cruising speed on the new heading. The decreasing bank angle, together with the decreasing airspeed during the second half of the Chandelle, maintains a constant turn rate. The turn needs to be kept coordinated by applying the correct amount of rudder throughout the maneuver. The aircraft can then be flown at low speed after establishing the new heading or normal cruise flight may be resumed.

Wing Over
The Wing Over is a maneuver used to reverse direction without changing altitude and to return to the pre-turn altitude and heading. Like the Chandelle, the pilot turns aircraft around, but by using pitch and rudder. The Wing Over is beneficial to multiple diving attacks on slow moving targets (bombers) that can't easily change their flight paths. To perform a Wing Over, the pilot applies pitch and throttle and moves into a steep climb that is much steeper than a Chandelle climb. Once the aircraft almost begins to stall, the pilot kicks the rudder sharply either left or right, causing the nose to yaw through 180°. This essentially swings the nose sharply up and over the topmost point of the turn, then drops it sideways toward the ground.

CHANDELLE TURN

A. Enter this shallow turn with a light, steady pressure of right or left aileron and minimal bank of the wings.

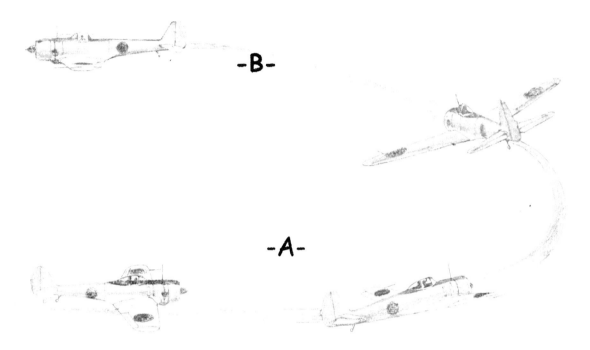

-B-

-A-

B. With a steady throttle position, a wide circle can be flown including the reverse of ailerons through a flat figure-8.

Hammerhead (Stall Turn)

The Hammerhead is often referred to as the Stall Turn or "Aerial Cartwheel," and is a favorite aerobatic maneuver at air shows. During a Hammerhead, a fighter flying straight and level enters a vertical climb at full throttle, loses airspeed, and appears to stop in midair (thus the name Stall Turn—a misnomer, because the aircraft never actually stalls). At the top of the climb, the fighter yaws left or right to point vertically towards the ground. As the fighter gains airspeed the pilot applies up elevator and straightens out to level flight. The Hammerhead is used to evade an enemy attacking at six o'clock and have him try to follow, and at the top of the maneuver get on the attacker's tail when he could not follow.

Immelmann Turn

Immelmann Turn, also known as a Roll-off-the-Top or simply as the Immelmann, was an energy-efficient method of reversing direction and placing the aircraft at a higher altitude but reduced overall airspeed. The WWI Immelmann Turn was probably used by Max Immelmann, but there is little verification that he originated it; it was definitely used by other WWI fighter pilots who named it after him. This maneuver is used when enemy aircraft passed overhead and were to be engaged or were suspected to be attackers. The Immelmann involves an ascending half loop (a vertical

180° turn) followed by an aileron roll at the top (half roll), resulting in level flight in the exact opposite direction at a higher altitude.

To successfully perform an Immelmann Turn, the pilot has to accelerate to a sufficient airspeed to complete a loop, then pull the aircraft into a climb and continue to pull back on the controls as the aircraft climbs. Rudder and ailerons have to be used to keep the half loop straight when viewed from the ground. As the aircraft passes over the point at which the climb started, it has to be inverted and then a half loop is to be completed. Sufficient airspeed has to be maintained to recover without losing altitude, and at the top of the loop the pilot then performs a half roll to regain normal, upright aircraft direction. Therefore, the aircraft would be at a higher altitude and had changed course 180°.

If the attacker had initial high airspeed he could modify the Immelmann by making a banked turn as he starts to come out of the half loop. This allows him to come out of the loop with a slightly different heading. Or, he could apply enough extra pitch to extend the loop into a dive. Either variation is useful if the pursued enemy makes an early break to one side or goes low.

After making a high speed diving attack on an enemy, the attacker would then zoom climb back up past the enemy aircraft and just short of the stall apply full rudder to yaw his aircraft around, placing his aircraft facing down

The WINGOVER

C. Lower the nose, throttle back and level off at your original altitude.

B. Execute an aileron turn banking a minimum of 60 degrees.

60 DEGREES

.....into a smooth pull-up.

A. Advance throttle at level flight & lift the nose.....

at the enemy aircraft and making another high-speed diving pass possible. This maneuver is difficult to perform correctly, as it required precise control of the fighter at low speed. This type of Immelmann was called Reversement by French pilots in WWI and a Wingover and the Hammerhead Turn in WWII.

Scissors

The Scissors is a series of turn reversals that forces the attacker's fighter into the enemy when both pilots are trying to gain an advantage over the other. The slower, more agile fighter flown by an experienced pilot is generally the victor. The Scissors usually occurs when both aircraft were flying parallel and in the same direction, with each pilot attempting to turn into the other and rolling back as their paths crossed. Once the opponent clears on either side, the pilot is to roll back into the enemy, turning as tightly as possible. To maintain a tight turn the pilot has to throttle back, but was to be aware of stalling.

Vertical Scissors

Vertical Scissors is basically the Scissors maneuver, except it is done while climbing or diving aircraft and trying to gain the better offensive position. The target most likely enters this maneuver because he has a disadvantage, in that the other aircraft has more speed. This maneuver causes the speed advantage to be canceled due to the pull of gravity slowing both aircraft

(i.e., ever diminishing thrust in climbing turns, plus the always present load). If the target executes this maneuver with better timing and technique, the defender will end up behind the attacker, allowing the target to become the attacker and placing the aircraft in a good offensive position. A descending vertical scissors combat is restricted by the certainty of increased load and the quickly approaching earth.

Blind Side Pass

The Blind Side Pass is considered the most deadly gunnery pass, as it is often the end of the inattentive enemy pilot. It is also called the Up and Under, the Belly Buster, the Gut Punch, or the Low Down. When attacking bombers or unsuspecting fighters, this maneuver exposes the enemy aircraft's belly, which is its most vulnerable area and also its blind spot. The attacker positions himself above or directly behind the oblivious target and dives to gain speed. Once under the target, the attacker pulls his nose up into the target's belly and fires.

Defensive Air Combat Maneuvers

In air combat, the objective is to see which pilot can maneuver into the best gun position to shoot down the enemy. Once coming under attack, a pilot immediately has to assess his fighter's performance against that of his attacker, then be able to employ any advantageous maneuvers to escape.

HAMMERHEAD STALL

.....STALL occurs.

B. Idle throttle until LIFT is negated by LOAD .....

A. Level flight proceeds a 90 degree vertical climb at full throttle.

C. With idle throttle, apply rudder & up-elevator to hold level as LOAD pulls the nose down.

Extending (Running Away)

Extending is basically "a determined effort to gain separation from the attacker;" best described as "running away." But this tactic is only of use if the attacked aircraft has a speed or climb/dive rate advantage. To achieve separation and extend the distance from the attacker, it is important to avoid turning, as each time a turn is made the attacker has an opportunity to decrease distance.

Generally, if the target could fly faster than the attacker then it should fly level toward safety, but if it could climb faster, then it should climb away. If the target had altitude advantage and its pilot thought he could out-dive his attacker, he was to drop the nose and dive away. A targeted pilot could try to lose his attacker by making a break turn, then following it up with a break turn in the reverse direction. However, each turn bleeds off some airspeed, and if the attacker matches the target turn for turn, the target could easily find himself in a Scissors situation, at which point it was

a contest for each to sustain enough speed to remain scissoring longer than the other and eventually one fighter is forced to break off the attack.

The Break

The Break is basically a determined, but temporary, emergency solution to elude an enemy following at six o'clock. As soon as the enemy is detected, the pilot applies maximum power while simultaneously rolling with hard aileron and rudder, increasing the Gs without going into a high-speed stall. The nose is kept down to maintain energy and the pilot has to make an effort to turn his head around against the G forces to find the enemy.

Break Turn

The Break Turn is also an emergency solution to an attack from behind. When using the Break Turn the pilot, if possible, has to turn into the attacker, as breaking away from an attack presented his tail to the enemy. The pilot

IMMELMANN TURN

B. Immediately half-roll back to level flight and quickly acquire your target.

.....through a half-loop to be fully inverted.

A. To attack a target directly overhead, accelerate and immediately pull the nose up.....

was to throttle back so he could turn tighter and roll toward the direction of the attacking aircraft (i.e., attack from the left then roll left) and then turns as tightly as possible into the attack. This maneuver is most effective when the attacker has great speed and can not make the turn with his target. However, the Break Turn depletes air speed and momentum and exposes the target if the attacker is able to turn with the break. In this case, the targeted pilot needs to go full throttle and lower his nose to gain more speed and continue to break into his attacker, if need be.

Barrel Roll Pass

The evasive Barrel Roll is a specific maneuver; a combination of a roll and loop used to get an enemy off a fighter's tail. The pilot flies a circle around a reference point on the horizon near his altitude and finishes at the entry point altitude. By corkscrewing, the fighter would lose airspeed and hopefully the attacker would fly by.

Split-S

The American Split-S—also called the Abschwung by the Luftwaffe and the Half-Roll and Dive, Tuck and Run, or Split-arse by the RAF—is a variation on the Loop. It is a half loop in reverse used as an air combat maneuver mainly to disengage from combat by reducing altitude and changing direction. It is almost an exact reversal of the Immelmann, and since it is essentially a dive, some airspeed is gained coming out of the turn. The Split-S maneuver contrasts to the Immelmann Turn, which is an ascending half loop that finishes with a half roll out, resulting in level flight in the exact opposite direction at a higher altitude. For this reason, the Split-S is also called a Reversed or Inverted Immelmann Turn.

To execute a Split-S, the pilot half rolls his aircraft and inverts and executes a descending half loop, resulting in level flight in the exact opposite direction at a lower altitude. The reason for initiating a Split-S from the inverted position is that when flying straight and level and the pilot pushes the fighter's nose down, he would experience negative Gs (weight lessening). The more he pushes the nose down, the more "weightless" he feels. The

DOUBLE IMMELMANN

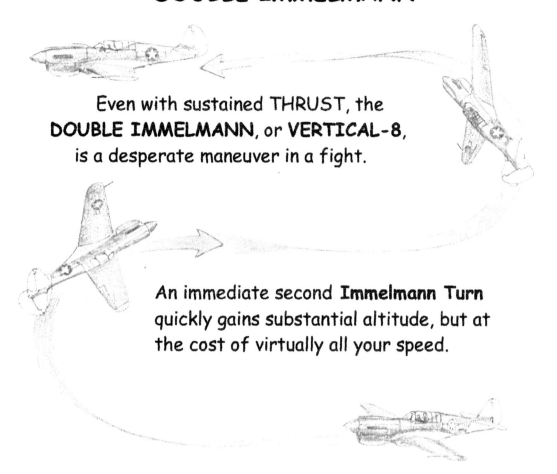

Even with sustained THRUST, the
DOUBLE IMMELMANN, or VERTICAL-8,
is a desperate maneuver in a fight.

An immediate second **Immelmann Turn**
quickly gains substantial altitude, but at
the cost of virtually all your speed.

effect of negative Gs is to push the pilot's blood up into his head—just the opposite of positive Gs. However, while the pilot's body could tolerate up to nine positive Gs without severe consequences, at two to three negative Gs the blood vessels in his eyes would begin to rupture, known as red out. Also, before going into a Split-S the pilot has to leave some margin of error between him and the ground. Occasionally, the increased airspeed in the dive could cause the control surfaces to freeze and the pilot would have to let the aircraft Fall and try to open the dive brakes or flaps to slow down.

The Split-S was a principal defensive maneuver for both sides, being a typical trade of altitude for speed combined with a directional change. Because the Split-S was a descending maneuver, the pilot had to always make certain he was beginning high enough to complete the half loop. The exact altitude needed depended on factors such as the aircraft's speed, weight, and maneuverability. The pilot could misjudge a Split-S from a lack of situational awareness or from an error in reading instruments. To use the Split-S, the P-38 required much more altitude than the P-40 and Corsair, while the Zero and Oscar required much less than all.

The Split-S can also be used as an offensive maneuver, with the pilot allowing the target to pass below, then Split-S onto its tail. Good judgment is essential when using it as an attack procedure. The attacking pilot has to be able to estimate where to begin the turn. If there is not enough separation

between him and the enemy aircraft, he could approach too quickly and overshoot or pass him by. Using the Split-S against targets with superior diving abilities is to be avoided. Rookie pilots often dove directly at lower targets head-on, which was not only a poor angle from which to hit the target, but also gave the target an equal opportunity to fire on the attacker.

Unpredictable Maneuvering

As a last resort when aggressively attacked from the rear, a pilot wants to minimize the attacker's opportunity to get off good shots by creating as much of a deflection angle as possible. The greater the angle between the attacker's guns and the target's flight path, the larger the margin for error. The means to successfully avoid a tailing attack is to be as unpredictable as possible to make it more difficult for the attacker to train his guns. It is important to have enough altitude when beginning any maneuver.

Skid

A Skid is nothing more than laterally braking in mid-air by using the rudders and ailerons, causing the aircraft to skid sideways. It is used to lose altitude without affecting airspeed or heading and force a pursuing aircraft to pass by and disrupt his aim. To perform a Skid, the pilot pushes the stick gently left or right to drop one wing, then turns the rudder in the opposite direction

Figure 25. **SCISSORS**

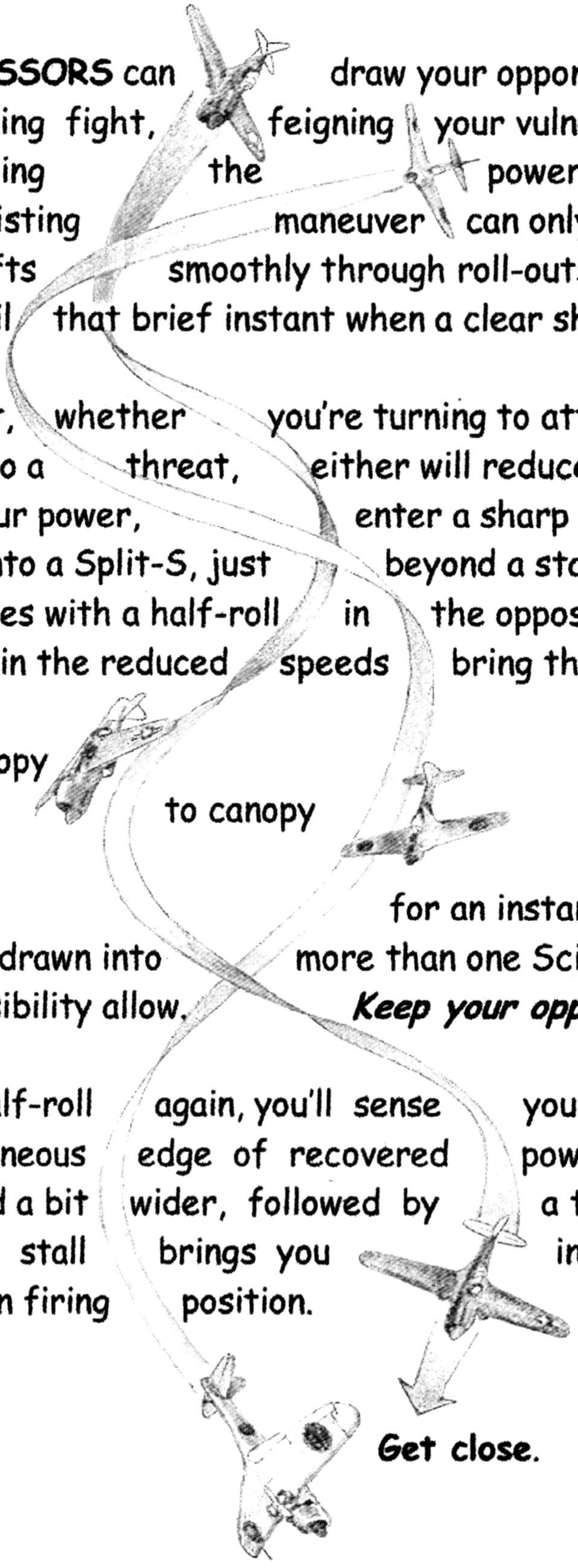

Using the **SCISSORS** can draw your opponent into a slower turning fight, feigning your vulnerability while steadily recouping the power spent in your turn. This twisting maneuver can only be used by a pilot who shifts smoothly through roll-outs, climbs and dives until that brief instant when a clear shot occurs.

A. At the onset, whether you're turning to attack, or you're breaking into a threat, either will reduce your speed.
B. To regain your power, enter a sharp half-roll and throttle up into a Split-S, just beyond a stall. Next, your opponent parries with a half-roll in the opposite direction. A rough parity in the reduced speeds bring the both of you

canopy

to canopy

for an instant.
You may be drawn into more than one Scissors as altitude and visibility allow. ***Keep your opponent in sight.***

C. As you half-roll again, you'll sense your P-40 has an instantaneous edge of recovered power. A swing downward a bit wider, followed by a throttle up just above a stall brings you into a high angle deflection firing position.

Get close.

BLIND SIDE PASS

A. If possible, put the sun at your back and *check behind you.*

B. Dive into the lower rear quarter below your target's flight path, the *blind side* and accelerate upward to optimal firing range at his "*deep 6 o'clock.*"

C. *DO NOT* overrun your target. Open fire and close to point-blank, then break away sharp at full throttle to recover your altitude.....and **check your "6".....AGAIN.**

BREAK TURN

The hard aileron-roll at reduced throttle is the last hope for a flyer suddenly caught in an opponent's gun sight. As you bear into the **aileron turn toward the threat** with back pressure on the stick, your speed will bleed off quickly.

Your opponent will briefly be out of view behind you. Throttle up to regain your speed and pull a hard reverse turn. Reacquire your adversary.....immediately.

BARREL ROLL PASS

Yet another variation of the Roll Away attack is the **BARREL ROLL PASS**. When properly executed, a turning escapee is caught after a somewhat shortened pursuit.

-B-

-C-

A. An opponent employs a break turn defeating your high speed attack.

-A-

B. To reduce your excess speed, execute a **BARREL ROLL** up and away from your fleeting target's escape course. As you reach fully inverted, immediately re-acquire your quarry.

C. The momentum of descending *"out of the barrel"* back to level flight will quickly place you in that fateful **6 o'clock** slot.

(moving the stick right and using left rudder, and *vice-versa*). Some altitude starts to bleed off and the aircraft would slide in the direction of the lower wing. Sometimes, the attacker would mistake this maneuver for a turn and attempt to follow it.

Jinking
Jinking—sometimes called Scissoring—is a series of quick, alternating breaking turns used when being tailed inside or close to gun range to force a faster flying attacker into passing. The pursued pilot jinks by pushing the stick left, then right, then left, then right again, etc., making loose turns, or he could tighten up the turn radius with the aid of the rudders. The objective is to avoid approaching gun or cannon rounds and disrupt the attacker's aim. Jinking is especially beneficial when the opponent is faster and trying to decrease distance. So if the attacker's airspeed is higher, he would have a difficult time holding his nose far enough into the turn and most likely pass and overshoot. With each successive turn, the attacker is forced to cut

the distance separating him and the target. As the shortest distance between two points is a straight line (a slight curve in this case) and the aircraft were the two points, to follow the target's turn and maintain it in his sights, the attacker had to cut the target's turn short.

Negative G Loop
During a stern attack, the target pilot would wait calmly for his attacker to commit to an attack. Once the attacker committed, the defending pilot would forcefully push his stick fully forward and drop down into an uninverted, negative-G loop. This tactic drew him below the attacker's line of sight in a near-weightless condition. Most attackers would be completely surprised by this audacious maneuver and not follow. This tactic could be carried further by adding rudder to kick the aircraft to one side, then throttle to speed up the uninverted loop, called "stuffing it all into the corner."

SPLIT-S

A. A snap half-roll to fully inverted, quickly followed by a full throttle, nose-down descent with the stick fully back.

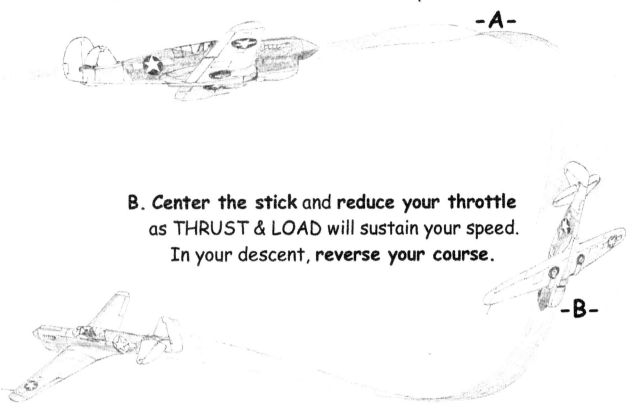

-A-

B. Center the stick and reduce your throttle as THRUST & LOAD will sustain your speed. In your descent, reverse your course.

-B-

The Vertical 8
The Vertical 8 is two half loops performed one immediately after the other and could only be executed with very high airspeed. If a slower attacker tries to follow and was not watching his airspeed closely, he would stall below and present himself as a good target.

High G Barrel Roll
This maneuver is executed by the target when the attacker overshoots the target and takes advantage of this change by placing the target behind the attacker. This is accomplished the target turning into the attacker's break, then executes a Barrel Roll parallel to his course and at the top of the Barrel Roll the target should be directly behind the attacker.

Constant Sideslip
A pilot attacked from the rear could persistently trim his aircraft so that it flew with constant sideslip, causing attackers to misjudge the direction of flight.

Combining Maneuvers
When attacked, a pilot could combine maneuvers to escape, such as combing a Loop interrupted by a Break Turn, or a quick Break Turn after any other maneuver.

Team Defensive Tactics

Thach Weave or Beam Defense Position
A report published in the Fleet Air Tactical Unit Intelligence Bulletin of 22 September 1941 described the Japanese Zero's amazing maneuverability and rate of climb. Soon U.S. Naval aviator Lt.Cdr. John Thach began to develop tactics to give the slower-turning F4F Wildcat fighters a chance of success when meeting the Zero in combat called "Beam Defense Position," which soon became known as the "Thach Weave." It was executed either by two fighter aircraft side-by-side or by two pairs of fighters flying together. When an enemy pilot chose one fighter as his target (the "bait" fighter; his wingman being the "hook"), the two wingmen turned in towards each other and crossed paths. Once their separation was great enough, they would then repeat the maneuver, again turning in towards each other, bringing the enemy plane into the hook's sights. A correctly-executed Thach Weave (assuming the bait was taken and followed) gave even the most maneuverable opponent little chance to escape. The tactic was first tested in combat by Thach during the Battle of Midway and soon the maneuver become standard not only among U.S. Navy pilots, but USAAF and USMC pilots also adopted it.

THACH WEAVE

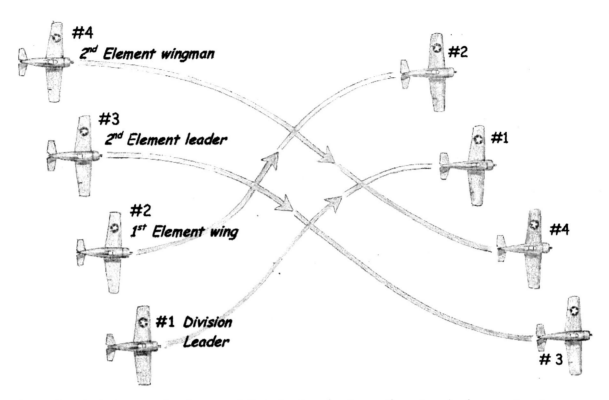

The Thach Weave deploys a 'division' echelon of paired elements, i.e., **Division Leader #1** and **Element #2** typically in a combat spread 100-150 yards from **Element Leader #3** and **Element #4**. Any opponent attacking one of these **Elements** will have two Wildcats countering from head-on. Reversing to confront this new dual-threat puts the intruder in front of the first F4F pair coming around for a deflection shot. Likewise, the paired Elements can assume the lead, or "weave" within their own 2-plane element.

The Lufbery Circle

The Lufbery Circle (rarely spelled "Lufberry," or less often, "Luffberry") is a defensive air combat tactic first used during WWI. In non-American sources it is usually referred to as a "Defensive Circle." While its name originates from leading Lafayette Escadrille ace Raoul Lufbery, he did not invent the tactic. How it got this name is unknown, but it may possibly be due to his use of the tactic when training incoming American pilots.

During WWI, the Lufbery was a simple concept, as the "wheel of wingmen" was a high-speed chandelle, nose to tail, that protected the 6 o'clock position of the pilot ahead. The tactic was devised to enable slower, less capable fighters to deal with attacks by an enemy flying superior aircraft and was sometimes used by light bomber formations. This tactic could only be used by formations of aircraft acting together, as it involved forming a horizontal circle that when attacked, the guns of each aircraft offered

protection to the others in the circle. The Lufbery as a whole had far fewer "blind spots," so that it was more difficult to attack an individual aircraft without being exposed to return fire from the others.

The Lufbery Circle, while generally effective against horizontal attacks by faster aircraft, was very vulnerable to attacks from fighters diving in high-speed hit-and-run attacks, providing vulnerable targets on a slow, predictable course in the Circle. Pilots also had to be careful in their decision to use it, as superior enemy fighters could get inside the Circle by circling in the opposite direction and firing, as the aircraft in the Circle could not bring their guns to bear. So it was essential for members of the Circle to make certain that enemy fighters could not interdict the integrity of the Circle or calamity was almost inevitable.

trim tabs during combat to maintain stability, the multitude relied on "feel" and getting into close range, yet the issue was vital.

When the attacking pilot pursued an enemy aircraft that was maneuvering he needed to be in stable flight before firing. Even in stable flight before shooting, the slightest change in direction by the enemy pilot could put the attacking aircraft slightly out of stable condition and cause yaw. For example, if the target began to bank, then the attacker would have to adjust his flight path for a shot that included both vertical and horizontal deflection.

The easiest shot was a zero deflection shot from directly behind the enemy and flying at exactly the same angle. The other zero deflection shot was a head-on attack, in which both the attacker and defender were closing directly at each other horizontally at very high speeds, so there was little time to aim and fire. The head-on pass was frequently used by American pilots with great effect, particularly by P-38 pilots firing their heavy array of nose-mounted .50 machine guns and 20mm cannon.

Thomas McGuire offered this Japanese reaction to the head-on pass:

"They don't like it and nine out of 10 will break first, even before they are in range. To be sure, the head-on attack cannot be recommended when flying a plane that has little armament, no convergence of lines of fire, and light armor, but what about this shout of "Banzai" and the suicide crash? Nothing about it because the Japanese aren't living up to dying for their propaganda. Instead they will break from the head-on pass in a vertical bank and try to come around for a tail attack. The P-38 pilot need only to keep on at the same speed or go into a shallow dive to defeat this tactic, for the enemy pilot loses speed in the bank and turn and will wind up too far behind to be a menace. In this case of the exceptional one, who does hold to a head-on pass, simply push over. The Japanese pilot will invariably go up. One thing you must not do when committed to a head-on pass, you must not turn until entirely clear."

A 20° shot from the front (11 to 1 o'clock) and the rear (7 to 5 o'clock) was considered a high probability shot, but was complicated by the fact that the attacker was either above or below the target; sometimes at large angles. If an attacking fighter was flying absolutely level at a faultless dead astern or head-on attack angle he could only miss to the left or right, but when making the same attack from above or below the attacker could miss left, right, up, or down. Most deflection shots were missed by being over or under, rather than by incorrect lead.

The most common gunnery mistake made by fighter pilots was not poor deflection shooting but firing too soon. Pilots were admonished about wasting long-range shots at high deflection because that would only warn the enemy pilot of an attack. Thomas McGuire's dictum for successful gunnery was to "go in close, then when you think you are too close, go on in closer."

7

Air Tactics Studies

Oswald Boelcke's Summary of Elementary Combat Tactics
Oswald Boelcke, an outstanding German WWI fighter pilot and arguably the best leader and tactician of that war, succinctly summarized the elementary tactics for dogfighting in his "Eight Commandments" for fighter pilots, known as "*Boelcke's Dicta*" and recapped as:

1) Take any advantages you can before you start an attack. Gain altitude and keep the sun behind you to blind your target.
2) After you commit to starting an attack, make sure you finish it.
3) Stick to close-range shots, and don't fire until you have the enemy well-lined up in your sights.
4) Constantly know where your opponent is. Don't glance away and let him fool you with his maneuvers.
5) Make your attack from behind if you can.
6) If an enemy is making a diving attack on you, don't evade it. Instead, trying climbing up to meet him.
7) When flying over enemy territory, remain aware of your escape route toward friendly lines.
8) Attack in numbers. If all pilots separate into individual battles, communicate and make sure no one is making a duplicate attack.

5th Fighter Command: Fighter Combat Tactics in the SWPA
In 1944, the 8th Air Force's Fighter Command published two manuals entitled *Long Reach* and *Down to Earth* which served as primers on air-to-air and air-to-ground combat, respectively, for the rookie fighter pilots recently arriving in the ETO. These manuals were compiled by VIII Fighter Command Staff Officers from the experiences of both the leading aces and veteran Fighter Group Leaders. These manuals were the motivation for the 5th Fighter Command to produce its own similar manual edited by Col. Roy Brischetto, Assistant Chief of Staff of 5th Fighter Command's General Staff Corps, who contacted a number of the leading aces in the Pacific, along with several Group Commanders and a few other less recognized, but no less qualified, front line fighter pilots. In its final form, the "Confidential" manual was published on 1 August 1945, containing written reports submitted by 26 pilots. Parts of some of these reports are included to give the reader insight into the tactics described in Individual Combat Reports.

First Hand Fighter Combat Tactics
When fighter aces were questioned about the most important factors that made them successful, two—luck and surprise—were mentioned most

frequently. Luck, or being in the right place at the right time, was something the pilot had no control over. Undoubtedly, many excellent pilots never became aces nor even scored a victory simply because they never had the luck to encounter any enemy aircraft. Conversely, many average pilots, utilizing surprise in their encounters with enemy aircraft, were successful.

The single most important controllable factor in successful air combat was surprise. It could be achieved by:
1) Attacking directly out of the sun (the most used means of surprise).
2) Attacking from the darker part of the sky as aircraft in the brighter part become silhouetted and more visible and the attacker less visible.
3) Attacking in the early morning or evening when lighting was problematical.
4) Making use of clouds, both offensively and defensively. When the enemy used the clouds, try to establish where the enemy aircraft were likely to emerge.
5) Making use of haze banks in Summer, as aircraft approaching on the same level are difficult to see if they attack from the side opposite the sun.

Other factors mentioned were more of a defensive, "stay alive," nature:
1) Awareness at all times was essential, as Navy ace and tactician James Flatley succinctly stated: "Eternal vigilance or eternal rest." The importance of developing a "rubber neck" was stressed. Before take off or landing, when an aircraft was most vulnerable, a search of the sky for enemy aircraft was essential. Other aphorisms included: "Watch your tail"; "Keep the sky under constant surveillance"; "Don't let the enemy slip out of the sun to get at you"; and "See the enemy first and report him to the rest of the flight."
2) "Rolling out and diving to escape when caught in a surprise bounce." This tactic was the credo of Gen. Claire Chennault when the P-40s of his AVG were outclassed and outmaneuvered by the nimble Japanese Zero. Chennault's Tigers were never to be jumped on deck, as they were to "always maintain an airspeed of at least 250mph and enough altitude so that if trouble developed there was enough diving height as an altitude advantage was a great asset as it could be turned into airspeed and surprise at the pilot's choosing."
3) "Turning into an attacking enemy aircraft if he was seen in time." Turning into an attack shortened the enemy's approach and made him turn more

rapidly and be forced to break away. ETO ace and tactician Col. Donald Blakeslee stressed to his pilots that if attacked they should "immediately turn into the enemy and meet him head-on and then under no circumstance break from this course." When asked by a young pilot "What if the German doesn't break either?" Blakeslee answered: "Well, then you earned your hazardous duty pay!"

4) When being chased, the pilot was to attempt to tighten a turn to gain the advantage and get into a position behind the enemy.

5) The Wingman System, the basic tenant of faith in the American fighter combat doctrine, allowed the Element Leader to concentrate on the attack with the confidence he was being covered from attack by his Wingman.

Once an enemy aircraft was seen and closed on, there was one common axiom for the attacking pilot: "Get in so close that you can't miss"; "Don't waste ammo at long range"; "Dive, hit hard, hit fast and get out"; and "Haul the stick back into your lap and use your excess speed to regain the altitude advantage."

Individual traits, such as excellent eyesight, natural judgment of height and distances, quick reflexes, and the aggressor mentality were essential for success. The fighter pilot's most important faculty was sharp eyesight, as the essential factor in all air combat was to see your enemy first, then continue to keep him in sight. It was demanding and tiring to remain continually observant for hours on end while sitting in a cramped cockpit unable to smoke, eat, or drink, and with the sunlight dazzling through your canopy and goggles for hours. Master tactician Hubert "Hub" Zemke of the 56FG in the ETO felt that to be successful, the fighter pilot must at all times have the inner desire to go into combat. Pilot attitude of being the hunter and not the hunted not only made the pilot confident, but also increased his survivability. The survival rate of the aggressive pilot was greater than that of the cautious pilot.

But also important was that the pilot had the understanding of the performance and handling capabilities and limitations of his fighter and those of the opposing enemy aircraft.

8

Fighter Formations

The principal motive for a fighter formation was management and discipline. In the interwar years, the United States favored the conventional fighter formation organized into Elements of three aircraft in a V formation that was favored by bombers. The V was discarded as soon as America entered the war and the British Leader/Wingman two-plane system was adopted. The RAF experience in the Battles of France and Britain caused them to be in turn influenced by the successful Luftwaffe "Schwarm" fighter formation techniques used there. The Luftwaffe had developed the technique during the Spanish Civil War, but later in WWII used the line abreast or "Wall" formation. The Japanese generally flew the Shotai, a division of three fighters arranged in Vics, in echelons or in a loose, staggered trail formation. The two wingmen would weave in loose formation behind their leader. When engaged the Shotai could stay together, Fall into trail, or brake with each aircraft fighting independently.

Paradoxically, during the air war in the Southwest Pacific, the Japanese and American fighter pilots swapped combat philosophy relative to their presumed national character. Japanese pilots grew up during a period when a militaristic establishment emphasized group principles into the Japanese national consciousness, but then developed tactics that emphasized the individual in air combat. Their American counterparts grew up in an environment that esteemed individualism, but then trained in well organized and disciplined small group air tactics.

The fundamental American fighter unit was two fighters, a Leader and Wingman ("No.2" in RAF parlance) known as an Element. The Leader's duty was to attack while the Wingman was to protect his Leader from interception from the rear throughout the mission. This technique was known as the "Wingman System" and was the key to survival and used with great success by American Air Forces. This two-plane Element was the basic unit of all larger combat formations.

Finger Four

A Flight was composed of two Elements and was led by the Leader of one of the Elements. It was considered the most effective fighter combat formation for attack and defense. It was adaptable to various combat situations, as each Element was easily able to assist the other. This formation was referred to as the "Finger Four" because from above the four fighters were in the position correlating to the finger tips when one looks down at the top of one's right hand. The Element Leader (No.1, or middle finger) was about 100 feet in front and to the right of his Wingman (No.2, or first finger),

while the second Element Leader (No.3, ring finger) was about 150 feet behind and to the right of the Element leader, and his Wingman (No.4, pinkie finger) was about 100 feet behind and to the right of him. The No.2 Wingman could fly to the left or right of the Leader, 100 feet behind and stepped slightly down for maneuverability. The second Element flew 150ft to the rear of the Flight Leader and crossed underneath with his Wingman on all turns. During the war, group tacticians were encouraged to develop and experiment with new formations, but the Finger Four continued as the fundamental combat tactical formation.

Two Flights made up a Section and was the usual component for bomber escort and support. Two Sections made up the typical Squadron of 16 fighters (that initially were organized into three four-plane Flights). Although there were variations in Section and Squadron tactics, the Finger Four remained the basis of all larger formations.

Echelon

When all four aircraft were on the same side of the Leader this formation was called an Echelon. The Echelon was entered by timed peel offs by the Leader's Wingman (to the right) or the Element (to the left), crossing over so all aircraft are on the same side of the Leader. The main use of the Echelon was to move to Trail Formation.

Trail

Trail was a formation where the four aircraft simply lined up one behind the other, each stacked a little below the aircraft in front with a separation of 175 to 250 feet between aircraft to avoid prop wash. Entering a Trail Formation was from an Echelon, with each aircraft peeling off (usually at three second intervals) following the Leader.
Formations and Tactics

General

The standard Fighter Squadron Formation was 16 aircraft in four-plane Flights, with the Flight being the basic component for both attack and defense. Each fighter within the Flight occupied a position on a line extending back at an approximate 45° angle from the Flight Leader, the fighters being spaced one to three aircraft lengths apart. The Wingman flew to the left or right and above the Flight Leader, usually on the opposite side from the Wingman. The Element Leader's Wingman could fly either above or below the Element Leader, but no matter the vertical variations, the one to three

FINGER-FOUR

Four USAAF fighter aircraft are typically called a *"flight"* and the flyers are designated *"elements"* likened to the fingers of an outstretched hand. The *flight* likewise bears a "call-sign," i.e., *Red Flight* with the mission leader being *Red Leader 1*, his wingman *Red 2*, the *Element Leader Red 3* and his wingman *Red 4*.

In the fight, *elements 1* and *3* were the primary gunmen with their corresponding wingmen in close support.

Elements 3 and *4* might well be sent up as high-cover if the logistics so demanded. The Flight's combat spread varied as affected by weather and visibility.

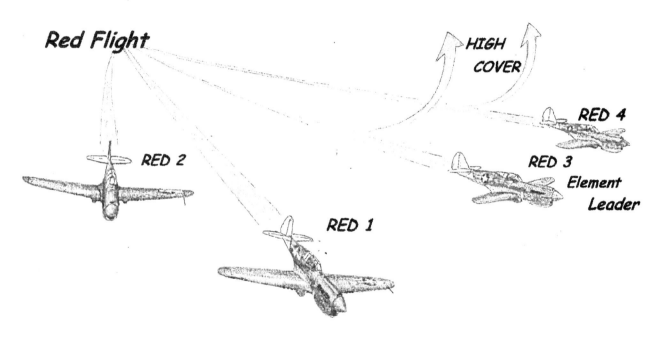

Red Flight — RED 2 — RED 1 — HIGH COVER — RED 4 — RED 3 Element Leader

aircraft length distance on the horizontal plane and the angle in reference to the Flight Leader was to be maintained.

This Flight Formation assured maximum visibility with complete coverage for each man in the Flight, allowing the Flight Leader to see that his Flight was remaining together and the other three pilots were to keep the Flight Leader in sight but not fly into the blind spot directly behind the Flight Leader. The formation was flexible enough to permit each pilot to maintain his throttle setting by weaving and crossing over when necessary without decreasing mutual support. It also was loose enough for the Flight Leader to maneuver freely without being overrun by his Flight or losing them due to an unanticipated turn, dive, or climb. This solely defensive formation was to remain unchanged regardless of whether the mission was an escort, patrol, or search, and would only change to line abreast or line astern except in combat.

The Squadron Formation had the same flexibility and visibility as the Flight Formation, with each of the following Flights being able to see the Squadron Leader and all other Flights ahead. The Lead Flight was ahead at lowest altitude, the second Flight was to the left or right and behind, the third Flight to the left or right and behind the preceding Flights (remaining on the opposite side as much as possible), and the fourth Flight was to the left and behind the third Flight, but not directly behind the first Flight. Each of the Flights was staggered upwards from the one immediately proceeding, the difference in altitude ranging from 500 to 1,000 feet. Within the Squadron Formation, the Flights would also weave and cross over when necessary to avoid changing throttle too much. This formation was used on all types of missions, as it assured it mutual protection if attacked, but was also the easiest to change to an attack formation.

Combat Formation

In combat, the Flight was also the fundamental component and its attack mode was basically to have the factions of the Flight drop into string, slightly staggered, with a three to six aircraft length interval between them. The Flights within the Squadron Formation also dropped into a string of Flights with an interval of half to a full flight's length between Flights,

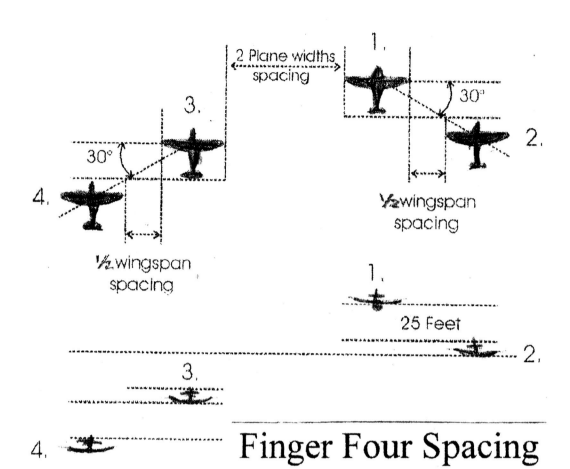

Finger Four Spacing

which were also slightly staggered. In both Flight and Squadron Formations, by dropping into a staggered string formation there was no risk of firing and hitting the fighter ahead when the formation concentrated its fire on a target. However, a Flight of four aircraft, much less a full Squadron Formation of 16 fighters, was usually unable to remain together after the first mutual attack. Usually, it was necessary for the Flights (or pilots of a single Flight) to break in different directions, either to attack or defend against the enemy fighters.

The four-plane Flight was to remain together for as long as possible, especially when attacking bombers, when there were no reasons for breaking formation. After making a firing pass, the Flight Leader attempted to remain in a shallow dive or climb so that his Flight could follow through normally and retain their relative positions, with the tail end man guarding the three flight members ahead and the Flight Leader in position to turn around to protect the tail end man if he was attacked.

If the combat became fighter versus fighter, then it could be necessary to break up into two-plane elements, but no further, as under no circumstances was a Wingman to leave his Element Leader.

Principal Mission of Fighter Pilots

The principal mission of fighter pilots was to either destroy or protect bombers, but opposing fighter pilots also had the same mission; as a result, fighter pilots faced one another with their objective being to destroy each other. American pilots entered the war in 1942 flying relatively advanced fighters for the time, but without the advantage of valid combat tactics, which had to be developed along the way. During WWI, pilots on the Western Front realized it was essential to approach the enemy "from an advantageous position using altitude, surprise, and concentration of force." However, once the enemy was met the situation developed into individual dogfights in which self control, marksmanship, and flying skill decided the victor. During the interwar years, air combat theory continued to emphasize inflexible, stylish formation flying for groups and elegant aerobatic maneuvers for individual pilots. The training for and the flying of intricate formations allowed aircraft of a unit to assemble quickly and properly with each other, then rendezvous with another unit elsewhere. During this period, the world political and military leaders were particularly anxious of the possibility of extensive bombing attacks on cities and fighters were developed almost completely in an anti-bomber role and were thus designated "pursuit" aircraft. The viability of comparably slow pursuit aircraft continued to be questioned by the self-styled "bomber will always get through" advocates. However, the development of very fast fighters in the late 1930s ended any doubts concerning the future of fighter aircraft and their ability to fly with or against bombers. Nonetheless, the emphasis on inflexible formation flying continued and all of the world's air forces used the three-plane section flying in V-formation (the "Vic") for their basic pursuit tactical component. The Flight Leader flew slightly in front of his two Wingmen, who were positioned to his right and left rear with all three planes flying close, almost wing tip to wing tip. It was assumed that the V-formation, especially the "V of Vs," was ideal for well coordinated, massed attacks on bombers. The world's air tacticians' fixation on bombers delayed the development of fighter tactics, especially when considering the large increase of speed and loss of maneuverability that resulted from the replacement of the biplane by the monoplane. Tacticians continued to presume that fighter combat would be flown by well-trained pilots in the small, elite, very well-trained fighter units flying spectacular aerobatic maneuvers in a series of one-on-one combats, most likely during patrol missions over the front lines.

By the late 1930s, American tactical air doctrine was similar to the flawed doctrine of the world's air forces. American observers in Europe during 1940, including Gen. George Kenney, saw the Allied air debacle in France and the desperate struggle during the Battle of Britain. They quickly realized that the AAF needed rehabilitation, and in the months before Pearl Harbor American aircraft designers greatly improved the oxygen system for the aircrews and designed and fitted self-sealing fuel tanks and improved armor in fighters. They also improved the design of the .50 caliber machine gun, increasing its rate of fire and efficiency. Fortunately, these designers were developing and improving aircraft systems just as they were also developing new aircraft designs in which to place them.

The Americans were also quick to note that the British V formation was much too rigid and mostly misused the skills of the wingmen. If the Flight Leader was forced to make a tight maneuver, the formation scattered and a collision between Wingmen was a continuous hazard. Luftwaffe tacticians, evaluating their experience in the Spanish Civil War, abandoned the V formation and adopted the famous four-plane Schwarm. The Schwarm consisted of a flight leader and his Wingman accompanied by a Section Leader and his Wingman. When flying in a Schwarm, the aircraft were separated by 600 to 1,000 feet, approximately equal to their turning radius, and were positioned almost exactly as four outstretched fingertips, causing the Americans to call their formation the "finger four." During combat, the Schwarm usually separated into two sections, with the section leader flying "the fighting plane," while his Wingman's primary duty was to protect his leader's tail. The Finger Four proved to be an ideal system for initiating inexperienced pilots, as their responsibility, though still dangerous, was much easier. As the Wingman became more experienced, he and his Leader developed more intricate offensive and defensive tactics, and so the AAF would become dedicated to the two-plane Element and stressed the importance of fighting as a unit.

A Squadron consisted of four (or five) flights—Red, White, Blue, and Green (and Yellow)—flying in a diamond formation. White Flight flew on the right flank slightly below and behind Red Flight. Blue Flight flew on the left flank above Red and behind White. Green Flight flew the top directly behind Red. The altitude difference between the low flight and top flight was not over 1,500 feet, while the space between flanks was about 3,500-4,000 feet. This configuration provided maximum visibility and protection, as when attacked, Red and White provided mutual protection, as did Blue and Green. A surprise bounce by enemy fighters was always a distinct possibility and every pilot in the formation searched the sky for attackers, particularly when clouds or the position of the sun were factors. If a Squadron had four Flights together, the last Flight might periodically weave behind the other three as a rear guard against an ambush. If the rear Flight was bounced it would dive toward the front of the formation while the lead Flight turned into the enemy attack, placing the attackers in their fire.

In the Flight of four, the third and fourth men would weave back and forth behind the first two. The Second Element Leader (the pilot in the third position) was always the second senior pilot, while the Flight Leader was the first senior pilot. The two Elements were not always aligned: sometimes slightly below, sometimes above, sometimes off to one side.

These Squadron/Flight arrangements were well suited to the air battles in the Pacific, which generally involved no more than 50 aircraft and occurred over a relatively small area, with most of the effective combat taking place at high speeds and at close range, usually inside 250-300 yards

9

5th Fighter Command Missions and Combat Tactics in the SWPA

Tactics of First- and Second-Generation American Fighters

Tactics for the 5th Fighter Command during the war fell into two pases. All first-generation American fighters, if the enemy was seen in time, were able to go into a high speed, curving dive that a Zero was unable to catch. Once the American pilot pulled out, he had difficulty regaining altitude but was safe. A lightly armored and incendiary Japanese aircraft caught in the fire of a fast-diving American fighter pass would probably experience severe damage and unless a cloud was nearby, diving away was often a fatal maneuver.

If U.S. second-generation fighters had the altitude advantage, their Japanese targets were doomed and American pilots could make a pass through a Japanese bomber formation, go into a shallow high-speed climb, and repeat the action before the enemy formation broke up or enemy escort fighters appeared. The ideal result of the first or second pass by fast U.S. fighters was to break up the Japanese bomber formation, making individual bombers vulnerable to attack by the American two-plane Element. If enemy escorts appeared, the P-38 could not turn with them and the American pilots had to keep their speed up and always try to get into an altitude advantage. If not, they would dive to keep airspeed always above 350mph so that an enemy pilot could not close. The enemy fighters could not match the Lightning's dives, climbs, and high altitude performance, and the American pilots were to never allow the enemy pilot to fight on his terms in a low altitude, turning dogfight. If the Japanese were about to attack, alerted radio-carrying American aircraft could all break off from a possible dogfight to gain speed and altitude and return to the attack.

Five Mission Types

Routine Patrol and Enemy Interception

The type of mission flown by a fighter pilot influenced the probability that he would encounter enemy aircraft. Generally, fighter pilots flew five types of missions, with the most common being the routine patrol, in which a small number of aircraft tried to prevent harassing attacks on air bases, locate and destroy enemy reconnaissance aircraft, and search for enemy naval vessels. The fighter patrol system was usually kept close to base, as other long-range aircraft were better suited for reconnaissance. Because enemy bases in the Pacific were at least 200 miles apart, a local patrol was unlikely to encounter the enemy and most patrols could be hazardous, because they caused fatigue and boredom, leading to flying accidents.

Bomber Escort

The second type of fighter combat mission was bomber escort, which was likely to result in engagements with the enemy. While the Marine and 13AF fighter pilots were protecting their bombers against the Japanese over Guadalcanal and intercepting attacking Japanese bombers, 5AF A-20 and B-25 strafers, dropping parafrag bombs, simultaneously began to systematically destroy Japanese air bases at Buna, Lae, and Salamaua, separating them from their western bases in New Britain. In the face of the destruction of every air base in New Guinea, the Japanese were compelled to intercept the American bombers and their escorts, which led to most fighter engagements in the SWPA.

Fighter Sweep

The third type of mission was a fighter sweep, usually coordinated with a bomber attack, in which fighters would lead the way over enemy bases, looking for combat with unwary enemy aircraft, enemy fighters taking off or landing, or to attack those on the ground. The fighter sweep in the Pacific was not as effective as that in the ETO, as the Japanese did not want to defy the odds and take on twelve or sixteen enemy fighters which had the advantage of numbers, surprise, and altitude.

Shipping Defense or Attack

The fourth mission, which was infrequent but likely to lead to air combat, was shipping defense or attack. During almost every Allied amphibious landing made after February 1942, Japanese aircraft attempted to attack shipping, with merchant and troop ships being the prime targets; however, warships often tempted their bomber formations. The Japanese sent out unescorted bomber formations, but after heavy losses soon discovered that their tactical and strategic bombers needed fighter protection. Convoy attack by escorted bombers then became a Japanese specialty, as Japanese bombers attacked American shipping and troops at Guadalcanal, New Georgia, Bougainville, and every step up the New Guinea coastal ladder. Some anti-shipping attacks led to the largest air battles in the Pacific.

Ground/Close Air Support

This last duty was yeoman-like and not glamorous. It was not only dangerous, but gained increased importance as the war continued, especially over the Philippines.

Tactics When Intercepting Japanese Bombers

Medium or High Altitude Bombers

The Japanese Air Forces had no true heavy bombers, such as the B-17 or B-24, as most would be classified as B-25 type medium bombers without low level capabilities. Enemy light bombers or torpedo bombers were not encountered very often by the 5FC.

Initially, the Japanese bombers flew in large, tight formations at higher altitudes using their standard bomber Chutai combat formation of nine bombers in a V formation of three Shotai of three bombers each. The largest formation was the Daitai of 27 bombers in a V composed of three Chutai, flying at over 23,000 feet or higher when heavy fighter opposition was expected. When enemy interceptors were encountered, the Japanese bombers went into a long line abreast formation formed by the Wingman in each Shotai, with the wing formations in progressively larger formations moving forward until they were almost abreast of the Leader. This maneuver gave a heavy concentration of defensive fire on the attacking interceptors, but the bombers at the very ends of the formation (known to the Japanese as "Komo" or "sitting duck") were the most vulnerable and suffered high casualties. By the beginning of 1943, excessive casualties caused the Japanese to abandon daylight V of V bomber formations and they concentrated their bomber attacks to medium and low altitude nighttime attacks by small formations and single bombers.

The Japanese held their tight formation pattern tenaciously, closing up if one of its bombers was shot down. The 5FC countered these bomber formations with a first pass of 16 fighters, attempting to break up the enemy formation by using the highest concentration of fire power and forcing the enemy to disperse his fire power. Once the enemy formation was scattered, the individual or bomber pairs were much easier to pick off for 5FC Flights or Elements. Generally, the 5th Fighter Command was able to break up these tight formations and keep the enemy bombers from reaching their target.

The most effective method for the fighter squadron to attack enemy bombers was to make a head-on pass from 45° left or right, breaking away to the same side as that from which the approach was made, then follow through the circle and swing ahead for another pass. The Squadron was to try to remain together as long as possible, but if enemy fighter intervention arrived and forced the Squadron to separate, then it was up to the Flights to make their attacks independently.

The 5FC also used the side attack from 90° high, coming down and breaking away when the angle of approach narrowed to approximately 45°. This attack mode kept the attacking fighters out of the arc of fire of that potent Japanese bomber 20mm tail stinger and it was also easier to keep the Squadron intact.

5FC pilots were instructed that as long as they could make passes on the bombers, they were not to engage enemy fighters, which could do no damage to the target, and that the enemy's air strength was undermined much more by the loss of a bomber than by the loss of a fighter. Enemy fighters were to be dealt with only when they could no longer be ignored.

Enemy fighters protecting their own bombers would typically linger well above the formation in a large loose, swarming cluster. As a rule, they did not make coordinated or combined passes and they were unable to prevent a determined interception, unless they greatly outnumbered the American intercepting force. The Japanese fighter pilots preferred to wait at the edges of combat, choosing lax opposing fighters that were completing passes or making a surprise attack from the clouds, then would pull back up into the cloud coverage as soon as possible after the attack.

Dive Bombers

Thomas McGuire: "Wheels-down dive bombers were so familiar that our pilots have almost a friendly feeling toward them….as these slow-moving, poorly armed, unarmored planes are the nearest thing to sitting ducks as will be found in modern warfare, and their strategy in action appears to be designed to have as many of them shot down as possible." After beginning their dives from 15,000 to 18,000 feet, Val dive bombers reached a maximum speed of 300-325mph and continued directly down at 55-60°, dropping their bombs at 1,500 feet, although veteran pilots would often hold their dives to 1,000 feet, where they broke formation and raced off for home in all directions, skimming just above the deck. Most 5FC fighters were able to follow them easily in their dives and often were able to force them to jettison their bombs before they could release them on the shipping that was their usual target. After having pulled out of its dive, a Val slowed down rapidly while skimming low over the water and the pursuing 5FC fighter would close and fire a fatal burst, with the best attack approach being from astern, but the attack could be varied to head-on or from the side under the right conditions.

When escorting dive bombers, Japanese fighter pilots were reluctant to make themselves vulnerable by following to low altitudes to protect them, but remained at altitude, waiting to have the Americans engage them there. The fast-diving American fighters followed the dive bombers and would seldom be intercepted by the Japanese fighter escorts.

Bomber Interception: Maneuvers

While the combined firepower of heavily-armed American bomber formations accounted for many enemy fighters that risked approaching too closely, Japanese bombers were comparatively lightly armed, mostly mounting only a few light machine guns. On both sides, bomber escort fighters presented the major danger to attacking fighters. The basic maneuvers used to attack an unescorted bomber, both Japanese and American, generally involved making attacks either high or low and off to one side to avoid gunner fire. Of course, when attacking a specific bomber the pilot would do well to be an expert on aircraft recognition and its armament.

High/Low Side Attack

When attacking bombers with tail guns, a pilot would choose a high and/ or low side attack that enabled him to stay out of that gunner's sights and gave him shots at the rear left and right quadrants of the bomber. The pilot needed to be an accomplished deflection shooter for this maneuver, which was approximately 35 to 45° off the rear of the bomber.

To make a high side pass, the pilot had to position his fighter about 1,500 feet above and slightly ahead of the bomber and laterally, keeping several wingspans of separation between him and the target. He would begin a steep dive and bank toward the rear of the target at approximately 45 lateral degrees. As he moved within firing range, he opened fire with a long leading burst, then broke off the attack and dove underneath the bomber.

After he cleared the target, the attacker pulled up out of the dive using the acquired diving speed and also to gain some lateral distance in preparation to make a low pass. He raised the nose and banked back toward the bomber, reversing the attack by banking inward and up toward the bomber's opposite rear quadrant. He fired another long burst, then pulled up and over the bomber, kept climbing, and repeated another high side attack.

This maneuver resembled a weave pattern, except that the pilot switched between high and low attacks, essentially flying an alternating high and low ribbon pattern around the bomber. The longer the pilot held the bomber in his sights before diving or climbing, the more he would have banked and the smaller his angle of deflection.

If the attacker did not have enough time to gain a 1,500 foot altitude advantage but was approximately 500 feet above the enemy bomber, the pilot could execute a low side pass. This attack basically involved the same tactic, except that the initial dive was necessarily shallower and would not have much power when the pilot went into the climbing portion of the maneuver. A low pass was used to make a lone pass on a bomber or to finish off a damaged bomber.

Opposite Attack

During frenzied combat conditions, a pilot did not always have time to position himself correctly for a tracking shot, so opposite attacks were a practical solution, as they allowed the pilot to fire off passing snapshots without being concerned with lead angles. A pilot could make an opposite attack while flying higher, lower, or head-on against a target. When attacking high, the attacker needed at least 2,000 feet above and below his intended target; a maneuver requiring room for both the dive and the recovery. The pilot went into a gentle dive in front and under his target and would have him in his sights only briefly to fire a spurt of bullets. The low attack was similar, except that the pilot climbed up and in front of the target. The most dangerous choice of attack was the level, head-on attack, which although it did not involve diving or climbing, it placed the attacker directly in front of the bomber for an extended length of time.

Overhead Pass

Some defensive maneuvers could be converted into offensive attacks against bombers. This variation of the Split-S was valuable if the bomber was flying toward the pilot and back-to-back Split-S and Immelmann turns could be used to make attacks on a bomber flying the same direction.

For an overhead pass on a bomber on a similar flight path, the pilot had to maneuver so that he was flying ahead, above, and considerably off to one side of the target. The pilot began a wide, banking descent toward the bomber, applying some rudder in the process to assist the turn. After he completed the 180° banking turn, he went into a half-roll to invert his fighter. He then pulled back on the stick to go into a half loop and toward the end of the loop he fired at the bomber. He then needed to immediately bank left or right to break out of the bomber's tail gunner's firing range.

The pilot could make a head-on version of this attack against an approaching bomber. As he closed, the attacker flew slightly above the bomber and once he passed overhead, he inverted his fighter and pulled back on the stick to fly a half-loop. As he came out of the loop he started to fire. He then made certain to bank hard in one direction to set up for another attack approach.

Bomber Escort

Initially, bombers flew in a mutually supportive boxed formation at staggered altitudes, using their turret and hand-held guns to protect one another. This defense was soon found not very effective, as attacking enemy fighters registered high victory totals. All combatants determined that a fighter escort was vital for the survival of a bomber mission. Range was the most significant escort problem, as the smaller fighters were unable to carry enough fuel for the entire mission. External auxiliary fuel tanks—underwing or belly—mostly alleviated this problem later.

Tactical concerns regarding bomber escort also needed to be resolved. The fighter escorts assigned to stay with the bomber group had much faster cruising speeds and often had to fly back-and-forth weaving patterns to avoid flying too far ahead of the bombers. The tactics used in bomber escort were "aggressive defense." On close cover with four Flights, the Flights were to weave over the bombers at 2,000 to 5,000 feet. When enemy fighters were definitely spotted, the Squadron Leader sent one or two Flights to break them up or shoot them down, but were not to pursue them too far away from the bombers. They were to return to the escort as soon as practical.

Allied Tactics against Enemy Aircraft Attacking Their Escorted Bombers:

Close Cover

Depending on the number of bombers escorted and the opposition expected, close cover for bombers usually had one Squadron assigned to each of the flanks, one Squadron ahead, and one Squadron behind. Formations of 24 or less bombers did not require four full Squadrons as escort, but with more than 24 the fighter numbers increased until, with a 100 or more bombers, there were three or four Squadrons as close cover, two Squadrons as medium and high cover, and a possible additional Squadron as top cover for the fighter and bomber formations as a whole. While a number of the enemy would attack from above, there would be others attacking from beneath when the close cover would descend somewhat and would separate into flights to fend off the single enemy passes.

Top Cover

Providing successful bomber top cover was difficult, because the Japanese made determined attacks from the most favorable positions. The Squadron on top cover was stationed at 4,000 to 8,000 feet above the entire bomber formation and the escorting fighter close cover and weaved to keep its true forward speed the same as that of the bombers below. If the bomber formation became disorganized, top cover was to guard over its perimeter to prevent enemy fighters from picking off stragglers. The Japanese seldom made an organized interception, instead trying to break up the bomber formation by attacking in pairs or more, but during or after the bombing run they would make haphazard individual or sometimes paired attacks. Usually, these attacks were from above as the enemy pilots half rolled into an overhead pass, diving and firing through the bomber formation, then clearing away to the side and regaining altitude. Because the Japanese did not attack in formation or numbers, the only feasible AAF counter tactic was to divide the top cover into flights and repel the attacks as soon as possible after the Japanese pilot had committed himself to his attack.

The preferred target for a Japanese pilot was the target of opportunity, so the fighter escorts had to be most vigilant when the bombers left the target area and damaged bombers began to straggle. To protect the crippled bombers on their return to base, the Squadron Leader assigned Flights to each of the stragglers within range of his cover.

Allied Tactics for the Escort of Low Level Strafers and Bombers

On a low level mission, the Squadron acting as close cover for medium bombers or strafers would generally be at slightly higher altitude (from 2,000 to 6,000 feet) than when escorting heavy bombers. The top cover would also be higher, staying at 8,000 to 10,000 feet above the close cover.

Since an attack from beneath was practically impossible on the low level bombers, escorting fighters were to break up Japanese attacks before they were well underway and before too many attackers could get within range of the strafers and bombers. Against strafers, the Japanese would dive either near or through the Allied formation in as nearly a vertical dive and climb as possible. Only a few enemy pilots would make courageous but foolhardy horizontal passes from that very disadvantageous position. The Squadron escort formation would again disperse in Flights to ward off individual enemy attacks, then would usually split up from Flights to Elements relatively early in the combat, because the defense would be more about protecting individual bombers on the perimeter, rather than covering the whole formation. It was a temptation for an escort pilot to chase enemy fighters after they made their passes and before they could regain altitude. This tactic was "foolish and futile," as it weakened both the Squadron and its Flights, but defeated the purpose of the escorts, which was to assure the bombers of an opportunity to bomb and/or strafe with as little interference as possible from enemy fighters.

Offensive Fighter Sweeps

Offensive Fighter sweeps were designed to penetrate an area and clear it of all enemy aircraft. They were relatively standard in planning and execution, with their variations governed by the known factors of terrain, enemy AA positions, targets, their expected opposition, and the nature of the mission. Offensive Fighter Sweeps were described in a combat narrative as raising "merry Hell with the Japanese Air Force, not to mention its morale."

An offensive sweep combat always began in one of two ways: either the Squadron descended to attack or was attacked, usually from above. On offensive sweeps, the diamond type Squadron formation was flown, with Flights dispersed to give maximum protection to all the aircraft involved. When only a few enemy aircraft were involved, the Squadron Leader sent one or two Flights down to contact the enemy, while the remaining Flights were positioned off to one side, into the sun, if possible, so that maximum coverage of the attacking Flights could be maintained. When a large number of enemy planes were sighted, the Squadron was instructed to only attack if it had the initial advantage. Once contact was made, it was impossible for a Squadron to maintain formation, at which time the combat broke down into Flights, and even further into Elements and individual combats. However, Flights were to make every effort to maintain a Flight formation, but Flights were often unavoidably separated, in which case the Elements were to remain intact and would attempt to rejoin into the Flight formation as quickly as possible. The Japanese were reluctant to attack a well maintained Flight, whereas invariably the Japanese would congregate on the lone fighter.

Usually, when a Japanese pilot was attacked he would most often go into a severe evasive turn. The Lead Element of the Flight would break away, thus giving the Second Element the better opportunity to fire, after which he too broke away and joined the Lead Element again. Pressing the attack for any length of time was not advised, because other enemy fighters would have time to arrive and make an unexpected attack. In this case it was desirable, if possible, to have one Flight held back for a while to act as top cover to protect against unseen enemy fighters attempting to join the fight.

When the Squadron was attacked from above, the only alternative to the top Flight was to dive away. However, the Squadron would never have so little warning that one of the lower Flights could not make a climbing turn into the attackers. When the formation was the typical diamond formation, the Flight that was the furthest away and below had the most time to avoid attack by turning and forcing the enemy into a head-on pass. The intermediate Flights may have had enough time to turn to fire a few bursts, which sometimes scared off the attackers. This tactic was not always successful, but the intermediate Flight could always dive away if the disadvantage became too great. When attacked from six o'clock at fairly close range, the U.S. fighter, because of its high roll and push over rates, was able to break away by having its pilot "shove the stick into the right hand corner." It was impossible for the enemy pilot, despite his fighter's great maneuverability, to apply sufficient lead to get a good shot. After the top Flight dove away, it was to do so under the other Flight's formation so that the other Flight to fend off the attack.

After the combat had continued for about 15 minutes, the Squadron Leader was to call for the Squadron to clear the area and reform. The Flight Leaders were to comply immediately to reduce the reforming time to a minimum in order to save fuel, which was very important when operating at extreme ranges.

Close Air Support

The important role of close air support was not given adequate attention in volumes one and two, which concentrated on the more glamorous air-to-air combat campaigns. ICRs were filed only if enemy aircraft were encountered during a mission and combat narratives usually gave brief, typically statistical descriptions of close air support. The following is a description and assessment of close air support in the SWPA and the Philippines.

New Guinea Campaign

In supporting the Allied advance along the coast of New Guinea with diversions to New Britain and the Admiralties, the Fifth Air Force slowly learned how to provide effective support to the ground forces. Their Douglas A-20s and North American B-25s, flying at tree top altitude, were deadly when used against enemy infantry, shipping, and parked aircraft. B-24 Liberators, bombing from medium altitude, could destroy fortifications if given enough time and a definite target. Once enemy air opposition had declined, every available type of 5th Fighter Command fighter aircraft (P-40s, P-39s, P-38s, and later P-47s) proved to be effective against ground targets. On short missions, the Thunderbolt and Lightning could carry bomb loads heavier than carried by A-20s and loads comparable to that carried by B-25s. In the New Guinea Campaign, 5FC fighters would gain experience in close air support which they would use to great effect in the Philippines.

During the Lae to Morotai operations target marking was optimally improved, although the marking of front line targets required more experience due to the proximity of friendly troops. Among the methods used for target identification were gridded oblique photographs, artillery and mortar smoke shells, large cloth arrows pointed toward the target, observation aircraft, and verbal descriptions by air-to-ground radio. To be certain of the correct targeting, usually two or more target indicators were utilized.

Air support communications were also improved, though in amphibious operations, it remained standard practice to request a mission the day before it was to be implemented. By mid-1944, Support Aircraft Parties (SAPs) had sufficient radio equipment, and in the late Summer the use of the DUKW amphibian vehicles in amphibious landing operations was preventing the damage of radio equipment by exposure to salt water. The Support Aircraft Request (SAR), originating at Hollandia, became a standard characteristic of each amphibious operation and provided a more rapid method of sending requests back to the executing agencies. The Support Aircraft Direction

(SAD) network was also available for each operation after Hollandia, but was little used after the end of the assault phase of the operation.

The direction of support aircraft from the front lines required improvement, but except in the fight for the Admiralties, ground fighting was never so critical that close support was essential against targets on which the pilots had not been briefed beforehand. In the Admiralties, support aircraft were directed to their targets by observers on the front lines who could spot both the aircraft and their targets. In later campaigns the Air Commanders, while always standing by to give whatever assistance they could to the ground forces, were hesitant to bomb within a few hundred yards of the front lines, as were Ground Force Commanders to request close support unless in almost desperate circumstances. In the absence of close bombing, ground-to-air radio direction was seldom an essential element of air support control and therefore the technique was not developed.

Another important advance was the command method for the control of close support aircraft in amphibious operations. This method was mostly based on the system employed by the Navy at Hollandia, which effectively provided aircraft in aiding ground troops to get ashore without interfering with the authority of the Air Commander. In planning for amphibious operations in SWPA, the Air Commander participated as a full equal to the Ground and Naval commanders. Thus, it was within his power to decide how much of his striking force he could employ to support the planned operation without becoming unable to perform other necessary missions. Once the degree of his contribution had been agreed upon, he could allow the attack and landing force commanders to control the support aircraft while these aircraft were in the objective area. To insure that these aircraft were employed prudently, this control was exerted through air officers who acted as Commanders Support Aircraft (CSA) and Air Coordinators. The Naval Attack Force Commander (NAFC) or the Landing Force Commander (LFC), after he had assumed command ashore, decided which targets in the objective area, if any, should be attacked by support aircraft. Then air officers aboard ships or on the beach, or in an aircraft overhead, directed the strike. This system was successful in SWPA during the period covered and for the remainder of the war.

Close support had been effective during these operations, but of course to varying degrees. At Shaggy Ridge, in the Finistere Range in northeastern Papua New Guinea, the terrain was unfavorable for air support, but the opposing ground forces were so evenly matched that only a comparatively small amount of close support turned the tide of battle. In the jungles north of Finschhafen, air attacks had certainly weakened the Japanese, but they were driven from the area by ground assault. At Momote, on Los Negros, Japanese troops concentrated across the airfield runway from the 1st Cavalry Division in mostly open terrain, and thus air support was highly effective. Against the enemy caves on Biak, bombs and strafing was basically another siege weapon used to wear down the defenders and air support was not considered decisive. However, at Noemfoor, air and sea bombardment of the beaches just previous to the landing was so effective that those Japanese who lived through it were too stunned to defend themselves. Against an enemy in open terrain, even though under cover, air power used in close support of ground forces could be devastating. Against an enemy sheltered in caves, as so many Japanese were to be later in the war in the Philippines, but more so at Peleliu, Iwo Jima, and Okinawa, close air support would be invaluable.

Philippine Campaign

Definite effects of Luzon close support strikes on enemy materiel and personnel were extremely difficult to determine, as pilots usually saw nothing but the explosion of their bombs and could report only unobserved results. When the infantry occupied an area immediately after an air attack, they could do an enemy body count, but had no means of determining whom had been killed by artillery, whom by infantry weapons, and whom by bombing and strafing. Bomb and shell fragments made similar wounds, and only an autopsy could determine whether a corpse charred by napalm had been dead previously to its fiery demise. Air attacks in support of Philippine guerrillas, who had no artillery, might have been a gauge of air support effectiveness, but their enemy casualty counts were notoriously exaggerated.

There were outstanding examples of attacks where tangible results could be established. After attacks on Mount Pinatubo, west of Fort Stotsenburg, on 29 and 30 March by 51 P-38s and P-51s, 600 dead Japanese were found in an area where most of them had certainly been killed by the air strikes. A strike by three flights of P-38s in support of I Corps on 11 May killed about 100 enemy troops above ground, destroyed several gun pits and trenches, obliterated a bivouac area, destroyed a store of mortar ammunition, and scored direct napalm hits on occupied caves. A strike in the Santa Fe area on 25 May by more than 200 P-38s, P-47s, and A-20s enabled the 126th Infantry to advance through the heavily fortified target area without resistance and cause the retreat of 150 frightened Japanese who had not been bombed and who could have inflicted heavy casualties on the advancing troops. Air attacks—many using napalm—in the Ipo Dam area from 10-16 June, when mopping-up operations were being carried out, were reported to have killed at least 800 enemy troops, with many others probably killed. A pillbox near Mankayan built of 20-inch reinforced concrete and covered with 20 feet of earth had survived 600 rounds of 155mm, 1,000 rounds of 75mm, and 100 rounds of 90mm artillery shells. It was then attacked by 32 P-38s, each carrying two 1,000 pound bombs. Three direct hits were made on the pillbox, killing 60 troops outside and trapping another 80 inside.

Interrogation of POWs contributed information about the effects of close support air strikes, though there was probably a tendency on the part of prisoners to exaggerate the ordeal they had undergone before being forced into the unthinkable act of surrendering. One of only several prisoners captured in the Shimbu Line stated that his unit of 255 men had suffered 80 casualties from bombing and strafing during the month before his surrender. All Japanese interrogated after the napalm attack at Ipo testified to the terror brought about by the fire bombs. An officer stated that 40% of the casualties suffered by his unit at Ipo had been inflicted by aircraft. A prisoner taken in the Eaglets Pass area on Luzon stated that only 40 men remained from an initial 350 in his unit, and that most of those lost had been killed by air action, which had also destroyed the horses and carts on which they depended for transportation.

A primary source for any evaluation of close support on Luzon comes from ground commanders who knew first hand the effects of air power mounted to support ground forces in accomplishing their mission. It is significant that in messages from ground commanders to air headquarters almost all Corps and Division Commanders considered air support of ground troops an important factor in the victory, with such phrases as "extremely accurate," "excellent support," "fine work," "telling effect," and "ample and effective" (from "Close Air Support in the Pacific" by Dr. Joe Taylor). That these Ground Commanders continued to request air support strikes is confirmation of their belief in its effectiveness.

There were instances of bombing and strafing of friendly troops, especially early in the campaign before air and ground had much experience working together. Many ground commanders had the philosophy that their troops had also experienced misdirected short rounds from friendly artillery. The common criticism of air support was that too often it failed to appear when scheduled, which placed the ground commander in a predicament. If he continued with his planned attack on schedule, he not only lost the benefit of the air strike, but also chanced exposing his men to a belated attack by friendly aircraft. Conversely, if he delayed his attack until the air support arrived and made the air strike, his troops possibly would not have time to execute the planned operations and could be exposed to enemy counterattacks against poor defensive positions. Allowing for poor weather and certain other uncontrollable, but infrequent, factors, and since air support requests were submitted the day before the strike, there was simply no satisfactory explanation for support flights arriving late so frequently. However, this problem in close support was almost remedied before the Philippine Campaign ended.

With a few exceptions, most Ground Commanders commended the SAPs. It was felt that one SAP officer should remain with a Division throughout the campaign, as they were "part of a combat team." It was also felt that the selection of SAP personnel "should permit evaluation of the officer's personality as well as his professional skill, because some SAP officers have distinguished themselves by their extraordinary skill and willingness to cooperate, while others have substantially handicapped smooth air-ground harmony by overemphasizing their prerogative of authority in the selection of air targets." Local Ground Commanders hesitated to take command action with respect to SAP personnel "in an effort to preserve harmony and insure the availability of support when it is needed." SAPs were to have command authority corresponding to the units to which they were attached (i.e., an Army SAP would command Corps SAPs and the latter would issue orders to SAPs with Divisions).

The AAF aircraft used for air support on Luzon generally had larger bomb carrying capacity than USN aircraft used in the Central Pacific, so more bombs and, more importantly, larger bombs could be employed. Napalm was certainly partly responsible for the success of aircraft against caves; it was used more extensively and in larger tanks than in the Central Pacific, and it was delivered against defenses immediately in front of the advancing ground troops. Whether or not it killed Japanese inside caves, it burned away camouflage and made pinpoint demolition bombing or direct artillery fire possible. The system of reducing caves on Luzon, in which air support played an important part, certainly resulted in lower casualties. The strength of the defensive installations must enter into any comparison of the efficacy of air support in the Philippine and Central Pacific theaters. The defenses of Iwo Jima were stronger than those encountered anywhere else in the Pacific, but the defenses of Saipan and Okinawa were not any stronger than those of the Shimbu Line, Zigzag or Balete Pass, or the Villa Verde Trail on Luzon (see volume 2).

Far East Air Forces (FEAF) commanders realized that the methods used during the Luzon and southern Philippines Campaigns were not suited to large-scale operations in a restricted area where air opposition was probable. At the end of the war, the 5th Air Force was developing the organization of tactical air commands of the ETO type. These commands, designed to control masses of aircraft engaged in the support of mass ground operations, were intended to function after Allied troops invaded the home islands of Japan.

The Pacific War established that almost any bomber or fighter could deliver effective close support. At the beginning of the war, medium (B-25s) and attack (A-20s) bombers were preferred, but as the requirement for fighters for defense against enemy aircraft declined they assumed the majority of close support missions. Heavy bombers were useful, however, when close support had to be conducted at long range, or when a large number of heavy bombs were needed to saturate an area.

Early in the Pacific war, light demolition bombs, fragmentation bombs, and machine guns were considered the best armament for close support attacks. These weapons continued to be used, but heavier bombs became favored as in the Philippines, where the 1,000 pound bomb became a staple. In the Central Pacific, partly because of the lesser carrying capacity of the mostly USN aircraft engaged there, smaller bombs were used to a greater extent. Rocket fire first complemented strafing during the invasion of the

Marianas and assumed greater importance in the Central Pacific as the war went on than in the Philippines. Napalm was an important addition to close support armament, but it was most effective when used in conjunction with fragmentation bombs, strafing, or ground fire.

Early in the war, the Buna and Tarawa operations plainly established that coordination and good liaison were essential to effective close support. Progress toward more absolute liaison was continual after these early battles, concluding in the complicated use of air and ground representatives in the Philippines. Close air support was most effective when closely coordinated with infantry action, artillery, and/or naval gunfire. Communications were probably the most important single factor contributing to successful close support. It was evident that close support improved as better communications became available. Once powerful High Frequency (HF) transmitters and receivers became available in greater numbers, they simplified the requesting and coordination of support missions. Very High Frequency (VHF) equipment made possible effective ground-to-air and air-to-air direction of attacks and better-trained personnel made it possible to keep these communications in efficient operation.

Visual markers were also important in close support air operations. Target marking was successfully realized by the use of smoke shells fired from artillery or mortars. Smoke rockets fired from aircraft and smoke grenades dropped from liaison aircraft were also successful target markers. Panels were used throughout the war for marking front lines, but when used alone they often were not seen from the air except by observation aircraft. Smoke grenades provided better results marking the lines for strike aircraft. The command systems for air support in the two major Pacific Theaters differed only superficially. In all amphibious operations, support aircraft were under the operational control of the Naval Attack Force Commander while in the objective area, but this control was always exercised through an air officer (Army, Navy, or Marine Corps) as Commander Support Aircraft (CSA) or Commander Air Support Control Unit (CASCU). In the Southwest Pacific, where ground operations were likely to continue long after the amphibious phase was concluded, the Air Commander regained operational control of support aircraft when the assault phase ended. This was not quite true in the Central Pacific, where the Tactical Air Force (TAF) on Okinawa came under the Tenth Army, but in practice TAF operated as much as the 5th or 13th Air Forces operated in the Philippines. The direct command of aircraft was always under the control of air officers everywhere in the Pacific.

Control of air support tended toward locally centralized control. In SWPA, the three 5th Air Force Bombardment Wings (including the 5th Fighter Command), the 13th Fighter Command, and the Marine Air Groups, Zamboanga (MAGSZAMBO), although originally established to permit decentralized control of air power in areas removed from air headquarters, were the means for locally centralized control of air support. Other agencies for centralized control of air support were the Commander Air Support Control Unit (CASCU), Landing Force Air Support Control Units (LFASCUs), Fire Support Control Centers (FSCCs), and the TAFs in the Central Pacific. As air and ground operations gained in scale and coordination became more and more essential, such centralization was obviously necessary. However, centralization of control was more important in the Central Pacific, where ground action was confined to small areas, than in the larger islands of SWPA and the Philippines.

Nevertheless, it was important that decentralized control be possible, for a strike by one flight of fighters in aid of a battalion of infantry could be as important to the outcome of the battle as an attack by a hundred aircraft in support of a division or corps. In the Central Pacific, the Air Liaison Parties (ALPs) failed to function effectively as an agency of decentralized control, though Ground Commanders wanted them to have this function. In SWPA, support aircraft parties and forward observer teams were more active than air coordinators in controlling support strikes.

Close air support was unquestionably effective in the Pacific. Ground Commanders, the true arbiters on ground support, gave it an almost unanimously favorable judgment. Close support was less effective against an enemy lodged in cave defenses than elsewhere, but even the caves were vulnerable to sustained air bombardment combined with infantry and artillery action, as was seen on Luzon. There is ample evidence that close air support inflicted casualties—sometimes very heavy casualties—on enemy troops, though it seems certain that air attacks on rear areas inflicted more casualties than attacks on the front lines. But even when enemy troops were not killed by accurate frontline strikes, they were often so stunned that a closely coordinated infantry attack could overrun their positions before they could resist. Unlike the ETO and MTO, where AA defenses and heavy ground fire were much more prevalent, close air support, though still dangerous, was much less so in the Pacific.

Air-to-Ground Tactics

Strafing

Col. Gwen Atkinson, CO of the 58FG, which specialized in ground support, stated: "We believe that surprise, speed, cover of approach, timing,

Atkinson

concentration upon a single target and a slipping, skidding breakaway on the deck are the essential factors necessary for successful strafing." Strafing could be done while diving or flying level at a very low altitude. Dive strafing attacks were best employed on long targets, while low strafing attacks worked well against smaller targets that were equally wide and long. But practically, the pilot would use whichever tactic was appropriate to the current combat situation.

"To make a strafing attack from a dive, the attack was started at about 5,000 feet and well to the side of the target, aligned along its length. The pilot pushed the stick forward to start the dive. Using the gunsight, the pilot acquired the target and fired, with the aircraft's inertia delivering the bullet stream along the length of the target as the pilot pulled out of his dive.

"The approach for a low strafing attack was started below 300 feet (the less altitude, the less time spent in enemy AA sights) and beyond the fighter's maximum .50 caliber range. The pilot positioned the nose on the target and the throttle was set to full. The pilot began to fire as soon as he was within his gun's maximum range and the target was in the gunsight. The pilot sprayed his bullets slightly to either side by turning the rudder left and right as he was firing.

"Every scheduled strafing attack required thorough planning, requiring the pilots to become totally familiar with the layout of the target itself, the geography around the target area (landmarks within a five mile radius needed to be memorized), and the best approach and withdrawal routes selected. The location of AA guns, in particular, had to be determined. Col. Atkinson stated:

"The enemy in many ways is cagey. He places his anti-aircraft guns in some of the damndest places, moves them frequently, and has accounted for many of our losses in just this manner. In concentrated areas, their medium and light guns are wicked. However, we have experienced little difficulty with their heavy stuff. We have no trouble turning away from or under it….. The Japanese are always full of surprises. One neat trick they have pulled on us is to plant land mines, and when we come in on our strafing runs, set them off in our faces."

An altitude of 15,000 feet was maintained on the way to the target area. The leader located the target and dropped to the deck with or without his wingman to check the target, particularly AA. The formation then turned 180°, setting course on the target, with flights dropping line astern at about 1,000 yard intervals. The approach was made at normal cruising speed at as low altitude as possible, trying to use a road or other landmarks to stay on target. About one mile from the target, the first flight pulled up to 100 feet, correcting their heading if necessary, and gave full rpm and throttle. The flight and element leaders concentrated on shooting up the target itself, while the wingmen acted as "anti-flak" aircraft, picking out gun positions and knocking them out. It was important to pick an "aimed target" rather than "hosing" the area. The pilot had to have his aircraft properly trimmed and know where his machine guns were harmonized to fire at correct range, putting as many rounds into the target while firing on it. Succeeding flights utilized similar tactics. Once past the target, all aircraft stayed on deck until the Formation Leader gave the signal to climb, usually five to ten miles away.

Another method of attack had the formation come around on the target at 4,000 feet, dive at high speed, shoot up the target, stay low and get away. It was a matter of the Leader's preference as to which method was to be used, but the on deck method was most common. A minimum airspeed of 250mph was advised because of the constant possibility of passing over unexpected AA positions while on the deck and the possibility of being bounced by enemy aircraft called to the area.

The guns of the fighter were harmonized for rounds to converge at a point ahead of the aircraft so that the rounds would impact the target together. The harmonization point was set for air-to-air combat at 250 yards, which was acceptable when strafing individual targets, such as soft or armored vehicles. Low level strafing attacks at this harmonization range were risky, as apart from the danger from AA and small arms fire, a small miscalculation or target fixation could cause the fighter to crash into the target or into trees or obstructions just beyond it. Also, if the target were carrying ammunition or explosives it could explode in the path of the attacker and damage it. The most accurate of all fighter bomber armament was the machine gun or cannon, as the great number of rounds fired assured more hits in an area, but the striking power of each round inflicted much less damage to the target than a hit or near miss by heavier ordnance, such as bombs or rockets, which were much less accurate. Pilots were advised to save about 50 rounds per gun during strafing missions to engage in air-to-air combat if necessary. In the P-51, a pilot could expend all the ammo in his out-board guns and have enough left in the two inboard guns to engage in combat.

If heavy AA fire was encountered only one pass was made, but if the target was undefended, the formation leader delegated at least one flight to fly top cover while the remainder of the formation flew another pass on the target. Top cover circled at 2,000 feet above the target in the opposite direction to the attacking aircraft to be able to intercede without delay if enemy aircraft attacked. The attacking formation often was disrupted after the first pass and afterward all aircraft had to beware of other aircraft and stay out of their fire and flight paths.

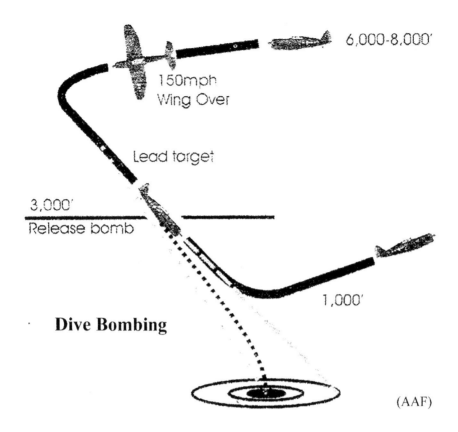

150mph Wing Over

6,000-8,000'

Lead target

3,000'
Release bomb

1,000'

Dive Bombing

(AAF)

If AA fire was heavy, pilots flying in line astern attacks needed to take evasive action in all but the last part of the attack: the firing run. On the way in, a slight pumping of the stick and small turns could confuse enemy gunners in determining the direction of the attacker's flight path. Once the pilot sighted the target he needed to end his evasive maneuvers and forget the AA fire until he finished his pass.

Most small arms ground fire had the tendency to not give enough lead when firing on low flying aircraft; consequently, most hits were on the aft portion of the attacker. Unlike the P-51, the P-40 and P-38 had all their coolant and radiators up front and close together with commensurate short coolant lines and were less vulnerable to ground fire.

Pilot Strafing Mistakes

Often the inexperienced pilot sighted the target through the gunsight pipper and then tried to correct his firing error by watching his strikes. The consequence was that at the start of his firing pass he would shoot below the target and then, when trying to correct, would spray the rounds above and around the target. The pilot could correct this fault by leaving the pipper above the target at the start of his run and as the range decreased allow the pip to drop on the target.

If the strafing approach was too steep or too shallow, it caused the pilot to split his concentration between hitting the ground with his fighter and hitting the target with his bullets. If the pass was too steep, the tendency was to open fire at too long range and to pull up at the optimum firing range when the concern about crashing into the target appeared. If the pass was too shallow, the tendency was to open fire too close to the target, snapping off quick, ineffective bursts, then pulling up too soon, again to avoid flying into the intended target. Instead of choosing one target and hitting it with a continual burst to destroy it, pilots tended to spray bullets at several targets in their view, missing or only slightly damaging them. Pilots also tended to continue firing as they pulled up past the target, wasting ammunition. In

any attack, the pilot would always have to pull up to avoid the target or its surroundings. After a while, a pilot developed the instinct to determine a good safety margin to clear his fighter of all ground obstacles in order to hold his fire until reaching a close and lethal range.

Dive Bombing

Dive bombing generally refers to all attacks between 70° (near vertical) and 90° (vertical), while at smaller angles it is usually termed glide or skip bombing. As a rule, the 90° vertical dive resulted in the best aim, because the pilot was flying straight down at the target, but the bomb had to be released earlier in order to pull out of the dive in time. Because of the angle of approach, dive bombing afforded the pilot a longer and more stable view of the target but gave the same opportunity to enemy defenses.

Dive bombing is a successive attack procedure that comprises four specific phases: a level approach, the dive itself, the bomb release, and the escape. The diving attack requires enough altitude to insure room for the diving portion of the attack, which will expend much of that altitude, and then room to pull out of the dive.

Approach: Once the target was spotted on the ground at about 6,000-8,000 feet altitude, the pilot would reduce his speed to 150mph and would line up the target slightly to one side with its longest aspect to give him more margin for error and also score multiple hits.

Dive: The pilot placed the target just in front of him at the start of the dive. When the target was about to pass under his wing tip, the pilot executed a wingover in the direction of the target, rather than pushing the nose over into a dive. The wingover permitted the pilot to keep the target in sight. He then dropped the nose by pushing the stick forward into a dive angle between 60 and 70 degrees below the horizon. He chopped the throttle completely, as excessive speed reduced accuracy, and by dropping his flaps the pilot could keep his airspeed under control, or he could use his dive brakes or spoilers if the aircraft was so equipped. The pilot dove toward the target at a 45 to 60° angle while aligning his nose with the edge of the target and maneuvered the aircraft to line the gun sight on the target and stabilized the aircraft. Once stabilized, the pilot judged the appropriate amount of lead.

Since most targets were stationary, the pilot had to lead the target slightly beyond where it was to hit. The correct amount of lead necessary depended on the dive angle (the steeper the dive, the less lead was required) and the range at which the pilot released the bomb (the farther away the bomb was released, the more lead was required). Also, the bomb would always travel further forward due to momentum, increasing the chance of one or more hits.

Release: The pilot released the bombs somewhere between 3,000 and 1,500 feet, being careful not to pick up so much speed that he could not concentrate upon his dive for fear of hitting the ground.

Pull out: The pilot immediately applied heavy back pressure on the stick and to level out above 1,000 feet, then flew away at full throttle. He tried to escape low, as the lower the altitude, the more difficult it was for enemy AA and ground fire to get a good shot.

Glide or Skip Bombing

The difference between glide bombing and dive bombing was in the approach angle. A glide bombing attack, often referred to as skip bombing, is a gently diving attack in which the pilot virtually "lobs" the bomb at a target. It is normally made at altitudes below 5,000 feet and at a dive angle less than 30°. This is perhaps the least accurate bombing method, as the inaccuracy of this type of attack is caused by the difficulty of estimating the correct release point.

Glide bombing was developed to allow bombing attacks by aircraft not equipped with bombsights and those carrying bombs with fuses too dangerous for release at low altitudes. The glide bomb technique was particularly well suited to attack targets located in rough terrain that prevented low level attack and could be used successfully on any targets vulnerable to all standard General Purpose bombs up to and including the 1,000 pound GP bomb.

Though the basic method of glide bombing execution was the same, there were as many variations of glide bombing as there were pilots using the method. It was critical that the pilot understood the limitations of his aircraft and knew the minimum allowable altitude of the type of bomb carried. The glide bombing attack began with an approach on the target at an altitude of 4,000 to 6,000 feet, depending on the height of the surrounding terrain and AA opposition. In order to minimize losses from AA, it was necessary to begin the dive no lower than 5,000 feet, and at 1,000 yards from the target the pilot fired continuously to reduce enemy return fire. The pilot was to close on the target slightly to the right, allowing an unobstructed view of the target throughout his approach. After setting up a dive angle of 25 to 35° to the target, a diving turn to the left was made, lining up on the target. Immediately upon rolling out of the turn and establishing an airspeed of about 300mph to maintain accuracy, the bombs were to be released when the attitude of the airplane was 20° or less below horizontal in the round out. The diving run was to be made at positive Gs to release the bombs accurately and was not to be too flat, causing the bombs to land short or even ricochet. As the bombs would Fall in the direction of the flight path, the pilot was to avoid using his rudder pedals when lining up the target (as yawing would not significantly change the flight path). The pullout began when the aircraft reached the lowest part of the round out no lower than the minimum altitude specified for releasing the bomb type carried (usually 500 to 700 feet). Evasive action from the target was determined by the surrounding terrain and enemy fire, but was to remain above 200 feet; this minimum altitude limit was not to be disregarded, but airspeed could be increased as required.

Rockets

The rocket was very simple in construction and employment. Because the rocket motor caused no recoil, the warhead could be much heavier and of a larger caliber than the airborne cannon shell. The rocket was self-propelled, so it would have a much greater impact velocity. As with dive bombing, rocket tactics were determined by target type, AA concentration, and weather/wind. The rocket was difficult to fire accurately and its deployment required a high degree of skill. In operations, the distraction of having to identify an often camouflaged or moving target under AA fire was reason enough to diminish accuracy. The rocket's weight and weight distribution caused it to have a curved trajectory, therefore it needed to be fired at a range of 1,000 to 2,000 yards, which put the pilot in jeopardy from AA and ground fire. Beyond that range the rocket's trajectory became too pronounced for any hope of accurate fire. The fighter bomber needed to remain stable as it launched the rocket. If the pilot skidded or turned the aircraft at launch, the rocket's low launching speed would cause a large error in aiming at a target. Pilots were likely to undershoot their targets, either because they launched their rockets at too long a range or flew too slowly at lower dive angles. Wind velocity and direction also needed to be considered accurately, as a 10mph wind could cause a 15 foot miss in line and a nine foot miss in range, which was the difference in scoring a hit or near miss, as in the case of a

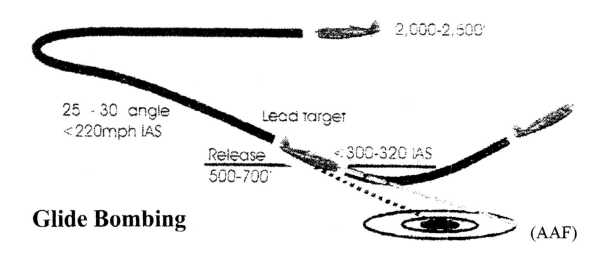

Glide Bombing

(AAF)

25 - 30 angle
<220mph IAS

Lead target

Release
500-700'

2,000-2,500'

<300-320 IAS

P-38 equipped with underwing rocket pods (AAF)

Filling napalm tanks (AAF)

Napalm tank underwing installation (AAF)

tank or gun position. The modification of the gyroscopic gunsight in late 1944 compensated for the gravity drop of the rocket and also for the effect of the wind and target movement.

For ground attacks with rockets, the principles of aiming are similar to those described for glide bombing ground targets: make a 30° or less dive, orient the nose toward the target, release the rocket, and pull out of the dive. The closer the attacker was to the target the more accurate the aim. With little or no AA fire, the optimum approach was to drop to below 1,500 feet and fly level, then make a gentle dive to a lower altitude and aim the nose toward the target and release the rockets at a range of 3,000 feet and pull out of the dive.

Against heavily defended targets, pilots were advised to make a steep 60° dive at 7-8,000 feet and fire all rockets in salvo at about 4,000 feet at a range of 5,000 feet. On these strongly defended targets, doctrine stated that they should only be attacked once. However, in practice, the pilots disregarded the prescribed tactics and developed their own tactics.

It was estimated that the salvo of all eight rockets would result in a one-in-twenty chance of hitting a target the size of a Panzer tank. Despite their inaccuracy, the rocket was more accurate than the free Fall bomb, but much less so than strafing with machine gun or cannon which, in turn, had much less striking power to inflict significant damage when hitting the target. The HVAR had the explosive effect of a 155mm shell. A rule of thumb on rocket targets stated that any target suitable for artillery fire was a suitable rocket target. Rocket attacks created a morale problem for the enemy which was more of a factor than the actual destructive damage they caused.

Napalm
Officially named the "Class C-Fire Bomb," they were usually referred to as "blaze bombs" or "fire bombs." Napalm was manufactured from the aluminum salts of naphennic and palmitic acids and ignited by a white phosphorous igniter. A P-38 or P-47 fighter bomber could carry three napalm tanks: 160 gallon on the centerline pylon and two 150-gallon on each wing pylon. Napalm tanks were usually painted flat yellow, although dark red and natural metal were common. Napalm tanks were hung on the fighter empty, then filled with petroleum jelly usually laboriously pumped from 50 gallon drums or more easily from a special fuel bowser.

Napalm tanks were used in the ETO and MTO on a limited basis, but much more extensively in the PTO. The pilot used the engine cowl as a sighting device, releasing the tanks when the end of the cowl came over the target. For best effect, the napalm tanks were to be tumbled onto the target. Initially, napalm was considered most effective for the incineration of entrenched enemy troops, but it was also used to destroy enemy camouflage and expose the target prior to rocket and bombing attacks. For this reason napalm tank(s) were mixed with bombs or rockets in attacks.

In attacking hilly or mountainous areas, the fighter bomber pilot dropped the napalm tank from a shallow angle, tumbling the tanks into enemy

positions that produced concentrated oval areas of fire on the ground. On flat terrain, napalm was dropped from level flight at minimal altitude that produced long swaths of fire that engulfed the selected target, such as trenches, foxholes, or gun positions. Napalm exploded with a large, intense fireball fueled by the gelled gasoline mixture, which would adhere to anything it touched as it spread forward upon impact. A 150 gallon tank of Napalm could burn out a 90x150 foot area and was extremely difficult to extinguish. Dropped napalm spread and rushed into the trenches and foxholes, causing horrific casualties. Napalm attacks on defensive positions made up of rubble and shattered buildings drove enemy troops into the open. Until napalm was introduced, troops in wooded jungle areas were attacked with fragmentation bombs, but their trenches and foxholes afforded them good cover. Concrete, stone, and steel-reinforced buildings and pillboxes were relatively immune to napalm, unless it engulfed the ventilation systems. It had a significant demoralizing effect on the troops defending the area around these fortifications and they were forced to take refuge inside them to escape the napalm. This allowed U.S. infantry to flank the fortifications and get to their rear to utilize satchel charges, pole charges, or grenades to neutralize them.

Col. Atkinson stated: "In the short time we have been using them (napalm), devastating damage has been delivered. They have definitely proved, through tests and results, to be a very effective weapon....Good results have been obtained.... To me, this method of warfare is only in its infancy. There is no limit to its utilization."

10

Japanese Aerial Strategy and Tactics

Japanese Grand Strategic Air Doctrine

General
Japanese Grand Strategy was to implement its national policy and the strategic function of all its armed services during its control of all occupied territory. The JNAF was initially organized as a highly effective striking force, flying light maneuverable high-performance aircraft that were well adapted to support rapid campaigns by amphibious forces. The function of the JNAF in these operations was to provide cover for the involved task forces, and, by swift surprise attacks, destroy the opposing enemy air force in the air or on the ground, clearing the way for landing operations. The JNAF was equipped to operate either from carriers or from land bases, and frequently assumed the permanent defense of land areas, while the JAAF provided support for the ground troops and conducted counter-air force operations.

Disposition
After Japan completed its planned conquests in mid-1942, the Army and Naval Air Forces were assigned to the strategic defense of the vast occupied areas. Once the threat of war with the Soviet Union diminished due to the Soviets' life and death struggle with Germany, Japan reduced its forces in Manchuria and Japan and spread them along the perimeter of the newly-conquered Empire according to a predetermined plan. This dispersal remained in place until mid-1942, when increased Allied pressure on several fronts forced realignment.

Mobility
The Japanese achieved great mobility for their Air Forces by building many new airfields throughout the occupied territories. Air units could be transferred quickly from one area to another on interior lines, and because of the availability of facilities in depth could readily be withdrawn from sustained combat when required.

Strategy
Both the JAAF and JNAF supported troops and naval forces only in defensive or offensive-defensive operations until crucial areas of the Empire were threatened to the point where their overall strength was seriously weakened. Then, consistent with this doctrine of strategic defense, the Japanese Air Forces abandoned their perimeter defense and reduced or ended their support of ground troops at outlying posts along the perimeter whenever the cost of such support became prohibitive. As the Empire shrunk, the ultimate strategic objective of the Japanese Air Force was to defend the Japanese Homeland and the Inner Zone.

Conclusion
Japan's aerial war effort suffered a predictable escalating deterioration, as the country lacked production numbers, quality, and the technological depth and expertise to continue what would become a war of attrition in the air. After the surprise of the initial Japanese victories had faded, the Japanese realized that they had pursued the wrong technological direction in the air war and did not have the ability to change. Consequently, Japan's air effort began losing momentum months before the Americans began deploying their second-generation fighters and improved bombers. The Japanese leaders had staked everything on their belief that Germany would defeat Russia and then at least neutralize England and America. Once Japan attacked Pearl Harbor, she was no longer fighting China but also America, Britain, Australia, and New Zealand. Japan was fighting alone in the Pacific against the overwhelming industrial and material capacity of the United States.

Japanese Fighter Tactics

Formations
Japanese fighter tactics against Allied fighters and bombers necessarily varied with the number and type of aircraft encountered, the conditions under which attacks were carried out, and the expertise of the Japanese pilots. The Japanese fighter tactical unit was normally a Squadron of nine fighters, subdivided into three Flights in either V or echelon formation. Earlier in the war, a V of three fighter aircraft had been employed, flanked by echelons of two fighters. Fighter formations usually flew at altitudes of 15,000 to 20,000 feet, but could operate effectively at altitudes of 27,000 feet or higher. However, by the beginning of 1944, the Japanese adopted the successful standard basic American fighter formation, consisting of two-plane Elements and four-plane Flights.

Characteristics of Japanese fighter tactics:

1) High cover was a Japanese fighter tenant, with their flights frequently taking off about a half hour apart, so that when one flight had expended its fuel a second flight would be available to take over.

2) Individual Japanese pilots seldom engaged Allied formations or even single aircraft and usually required numerical superiority before attacking.

Fighter vs. Fighter Tactics

Attacks against Allied fighters were frequently made from above and the side, and if possible out of the sun. Head-on attacks against Allied fighters were generally avoided by Japanese pilots because of the heavy fire power of Allied fighters, particularly the P-38, and because of the lack of pilot armor protection in Japanese fighters. Japanese fighter pilots attempted to draw their adversary up into a steep climb and into stalling position, after which they would execute a quick wingover or snap-loop back on their opponent's tail. Evasive tactics were characterized by abrupt and violent skids, turns, and rolls in their maneuverable fighters. The favorite evasive maneuver of Japanese fighters was a Split-S, which was a downward half snap-roll followed by a pull-out to normal flight, thus obtaining a 180° change in direction with loss of altitude.

In January 1945, Headquarters AAF issued an Intelligence Report (No. 45-10**1**) entitled "Japanese Fighter Tactics" to be distributed to Squadron Intelligence Officers and in summary stated:

"Head-on attacks against Allied fighters were usually avoided because the Japanese armor protection was inadequate against the heavy Allied fighter fire power, especially the four .50 caliber machine guns and 20 mm cannon of the Lightning or the eight .50s of the Thunderbolt. Attacks were usually made from high astern or from above and the side. The gun aiming of inexperienced pilots flying the lightweight Zeroes and Oscars were particularly affected by their opponent's slip streams in a stern attack. However, Japanese fighter pilots preferred the head-on attack against heavy bomber formations but could often be turned away from a bomber formation that fired long bursts at maximum range. Surprisingly, the Japanese rarely used ramming tactics until later in the war. Japanese fighter pilots attempted to draw their opponents into a steep climb and into a stalling position and then go into a quick stall turn or loop back onto their opponent's tail. Rather than initiate an attack, Japanese fighter pilots often elected to make the most of their superior maneuverability to execute a quick turn to get on the enemy's tail. Their choice evasive tactics were to Split-S, half roll and dive away, or to go into steep turns and climbs."

Fighter vs. Bomber Tactics

Japanese fighter attacks against Allied bombers came from all directions, with a decreasing trend in frontal attacks as frontal armament increased in the B-24s and B-25s. Frequently these attacks were coordinated by two fighters on each side, with one coming in from above the wing while the other passed below, each peeling off to fire at the American bomber.

The degree of Japanese fighter coordination varied greatly and many times attacks were not coordinated, especially later in the war when pilot quality declined. However, in missions flown by veteran pilots a high degree of coordination was achieved, particularly in frontal and waist attacks. The Japanese greatly relied on the maneuverability of their fighters, and while their early tendency towards acrobatics steadily diminished, they employed an increased variety of attacks. Against perceived cultural stereotypes, ordinary Japanese fighter pilots were not particularly steadfast in pressing home their attacks unless they were on a Kamikaze mission. Japanese pilots were especially alert for any damaged enemy bombers and took quick advantage of stragglers, which were to endure their concentrated attacks. When a tight formation was maintained by American bombers, the Japanese attacks were usually concentrated on the bomber formation leader.

A B-25 under attack by a Zero. (AAF)

A Japanese report on attacking U.S. bombers captured in February 1944 stated:

1) The Flight or Squadron Commander must always be followed and against an Allied bomber formation a simultaneous attack was to be made.

2) Keep out of the field of fire of revolving turrets on Allied bombers.

3) Remain clear of the 30° cone of fire behind the tail.

4) Attack from the upper or lower rear or from the beam.

5) Use a frontal attack only in an unavoidable situation, in which case attack from above or below.

6) In the case of attacks made on both the left and right sides of a bomber, when one side had finished its attack, the other was to immediately take up the attack. The Flight on each side was then to repeat its attack.

Night Fighters

During 1943, American heavy bombers, operating at night over enemy bases in New Britain and the Upper Solomons, encountered increased fighter opposition, as the Japanese concentrated greater efforts on night interceptions in order to oppose these bombardment missions.

Air-to-Air Bombing

The Luftwaffe experimented briefly with air-to-air bombing as a means to break up the American heavy bomber formations, relying on blast and shrapnel effect to down the bombers. As early as 1939, the Japanese had developed special small air-to-air bombs and the first use against American bomber formations was reported in May 1942 in the SWPA and persisted with this method of attack throughout the war.

The Japanese air-to-air bombs, released both singly and in pattern arrays, were accurately timed and mechanically fused to explode after a set time, with the explosion scattering a large number of steel pellets filled with phosphorus downwards in a cone. If a steel pellet penetrated the skin of a bomber the phosphorous, which had ignited automatically on contact with the air, would set fire to anything flammable that it touched. The attack was made head-on and the bomb released between 1,000 and 2,000 feet above the bomber formation. Often the Japanese positioned a spotter plane flying at the level of the formation to be attacked.

Japanese air-to-air bombing was summarized by the British Directorate of Air Tactics in early 1943:

"Although losses have been caused to Allied aircraft by Japanese aerial bombs, the Japanese persistence in this type of attack cannot be said to pay good dividends. The greater danger appears to be the effect on a formation of disturbing it so that enemy fighters may be able to pick off any resulting straggler by more normal methods attack."

A B-24 flying through an exploding phosphorous air-to-bomb. (AAF)

Major Japanese Fighter Maneuvers

Split-S (Half Roll)

The loop and tight turn were fundamental Japanese maneuvers and the Split-S was a variation. The Split-S, referred to as the Half Roll by the Japanese, was the most widely used evasive maneuver by Japanese fighter pilots to disengage from combat from head-on and stern attacks and at all altitudes. To execute a Split-S, the pilot half rolled his aircraft inverted and executed a descending half loop, resulting in level flight in the exact opposite direction at a lower altitude. The highly maneuverable enemy fighters were able to complete this maneuver at extremely low altitudes and also at combat speeds that compared to Allied fighters.

The Loop and Tight Turn

When AAF fighters closed on the tails of enemy fighters, the Japanese pilots used their highly maneuverable fighters to execute a quick loop or a steep climbing turn, trying to encourage the American fighters to follow. If an AAF pilot followed, he soon found the more agile enemy fighter on his tail. To counteract these sudden enemy maneuvers, Allied fighter Flights spread up or down, which caught enemy pilots who moved to the right or left to evade attacks from astern.

Timed Attacks on Weaving Fighters

The Japanese used this attack for use against AAF fighters that were weaving in Elements or in Flights. The enemy pilots followed in line astern, working in teams, closing quickly to make well-timed attacks on AAF aircraft while they were on the outside of their weave. The Japanese fired a burst and broke off by zooming to altitude or by a sudden 90-180° turn. The attack was timed so that Japanese pilots could fire at a time when opposing fighters could not give each other effective mutual protection. The Allies suffered heavy losses from these well-timed enemy attacks when they were pressed home with determination.

Inverted Head-on Attack

Veteran Japanese fighter pilots would make head-on passes at enemy fighters, rolling over and firing while inverted, then diving under the opposing fighter, Split-Sing to come back on the tail of the AAF fighter as it attempted to climb away. In a slight variation, the Japanese pilot was also in position to attack if the AAF fighter tried to dive away. This tactic was used repeatedly in the first years of the war by veteran Oscar and Zero pilots against single AAF fighters—particularly P-40s, which had a comparatively slow rate of climb. This tactic was used mainly at comparatively low altitudes, where the more maneuverable types of enemy fighters had the altitude advantage.

Scissors: Japanese Style

If there was enough time and conditions were right, a pair of Japanese pilots could trap an attacker by crossing each other's path in a "scissors." In the scissors, the defender banked in the direction of his Wingman but at a much lower angle, attempting to maintain speed. If the Wingman was close enough, he would be turning toward the attacker and trying to close on its rear quarter, causing the attacker to break off or risk an attack on himself.

The Japanese used the Vertical Scissors to counter frontal attacks when an AAF Element climbed to attack the standard V of three enemy fighters with their favored head-on pass due to their heavy machine gun and cannon firepower. As soon as the AAF fighters reached firing range, two of the enemy fighters dove straight down, while the third pulled up in a sudden zoom, half rolling at the top. If the American fighters followed the lower Zeros, the Zero on top dove on their tails. If they attempted to pull up and fire at the top Zero they were attacked by Zeros from below. The maneuver was compared to the closing of two jaws of a trap, with the direction of closure being in the vertical plane.

Over and Under Bracket Defense

The Over and Under Bracket Defense was a variation of the Vertical Scissors. When two Japanese fighters were attacked from astern by enemy fighters, one Chandelled up while the other dove. If the enemy fighters split up in their pursuit, the high Japanese pilot turned his Chandelle into a loop and came down on the tail of the diving enemy fighter. If the enemy fighters stayed together and pursued a single Japanese fighter, the other Japanese pilot was left to come around for an astern attack.

"Prince of Wales" Maneuver

The Japanese "Prince of Wales" maneuver was a three-plane maneuver where the *Shotai* Leader would wait until the attacker was almost in range, then pull into a loop while his two Wingmen turned abruptly toward the attacker. If the American continued forward at very high speed, one of the three Japanese fighters would get a good shot.

Japanese Fighter Escort Tactics

Early in the war, the Japanese appeared to have no standard plan of fighter formations nor tactics for escorting their bombers. At times, Japanese escort fighters could be lured away from their bomber formations by the attacks of small groups of AAF fighters, which allowed other groups of their fighters to attack the bombers with devastating results. After a while, Japanese fighter escorts became more resolute and remained close to the bombers, refusing to be drawn away. Nevertheless, there were many occasions when the Japanese sent out bombers without escorts, or the escorts just did not make the rendezvous with the bombers, again with very undesirable results.

When Japanese fighters did fly escort, they flew in flights of six in flat three-plane V formations. One flight flew slightly ahead of the bombers, two flights flew on each flank, and another flight was slightly astern of the bombers. These six flights flew at the same level as the bombers, providing close cover. Japanese top fighter cover was positioned at 10,000 feet above the main bomber force. There was no medium altitude cover. The Japanese escort flights flew on a straight course with the bombers until enemy fighters were sighted, then the flights went into line astern, stepped down, and started sweeping S-turns. The low cover stayed with the bombers and attempted to loop onto the tails of the AAF fighters when they made stern attacks. If one flight was attacked, they formed a loose Lufbery circle and any Japanese fighter that was attacked would dive out, leaving the others in a position to protect it if AAF fighters dove after it. After the dive, the

Japanese fighter would go into a steep climbing turn and pull back into position in the defensive circle. The top cover Japanese fighters did not commit until the enemy fighters had separated, then made diving attacks out of the sun on individual planes. However, the Japanese used extremely high top cover and sometimes the fighters in the top cover were so far above the bombers that they failed to see the attacks on the bombers and failed to protect them.

Japanese Tricks and Decoys

Single-Plane Decoy
The Japanese would send out a lone fighter to fly straight and level, apparently vulnerable to attack, while one or more fighters would hide in the sun or clouds, ready to bounce on any enemy fighter who would take the bait.

Acrobatic Decoys
A group of enemy fighters would attract attention to themselves by performing various acrobatic maneuvers, appearing to be entirely unaware of the proximity of AAF fighters. Meanwhile, other Japanese fighters would be staked out above for an attack from the sun and dive on the AAF fighters as soon as they committed themselves to attack the decoys.

Fake Dogfight Decoys
This ploy was used when AAF fighters were escorting bombers, as the Japanese would feign a dogfight in the distance with the intention of luring the escorts away from the bombers. The AAF pilot who left the bombers planning to help his comrades in the supposed dogfight would find himself seriously outnumbered and in trouble.

Uncamouflaged Decoys
Occasionally, the Japanese flew uncamouflaged maneuverable fighters at one altitude and camouflaged fighters with good diving speed (e.g., Tony and/or Tojo) at a higher altitude. The silver decoy fighters could be seen plainly glinting in the sun, while the fighters at higher altitude were difficult to see because of their camouflage. When Allied fighters descended on the decoys, the camouflaged fighters were in a favorable position for attack.

Late Take Off Decoys
A number of Japanese fighters waited to take off from their airdromes until after Allied fighters were in sight in order to create the impression that they were vulnerable while they took off and were at low altitude. These fighters were actually decoys for other fighters who had taken off earlier and were hiding in the sun.

Low Lufbery Decoy
This maneuver was intended to take advantage of the higher rate of climb of the Japanese fighters from low speed. Japanese fighters formed a Lufbery Circle, milling around on the deck, and when Allied fighters attacked from above, the Japanese waited until the Allied aircraft lost their diving speed, then they immediately climbed to gain an altitude advantage and position for attack.

Flank/Sun Attack
A Japanese fighter (or fighters) would be in position on either flank of the American bomber formation to feint an attack while others were positioned up sun, ready to attack. One would dive out of the sun and after his attack would take up a flank position, then one of the flank fighters would move up into the sun and the procedure would be repeated in constant rotation.

Fake Radio Calls
The Japanese used false radio calls in English in an attempt to lure enemy fighters to lower altitudes, where they were outnumbered.

Low Level AA Traps
During low altitude combat, a Japanese pilot would fly slowly and apparently unconcerned over his home base in an attempt to have an enemy pilot close on him, but in reality to set up him up as a close range target for small and medium anti-aircraft batteries or automatic weapons. When over or near their own anti-aircraft batteries, the Japanese pilots sometimes zoomed up and attacked enemy fighters after they had been forced to break off due to the anti-aircraft fire. At tree top combat, a veteran Japanese pilot would allow an over-eager enemy pilot to dive and follow him for an easy shot and zoom up at the last moment, hoping that enemy pilot would forget how close he was to the ground and auger in. The Japanese pilot could also roll or turn his nimble fighter just above the deck, tempting the enemy pilot to follow him in a maneuver impossible to follow at low altitude.

Japanese AA Defenses
AA defenses varied with the target's type and importance, as did the accuracy and intensity with which the Japanese defended them. Japanese heavy guns were generally sited within a mile radius of the target, but the medium AA batteries were invariably located much closer to where they were most effective against diving and strafing fighters and medium bombers (B-25s). Medium batteries were laid out in one of four patterns: a line, an arc, a triangle, or a quadrangle. The linear pattern could consist of two to 12 guns, the arc from three to 10 guns, and triangular and quadrangular from three or four guns.

The mission of the 5FC was to not only destroy Japanese aircraft in the air, but also on the ground and airfields, and their parked aircraft became a major target. When airfields were approached by low level fighters and bombers, the Japanese tried to withhold their AA fire until the attacking aircraft were in effective range. Then they opened up with every available weapon, including rifles and even trench mortars. Thus, the best chance for success was to surprise the AA defenses using the cover of hills and trees. However, on the second attack the AA fire became much more deadly.

Japanese AA defense consisted of Regiments (24 guns + 20mm AA cannon and 7.7mm and 13mm machine guns) which were all manned by Army troops with two Battalions (12 guns + 20mm AA guns and 7.7mm and 13mm machine guns) normally being the tactical unit.

Medium flak was the most dangerous flak defense encountered by the 5th Fighter Command and ranged from 20mm to 40mm. The Army 20mm

Field AA Model 98 Machine Cannon (1938) was a single mount with a rate of fire of 120 rounds per minute (rpm) and an effective range of 5,000 to 8,300 feet (tracer burn out altitude). It was the most effective and widely used of Japanese medium AA guns and the most encountered in the SWPA. The Navy 25mm Field AA Gun Model 98 Machine Cannon (1936) could be a single, twin or triple mount firing 175 to 200rpm per barrel with an effective range of 8,000 to 10,500 feet. It was used on all the important islands of the Japanese perimeter defense and later moved to the Homeland, but was not widely used there. The Army 40mm Field AA Gun was a single or twin mount firing 60 to 100rpm per barrel with a range of 5,000 to 8,500 feet. The Japanese Army also acquired 200 British 40mm Bofors guns during the capture of Singapore and continued to use them. The Japanese Navy used a twin-mounted copy of the 1931 British Vickers-Armstrong gun, but it was not used in large numbers. The fire control of medium guns depended on tracer observation (largely in the daytime and entirely at night). The medium AA shells were not time fused and exploded on impact; failing to hit a target, they exploded at the burnout of the tracer. Medium flak damage was characterized by a small entry hole and a large exit hole and caused major damage.

Heavy AA guns were encountered during the missions over Rabaul. The Army 75mm Field AA Gun Type 88 was one of the most prolific of all Japanese AA guns. It was issued to most Japanese Army units in the field, but as the war continued many were withdrawn to the Japanese Homeland. The design originated in 1928 and was simply constructed from easily machined parts. The gun was mounted on a pedestal that attached to five outrigger legs. Compared to other WWII AA guns, this gun was a substandard performer, having a maximum effective range of 24,000 feet, but it was the best Japanese high-altitude flak gun. Heavy flak was director-controlled and time fused, and exploded into flying fragments that caused generally minor damage. The continuously pointed fire was the predominate type of heavy flak fire, but predicted concentrations, barrages, and "creeping barrages" were also used. Because their fire control equipment was inadequate, the Japanese used the predicted concentration and barrage fire to greatest effect.

Japanese Gun-Laying Radar
Japanese gun-laying radar first appeared in 1943, and was copied from captured British SCL, GL Mark II, and U.S. SCR 268 sets. Because the American set was so complex to copy, the Japanese chose the British sets as an example. The first two Army sets were the Tachi 1 and 2 developed from the SCL and were superseded by the Tachi 4. These units had a transmitter and receiver on the same mount, but the set had poor accuracy and was too difficult to use. The 78 Mc Tachi 3 was refined from the British GL Mark II unit and became the standard Army radar unit. The Navy developed the large and difficult to use S-set that was replaced by the smaller, simpler, and more accurate 75 Mc S-24. The Tachi sets were used only for Home Island defense and during B-29 operations, U.S. intelligence found that the Japanese had few radar-controlled guns in use. During raids in 8/10 to 10/10 overcast, the AA fire was sparse and inaccurate, indicating that the guns were not radar controlled. Also, during night attacks the gun-laying radar was probably not used, as only B-29s caught in a searchlight beam were fired upon.

Use of Airfield Camouflage
Generally, the Japanese made little use of camouflage on airstrips. When camouflage was used it consisted of natural foliage covers, nets to cover or break up an aircraft outline, and aircraft dispersal in nearby wooded areas. Aircraft were also painted in camouflage and parked along the peripheries of airfields.

Camouflaged JAAF Ki-49 Helen. (AFHRC)

Camouflaged JAAF Ki-43 Oscar. (AFHRC)

A close look will reveal aircraft dispersed among the trees in a coconut plantation. (AAF)

Use of Dummy Aircraft and Other Targets
Dummy or wrecked aircraft and barges, and even dummy trains and truck convoys, all well protected by anti-aircraft guns, were used by the Japanese as bait to lure strafers. Intact but unserviceable or dummy aircraft were

lined up on main or satellite airfields to suggest that these airfields were still in use, while wrecked aircraft were lined up on fields in service with serviceable aircraft dispersed and hidden. The Japanese also used anti-strafing cables suspended between trees or hills.

Japanese Bombing Tactics

Formations
Bombers usually flew in multiples of nine in a V of Vs, although occasionally attacks were made in line abreast, with fighters weaving in loose escort formations. Until the beginning of 1944, Japanese bomber formations were flown in six separate flat Vs, occasionally with one or two vacancies and frequently with one bomber at the rear of the apex of the V; or in a large V of three nine-plane Vs, with the leading V flying 50 or 100 feet above the others, changing to a slightly staggered formation of one V approaching seven or ten miles from the bomb release point; or in three flights of nine bombers, successively stepped up 250 feet from port to starboard and in line with fighters weaving about the formation; or in two nine-plane V of Vs, with the leading echelon highest and the left echelon next highest.

Japanese Bombing Tactics
Japanese bombing tactics demonstrated some of their supposed cultural characteristics: courage, disregard for losses, and adherence to inflexible plans. Initial Japanese bomber attacks were characterized by a long approach in close formation, unwaveringly held regardless of anti-aircraft fire and/ or fighter opposition. Bombs were usually dropped on a signal from the leader at altitudes ranging from 7,000 to 26,000 feet, depending on the type of target and the opposition. Typically, the bomber formation was well maintained until the bombs were dropped, when it was opened up somewhat going into a series of undulations, losing and gaining about 500 feet in altitude.

The Japanese usually preceded long distance bombing missions by aerial reconnaissance of the intended target, along with an alternative objective. Bomber operations against important targets (airfields were given highest target priority) were characterized by repeated attacks and follow up missions. Many of these attacks were made along the same route and at the same time each day, which made them predictable and more vulnerable.

By the end of 1943, the Japanese were on the defensive in most theaters and were forced to change their bombing tactics. They had to virtually forsake daylight horizontal bombing attacks on Allied land bases or convoys with air cover and implement dawn and dusk bombing by fighters and night bombing by medium, torpedo, and dive bombers. They also had to improve efficiency and coordination in night torpedo and bombing attacks against Allied shipping en route and at anchor in advanced bases.

Japanese Bombing Attacks on Airfields
Early in the war, the Japanese took full advantage of the weakness of Allied air and ground defenses. Japanese fighters operated in conjunction with dive bombers that attacked AA positions and ground installations, with fighters strafing aircraft on the ground from low level. After the Allies increased the strength of their air interception and ground defenses, the Japanese were forced to change their bombing tactics when attacking airfields. Bombers took evasive tactics against anti-aircraft fire by maintaining altitude above the AA's effective range, by occasionally changing altitude, and by weaving in formation. Fighter escort on bomber missions varied according to the opposition expected and the number of fighters available, and often did not involve strafing, which had become too dangerous in the face of increased Allied AA defenses. These bombing attacks from higher altitudes yielded much poorer results. By the start of 1943, the typical Japanese airfield attack was by night, by a single bomber or by small to

medium formations. Occasionally the Japanese reverted to daylight attacks, attacking aircraft based on newly-occupied forward strips that were supporting Allied ground forces in New Guinea. Initially, these forward bases were typically lightly defended by AA and had poorly developed warning systems.

Dive Bombing
Japanese dive bombing attacks, which were most frequent and effective during the early months of the war, were chiefly directed against shipping and equipment on beachheads. The accuracy of Japanese dive bombing was not particularly outstanding and was affected by AA fire and fighter interception. The usual Japanese dive bombing formations were in multiples of three: three-plane Vs in line astern; in six or nine-plane Vs; or in Vs of Vs. The number of dive bombers employed varied with the type of target; for example, larger formations were employed against warships, rather than against merchant ships, which the Japanese considered less important and could be easily dealt with after the warships had been dispatched. The Japanese attempted to saturate enemy defenses by increasing the number and concentration of attacking aircraft. Once the Allies were capable of providing fighter opposition, the enemy dive bombers usually approached the target at altitudes of 12,000 to 18,000 feet and immediately before the initial dive, they altered their formations to one of loose echelon or string. After this change, the dive bombers initiated individual dives of 45° or steeper in quick succession usually from up sun, from areas of restricted visibility, or from coordinates exposing them to minimum anti-aircraft fire. The bomb release point varied from 500 feet to as high as 3,000 feet, often depending on the intensity of AA fire. The bomb release point was generally higher during dives approaching the vertical, where higher speeds had been achieved. When larger formations were employed, enemy dive bombers frequently divided their strength into smaller forces and attacked the target simultaneously from different directions.

Glide Bombing
The majority of Japanese bombing attacks were made by a powered glide at an angle of 45-50°, beginning well coordinated dives at an altitude of 3,000 to 5,000 feet and usually from out of the sun. The bombers followed each other down, releasing their bombs on the target, and subsequently fired their machine guns against ground installations. They withdrew at high speed with evasive action usually limited to short climbs and dips.

Torpedo Bombing

Daytime
Daylight torpedo bombing approaches were usually made in a close wedge or loose diamond formation at medium altitude or in small groups that separated to attack individual objectives from different directions. The approaches were made at an angle of 40 to 45° and the torpedoes were dropped from an altitude of 200 to 300 feet at a range of 500 to 1,200 yards from the target. In planning the attack, the approaches were to be made from the direction of the least expected AA fire concentration and advantage of the position of the sun and cloud formations was considered.

Nighttime
Japanese nighttime torpedo attacks (including dawn and dusk) were highly developed and generally followed the same pattern. Reconnaissance aircraft dropped variously colored flares to reveal the course of the convoy and identify the targets by types. Torpedo planes then attacked singly, with most of the force approaching from one direction, while a few attempted to approach from another course. The attackers skimmed the surface of the water, dropped their torpedoes at less than 1,000 yards, and evaded on their retreat with S-turns and roller coaster maneuvers

PART 5:
Logistics and Airfields

1

AAF Logistics: Supply, Transport, and Maintenance

From the time that the first U.S. forces arrived in Australia on 22 December 1941, the Southwest Pacific would continue to be an area of operations in which logistic plans needed to be quickly altered to meet the requirements of volatile and rapidly changing conditions. Important areas were unexpectedly bypassed and once vital installations constructed to meet future requirements became redundant. For both the Allied and Japanese, these changes necessitated significant modifications in their planning and construction of airfields and bases.

Operations in the Southwest Pacific were characterized by:
1) The long distances involved in both combat and supply endeavors;
2) The tactical leap-frogging method of advance;
3) The especially unfavorable conditions, such as rugged terrain, primitive jungle, and torrential rainFall;
4) The total lack of existing facilities that could be adapted to military requirements;
5) The primary tactical importance of air power;
6) The primary logistical importance of seaborne transportation;
7) The dependence of both shipping and air support on construction to provide operating facilities;
8) The continual critical shortages of construction manpower and materiel;
9) The continual and imperative need to improvise.

Supply
Supply or Logistics, or getting what is needed, where it is needed, and when it is needed, is a significant factor in strategic planning. From the beginning of the war, the AAF attempted to standardize and simplify supply procedures. Standard tables of equipment requirements were prepared for each man, each aircraft, and each unit. Rates of consumption were used to predict future requirements. Combat supply tables based upon estimated requirements for units in combat were used to determine the initial supply of these units overseas. To maintain unit stocks at a sufficient level, perpetual inventory systems and records were used by supply agencies. Supply tables and procedures underwent constant revision to manage the constantly changing situations in the theaters. Unlike the ground forces, whose supply gradually moved forward with the attacking army, Air Force units advanced in a series of leaps. Between such leaps supply operations at a base could become routine, but when a new base was captured, the movement of supplies forward became a high priority period of intense activity. Supply personnel

were to make use of the available materiel in their theater as much as possible, but in the SWPA this was limited to basic building materials and some captured enemy equipment. Allied countries used as bases, such as England and Australia, provided millions of dollars worth of supplies facilitated by reverse Lend-Lease.

Aerial planners had to consider that the continuing effectiveness of air power depended on an uninterrupted flow of supplies to an air base. Supplies had to be transported mainly by surface transportation to units that often were thousands of miles away. Many of these supplies, such as fuel, ammunition, and spare parts, were required in huge quantities; some were very specialized, while others were needed ASAP.

Although a bomber and its crew could be flown from the U.S. to the SWPA via Hawaii and the Pacific islands on the way to Australia, a shorter-range fighter aircraft had to be crated or placed upon the deck of a transport ship. Although fighter pilots could be air transported, the ground crews and supplies required weeks or even months to reach the combat theater via shipping across the Pacific. Thus, logistical planning had to be completed months in advance of major air operations.

Commands Responsible for AAF Supply, Transport, and Maintenance

Air Service Command (ASC)
The ASC operated within the Continental U.S., receiving all aircraft and aircraft equipment and supplies; making certain that necessary stocks were adequate and available; provided for overhaul and heavy repair work; and salvaged damaged or excess material. The ASC scheduled the equipment and supplies required by units in the U.S. and by all the overseas Air Forces so that they could be ordered, delivered, and stocked. ASC was organized into eleven subordinate Air Service Commands, each operating in a designated area of the U.S.

AAF Air Service Commands
These AAF Air Service Commands, under the control of the Air Force Commander, conducted supply and maintenance functions similar to those of the ASC, but in overseas theaters of operations. Each Air Force Air Service Command depended on the ASC in the U.S. for its stocks of supplies and for technical instructions and guidance as to maintenance. In a large operational theater, the Air Force Air Service Command could be subdivided into subordinate area Air Service Commands.

Air Transport Command (ATC)

The ATC provided all air transport for the War Department of cargo, personnel, and mail to, from, and between theaters of operations and within the Continental U.S. Through its ferrying division, it ferried aircraft within the Continental U.S. and overseas.

Air Force Troop Carrier Commands (or Wings)

The chief duties of the Air Force Troop Carrier Commands were to provide air transportation both for air and ground personnel and for cargo in combat areas.

Army Service Forces (ASF),

In addition, the AAF relied greatly upon the Army Service Forces (ASF), with its seven supply services for materiel common to the entire Army and for certain special supplies, such as bombs. The Army Transportation Corps, which was part of the ASF, was responsible for Army land and water transport and transported the bulk of AAF materiel overseas.

During the early months of the war, the main AAF supply problem was one of production. As production gradually met requirements, except for certain critical items, the supply/distribution problem increased greatly. Supply levels had to be maintained in each theater, with adequate quantities available for anticipated requirements in addition to maintaining a reserve, but without having an excess in any one theater.

There were four major groups of supplies required by AAF units:

1) **Aircraft:** The supply of aircraft and their allocation to the different combat theaters was determined by the strategic and tactical plans for the air war. The allocation of aircraft significantly determined almost all other types of AAF supply requirements.
2) **Spare parts, maintenance equipment, and specific aviation equipment and supplies:** An aircraft was constructed of many thousands of individual parts, any of which could necessitate replacement due to battle damage or normal wear. The Air Service Command had to have an enormous assortment of over a half million items stored and available at locations around the world where they would be needed.
3) **"Consumable supplies"** required by combat aircraft, such as aviation fuel, bombs, and ammunition.
4) **Materials procured by the Army Service Forces to fulfill the requirements of daily existence.** The major types of these supplies were:

Quartermaster: food, water, and other subsistence supplies, clothing, personal equipment, general supplies (such as beds, blankets, cooking utensils), fuel and oil for vehicles.

Medical Corps: medical supplies and equipment.

Ordnance: bombs (other than chemical bombs) and ammunition, weapons, and general purpose motor vehicles.

Chemical Warfare: incendiary bombs, smoke bombs, smoke, gas masks, decontamination equipment and supplies

Signal Corps: communication systems (telegraph, telephone, ground and airborne radio, radar, teletype, pigeons).

Corps of Engineers: construction equipment and supplies (graders, bulldozers, concrete, lumber, landing mats, brick), searchlights, barrage balloons.

Transportation: rail equipment (railroad cars), boating equipment (boats and barges), and pier equipment.

Domestic Supply

There were Air Depots located near the centers of each of the eleven Continental Air Service Command areas. An Air Depot was a large warehouse, usually stocked with two months' supply of the types of supplies required

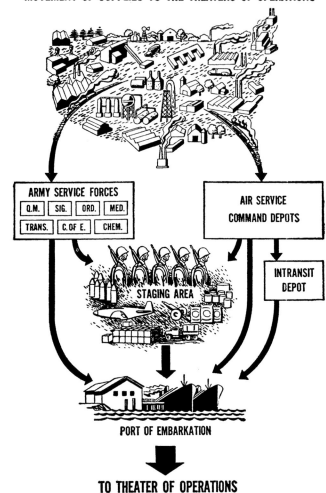

MOVEMENT OF SUPPLIES TO THE THEATERS OF OPERATIONS

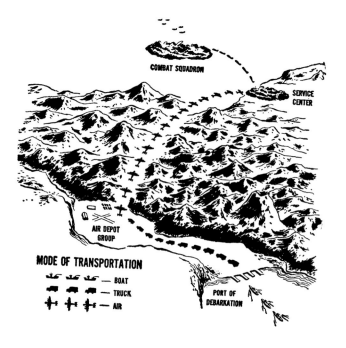

in its area. It also performed heavy aircraft maintenance. Working closely with the Air Depot was a Base Supply organization under the Base Commander at each of the major U.S. airbases. It provided air supplies from a 30-day supply to all units located there. When a unit stationed at a base required a part for an airplane, it requisitioned Base Supply. Base Supply then provided the part and when necessary replenished its own stock from its Air Depot, or from one of the ASC specialized depots that maintained central stocks of certain specialized types of equipment. Air Depot stocks were maintained by deliveries from manufacturers and from ASC Specialized Depots. Continuous stock controls were maintained at all these facilities, making it possible on short notice to remedy the shortages that arose in one area by requisitioning Depots in another area and shipping the scarce item by air.

Overseas Supply

The Air Service Command obtained and issued initial equipment and supplies to units transferring overseas and maintained supply levels in each theater with continual replenishments upon requisitions from the theaters. Once supplies were received in the theater, however, the Air Force Air Service Command of that theater had the express responsibility for them. The system for supplying Air Force combat units in a theater was basically comparable to domestic supply, except that the need for mobility and flexibility was more definite. During a tactical campaign, when air combat units were to rapidly advance, supply units had to be prepared to leap frog from airfield to airfield, as fixed bases with permanent facilities were found only in areas well to the rear.

Each theater included at least one Air Force General Depot that provided a comprehensive center for AAF technical supplies, as well as supplies

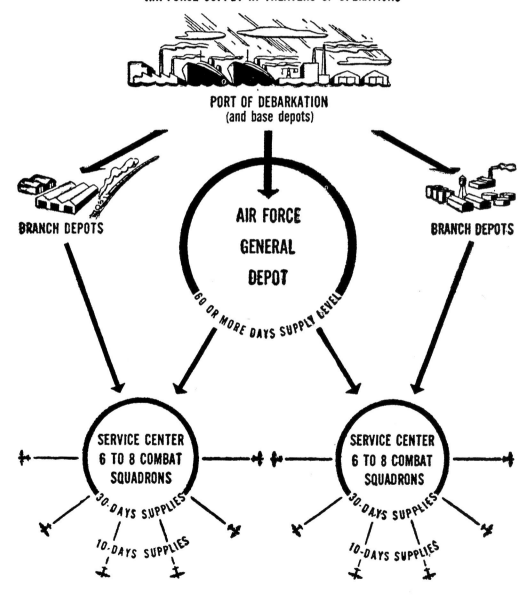

AIR FORCE SUPPLY IN THEATERS OF OPERATIONS

PORT OF DEBARKATION
(and base depots)

AIR FORCE GENERAL DEPOT

60 OR MORE DAYS SUPPLY LEVEL

BRANCH DEPOTS

BRANCH DEPOTS

SERVICE CENTER 6 TO 8 COMBAT SQUADRONS

SERVICE CENTER 6 TO 8 COMBAT SQUADRONS

30-DAYS SUPPLIES

30-DAYS SUPPLIES

10-DAYS SUPPLIES

10-DAYS SUPPLIES

NOTE: SUPPLIES FROM DEPOTS MAY BY-PASS SERVICE CENTERS AND GO DIRECT TO COMBAT SQUADRONS.

procured by Army Service Forces and also provided heavy maintenance. A number of Branch Depots that stored and issued supplies which required special methods of handling and storage were operated in connection with the Air Force General Depot and also under the command of the Air Force Air Service Commander. They included an aviation gas and oil depot, an ordnance ammunition depot, and a chemical ammunition depot. In addition, the following Branch Depots, which provided supplies used by both ground and air forces, were established if suitable Ground Force Depots were not conveniently located. Examples of Branch Depots included the Quartermaster Class I Depot (for consumable supplies, such as food), Quartermaster Class III depot (for motor fuels), and Engineer Depot (for construction and camouflage materials).

The providers of supplies were the Service Centers, which were generally similar to the Continental Base Supply organizations. Service Centers, located closer to the front lines than Depots, provided supplies and repair services for all types of equipment. Sections could be detached from the Service Center and assigned to advanced areas or could operate as a unit at the Service Center. A Service Center was able to service as many as eight combat squadrons. Its supplies were restocked by deliveries from the Air Force General Depot and Branch Depots.

Once freighters were unloaded, the supplies were stored in large warehouses, such as this Quonset located in Sydney, Australia. (AAF)

Huge **Quarter Master Depot** located at Base B at Oro Bay, New Guinea. (AAF)

The general configuration of overseas supply systems was adapted to the particular military and geographic features of each theater. In the ETO, Service Center personnel were merged with the supply and maintenance sections of combat units, while Air Force General Depots were not located far from the front lines. Service Center organizations in the Pacific had to

be adapted to the leap-frogging SWPA and Central Pacific island campaigns by dividing them into sections for rapid movement to advanced bases.

AAF supply and maintenance organizations included components that were thoroughly familiar with the equipment and supplies procured by the Army Service Forces. The Service Center provided for supply and maintenance of materiel originally acquired by Army Service Forces for AAF use as well as for AAF procured materiel. Similarly, the AAF provided the Ground Army with such aviation supplies as liaison aircraft, parachutes, aerial delivery containers, and cargo chutes. In advanced areas, or in theaters in which no ground establishments were established, the Air Force Air Service Command was responsible for all duties usually performed by the Army Service Forces.

Transportation
America's military effectiveness relied on transportation resources to dispatch personnel and supplies thousands of miles to the combat theaters. The large early shipping losses due to German U-Boats were surmounted by shipbuilders and Merchant Marine. Domestic railroads and other commercial carriers fulfilled the heaviest demands in their history. The Army, through its Transportation Corps, coordinated transportation by land and sea for all troops and supplies, while the AAF, through its Air Transport Command, operated the largest air transport service in history.

Unlike most other military organizations, many air combat units had to be divided for movement. In the SWPA, part of a fighter unit, for example, flew in its own aircraft to its new base while the ground crews were usually transported by transport aircraft, or if the new base was not too distant, by sea. Other non-flying personnel were usually transported by sea.

Moving AAF Units Overseas
When the training of an AAF unit was completed and it was ready for combat operations, it was processed for movement overseas. Fighter units whose aircraft had limited ranges were usually shipped by sea, while both the air and ground echelons were transported by water transport. The volume of shipping required to move an AAF unit depended on whether its equipment was dismantled and crated or was shipped uncrated on the decks of cargo vessels; this in turn depended on the facilities available at the destination. Early war shipments were normally crated to save space if destined for an established area such as Australia, where facilities for uncrating and assembling equipment were sufficient. However, equipment, except aircraft, destined for a newly-captured base in the Pacific was generally shipped fully assembled and ready for immediate operation. Because of their relatively light weight and bulky shape, aircraft created a special shipping problem. Twenty or more fighters could be carried on a light spar deck built several feet above the deck of an oil tanker. Propellers, wing tips, and several other parts were removed and the surface of the rest of the fighter was specially treated and joints taped to protect it from damaging salt water moisture. As a result, the long and expensive process of disassembling, crating, and reassembling the airplane was avoided while the fuel carrying capacity of the tanker was not affected.

Procedure for Overseas Movement
For the purpose of handling, directing, and processing the enormous volume of equipment and numbers of troops en route to overseas theaters, the War Department, through its Transportation Corps, established eight large installations known as Ports of Embarkation that were supplemented by a number of sub-ports. These ports, which are located adjoining key harbors such as New York, New Orleans, and San Francisco, were huge installations that included staging areas for troops and large numbers of depots and warehouses for the storage of supplies.

All AAF personnel, supplies, and equipment not flown to their destination passed through one of these ports en route to their theater destination. Personnel were transported by rail or truck to a staging area near a Port of Embarkation, where they were checked on such matters as their physical state, inoculations, pay, personnel records, insurance, and individual equipment. Only after it was established that each man had met all requirements for shipment did the Port Commander assign the unit to a specific ship.

While flying personnel often ferried their aircraft to combat areas, enlisted men were mostly moved in troop transports or LSTs. (AAF)

Since fighter aircraft had short ranges, they could not be flown from California to Australia and were lashed down to the tops of freighters, as were these P-47s. (AAF)

Water transportation, though relatively slow, was an economical use of manpower and fuel and indispensable to move the bulk of personnel and materiel overseas. The turnaround time required to load a ship in San Francisco, move it to Australia, unload and reload, then return to America to unload, with an allowance for normal repairs, was 70 days for a transport ship and 120 days for cargo vessels. Once in Australia, rail and road transportation was only utilized until the New Guinea Campaign began, when ships or aircraft were used to move supplies there depending on bulk and urgency. Because the cargo carried by an individual aircraft was limited, air transport was reserved for priority transport, such as for key personnel, emergency supplies and equipment, rapid evacuation of the sick and wounded, and the all-important mail. Air transport provided access in New

Guinea over regions controlled by the Japanese; by natural obstacles, such as the Owen Stanley Mountains; or where roads and railroads did not exist, which was most everywhere. Large quantities of supplies could be moved over moderate distances with the greatest speed by utilizing all available cargo aircraft,

Procedure for Moving Air Echelons Overseas

The AAF was responsible for processing and monitoring all air shipments to overseas destinations through its Air Transport Command, which operated eight Ports of Aerial Embarkation and a number of sub-ports, that performed essentially the same functions as the water ports, but on a much smaller scale. Aircrews passing through these ports were checked, processed, and then briefed for their over water journey. At each Port of Aerial Embarkation, the Air Transport Command operated an air freight terminal that handled, stored, and repacked air cargo.

Debarkation

At the end of their voyage, troops and supplies were unloaded at the theater Ports of Debarkation. At a number of these Ports of Debarkation, Air Depots, sometimes called Ex-Transit Depots, were maintained by the theater Air Force Air Service Commands.

Shipment of Supplies and Replacement Equipment

Once the air unit had been transported to and established at its theater base, it required immediate and continuous support via the supply of consumable supplies and replacement equipment. As the forces in the theater increased, these replacement supplies utilized an increasing proportion of total shipping requirements to the theater. Except for gasoline and oil, which were usually shipped directly from refineries, such supplies passed through Ports of Embarkation (water or air) and were managed like original shipments.

Of all the supplies coveted by men overseas was the mail, seen here being sorted in a large sorting facility. (AAF)

Ordinary supply requirements for units overseas, other than aviation fuel, bombs, ammunition, and aircraft, averaged about one ship ton per man per month. To maintain an air force of 100,000 men supplied with food, clothing, replacement vehicles, and their gasoline, parts, and similar items for one month required about 100,000 ship tons. In late 1944, the consumption of aviation fuel by the AAF in all theaters was nearly 150 million gallons per month, or 35 oil tanker loads (at 100,000 barrels per tanker). In the SWPA, large bases were equipped with pumping and storage facilities, but for newly-established bases' immediate fuel requirements were met by gasoline shipped in drums in cargo vessels.

In the combat areas of the SWPA, port facilities were very rudimentary and long jetties and oil pipelines had to be constructed out to the waiting tankers, as here at Lae, New Guinea. (AAF)

The AAF, through the **Air Transport Command** (ATC), was responsible for all transport by air of cargo and personnel for the War Department. (AAF)

Transport within Theaters

The SWPA campaigns relied largely upon air and water transport. To a considerable extent, the existence of transportation facilities determined the location of Depots, Service Centers, and Advanced Airbases. For a large-scale action, it was critical that the Depot be connected with all its Service Centers and that the Service Centers be located at, or be within a few hours distance of the bases they supported. In areas where such facilities were limited or where distances were great, the importance of air transport within the theater increased. Cargo plane units were sometimes assigned to the Air Force Air Service Command to provide fast air freight service between Depots and Service Centers and between Service Centers and bases.

Air Transport Command (ATC)

The AAF, through the Air Transport Command (ATC), was responsible for all transport by air of cargo and personnel for the War Department. In addition, it provided air transport services for other governmental agencies and for the governments of the Allies. The ATC's principal transport functions were the operation of air transport services within the U.S., between the U.S. and all of the theaters of operations, and between different theaters of operations. The ATC operated scheduled flights over AACS routes, but

much of its unique importance arose from the speed and mobility with which it met emergency demands in combat operations. It operated over air routes in the U.S. totaling 35,000 miles and overseas air routes totaling more than 95,000 miles. More than 200 bases along these routes were established by the AAF, as well as a world wide communications network and necessary weather forecasting units. For example, during December 1943, ATC operations totaled more than 35,000,000 ton miles of cargo and almost 100,000,000 passenger miles, of which more than 90% were over foreign routes.

With the development of ATC and the need for military air movement to all regions of the world, it was necessary to militarize many of the existing commercial airlines. A number of civil carriers entered into contracts with the government, under which they operated scheduled transport services with aircraft allotted to them by the AAF. Large numbers of flight and ground personnel of these air carriers were absorbed into the AAF and the carriers also trained military pilots for air transport operations.

Troop Carrier Operations

Air transport of cargo and personnel by Troop Carrier units was an important element in combat areas, particularly in the Pacific. These operations included the transport of key personnel and troops and rush orders of spare parts and freight to advanced units, both air and ground. Supplies carried to areas before landing fields were available were specially packed and dropped from low altitude, usually by parachute. Troop Carrier aircraft enabled fighter units to leap forward rapidly to advanced airfields by flying in engineer and maintenance units first. It was their job to prepare the landing fields and service aircraft. Evacuation of casualties from the front lines was another important function of Troop Carrier units, as air evacuation provided the greatest possible speed in carrying casualties to hospitals, where they could be quickly and properly treated. Medical evacuation units composed of medical officers and nurses and enlisted men were trained to take care of casualties while in flight. During 1945, more than 173,000 wounded and sick were evacuated by air by troop carrier and other AAF units.

Port Facilities

The major Allied objective in each SWPA operation was to advance the fighting line farther and farther into enemy-held territory. Establishing air facilities in forward areas, which helped make this advance possible, was a foremost engineer mission. Airfields had to be prepared first in Australia, then around the southern tip of New Guinea and along its northern coast, and on many related islands, including New Britain and the Admiralties,

Developed deep water ports in the SWPA were non-existent and sleepy peacetime ports, such as **Port Moresby** (shown), had to be developed to handle supplies shipped in from Australia or America. (AAF)

After an area was invaded and captured, landing areas and ports had to be quickly made available to land additional troops and supplies, such as at **San Fernando, Lingayan, Luzon**. (AAF)

and then in the Philippines. However, construction of an airfield and its nearby supporting facilities was inadequate, as these airfields needed a sufficient supply of the numerous items essential to keeping aircraft operational. Therefore, the typical Southwest Pacific airfield had to be connected by supply roads to extensive base installations and port facilities, where large ships could efficiently unload the several thousand tons of supplies required daily at the airfield. A substantial additional tonnage had to be unloaded to meet the concurrent engineer construction requirements and also the requirements of ground and naval units assigned to security and the projected tactical responsibilities in the area. Thus, the acquisition of harbors and the early construction of port facilities played a very significant part in all planning.

No doubt due to their low logistical requirements, Japanese occupation forces made little or no effort to develop port facilities. Although deep water was found close to shore in many areas of the Southwest Pacific, there were no major ports to be found between Brisbane, Australia, and Manila, in the Philippines. Almost all islands and much of the New Guinea coast were surrounded by reefs that rose to within a few feet of the surface of the water and entrance channels through these reefs were narrow and difficult to negotiate. In addition, once makeshift harbors were established they were often unprotected from winds and high surf.

Open Storage areas, such as at **Dreger Bay, Base B, New Guinea**, were necessary and convenient. (AAF)

Maintenance

Even in peacetime, aircraft required continuous maintenance, and in wartime, maintenance requirements multiplied due to battle damage and the increased attrition due to combat operations. AAF maintenance problems were increased by geographic and climatic conditions. In the South Pacific tropics, maintenance was increased by humidity, corrosion of metal surfaces, condensation of moisture within instruments, leakage, and the short circuit of wiring and electronic systems. The aircraft in service rate improved as the war progressed and was always much higher when compared to that of the Japanese.

Aircraft maintenance in the SWPA was mostly done outdoors in adverse tropical, geographic and climatic conditions. (AAF)

Echelons of Maintenance

The main objectives of the AAF maintenance system were the maximum serviceability of aircraft for the combat unit and the economical use of specialized personnel and repair equipment. AAF maintenance was divided into echelons, or levels, ranging from repair work done by the aircrew to complete overhaul by an Air Depot. The maintenance echelon organization was flexible, especially under combat conditions on quickly changing battle fronts.

The Echelons of Maintenance were:

First Echelon: Maintenance responsibilities performed by the air echelon of the combat unit consisted of servicing aircraft (fueling) and equipment;

preflight and daily inspections; minor repairs (tightening of nuts and bolts, hose clamps), adjustments, and replacements. All essential First Echelon tools and equipment were transportable by air.

Second Echelon: Maintenance responsibilities performed by the ground crew of the combat unit and by Airbase Squadrons, Airways Detachments, and Airdrome Squadrons consisted of servicing aircraft and equipment, periodic preventive inspections, and those adjustments, repairs, and replacements that could be done with hand tools and mobile equipment (such as checking timing, adjusting valves, engine changes, etc.). Most repair equipment could be transported by air, but certain items necessitated surface transportation.

Third Echelon: Maintenance performed by the Base Maintenance organization in the U.S. and the Service Center in overseas theaters. Responsibilities consisted of repairs and replacements requiring mobile machinery and equipment that necessitated ground transportation. It included field repairs and salvage, removal and replacement of major unit assemblies, fabrication of minor parts, and minor repairs to aircraft structures. Normally, Third Echelon maintenance incorporated repairs that could be completed within a limited time.

Fourth Echelon: Maintenance responsibilities performed by the Air Depot included complete restoration of worn or damaged aircraft, periodic overhaul of assemblies and accessories, fabrication of such parts as may be required to supplement normal supply, accomplishment of technical modifications as directed, and final disposition of reclaimed and salvaged materials.

Mobility in Maintenance

Service Squadrons, which were a part of the Service Group, could operate at the Service Center Base or with the combat squadrons at forward bases. Service Center functions could be carried out at permanent installations with hangars and fixed machinery. However, under rapidly moving combat situations, Service Center organizations were able to move swiftly and operate in the field away from their Headquarters, sometimes for extended periods. The Service Squadron included mobile units that had the function of operating in advanced areas or at dispersed fields and making Third Echelon repairs on aircraft that had crashed or were unable to return to their base. The Service Center consisted of one or more of the following: a Machine Shop to make spare parts and an Instrument Repair Shop, both housed in heavy duty vans; an Electric Shop; a Paint and Fabric Shop; a Propeller Shop; a Sheet Metal Shop; and a Cabinet Shop for woodwork. Most of these shops were accommodated in tents and could be transported by truck and set up quickly.

Units created to increase the mobility of aircraft maintenance included the Airdrome Squadron, which performed Second Echelon repair. It was used in leapfrogging operations to provide immediate service and repair for combat units without waiting for the regular ground crews of that unit to arrive. It was capable of supporting one to three combat squadrons for a week to ten days.

Maintenance Methods

AAF maintenance was based on established industrial production line practices. In the First and Second Echelons, ground crews were grouped into specialties so that maximum use could be made of their specialized training and so that many men could work on each aircraft at the same time. For example, in servicing an aircraft, one group could be checking the spark plugs while another was checking radios, another the landing gears, and another fuel and oil levels. Further specialization in both men and equipment occurred in Third Echelon maintenance, and where possible, Fourth Echelon maintenance was set up on a production line basis. However, under combat conditions maintenance depended heavily on the ingenuity and inventiveness of ground personnel who could not wait for overhaul or replacements.

Preventive Inspection

The foundation of the AAF maintenance system was the inspection of all parts to prevent accidents, damage, or part failure before it occurred. A detailed and systematic inspection procedure was prescribed and definite responsibility was fixed for different phases of each inspection. The Maintenance Inspection Record was a complete logbook of each aircraft's air operation and maintenance. It contained the record of flying time and determined when the oil and engines should be changed. Inspections were made before every flight; daily; after 25, 50, and 100 hours of flight; at time of engine change; 25 hours after engine change; and at special periods as required by the particular model aircraft. These inspections were progressively more detailed and thorough, and by the time an aircraft completed 500 flying hours, every part and every accessory had been checked. Because lives and the success of the missions depended on these inspections, they were done with great attention.

Technical Orders (TOs)

To distribute adequate, authentic, and uniform technical instructions for the operation and maintenance of all AAF equipment throughout the world, the Air Service Command issued a series of publications known as Technical Orders or Tech Orders. These ranged in size from one page to a book, and a complete set consisted of about 190 volumes. Tech Orders covered every type of aircraft and each of its parts and accessories. They provided detailed, illustrated instructions of maintenance methods for all the various skills and trades required in aircraft maintenance. Four Tech Orders were issued with each aircraft as it left the assembly line: Handbook of Operations and Flight Instruction; Handbook of Service Instruction; Handbook of Overhaul Instruction; and Illustrated Parts List. Tech Orders were constantly revised and supplemented as improved maintenance methods and modifications in aircraft and equipment occurred.

Manufacturers' Representatives

Aircraft, engine, and aircraft accessory manufacturers were under contract to the AAF to furnish technical personnel in the combat theaters for supervision and instruction in the maintenance and operation of their company's equipment. These men were responsible to the Air Force Air Service Commander, who usually requested them and to whom they were required to make weekly reports. Manufacturers' Representatives were subject to military law, were lawful belligerents, and could be treated as prisoners of war if captured. Their privileges were the same as those of Commissioned Officers and they wore the same uniforms, but without insignia of grade, arm, or service.

Reclamation and Salvage

Wherever possible, a damaged aircraft was repaired and put back in the air. In most theaters, a principal source of parts was from aircraft so badly damaged in action that they could not be economically repaired. Usable parts were stripped (cannibalized) and either used immediately on other aircraft, or were stocked in a process called reclamation. If possible, whatever remained after an aircraft had been stripped for parts was returned to the Depot, where it could be melted down for use in fabrication or sold for its basic materials in a process known as salvage. Reclamation and salvage in the U.S. and England assumed such large proportions that organizations were sometimes detailed for the purpose. Salvage was not possible in combat areas, particularly the Pacific, and stripped aircraft were abandoned and claimed by the jungle after the Allies leapfrogged to a new base.

2

AAF Airfields

Background

WWII was the first war in which extensive employment was made of air power. Because aircraft were the principal tactical weapon in SWPA, the construction of airfields and associated facilities were the most important construction priority. From 15 February 1942 to VJ-Day, more than 200 runways and innumerable supporting facilities were constructed extending from Australia to Okinawa. During the war, the Japanese mostly built rudimentary airfields and then were barely able to maintain and repair them. Meanwhile, the Allies captured and improved existing Japanese airfields, but more often than not, constructed new airfields quickly and efficiently, then were able to supply, maintain, and repair them. This advantage in superior airfields was the primary reason for Allied air power dominating the Pacific Theater.

As the war progressed, the Construction Engineers became more proficient, as the base at **Tacloban**, Leyte, Philippines, demonstrates with its long well-graded and surfaced runways and taxiways leading to multiple hardstands. (AAF)

Early and captured airfields were characterized by quick, basic construction, such as **Tadji Airfield**, New Guinea, which was captured from the Japanese. In this photo pyramidal tents pitched among standing water are seen. (AAF

The leapfrogging, stepping stone advances, beginning in early 1943 with the Japanese defeat at Buna, consisted of the dislodgment forward or to either flank of the enemy under air cover and development of the captured area: first as an air base, then as a port and supply base for the support of the next offensive leap. Often, forward movement was brought about by a flanking action which cut or disrupted every line of air and sea communication to an intended forward enemy-held objective. Subsequently, with the objective secured, flank protection to that area was provided. For example, the Allied base at Saidor, in addition to constituting a stepping stone in the Allied advance, flanked the Admiralty Islands and protected that important operation from attacks launched from the Japanese at Hollandia, both in the course of seizure and then in the subsequent consolidation and base construction in those islands. Likewise, the Admiralties later protected Allied-held Hollandia from invasion by Japanese naval forces from the east and northeast. As the advance along the New Guinea coast to the west succeeded, the rear most stepping stones became of less and less use and were eventually abandoned, so the many major installations in southern and southeastern Australia that were planned and constructed in the early years of SWPA operations were abandoned shortly after completion.

As the Allies went on the offensive and the Japanese were unable to staunch even weak Allied drives, the Allied advance progressed much more rapidly than predicted. The speed of the advance, along with the distances involved, made it necessary for the Allies to construct new and large facilities forward for use, replacing those left far in the rear.

Construction in the SWPA

During the war, construction in the SWPA went through many stages, all of which necessitated the development of engineering design and construction methods to meet unusual situations, many of which had not previously been encountered by military engineering. Throughout SWPA operations there were acute shortages in manpower, materials, and equipment. The future success of tactical operations was largely dependent on the rapid completion of air, ground, and naval bases, and often the engineers were forced to improvise and adapt, but the fundamental doctrines of military construction needed to be observed:

1) Rigid adherence to "first things first";
2) Concentration of effort on the vital task or portion of that task;
3) Completion of the vital portion of each task to usable condition at the earliest moment, then concentration on the next controlling item;
4) Stringent economy of effort and material;
5) Utmost simplicity of design.

The Corps of Engineers had gained great experience completing civil works construction during the 1930s and made a great effort to modernize its military construction techniques and to change troop construction methods from employment of hand labor to use of mechanical equipment. But prewar, very inadequate appropriations made for new equipment and poor staff decisions which emphasized mobility in the limited number of this new construction equipment appropriated were made at the expense of their effectiveness and durability. Therefore, at the beginning of the war, military engineering procedures, doctrines, training, organization, and equipment were based on the circumstance that many of the tasks to be performed by either engineer combat or engineer construction troops would still largely be completed by manual labor, supplemented by small numbers of highly mobile but lightweight and inadequate equipment.

When the war began, the insubstantial, low capacity equipment, when it reached the construction area at all, was usually unable to completely accomplish its intended use, which led to overuse and, being fragile, consequently led to rapid breakdowns. All engineer units demanded more heavy equipment, but until heavy duty bulldozers, graders, scrapers, and shovels were shipped to the SWPA picks and shovels and the few pieces of heavy equipment available, both American and captured Japanese, then served as the primary construction procedures. Once superior heavy equipment arrived it very effectively performed their construction goals, stopping only for maintenance.

Airfield Construction Priorities

Specific construction priorities were established for the building of an airfield:

First Priority (the various items listed below were to be implemented concurrently):

1) Initial beach landing and docking facilities;
2) Initial road access from the docks to supply areas;
3) Initial airdrome facilities to provide, in order:
    a) Landing strip for transport aircraft;
    b) Landing strip for fighter aircraft with alert and dispersal facilities;
4) Water supply points;
5) Minimum storage;
6) Defense installations (normally by tactical forces with the technical assistance of assigned or attached combat engineer troops).

Second Priority (various items listed below could be executed concurrently and completed but with priority of effort listed in relative order):

1) Complete hospital facilities;
2) Complete wharves and docks;
3) Complete water supply installations;
4) Complete necessary runways and dispersal areas for fighter and heavy bomber aircraft, and necessary operations buildings;
5) Complete roads;
6) Complete warehousing;
7) Complete bulk petroleum storage and distribution facilities;
8) Complete revetments in dispersal areas for the protection of aircraft.

Third Priority: Construction of minimum administrative and service installations and of utilities other than those included above, which were considered essential.

Airfield Construction

The SWPA was the first theater of operations in which the AAF had to operate from bases located in the combat zone, often constructed and operated under enemy action in remote areas on undeveloped and primitive terrain that was usually covered with jungle. This unique situation presented both air and engineer personnel with many unique problems. Previous concepts, techniques, and machinery had to be abandoned, modified, or completely transformed to meet these conditions.

From the onset, it was obvious that the construction of airfields in the SWPA would be a daunting undertaking. The construction forces were too small and the environment so unfavorable that it was considered impossible to construct airbases under the existing regimen and a complete reanalysis of the undertaking would be necessary. This rethinking would begin with the Engineering Officer in the field, who had to proceed without any specific direction except to use basic military engineering principles. These Engineer Construction Regiments and Battalions had to pioneer methods and standards of design and build accordingly. The failures and then successes of these early ventures led to the standardization of theater-wide principles of airfield construction.

Upon embarking on a new project, these early construction units first had to establish the primary purpose of the airbase, then determine the absolute minimum amount of work required to achieve that purpose. Airbase fundamentals defined an airfield as "a runway suitable for aircraft landings and takeoffs, with facilities for commanding, parking, supplying, and servicing aircraft and the aerial units which flew and maintained them. In forward areas, protection of the installation from hostile aircraft, provision for crash landings, and provision for repair of bomb damages were additional elements." New construction criteria required a major alteration in conditions under which the air arm had previously operated.

New Airfield Design and Construction Criteria

Prior to 1942, design doctrine for military airfields included clearings at least 1,000 feet wide, with paved runways 300 to 400 feet wide along the center line of the clearing, and three intersecting runways in the directions of the three prevailing winds. The lengths of the runways were determined by the type of operations from the runway: fighters, 3,000 feet; medium bombers, 4,000 feet; and heavy bombers, at least one runway of 5,000 feet. All landing surfaces were designed to resist stress due to landing with the entire weight of the aircraft concentrated on one wheel, plus 50% additional for impact. Also, it was considered necessary that surfaces be designed to prevent fatigue failures due to repeated maximum loadings on a single pair of wheel tracks. Some specifications were immediately modified in the SWPA to meet existing conditions and with further experience, other important modifications were made. Among these changes were:

Type of Airfield: During the first nine months of 1942, the tactical situation was very fluid and it was found unfeasible to designate any particular airfield exclusively for use of one type of aircraft. An airfield built for use by fighters was often used almost immediately by medium or heavy bombers, so it was necessary to adapt the plans of the Theater to meet that situation. Consequently, any airfield had to be designed to accommodate the heaviest loads.

Length of Runway: There were a number of factors that imposed a change in the specified length of runways. Runways in the SWPA were often built to accommodate fighters and transports that were necessary to protect and supply and lend support to the infantry. Later, these runways were lengthened or a secondary longer and better constructed runway was begun to accommodate medium and heavy bombers (see Runway Layout below). All aircraft in SWPA operated against targets at such great distances that overloading with fuel and ordnance was a critical necessity, requiring long runways and long approach areas beyond the ends of those runways.

Width of Runway: It was soon acknowledged that a runway 7,000 feet long by 100 feet wide had several construction advantages over one that was shorter but 200 feet wide. The lesser width of the runway and shoulders reduced much of the grading which would have otherwise been necessary. Since road graders and paving equipment normally moved along the long axis of a runway, they did not lose as much time in turning and backing up on the narrower runways as they did on the wider runways. This concentration on length rather than width resulted in much more actual working time and freed equipment to build additional airfields with the few men and machines available.

Runway Layout

Both in the UK and U.S., crossing runways in the direction of the three prevailing winds was a routine specification. In the SWPA, however, winds were generally gentle, seldom exceeding 15 miles per hour, and were generally in the same direction. Where practicable runways were oriented into the diametrically opposite prevailing wind directions, such orientation was not entirely essential and it was possible to use other orientations to meet criteria of the surrounding terrain and the availability of engineer manpower and equipment. Except in areas very near the Equator, where trade winds prevailed, these mild winds could be expected to blow from diametrically opposite directions during the respective seasons, with very mild winds of erratic direction occurring between the two seasons. For instance, in southern New Guinea, during June through September, these winds were entirely from the southeast, whereas during November through April they were almost entirely from the northwest. This circumstance made it possible to orient one runway northwest-southeast and eliminate cross winds of any magnitude. Occasionally due to geography, the runways had to be located between hills, regardless of wind direction. However, due to the high landing and takeoff speeds inherent in the new combat aircraft at that time, it was found that the side winds had only minor effect. These aircraft did not stall into a three point landing but flew in until two wheels touched the runway.

The crossing of runways was abandoned for two reasons: an enemy bomb dropped at the point of intersection would put both runways out of commission; and second, by not crossing the runways, each runway could be located to make optimum use of the terrain, regardless of the grade of a possible intersection.

It was also found that greater efficiency in construction and combat operations was achieved using parallel runways. The first runway constructed was intended for immediate use by fighter aircraft, but did not receive its final surface treatment at that particular time. With increased operational demands a second runway, usually paralleling the first, was built 200 feet or more away and completely drained and paved, then the first runway was drained and paved. In addition, it was common to provide a smooth, compacted, unpaved crash strip somewhere in an area to receive damaged aircraft returning from combat.

Surface Materials

The criteria to land with the entire weight of the aircraft concentrated on one wheel plus 50% additional for impact was found to be incorrect. At the moment of landing, an aircraft was airborne, as its weight was carried by the wings, and the impact on the surface material at the instant of touch down was almost entirely due to the unsprung weight of the landing gear alone. The weight sustained by the runway at the instant of impact was transmitted by the aircraft tires. Theoretically, tires inflated to 70psi could not exert more ground pressure than 70psi. Surfaces capable of sustaining 100 to 150psi over a 1,000 square inch area were judged to be safe for nearly all conditions and by all heavy bombers. The surface suffered most severe stress near the end of a landing run, when the aircraft was no longer running fast enough to have much weight carried on its wings and on taxiways; in warm-up areas; in hardstands or dispersal areas; and at the apron before take off.

Time and Effort Saving Expediencies

During the first nine months of 1942, over 40 battalion months were saved by eliminating drainage and sometimes paving specifications in the construction of a number of airdromes in Australia and some in New Guinea. As the occupancy and use of these installations was not certain, the expenditure of time, materials, and effort to drain them was not justified. Instead, more airdromes were constructed with the inadequate engineer manpower and equipment available. This construction was started at the beginning of the dry season (nine months long in most of Australia), when no major drainage was needed, but was authorized to be added shortly before the wet season would begin. The paving of many of these runways was not specified, which also proved to be another correct assessment. Some of these airdromes were never occupied for tactical operations, while other forward airdromes were adequate without surfacing and met their requirement over their critical period of operations. Some airdromes were constructed with the knowledge that they would have to be abandoned once the rainy season began.

Airfield Types

During early airfield construction in the SWPA there were no airfield type guidelines which laid out various design and specifications for the aircraft operating from them. However, with the advance along the north coast of New Guinea the pattern of operations, while not routine, was apparent, and GHQ, SWPA issued standard diagrammatic plans for airfields to be used by different types of aircraft.

Type A (AAF)

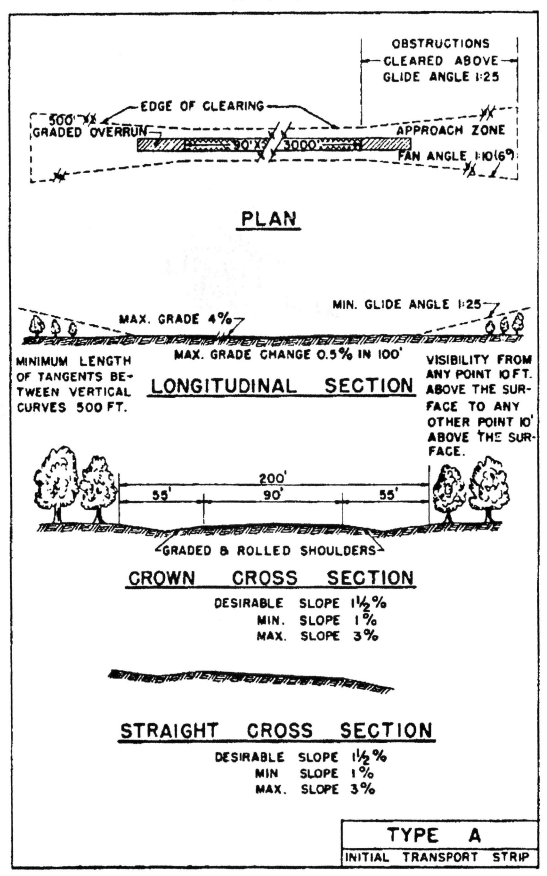

Type B (AAF)

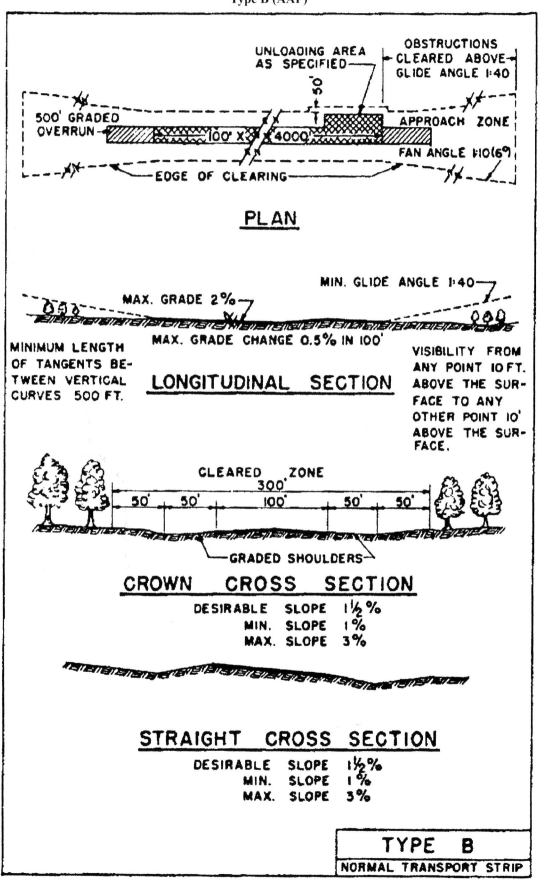

Type C (AAF)

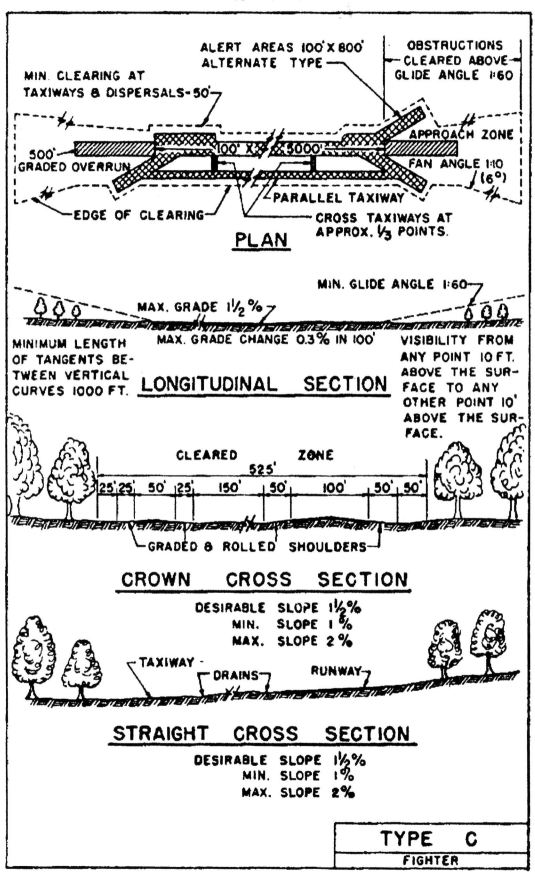

Type D (AAF)

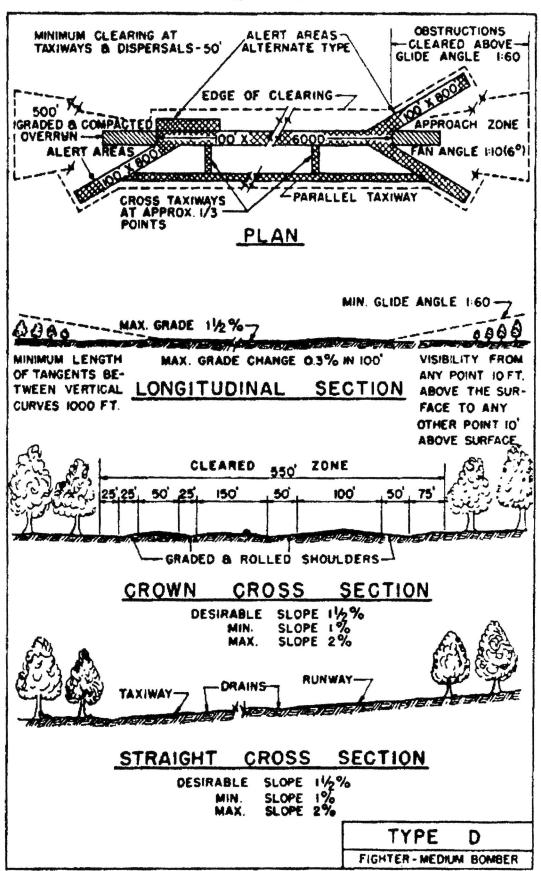

Type E (AAF)

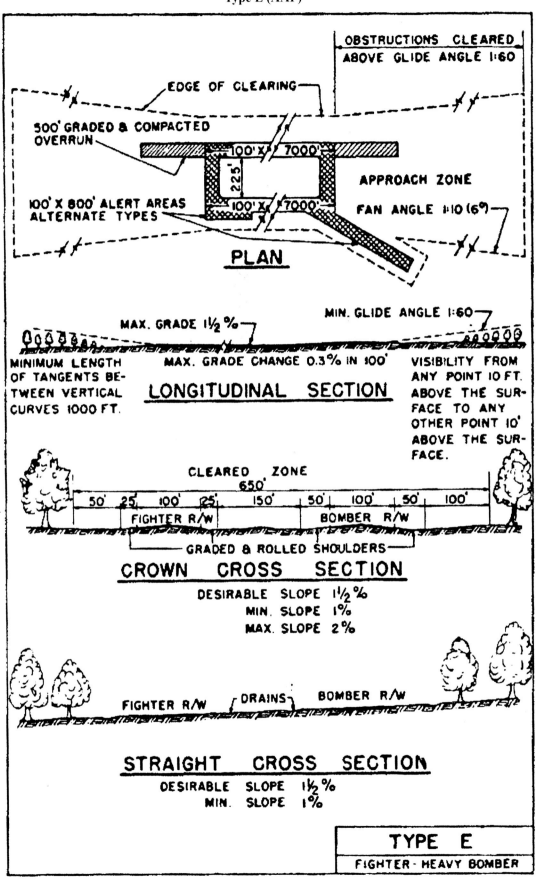

PLAN

LONGITUDINAL SECTION

CROWN CROSS SECTION

STRAIGHT CROSS SECTION

TYPE E

FIGHTER - HEAVY BOMBER

The standard airfields were: Type A: Initial Transport Strip; Type B: Normal Transport Strip; Type C: Fighter; Type D: Fighter and Medium Bomber; and Type E: Fighter and Heavy Bomber. These plans were drawn so that an airfield built initially for transports could be developed in turn for use by fighters, medium bombers, and finally heavy bombers with a minimum of effort and without wasting previous construction efforts. In addition, standard plans were issued for dispersals and taxiways; however, the construction organization in the field was authorized to adapt these standard plans to meet their requirements. During mid-1944, the Office of the Chief Engineer (OCE), GHQ, SWPA, conducted several studies of dispersal layouts, seeking a means to further reduce both construction time and effort required to place an airfield into operation. However, due to pressing aircraft combat operational requirements, it was necessary to continue the use of the standard plans already issued.

Site Selection and Construction
In July and August 1942, GHQ, SWPA formalized and standardized specifications governing procedures for the selection of sites and the coordination of airdrome construction in Australia. During the New Guinea Campaign airdrome sites were chosen, theoretically by Task Force Commanders, and after approval by a local representative of Allied Air Forces, construction was initiated. However, sites were actually selected by the Task Force Engineer and then approved by a Fifth Air Force representative, or the selection was made jointly. Fifth Air Force decisions regarding such matters as airdrome layouts and the locations of hardstands were final, apart from any differences in the views of Fifth Air Force and Allied Air Forces. Immediately before the Philippine Campaign, Allied Air Forces insisted that the GHQ, SWPA grant them responsibility for selection of airdrome sites, but they did not have adequate reconnaissance and survey parties to collect pre-invasion information as a basis for its site location decisions. On 15 October 1944, only a few days prior to the initiation of the Leyte operation, responsibility for selection of airdrome sites was returned to the Task Force Commanders.

The geography of New Guinea had two prevailing features which were the most adaptable for the location of airfields. These were the low, sloping lands near the sea and the higher benchlands between these lowlands and the mountains. In the lowlands, the best locations were usually found in existing coconut groves. On the benchlands, the most likely locations for airfield development were in areas where kunai grass was the most prevalent vegetation. In these areas, it was often possible to land transport aircraft after the grass had been cut and a few boulders were removed and holes filled. However, it was not feasible to spread cut kunai grass back over the stubble, as there was no way of anchoring the material against propeller blast without disturbing the underlying sod surface. Also, it was not practical to store the cut grass for use as a dust preventative if the runway was later to be further developed, as it would quickly rot in the climate.

Often, depending on the tactical situation, it was necessary to construct small transport aircraft runways to supply advance units which were located in areas inaccessible to other means of resupply. These advanced landing fields seldom had a runway length of more than 3,000 feet and were crudely constructed with limited safety requirements. Local native labor was recruited for clearing and leveling. Construction mostly consisted simply of cutting and burning kunai grass and filling and packing holes. Drainage requirements could be mostly ignored, as it was usually possible to select sites which, except during heavy rains, drained naturally. When all weather landing fields were required, engineer units and local troops were assigned to improve runways, as at Nadzab and Gusap, located northwest of Lae, New Guinea. These early transport fields were often initially selected as the basis for subsequent construction of complete operational airdromes.

When a suitable site was selected for the development of air facilities,

one or more Engineer Aviation Battalions or General Service Regiments were assigned to the construction of the project. Theoretically, the development of air facilities followed a pattern. Initially, the selected area was cleared and leveled as a sod runway for transport aircraft and soon minimum facilities were added to accommodate fighters. This runway was lengthened and surfaced as an advanced fighter airfield; dispersal facilities were enlarged and the runway further lengthened for use by medium bombers; and, if required, the runway was further extended to 7,000 feet for use by heavy bombers. If the base was to be fully developed, facilities for depot and repair units were constructed. Airfields with 7,000 foot runways were seldom built, as B-17 and B-24 heavy bombers were able to operate satisfactorily from 5,000 to 6,000 foot runways. When each successive aircraft type was moved in, the preceding type moved forward to another, more advanced location where the same base development was taking place. An example of this phased development took place in April 1944, when heavy bombers were based at Dobodura; medium bombers at Nadzab; fighters at Finschhafen, Saidor, and Cape Gloucester; and transport aircraft moved supplies to the newly-seized runway on Los Negros, in the Admiralty Islands.

Clearing
Clearing of airfield sites in the SWPA varied from the relatively simple hand cutting or mowing of thick kunai grass to the removal of extensive rain forests. The width of necessary clearing depended upon several factors, including tree height and density and local conditions, such as cross winds, obstructions, and the direction of runway regarding the prevailing winds. In Australia's Northern Territory, clearing operations were relatively simple, where a one inch cable was stretched across the proposed runway and attached at each end to a bulldozer. As the two dozers moved forward across the future runway area, nearly all the trees, which averaged about 12 inches in diameter (with very few exceeding 18 inches), were completely uprooted, making it only necessary to remove the cut tree trunks and branches and the uprooted stumps. An area 100 feet wide by 5,000 feet long could be cleared in ten hours by a crew of ten men. However, as the dry season became well advanced, the ground became so hard in some areas that many trees broke off near the base instead of being uprooted.

The local native population, called "Fuzzy Wuzzies", was used extensively for rudimentary clearing operations. (AAF)

The removal of coconut palm trees by conventional methods could be extremely difficult because of their large root mass. After trying several methods, a D-8 bulldozer with a low front scoop loosened the root ball on one side and, then dug deeply under the root ball on the opposite side. Getting low under the root ball on this side and with a heavy pushing lift,

Bulldozers towing **Carry Alls** behind greatly speeded airfield construction. (AAF)

the dozer removed the tree and root ball quickly and effectively. Because this method was inherently dangerous and also loosened the coconuts from the tops of trees, these pieces of equipment were later equipped with a cab or overhead protection.

Clearing operations in the extremely dense New Guinea rain forests required much effort, both in man- and equipment-hours. During their initial duty in dense rain forests, several engineer units mistakenly assumed that tree clearing there could be carried out similarly to lumbering in America by cutting down the trees; that was until they attempted to pull out the tenacious stumps. These units quickly learned to use the weight of the tree itself to pull the stump. A short trench alongside the tree was dug by hand, blown by explosive, or gouged out by heavy equipment. With larger trees, a bulldozer was used to scoop up an earth platform on the other side of the tree from the trench. When these preparations were completed, a D-8 was moved to the platform to push as high up on the trunk as possible. With difficult trees a cable was fastened high in the tree and pulled down by a heavy truck or tractor. At Cape Sansapor, it was found that approximately three trees per acre were of such large size that they had to be blown down by explosives, cut into several pieces, then removed by bulldozers working in pairs.

Drainage
Engineer units in the Southwest Pacific had to learn largely from field experience both the extent of the need for and the methods of providing adequate drainage for surface water on airfields. The basic premise for drainage was "in almost every case, it was much easier to reduce the surface and ground water table down by a foot or more by adequate drainage than it was to haul in and place 1,000s to 100,000s of cubic yards of selected materials to build up the roads, airdromes and hardstand areas on a soft and unstable foundation above the water table. Relatively little effort spent on such drainage relief will effect major savings not only in the overall initial construction but also in subsequent maintenance."

When airfields were developed on new sites in forward areas, initial consideration was only given to providing an operational runway with limited aircraft dispersal facilities while expending minimal time, labor, and materials. The runway and dispersal areas usually covered about 2,000 acres of dense jungle that concealed minor topographical variations which would be the determining factors in proper drainage design. Often a runway was needed to be operational even before a topographic survey of the entire area could be completed; thus, only the major drainage system was established in time to be included in the construction of the runway. In these remote areas, rainFall records were never kept and made planning of drainage

capacity difficult. The key to successful airfield construction was a comprehensive drainage system; however, during the early stages of construction, in order to meet immediate tactical requirements, inadequate consideration was given to drainage and much drainage work was bypassed. As the airfield was further developed, the drainage system was enlarged and improved. As a result of this two-stage method of completing an airfield the total man-hours of work were increased, but this method fulfilled the initial tactical requirements with a minimum of time and effort.

Of course, wherever possible airfields were located in areas where it would not be necessary to divert large quantities of water. However, after clearing a site, it was often found necessary to excavate drainage ditches parallel to the runways in order to drain the water from the surface and subgrade. These ditches were cut by grader, ditching machine, bulldozer, carryall, and/or dragline. If an airfield site had been well selected it was possible to cut ditches to the required depth and size with a grader. To divert major streams, ditches needed to be of a large cross section and were usually excavated with carryalls. In a few cases, in which soil conditions were such that neither graders nor tractors could operate efficiently, draglines were used to excavate these main ditches.

Airfield construction in New Guinea, especially at Embi, Merauke, Hollandia, and Cape Sansapor, was often complicated by the saturation of the subgrade, together with a high water table. At these locations, it was necessary to dig large ditches by dragline in order to drain the area under construction. At Jackson Drome, near Port Moresby, underground Springs in the runway area developed at the start of the rainy season and it was necessary to install an elaborate system of herringbone French drains and cross-runway drains.

As arid Australia was left behind and the Allies advanced into areas of intense tropical rainFall, the necessity for an adequate drainage system and for continuous drainage maintenance was stressed. Drainage facilities were designed in the field to fit local conditions and in early operations no specific formula was standard. It would not be until June 1944 that Maj.Gen. Hugh Casey, Chief Engineer, finally became so fed up with the lack of adequate drainage at various bases he stated in a Memorandum: "Failure to provide adequate drainage as one of the earliest features of any construction project indicates a basis lack of engineering knowledge….the need for continuous drainage maintenance can not be overstressed."

Runway Base Course
During the construction of airfields in the rain forests and coconut groves of New Guinea and nearby islands, it was generally necessary to first strip off and then dispose of the layer of humus, varying in thickness from one to two feet or more, thus uncovering the relatively firm subsoil. After the removal of the humus, the base courses for runways, taxiways, and hardstands were constructed of local materials, usually mixtures of sand, clay, and gravel. Where relatively soft coral or suitable bank gravel was available, it was used in preference to other materials. Where coral or bank gravel was not available, it was often necessary to mix gravel from stream beds or beaches with sand-clay from bank sources. Beach and stream gravels usually consisted of large stones and sand without sufficient fines or binder material and rock crushers were used extensively to break down the large stones to create sufficient fine material.

Runway Surfacing
In the SWPA, during the course of airfield development in forward areas, a runway could have a successive a number of different types of surface. If the runway were located in a kunai grass area, the initial surface was usually of sod, suitable for early use by transport aircraft. When the field was improved for fighter use, the runway was normally surfaced with coral or mixtures of sand, clay, and gravel obtained locally. If surfacing materials

RUNWAY CONSTRUCTION AND DRAINAGE

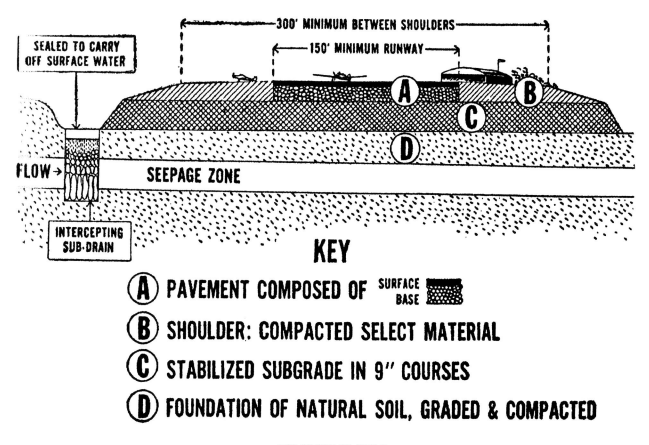

KEY

Ⓐ PAVEMENT COMPOSED OF ᵁᴿᶠᴬᶜᴱ BASE

Ⓑ SHOULDER: COMPACTED SELECT MATERIAL

Ⓒ STABILIZED SUBGRADE IN 9" COURSES

Ⓓ FOUNDATION OF NATURAL SOIL, GRADED & COMPACTED

NOT DRAWN TO SCALE

were not available locally, the runway was covered with pierced steel plank landing mat. Later airfields were seldom improved beyond requirements for fighter aircraft, but when bomber operations were planned, a bitumen seal coat was normally added to runways surfaced with local materials.

For the construction of all weather runways for early operations in Papua, a base course of four to five inches of compacted decomposed shale, granite, or even clay-sand-gravel was first laid. However, since the depth of the base course had to be varied according to the type of soil and bearing capacity of the subgrade, there were many instances where a much thicker base course was necessary. On the more developed type fields, this base course was primed with a 50% tar and 50% mixture of diesel oil and gasoline. Tar, which could be obtained in quantity in Australia, was used instead of bitumen for priming to conserve shipping space. After several fires had started from the use of gasoline in cutting back the tar, only diesel oil was used for that purpose. On top of the priming layer the following were laid, in order: a thin layer of hot asphalt, a layer of 3/4 inch stone chips, another layer of hot asphalt, a layer of 5/8 inch stone chips, another layer of asphalt, and, if available, screenings and dust. A large number of man-hours were saved in quarry and rock crusher work and in runway construction using this construction method. On some runways, two layers of asphalt were placed instead of three; one coarse layer and one fine layer. The wheels of a heavy aircraft or propeller blast at take-off occasionally picked up this thin surface layer, but these small areas were easily repaired with patches. Runways with this type of base course and surface were used at Port Moresby, Dobodura, and Nadzab, and were in maximum operation under heaviest load and tropical rainFall conditions for more than 18 months without requiring excessive maintenance.

Pierced Steel Planking (PSP) landing mat was used on many runways in the SWPA, but it was necessary to have a well compacted subgrade and often a layer of surfacing material under the mat. PSP was used to construct satisfactory runways in areas where only sand-gravel surfacing material was found and could not be used alone because of lack of a binder. Landing mat was also placed on beach sand subgrades, under which were only two inches of coral or similar material. At Lingayen Airfield, on the shores of Lingayen Gulf, PSP was placed atop a compacted beach sand subgrade with only palm leaf thatch or woven bamboo mats between the landing mat and the subgrade. The palm leaf and bamboo prevented the non-cohesive sand from working its way up through the holes in the mat and kept down the dust. This surface functioned very effectively under continuous use by fighters and medium bombers for two months of the decisive operational period. At Gurney Drome, Milne Bay, runways needed to be quickly constructed to stave off impending Japanese landings and the mat was placed directly on a subgrade that had not been thoroughly consolidated and drained. The runways were used successfully, but after heavy rains,

Coral for airdrome construction became more common as the Allies advanced northwest. (AAF)

Pierced Steel Planking (PSP) landing mat was used on many runways in the SWPA. (AAF)

mud oozed through holes in the mat and several aircraft skidded on landing and were damaged. To remedy the situation, the PSP was removed and the base was treated with bitumen and the mat reinstalled.

Coral for airdrome construction became more common as the Allies advanced northwest along the coast of Netherlands New Guinea. When coral deposits could be easily quarried, it was an excellent concrete-like surfacing material. Coral was placed on the runway and rolled, sprinkled, scraped, then rolled through several cycles into a dense hard surface. However, at Cape Sansapor and on Morotai Island, the coral deposits were so hard that they could not be used and substitutes had to be found. At Tacloban Drome, on Leyte, a hydraulic pipeline dredge pumped sand from the adjacent bay in order to supplement the inadequate quantity of coral quarried ashore. Coral surfaces did have the disadvantage of being subject to damage by propeller blast. This was minimized by the application of bitumen and the placement of steel mat at each end of the runway, where damage was most likely to occur.

Runway surfaces normally resisted heavy use, but minor failures occurred due to the poor choice of surfacing materials and improper drainage, along with inadequate repair of bomb craters. At Port Moresby in 1942, when construction work was begun on the surrounding airfields, Japanese air raids caused bomb craters that were hurriedly filled by bulldozing the displaced ground back into the crater, then compacting it with sheepsfoot rollers. Craters refilled by this method settled under traffic, making it necessary to empty and square up each crater, to backfill it with rock, tamping and compacting as the backfilling process continued, then to resurface it.

While at Kiriwina Island, Engineer units in the field developed the "gradient" method of airfield construction for the precise final grading of a runway surface. By the use of a target attached to the blade of a grader, a surveyor using a transit was able to signal and guide the grader operator in obtaining a very smooth surface. This method expedited airfield construction and reduced future maintenance, especially after daily rains, when the runways dried out evenly because no water collected in low spots and ruts.

Taxiways and Dispersed Hardstands and Revetments.
Providing taxiways and dispersed hardstands at airfields in forward areas required much more construction work than the preparation of the runways. Normally, a separate dispersal point was provided for each aircraft on an airfield, but initial requirements were to be one heavy bomber, or two medium bombers, or three fighter aircraft for each dispersal point. It was necessary that all dispersals be connected to runways by a system of all

weather taxiways. In order to reduce construction time and effort, the width of taxiways to fighter and medium bomber dispersals was reduced from 50 feet to 40 feet, while the normal 50-foot width was used only where heavy bombers were to be dispersed.

Dispersal areas were located along the taxiways so that their centers were spaced a minimum of 300 feet apart. In addition, these centers were placed 110 feet from the center line of the taxiway for use by fighters and 120 feet for bombers. During early New Guinea operations, circular dispersals were constructed with a diameter of 60 feet for fighters, 80 feet for medium bombers, and 100 feet for heavy bombers. In early 1944, GHQ, SWPA, issued plans for standard dispersals. A Type 1 fighter or medium bomber dispersal had an increased diameter of 80 feet, while the diameter of Type 2 heavy bomber dispersals remained at 100 feet. The minimum distance between centers was increased to 450 feet.

Construction of taxiways and dispersed hardstands was similar to that of runways. The humus top layer, if present, was stripped off and a base of locally occurring material was used. Surfacing material usually consisted of a thin layer of crushed rock or gravel bound by asphalt emulsion (asphalt dispersed through water and chemically stabilized) or cutback (blend of asphalt cement with petroleum solvent), and was to be laid at the minimum required to eliminate dust and reduce maintenance. A revetment was any type of sheltering wall or bank either above or partially below ground to protect dispersed aircraft against bomb blasts and shrapnel.

Revetments were usually built of earth and timber, but occasionally of sandbags, coconut logs, and earth-filled oil drums. For the construction of earth revetments at Port Moresby's Jackson, Wards, and Kila Dromes, a team of one bulldozer and two, or even three carryall scrapers was the most efficient equipment arrangement. The bulldozer was used to widen the piles of earth dropped by the carryalls; otherwise, the fill rapidly became too narrow for carryall operation. A grader was employed later and the usual paving and drainage equipment was used to pave and drain the protected hardstands within the revetment. The standard earth fill revetment was semicircular and its size varied with the type of aircraft which it was to protect. For fighters, the fill was eight feet high and the inside bottom edge was 45 feet from the center point of the dispersed hardstand. For bombers, the earth fill was 14 feet high, while the distance from the center point of the hardstand to the inside bottom edge was 50 feet for medium bombers and 75 feet for heavy bombers. Earth revetments never received more than an intermediate priority rating on early airfield construction projects, and by July 1943 their construction was given a low priority because of the increase in Allied airfield defenses and the decrease in Japanese air attacks.

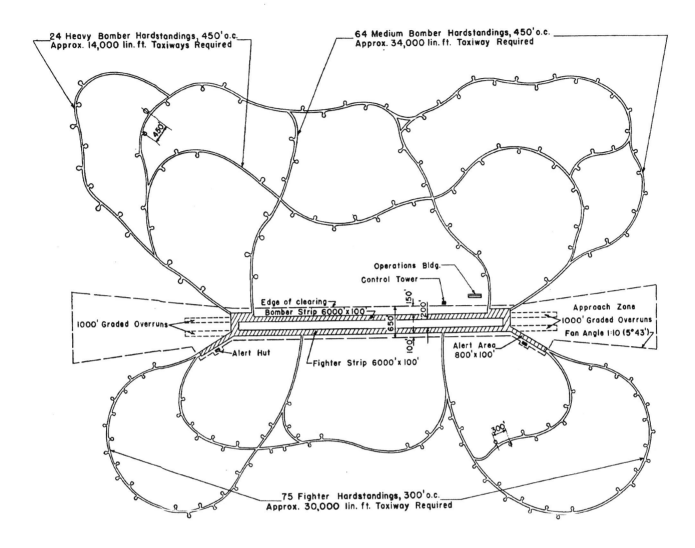

After October 1943, due to the large construction program and the improved overall situation in the air war, revetments were omitted as a calculated risk.

Soil Stabilization and Dust Control

Gravel and dust whipped up by the air stream from whirling propellers could damage aircraft and their engines, so to minimize this damage soil stabilization was contemplated in early SWPA construction. Soil stabilization also improved load bearing properties, reduced the water holding capacity, and increased plasticity of soil. After field testing various mixtures (including molasses!) and wire mesh mats for soil stabilization, a bituminous cutback with 20% to 30% diesel oil surface coat was found to be the most effective when spread at approximately 0.2 gallons per square yard. This mixture was spread on coral runways, which had a tendency to become dusty during dry weather. It was also used on the runway surface prior to laying PSP mat and then on top of or through the mat.

Maintenance

Wherever bituminous surfaces were used, frequent daily maintenance was necessary on heavily used areas, especially near the ends of the runways and at points on the taxiway where aircraft turned. These surface abrasions required immediate correction, because deeper wear required removal of the surface material and replacement with premixed bituminous patching

material. In order to make repairs efficiently, centrally located premixed asphalt plants were constructed. Preheated asphalt was mixed with coral aggregate at a rate of 18 gallons per cubic yard of coral. Before making the patch, the damaged portion of the surface was removed and the outline of the area to be patched was cut in straight lines parallel and perpendicular to the paved center line. Then the edges were trimmed vertically and before placing the hot mix, these edges were painted with asphalt to improve the bond between the old and new materials. The patching material was then evenly spread and leveled with fine dry coral sprinkled over the patched area. Immediately after sprinkling the coral, the surface patches were compacted to grade by a five- to eight-ton roller in a longitudinal direction, beginning at the outer edge of each patch and working toward the center, with each pass of the roller overlapping the previous one by one half the width of the roller.

Personnel Facilities

Housing

The dwelling specifications stipulated that General Officer dwelling space was not to exceed 400 square feet per Officer, Field Grade Officers not to exceed 80 square feet, Company Grade Officers 60 square feet, and 50 square feet per enlisted man. "All housing will be designed to provide the minimum necessary shelter essential to the health and well being of a command, and will ordinarily be provided initially by tents, except where quarters for General Officers are authorized." Huts or existing shelters where available could be used. Lumber was used for flooring and framing tents and other dwellings was only authorized if it were not authorized for higher priority uses. However, Operations Instructions did state that "care should be taken in the location of tents to eliminate the need for flooring."

Mess Hall and Kitchen Facilities
Combined Mess and Kitchen construction was on the basis of 12 square feet per man served. They were to be "Hut Type" buildings, "properly" fly proofed, have "thin" (not more than two inch thick) concrete floors, "proper" grease traps, and other sanitary facilities.

Latrines and Showers
Showers were authorized on the basis of one for every 20 men with necessary faucets, wash troughs, and connections to provide laundry and washing water. Latrines were to be properly fly proofed shelters and one hole was to be provided for every 14 men. Water borne sewage facilities were to be provided only with authorization. After sewage holes were filled they were to be covered and the latrine facilities moved to a new location.

Water Supply
Water supply systems without sewage removal were designed on the basis of 15 gallons per man per day and 30 gallons per hospital bed per day. Sufficient water storage was to be 50% of the average daily requirements. Water was to be piped to kitchens, hospitals, showers, and other "principal" installations.

Lighting
Electricity was to be used primarily to supply light and power to hospitals, essential shops, warehouses, offices, kitchens, messes, and other necessary operational facilities. Once these higher priority electrical requirements were met then lighting for base camps was authorized not to exceed one outlet with a 60 watt bulb per pyramidal tent.

Recreational Facilities
Recreational Facilities were "an important factor for the health and morale of the troops" and were to be provided at the "earliest practicable time" without interfering with the "prescribed" base development.

Headquarters and Administration buildings were housed in captured Japanese buildings or large native-built dwellings. (AAF)

The ubiquitous tent was the standard bivouac in the SWPA, often with wooden floors and a single 60 watt bulb. (AAF)

Showers were authorized for every 20 men. (AAF)

Recreational Facilities were "an important factor for the health and morale of the troops". (AAF)

3

Warning and Control Systems in the SWPA

AAF Fighter Communications, Warning, and Control

AAF Aircraft Radio Communication

The reliance on radio communication between the Allies and the Japanese was considerably different. The Allies used voice radio for local air traffic control at their air bases, en route navigation, and voice communications between aircraft. For this use, multi-channel VHF radios with eight push button, pre-selected channels and multiple frequencies that could be changed in flight were required. VHF waves were limited to use in short range, line-of-sight communications, but their reception was reliable and not impaired by the static of longer wavelengths. Because of their limited transmission range, VHF signals of the same frequency could be used by transmitters several hundred miles apart without interfering with one another. Until these radios became available in 1943, frequency changes were made with the hand-cranked frequency tuner for the transmitter and another for the receiver, making radio tuning a tiresome task while flying a single-seat aircraft.

On early hand held aircraft microphones, a microphone button that was left on or jammed during the flight caused an open circuit which only that pilot could use, but he would not realize anything was wrong and so no other pilot could use that circuit to communicate with the rest of the formation. The Type T-30 Throat Microphone was a vibration receptive carbon-type microphone that was a small round disk about three-quarters of an inch in diameter. A brown elastic strap with a snap at the end held the vibration receiving unit in place on one side of the larynx (Adam's Apple) and was activated by mechanical vibrations from the throat area during speech. By late 1943, the throat microphones were replaced by the much more comfortable face mask microphone.

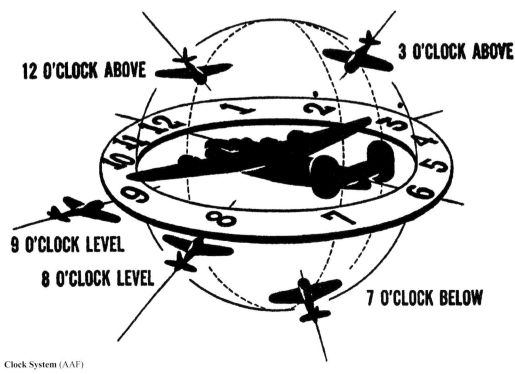

Clock System (AAF)

AAF Radar

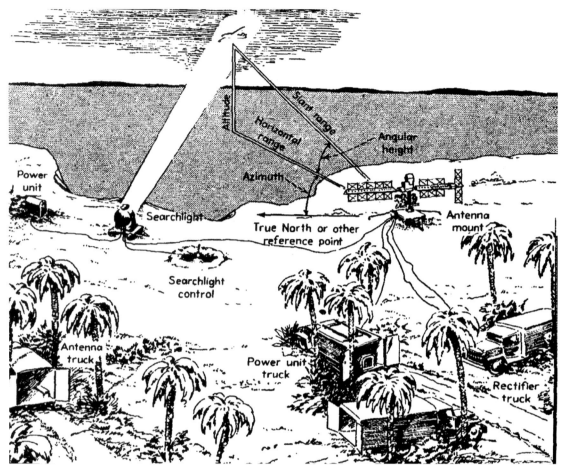

SCR-270/Searchlight Unit (AAF)

SCR-268 (AAF)

SCR-270 (AAF)

5-3-5 SCR-584 with Gun Battery (AAF

Radios installed in WWII fighters were essential in the Finger Four and the two-plane element system to permit coordinated maneuvers not only prior to but also during combat. While flying in a standard Finger Four formation, pilots were constantly searching every quadrant of the sky and once one of the four pilots spotted a bogey, it was essential that each pilot in the formation be able to simultaneously hear the call to determine the clock system position of the enemy.

An ingenious and effective method of radio terminology called the Clock System was developed to describe the three dimensional location of an aircraft. When flying in formation, an imaginary clock was used as a horizontal reference with the pilot in the center of the clock, 12 o'clock directly ahead, and 6 o'clock directly behind. For example, a target at nine o'clock was directly to the left while "low" and "high" simply meant that the aircraft was above or below the flight (a "bogey" was an unidentified aircraft while a "bandit" was a definitely identified enemy aircraft; but in practice in the Pacific these terms were often intermingled). A pilot's call of "bandits at twelve o'clock low" meant that enemy aircraft were directly ahead and below the flight and in an ideal position to be attacked. On the other hand, the call "Zeros at six o'clock high" meant that enemy fighters were above and to the rear of the flight and the flight was in grave danger and needed to react immediately. Because of the inherent danger, after a while "six" became the general description for the entire area behind an aircraft. Pilots regularly used their radios for defense and attack, but any defensive maneuver was best prompted by a radio call. If a pilot's Wingman called for him to "break right" he would immediately go into a sharp defensive right turn, no matter if he saw the attacker or not. If a pilot saw an attacker closing from the rear, he would radio his Wingman to "clear my six."

AAF Aircraft Warning and Control System

During the Battle of Britain, the great benefits of fighters controlled by large, permanent, ground based radar became evident. Led by British and then American research, the development of radar progressed rapidly, and by Pearl Harbor key USN warships, particularly carriers, were equipped with air search radar and as time passed America built large radar bases throughout the Pacific.

During the New Guinea Campaign, terrain and distance influenced the operation and organization of Allied aircraft warning and air defense. The rugged terrain of the northern coast of New Guinea blocked line of sight radar transmissions and the continuity of early warning from early warning radar sets located inside Allied defense perimeters. Adequate early warning often could only be established by ground troops capturing enemy territory miles beyond the air base perimeter and locating radar stations there, or by claiming sites from the jungle. These additional, newly-sited sets removed unprotected enemy aircraft approach areas that were located behind beam blocking terrain. The protection of the 5AF airdromes in the Markham Valley (Lae, Nadzab, and Gusap) are an example of these operations. At the time, the Japanese held the Huon Peninsula and the mountains there blocked Allied radar transmissions and allowed Japanese aircraft to approach along the north coast, then fly through the valleys that blocked radar detection and the Allies' first warning was the explosion of enemy bombs.

Radar was most beneficial when the Allies were on the defensive early in the war, as it allowed ground controllers to vector fighter units toward targets. The radar available was rudimentary by later standards, but gave defenders the range and bearing of the attackers, and by judging how soon the contacts appeared on the sets, an approximate idea of altitude. Fighter Squadrons could then be scrambled and directed to the target by ground controllers, allowing time for the early slow-climbing AAF fighters to reach the altitude of the high-flying Japanese bombers and their fighter escorts (if they were able).

At the time of American involvement in New Guinea and Guadalcanal, Allied units were equipped with Australian radar sets and the first portable U.S. sets, which were fragile and required skilled operators. The SCR-268 and SCR-270 sets—weighing about 3,000 pounds—and their operators and technicians could be air transported or landed by amphibious vessels and then situated by gouging sites out of the jungle. The placement of these sets often had to be a compromise and their full capability was not realized. Their range was about 150 miles and individually would have been much less valuable without the invaluable support of the celebrated Australian Coast Watchers, who manned 140 outposts by mid-war.

Initially, the Allied radar network at Moresby was of little value, as the Owen Stanley Mountains blocked long-range acquisition of approaching enemy formations. At the time, Australian P-40s needed some degree of advanced warning to reach the altitude of the attackers and even when able to arrive at combat altitude, the Japanese often were headed back over the mountains toward home. The slow climbing and altitude impaired American P-39s could never hope to reach the Japanese bombers, and for a while it was standard operating procedure for the Cobras to take off seaward to escape destruction by bombs while on the ground, giving them the soubriquet the "fishing fleet." However, once the Australian infantry chased the Japanese back over the Owen Stanleys and the Allies established bases at Dobodura the situation changed; radar sets stationed at Dobodura could cover approaches to Moresby as well as Japanese attacks on Allied forces attacking Buna.

Operation of the Allied radar screen involved the radar controller vectoring fighters to a target and keeping track of the friendly aircraft flying in and out of the area. So when Signal Corps radar reported a plot, it was placed on the plotting board, where trackers followed friendly aircraft and informed controllers about the incoming movement on their board. If any incoming movement could not be accounted for then the controller was to scramble fighters and vector them to the potential targets. Hypothetically, the controller also was to control AA, and once the incoming aircraft were identified as hostile he was to instruct the flak batteries to fire at will.

Until the introduction of modern FM radio equipment later in the war, the efficiency of aircraft warning from radar bases to control centers was decreased by the manually operated high frequency radio telegraph circuits that were utilized for warning purposes. In addition, equipment available for this intention was unsuited to installation and operation at remote and isolated locations in the tropical jungle due to moisture and excessive humidity and the bulk of the equipment itself. In addition to short-range radio sets, American fighters carried long-range sets that allowed them to communicate with controllers operating radar units on the ground.

The Royal Australian Air Force developed lightweight radar sets (LW/AW) which could be completely dismantled for air transport to relatively distant sites. America, which did not have a comparable radar set, adopted and procured these sets in quantity to reinforce their early heavy SCR-268 and SCR-270 warning screens by locating them in previously inaccessible terrain.

Japanese Aircraft Warning, Control, and Communications System

Japanese Aircraft Radio Communication

Although the Japanese were preeminent in postwar consumer electronics, Japanese airborne communications experienced a prewar gap in development due to a lack of funding and the shortage of engineers and resources. While all early WWII aircraft radios were deemed problematic, the early Japanese radios were considered several years behind Allied and Axis technology, being particularly poorly designed and constructed and very fragile, causing a very high failure rate. The standard fighter radio was the Type 96 Air Mark I Radio Telephone, which was small, uncomplicated, and lightweight.

However, its manufacture was of poor quality, particularly the vacuum tubes, which were of American design and manufactured under license in Japan but were unreliable due to below standard materials and poor factory quality control. The radio's installation was substandard and it was difficult to maintain in the field. In harsh frontline conditions, the radio's failure rate was high and with experienced radio repair technicians lacking and replacement parts regularly unavailable, many fighter pilots removed their useless radios. Early Japanese radios suffered from chronic static interference due to the distance from the base transmitter to the aircraft receiver, due to weather, and from unshielded spark plugs. Japanese Receiver/Transmitters had a single pre-tuned channel which relieved the Japanese pilot of having to tune the radio during flight. Japanese air combat philosophy stressed radio silence, so only one channel was needed for reduced voice radio traffic. The only legitimate need for a radio was to warn of an enemy attack, give orders to make an attack, and to report the sighting of the enemy. Often only the *Shotai* leader would have a single channel air-to-ground radio for communications with base, but aircraft-to-aircraft radios in a flight were often absent or inoperable, forcing Japanese pilots to rely on traditional visual signals. Also, with only one channel Allied jamming would render any control useless. Because Japanese airborne radios were so poor vectoring was difficult, so instead the Japanese had to rely on standing defensive patrols, hoping that they would be in the right place at the right time. The Japanese flew large unstructured fighter formations without any obvious mutual aircraft-to-aircraft support into combat, which then led to the uncoordinated "swarming" tactics described in many AAF combat reports and were probably the result of their poor aircraft-to-aircraft communications. The one advantage in flying in these formations was that it allowed all Japanese pilots to observe the entire sky, and once they sighted the American formation, using conventional hand and wing signals they could prepare for the defense or prepare for a swarming attack. In 1943, the Japanese still had veteran pilots, many from newly-arrived and rebuilt units at Rabaul, and this swarming attack strategy could be beneficial. The Japanese could take advantage of maneuverability of their fighters to try to break up AAF fighter formations that were usually flying bomber or transport escort. The Japanese pilots rushed in and out, using random maneuvers, hoping to lure the AAF fighters away and any that tried to follow could be swarmed by veteran pilots. Eventually, attrition took its toll on these Japanese veterans and the Americans would encounter Japanese replacements with ever decreasing training time and skill. The Japanese continued to fly in large uncoordinated formations using Zeros and Oscars that could remain on standing patrol for extensive periods. American fighters would dive through these patrolling fighters and scatter them using coordinated or two-plane element tactics. They would then pick off the stragglers, who often lost their wingmen, or catch them at low levels when they were forced to return to base to refuel. Due to their inadequate warning system many Japanese aircraft were also caught on the ground.

However, by late 1943, the Type 96 Fighter Radio was replaced by the Type 3 Air Mark 1 Radio Telephone, which had an output of 15 Watts and a range of 50 miles and was an improvement, with some contemporary electronic features and a design augmented by good to excellent construction. These radios still did not have an auto tune feature and were supplied with two to four crystals installed before the mission. The new Japanese throat microphone was considered to be superior to Allied types. In 1944, using these improved radios, many Japanese fighter units, particularly over the Philippines, attempted to change to the American Finger Four method of formation flying, which depended on radio transmissions. However, by this time it was too late, as the inexperienced, ill-trained Japanese pilots would scatter as soon as combat began. Units equipped with the older and slower Oscar also used this new formation, but some of their veteran pilots continued

Tachi-4 Receiver. (Author)

to use the original three aircraft formation which had been effective to break up Allied formations.

Japanese Aircraft Warning and Control System

While the Japanese communications network often performed adequately, it was comparatively crude. The Japanese did not use indigenous Coast Watchers, but established numerous observation posts in advantageous positions on the many islands in the Solomons and along the coasts of New Guinea and the Bismarcks. These outposts were placed as close as possible to Allied airfields (even within the enemy lines), usually on high terrain. Their equipment for observation was usually limited to binoculars and sometimes trumpet-type sound locators, although they were not very effective against high-speed, high-flying aircraft. Japanese ground-to-ground radios were very good, so a visual sighting could be quickly relayed to a base likely to come under attack. Because of the relative lack of targets in the South Pacific, it did not require too much speculation to determine which base or facility was going to come under Allied air attack.

Although Japan had joined Germany and Italy in a Tripartite Pact in 1936, there essentially was no exchange of technical radar information for about five years. In January 1941, IJN engineers visited Germany and were shown German radars and a captured British MRU (their earliest searchlight

JAAF 1.5m Tachi-2 AA/Searchlight Radar. (Author)

JAAF 4m Tachi-6 Antenna hidden in a tree. (Author)

control radar). German-educated Yoji Ito, leader of the Navy delegation, obtained detailed information and work was begun by the Navy on Japan's first true radar. From this point Japanese radar development was rapid, aided by the capture of British GL Mk-2 radar and a Searchlight Control (SLC) at Singapore and two U.S. Army radars (an SCR-268 and a SCR-270 at Corregidor). In a rare collaboration, the Japanese Army and Navy conducted reverse engineering on the Allied sets. But progress in development was slow due to a shortage of radar qualified engineers and the Japanese High Command's lack of appreciation of the value of radar and subsequent lack of support for the project. Once the radar was developed its use was limited to the larger important Japanese bases, particularly in Korea and Japan. But this radar was unreliable, as the manufacturing of the components was notoriously poor (especially the American-copied vacuum tubes). But even when it functioned properly, this radar had a range of about 90 miles, which was able to only detect large Allied attacks, particularly if they included heavy bombers flying at medium altitudes.

The major problem with the Japanese visual or radar warning system, even when it was successful, was its lack of adequate communications between ground control and the patrolling aircraft for directing the interception. However, it was against the devastating low level, "under the radar" attacks by Allied medium bombers and fighters that the large Japanese bases, such

as those at Wewak and Hollandia, were the most vulnerable. All too often the only warning a Japanese airfield received was from the airbase gun crews beginning to fire at the B-25s and P-38s swooping in for the attack.

PART 6:
The Air War in the SWPA:
Japanese Perspectives
and Turning Points

1

History and Perspective

The Origins of the Imperial Japanese Navy Air Force

After the *Meiji* Restoration in 1868, the Japanese military scrupulously followed Western military and technical developments. Japan's interest in aviation began in 1909, when a small delegation was sent to France and Germany for pilot training and to purchase a small number of aircraft. Two years later, these pilots and aircraft returned and began flights over Japan. In 1910, the Japanese acquired a primitive airplane similar to one designed and flown by the Frenchman Henri Farman and placed it into limited production at the Tokugawa Balloon Factory in 1911.

In 1912, the Imperial Navy sent delegations to America and France to acquire a few seaplanes for evaluation, and in Fall 1914, four Japanese seaplanes bombed the German concession at Tsingtao, China, and sank a German minelayer. Although this single air action comprised Japan's employment of military aviation during WWI, the Japanese paid close attention to the air war over Europe. During WWI, Japan acquired several Allied military aircraft for study, including French Nieuport fighters and Salmson 2A-2 bombers. During the 1920s, a British Royal Navy aviation delegation visited Japan and recommended that Japan establish the Imperial Japanese Navy Air Force and assisted in its organization and the training of some of its first officers. The Army had reorganized its air arm and in 1919, it was officially recognized as the Army Air Service. Seeing the rise of Army aviation, the Japanese Navy promptly developed its own air arm, which eventually became the largest component of the Imperial air arsenal.

During WWI, the Japanese had foreseen the potential of aerial attack on civilian targets and in the early 1920s, when the world's great naval powers negotiated a naval limitation treaty, the Japanese suggested the exclusion of or structural restrictions on the development of aircraft carriers but were refused. This treaty was to be short-lived, and in 1922, the IJN launched the Hosho, the world's first purpose-built aircraft carrier, while other navies had experimentally retrofitted various types of vessels with a flight deck. In 1921, the Navy met with a large British delegation that included several of their eminent naval aviation experts. Herbert Smith, one of the head designers at Sopwith during WWI, assisted in designing some of Japan's first modern naval aircraft. In 1927, the Naval Air Division was established and officially Japanese naval air power became part of the Japanese war machine.

The IJNAF was very traditional, and consequently, many of its operational procedures and tactics in WWII were those which they had adopted from the Royal Navy twenty years earlier. A representative example was its extensive use of float planes and flying boats during the war in a way that the Royal Navy had commonly used during WWI and the 1920s. At that time no water-based aircraft was able to exceed 100mph and only a few multi-engined, land-based aircraft could exceed 100mph. But this speed equality totally changed in the 1930s, and the British had found their float planes and flying boats became too slow to be of military worth. However, the Japanese continued to depend on a considerable number of float planes and flying boats during the war, including two float plane fighter types (the Kawanishi N1K1 Rex and the Nakajima A6M2 Rufe) that were comparable to a float Spitfire.

Although the first Japanese aircraft carrier appeared in the 1920s, at that time the JNAF, like the U.S. Navy, believed that the battleship was supreme and that the aircraft carrier could possibly be used as a reconnaissance or an attack element, but also like the USN, the IJN had difficulty integrating their carriers into their tactical format. Few naval tacticians in either country at that time forecast that navies in the future would be built around the aircraft carrier, with the battleships providing anti-aircraft cover and also mobile artillery against land targets during invasions of enemy held territory.

The Origins of the Imperial Japanese Army Air Force

After the 1918 Armistice, the Japanese Army's air arm was reorganized and transferred from the Transport Command in 1919 and designated as the Army Air Service. After the war, the French and British, burdened with large surpluses of aircraft, thousands of trained personnel, and a ruinous wartime debt, deployed delegations to Japan to sell aircraft and know how. To establish the Army's fighter arm, the Japanese purchased a number of the renowned French SPAD XIII pursuit aircraft, along with a license to manufacture selected training and reconnaissance aircraft. By 1925, the Japanese Army Air Corps, possessing an impressive 500 aircraft, was created and granted an equal standing to that of the older and more influential branches of the Army, such as infantry and artillery.

During the 1920s, Germany also sent an aviation delegation to Japan to organize and train the fledgling Imperial Japanese Army Air Force. Like the German Air Force in WWI, the IJAAF was directly connected to the Army and its operations and it developed those roles which would later be designated as interdiction and close support in the USAAC. By 1939, the Luftwaffe was beginning to develop a role independent of the needs of the German Army, but for all practical purposes, the JAAF never disengaged from the Army and so was always regarded as the secondary of Japan's two air forces.

Changes in the JNAF and JAAF in the 1930s
By the early 1930s, neither of the Japanese Air Forces had yet to establish a branch that was able to conduct long-range operations inside enemy airspace, nor did they have any clear plan for protecting air bases and air strips from aerial attack. Additionally, the JAAF and the JNAF had different, even incompatible, tactics and operating procedures.

Until the early 1930s, the JAAF and the JNAF were primarily equipped with obsolescent foreign aircraft models that were either imported or built in Japan under manufacturing licenses. Soon, Japanese aircraft designers began to produce aircraft that were better adapted to their own operational requirements and were equal to contemporary standards. Because of Japan's relative isolation across the vast Pacific and the general secretiveness of the Japanese government and society, this important transformation in the Japanese aviation industry was not realized in the West. Indeed, even by Pearl Harbor this was not fully recognized by the American aviation establishment, which assumed that Japan's air forces would consist of, at most, a few hundred aircraft, mainly imitations of older and obsolete European and American designs. In fact, the widely respected Jane's All the World's Aircraft for 1941 illustrated contemporary Japanese aircraft as consisting of a number of outdated older foreign designs and a few indigenous and also outdated designs.

Either for racist reasons or on the basis of supposed better numbers and equipment, American pilots (AAC or USN) assumed that the Japanese were not particularly good pilots and that they would prevail over the enemy in many one-sided air combats. This expectation was more or less reasonable in terms of the representation which they had been given of Japanese aviation. An early-war AAC intelligence report actually stated that Japanese pilots could easily be attacked from the side or behind because their "slanty" eyes gave them poor peripheral vision!

The China "Incident"
In 1937, Japan began a campaign to conquer China and captured and brutally decimated its (then) capital city of Nanking, the coastal provinces, and many of its larger inland river valleys. In the conflict, the JNAF was assigned new duties. From bases on Taiwan, its long range, land-based Type 96 Nell Bombers bombed Chinese targets while to support both Army and Navy operations in China, JNAF fighter aircraft were also assigned to land bases on the Chinese mainland. The Japanese Navy had gained precedence with the Japanese High Command and had the choice of China operations; it was supplied with the personnel and equipment necessary to perform them. Since it had long range bombers and the best fighters, the JNAF was assigned to bomb targets on land and to protect all Japanese air bases—both those of the Army and its own—from enemy attack. This daunting new extension of duties was handled without a problem by the JNAF until Pearl Harbor, when the war expanded greatly from its China confines.

During the China Campaign, Japanese pilots gained valuable combat experience, but against ill-trained Chinese pilots who were flying obsolete aircraft. The JNAF introduced the Zero, one of the war's great dogfighters, while the JAAF introduced the agile Oscar, both of which totally outclassed the Chinese. Unfortunately, the success encouraged the Japanese to place too great an emphasis on the individual pilot and his dogfighting skills flying light maneuverable fighter aircraft. Tactically, the Japanese did develop a significant modification to the standard V formation, as their three-plane section, the Shotai, was much more flexible than other types of the V. Instead of flying in rigid position behind their leader, the two Wingmen flew much farther behind. While the Flight Leader flew on a steady course, watching for an enemy to engage, his Wingmen weaved to

the right and left and up and down behind him, giving the formation a much better defense against surprise attack because the weaving fighters were able to check blind spots. The Zero's and Oscar's bubble canopies enhanced the viability of the V formation, as it gave the pilot excellent visibility, as it would on later model AAF P-47s and P-51s. When the Flight Leader engaged, instead of attacking and firing simultaneously, the Wingmen trailed the Leader, with each attacking in succession. When several Shotai followed in the same attack against a target the result could be overwhelming. However, once engaged, or if the Shotai came under attack, the Japanese pilots would fight individually. The method succeeded for several years and the Japanese failed to see its defects and importantly, would not develop disciplined techniques for deployment at the Squadron and Group levels.

The Imperial Japanese Air Forces in the Pacific War
In hindsight, it is obvious that the JNAF and its control of the air were essential to Japanese naval operations during the war. However, this factor was not wholly appreciated by either combatant until after Pearl Harbor and the "naval" battles of Coral Sea and Midway, both of which were determined by air power launched from aircraft carriers. Before these battles, many prominent Japanese and American naval officers believed that the battleship armed with multiple AA guns and its decks and waterline protected by steel armor would be invulnerable to attack by dive and torpedo bombers launched from aircraft carriers. Meanwhile, the aircraft carrier was a lightly protected, high-priority target and was especially vulnerable and required protection by cruisers, a destroyer screen, and perhaps a battleship, as well as air cover.

Japanese grand and aerial strategy and tactics for the war were based on a short war, lasting a year or less, when the Japanese expected America to acknowledge Japan's "right" to a sphere of influence in the Far East and sign an armistice, especially after their devastating losses at Pearl Harbor.

The Japanese Pacific War from Pearl Harbor to Midway
From Pearl Harbor and during the first six months of the war, Adm. Isoruku Yamamoto led the Japanese Fleet and the JNAF, providing his nation with a succession of spectacular victories that established Japanese authority in the Far East and Pacific. But, then, on 6-8 June 1942, the Japanese Navy lost over 300 pilots and four of its largest aircraft carriers at Midway; a catastrophe from which the JNAF and Japan itself never completely recovered. Furthermore, any possibility for Japan winning a short war also disappeared and Japan had formulated no plans for and did not have the resources to stay in a lengthy conflict. After the contemptible Japanese attack on Pearl Harbor, the Americans would never accept anything other than an unconditional surrender.

During 1942, the Japanese Navy concentrated on the production of existing aircraft and introduced just three new aircraft types: a flying boat, the Type 2 Emily; and two recon aircraft, the Nakajima J1N1 Irving and the Aichi D4Y1 carrier-based Judy. A number of new or experimental aircraft became operational as the war continued, but these new aircraft, at best, supplemented the older types, and most of the operational types with which the JNAF began the war in December 1941 remained as first line equipment when the war ended in August 1945. Meanwhile, the USAAF and the USN introduced new and much improved types to replace older ones.

1942: Japanese Air Operations in New Guinea

General
From early February 1942 until July 1944, the air forces of the United States, Australia, and Japan fought a war of attrition in New Guinea, the Solomon Islands, and the Bismarck Archipelago. The first stage of the

Japanese air campaign over New Guinea was the Navy's offensive against Port Moresby, from May until October 1942. During the next stage, lasting from early 1943 until June 1943, the Japanese Army assumed the air war over New Guinea, as the Navy's air forces were increasingly committed to the Solomons Campaign. The Japanese had intended that this stage be offensive, but it became increasingly defensive as Allied air power increased. The third stage was a short period in the Summer of 1943, in which the JAAF allocated a more active responsibility to its air forces in New Guinea, only to see the bulk of that force destroyed in a single air attack. Finally, the JAAF fought a low key defensive campaign for approximately a year, from the Summer of 1943 until their army was pushed out of New Guinea and the war moved to Philippines and the Marianas.

Occupation of Rabaul and the
Beginning of Air Operations against New Guinea
In 1941, when the Japanese planned for a war in the Pacific, the islands of the Bismarck Archipelago, particularly Rabaul on New Britain, were a primary objective. Australian-occupied Rabaul, with its excellent natural harbor, was seen as a potential threat to the large naval base the Japanese planned to develop on Truk Island in the Carolines, almost 700 miles to the north in the central Pacific Ocean. The Japanese plan was for the Japanese Army's South Seas Force to first seize Guam and then the airfields in the Bismarck Islands. The Navy's Special Landing Forces were to occupy Guam, after which they would cooperate with the Army in occupying Rabaul. While these operations were being conducted, the operations in the Philippines, Malaya, and the Netherlands East Indies were rapidly and unexpectedly successfully concluded and the Japanese Army and Navy were forced to quickly decide on their next offensive. The invasion of Australia was rejected because it would have required excessive resources, so the Navy High Command ordered the 4th Fleet and the 11th Air Fleet to attack Lae and Salamaua on New Guinea, Port Moresby on Papua, and the Solomon Islands.

Zero fighters of the Chitose Air Corps moved to Rabaul on 31 January 1942. On 2 and 5 February, Mavis flying boats of the Yokohama Air Corps bombed Port Moresby for the first time to begin the air war over New Guinea. On 9 February, Gasmata, on New Britain's southern coast, was occupied and work begun on an airstrip. To carry out further operations, the 4th Air Corps was created and headquartered in Rabaul with a nominal strength of 27 fighters and 27 bombers, and on 24 February, it began bombing Port Moresby.

On 7 March 1942, the Japanese High Command decided upon the second stage of their South Pacific operation, which focused on the continuation of major offensives. As part of this new strategy, the decision was made to continue the advance in the Solomons and New Guinea area with the intention of eventually interrupting the supply route between the United States and Australia. Lae and Salamaua, on the northeastern New Guinea coast, were occupied on 8 March. Two days later, the Tainan Air Corps sent eleven Zero fighters to Lae, which became an extremely busy advanced airbase.

Deployment of the JAAF
Meanwhile, JAAF units were withdrawn from the Far East and based at Rabaul and Lae. Until the end of July 1942, these JAAF units conducted intensive missions across the Owen Stanley Mountains to attack the Allied Port Moresby airfields and other bases on the New Guinea mainland. Meanwhile, Allied air attacks on Japanese air bases required the Japanese to import more aircraft to defend them. Although the Allies often lost more aircraft in individual air battles, their air strength did not diminish significantly. Conversely, the Japanese endured fewer losses, but showed a slow decline in the quality of their air forces, as highly trained and experienced pilots

were lost and replaced by increasingly less experienced pilots from other theaters, then by less well trained novice pilots. During this time, neither side was able to achieve air superiority and significantly, the Japanese failed to drive the Allied air forces out of New Guinea before they could be reinforced by a seemingly unending supply of new aircraft and well trained pilots.

Additional JAAF Deployment to and
JNAF Withdrawal from New Guinea Operations
The next stage in Japanese air operations over New Guinea involved the deployment of additional JAAF units withdrawn from other theaters to the New Guinea mainland. After the Americans landed on Guadalcanal on 7 August 1942, the JNAF based on Rabaul were forced to fly increasingly more missions to the Solomons while continuing their air campaign against New Guinea. So, as the Navy's commitment escalated over the Solomons, the JAAF would have a larger responsibility over New Guinea. On 11 November, Hattori Takushiro, of the Army General Staff, deployed the JAAF at Rabaul to New Guinea to regain air superiority, which would be a significant undertaking, with 25,000 American Army, Navy, and Marine first line aircraft projected to be operating in the South Pacific by the end of 1943.

Loss of Guadalcanal and the Fight to Save New Guinea
Faced with a looming defeat on Guadalcanal and with the withdrawal of their forces from Port Moresby along the Kokoda Track, the Japanese military finally decided to commit more of its air forces to the SWPA. On 18 November, the Japanese Army and Navy agreed on operations in the SWPA, committing the 6th Air Division of the JAAF to the New Guinea front. Sixty Oscar fighters of the 11th *Sentai* reached Rabaul via Truk on 18 December, and almost immediately became involved in air defense operations. By the end of the month, they were flying missions against targets on mainland New Guinea. On 29 December, JAAF heavy bomber units were ordered to deploy from Burma to New Guinea.

1943: Japanese Air Reversals in the SWPA
It was the Japanese air policy to deploy its most capable units to its outer defense perimeter, especially the Solomons, Rabaul, and then New Guinea, and then to feed first line replacements of aircraft and personnel into the desperate lost battles which first sapped the strength of the JNAF and then the JAAF. In November 1942, the JNAF was ordered to retire from the SWPA for refurbishing and refitting and the air responsibility for the theater passed to the beleaguered JAAF.

The Introduction of New American
Fighter Types and the Japanese Response
Even against first generation U.S. fighters such as the Navy's F4F Wildcat and the P-40, the Japanese suffered serious losses. As inferior as early U.S. aircraft were on paper, it was they who blunted the Japanese advance and were beginning to reverse America's fortunes prior to the arrival of the new and much improved aircraft coming off America's drawing boards and production lines. So by mid-1943, Japanese aircraft no longer dominated Pacific skies and after that time would fight defensively to protect their shrinking empire against these new enemy fighters.

The USMC had introduced the formidable F4U Corsair, and in August, USN carrier units began to operate the new F6F Hellcat. Meanwhile, later model AAF P-38s, while less maneuverable than the F4U or the F6F, used their superior speed and ceiling advantage to defeat the Japanese Air Forces in the last air battles over New Guinea and later over the Philippines. With superior aircraft, experienced pilots followed by a good supply of capable replacement pilots, and skilled mechanics with adequate tools and spare parts, the American units could enter combat against the JNAF or JAAF with a high degree of confidence.

In response to these new American fighters, Japanese aircraft designers, influenced by European and American fighter development, changed their design concept from acrobatic maneuverability to increased speed and rate of climb and diving ability. During 1943, the Japanese Navy introduced some newer, more capable aircraft types, including the J2M Jack and the B6N Jill. The Jack (Raiden) was designed mainly as a bomber interceptor, and on the infrequent occasions when it was flown by a competent, experienced pilot, it was considered a respectable opponent for most Allied fighters. The planned production of the Jack never reached projected rates, thus the Jack did not replace the outmoded Zero, whose total wartime production was to be somewhat over 10,000. The Jill (Tenzen) was a torpedo bomber that improved on the earlier, slower Kate, but it did not entirely replace the Kate, nor did a new dive bomber variant, the Judy, introduced in late 1943. The JNAF also attempted to modify their aircraft, but the results were considered negligible at best. For instance, the wingspan of the Model 52 Zero was reduced to give it increased rolling performance, but it remained basically the same Zero but no longer intimidated Allied fliers.

The JAAF was somewhat better off than the JNAF, as their combat losses, while high, were less, and at least their airfields had not been sunk along with the related loss of highly trained and experienced pilots. By 1942, the Ki-43 Oscar became the backbone of the JAAF with a performance comparable to the Zero. Like the Zero, as the war continued, it was progressively modified and up-gunned, but with the exception of its turning facility, it would never approach the performance of its enemies. The Ki-44 Tojo and the Ki-61 Tony entered JAAF service in late 1942. These new fighters were comparable to contemporary Allied fighters in performance (speed, climb, and dive) and had some pilot and fuel tank protection. Also, to utilize these new fighters to their best advantage, the Japanese adopted the standard American Finger Four fighter tactical scheme at the end of 1943. However, all these advantages were negated when flown by inexperienced pilots.

1943: New Guinea Air Operations

On 4 January 1943, the Japanese Army and Navy High Commands signed an Army-Navy Central Agreement that ordered operations on New Guinea to be continued to "secure a position of superiority." Lae, Salamaua, Wewak, and Madang on New Guinea were to be strengthened or occupied, and the area north of the Owen Stanleys was to be secured so that it could function as a base for operations aimed at Port Moresby. The JNAF continued to refit from its harrowing air battles over the Solomons and Japanese air operations over New Guinea were conducted principally by the Army.

By 25 March 1943, the importance of the New Guinea Front to Japan's war efforts was realized and a revised Army-Navy Central Agreement ordered a substantial commitment to the defense of Lae and Salamaua and the strengthening of bases along the northern New Guinea coast, while a delaying operation would be fought in the Northern Solomons. The assault on Port Moresby, while officially continuing as a long term objective, was for all practical purposes abandoned.

Reflecting this revised strategy, the Army decided to strengthen its Air Forces in the New Guinea area. The 68th and 78th Sentai of the 14th Air Brigade, flying the Tony fighter, arrived in Rabaul in late April and were deployed to New Guinea. The 13th Sentai, flying the Nick twin-engine fighter, and the 24th Sentai flying the venerable Oscar began arriving in Rabaul in late May.

The situation changed further when the Japanese discovered that the Allies were constructing airfields in the New Guinea highlands which threatened the Japanese airfields at Madang and Wewak. Ground operations

to neutralize these new threats were immediately planned. To provide further support, the 7th Air Division, which was formed in late January 1943, was deployed to Wewak on 19 June. While the actual deployment of these air units was delayed due to insufficient readiness of bases in New Guinea, JAAF air strength, at least on paper, was gradually reinforced during this period. The Army made another organizational change during this time when it created the 4th Air Army to implement overall command over the 6th and 7th Divisions. The new Air Army was formed in mid-June, and its Headquarters was deployed to Rabaul by 10 August. Eventually, about a quarter of the Army's Air Forces would be committed to the South Pacific. Most of these units were the most elite that the Army possessed and would be exposed to losses of approximately 50% per month, making this a major commitment. The main 7th Air Division units deployed from its Headquarters to Wewak, New Guinea, in July 1943, were the 59th Sentai (fighters) and the 5th, 7th, and 61st Sentai (all heavy bombers). With these new deployments, it seemed that the JAAF had evened the disparity between the Japanese and the Allied Air Forces. However, the Army finally had to face reality and agreed on a plan for New Guinea Area operations with the Operations Section of the Navy High Command that called for a holding strategy in New Guinea. While this meant that the capture of Port Moresby was finally and formally cancelled, the JAAF in New Guinea had the task of neutralizing the Allied air bases there. In addition, they had to defend their own air bases and provide escort for convoys attempting to supply the Japanese garrisons on New Guinea.

In June 1943, with the Japanese preparing for the New Georgia Campaign, the Fifth Air Force received its only lull in battle until early 1945. After mid-1943, both theaters were usually zealously contested. The most eventful period was the first two weeks of December 1943, when the 5AF was active over Cape Gloucester and Wewak with the 13AF in the Solomons attacking Rabaul.

From the invasion of Guadalcanal until the abandonment of Rabaul and nearby bases, the Japanese had to wage a fierce two-front war, causing Japanese Navy units to often move air units from one threatened sector to another until they became depleted by attrition, after which Japanese Army units ultimately faced the Fifth Air Force with little Navy support and suffered greatly. But for most of the period between Spring 1942 and until the final weeks of Winter 1943-1944, neither the Allies nor Japanese prevailed in the air. After the Japanese lost Guadalcanal, there were only two periods of two weeks between February 1943 and May 1943 when Allied kill claims were minimal. During these slack times weather kept aircraft grounded, no doubt to the great relief of pilots of both sides, and on other days small engagements took place in which each side took few or no losses. Gradually, the Allies gained air superiority, as their tenacious defensive responsibilities had exhausted much of the Japanese Army's air strength.

By early August 1943, due to widespread illness and the lack of replacement aircraft, the 4th Air Army had an operational strength of just one-third of its nominal strength. Nevertheless, the Japanese attempted to fulfill their plan to regain air superiority. On 12 August, the 4th Air Army began air raids on the Mt. Hagen area, Bena Bena, Wau, Salamaua, and elsewhere. This plan came to an abrupt halt on 17 August 1943, when Allied Air Forces surprised the Wewak area—home to the JAAF's principal air bases on New Guinea—and destroyed over 100 aircraft, reducing the 4th Air Army to a handful of operational aircraft. A major cause for this devastating air defeat was the lack of sufficient aircraft revetments and an adequate air warning system. The Japanese had continued to rely almost completely on a visual warning system that did not provide enough time for their aircraft on the ground to either be hidden or scrambled. The primitive condition of the Japanese airfields did not allow the quick scrambling of a large number of aircraft. A major tactical error was made when all of the 4th Air Army's aircraft were based at front line air bases around Wewak. Instead of placing all its strength on the front line, the 4ᵗʰ Air Army, along with the 6ᵗʰ and 7ᵗʰ Air Divisions, had wanted to deploy its units in more depth, with a number of aircraft more safely based at airfields further to the rear. However, both the Army High Command and the 8ᵗʰ Area Army had insisted that as many aircraft as possible be based at airfields at the front to make them more available to use in operations.

After the debacle at Wewak, the JAAF tried to reconstitute there while strengthening its airbase at Hollandia. Meanwhile, the Allied infantry pushed the Japanese back from their positions at Lae and Salamaua, and on 22 September, they landed near Finschhafen, on the northeastern coast of New Guinea, further reducing Japanese air strength. By late September, although they had two Air Divisions (the 6ᵗʰ and 7ᵗʰ) in the area on paper, they actually had only 60 or 70 operational aircraft.

Faced with these developments, the Japanese High Command was finally forced to make a major strategic change. On 15 September 1943, the concept of the Absolute National Defense Zone was adopted as policy, under which a delaying action would be continued in the South Pacific while a new line of defense was prepared along the Marianas-Carolines-Philippines arc. From these new positions, the Japanese planned to launch counteroffensives and if circumstances permitted, offensive operations in New Guinea would be resumed in mid-1944 or later.

On 30 September, the Japanese Army and Navy High Commands adopted new strategies based upon their new plan. The 6ᵗʰ Air Division, using its remaining few aircraft, continued its mostly defensive operations out of Wewak. When the Allies landed at Saidor on 2 January 1944, they sealed off the vital Dampier Strait sea lane between New Guinea and New Britain, which meant that Rabaul was isolated from New Guinea. In response, the 4ᵗʰ Air Army launched a maximum effort counterattack, but by this time, it had less than 100 operational aircraft and was only able to fly 160 total sorties, all on five separate missions. Not only did these air raids have a negligible effect on the Allied landing force, but mission losses depleted the 4ᵗʰ Air Army to less than 50 operational planes.

Toward the end of 1943, the AAF 5ᵗʰ and 13ᵗʰ Air Forces, joined by USN carriers, often attacked targets in the SWPA, usually Rabaul. As the war continued, the 13ᵗʰ and 5ᵗʰ Air Forces, with more men and aircraft, increased the tempo of their attacks. The 13AF continued its attacks on Rabaul and adjacent areas while the 5AF moved west towards the Philippines. The Japanese Air Forces bore the brunt of these battles, taking heavy losses which they were now unable to replace with newly trained pilots and aircraft or by pilots and aircraft they stripped from other areas in the Pacific.

1944 Withdrawal from New Guinea and Defense of the Philippines

New Guinea

At the end of January 1944, in order to improve its position, the Japanese Army High Command decided to move the 4ᵗʰ Air Army's Center of Operations further westward than Hollandia. The High Command also decided at this time to temporarily reinforce the 4ᵗʰ Air Army with 2ⁿᵈ Area Army fighter and bomber units. While they would remain under 2ⁿᵈ Area Army control, these units were to cooperate with the 8ᵗʰ Area Army.

The Japanese Navy had also launched unsuccessful attacks against the Allied Saidor invasion force from Rabaul and by mid-January, the plight of the Japanese Air Forces in New Guinea-Solomons area had become desperate, with only 100 planes operational across the entire region. The JNAF was finally forced from both New Guinea and the Solomons. On 17 February 1944, U.S. Navy carriers launched a massive raid on Truk, the key Japanese base in the central Pacific, destroying over 200 Japanese aircraft and causing heavy damage to shipping and installations. Since Truk

was now directly threatened, the Japanese Navy had to replace its air losses with the only air forces available, which were those at Rabaul. Three days after the attack, all remaining naval aircraft of the Japanese 2ⁿᵈ Air Flotilla at Rabaul were flown to Truk and the JNAF left the New Guinea-Solomons area permanently

On 25 March 1944, the 4ᵗʰ Air Army was transferred to the 2ⁿᵈ Area Army and its Headquarters arrived in Hollandia. As an airbase, however, Hollandia remained inadequately prepared, as facilities were not completed and radar and other warning and intelligence networks were only being readied. Hollandia was as vulnerable as Wewak had been, and by the end of March, the JAAF had amassed approximately 300 aircraft, but only about 150 were operational.

In a repeat of its earlier catastrophe at Wewak, the majority of Japanese aircraft at Hollandia were destroyed in a two-day attack on 30-31 March 1944, when over 150 planes were destroyed on the ground. On 22 April 1944, before the Japanese could recoup their losses, the Americans landed near Hollandia, forcing surviving 6ᵗʰ Air Division personnel and pilots to abandon their 100 remaining aircraft. They retreated west overland and arrived at Sarmi by early May, but the Division was never reconstituted and was disbanded in August 1944.

Only the 7ᵗʰ Air Division remained operational, primarily from bases in the East Indies, but this Air Division, too, was nearly annihilated; on 25 May 1944, its operational strength was only 87 aircraft. When the Americans landed on Biak Island two days later, the 7ᵗʰ Air Division attempted to support Japanese Infantry there, but since it had too few aircraft, it concentrated on convoy escort and air defense, which it effectively accomplished. By early July, the Japanese Biak garrison had been eradicated and the JAAF had fought its last action over New Guinea.

The Philippines

The Battle of the Philippine Sea and Its Aftermath

The Battle of the Philippine Sea of mid June 1944 was the next major naval engagement in the Pacific, occurring two years after the Battle of Midway. In June 1944, a large American task force approached the Marianas Islands to cover amphibious landings on Guam, Tinian, and Saipan, which were potential bases for B-29 missions against the Japanese Home Islands. The Japanese Navy had no option but to send six carriers with 473 aircraft into a one-sided battle the Americans called the "Marianas Turkey Shoot." The two-day battle was the largest pure carrier *vs* carrier battle in history and was to be the last. For the second time in two years, the JNAF incurred horrendous losses: three carriers and nearly 500 carrier and land based aircraft, including its few remaining veteran pilots and many pilots who had just seen their only aerial combat. The majority of the INJ aircrew were so poorly trained and American pilots and aircraft so superior that entire Japanese Air Groups were annihilated.

The immediate consequence of the Japanese defeat was the U.S. capture of the Marianas, breaking the Japanese inner line of defense. As a result of their huge losses of aircrew during the battle, the remnants of the Japanese carrier air groups were never again able to challenge the American fleet. During the Battle of Leyte Gulf four months later, the Japanese carrier force, which had once dominated the Pacific War, was relegated to being decoys, while the Imperial Navy's battleships and their associate cruisers and destroyers were assigned the primary attacking role. The loss at the Philippine Seas was so catastrophic that the Japanese Cabinet headed by Hideki Tojo, which was responsible for starting the war, was removed and the Japanese could now only wait for the devastating B-29 bombing attacks that would be staged from these new Marianas bases.

1944-45: Philippines Air Operations

The shattering air losses that the Japanese suffered in the Battle of the Philippine Sea in June 1944 marked the end to any serious Japanese air resistance over New Guinea. Pre-invasion USN air strikes on the Philippines, Formosa, and Okinawa further devastated Japanese air power and paved the way for the Philippines Invasion in October. On 11 October, Adm. Halsey's USN 3rd Fleet struck Luzon and moved on to attack Formosa from 12 through 15 October. The Formosa attacks disabled or destroyed nearly all of the 230 fighters that the JNAF had available there. Other pre-invasion air operations included the bombing of Hong Kong, Dutch East Indies, and Mindanao. Postwar analysis estimated that during the American invasion preparation operations in the Formosa-Ryukyu Islands-Luzon area, the Japanese losses were between 300 and 500 aircraft. The Japanese inaccurate intelligence reports had profound impact on Imperial Army strategy. Believing their first hand accounts that the American fleet had been severely weakened and would be unable to sustain the long supply routes to the Philippines, Japanese Army Command decided to confront the American invasion at Leyte, rather than Luzon, where they would have had a greater tactical advantage, so during the Philippines Invasion, instead of over 20 major USN warships sunk and hundreds of aircraft shot down as the Japanese expected, the Allies only suffered two damaged warships and 89 aircraft lost.

Battle of Leyte Gulf: 23-26 October 1944

Once the Americans landed at Leyte, the Japanese High Command decided to send the Imperial Fleet to interdict and destroy the USN invasion fleet. However, the naval battle was the third and foremost disaster the INJ would suffer during the war. In the fighting at Leyte Gulf, the Japanese lost four aircraft carriers, three battleships, eight cruisers, and twelve destroyers, as well as 10,000+ killed. Allied losses were dramatically less and included 1,500 killed, as well as one light aircraft carrier, two escort carriers, two destroyers, and a destroyer escort sunk. Crippled by their losses, the Battle of Leyte Gulf marked the last time the Imperial Japanese Navy would conduct large scale operations during the war.

The victory at the Battle of Leyte Gulf secured the beachheads of the U.S. Sixth Army on Leyte against attack from the sea and eventually opened the door for the liberation of the Philippines. However, much hard fighting would be required before the island was completely in Allied hands at the end of December 1944. The land battle for Leyte was fought in parallel with an air and sea campaign, in which the Japanese reinforced and resupplied their troops on Leyte, while the Allies attempted to interdict them and establish air-sea superiority for a series of amphibious landings in Ormoc Bay, engagements collectively referred to as the Battle of Ormoc Bay.

Battle of Ormoc Bay: 11 November to 21 December 1944

Even after their defeat in the decisive Leyte Gulf Battle, Japan still tried to run reinforcements and supplies down from Manila to Leyte aboard fast warships. The under-appreciated Battle of Ormoc Bay saw American air superiority over Ormoc Bay virtually prevent the Japanese landing of significant numbers of troops and tonnage of supplies. Without adequate air escort, six Japanese convoys and their destroyer escorts were decimated and auxiliary American landings on Leyte were interdicted only by light, ineffective Japanese air attacks.

Loss of Leyte: Consequences

American air superiority over Ormoc Bay ensured the American victory over Leyte, which was the stepping stone to the invasion and capture of the other Japanese-held Philippine Islands. After January 1945, the Japanese air response in the Philippines was negligible and the 5FC was allowed to roam the Philippine skies at will in a devastating ground support role that

would become a "back water" theater and the glory days of the Fifth Fighter Command were over.

At Leyte, the Imperial Japanese Navy suffered its greatest loss of ships and crew ever. For the remainder of the war, major IJN surface ships returned to their bases to languish, entirely or almost entirely inactive due to the shortage of fuel and were unable to impose themselves on the Okinawa landings (except for Operation Go-Ten and the Kamikaze mission of the super battleship Yamato in April 1945).

The loss of Leyte meant the inevitable loss of the Philippines, which in turn meant that Japan would be all but cut off from its occupied territories in Southeast Asia, which provided resources that were vital to Japan, particularly the oil needed for its ships and aircraft. Also, manufactured commodities located in Japan, such as refined oil and gasoline, supplies, equipment, and ammunition could not be shipped back to the battle fronts. Finally, the loss of Leyte opened the way for the invasion of Okinawa in 1945.

1945: The War Winds Down

During the last six months of the war, the remaining units of the JAAF stationed outside the Home Islands in the Philippines, Celebes, and Halmaheras were largely cut off and powerless, without any prospect for deliveries of aviation gasoline, spare parts, or ammunition. Even as the Japanese Empire lurched toward total collapse, the majority of operations and resources continued to be assigned to the JNAF, which was to assume the majority of the defense of Okinawa and the Home Islands.

During the Battle for Okinawa, the Japanese would expend large numbers of aircraft for their Kamikaze operations, during which the USN lost 34 ships (or as many as 47, depending on the source), had 368 damaged, and suffered 4,900 killed and 4,800 wounded. The Japanese lost over 2,800 aircraft, but nearly 14% percent of Kamikazes survived USMC and USN interceptors and concerted AA fire to score a hit on a ship and nearly 8.5% of all ships hit by Kamikazes sank.

A schedule of determined B-29 attacks on Japanese targets would not begin until January 1945, due to delayed base construction and some difficult flying weather, which finally gave the JNAF some respite. The initial B-29 attacks concentrated on airframe and aircraft engine plants on the Home Islands and were successful in destroying most of Japan's established aviation industry. To escape this heavy concentrated bombing, the Japanese attempted to disperse their war industries into widespread small neighborhood machine shops and factories, particularly those connected with military aircraft production. So beginning in mid-March, the B-29s began low altitude incendiary bombing at night to destroy Japanese neighborhoods that were largely constructed of wood. Once these nighttime attacks began, the totally inadequate Japanese night fighter force and AA/searchlight/radar defenses left Japanese cities vulnerable to total destruction. While these incendiary raids were a response to this industrial dispersal, in the postwar, antiwar revisionists argued that they were purely an unnecessary morale-breaking psychological campaign against the Japanese population. The resulting firestorms killed many thousands and burned out large portions of Japan's inflammable wooden cities, and after the first few months, there was a shortage of large, built up areas left for the Americans to bomb.

In anticipation of the Allied invasion of the Home Islands, during the Summer of 1945, the JAAF joined its meager force of 1,000 to 1,500 aircraft with the JNAF's 3,500 aircraft on Kyushu for the "final battle." The Japanese estimated that this number of aircraft, mostly used as Kamikazes, was sufficient to sink or damage 1,000 ships of an invading fleet. However, these aircraft were mostly grounded and kept in reserve along with stocks of aviation gasoline, where they remained until the atomic bombs ended the war, preventing an invasion that was certain to be fierce and bloody.

2

The Japanese Air Forces:
Reasons for their Defeat

The Japanese High Command's
Failure to Understand American Capacity

Japanese Grand Strategy, and thus its aerial strategy and tactics, were based on a short war, lasting a year or less, when the Japanese expected America to acknowledge Japan's "right" to a sphere of influence in the Far East and sign an armistice, especially after their devastating losses at Pearl Harbor. The Japanese Air Force's High Commands did not comprehend or refused to acknowledge that industrial and personnel superiority and logistics would determine the war's outcome. Soon they were overwhelmed by American aircraft industrial technology and productivity; by its augmented pilot and aircrew training programs; and by its developments in superior operational procedures and tactics. Although the Japanese aircrews and ground crews performed to the best of their ability, the balance of power turned against them in late 1943, and they had no hope of reversing this situation.

The Japanese High Command's
Failure to Understand Warfare in the SWPA

In their planning, the Japanese (and initially, the Allies) did not recognize what the war in the SWPA would entail, as the area was among the world's most unknown, primitive, and hostile. There were no tangible strategic objectives, cities, or resources to seize. The area's only value for the Japanese was in its geography as a possible portal to Australia and as an anchor on the defensive perimeter of its newly-won empire. It was not long before both sides realized that air power would determine the course of the war in that area and that the establishment of airfields would become the primary strategic objective of the planning and fighting. Each side soon found there was an additional enemy in the environment, with its forbidding terrain, torrential tropical weather, and debilitating jungle diseases.

Progressive Lack of Air Resources and Personnel

The IJN and its IJNAF had gained primacy with the Japanese High Command in the mid-1930s, and during the Campaign in China in the late 1930s, were given a greatly expanded role and the resources to assume that role. Once the Americans and their Allies were drawn into the war, the IJN and the IJNAF saw their responsibilities greatly increase, as their combat sphere moved from China to the SWPA and the Central Pacific. From the middle of the Pacific War, this increase of duties impacted the JNAF greatly, as the required personnel and equipment were just not available to perform them.

While the JAAF had fewer operational responsibilities, it was also provided fewer resources than the JNAF. Additionally, the JAAF had been assigned, without Navy support of any kind, to oppose the enemy air forces in China, Burma, and India, while the JNAF had responsibility for almost all of the remainder of the Pacific War, later including the defense of the Japanese Home Islands. However, this burden would take its toll on the JNAF over the Solomons and New Guinea, and the JAAF had many units withdrawn from the Far East to be thrown into the bloody New Guinea air battles. The efforts of both Japanese air services in the South Pacific were to no avail in the face of ever-diminishing resources.

Failure of JNAF-JAAF Cooperation and Standardization

Unlike Britain, France, and Germany, the Japanese did not establish an independent air force, but like America, their Army and Navy each developed their individual aviation divisions. Also, while the Japanese recognized that large scale terror bombing could undermine enemy morale, Japan's strategic situation discouraged the bomber faction in Japan. The Army controlled the Japanese military, and in the 1930s, also extended its control to the Japanese government. So began the constant rivalries and intrigues between the Japanese generals and admirals over their air wings and consequently, there was no centralized command for Japanese air operations. Both the Army and Navy maintained separate "Air Headquarters" in Tokyo, but their responsibilities were administrative, not operational. JNAF Air fleets were assigned to various theaters or aircraft carriers and placed under the command of base or fleet commanders. The Japanese Army Air Force had no counterpart of USAAF's General Hap Arnold, but the Japanese Navy Air Force and the U.S. Navy command structure were similar, with operational control delegated to the commanders of carrier task forces.

So in the South Pacific and SWPA campaigns, along with the lack of cooperation between Japanese air, land, and sea forces, the JAAF and the JNAF had different and even incompatible tactics, operating procedures, and equipment. Throughout the war, there were numerous examples of a lack of cooperation between the two Japanese Air Forces. Non-standardization of equipment was the major problem created by this non-cooperation. Examples were:
• The JAAF used a 24-volt electrical system from 1938, while the JNAF would not convert to it until April 1945, and then it equipped only two aircraft types.

- Aircraft machine guns and cannon ammunition of the same caliber could not be mutually used due to differences in gun barrel chamber dimensions. There are stories of JAAF units out of ammunition being unable to use the like caliber ammunition from the well-stocked dumps of nearby JNAF units. Also, design variations in gun mounts prevented the joint use of most guns, cannons, and rockets.
- The differences in range of Army and Navy aircraft disrupted coordinated operations. This factor was particularly evident when shorter range JAAF fighters were assigned cover for naval sea operations or for escort of JNAF bombers.
- There were major differences in radio equipment and thus poor communications between the aircraft of the two air forces. The differences in IFF equipment made accurate identification of JNAF and JAAF aircraft difficult and often impossible.

In 1943, the situation became so critical for Japanese manufacturers, facing a shortage of raw materials, that an Army-Navy Technical Committee was formed to present proposals for joint research, design, and production of aircraft, weapons, and equipment. But, aside from a few of the committee's proposals accepted in research, their other proposals met the persistent disagreement between the two air forces.

A request was made late in the war for a determined effort for complete Army-Navy cooperation, going so far as designing and using common aircraft. However, cooperation was hindered by the need for retooling factories, modifications of existing equipment and installations, and the retraining of personnel in its operation and maintenance. The large stocks of existing supplies and equipment would have had to be used and replaced with the substituted supplies and equipment, which would have burdened an already complicated supply system. If the two services integrated their aircraft and equipment, existing tactics would have had to be revised. However, the decades-long rivalry and friction between the two air forces would continue and hampered the development of promising jet and rocket-powered aircraft, so the Japanese war effort was chronically hindered, as the Japanese High Command never convened a high level meeting to resolve JAAF/JNAF differences and to make the most of the assets each service.

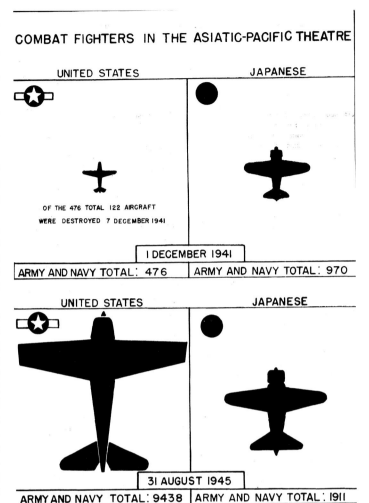

COMBAT FIGHTERS IN THE ASIATIC-PACIFIC THEATRE

UNITED STATES — JAPANESE

OF THE 476 TOTAL 122 AIRCRAFT WERE DESTROYED 7 DECEMBER 1941

I DECEMBER 1941

ARMY AND NAVY TOTAL: 476 | ARMY AND NAVY TOTAL: 970

UNITED STATES — JAPANESE

31 AUGUST 1945

ARMY AND NAVY TOTAL: 9438 | ARMY AND NAVY TOTAL: 1911

Failure of Command at Unit Level
Generally, Japanese flying units were commanded by a non-flying officer who would issue detailed orders to be carried out, without deviation, by the flying commander. If their attack plan was disrupted, the formations often became confused and were unable to go to a (non-existent) Plan B.

Failure of Japanese and Success of the Allied Intelligence Systems
The Japanese Air Forces lacked a dedicated intelligence system that extended from front line units to Headquarters. Pilots and crews were not debriefed to obtain an impartial account on aerial victories and losses and on the successes or failures of the mission. Thus, the Japanese had no accurate information on the effectiveness of their air attacks, tactics, and equipment. Only a few Japanese fighters were equipped with gun cameras to verify victory claims and to evaluate combat tactics. Headquarters depended on verbal reports, which led to exaggerated victory claims and to overconfidence in the success of Japanese air tactics. Of course, for political and public relations motives the Japanese and, to a lesser extent, the Allies (early in the war) issued exaggerated reports of success to their populations.

An example of a significant breakdown between Japanese Air Intelligence and Air Operations occurred during the critical weeks when the Allies depended almost completely on air supply flown over the Owen Stanleys to their Dobodura airfields. These supply flights had to be flown at regular times dictated by daily weather conditions, and the unarmed transport aircraft, even with fighter escort, would have been easy targets for determined Japanese fighter operations. But neither the JNAF nor JAAF made any serious effort to halt this vital flow of transport aircraft from Port Moresby, despite the knowledge of their existence, but apparently, not their importance.

A significant factor in Allied success was their ability to intercept and decipher Japanese radio traffic. The Japanese High Command was confident that no one could break their ironclad codes and that foreigners could not learn Japanese well enough to make use of any information that was collected. But the Allies were able to break enemy codes, both in the Pacific and in Europe, and once the deciphered messages were verified, enemy objectives and strengths became known and then judiciously and effectively attacked.

Failure of Japanese Industry to Maintain Aircraft Manufacturing Quantity and Quality
Japan emerged into the twentieth century with an impressive victory over Russia in 1905, and its small but successful role on the side of the Allied Western nations in WWI placed Japan among the world's military powers, but its victories were due to the use of Western equipment. The Japanese realized that to be a genuine world power, they would have to develop into an advanced industrial/military power like Britain or the United States. However, the Japanese also appreciated that their economic base when compared to the Western Powers was extremely deficient and was rooted in a long-established agrarian society. Consequently, the Japanese needed to first develop the important sectors of a new industrial economy as soon as possible, using Western technology, but while considering and making

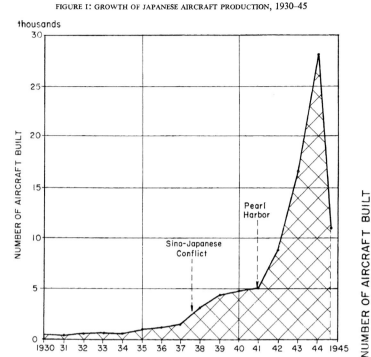

FIGURE I: GROWTH OF JAPANESE AIRCRAFT PRODUCTION, 1930–45

FIGURE II : JAPANESE AIRCRAFT PRODUCTION BY CLASS OF AIRCRAFT, 1941–45

TABLE I: JAPANESE AIRCRAFT PRODUCTION, 1930–45

Year	Number of Aircraft	Year	Number of Aircraft
1930	445	1938	3,201
1931	368	1939	4,467
1932	691	1940	4,768
1933	766	1941	5,088
1934	688	1942	8,861
1935	952	1943	16,693
1936	1,181	1944	28,180
1937	1,511	1945	11,066

use of what was available from their agrarian sector. Japan used exports to increase its foreign currency reserves in order to purchase Western technology and to send its best students abroad to study. Unlike most Asian countries, Japan used its purchase of foreign military technology to examine and then use as a basis for future development, rather than for immediate use. Thus, the Japanese were able to develop only key areas of an industrial economy, and in doing so were able to quickly embrace and even improve upon imported technology. But this came at the price of developing a seriously one-sided prewar industrial economy, as they used a large proportion of their gross national product in developing and supporting its military. Ultimately, Japan would find itself unable to continue a broadening base of outstanding manufacture and innovation, and both the quantity and quality of armaments deteriorated.

As in pre-WWII America, private industry developed aircraft in Japan, with three large companies controlling the industry. Seeing the potential of aviation during WWI, the mammoth industrial cartels Mitsubishi and Kawasaki established aviation divisions and were shortly joined by Nakajima, which was a dedicated aviation company. Even though Nakajima was smaller, its specialization in aircraft eventually made the company Japan's leading aircraft supplier. These three companies appropriated foreign technology and used their large work forces to perform the labor intensive work with wood and canvas to build their early aircraft. Development of aircraft engines proved to be a difficult problem for the Japanese and would continue to plague them until the end of the war. By the early 1930s, spurred by R.Adm. Isoroku Yamamoto, then the head of the Technical Division of

the Technical Aviation Department, Japan decided that it had progressed satisfactorily in its aviation development to become self sufficient in aircraft production. The first lot of Japanese-manufactured aircraft was mediocre, but by 1935, the Navy was developing world class warplanes. While the Army's aviation division trailed the Navy, it was flying Japanese-made aircraft upon the outbreak of war with China in 1937.

Failure of Japanese Air Research

Japanese air research encountered the same problems that were common to many areas of Japanese technology. The Japanese Army and Navy typically conducted research independently, with little if any coordination of their efforts, and even lacked an effective exchange of information of their respective developments. The Japanese military had something of an antipathy for university-based research. With a few noteworthy exceptions, the Japanese generally did not wholly exploit the capabilities of the Japanese academic research sector. While individual industrial companies did have good relations with the academic community, generally, the efforts of industry and academia were disorganized and isolated from each other and the military. So when the need to improve defensive protection became apparent, the response of Japan's research and production efforts was too late to have a decisive effect.

Failure of the Timely Development and Deployment of New Improved Fighters

The Japanese wrongly attributed the early success and low loss rates of their air forces to the invincibility of the Zero and Oscar fighters, rather than to their numerical superiority, well trained pilots, and the poor quality of its opponents' aircraft and pilots. The Japanese General Staff zealously adhered to the concept of aircraft maneuverability, despite the handicaps it imposed on armament and protective armor. This continued belief in light, maneuverable fighters led to irrational demands when modifying these operational types. The consequence was multiple problems resulting from these modifications. Japanese technical research was directed to modifying old models, and the planning and development for new fighter types was critically delayed until mid-1943, when Japanese fighters no longer had air superiority. After that time, Japanese fighters would need to fight defensively to protect their conquered territories. Influenced by European and American fighter development, Japanese designers were capable of designing second generation fighters that could equal American second generation fighters by changing their aircraft design philosophy from maneuverability to increased speed and rate of climb and diving ability. The cost of these new designs was an inherent increase in gross weight and drag that decreased agility and performance. To compensate for reduced performance, engine power needed to be increased. The Japanese attempted to modify their existing power plants, which caused an increase in field maintenance time and more importantly, an increase in production time. Finally, the Japanese decided to develop new improved engines, which then further delayed the arrival of new aircraft types.

In the end, the Japanese aircraft industry was unable to match the Americans in quantity or quality. Even when a basic fighter design was considered adequate, the product of mass production was often of poor quality. The Japanese were unable to manufacture the intricate aviation subsystems that required precise tolerances, so the reliability and performance of a new fighter design was degraded. Once aluminum became scarce, the use of substitute materials, especially wood, was mandated. Even though the Japanese woodworking industry was known for its craftsmanship, there was not enough special woodworking machinery available for mass production of aircraft parts. Second generation Tonys, Georges, and Franks were never produced in large numbers, as the venerable Zero and Oscar continued in mass production. Also, any advantages afforded by these improved fighters (e.g., Franks and Georges) were negated when flown by ill-trained and inexperienced pilots.

The Question of Japanese Aircraft Vulnerability and Protection

The issue of Japanese aircraft vulnerability as a primary reason for their defeat is more complicated than "we had armor and self-sealing fuel tanks and they didn't." The efficacy of defensive measures for aircraft increased with increases in aircraft performance, armament, and the efficiency of ammunition. During the war, the Japanese were slow to grasp the increasing need for defensive measures.

Air combat in 1939-1940 over Europe established the importance of aircraft fuel tank and armored crew and equipment protection. The American Air Forces, though not early leaders in the field, soon recognized these advantages. That the Japanese were slow to learn the lessons of the European war in 1939-1940 is quite understandable, since they had their own war in China to provide more immediate lessons that led them to different conclusions than those of the Allies. Thus, learning from its combat experience in China, the Japanese Air Forces took a different position on pilot/aircraft protection and their air forces were somewhat confused in recognizing whether aircrew/aircraft protective issues were a high priority concern for its combat aircraft.

When the Pacific War began, only a relatively small number of the latest

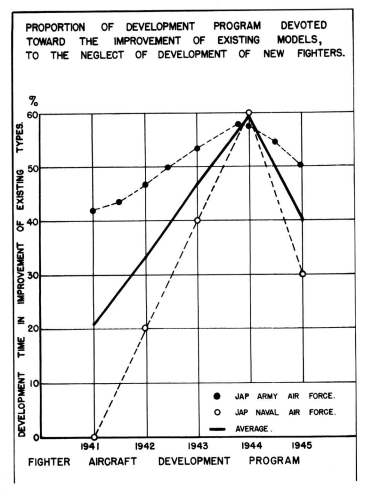

PROPORTION OF DEVELOPMENT PROGRAM DEVOTED TOWARD THE IMPROVEMENT OF EXISTING MODELS, TO THE NEGLECT OF DEVELOPMENT OF NEW FIGHTERS.

FIGHTER AIRCRAFT DEVELOPMENT PROGRAM

Allied aircraft were well equipped with crew/fuel tank protection, while a substantial proportion were equipped with little if any protection. Notwithstanding the Zero armed with cannon and the P-40 with six .50 caliber guns, neither side had the aircraft munitions available to penetrate aircraft structures and to cause critical damage.

While fuel tank and pilot protection had become virtually standard in many frontline Allied aircraft by late 1942, the Japanese combat experience of the first period of the Pacific War was a general pattern of success, but the few increasing aerial disasters perhaps should have been a warning against Japanese complacency regarding aircraft protection.

The JAAF was the first to begin to include armor and rudimentary fuel tank protection in a small fraction of its aircraft. The Army's fuel tank protection approaches were similar to those of the RAF's "first generation" tank protection, which afforded some protection from rifle caliber (.30) fire and small anti-aircraft shrapnel. At the same time, JNAF flew without any protective features, as it belatedly expanded its preliminary fuel tank protection research and considered armor plate for some of its aircraft. It is doubtful whether either the JAAF or JNAF was at a corresponding technological stage to be able to match the recent construction developments in protected fuel tanks then being installed in American, British, and German aircraft. The Japanese trailed in developing the synthetic materials that were optimal for use as the inner lining of self-sealing fuel tanks, and besides, they had not yet developed the manufacturing capabilities required to produce essential tank materials. So, unlike the combatants in the ETO, the Japanese had not developed any uniform policy concerning crew/aircraft protection, much less developed any standards for crew/aircraft protection.

Actually, at that time, the Japanese were at no great disadvantage due to their lack of aircraft protection; it was the Allies who were at a disadvantage. While not considered to be well armed, Japanese aircraft armament (both the JAAF Oscar's 12.7mm (.50 caliber) machine gun and the JNAF Zero's 20mm cannon) could inflict serious damage to most Allied aircraft of the time, which were no better protected than Japanese aircraft. Those Allied aircraft that were equipped with crew/aircraft protection often suffered reduced performance. The P-39 and P-40 had the horsepower advantage over the Oscar and Zero, which was significantly counteracted by the increased weighty structural integrity and protective features. During the early New Guinea Campaign, poor maintenance and rough handling of the few self-sealing tanks on hand reduced the number available for installation at this critical time when the Allies were at a numerical disadvantage. Also, the type of tank lining for use with high aromatic content gasoline used overseas was incorrect and caused initial problems until rectified. During the Battle of the Coral Sea, USN squadrons could have had more or worse less aircraft available, each with different results in this pivotal first carrier battle of WWII that was essentially considered a draw.

In early 1942, the quantity and quality of Japanese aircraft, along with aircrew experience and proficiency, was usually sufficient to overwhelm Allied air power. Based on initial combat experience, the JAAF's first generation of protective measures appeared to be "adequate." Ultimately, it would be of limited value and gradually lagged behind the increasing effectiveness of Allied armament, as it was designed to protect against rifle (.30) caliber fire of early Allied aircraft (the cannon on the P-39 was considered useless by its pilots). Throughout 1942, an increasing number of Allied aircraft were armed with .50 caliber machine guns (the P-38 mounted a 20mm cannon) and improved ammunition that could easily overcome the limited Japanese fire proofing measures and destroy the light-gauge aluminum stressed skin construction of Japanese aircraft.

The American requirement for a high degree of crew/aircraft protection proved to be somewhat of a handicap during the early war. The weight of armor added to U.S. fighter aircraft, such as the P-39 or USN F4F, reduced their climb rate, range, and other performance perimeters that these marginal first generation fighters would find they needed when in combat with Japanese Zeros or Oscars. Early model P-40s, with high altitude performance, were withheld from combat during the critical early days of the air war, when such fighters were in short supply to intercept high altitude Japanese bombers and their escorts.

From these early operations, the Japanese found that their aircraft were capable of defeating Allied fighters, but with a much higher loss rate than found earlier in China. The Japanese suffered several disastrous air combats that revealed a significant vulnerability of particular aircraft under specific tactical conditions. Nonetheless, the Japanese reaction was to continue the status quo, with the JAAF and JNAF upgrading the quality and augmenting the number of their aircraft, but separately and without any sense of urgency.

By mid-1942, the Japanese had captured a number of Allied aircraft equipped with various protective features and had also seen the vulnerability of their own aircraft, but they failed to see any potential threat. The Japanese saw that both protected and unprotected aircraft had their vulnerabilities and both could be and were shot down. It would not be until the Allies' progressive introduction of higher performance aircraft, such as the P-38 and P-47, with superior ammunition and heavier armament that the relative balance of air combat changed, but the change was to be incremental, rather than significant.

In combat, Japanese fighters, without any protection, were more than able to evenly compete against Allied fighters throughout 1942. Like the P-39 and P-40, the early Zero had only a single-stage supercharger, and yet it appreciably outperformed the American fighters at high altitudes and also had important advantages at low and medium altitude. The introduction of the P-38, while superior to the Japanese at high altitude, did not initially

give the Allies any decisive advantage. The introduction of relatively heavy fighters with huge engines up to 2,000hp was significant. The P-47 was more than twice as heavy as the Zero and the P-38 three times as heavy. The weight penalty of crew/aircraft protection, considering the reduced performance and altering of the center of gravity, was relatively less in these heavier fighters than it had been on the earlier, lighter P-39s and P-40s. These second generation American fighters gained in performance without sacrificing in protection and eventually, improved tactics and better training led to a growing parity and then advantage in relative pilot experience which gave the Americans a definite performance advantage that was to have a decisive consequence.

Throughout 1942, the vulnerability of Japanese bombers became increasingly evident over Guadalcanal and New Guinea. Low level torpedo attacks, in particular, met the heaviest opposition and suffered the greatest losses, but medium and high altitude attacks suffered steady attrition and exposed the vulnerability common to Japanese bombers, even when escorted and opposed primarily by fighters, rather than close range concentrated anti-aircraft fire. American fighters in steep diving attacks were under little threat from the defensive fire of Japanese bombers and could fire at will at the bombers, including their vulnerable engines and fuel tanks. JNAF bombers were forced to switch progressively from day to night operations.

Through the first three quarters of 1942 in the Pacific war, with a few exceptions, the lack of aircrew and fuel tank protection had negligible unfavorable effect on Japanese air operations. On the other hand, the extra weight of armor, self-sealing tanks, and other protective additions on AAF fighters made them less able to effectively combat the highly maneuverable Japanese fighters. However, these same protective features on American bombers made them more combative and survivable than Japanese bombers.

From late 1942, when there should have been an urgent effort to improve aircraft protection, Japanese efforts were uneven at best, as was the upgrading aircraft armament. The consequences of failing to provide defensive measures for aircraft were first apparent in the bomber force and as early as the beginning of 1943, had greatly reduced the flexibility of Japanese bomber employment. High fighter and bomber aircrew casualties beginning in 1942, caused in a significant degree due to inadequate protection, gradually undermined one of the strengths of Japanese air power, specifically the high operational efficiency of its aircrews.

Despite some improvements, by the beginning of 1943, the deficiencies of the Japanese Air Forces were becoming more apparent. JAAF aircraft were appreciably behind their Allied counterparts in both fire power and defensive measures, while the JNAF was totally negligent in equipping its fighters with defensive features and fell behind the Army in fire power. Once the intrinsic problems in inadequately protecting their crews and aircraft began to become obvious, the Japanese found themselves unable to quickly remedy this shortcoming. Implementation of effective defensive measures was slowed by the Japanese Air Force's lingering conviction that defensive measures were ineffective, the inherent fatalism in mass and individual military psychology, the technological and manufacturing limitations of Japanese military industry, deficiencies in industrial and military research, and the general lack of understanding of the problem at High Command levels.

By mid-1943, several factors made defensive measures increasingly necessary for Japanese aircraft. The Allied Air Forces were increasing in strength weekly, clearly outnumbering and bringing the combat to the Japanese, who were thus forced into a defensive position. When fighting defensively, aircrew and aircraft protection became even more imperative. The new American high performance, high altitude fighters were more liable to catch Japanese aircraft by surprise and no amount of maneuverability would help the unaware Japanese pilot take effective evasive action when fired upon by surprise. Japanese losses began to take their toll, and when veteran pilots were lost, the general proficiency of Japanese pilots began to decline. These less skilled pilots were less able to evade enemy fire and would profit more from defensive features.

By the middle of 1943, the Japanese Army had developed an improved fuel tank for its fighter aircraft, but they failed to equip many production aircraft with these new tanks; when tanks had to be replaced sometimes unprotected metal tanks were installed. Older aircraft were apparently seldom retrofitted with the improved tanks. JAAF fighters also received improved armor, while their bombers were incrementally equipped with improved protection and defensive armament, but nonetheless, both lagged behind American standards.

By the end of 1943, while the JAAF had appreciably improved both fire power and protection in many of its combat aircraft, the JNAF's situation was virtually unchanged in broaching the aircraft vulnerability problem. It is incomprehensible that the Zero did not receive basic protection, such as a carbon dioxide fire suppression system and an armored windshield, until a year later than when these items were available. The relatively easy matter of installing pilot armor in the Zero was also delayed. To offset the added weight of this armor, an obvious trade off would have been to reduce the fuel load, as from mid-1943, the Zero seldom flew the long range missions that had typified its earlier combat. But by and large, by this time the Japanese had lost the air war and any defensive changes in their aircraft would make no difference in the outcome. It has been documented that many Japanese pilots chose aircraft without armor or had it removed to give their aircraft increased performance.

Many factors contributed to the eventual outcome of the Pacific air war. The Japanese trailed the Allies in providing aircraft protection until the end of the war, partly due to their lingering failure to dispose of any positive or negative notions of combat learned in China and partly due to an inadequate research and production system. Japanese aircraft were relatively more vulnerable than Allied aircraft throughout the Pacific air war, and this vulnerability was not always obvious, nor was it always a particular handicap, especially during the early days of the war, when Japanese aircraft performance and pilot skill were usually more than enough to offset any advantage superior aircraft protection gave the Allies.

Despite numerical superiority and improvements in aircraft, the introduction of better tactics and increased pilot training and skill, the Allies had yet to decisively defeat the Japanese in the air in 1943. The high losses among Japanese aircrew during that year, however, led to a collapse in Japanese air power in 1944, despite greatly increased aircraft production and numbers of pilots being trained. The vulnerability of Japanese aircraft ultimately led to disastrous aircrew losses, which was a major factor in tipping the balance of the air war against the Japanese.

The Failure of Engine
and Turbo-Supercharger Development and Production

Poorly performing, underpowered aircraft engines were always the Achilles Heel of the Japanese aircraft industry. Inadequate engine designs were made even more unsatisfactory when put into poor quality Japanese mass production. It was not until 1940 that the Japanese began research on high altitude turbo-superchargers, but development always lagged behind increased performance demands. The effectiveness of a turbo-supercharger was handicapped when installed in poorly performing engines, while the use of low octane fuels further decreased engine performance. Even when copying captured Allied models, the Japanese never developed a quality turbo-supercharger during the war and Japanese fighters were unable to cope with high-flying B-29 bombers and their Mustang escorts.

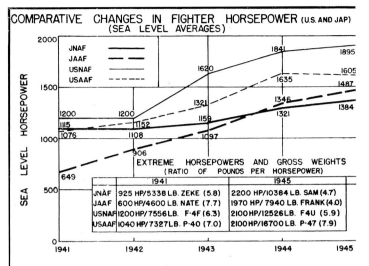

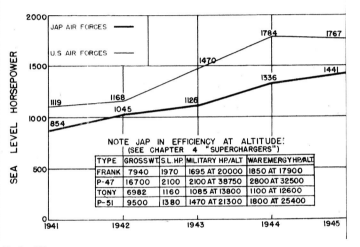

Engine HP

Failure of the Japanese Bomber Force

The earlier successes in China and the aerial triumphs during the early months of 1942 led the Japanese to continue to believe that their bomber aircraft and tactics, the organization of their bomber units, and their logistical support would be sufficient to remain victorious. In these previous victories, air attacks had been followed by rapid and easy advances by Japanese naval and army forces against poorly equipped, inexperienced enemies.

Japanese bombers that had been good enough for the campaigns in China and Southeast Asia were not good enough for operations against the Allies in the South Pacific. The bombers had serious defensive weaknesses, mainly in defensive firepower and ability to withstand battle damage. Offensively, the greatest fault in their design was their small bomb load and the number of crew required to carry such a small load. Allied fighters, such as the P-47, were able to carry as much or more bomb weight than some Japanese bombers. What the Japanese needed was a true heavy bomber, such as the B-24, which was able to fight in formation through strong defenses and deliver a heavy bomb load. Nor did the Japanese develop a medium bomber such as the B-25, which could deliver devastating low level strafing and bombing attacks on enemy airfields that were so effective in the SWPA.

Tactically, the Japanese Air Forces rarely returned to bomb a target more than once or twice, and thus failed to achieve long term destruction, especially of Allied airfields and parked aircraft. The Allies later relentlessly bombed and strafed the Japanese airfields at Rabaul, Wewak, and Hollandia to utter obliteration. The Japanese also developed the habit of sending a reconnaissance flight over a target, which alerted the Allies that an attack would follow in one or two days and to have defending fighters ready.

The development of four-engine heavy bombers was basically abandoned in December 1941 with the failure of the Liz heavy bomber. The exigencies of the Pacific War then required the production of fighter and medium bombers. The Japanese later attempted to develop the Rita four-engine bomber, but found that it was beyond the scope of production facilities.

Failure of the Timely Development and Deployment of New Improved Reconnaissance Aircraft

The lack of suitable fast, high-flying, long range recon aircraft was first felt by the JNAF over the Solomons. The only suitable recon aircraft was the JAAF Dinah, which was then employed to gather information, but the dependant Navy maintained that the JAAF aircrew navigation training was inferior and that inaccurate fixes of Allied Task Forces at vital times caused uncertainty, resulting in a slow or wrong reaction for a JNAF attack. Once the war turned from offensive to defensive for the Japanese, the need for a very long reconnaissance aircraft became less important to cover their shrinking empire.

Failure of the Logistics and Maintenance Organizations

Geographically, the Japanese theoretically should have had superior logistics, as the South Pacific was much closer to their major bases at Rabaul, Truk, the Philippines, and Formosa than Australia and New Guinea were to California for the Americans. Japan lost much of this advantage, however, by the overextension of its war effort, with active fronts in the South Pacific and in the China and Burma Theaters. They also had to consider the possibility that the Americans would soon move toward the Central Pacific and that Russia would eventually overcome Germany and have the reserves to strike toward Japan through Manchuria and Korea. Consequently, after their initial deployment of ground and air units to the South Pacific, the Japanese were hard pressed to supply and keep these units up to strength. The Japanese Navy generally flew fighters and bombers in from Truk to the SWPA, although at times old carriers were utilized to ferry Zeros some of the distance. The JAAF reinforced New Guinea via Southeast Asia, Formosa, and the East Indies. JNAF ferrying losses into Rabaul due to accidents were estimated at 3-5%, as the airfields there were very good. However, the situation for the JAAF in New Guinea, where airfields were of much lower quality, was much different and the accident rate was much higher.

Of the aircraft sent to the South Pacific from Japan, ferrying losses were estimated throughout the war to approximate 50%. (Losses were considered to be an airplane that did not arrive at the front when intended, not one destroyed.) The highest losses occurred between Kyushu (Japan) and Formosa, and of those damaged only half could be repaired. Though the distance from Japan to Formosa was relatively short, the losses on this route were high because of engine failure, as the run-in time for engines and flying tests was steadily reduced beginning from the early war. The lack of high grade fuel also contributed to the high loss rate. On the remainder of the ferry route to the South Pacific weather played a large part in the losses, especially the ferried planes, which where guided by a navigation aircraft, and if anything happened to it, the followers were in definite peril, especially JAAF pilots, who were chronically deficient in over water navigation ability.

The early war rates of mechanical failure were low, but later, as manufacturing quality control decreased the risks increased. After Spring 1942, ferry pilots were not the best pilots available, as the best ferry pilots were transferred to combat units as bomber or fighter pilots. There was also a decline in maintenance, as the best maintenance men had been sent to forward areas and were generally abandoned there, as they could not be

Maintenance personnel had been sent to forward areas and were generally abandoned there, as they could not be evacuated by sea or air due to Allied air superiority. (Author)

evacuated by sea or air due to Allied air superiority. Thus, any aircraft delayed in route to the front because of the poor status of the Japanese maintenance organization many times would not reach the front at all.

Poor Quality of Airbases

The Japanese Air Forces in the Pacific were not effectively supported with a logistical organization capable of building and maintaining air bases in the tropics and repairing them after attack. Except for the airfields surrounding Rabaul, the other Japanese air bases in the SWPA generally had very rudimentary grass, gravel, or coral runways, poor AA and early warning defenses, poor dispersal and constructed aircraft protection, and poor personnel accommodations, medical facilities, and food. Many of the JNAF's aircraft carriers, the vaunted "floating airfields," were sunk at Midway, and after the loss of Guadalcanal, IJN carriers did not approach the SWPA again. Meanwhile, the Allies built a network of large and small bases that were well supplied and well protected by AA fire and fighter cover. Japanese bombers were incapable of destroying these Allied bases, while 5AF bomber and fighter bomber units destroyed most Japanese bases and forced the Japanese Air Forces to continually retreat out of AAF bomber range (for the time being, until the Allied advance placed their bombers in range to attack these bases).

Japanese airbases in the SWPA generally had very rudimentary grass, gravel, or coral runways that required extensive rehabilitation after their capture by Allied forces. (AAF)

The Allies' Increased Weather Forecasting Proficiency

The Japanese took advantage of bad weather in the mid-Pacific to screen their approach to Pearl Harbor in December 1941. The Japanese developed an efficient weather service with widely dispersed reporting stations augmented by submarine reports from inside Allied territory. In the early war, the weather favored the Japanese, as the thrust of their advance was south and they were in possession of the area of forming weather. They used local weather fronts that rapidly formed in their territory for planning daily local operations and the larger more well defined approaching weather conditions to cover longer term operations, particularly those by sea, such as convoy cover. However, in January 1943, a weather forecast miscalculation was disastrous when the storm under whose cover their convoy sought to reinforce Lae, New Guinea, dispersed and the Fifth Air Force destroyed the convoy during the Battle of the Bismarck Sea. As the Allies went on the offensive, the Japanese requirement for long range forecasts decreased, since most Japanese air operations became local in defense of their airfields.

The swift and sweeping southward thrust of Japanese forces after Pearl Harbor closed a vast area of major weather significance in the Pacific Ocean to all Allied reporting. Until mid-1943, the operations of the AAF weather services in the Pacific were conducted relatively conventionally. The 15th Weather Squadron served both the 5th Air Force and MacArthur's forces in the SWPA. Initially, the Squadron was limited to weather reports from a few outlying reporting stations and from enemy territory via aerial weather reconnaissance reports, along with sporadic reports from Guerilla stations in the Philippines. Some help was received from interceptions of Japanese reports from Truk and Rabaul, and later, when Allied Intelligence became better developed from direct intercepts from Japan. However, until that

difficulty was solved, initial Allied communications problems frequently caused lost or delayed weather data. Despite close cooperation with the Navy and Marines in the operation of shared weather centrals, AAF units primarily provided weather data for the needs of their own forces.

As the Allies advanced from New Guinea in the Southern Hemisphere towards the Equator, new weather forecasting requirements developed. The need for long range forecasting increased, as did the understanding of tropical and sub-tropical Pacific weather to aid operational planning. Especially important to forecasting was the arrival of additional mobile weather detachments with better trained weather personnel that were based over the area. Increased weather reconnaissance flights were regularly flown over large areas of Japanese controlled territory. Finally, accurate weather forecasting became both an art and a science that could be relied on. The number of weather aborted air missions decreased constantly as the Allied advance progressed. During the Leyte Campaign, the number of aborted missions decreased to only 7%. After mid-1944, there were no more Black Sunday weather disasters (see Part 3/Chapter 3).

Diminishing Quality of Japanese Pilots

Tactical and Technical Trends: No. 15 of 31 December 1942, issued by the Military Intelligence Service of the War Department, stated the following about the quality of the Japanese pilot after one year in the Pacific War:

"The first line Japanese pilot is well trained and resourceful, and handles his plane in a skillful manner; he will initiate attack, is aggressive in combat, and is a fighting airman not to be underestimated. It is also noteworthy that they will change their methods with alacrity whenever they find their aerial operations successfully countered. They are alert, and quick to take advantage

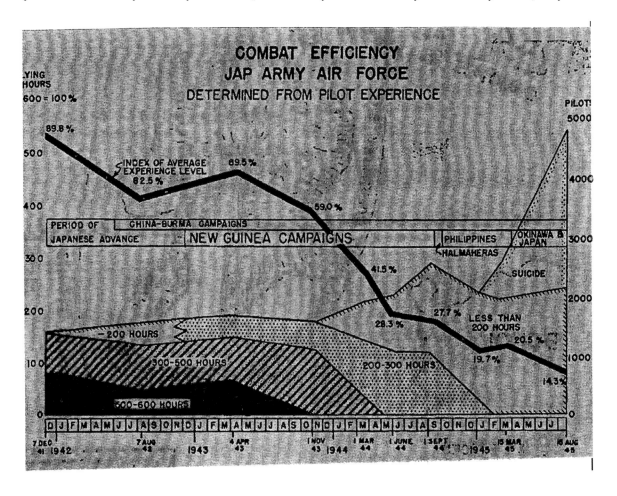

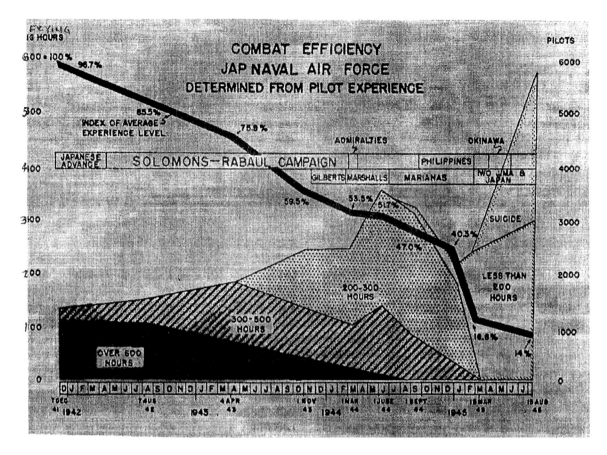

of any evident weakness. A disabled plane will receive more fire than other planes in formation. Stragglers are sure to be concentrated on, and a gun not firing is a sure point of attack…..

"In Japan it has been the tradition that Naval officers are of a higher type than those of the Army, and it has been observed that in planes of corresponding type, the naval pilot is much harder to combat, and that apparently the materiel, quality of personnel, and training in the Naval Service are of a higher standard than in the Japanese Army Air Forces. However, morale is undoubtedly high in both services."

However, this bulletin noted that the Japanese had divided their pilots into "Division I and Division II," with Division I pilots being veterans of China with four years of experience, while Division II pilots were newly trained and much less experienced. The dwindling number of Division I pilots were assigned to lead the more numerous Division II pilots into combat to conserve the number of experienced pilots and to give Division II pilots leadership and a better chance to survive.

A little more than a year later, in 1944, ace Gerald Johnson commented on the diminishing quality of Japanese pilots:

"The Jap fighter planes have all been very maneuverable and when flown by an experienced pilot become a most difficult target to destroy. Fortunately, however, the majority of Japanese pilots encountered are not of this caliber. They are excellent stick and rudder men, but their weakness is that all their maneuvers are evenly coordinated. They make use of sharp turns and aerobatic maneuvers, seldom using skids, slips, or violent uncoordinated maneuvers in their evasive tactics. Another characteristic of the younger pilots is their definite lack of alertness. In many recent instances we have engaged enemy fighters and they have made no effort to evade our initial attack, evidently because they didn't see us. Pilots have reported that in addition to being surprised, many of the Jap pilots are either frightened or bewildered once their formation has been split up, and they make little or no effort to evade attack. I have destroyed several fighters recently when they have tried to dive away or make shallow climbing turns. Any of these could have taken a shot at me if he had utilized his superior maneuverability and climb."

As discussed in detail earlier, while much of the decline in Japanese pilot quality could be attributed to reduced training standards, some was the direct result of debilitating diseases, especially Malaria and Dysentery, along with physical and mental exhaustion due to poor diet, lack of rest, and the stress of unremitting combat.

Japanese leaders and culture assumed that every soldier would do his duty and death would be an honor, so there was no policy of relieving units or individual pilots. In contrast to AAF practice, the JAAF did not typically rotate land based air units; instead, they attempted to maintain strength by constant reinforcement from other areas. Meanwhile, the JNAF often had to reinforce threatened areas with carrier based units that were initially manned by elite pilots. Exhausted units were reinforced with newly-trained pilots, while decimated units had their remnants sent to Japan for building new units or supplying under-strength units. This system continually diminished pilot numbers and steadily weakened the Japanese position. Without a rotation policy, the number of experienced Japanese pilots KIA or lost through illness increased and newly-trained replacement pilots, instead of being eased into combat, were forced into difficult and often fatal missions, flying outmoded aircraft increasingly in poor repair. The result was a serious decline in pilot quality, which became much more severe as the Allies deployed superior aircraft flown by well trained replacement pilots. Even though Japanese factories produced more and somewhat improved aircraft as the war progressed, the numbers needed to slow the Allied advance through the Pacific did not arrive at the front.

Japanese/American Mutual Hatred

Japanese

With the rise of militarism in Japan in the 1930s and the Emperor's unwillingness to lead his subjects away from armed conflict, war was presented "as purifying" and death "as a duty, a spiritual shield to let soldiers fight to the end." In issues involving Asia, Japan believed it had a sovereign right to rule, to become the "Light of Greater East Asia" and ultimately the "Light of the World." The Japanese Army believed it was descended from the gods, "the divine blade; an embodiment of the Emperor's will" and was "destined to take dominion over the lesser peoples of the world." Just as the Nazis considered the Jews, Russians, and Gypsies as *Untermenschen*, the Japanese considered the Chinese and Koreans inferior. While the Allies portrayed the Japanese as inferior, yellow-skinned, buck-toothed Orientals, the Japanese soldier was led to believe the Allies were "Colonials akin to a mystical fiend against whom their Divine Emperor had declared a holy war." While the Japanese signed the 1929 Geneva Convention that protected prisoners of war and civilians, they did not ratify it, but in 1942, gave a qualified promise to abide by the rules of the Geneva Convention; as described in Chapter 1, they never did so.

The quality and strength of the Japanese Air Services at their peak owed much to the martial spirit instilled into its fighting men. Boys became desensitized at an early age as they played endlessly in pretended wars, tolerated a strictly disciplined school system, and were ingrained with the belief that their life belonged to the Emperor. They were taught from childhood that Japan had never lost a war against a foreign enemy and that the nation was protected by the gods. Thus, they went into combat with an absolute conviction in final victory that continued even when they were fighting against overwhelming odds.

Military training imbued the ideologies of the Samurai ("Those who serve") and its progeny, Bushido ("The Way of the Warrior"), which left no opportunity for compassion and the ruthless military regimen unfailingly smothered any individualism. Any apparent failure, disobedience, or insufficient devotion to the Emperor would often instigate punishment, frequently physical. In the belief that such punishments were merely the proper technique to deal with the infraction, officers would berate and beat enlisted men, who would then in turn do the same to men in the lower ranks.

Bushido, which the Japanese acclaimed to be the essence of the Samurai spirit, was basically a myth, as it was a modern creation based on the beliefs and writings from the end of Japan's feudal period, in which the warrior class wished to justify its future existence in a peaceful society. It did not encompass the previous centuries of the Samurai character and behavior, but instead projected an idealized version of the Samurai Code that emphasized steadfast allegiance to one's master and glorified sacrificial death. To die for the Emperor was considered the ultimate virtue and death in battle was an unvarying ideal that was fundamental in the life of Japan's WWII warriors. During training, the Japanese recruit was admonished to determinedly avoid capture; a virtue which was formalized in January 1941 by the Senjinkun (Instructions for the Battlefield). The Japanese reluctance to implement self-sealing fuel tanks and cockpit armor plate on their aircraft can be attributed, in part, to the Bushido Code. Acts of Jibaku (Self Destruction) by aviators in severely damaged aircraft and the refusal by many airmen to wear parachutes on combat missions were obvious expressions of this philosophy. There are numerous reports of Japanese pilots and crew who jumped without parachutes from slightly damaged aircraft over Allied territory so as not to be captured. Subsequently, in the face of defeat, the psychological basis of the Kamikaze Special Attack Corps had already been firmly established and recruiting to these suicide units was easy and numerous. But ultimately, in a modern war against a numerically and technologically superior enemy, the Bushido tenets proved to be antiquated and self defeating, especially against the Allied enemy, who valued life so highly.

The Japanese High Command's indifference toward their own soldiers; ancient hostilities and racist attitudes; and the ingrained Bushido Code led to the ensuing butchery that became common for both sides during the war. The Japanese gave no quarter on the battlefield and expected none, and the battles in China became particularly brutal. After Pearl Harbor, the Japanese conquests of the Philippines and the Netherlands East Indies were cruel and unyielding, and reports of pitiless mistreatment and executions of prisoners emerged, as did the machine gunning of parachuting pilots. Tales of the horrific Bataan Death March emerged relatively early in the war, as did tales of the savagery of the Japanese soldier in battle. The concept of death rather than surrender, the Banzai attack, and the later Kamikaze suicide attacks were foreign to Western culture, but were an accepted part of the Japanese Bushido and Samurai Codes.

American

Racial prejudice and hatred were part of American military training early in the war. The booklet *Combat Lessons: Battle Leadership*, issued by the U.S. War Department in September 1942, contained a paragraph with the following admonishment: "HATE YOUR ENEMY! Our men do not ordinarily hate. They must hate. They are better soldiers when they hate. Hate can be taught by meticulous example."

In the Know Your Enemies Series, "The Jap Army," distributed by the Army Orientation Course in 1942, racism was blatant, as seen in the following excerpt:

"The Jap has the extra disadvantage of being a runt....His runtiness makes him cocky and makes him hate all the taller races of the earth. The little brown Jap is taught from his childhood that he is the superior race on earth, that white men are bragging scum unfit to step on the ground where the sun also rises. The Jap looks down on the white man in his mind as he looks up at him with his eyes."

Shooting of Parachuting Air Crew and Other Mayhem

In the European Air War, Luftwaffe and Allied fighter pilots respected the unofficial code of air chivalry and usually allowed parachuting pilots to descend unmolested. Luftwaffe fighter pilots, including many Luftwaffe aces, were shot down several times over their own territory and would fly again to shoot down many more Allied aircraft. On the other hand, the Luftwaffe, except in very isolated instances, did not shoot at the many hundreds of Allied fighter pilots and thousands of Allied bomber crews that would parachute into German captivity. Thus, not killing parachuting aircrew in the ETO was of mutual preservation, particularly for the far larger numbers of Allied aircrews shot down. From the beginning of the Pacific War, the Japanese routinely shot at parachuting Allied pilots and continued to do so throughout the war. Japanese fighter pilots were intelligent young men who were indoctrinated in the so-called "cult of death" that pervaded the Japanese military culture. Surrender was considered treason and, even worse, cowardice. Kamikaze-type aerial suicide in the early stages of the war was rare for Japanese pilots and most carried parachutes, realizing that they could land in friendly territory. Japanese pilots felt that an honorable death was preferable to captivity, and thus destroying enemy aircraft and crew, even if parachuting, was equally acceptable, because these victims had sacrificed their honor. There are many American references, many very callous and some jubilant, in the Individual Combat Reports (ICRs) to the shooting of Japanese aircrew in their parachutes. The days of air chivalry certainly never occurred in the Pacific, as neither side gave any quarter to the other.

On 4 March 1943, during the Battle of the Bismarck Sea, Gen. George Kenney ordered Allied patrol boats and aircraft to attack Japanese rescue vessels, as well as the survivors from their sunken vessels on life rafts and swimming or floating in the sea. This was later justified on the grounds that the Japanese would have been quickly rescued and returned to duty. However, Kenney's orders violated the 1907 Hague Convention that banned the killing of shipwreck survivors under any circumstances and could be considered a war crime.

The collection of Japanese hand guns, flags, and other souvenirs was a common and accepted practice on the battlefield. The collection of skulls and gold teeth began quite early in the war, bringing about an order in September 1942 for stern disciplinary action against such souvenir taking. However, after the war, when Japanese remains were repatriated from the Marianas Island battles of the Summer of 1944 a large number were missing their skulls.

The animosity of American pilots toward the Japanese persisted well beyond the end of the war. During my talks with some aces they insisted that they would never buy a "Jap" car or TV. During an Air Show in Miami in the 1980s, I saw Pappy Boyington selling his books (autographed $20 extra!) from the rear of his station wagon and about 100 feet down the way, Japanese pilot Mike Kawato was selling his book, *Flight into Conquest* (already autographed), in which he claims to have shot down Boyington. After a number of beers in the hot Florida sun, Pappy decided to confront "that lying Jap" and had to be restrained.

During the postwar, the Japanese government and people have failed to recognize or apologize for the widespread atrocities that were committed during the war and have been accused of covering up their war crimes. Now that Allied countries such as America and Australia no longer teach history as a major subject, this issue is likely to fade there. However, Asian countries that suffered most from Japan's brutal militarism from 1937 to 1945, such as the emerging Asian Goliaths, China, and Korea have not let these important issues disappear.

Japanese propaganda poster depicting President Roosevelt as Franekstein. It was the ancient code of Bushido and the Samurai that led to Japanese atrocities.

An American propaganda poster of a stereotypical Japanese soldier with thick-lensed glasses, mustache, and buck teeth carrying a ravaged Caucasian woman through Hell.

PART 7:
Glossary and Abbreviations

A-1	Personnel Officer or Section
A-2	Intelligence Officer or Section
A-3	Operations or Training Officer of Section
A-4	Supply Officer or Section
AAC	Army Air Corps
AAF	Army Air Force
AA	Anti-aircraft
Abort	Turn back from a mission due to mechanical problems or weather
A/C	Aircraft
ACC	Assistant crew chief
ACG	Air Commando group
A/D	Airdrome
AF	Air Force
A/F	Air Field
AFB	Air Force base
AFC	Air Force Cross
AFM	Air Force Medal
Aileron	Hinged or movable portion on the trailing edge of the wing which function is to cause roll
Airfoil	Any surface (e.g. wing, aileron, rudder) designed to effect a reaction from the air through which it moves
Air Group	(AG) Unit with two or more Squadrons
Air Scoop	A scoop or hood designed to catch air and maintain air pressure usually to the engine
Angels	One thousand feet altitude
AP	Armor-piercing ammunition
API	Armor-piercing incendiary ammunition
Armor	Bullet-proof or bullet deflecting metal plating shielding the pilot or essential aircraft parts from enemy fire
Armorer	Ground crewman who repairs, loads, handles a/c armament and bombs
Attitude	The position of an aircraft in reference to the earth
AVG	American Volunteer Group "Flying Tigers"
BC	Bomber Command
B/F	Bomber Force
Bandit	Enemy aircraft
Bank	To incline an aircraft laterally as in rotating it around its longitudinal axis
BB	Battleship
Beat up	Thorough buzz job, strafing run, ground attack
Belly-in	To land wheels up
BG	Bomb Group
Bird	Airplane
Blower	Supercharger
Bogey	Unidentified aircraft that is probably enemy
Bounce	Attack on an enemy aircraft usually from above
Briefing	Pre-take off instruction session
Browned off	Become angry or upset
BS	Bomb Squadron (M = Medium)

BSM	Bronze Star Medal
BuAer	Bureau of Aeronautics
Bug	Cluster to a decoration
Buttoned Up	Ready to go, fly.
Buzz	Fly low over the ground especially the base
BW	Bomb Wing (M= Medium/H= Heavy)
CA	Heavy cruiser
CAP	Combat air Patrol
CBI	China Burma India Theater
CC	Crew Chief
Ceiling	Maximum altitude for flying (or base of cloud cover)
CG	Aircraft center of gravity
Chandelle	An abrupt climbing turn to almost a stall in which the momentum of the aircraft is used to obtain a higher rate of climb than would be possible in unaccelerated flight. The purpose is gain altitude at the same time that the direction of flight is changed.
Chutai	Japanese unit Falling between AAF Squadron and Flight
CinCPac	Commander in Chief Pacific Fleet
MH	Congressional Medal of Honor
CL	Light Cruiser
Clearing	Visually inspecting all surrounding quadrants before beginning a maneuver
CO	Commanding Officer
CominCH	Commander in Chief US Fleet
Control Stick	Vertical lever that operates the longitudinal and lateral control surfaces of the aircraft. The elevator is operated by the fore and aft movement of the stick while the ailerons are controlled by the side to side movement.
Control Surface	A movable airfoil designed to be rotated or otherwise moved by the pilot in order to change the attitude of the aircraft
Cowling	Removable cover as around an engine
Cowl flap	Controllable louver for regulating airflow through the engine.
CNO	Chief Naval Operations
CP	Command Pilot
CTF	Commander, Task Force
CTG	Commander, Task Group
CTU	Commander, Task Unit
CV	Aircraft Carrier
CVE	Escort Carrier
CVG	Carrier Air Group
CVL	Light Carrier
CWO	Chief Warrant Officer
D	Died
Daitai	Japanese Battalion
Damaged (D)	Claim in air combat in which an aircraft is partially destroyed but Returns to base and is repairable
DB	Dive Bomber
DD	Destroyer
DE	Destroyer Escort

Deck	The ground or flying just above the ground
Deflection	Shooting at the target from an angle
DFC	Distinguished Flying Cross
Dihedral	The angle the wing rises from perpendicular from the fuselage
Ding	An aircraft accident
Dispersal	Squadron huts on edges of airfields used for dress
Ditch	To force land in the water with the intention of abandoning the aircraft
Division	A Japanese unit of four to nine aircraft
Dokuritu	Independent (Japanese)
DOW	Died of Wounds
DSC	Distinguished Service Cross
DUC	Distinguished Unit Citation
Duff	Bad or unreliable
E/A	Enemy Aircraft
Eager	Pilot volunteering for combat missions
Element	Two aircraft, leader and Wingman
Elevator	A movable airfoil hinged to the stabilizer, which causes pitch
ETO	European Theater of Operations
FBG	Fighter Bomber Group
FBW	Fighter Bomber Wing
FEW	Fighter Escort Wing
FD	Fighter Director
FDO	Fighter Director Officer
FG	Fighter Group
Firewall	To accelerate (e.g. push stick forward toward firewall)
Flak	Anti-aircraft guns and fire
Flap	A hinged or pivoted airfoil forming the rear portion of an airfoil, such as the wing
Flap	Any excitement, action
Flat Out	Full speed
Flight	Eight fighters made up in two sections
FS	Fighter Squadron
FS(P)	Fighter Squadron (Provisional)
G	A unit to express the pull of gravity (i.e. 2 Gs causes a double in weight)
Gaggle	A group of aircraft
GCI	Ground Control Intercept. A Ground radar station capable of directing a fighter toward and enemy aircraft
Gen	Information, usually rumor or hearsay
Gong	Decoration or medal
Group	48 and later 72 fighters = 3 Squadrons (bomber groups = 4 Squadrons)
Hiko	Flying (Japanese)
Hikodan	Japanese Brigade above Sentai
Hikotai	Japanese Flying Unit
HQ	Headquarters
HVAR	High Velocity Aerial Rocket

IAS	Indicated air speed
IFF	Identification, Friend or foe
Immelmann	A maneuver made by completing the first half of a normal loop; from inverted position at the top of the loop, half rolling the aircraft to the level position, attaining a 180-degree change in direction simultaneously with a gain in altitude.
Initial	The approach leg to the overhead pattern
IO	Intelligence Officer
IP	Initial Point the start of a bomber's run to target
Jackpot	Airdrome strafing in a predetermined area
Jink	Rapid, random movements to avoid an enemy attack
KIA	Killed in Action
KIFA	Killed in Flying Accident
Kite	Aircraft
Knot	Velocity of one nautical mile per hour.
Koku	Air, Aviation (Japanese)
Kyodo	Japanese Operational Training Unit Hikotai
Kyoiku	Japanese Training Unit Sentaizuk
Let down	Gentle reduction of altitude as opposed to a dive
Loop	A maneuver in which the aircraft follows a closed curve approximately in a vertical plane.
Lufbery	Aircraft formation in which two or more aircraft follow each other in a vertical spiral or a horizontal circle in order to protect one another and also to be in a position to face attacking aircraft.
Mach	The relationship of the speed of an aircraft to the speed of sound
Maneuver ability	Quality in an aircraft that determines the rate at which its attitude and direction of flight can be changed.
May Day	Warning of imminent bail out, please plot position
MIA	Missing In Action
Military	2nd highest throttle setting (after War Emergency) to be used for a Power maximum of 15 minutes
Monocoque	A fuselage construction which relies on the strength of the skin or shell mounted on vertical bulkheads for its strength.
MTO	Mediterranean Theater of Operations
NFS	Night Fighter Squadron
NMF	Natural Metal Finish
NYR	Not Yet Returned
OCS	Officer Candidate School
O/D	Olive Drab (color)
OD	Officer of the Day, 24-hour duty in charge of station
OLC	Oak Leaf Cluster
Oleo	Shock absorbing, telescopic landing gear strut
Ops	Operations, active duty
OS	Observation Squadron
OTU	Operational Training Unit
Overshoot	To fly over or past the enemy when following through the attack
Peel off	Diving away from a formation to make an attack or land
Pedals	Foot (rudder) bar by which the control cables leading to the rudder are operated
PG	Pursuit Group

Pipper	The dot of light at the center of the image on the windshield by the gunsight
Pitch	The angle of motion from the lateral axis
Port	Left side
POW	Prisoner of War
PPS	Pursuit Squadron (Provisional)
PS	Pursuit Squadron
Prang	Wreck an aircraft
PRG	Photo Reconnaissance Squadron
Probable (P)	A combat claim in which it was not known if the aircraft crashed but was so badly damaged as to make a crash probable
PRO	Public Relations Officer
PRU	Photo Recon Unit
PTO	Pacific Theater of Operations
Rack	To make a sudden violent maneuver
RAF	Royal Air Force
Ramrod	Bomber escort mission
Recce	Reconnaissance
Rentai	Japanese Regiment
Red Line	Red mark on the air speed indicator showing safe maximum speed
Roll	Maneuver in which a complete revolution about a longitudinal axis is made, with the horizontal direction of flight maintained.
Rudder	A hinged or movable auxiliary airfoil which causes yaw.
Rudder Bar	Foot bar (or pedals) by which the control cables leading to the rudder are operated.
R/T	Radio Telephone
RV	Rendezvous
Salvo	Dropping bombs or firing rockets simultaneously.
SE (S/E)	Single engine aircraft
Scramble	Hurried launch of fighter aircraft
Section	Four aircraft made up into two Elements (coded by colors)
Service Ceiling	The height above sea level under standard air conditions and normal rated load that an aircraft in unable to climb faster than a specified rate (i.e. 100 feet per minute).
Sentai	Japanese Regiment equivalent to AAF Group
Shiden	Division (Japanese)
Side Slipping	Motion in which the aircraft moves inward of its intended direction of flight as the nose is held too high during a turn. It is the opposite of skidding.
Six	Most commonly used Clock term indicating the area behind an aircraft.
Skidding	Sliding sideways away from the center of the direction of intended direction of flight in a turn. It is caused by not banking enough and is the opposite of side slipping.
Slipstream	The current of air driven aft by a propeller.
Slow time	Engine breaking in period
Snap roll	A roll done by a quick movement of the controls, in which executes a complete revolution is made.
Sortie	A single aircraft on one mission
Spin	A maneuver in which an aircraft descends in a small spiral at a large pitch.
Spinner	A fairing covering the propeller hub

Split-S	High-speed maneuver in which the aircraft makes a half roll onto its back and then dives groundward leveling off going in the opposite direction at a much lower altitude
Squadron	12 to 20 fighter aircraft out of 25 on base (AAF), 18 to 36 fighters (USN)
SS	Silver Star
SS	Submarine
Stabilizer	Any airfoil whose primary function is to increase the stability of an aircraft. It refers to the horizontal tail surface and the vertical tail surface.
Stall	The aircraft loses lift and drops because of too low flying speed or excessive climb.
Starboard	Right side
Strattle	Bracketing a target with near hits without scoring a hit.
Strafe	To fire on a ground target
Supercharger	A pump for supplying the engine with a more air than prevailing atmospheric pressure.
Tab	A small airfoil attached to the control surface for the purpose of reducing the control force or trimming of an aircraft.
TAC	Tactical Air Command
TAF	Tactical Air Force
Tally-ho	Making enemy contact
Tail end Charlie	Last plane in formation
TDY	Temporary Duty
TE (T/E)	Twin engine aircraft
10/10 Cloud	Completely overcast. Percentage of overcast expressed in 1/10th of the obscured by cloud.
TF	Task Force
TFS	Tactical Fighter Squadron
TFW	Tactical Fighter Wing
TG	Task Group
Tokushu	Japanese Special Attack Unit Kogekitai
Tour	Specified time or course of duty at a given assignment or place
Tracer	Visible bullets (every 3rd or 4th bullet)
Tractor	Aircraft with propeller(s) forward of the main supporting surfaces
Trim	The level attitude of the wings and fuselage with all controls neutral.
TRS	Tactical Reconnaissance Squadron
TRW	Tactical Reconnaissance Wing
TU	Task Unit
T/O	Take Off
U/I	Unidentified
USAAC	United States Army Air Corps
USAAF	United States Army Air Force
USMC	United States Marine Corps
USN	United States Navy
VB	Dive bomber Squadron (Navy)
VBF	Fighter bomber Squadron (Navy)
VC	Composite Squadron (Navy)
Vector	Direct to area (on a magnetic heading)
VF	Fighting Squadron (fighter USN)

Vector	Heading given to an intercepting aircraft by the GCI radar station
Vic or V	A V-formation of 3 aircraft
Victory (V)	A plane that is seen descending completely enveloped in flames away from the fuselage or if a single seat a/c whose pilot bails out
W/A	Wounded in Action
War Emergency Power	Highest throttle setting for use in emergency situations, it produced more than 100% of the engine's normal rated power for a limited amount of time, often about five minutes (also called Combat Power).
Water Injection	The injection of water into a combustible mixture of an engine to improve combustion or to improve cooling.
WIA	Wounded in action
Wing Loading	The aircraft gross weight divided by the wing area
Wingover	A climbing turn to the brink of a stall, the nose is allowed to drop, followed by a diving half roll but returning to normal flight after the dive in the reverse direction.
Wingroot	Area where the wing joins the fuselage
Write off	Total wreck, beyond repair
XO	Executive Officer
Yaw	Movement of an aircraft around its vertical axis.
ZI	Zone of the Interior, the USA

Bibliography

Microfilm and CDs*

NARA: M-1065: CD 1: Unit Narrative Combat Reports
NARA: M-1065: CD 2: Mission Reports: 8FG
NARA: M-1065: CD 3: Operations Orders
NARA: M-1065: CD 4: Mission Reports 431FS and 432FS
NARA: M-1065: CD 4: IRCs: HQ Squadron; 5FC
   IRCs: 35FG
   IRCs: 3ACS
   IRCs: 6NFS
   IRCs: 7FS
NARA: M-1065: CD 5: IRCs: 7FS
   IRCs: 8FS
   IRCs: 9FS
NARA: M-1065: CD 6: IRCs: 35FS
   IRCs: 36FS
   IRCs: 39FS
   IRCs: 40FS
   IRCs: 41FS
   IRCs: 69FS
NARA: M-1065: CD 7:   IRCs: 80FS
   IRCs: 310FS
   IRCs: 311FS
   IRCs: 340FS
   IRCs: 341FS
   IRCs: 342FS
NARA: M-1065: CD 8:   IRCs: 388BS
   IRCs: 416NFS
   IRCs: 418NFS
   IRCs: 419NSF
   IRCs: 421NSF
   IRCs: 431FS
NARA: M-1065: CD 9: IRCs: 432FS
   IRCs: 433FS
   IRCs: 460FS
   IRCs: 547NFS
(**Note:** IRC=Individual Combat Report)
AFHRC: History of the 8th Fighter Group: Reel: B0062
AFHRC: History of the 24th Fighter Group: Reel: B0093
AFHRC: History of the 35th Fighter Group: Reel: B0116
AFHRC: History of the 49th Fighter Group: Reel: B0143
AFHRC: History of the 58th Fighter Group: Reel: B0175
AFHRC: History of the 348th Fighter Group: Reel: B0302
AFHRC: History of the 475th Fighter Group: Reel: B0632
USAAF Historical Studies #9: The AAF in Australia to the Summer of 1942
USAAF Historical Studies #13: 5AF in the Huon Campaign, January-October 1943
USAAF Historical Studies #16: 5AF in the Huon Peninsula Campaign, October 1943-February 1944
USAAF Historical Studies #17: Air Action in the Papuan Campaign, 21 July 1942 to 23 January 1943
USAAF Historical Studies #43: 5AF in the Conquest of the Bismarck Archipelago, November1943-March 1944
US Army Air Forces, Far East, Military History Section:
Java-Sumatra Air Operations Record, Japanese Monograph #69, Tokyo, 1962
Philippines Air Operations Record, Japanese Monograph #11, Tokyo, 1962

Books, Papers, and Pamphlets

Abacus, Pacific Theater, Abacus, MI, 1999
Air Classics (eds.), *Air Aces of the Pacific War*, Air Classics, CA, 1983
Air Classics (eds.), *P-38 Lightning Aces*, Air Classics, CA, 1993
Alcorn, John, *The Jolly Rogers,* Historical Aviation Album, CA, 1981
American Fighter Aces Association, *Fighter Aces Album*, AZ, 1978
Anders, Curt, *Fighting Airmen*, G.P. Putnam, NY, 1966
Angelella, Salvadore, *A Prototype JFACC: General George Kenney*, Air U, AL, 1994
Arnold, Elliott, and Hough, Donald, *Big Distance*, Duell, Sloan and Pearce, NY, 1945
Arnold, Gen H.H., *Global Mission*, Harper and Brothers, NY, 1949
Barr, James, *Airpower Employment of the Fifth Air Force in the World War II Southwest Pacific Theater*, ACSC, AL, 1997
Bartsch, William, *December 8, 1941: MacArthur's Pearl Harbor*, Texas A&M, TX, 2003
Bartsch, William, *Doomed at the Start*, Texas A&M, TX, 1993
Bartsch, William, *Every Day A Nightmare*, Texas A&M, TX, 2010
Bauer, Dan, *Great American Fighter Aces*, Motor Books, WI, 1992
Bergerud, Eric, *Fire in the Sky*, Westview, CO, 2000
Birdsall, Steve, *Flying Buccaneers*, NY, Doubleday 1977
Bong, Carl, *Dear Mom, So We Have a War*, Burgess, WI, 1991
Bong, Carl and O'Conner, Mike, *Ace of Aces*, Champlin, AZ, 1985
Bowman, Martin, *USAAF Handbook: 1939-1945*, Sutton, UK, 1997
Bozung, Jack (ed.), *The 5th Over the Southwest Pacific*, AAF Publications, CA, 1945
Brayley, Martin, *The USAAF Airman: Service & Survival*, Crowood, UK, 2007
Brereton, Lewis, *The Brereton Diaries*, Wm. Morrow, NY, 1946
Bright, Charles, *Historical Dictionary of the US Air Force*, Greenwood, NY, Press, 1992
Bruning, John, *Jungle Ace*, Brasseys, Wash. DC, 2001
Burton, John, *Fortnight of Infamy: Collapse of Allied Airpower West of Pearl Harbor*, NIP, MD, 2006
Caidin, Martin, Ragged, *Rugged Warriors*, E.P. Dutton, NY, 1966
Cannon, M.H., *US Army in WW II: The Pacific: Leyte, the Return to the Philippines*, Office of the Chief of Military History, Wash DC, 1954
Carter, Kit, and Robert Mueller (eds.), *Combat Chronology: 1941-1945*, Center for Air Force History Washington, DC, 1991

Cea, Eduardo, *Fighters of the Imperial Japanese Army 1939-1945*, AF Editions, Spain, 2009

Cea, Eduardo, *Fighters of the Imperial Japanese Navy: Carrier-based Aircraft 1922-1945 (I)*, AF Editions, Spain, 2009

Cea, Eduardo, *Fighters of the Imperial Japanese Navy: Carrier-based Aircraft 1922-1945 (II)*, AF Editions, Spain, 2009

Cea, Eduardo, *Fighters of the Imperial Japanese Navy: Land-based Aircraft 1929-1945 (I)*, AF Editions, Spain, 2010

Cea, Eduardo, *Fighters of the Imperial Japanese Navy: Land-based Aircraft 1929-1945 (II)*, AF Editions, Spain, 2010

Cea, Eduardo, *Bombers of the Imperial Japanese Army 1939-1945*, AF Editions, Spain, 2010

Chiu, Ben, *Combat Flight Simulator*, Microsoft, WA, 1998

Claringbould, Michael, *Black Sunday*, Aerothentic Publications, Australia, 1998

Claringbould, Michael, *The Forgotten Fifth*, Aerothentic Publications, Australia, 1997

Coll, Keith & Rosenthal, H.H., *Corps of Engineers: Troops and Equipment*, Dept. of the Army, GPO, Wash. DC, 1958

Collier, Basil, *Japanese Aircraft of World War II*, Mayflower, NY, 1979

Copp, Dewitt, *A Few Great Captains*, Doubleday, NY, 1980

Copp, Dewitt, *Forged in Fire*, Doubleday, NY, 1982

Cortesi, Lawrence, *Operation Bismarck Sea*, Major Books, CA, 1977

Cox, Douglas, *Airpower Leadership on the Front line: Lt.Gen. George H. Brett and the Combat Command*, Maxwell AFB, Air University Press, AL, 2006

Crabb, B.Gen. J.V., *Fifth Air Force Air War against Japan*, 5AF, Feb. 1946

Craven, W.F. & Cate, J.L, *The Army Air Forces in World War II, Volumes I-V*, University of Chicago Press, IL, 1948

Dean, Francis, *America's Hundred Thousand: US Fighter Production of World War Two*, Schiffer, PA, 1997

Dod, Karl, *The Corps of Engineers: War against Japan*, Center of Military History, Wash. DC, 1966

Doyle, David, *P-38 Lightning in Action,* Squadron/Signal, TX, 2011

Dyess, William, *The Dyess Story*, Putnam, NY, 1944

Edmonds, Walter, *They Fought with What They Had*, Little Brown, MA, 1951

Falk, Stanley, Liberation of the Philippines, Ballantine, NY, 1971

Ferguson, S.W. and Pascalls, William, *Protect & Avenge: 49th Fighter Group in World War II*, Schiffer, PA, 1996

Fifth Air Force, *Fifth Air Force Air War against Japan: September 1942-August 1945*, Pvt. Printing, 1946

Fifth Air Force, *Fifth over the Southwest Pacific*, AAF Publications, CA, 1947

Fifth Air Force, *Menace over Moresby*, Newsfoto, TX, 1950

Fifth Air Force, *Pacific Sweep*, Johnston, Australia, 1945

Fogerty, Robert, *Biographical Data on Air Force General Officers*, Maxwell AFB, AL, Air University Press, 1953.

Forrester, Randy, *Fifth Air Force*, Turner, KY, 1994

Francillon, Rene, *American Fighters of World War Two: Volume One*, Hylton Lacy, UK, 1968

Francillon, Rene, *American Fighters of World War Two: Volume Two*, Hylton Lacy, UK, 1968

Francillon, Rene, *Japanese Aircraft of the Pacific War*, Funk & Wagnalls, NY, 1970

Furbank, Jeffrey, *Critical Analysis of the Generalship of General Douglas MacArthur as Commander in the Pacific During World War II*, Air University, AL, 1990

Gailey, Harry, *MacArthur Strikes Back*, Presidio, CA, 2000

Gamble, Bruce, *Fortress Rabaul*, Zenith, MN, 2010

Gann, Timothy, *Fifth Air Force Light and Medium Bomber Operations during 1942 and 1943*, Air U, Al, 1993

Caygill, Peter, *Flying the Limit,* Pen & Sword, UK, 2005

Goldstein, Donald, Ennis C. Whitehead: *Aerospace Commander and Pioneer*, University of Denver, CO. 1970

Green, William, and Swanborough, Gordon, *Japanese Army Fighters, Vol. 2*, Aero, CA, 1978

Griffith, Thomas, *MacArthur's Airman*, U. of Kansas Press, Lawrence, KS, 1998

Gurney, Gene, *Five Down and Glory*, Ayers, NY, 1972

Hammel, Eric, *Aces against Japan Vol.1*, Pacifica, CA. 1992

Hammel, Eric, *Aces against Japan Vol.3*, Pacifica, CA. 1996

Hata, I., Izawa, Y., & Shores, C., *Japanese Army Air Force Fighter Units and Their Aces*, Grub Street, UK, 2002

Hata, I., Izawa, Y., *Japanese Naval Aces and Fighter Units in World War II*, NIP, MD, 1989

Haugland, Vern, *AAF against Japan*, Harper, NY, 1948

Haulman, Daniel & Stancik, William, *Air Force Aerial Victory Credits, WW I, WW II, Korea & Vietnam*, USAFHRC, Maxwell AFB, AL, 1988

Hess, William, *America's Aces in a Day*, Specialty, MN, 1996

Hess, William, *49th Fighter Group*, Osprey, UL, 2004

Hess, William, *Pacific Sweep*, Doubleday, NY, 1974

Holmes, Tony (ed.), *Twelve to One: V Fighter Command Aces of the Pacific*, Osprey, UK, 2004

Ichimura, Hiroshi, *Ki-43 Oscar Aces of World War II*, Osprey, UK, 2009

James, D. Clayton, *Years of MacArthur: 1941-45*, Houghton-Mifflin, MA, 1975

Janes, *Combat Simulations*, Janes, UK, 1998

Jones, Laurence, *Defense of the Philippines to the Battle of Buna: A Critical Analysis of General Douglas MacArthur*, Air University, AL 1989

Kenney, George C., *General Kenney Reports: A Personal History of the Pacific War*, Sloan & Pearce, NY, 1949

King, Carl, *Journal of S/Sgt. Carl King; 475th Fighter Group*, Pvt. Printing, 1996

Kolin, Jeff, *421st Fighter Squadron in World War II*, Schiffer, PA, 2001

Kupferer, Anthony, *The Story of the 58th Fighter Group in WW II*, Taylor Publishing, TX, 1989

Lindbergh, Charles, *Wartime Diaries of Charles A. Lindbergh*, Harcourt, Brace, NY, 1970

Lundstrom, John B., *The First Team and the Guadalcanal Campaign: Naval Fighter Combat from August to November 1942*, Naval Institute Press, MD, 2005

MacIssac, David (ed.), *Strategic Bombing Survey*, Garland, NY, 1976 (various volumes)

Maloney, Edward (ed.), *Fighter Tactics of the Aces*, WW II Publications, CA, 1978

Marin, Charles, *Last Great Ace*, Fruit Cove, FL, 1998

Mason, Herbert, *Operation Thursday: Birth of the Air Commandos*, AAF, Wash. DC, 1994

Maurer, Maurer, *Air Force Combat Units of World War II*, USGPO, Wash., DC, 1961

Maurer, Maurer, *Combat Squadrons of the Air Force World War II*, USGPO, Wash., DC, 1969

McAuley, Lex, *Battle of the Bismarck Sea*, St. Martins, NY, 1991

McAuley, Lex, *Into the Dragon's Jaws: Fifth Air Force over Rabaul*, Champlin Fighter Museum Press, AZ, 1986

McAuley, Lex, *MacArthur's Eagles*, NIP, MD, 2005

McDowell, Ernest, *49th Fighter Group*, Squadron Signal, TX, 1989

McGuire, Thomas, *Combat Tactics in the SWPA*, FEAF, 1944

Mellinger, George and Stanaway, *John, P-39 Airacobra Aces of World War II*, Osprey, UK, 2001

Microsoft, *Microsoft Combat Flight Simulator*, WA, 1998

Mikesh, Robert, *Japanese Aircraft: Code Names & Designations*, Schiffer, PA, 1993

Mikesh, Robert, *Japanese Aircraft Equipment: 1940-1945*, Schiffer, PA, 2004

Molesworth, Carl, *P-40 Warhawk Aces of the Pacific*, Osprey, UK. 2003

Molesworth, Carl, *P-40 Warhawk vs. Ki-43 Oscar*, Osprey, UK. 2008

Morehead, James, *In My Sights: Memoir of a P-40 Ace*, Presidio, CA, 1998

Morgan, Hugh and Seibel, Jurgen, *Combat Kill*, PSL, UK, 1992

Nakireru, Omaviekovwa, *The Fighter Pilot Who Refused to Die*, iUniverse, NY, 2003

Nijboer, Donald, *P-38 Lightning vs. Ki-61 Tony: New Guinea 1943-44*, Osprey, UK, 2010

Nila, Gary, *Japanese Naval Aviation Uniforms and Equipment: 1937-45*, Osprey, UK. 2002

Northern Territory Government, *Signs of History*, NTG, Australia, 1990

Obert, David, *Philippines Defender*, Levite, OK, 1992

Odgers, George, *Air War against Japan*, Australia, 1957

Okumiya, Masatake, Horikoshi, Jiro, and Caidin, Martin, *Zero!*, E.P. Dutton, NY, 1956.

Oliver, William and Lorenz, Dwight, *The Inner Seven*, Turner, KY, 1999

Olynyk, Frank, *USAAF (Pacific Theater) Credits for the Destruction of Enemy Aircraft in Air-to-Air Combat World War II*, Pvt. Printing, OH, 1985

Olynyk, Frank, *Stars and Bars*, Grub Street, UK, 1995

Paloque, Gerard, *The 5th Air Force*, Historie & Collections, France 2009

RAF Office of Intelligence, *Japanese Air Forces in World War II*, Hippocrene, NY, 1979 (reprint of 1945 report)

Rearden, Jim, *Koga's Zero: The Fighter That Changed World War II*, Pictorial Histories, MT, 1995

Rodman, Matthew, *Flexible Airpower: Fifth Air Force in WW II*, Texas Tech U, TX, 1998

Rodman, Matthew, *War of Their Own: Bombers over the Southwest Pacific*, Air U, AL, 2005

Rottmann, Gordon, *World War II Pacific Island Guide*, Greenwood. CO, 2004

Rust, Ken, *Fifth Air Force Story*, Historical Aviation Album, MN, 1973

71st Reconnaissance Group, *May 44-August 45: 71TRG History*, Pvt. Printing n.d.

Safford, Gene, *Aces of the Southwest Pacific*, Squadron/Signal. TX, 1977

Sakai, Saburo; Caidin, Martin; and Saito, Fred, *Samurai!*, Bantam, NY, 1985

Sakaida, Henry, *JAAF Aces: 1937-45*, Osprey, UK, 1997

Sakaida, Henry, *JNAF Aces: 1937-45*, Osprey, UK, 1998

Sakaida, Henry, *Winged Samurai*, Champlin Fighter Museum Press, AZ, 1986

Scott, Peter, *Emblems of the Rising Sun*, Hikoki, UK, 1999

Shores, Chris, Cull, Brian and Izawa, Yashuo, Bloody Shambles: Volume I, Grub Street, UK, 1992

Shores, Chris, Cull, Brian and Izawa, Yashuo, *Bloody Shambles: Volume II*, Grub Street, UK, 1993

Sinton, Russell (ed.), *Menace from Moresby*, Battery Press, TN, 1989 (reprint of 1946)

Smith, Robert, *Approach to the Philippines*, Dept. of the Army, Wash, DC, 1953

Spector, Ronald, *Eagle against the Sun*, Free Press, NY, 1984

Spick, Mike, *Air Battles in Miniature*, PSL, UK, 1978

Spick, Mike, *Fighter Pilot Tactics*, Stein and Day, NY, 1983

Stanaway, John and Hickey, Lawrence, *Attack & Conquer: 8th Fighter Group in World War II*, Schiffer, PA, 1995

Stanaway, John, *Cobra in the Clouds*, Historical Aviation Album, CA

Stanaway, John, *475th Fighter Group*, Osprey, UK, 2007

Stanaway, John, *Kearby's Thunderbolts*, Schiffer, PA, 1997

Stanaway, John, *Kearby's Thunderbolts*, Phalanx, MN, 1992

Stanaway, John, *Mustang and Thunderbolt Aces of the Pacific and CBI*, Osprey, UK, 1999

Stanaway, John, *Peter Three Eight: The Pilot's Story*, Pictorial Histories, MT, 1986

Stanaway, John, *P-38 Lightning Aces of the Pacific and CBI*, Osprey, UK, 1997

Stanaway, John, *Possum, Clover & Hades*, Schiffer, PA, 1994

Stevens, Joe, *One More Pass before Seeking Cover*, Pvt. Printing, TX, 1992

Susedik, Tina, *Ruff Stuff*, Pvt. Printing, WI, 2006

Sweeting, C.G., *Combat Flying Clothing*, Smithsonian, Wash. DC, 1984

Sweeting, C.G., *Combat Flying Equipment*, Smithsonian, Wash. DC, 1989

Taafe, Stephen, *MacArthur's Jungle War*, U. of Kansas, KS, 1998

Tacitus, *Fighter Combat Comparisons*, Tacitus, NJ, n.d.

Tagaya, Osamu, *Imperial Japanese Naval Aviator, 1937-45*, Osprey, UK, 2004

Thorpe, Donald, *Japanese Army Air Force Camouflage and Markings of World War II*, Aero, CA, 1968

Thorpe, Donald, *Japanese Naval Air Force Camouflage and Markings of World War II*, Aero, CA, 1977

Toll, Henry, *Tropic Lightning*, Sunflower University Press, KS, 1987

US Army, *Leyte*, Wash. DC, 1995

US Army, *Luzon*, Wash. DC, 1995

US Army, *New Guinea*, Wash. DC, 1995

US Army, *Papua*, Wash. DC, 1995

US Army, *Southern Philippines*, Wash. DC, 1995

US Navy, *Building the Navy's Bases in World War II*, GPO, Wash, DC, 1947

US War Department, *The Admiralties*, Wash. DC, 1945

US War Department, *Papuan Campaign*, Wash. DC, 1945

Wagner, Ray, *American Combat Planes*, Doubleday, NY, 1968

Wiley, Katherine (ed.), *Strafin' Saints: 71st Tactical Reconnaissance Squadron: 1943-45*, Pvt. Printing, TX, 1995

Willoughey, Charles & Chamberlain, John, *MacArthur: 1941-1951*, McGraw-Hill, NY, 1957

Wills, Jonathon, *How the Southwest Pacific Area Operations in WW II Influenced the Royal Australian Air Force*, ACSC, AL, 1997

Wolf, William, *US Aerial Armament of WW II: Vol. 1 Guns, Ammunition, and Turrets*, Schiffer, PA, 2010

Wolf, William, *US Aerial Armament of WW II: Volume 2: Bombs, Bombsights, and Bombing*, Schiffer, PA, 2010

Wolf, William, *US Aerial Armament of WW II: Volume 3: Air-Dropped, Air-Launched, and Secret Weapons*, Schiffer, PA, 2010

Wolf, William, *Victory Roll: The American Fighter Pilot and Aircraft in World War Two*, Schiffer, PA, 2004

Wolk, Herman, *Cataclysm: Hap Arnold and the Defeat of Japan*, U. North Texas Press, TX, 2010

Y'Blood, William, *Air Commandos against Japan*, NIP, MD, 2008

Yenne, Bill, *Aces High*, Berkeley Caliber, NY, 2009

Young, Edward, *Air Commando Fighters of World War II*, Specialty, MN, 2000

Yoshino, Ronald, *Lightning Strikes*, Sunflower University Press, KS, 1988

Zbiegniewski, Andre, *421 NFS: 1943-47*, Kagero, Poland, 2004

Zbiegniewski, Andre, *475FG: 1943-45*, Kagero, Poland, 2003

Manuals, Reports, Papers, Letters, and Memorandums

35th Fighter Group, Group Historical Officer, "Offensive Sweeps for the P-47 in the SWPA," March 1945

35th Fighter Group, Headquarters, "Group Medical and Sanitation Report," 1943

204th Air Group JNAF, Combat Guide, 21 October 1943

342nd Fighter Squadron, Roth, 1st Lt, Bernard: Telegram to the Commanding General of the Fifth Air Force, 12 October 1943

Air Intelligence Group/USN, *Performance Characteristics Data: Japanese Aircraft, USN*, 1944

Army Air Corps Field Manual I-40, 9 September 1940, "Intelligence Procedures in Aviation Units"

British Air Intelligence, *Japanese Air Forces in WW II: Organization of the Japanese Army & Naval Air Forces 1945*, Hippocrene, NY, 1979 (reprint 1945)

Crabb, J.V., *Fifth Air Force Air War against Japan*, Fifth Air Force, 1946

First Demobilization Ministry, *Historical Data of Japanese Air Units, First Demobilization Ministry*, April 1946

GHQ, SWPA, Special Technical Memorandum No. 1 (7 June 1944): "Drainage," Maj.Gen. Hugh J. Casey.

Headquarters AAF, Japanese Fighter Tactics Intelligence Report (No.45-101), Washington DC, January 1945

Informational Intelligence Summary 59, Akutan Zero

Informational Intelligence Summary 85, Akutan Zero

Joint Fighter Conference, "Report of the Joint Fighter Conference," NAS Patuxent River, MD, 16-23 October 1944

Krueger, Lt.Gen. Walter: Letter to Gen. Ennis Whitehead, 17 March 1945

Lockheed Aircraft Corp., "Contract Model Specifications of the Lockheed Lightning (Report 2338)," Lockheed, CA, August 1942

Maxwell AFB, USAF Credits, Maxwell AFB, AL, 1978

McGuire, Maj. Thomas, "Combat Tactics of the Southwest Pacific Area," FEAF A-3 Training Section, October 1944

Military Analysis Division, *Air Campaigns of the Pacific War*, USSBS, GPO, Washington, DC, 1947

Military Analysis Division, *The Allied Campaign against Rabaul*, USSBS, GPO, Washington, DC, 1947

Nakagawa, Yasuzo, Japanese *Radar and Related Weapons of World War II*, Aegean Park, Press, CA. 1997

Office of the Chief Engineer, *Airfield and Airbase Development: Vol. VI*, GPO. 1951

Office of the Chief Engineer, *Engineers in the Southwest Pacific: 1941-45, Vol.1: Engineers in Theater Operations*, Wash. DC, GPO 1947

Rand Corp., *Aircraft Vulnerability in World War II, USAF*, Project Rand, Rand Corp, CA, 19 May 1950 (Copy 15)

Reinburg, Joseph, *Air-to-Air Combat in World War II: A Quantitative History, Institute for Defense Analysis*, VA, 1966

Tactical and Technical Trends, "Akutan Zero," No. 5

Tactical and Technical Trends, "Japanese Aerial Burst Bombs," No. 47, 1 June 1944

Tactical and Technical Trends, "Japanese Anti-aircraft Fire," No. 42, 12 January 1944

Tactical and Technical Trends, "Japanese Anti-aircraft Installations" No. 31, 12 August 1943

Tactical and Technical Trends, "Japanese Camouflage and Deception Methods on Airfields," No. 29, 15 July 1943

Tactical and Technical Trends, "Japanese Fighter Aircraft," No. 19, 25 February 1943

Tactical and Technical Trends, "Japanese Fighter Tactics," No. 20, 24 September 1942

Tactical and Technical Trends, "Japanese Pilots," No. 15, 31 December 1942

Tactical and Technical Trends, "Notes on Japanese Air Tactics," No. 8, 11 March 1943

Technical Aviation Intelligence Brief #3

TAIC: "Japanese Air Services and Japanese Aircraft," Intelligence Information Memorandum No. 12, September 1942

US Army Orientation Course, "The Jap Army," Infantry Journal, 1942

US Army Air Force, *Official Guide to the Army Air Forces*, Simon & Schuster, NY, 1944

US Navy, Fleet Air Tactical Unit Intelligence Bulletin, 22 September 1941

US War Dept., Material Division, "P-47B Acceptance Performance Report," June 1942

US War Department, *Handbook on Japanese Forces: Chapter IV, Japanese Air Service*, TM-E30-480, 1 October 1944

US Strategic Bombing Survey, *Air Campaigns of the Pacific War*, GPO, Wash, DC, 1947

US Strategic Bombing Survey, *Air Forces Allied with the US in the War against Japan*, GPO, Wash, DC, 1947

US Strategic Bombing Survey, *Allied Campaign against Rabaul*, GPO, Wash, DC, 1947

US Strategic Bombing Survey, *Japanese Air Power*, GPO, Wash, DC, 1947

US Strategic Bombing Survey, *Japan's Struggle to End the War*, GPO, Wash, DC, 1947

US Strategic Bombing Survey, *Japanese Air Weapons and Tactics*, GPO, Wash, DC, 1947

US Strategic Bombing Survey, *Summary Report (Pacific War)*, GPO, Wash, DC, 1947

US War Department, *Pilot's Information File (Form 24)*, Wash, DC, 1944

US War Department, *Combat Lessons No. 1, Battle Leadership*, September 1942

Wagner, Lt.Col. Boyd to the Commanding General, USAFIA, Melbourne, "Report on first action against Japanese by P-39 type airplane," 1 May 1942

Willits, Pat (editor), *Jeppesen Sanderson Private Pilot Manual*, Jeppesen Sanderson, CO, 1998

Personnel Index

Durham, Jasper: 638, 790, 819, 834
Dutton, Al: 62, 82
Dwinell, William: 563
Dwyer, William: 500, 514, **515**, 627
Dyess, William: 19, 22, 32, 33, 39, 40, 44, 45, **45**, 46, **47**, 48

E

Eagleston, Glenn (AAF): 916
Eason, Hoyt: 212, 213, **214**, 227
Easterling, Ralph: 700, **701**
Eastham, David: 291, 721, 772
Ebert, John: 883
Economoff, Gerald: 752, 807, 866
Edmonds, Robert: 806
Edesberg, Edward: 729, 804
Egan, James: 149, 153, 154, **154, 158**, 159
Egan, John: 92
Egenes, Hubert: 62, 63, 74, 82
Egusa, Takashige: 67
Ehlinger, John: 320, 406, 473, 516, 552
Eichelberger, Gen, Robert: 195, 207, 208, **208**
Eisenberg, Monty: 102, 105, 111
Eissman, Gilbert: 572
Ekdahl, Wilson: 597, 628, 651, 723, **723**, 748
Ellenberger, Blaine: 790, 791
Ellis, Frank: 790, **806**, 807
Ellis, Herbert: 28, 29, **29**
Elofson, Elferd: 278, 351, 352, 436
Else, Merle: 159
Elsmore, Raymond: 43
Ellenberger, Blaine: 790, 822
Ellings, George: 796, **796**
Elliott, Vincent: 354, 355, 398, 398, 404, 405, 410, 411, 492, 495, 496, 517, 527, 639
Elliott, William: 397, 629
Ellis, Frank: 790, **806**, 807
Ellstrom, George: 28
Elvey, George: 889
Eltien, Clifford: 739, 759, 797
Emrich, Hubert: 790
Endo, Masuaki: 1008, 1008
Epling, Fenton: 530, 590
Erdman, Orville: 301, 616
Ericsson, Jack: 439, 501, 501
Erickson, Charles: 810
Erickson, Edward: 33
Erickson, Irving: 149, 150, 151, **151**, 152, 154, 155, 157, **158**, 159
Erzen, Leonard: 526
Estes. Carl: 609
Estes, Harney: 884
Eubank, Eugene: 21, 22, **22**, 54, 58, 76, **76**, 77, 80, 100
Evans, John: 795
Evans, Raymond: 526, 790, 816, **816**
Evanski, Harold: 809
Everhart, Lee (Leo): 500, 514, **515**, 627, 659
Everhart, Sylvester: 834
Evers, Willis: 414, 426, 427

Ewers, Benjamin: 434
Excell, Gerald: 776

F

Fagan, James: 353, 437
Faikus, Anthony: 538, 761, 860, **860** (A/C)
Fairbanks, Leo: 833
Fairweather, George: 885
Falletta, Charles: 154, 155, 156, **157**, 159
Fanning, Grover: 261, 268, **268**, 269, 278, 279, 317, 319, 344, 396, 407, **407**
Fariello, Frank: 661
Farley, Thomas: 278
Farrell, Roger: 527, 530, **530**
Farris, James: 334, 364, 400, 418, 489, 493, 518, 639
Ford, Francis: 706, 771, **771**
Fostakowski, Theodore: 472
Foster, Paul: 707, **707**
Faurot, Robert: 206, 226, 227, 228
Feallock, William: 31, 33
Featherstone, Frederick: 149, 150
Feehan, Robert: 338
Feiler, William: 208, **208**, 209
Felts, Marion: 528, 529, 550, 591, 700, 701
Fenn, George: 423
Fennimore, John: 522, 592
Fernandez, William: 732, 748, 845
Fenske, Robert 806
Ferris, William: 419
Ferryman, Glenn: 291
Fields, Quanah "Chief": 71, **72**, 82
Finberg, Floyd: 193, **193**, 261, **261**, 262, 278, 279
Finney, Herbert: 875
Fish, Owen: 103
Fischer, Jerome: 403, 503
Fisher, Donald: 608
Fisher, John: 109, 110
Fisher, William: 70, 77, 80
Fisk, Jack: 406, 406, 417, 417, 438
Flack, Nelson: 318, 360, 436, 436
Fleischer, Richard: 503, **504**, 526, 545, **545**, 608, **608**
Fletcher, Bud: 558, 560, 562, 773
Florence, John: 264
Fogarty, John: 394, 427, 430, 473, 511
Ford, Francis: 706, 771, **771**
Ford, Samuel: 790
Forgey, John: 819, 828
Forrester, Rolland: 568, 612, 713
Forster, Joseph: 437, 456, 456 (2), 473, 474, 481, 489, 563, 563, 564, 664, 664, 696, 697, 697, 709, 709, 712, 744, 744, 783, 783, 882
Fortier, Durward: 877
Foss, Joseph: 915, 923-927, **924**, 931, 1016
Fosse, James: 27
Fostakowski, Theodore: 370, 427
Foster, Paul: 707
Foster, Oliver: 790, 792
Fotheringham, William: 289, 290, **290**, 310, 333, 349
Foulkes, Robert: 790, 792
Foulois, Gen, Benjamin: 92
Foulis, William: 505, **505**, 552, 576. 778, **778**, 780

Gustavson, Robert: 657
Guttel, John: 337, 338

H

Hadley, Robert: 489, 517, 618
Hagan, Virgil: 401, 406
Hagerstrom, Robert: 259
Hagerstrom, James: 265, 266, **266**, **318**, 384, **384**, 403, 522, **523**(2), 942, 966 (Bio), **966,** 973, 975
Hague, Jesse: 61, 62, 64, 70, 71, **71**, 73, 74, 82, 165
Haher, John: 522, 550, 592, 689, 690, 693, 700, 714, 716, 742, 751, 767
Haigh, Robert: 761
Hailey, Albon: 193, 340, 354, 356, 426
Hailey, William: 519
Hall, Burton: 750
Hall, Gen. Charles: 863
Hall, Francis: 778
Hall, Jack: 40, 41, 42, 149
Halsey, Adm. William: 460, 532, **536,** 555, 645, 669, 672, 673, 675, 677, 705, 708, 733, 763, 798, 802, 809, 813, 819, 827
Halvorson, Max: 27
Hamblin, Robert: 696, 789, 790
Hamlin, Robert: 828
Hamburger, Robert: 608, 609, 701
Hamilton, James: 58
Hamilton, Thomas: 699, 713, 724
Hammett, Henry: 731, 739, 748
Hammond, Robert: 821
Haney, William: 249, **249**, 250, 260, 261, 277, 279, 300, 312, 410, 421, 431
Haning, William: 193, **193**, 213, 258, **258**, 259, 319, 320, 330, **340**, 355
Haniotis, George: 403, 421, 432, 437
Hanisch, John: 689
Hannan, John: 517, 563, 712, 716, 744, 746
Hanover, Donald: 288, 304, 305, 338, 348, **348**, **426**, 427
Hansen, Robert: 822, 889
Hanson, Ferdinand: 473, 484, 517
Hanson, John: 360, 436, 437
Hanson, Robert: 33, 35, 319, 335, 473, 481, 484, 491
Hanson, Robert (USMC): 926, 926
Harbour, David: 242, 243, 353
Harding, Gen. Edwin: 195, 207, **207**
Harding, Wallace: 622, 760, 780, **780**, 845
Harper, Jean: 786
Hart, Kenneth: 635, 718, 727, **728**, 737, 747, 850, **851**
Hart, Adm. Thomas: 53, **54**
Hart, Wallace: 822
Hartz, Paul: 886
Harries, Fred: 539
Harringer, Robert: 149, 893
Harris, Bruce: 108
Harris, Ernest: 207, 224, 225, **225**, 226, 252, 263, 265, **266**, 280, **280**, 281, 303, 304, 317, 351, 360, 404, 435, 436, 437, 471, 476, 915, 957, 962 (Bio), **962**, 973
Harris, Frederick: 334, 340, 359, 362, 363, 364, 370, 400, 401, 404, 407, 418, 423
Harris, Harold: 694, 714, 731, 748, 773, **Profile #11/2** (P-38)
Harris, James: 12, 310, 311, 317, **317**, 318, 365, 407, **407**, 413
Harris, Orland: 789
Harris, Russell: 808

Harris, William (Bruce): 191, 206, **206,** 265, 266, 269, 278
Harrison, Robert: 479, 630, 644
Hart, Douglas: 592, 702
Hartley, Ralph: 761, 836
Hartmann, Dirck: 267
Harvey, Clyde: 96, 97, **97**, 111, 261, 262, 265
Hashiguchi, Takashi: 67
Hasty, William: 516, 611, 889
Hatfield, Hugh: 713
Hawkins, Alva: 155, 157
Hawley, R.G: 488
Hawke, Marion: 522
Haws, Eugene: 821
Hawthorne, Martin: 519
Hay, Charles: 291
Hayes, Thomas: 61, 62, 72. 73, **73**, 82, 970, **970**
Haynes George: 61
Heckerman, Arthur: 501
Heinz, Eugene: 270
Hedrick, Edward: 339, 370, 398, 405
Hedrick, Howard: 319, 363, 411, 419, 427, 430, 437, 438, 492, 517
Heiden, Ralph: 608
Heins, Lt.: 475
Helterline, Frederick: 551, 608, **609**, 610, 659
Henderson, Dwight: 845
Henderson, Milburn: 322, 477, 505
Henkes, Lawrence: 776, 861
Hennon, William: 36, 41, 57, 60, **60**, 61, 63, 64, 73, 74, 77, 78, **78**, 80, 82, 92, 103, **105**, 106, 107, **107**, 173, 175
Henry, John: 514
Henze, Irvin: 475
Herbert, James: 209
Herman, Christopher: 472, 473, 483, 616, 742, 786, 804, **804**
Herman, Robert: 411, 433, 497, 627
Herring, Gen. E. F.: 175, 195, 233
Hewitt, Air Commodore J.E.: 13, 100, 186
Hickok, Walter: 719
Hilbert, George: 321
Hilbig, Randall: 291, 490, **490**
Hill, Allen: 356, **356**, 402, 423, **423**, 426, **426**, 427, 431, 433. **433**
Hill, Francis: 691, 755, 756, 775, 777, 803, 822
Hill, Glade: 12, 311, 421, 431
Hill, Herbert: 205
Hill, Player: 890
Hilliard, Raymond: 280
Hnatio, Myron: 503, **504**, 516, **516**, 544, **545**, 546
Hochuli, Robert: 869
Hodge, Idon: 793, **793**, 821, 835
Holder, Glendi: 362, 494, 500, 514, **515**
Holze, Harold: 265, 339, 340, 411, 422
Hollabaugh, Simpson: 308
Holladay, Dan: 784
Hollingshead, Billy: 513
Hollister, Dwight: 891, **891**
Holstein, Thomas: 529, 700, 701, 736, 787, 822
Homer, Cyril: **518**, 519, 520, **520**, **558**, 559, 560, 562, **563**, **597**, 619, 626, **627**, 712, **713**, 869, **870,** 942, 955-956 (Bio), **955**, 972, 975, 981, Aircraft **995(2),** 1045
Honda, Minoru: 1009, 1009
Hood, John: 209, **210**, 243, 319, 320, **340**, 353, 355, 357, 369, **370**

Malone, Lt, ? (71TRG): 811
Malone, Thomas: 556, 723
Manes, Hubert: 709, 716, 730, 731
Mangas, John: 212, 223
Mann, Clifford: 355, 418, 535, 563, 565, 612
Manning, George: 106, 190, 213, 223, 244, 265, 277, 299, 317
Mansfield, Harry: 775
Marble, Hugh: 37, 48
Marett, Samuel: 19, 22, 31, 32
Marion, Elroy: 835
Markey, Walter: 223, 261, 352, 478
Markham, Kenneth: 714, 732, 751, 784
Marks, Leonard: 149, 154, 155, **155**, 157
Marlatt, Wilmot: 247
Marling, Milby: 352, 397, 413
Marman, George: 709
Marshall, Gen. George C.: 21, 22, 37, 53, 75, 86, 87, 148, 166, 216, 217, 219, 274, 275, 315, 319
Marshall, Gen. Richard: 178-81
Marston, Arthur: 526, 790, 868
Martin, Charles: 790, 791, 810
Martin, Harold: 95
Martin, Harvey: 102, 103, 108
Martin, James: 102, **102**, 252
Martin, Louis: 480, **480**, 549
Martin, Ralph: 162, 164
Martin, Robert: 409, 471
Martin, Thomas: 747, 781, 835, 851, **851**
Martin, Troy: 612
Martin, William: 175, 205, 213, 223, 244, 253, 254, 265, 266
Marvin, Jack: 538, 707
Martin, Roy: 608, 848
Mastilock, John: 753
Matsuda, Maj.Gen. Iwao: 460, 495
Mathers, Leonidas: 171, 228, 267, 288, **288**, 289, 332, 338
Mathis, Ross: 827
Mathre, Milden: 691, **691**, **749**, 750, 767, 773, 803, **803**
Mayo, Leo: 259, 278, 279, 400, 401, 427, 430
Max, Howard: 848
Maxwell, Edward: 307
Maxwell, Glenn: 748, 784
Mazur, Joseph: 713
May, E.V.: 700
Maynard Robert: 698, 770, 797
McAfee, Oliver: 489, 496, 513, 618
McAlpin, Robert: 819
McCabe, Leighton: 638
McCallum, Gerald: 57, 60, 62, 63, 74, 75
McCallum, Robert (Bo): 77, 78
McCampbell, David (USN): 916, **928**, 929, 930, 931, 1016
McClelland, Harold: 164, 361, **361**, 362, 494, **499**, 500, 505, **506**, 615, 627, 640
McComsey, Robert: 106, **106**, 262, 645, **645**, 688, 692
McConnell, William: 193
McCowan, Morgan: 32
McCoy, Bennett: 362, 470, 615
McCoy, Frank: 13, 14, **14**
McCoy, George: 92
McCrary, James: 755

McCullough, Harry: 360
McDaris, Robert: 223, 302, 303, 550 **551**
McDonald. Joseph: 790
McDonough, William: **240**, 241, 528, 531, **531**, 539, **539**, 556, 568, **568**
McDougal, Miles: 641
McElroy, Charles: 407, 437, 598, 608, 636, 691, 722, 739, 740, 748, 750, 750
McGee, Donald: 149, 150, 151, **151**, 152, 155, 158, **158**, 271, **271**, 310, 337, 357, **357**(2), **444**(Aircraft Profile)
McGovern, David: 149, 151, 155
McGuire, Eugene: 418, 437, 472, 473
McGuire, Thomas: 320, 330, **330**, 331, **335**, 336, 339, **339**, 340, 354, 370, **370**, 394, **398**, 399, 401, 405, 408, 416, 418, 437, 483, 492, 495, **495**, 511, 528, 560, 597, **597**, 598, **598**, 616, **617**, 618, 628, **628**, 631, 634, 659, 662, **662**, 691, **691**, 694, 695, **695**, 712, **712**, 717, **717**, 746, **746**, 759, **759**, 767, 780, **781**, 786, **786**, 801, 810, **810**, 818, 927, 929-930, **929(2)**, 937, 943, 947-948 (Bio), **947**, 949, 959, 974, 975, **978**, 981, 985, 987-988 (Aircraft), **987(2)**, **988(4)**, 991, 1016, 1017, 1019, 1020 (MoH), **1020**, 1030, 1050, 1152, 1162, 1201, 1209
McGuire, Marilyn: 811
McHenry, Joseph: 784, 785
McHale, Robert: 252, 253, 523, 530, 531, 590, 593, 608, **609**
McIlvride, Robert: 805
McInnis, Laurence: 592
McKay, Paul: 813
McKeon, Joseph: 164, **208**, 209, 286, **346**, 347, **364**, 367, **367**, 401, **401**
McKenzie, Albert: 710, 713, 718, 745
McLain, James: 719, 789, 790
McLaughlin, James: 301, 301, 434, 501, 553
McLendon, Andrew: 704
McLean, John: 12, 310, 312, 397, 413, 421, 641
McLeod, Robert: 264
McMath, Paul: 800, 810
McMahon, David: 810
McMahon, Robert: 32, 33, 39, 79, **79**, 161, **161**
McMillen, Rolland: 627
McMullen, Harry: 532
McMurry, George: 299
McNaulty, Robert: 775
McNay, Joseph: 93
McNeill, Robert: 967
McPeak, Robert: 848
McQueen, James: 812
McQuire, James: 612
McWherter, Robert: 61, 62, 63, 80, 82
McWhorter, Thurman: 828
Meech, Donald: 875
Meeks, James: 760, 761
Melikian, Raymond: 82, 109, 110, 111, 193, 223, 254, **254**, 277, **277**, 302, 317, **317**, 397, 407, 419, 440, 476
Melville, William: 423
Menger, James: 590, 592
Menter, Marvin: 829
Meschino, Albert: 713, 784, 895, 818, 845
Mettler, William: 307
Meuten, Donald: 471, 526, 527, 550
Meyer, Dale: 347, 406. 412, 438
Meyer, Floyd: **478**, 544, **608**
Meyer, Raymond: 891, **Profile #24/2** (P-38)
Meyer, Walter: 693, 751, **751**

O

Oakes, Roy: 813, 875, **875**
Obert, David: 41, **41**, 42, 48
O'Brien, William: 483, 492, 513, 597, 616, 635, **635**, **716**
O'Connor, Joseph: 265, 480
Odell, William: 639
Odgers, Robert: 696
O'Donnell, Gen. Emmett: 64
Odren, Harry: 588, **790**, 791, 834, 875
Oehlbeck, Maynard: 704
Oestreicher, Robert: 67, 68, 69, **69**, 82
Ogawa, Shoichi: 67
Ogden, Kenneth: 867
Oglesby, Harold: 662, **662**, 701, **701**
Ogura, Mitsuo: 1006, 1006
O'Hare, Edward "Butch" (USN): 922, 923, 929, 930, 1016
Okano, Hiroshi: 1010, 1010
Oki, Yoshio: 1010, 1010
Oksala, Frank: 291, 402, 432, 477, **477**, **608**
Oliver, Bennett: 319
Oliver, Bernard: 62, 63, 74, 82
O'Leary, James: 790, 818
O'Neill, Cyril: 891
O'Neill, James: 510, 549, 590, 730, 758
O'Neill, John: 253, 262, 262, 397, 398, 407, 413, **413**, 421, **421**, 433, **935**, 944, 973, 974, 976, 977, **980**, 983
O'Neill, Lawrence: 354, **354**, 502, **502**
Onozaki, Hiroshi: 1006, 1006
O'Riley, Frederick: 112
O'Rourke, John: 852, **852**
Olson, Arvid: 801, **802**, 843, 858
Olson, Dean: 664, 710, **711**
Olson, Jack: 723
Olster, Mortimer: 739
Orr, George: 503, 600, 612, 613, 622
Osborne, Allen: 419
Ota, Toshio: 1011, 1011
Overbey, William: 610, 612, 757
Oveson, Keith: 258, 261, 279
Owens, Harrold: 565, 712, 718, 783, 852
Owens, Roy: 271
Oxford, Thomas: 727, 781
Oxley, Gilbert: 155, 164
Ozaki, Takeo: 67
Ozier, Joseph: 892

P

Page, Jack: 845
Pahlka, David: 636
Palmer, James: 271,
Pardy, David: 321, 475, 539
Pare, Roger: 405, 406, 433
Park, Edward: 539, 707
Parkansky, John: 320, 347
Parker, Gerald: 894
Parker, Robert: 470
Parlett, Lakin: 709, 712, 733
Paris, Joel: 550, **551**, 590, **590**, 750, **750**, 757, **758**, 774, 784, **785**, 803, **803**, **844**, 845
Parsons, Douglas: 547, 557, 635, 708

Parsons, Lynn: 738, 753, **753**
Partridge, Lloyd: 722
Patterson, Donald: 659
Patterson, Henry: 720
Patterson, Robert: 821
Patterson, Sec. War Robert: 18
Payne, Walter: 720
Pearson, Merle: 561
Peaslee, Jesse: 173, 189, 244, 265, 277, 279, **443** (Aircraft profile)
Peck, Edward: 299, 396, 590, 593, **593**, 619, 630, 688, 713, 803, 837
Peirse, Richard: 53, **53**, 60, 75, 82
Pell, Floyd: 65, **65**, 67, 69, 70, 82
Peregoy, Arthur: 358, 423, 427, 473, 474, 489, 517, 518, 561
Peress, John: 68, 70, 82
Perkins, John: **501**, 502, 553, 707
Perrin, Edwin: 100
Perry, Elton: 100
Peters, Paul: 552, 556, 611
Peters, Robert: 713
Petersen, Carl: 523
Petersen, Charles: 436
Peterson, Clay: **105**, 106, 208, 209, 261
Peterson, Harry: 282, 283, 306
Peterson, Herbert: 810, 835
Peterson, Howard: 208, **208**, 209, 282, 306
Petrovic, John: 731, 837, **837**
Peugeot, Francis: 533, 808
Pew, Robert: 735, **735**, 849
Pharr, Walter: 535, **535**
Phillips, James: 33
Phillips, Chester: 299, 353
Pickens, John: 423
Pierce, Sammie: 265, **266**, 280, 281, 403, 404
Pietscher, Reed: 861
Pietz, John: 628, 727, **728**, 781, **781**, 403, **403**
Pine, Irving: 860, 881
Pitchford, Joel: 503, **504**
Pitchford, John: 157
Pitonyak, Francis: 423
Pixey, Victor: 92
Planck, Carl: 212, 213, **213**, 214, 224, 258, **260**, 272, 430, 431
Plunkett, Gentry: 93. 159
Poleschuk, Stephen: 96, **96**, 97
Polhamus, Richard: 359, 531
Pollock, Lemuel: 530, 549, **549**
Pool, Kenneth: 514, 637, **637**, 695, 705, **705**, 719
Poorten, Adm. Hein ter: 53, **53**
Popek, Edward: 291, 409, **409**, 507, **507**, 611, 886, **887**(2), **Profile #20/2** (P-51)
Porteous, John: 531
Porter, James: 97, 245, 263, 303, 396
Porter, Philip: 651, 796, **796**
Portmore, Gilbert: 107, 109
Posey, Charles: 821
Poston, James: 608, 609, 698, **699**
Posten, John: 32, 33, 40, 41, 42, 43, **43**, 44, 110, **110**, 111
Posvistak, Walter: 362
Poteet, Linfield: 656
Powell, George: 175, 213, 292
Powell, Ormand: 496

Thompson, William: 723, 743 755, 767, 773, 784
Thorne, Henry: 19, 22, 23, 48, **48**
Thornton, Stuart: 713
Thorson, Harold: 833
Thorvalson, Joel: 267, 471
Thropp, Douglas: 739, 747, **747**, 804, 810,
Tice, Clayton: 109, 111, 213, 248, **248**, 249, **287, 859**, 872, 885, **885**
Tilley, John: 483, **483**, 496, 517, 597, **597**, 717, 739, 755, **755**, 780, **781**, 787, **787**, 835
Tillou, John: 873
Toll, Henry: 710, **711**, 734, 862
Tomberg, Robert: 319, 406, 488, **488**, 513, 571, 572, 793
Tomkins (Tompkins), Franklin: 284, 319, 320, 332, 355, 400, **400**, 401, 411, 416, 418, 473, 474, 511
Tompkins, Bertram: 753, 794, 795
Trabing, Donald: 625, **625**, 820
Treadway, Willis: 598, **598**, 751, **751**
Triplehorn, Gerald: 724
Tobre, Perry: 736
Trout, Chester: 57, 162
Trout, Marcus: 707, 822, 832
Troxell, Clifton: 157, **157**, 158, **158**, 357, **357**, 498, **499**, 626, 627, 945, 971, **971**, 972, 983
Tubre, Perry: 722
Tudor, William: 811
Tueche, Eli: 821
Tuman, Howard: 474, 484, **486**, 532, 808, 809
Turick, Henry: 250
Turnbull, Gladson: 696
Turner, William: 61, 62, 74, 172, 439, 627, 698, 771, 797
Tuttle, Randall: 800, 810
Tuuri, Eugene: 300, **446 (P-39 Profile)**, 501, 502, 553
Tyler, Gerald (AAF): 916

U-V
Uehara, Sadao: 1012
Upton, William: 403
Uto, Kazushi: 1012, 1012
Van Auken, Robert: 92, 95, 98, 99, 101, 104, 105
Van Patten, Everett: 627, 640
Varland, Erling: 727
Vasey, Gen. C.A.: 195, 207, **208**, 380
Vattendahl, Marge: 556, 658
Vaughn, Harold: 761
Vaught, Robert: 82, 97, **97, 209**, 210, 254, **254**
Vejtasa, Stanley (USN): 928, 928
Vetort, Francis: 270, 475
Viet, George: 433
Villemor, Jesus: 22, 33, **33**, 42
Vining, Leland: 339, 421
Vinzant. Mark: 872
Vodra, Richard: 365, 278, **278**, 279, 404
von Richtofen, Manfred: 915
Voorhees, Irving: 205, 207

W
Wacker, George: 850
Wade, Charles: 891
Wagner, Barrett: 858, **858**

Wagner, Boyd: 19, **19**, 22, 27, **27**, 29, 31, 32, 34, 35, **35**, 36, 39, 48, 57, 58, **58**, 82, 92, 96, **99**, 114, 149, 150, **150**, 152, 153, 160, 193, 194, 198, 204, 206, 209, 922, **923**, 931, 945, 975, 1045, 1062
Wagner, Furlo: 205, 529, 539, 589, 610, 630
Wagner, Lucas: 709
Wahl, Gene: 74, 77, 157, **157**, 161
Wainwright, Gen. Jonathan: 45, 113
Walcott, Philip: 552
Waldman, William: 319, 331, 334, 340, 359, 363, 411
Waldron, Gen. Albert: 195
Walker, George: 610, 629, 630, 645, 656, **656**, 688, 690, **691**, 714,716, 748, **749**, 773
Walker, Gen. Kenneth: 183, 184, 185, 186, 228, 233, 349
Walker, William: 68, 69, 70
Wallace, Jamie: 407, 475
Wallace, John: 538, 552
Wallace, William: 527, 754
Wandrey, Ralph: 8, **8**, 308, **308**, 312, 404, 405, 413, 439
Walters, Allen: 100, 186
Walters, James: 227, 254, 415, **415**
Wandrey, Ralph: 8, **8(2)**, 308, **308**, 312, 404, 407, 413, 439, 478, 479, 551, **551**, 573
Ward, James: 847
Warner, John: 843
Warrick, Thomas: 475
Watkins, James: 10, 11, **11(ICR)**, 12, 210, 279, 287, 288, 310, 311, **311**, 312, 313, 317, **317**, 318, 958-959 (Bio), **958**, 973, 975, 984, Aircraft **997(2), 998**
Watson, Ralph: 748, 785, 803
Wavell, Gen. Archibald: 37, 46, 51, **51**, 53, **53**, 60, 75, 76, 82, 181, 182
Wayne, Howard: 591
Webster, Cutler: 819
Weaver, Carl: 438, 439, 505, 506, 615
Weaver, Ira: 707
Weber, John: 242, 355, 411, 427
Weeks, Arthur: 291
Weisfus, Walter: 648
Welch, George: 164, 208, 208, 209, 286, 290, 290, 332, 333, 342, 342, 408, 922, 923, 930, 945, 953-954 (Bio), 953, 971, 972, 976, 981, 994, 1017, 1061
Weldon, John: 517, **517**
Wells, Howard: 815
Wells, Selmon: 510
Wenige, Arthur: 210, **242**, 268, 319, **323**, 324, 411, 428, 429, 430, 433
Werner, Richard: 103
Wertin, Vincent: 753, 794
Wesley, Bryant: 210
West, Richard: 362, 464, 470, **470**, 615, 616, **616**, 626, **626**, 666, 695, **695(2)**, 705, **705**, 719, **720**, 721, **Profile #8/2** (P-38), 957 (Bio), **957**, 972, 975, 984, Aircraft **996**, 1066 (Flying P-40), **1066**
Whistler, Charles: 721, 754, 771
White, James: 885
White, Kiefer: 40
White, Gen. Miller: 180
White, Robert: 252, **252**, 278, 279, **279**, 351, 352, **352**, 436, **436**
White, Varian 33, 36, 43, 44
White, William: 861
Whitehead, Gen. Ennis: 173, 183 (Bio), **183**, 185, 186, 190, 192, 195, 212, 214, 220, 227, 233, 234, **234**, 235, 238, 257, 292, 373, 373, 383, 408, 409, 418, 420 440, 642, **815**, 848, 849, 869

General Index

Note: General Index subjects only include those discussed in a long paragraph or more

A

Abbreviations: 14
Aces: History: 914, Race/Pacific: 922-933, 5th Fighter Command: 540-545, 5th Fighter Command Aces with 10+ Victories: 946-964, Group and Squadron Aces: 972-974
Aiming and Firing: 1200-1201
Aircraft of the Aces: 975-978, Japanese: 1002-1015
Aircraft: 5FC: 1057-1097, Japanese: 1097-1149
Airfields: Australia 115-116, Port Moresby 117-120, life on: 468, health: 468-469, AAF: 1233-1246
Airfield Construction: 134-140, 293-294
Air Tactics and Combat: 1180-1199, Studies: 1202-1203, Japanese: 2018-1224
Aitape/Tadji Airfields: 578
Alexishafen Airdrome: 462, **463**
American-British-Dutch-Australian Command (ABDACOM): 51 formation, **51** (map)
Armament and Equipment (Fighter): 1152-1162
Armor: US: 1163, 1163, Japanese: 1169
Australia: 85-86 early situation, 86-87 developed as a base, ferry route 115-116
Awards and Decorations: US: 115-121, Japanese: 1021-1022

B

Backhander: Operation: 460, 495
Bell P-39 Airacobra: 1057-1062, 1057, 1059(2), 1060
Berry Drome (12 Mile Drome): 130-131
Betty/Mitsubishi G4M: 1115-1117, 1115, 1117
Biak Island-Base H: 600
Biak Invasion: 599-602
Bougainville Landings: 460
Brereton Route: 56-57, 56(map)
Brewer, Operation: **534**
Bullet-Proof Windscreens: 1164, 1164
Buna: 163 invasion
Buna-Gona Campaign: 194

C

Cape Gloucester Airdrome: 464. **464**
Cartwheel, Operation: 460
Coral Sea, Battle of the: 153
Chronicle, Operation: 294
Code Names for Major Japanese Aircraft: 1097-1098
Communications, Warning, and Control (AAF Fighter): 1247-1251
Curtiss P-40 Warhawk: 1062-1068, 1062, 1064(2), 1066
Cutthroat, Operation: 519

D

Darwin: 65-68 Australia's Pearl Harbor, 66 (3+ maps), 88-89 description, 105-112 air raids
Daugo Island Emergency Airfield: 134
Dengue Fever: 146
Designations Japanese Aircraft: 1097-1100, Manufacturer's Code letter: 1100, Ki Number System: 1101, Popular Names: 1102
Dexterity, Operation: 460, 462, 465, 477
Dinah/Mitsubishi Ki-46: 1141-1142, 1141, 1142
Director, Operation: 460, 482
Dobodura and Oro Bay Airfields: 198-204, 255
Drop Tanks: 1168, 1168
Dumpu Drome: 465
Durand Drome (17 Mile Drome): 132
Dysentery: 146

E

8th Fighter Control Squadron: 167
8th Fighter Group: 92-93 history, 1044
Elkton Plan: 217-222, 284-285, 314-316 Reno, 381-382 Montclair

F

49th Pursuit Group: 92 history, 1046
58th Fighter Group: 473 history, 1046
475th Fighter Group: 318 history, 1049
421st NFS: 512 history
Far East Air Force (FEAF): 19 order of battle, 22 description, airfields 19-20
Fighter Comparisons USAAF: 1093-1095
Finschhafen (Base F/Dreger Field): 465, 466-467, **466**, **467 maps** (2)
Food: 235
Formations Fighter: 1204-1207
Frank/Nakajima Ki-84: 1131-1132, 1131, 1132
Fuels: US: 1169, Japanese: 1170

G

George/Kawanishi N1K1-J: 1145, 1145
Gun Camera: 920-921, 920, 921(2)
Gusap Drome: 380-383

H-I

Health: 235-236
Helen/ Nakajima Ki-49: 1137-1138, 1137, 1138
Hollandia: 447 (Air Battle), 554 (Campaign), 578-587 (Airfields)
I-Go, Operation: 265, 273
Individual Combat Report (ICR): 9, **9** (3)
Intelligence Officer: 916-917
Irving/Nakajima J1N1: 1111-1112, 1111, 1112

Airfield Index

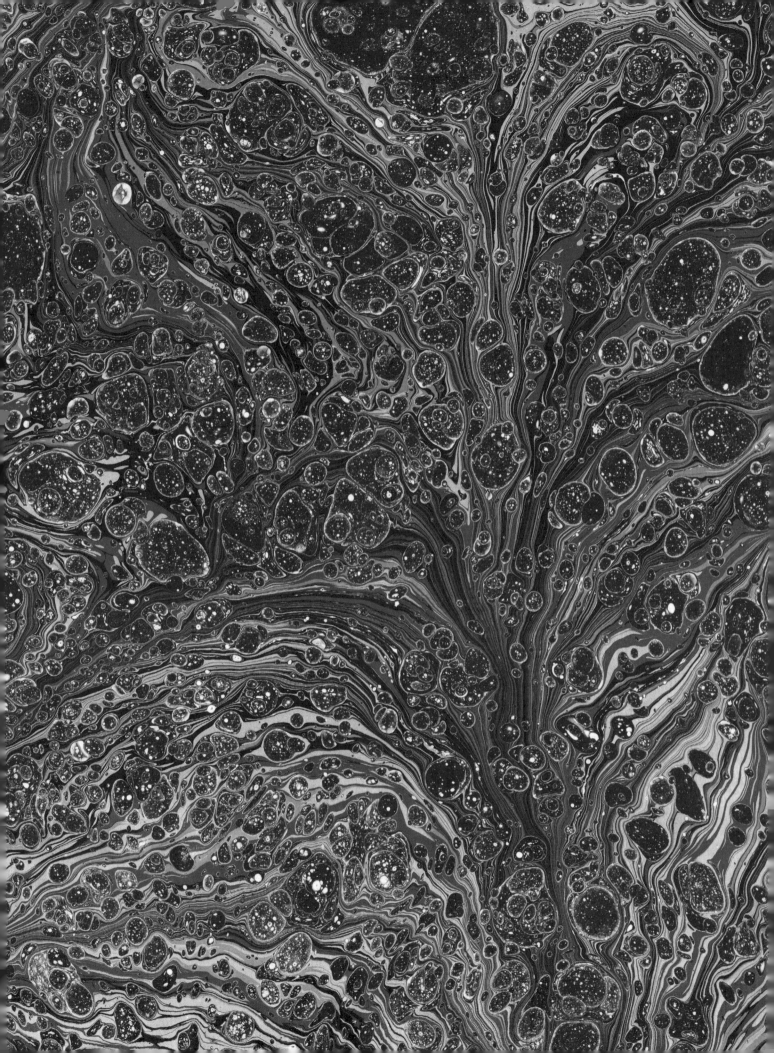